Apache Server 2 Bible

Apache Server 2 Bible

Mohammed J. Kabir

Hungry Minds™

Best-Selling Books • Digital Downloads • e-Books • Answer Networks • e-Newsletters • Branded Web Sites • e-Learning

New York, NY✦ Cleveland, OH ✦ Indianapolis, IN

Apache Server 2 Bible

Published by
Hungry Minds, Inc.
909 Third Avenue
New York, NY 10022
www.hungryminds.com

Library of Congress Control Number: 2001092889

ISBN: 0-7645-4821-2

Printed in the United States of America

10 9 8 7 6 5 4 3 2 1

1B/RT/QT/QS/IN

Distributed in the United States by Hungry Minds, Inc.

Distributed by CDG Books Canada Inc. for Canada; by Transworld Publishers Limited in the United Kingdom; by IDG Norge Books for Norway; by IDG Sweden Books for Sweden; by IDG Books Australia Publishing Corporation Pty. Ltd. for Australia and New Zealand; by TransQuest Publishers Pte Ltd. for Singapore, Malaysia, Thailand, Indonesia, and Hong Kong; by Gotop Information Inc. for Taiwan; by ICG Muse, Inc. for Japan; by Intersoft for South Africa; by Eyrolles for France; by International Thomson Publishing for Germany, Austria, and Switzerland; by Distribuidora Cuspide for Argentina; by LR International for Brazil; by Galileo Libros for Chile; by Ediciones ZETA S.C.R. Ltda. for Peru; by WS Computer Publishing Corporation, Inc., for the Philippines; by Contemporanea de Ediciones for Venezuela; by Express Computer Distributors for the Caribbean and West Indies; by Micronesia Media Distributor, Inc. for Micronesia; by Chips Computadoras S.A. de C.V. for Mexico; by Editorial Norma de Panama S.A. for Panama; by American Bookshops for Finland.

For general information on Hungry Minds' products and services please contact our Customer Care department within the U.S. at 800-762-2974, outside the U.S. at 317-572-3993 or fax 317-572-4002.

For sales inquiries and reseller information, including discounts, premium and bulk quantity sales, and foreign-language translations, please contact our Customer Care department at 800-434-3422, fax 317-572-4002 or write to Hungry Minds, Inc., Attn: Customer Care Department, 10475 Crosspoint Boulevard, Indianapolis, IN 46256.

For information on licensing foreign or domestic rights, please contact our Sub-Rights Customer Care department at 212-884-5000.

For information on using Hungry Minds' products and services in the classroom or for ordering examination copies, please contact our Educational Sales department at 800-434-2086 or fax 317-572-4005.

For press review copies, author interviews, or other publicity information, please contact our Public Relations department at 317-572-3168 or fax 317-572-4168.

For authorization to photocopy items for corporate, personal, or educational use, please contact Copyright Clearance Center, 222 Rosewood Drive, Danvers, MA 01923, or fax 978-750-4470.

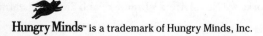

Hungry Minds™ is a trademark of Hungry Minds, Inc.

Credits

Acquisitions Editor
Terri Varveris

Project Editor
James H. Russell

Technical Editor
Gregory W. Stephens

Copy Editor
Richard H. Adin

Editorial Managers
Kyle Looper
Ami Frank Sullivan

**Vice President & Executive
Group Publisher**
Richard Swadley

Vice President & Group Publisher
Bob Ipsen

Editorial Director
Mary Bednarek

Project Coordinator
Regina Snyder

Graphics and Production Specialists
Beth Brooks
Melanie DesJardins
Joyce Haughey
Betty Schulte
Jeremey Unger

Quality Control Technicians
Laura Albert
John Greenough
Andy Hollandbeck
Angel Perez

Media Development Specialist
Travis Silvers

Illustrator
Kate Shaw

Proofreading and Indexing
TECHBOOKS Production Services

Cover Image
Kate Shaw

About the Author

Mohammed Kabir is the founder and CEO of Evoknow, Inc. His company specializes in CRM software development. When he is not busy managing software projects or writing books, he enjoys traveling. Kabir studied computer engineering at California State University, Sacramento. He can be reached at kabir@evoknow.com.

To the memory of my mother, Nazma Bathen.

Preface

Welcome to Apache Server 2.0. Chances are that you already have heard about Apache server. In fact, more than 60 percent of all Web administrators use Apache. Apache is the most powerful, open-source, Web-server platform in the world.

As a practicing Web developer, researcher, and administrator, I find Apache to be the perfect fit for most Web sites. Apache 2.0 is a major revision of Apache server. Apache Group originally created a highly configurable Web server in the first version, which became popular very fast; in version 2, Apache Group focused on scalability, reliability, and performance. Major code revisions were done to create a very scalable Apache architecture.

Today, Apache stands tall as the most widely used Web platform. Every day an increasing number of corporations accept this open-source marvel into their IT infrastructure. Many large IT companies, such as IBM, have embraced Apache in their product offerings. The future of Apache looks great. Whether you're new to Apache or are already a practicing Apache administrator, now is the perfect time to get started with Apache 2.0. This book will help you do just that.

How This Book Is Organized

The book has six parts. Very short descriptions of each part follow.

Part I: Getting Started

With a brief introduction to the world's number one Web server, in this part I guide you through the process of obtaining and compiling Apache. I show you how to get Apache up and running with minimal changes to the default configuration files so that you can get Apache up and running on your system as quickly as possible. This part ends with complete references to the Apache core directives and standard modules so that you can get ready for serious Apache administration tasks.

Part II: Web Site Administration

This part focuses on typical Web administration tasks such as virtual Web-site creation, user authentication and authorization tasks, monitoring, logging, rewriting and redirecting URLs, proxy service, and the like. You learn a great deal there is to know about creating and managing virtual Web sites. You master various methods of user authentication, authorization, and access control techniques. You learn to monitor Web servers and to customize log files for analysis.

Part III: Running Web Applications

This part focuses on the ways in which you can serve dynamic contents using Apache. It covers Common Gateway Interface (CGI), Server-Side Includes (SSI), FastCGI, PHP, mod_perl, and Java servlets. You quickly learn to use these technologies with Apache.

Part IV: Securing Your Web Site

Any computer on the Internet is subject to abuse or attempts of misuse. It is always a good idea to play it safe and to take precautionary measures. In this part, you learn to make your Web sites more secure and resistant to hacker attacks. You are also introduced to the potential risks of running SSI and CGI programs and how to take preventive measures to avoid these risks. You also learn to enable Secure Socket Layer (SSL) service using Apache modules to enable secure e-commerce.

Part V: Running Apache on Windows

Apache on Windows (Win32) platform has become very popular; more and more people are trying Apache on Windows platform. With Apache 2.0, the performance of Apache Web server under this platform has become very promising. In this part, you learn how to install and configure Apache on Win32 platform.

Part VI: Tuning for Performance and Scalability

In this part, I discuss how you can speed up Apache by tuning your Web server system and by optimizing various Apache server configuration. The chapter provides a great deal of information on how to benefit from high-performance hardware, how to tune hard disks and file systems under Linux to enhance system performance. It also covers Web caching and tuning issues related to Perl-based Web applications.

Conventions Used in This Book

You don't have to learn any new conventions to read this book. Just remember that when you are asked to enter a command, you need press the Enter or the Return key after you type the command at your command prompt. A monospaced font is used to denote configuration or code segment.

Also, pay attention to these icons:

 The Note icon indicates that something needs a bit more explanation.

 The Tip icon tells you something that is likely to save you some time and effort.

 The Caution icon makes you aware of a potential danger.

 The On The CD-ROM icon clues you in to files, programs, and other goodies that are on the CD-ROM.

 The Cross=Reference icon helps you navigate the book better, pointing you to topics that are related to the one you're currently reading about.

Tell Us What You Think of This Book

Both Hungry Minds and I want to know what you think of this book. Please register this book online at the Hungry Minds Web site (www.hungryminds.com) and give us your feedback. If you are interested in communicating with me directly, send e-mail messages to kabir@evoknow.com. I will do my best to respond promptly.

The Book Web Site

This book has a Web site at http://www.evoknow.com/kabir/apache2. You can visit this Web site for updated contents, errata, and FAQ.

Acknowledgments

I would like to thank the Apache Group for creating the most powerful, extensible, and modular Web server in the world. I give special thanks to Ralf S. Engelschall. Ralf, the author of the `mod_rewrite` module, provided a great deal of support in the development of Chapter 9 on URL rewriting rules. The practical examples in that chapter are derived from his personal collection, which keeps growing at his Web site `www.engelschall.com/pw/apache/rewriteguide`.

I also thank the Hungry Minds team, who made this book a reality. It is impossible to list everyone involved but I must mention the following kind individuals:

James Russell, the project development editor, kept this project going. I don't know how I could have done this book without his generous help and suggestions every step of the way. Thanks James.

Terri Varveris, the acquisitions editor, provided me with this book opportunity and made sure I saw it through to the end. Thanks, Terri.

Sheila Kabir, my wife, had to put up with many long work hours during the few months it took to write this book. Thank you, sweetheart.

Contents at a Glance

Contents

Part II: Web Site Administration   157

Chapter 6: Hosting Virtual Web Sites 159

Chapter 7: Authenticating and Authorizing Web Site Visitors 181

Part III: Running Web Applications   319

Chapter 12: Running CGI Scripts 321

Getting Started

In this part, I show you why Apache is a great Web server; where to get it from, and how to install and configure it. I also get you up to speed with the Apache code directives and the many popular modules that make Apache the most configurable Web server on the planet.

Apache: The Number One Web Server

Welcome to Apache—the number one Web server in the world. If you are toying with the idea of running Apache, you are in the right place! This chapter introduces the Apache way of running a Web server.

More than 60 percent of the Web servers in the world use Apache, according to a prominent Web server survey company called Netcraft (www.netcraft.co.uk/Survey/). Netcraft publishes the Top Server statistics periodically. Table 1-1 shows the Top Server statistics that was available at the time of writing this chapter. If you want to put faces to the numbers, you can visit www.apache.org/info/apache_users.html.

Table 1-1
Top Server Statistics by Netcraft

Server	Nov 2001	Percent	Dec 2001	Percent
Apache	7750275	61.88	8588323	63.34
Microsoft IIS	3307207	26.40	3609428	26.62
iPlanet	431935	3.45	383078	2.83
Zeus	174052	3.45	172352	1.27

Apache Rocks On

What Apache has accomplished is simply amazing! Who knew that an open source Web server could consistently beat two major commercial competitors, Microsoft and Netscape as a Web server platform! Everyone has his or her own reason for why Apache is so popular. Here are mine:

✦ **Apache is a highly configurable Web Server with a modular design.** It is very easy to extend the capabilities of Apache Web server. Anyone with decent C or Perl programming expertise can write a module to perform a special function. This means that there are tons of Apache modules available for use.

✦ **Apache is a free, open source technology.** Being free is important but not as important as being open source.

✦ **Apache works great with Perl, PHP, and other scripting languages.** Most Web applications are still scripts. Perl excels in the script world and Apache makes using Perl a piece of cake with both CGI support and mod_perl support.

✦ **Apache runs on Linux and other Unix systems.** Linux used to be an underdog operating system, which has now found itself in enterprise computing arena. Linux and Apache go hand-in-hand in the enterprise world today. I believe Linux's acceptance in the business world has made Apache's entry into such territory easy. However, there are people who would argue that it was Apache's fame that made Linux find its way into the business world easier. Either way, Apache and Linux is a powerful combination. Other Unix systems such as FreeBSD and Solaris, and the new Mac OS X also play a great role in expanding Apache's user base horizon.

✦ **Apache also runs on Windows.** Although Apache will run much better on Windows platform with version 2.0, Apache was already in Windows market with Version 1.3.*x*. We will see a lot of Windows systems switching to Apache from Microsoft Internet Information Server (IIS) because Apache 2.0 architecture gives it the power it needed to compete natively.

Apache: The Beginning

Here is a bit of Apache history. In the early days of the Web, the National Center for Super Computing Applications (NCSA) created a Web server that became the number one Web server in early 1995. However, the primary developer of the NCSA Web server left NCSA about the same time, and the server project began to stall. In the meantime, people who were using the NCSA Web server began to exchange their own patches for the server and soon realized that a forum to manage the patches was necessary. The Apache Group was born. The group used the NCSA Web server code and gave birth to a new Web server called Apache. Originally derived from the core code of the NCSA Web server and a bunch of patches, the Apache server is now the talk of the Web server community. In three short years, it acquired the lead server role in the market.

The very first version (0.6.2) of publicly distributed Apache was released in April 1995. The 1.0 version was released on December 1, 1995. The Apache Group has expanded and incorporated as a nonprofit group. The group operates entirely via the Internet. However, the development of the Apache server is not limited in any way by the group. Anyone who has the know-how to participate in the development of the server or its component modules is welcome to do so, although the group is the final authority on what gets included in the standard distribution of what is known as the Apache Web server. This allows literally thousands of developers around the world to come up with new features, bug fixes, ports to new platforms, and more. When new code is submitted to the Apache Group, the group members investigate the details, perform tests, and do quality control checks. If they are satisfied, the code is integrated into the main Apache distribution.

The Apache Feature List

One of the greatest features that Apache offers is that it runs on virtually all widely used computer platforms. At the beginning, Apache used to be primarily a Unix-based Web server, but that is no longer true. Apache not only runs on most (if not all) flavors of Unix, but it also runs on Windows 2000/NT/9x and many other desktop and server-class operating systems such as Amiga OS 3.x and OS/2.

Apache offers many other features including fancy directory indexing; directory aliasing; content negotiations; configurable HTTP error reporting; SetUID execution of CGI Programs; resource management for child processes; server-side image maps; URL rewriting; URL spell checking; and online manuals.

The other major features of Apache are:

✦ **Support for the latest HTTP 1.1 protocol:** Apache is one of the first Web servers to integrate the HTTP 1.1 protocol. It is fully compliant with the new HTTP 1.1 standard and at the same time it is backward compatible with HTTP 1.0. Apache is ready for all the great things that the new protocol has to offer.

For example, before HTTP 1.1, a Web browser had to wait for a response from the Web server before it could issue another request. With the emergence of HTTP 1.1, this is no longer the case. A Web browser can send requests in parallel, which saves bandwidth by not transmitting HTTP headers in each request. This is likely to provide a performance boost at the end-user side because files requested in parallel will appear faster on the browser.

✦ **Simple, yet powerful file-based configuration:** The Apache server does not come with a graphical user interface for administrators. It comes with single primary configuration file called `httpd.conf` that you can use to configure Apache to your liking. All you need is your favorite text editor. However, it is flexible enough to allow you spread out your virtual host configuration in multiple files so that a single `httpd.conf` does not become too cumbersome to manage with many virtual server configurations.

✦ **Support for CGI (Common Gateway Interface):** Apache supports CGI using the `mod_cgi` and `mod_cgid` modules. It is CGI 1.1 compliant and offers extended features such as custom environment variables and debugging support that are hard to find in other Web servers. See Chapter 12 for details.

✦ **Support for FastCGI:** Not everyone writes their CGI in Perl, so how can they make their CGI applications faster? Apache has a solution for that as well. Use the `mod_fcgi` module to implement a FastCGI environment within Apache and make your FastCGI applications blazing fast. See Chapter 14 for details.

✦ **Support for virtual hosts:** Apache is also one of the first Web servers to support both IP-based and named virtual hosts. See Chapter 6 for details.

✦ **Support for HTTP authentication:** Web-based basic authentication is supported in Apache. It is also ready for message-digest-based authentication, which is something the popular Web browsers have yet to implement. Apache can implement basic authentication using either standard password files, DBMs, SQL calls, or calls to external authentication programs. See Chapter 7 for details.

✦ **Integrated Perl:** Perl has become the de facto standard for CGI script programming. Apache is surely one of the factors that made Perl such a popular CGI programming language. Apache is now more Perl-friendly then ever before. Using its `mod_perl` module, you can load a Perl-based CGI script in memory and reuse it as many times as you want. This process removes the start-up penalties that are often associated with an interpreted language like Perl. See Chapter 16 for details.

✦ **Support for PHP scripting:** This scripting language has become very widely used and Apache provides great support for PHP using the `mod_php` module. See Chapter 15 for details.

✦ **Java Servlet support:** Java servlets and Java Server Pages (JSP) are becoming very commonplace in dynamic Web sites. You can run Java servlets using the award-wining Tomcat environment with Apache. See Chapter 17 for details.

✦ **Integrated Proxy server:** You can turn Apache into a caching (forward) proxy server. However, the current implementation of the optional proxy module does not support reverse proxy or the latest HTTP 1.1 protocol. There are plans for updating this module soon. See Chapter 10 for details.

✦ **Server status and customizable logs:** Apache gives you a great deal of flexibility in logging and monitoring the status of the server itself. Server status can be monitored via a Web browser. You can also customize your log files to your liking. See Chapter 8 for details.

✦ **Support for Server-Side Includes (SSI):** Apache offers set of server side includes that add a great deal of flexibility for the Web site developer. See Chapter 13 for details.

✦ **Support for Secured Socket Layer (SSL):** You can easily create an SSL Web site using OpenSSL and the `mod_ssl` module for Apache. See Chapter 19 for details.

Understanding Apache 2.0 Architecture

Apache Server 2.0 makes Apache a more flexible, more portable, and more scalable Web solution than ever before. The new 2.0 releases offer many improvements; the major improvements are discussed in the following sections.

Multiprocessing modules

The first major change in Apache 2.0 is the introduction of multiprocessing modules (MPMs). To understand why MPMs are created, you need to understand how Apache worked before. Apache Version 1.3 or earlier used a preforking architecture. In this architecture, an Apache parent process forked a set of child processes, which serviced the actual requests. The parent process simply monitored the children and spawned or killed child processes based on the amount of requests received. Unfortunately, this model didn't work well under platforms that are not process-centric such as Windows. So, the Apache Group came up with the MPM-based solution.

Each MPM is responsible for starting the server processes and for servicing requests via child processes or threads depending on the MPM implementation. Several MPMs are available. They are discussed in the following sections.

The prefork MPM

The prefork MPM mimics the Apache 1.3 or earlier architecture, creating a pool of child processes to service requests. Each child process has a single thread. For example, if Apache starts 30 child processes, it can service 30 requests simultaneously.

If something goes wrong and the child process dies, only a single request is lost. The number of child processes is controlled using a minimum and maximum setting. When the number of requests increases, new child processes are added until the maximum is reached. Similarly, when the requests fall, any extra child processes are killed.

The threaded MPM

This MPM enables thread support in Apache 2.0. This is like the prefork MPM, but instead of each child process having a single thread, each child process is allowed to have a specified number of threads. Each thread within a child process can service a different request. If Apache starts 30 child processes where each child is allowed to have at maximum 10 threads, than Apache can service $30 \times 10 = 300$ requests simultaneously.

If something goes wrong with a thread, for example, an experimental module causes the thread to die, then the entire process dies. This means that all the requests being serviced by the threads within the child process will be lost. However, because requests are distributed among threads on separate child processes, it is likely that a child's death will take down at maximum of $1/n$ of all the total connection, where n presents the number of all simultaneous connections.

A process is added or removed by monitoring its spare-thread count. For example, if a process has less than the minimum number of spare threads, a new process is added. Similarly, when a process has a maximum number of idle threads, it killed.

All processes run under the same user and group ID assigned to Apache server.

Because threads are more resource efficient than processes, this MPM is very scalable.

The perchild MPM

This is also new in Apache 2.0. In this MPM model a set number of child processes are started with a specified number of threads. As request load increases the processes add new threads as needed. When request count reduces, processes shrink their thread counts using a minimum and maximum thread count setting.

The key difference between this module and the threaded MPM is that the process count is static and also each process can run using a different user and group ID. This makes it easy to run different virtual Web sites under different user and group IDs. See Chapter 6 for details.

The winnt MPM

This is the MPM for the Windows platform, including Windows 2000, Windows NT, and Window 9x. It is a multithreaded module. Using this module Apache will create a parent process and a child process. The child process creates all the threads that services the request. Also, this module now takes advantage of some Windows-only native function calls, which allows it to perform better than the earlier versions of Apache server on Windows platform.

Filtering I/O

Apache 2.0 now provides architecture for layered I/O. This means that one module's output can become another module's input. This filtering effect is very interesting. For example, the output produced by CGI scripts, which is processed by the mod_cgi module, can now be handed to the mod_include module responsible for SSIs. In other words, CGI scripts can produce output as SSI tags, which can be processed before the final output is sent to the Web browser. Many other applications of filtering I/O will be available in the future.

New CGI daemon

Because many of the MPM modules use threads, executing CGI scripts become cumbersome when a thread gets such a request. The mod_cgi module still works, but not optimally for threaded MPMs, so mod_cgid was added. The mod_cgid module creates a daemon process, which spawns CGI processes and interacts with threads more efficiently. Figure 1-1 shows how a CGI request for a script called myscript.pl is serviced.

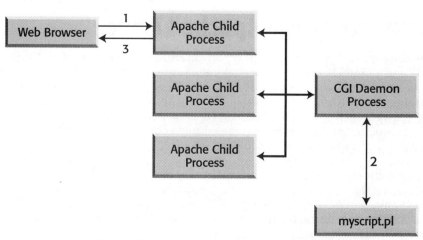

Figure 1-1: How the CGI daemon works with Apache child processes.

Here is how the CGI scripts are executed:

1. When the CGI request comes to a thread within a child process, it passes the request to the CGI daemon.

2. The CGI daemon spawns the CGI script and outputs the CGI script-generated data to the thread in the child process.

3. The thread returns the data to the Web browser.

When the main Apache server starts, it also starts the CGI daemon and establishes a socket connection. So, when a new child process is created, it inherits the socket connection and therefore does not have any need to create a connection to the CGI daemon for each request. The entire process improves CGI execution in the threaded environment.

Apache Portable Run-Time

In furtherance of the Apache Group's vision to create the most popular Web server in the world, it became clear that Apache's portability needed to be addressed in Apache 2.0. Prior to the current release, Apache had been dealing with portability internally, which made the code base less manageable. So, Apache Group introduced the Apache Portable Run-Time (APR). APR's purpose is to provide a single C interface to platform-specific functions so that code can be written once.

This enables Apache to run more natively on platforms such as Windows, BeOS, Amiga, and OS/2. Because of APR, many programs, such as ApacheBench, can run on these platforms.

Understanding the Apache License

Free software such as Apache, Perl (Practical Extraction and Reporting Language), and Linux (an *x*86-based Unix clone operating system) are getting a great deal of press because of Netscape's decision to make Netscape Communicator, one of the most popular Web browsers, available for free with its Mozilla project. Unfortunately, free software such as Apache, Perl, and Linux do not share the same licensing agreements, and so the media has created some confusion by associating these packages in the same licensing category.

All free software is intended to be, well, free for all. However, there are some legal restrictions that the individual software licenses enforce. For example, Linux, which is made free by GNU Public License (GPL), requires that any changes to Linux be made public. Apache, on the other hand, does not require that changes made to Apache be made public by anyone.

In short, think of Apache as free, copyrighted software published by the Apache Group. It is neither in the public domain nor is it shareware. Also note that Apache is not covered by GPL. The Apache Software License document is listed in Listing 1-1 for your convenience.

Listing 1-1: **Apache Software License**

```
/* ========================================================================
 * The Apache Software License, Version 1.1
 *
 * Copyright (c) 2000-2001 The Apache Software Foundation.  All rights
 * reserved.
 *
 * Redistribution and use in source and binary forms, with or without
 * modification, are permitted provided that the following conditions
 * are met:
 *
 * 1. Redistributions of source code must retain the above copyright
 *    notice, this list of conditions and the following disclaimer.
 *
 * 2. Redistributions in binary form must reproduce the above copyright
 *    notice, this list of conditions and the following disclaimer in
 *    the documentation and/or other materials provided with the
 *    distribution.
 *
 * 3. The end-user documentation included with the redistribution,
 *    if any, must include the following acknowledgment:
 *       "This product includes software developed by the
 *        Apache Software Foundation (http://www.apache.org/)."
 *    Alternately, this acknowledgment may appear in the software itself,
 *    if and wherever such third-party acknowledgments normally appear.
 *
 * 4. The names "Apache" and "Apache Software Foundation" must
 *    not be used to endorse or promote products derived from this
 *    software without prior written permission. For written
 *    permission, please contact apache@apache.org.
 *
 * 5. Products derived from this software may not be called "Apache",
 *    nor may "Apache" appear in their name, without prior written
 *    permission of the Apache Software Foundation.
 *
 * THIS SOFTWARE IS PROVIDED "AS IS" AND ANY EXPRESSED OR IMPLIED
 * WARRANTIES, INCLUDING, BUT NOT LIMITED TO, THE IMPLIED WARRANTIES
 * OF MERCHANTABILITY AND FITNESS FOR A PARTICULAR PURPOSE ARE
 * DISCLAIMED.  IN NO EVENT SHALL THE APACHE SOFTWARE FOUNDATION OR
 * ITS CONTRIBUTORS BE LIABLE FOR ANY DIRECT, INDIRECT, INCIDENTAL,
 * SPECIAL, EXEMPLARY, OR CONSEQUENTIAL DAMAGES (INCLUDING, BUT NOT
 * LIMITED TO, PROCUREMENT OF SUBSTITUTE GOODS OR SERVICES; LOSS OF
 * USE, DATA, OR PROFITS; OR BUSINESS INTERRUPTION) HOWEVER CAUSED AND
 * ON ANY THEORY OF LIABILITY, WHETHER IN CONTRACT, STRICT LIABILITY,
 * OR TORT (INCLUDING NEGLIGENCE OR OTHERWISE) ARISING IN ANY WAY OUT
 * OF THE USE OF THIS SOFTWARE, EVEN IF ADVISED OF THE POSSIBILITY OF
 * SUCH DAMAGE.
```

Continued

Listing 1-1 *(continued)*

```
*  ========================================================================
*
* This software consists of voluntary contributions made by many
* individuals on behalf of the Apache Software Foundation.  For more
* information on the Apache Software Foundation, please see
* <http://www.apache.org/>.
*
* Portions of this software are based upon public domain software
* originally written at the National Center for Supercomputing Applications,
* University of Illinois, Urbana-Champaign.
*/
```

✦   ✦   ✦

Obtaining and Installing Apache

Although compiling your own Apache binaries may seem like a bit of work, it's worth the effort. As you become more familiar with Apache, you will learn that it is the only Web server that provides virtually all (if not more) of the functionalities of a full-blown commercial server, while letting you look at how these functionalities are implemented in the source. I find this aspect of Apache fascinating.

For people who are not C programmers but who still need a powerful, free, Web server, however, playing around with a lot of ANSI C code may not exactly be a favorite pastime. Fortunately, there's nothing to worry about—Apache comes in both source code and in prebuilt binary packages. This chapter discusses installing Apache from source code and from prebuilt binaries.

The Official Source for Apache

Whenever you obtain free software (source code or binary files) from the Internet, make sure you're not getting it from an unknown Web or FTP site. What I mean by an unknown can be better understood by use of an example. Say you want to obtain free Java-based Web browser software developed by Sun Microsystems. You need to be able to do some sort of authenticity check, which is often difficult on the Internet; therefore, you should stick with sites that are widely used. For example, you don't want to get it from an FTP site with hostname such as `dialup-666.someforeignisp.net.ch`; you should probably look for it somewhere on the `java.sun.com` site instead, because you can't be sure that `666.someforeignisp.net.ch` has completely checked the software for any hidden dangers. You get the idea.

Lucky for us, Apache developers and supporters made sure an official place was set up for obtaining Apache software. The official Apache Web site is www.apache.org. This site contains the latest stable version of Apache, the latest release version of Apache, patches, contributed Apache modules, and so on. This is where you want to go for all your Apache needs — although you might be directed to a mirror site that is geographically near you to help cut down on bandwidth and network congestion. You can also use the Pretty Good Privacy (PGP) signatures offered on the site to verify the authenticity of the source code. If you do not know how to use PGP, check out www.pgp.net.

Note   Windows users: Please read Chapter 20 for details on your platform. This chapter is primary geared towards Unix installation and uses Linux as the sample platform. Instructions in this chapter apply to most Unix systems.

System Requirements

Apache runs on just about any platform in use today, including Linux; FreeBSD; OpenBSD; NetBSD; BSDI; Amiga OS 3.x; Mac OS X; SunOS; Solaris; IRIX; HPUX; Digital Unix; UnixWare; AIX; SCO; ReliantUNIX; DGUX; OpenStep/Mach; DYNIX/ptx; BeOS; and Windows.

Requirements for building Apache from source distribution

If you are planning on building Apache from source, which is what I highly recommend since compiling your own will give you a very lean and mean server, then you need to make sure that your system meets the requirements stated in Table 2-1.

Note   These requirements are for building Apache from the source code only. For running Apache on your system, browse the requirements in the next section.

Table 2-1
Requirements for Building Apache from Source

Resource	Required?	Requirements
Disk Space	Mandatory	Approximately 12 MB of disk space is needed to compile and install Apache from source distribution. However, if you add many modules that are not part of the standard source distribution, then your space requirements will increase.
		After it is installed, Apache only needs approximately 5 MB of disk space. However, I highly recommend that you maintain the source code on your hard disk until you finish reading this book.
ANSI C Compiler	Mandatory	ANSI C compiler is required. For most systems, the GNU C compiler (GCC) from the Free Software Foundation is highly recommended. The version you should have is 2.7.2 or above. GCC can be found at `www.gnu.org`. Most Linux systems, such as Red Hat Linux, comes with the latest stable version of the GCC compiler.
Perl 5 Interpreter	Recommended	You do not need Perl for compiling Apache, but some of the support scripts, such as `apxs`, `split-logfile`, `log_server_status`, and `dbmmanage`, which are found in the support subdirectory of your source distribution, are Perl scripts. You need Perl only if you plan to use those scripts. I highly recommend that you install Perl on your system. Perl version 5.003 or above will work fine.

Continued

	Table 2-1 (continued)	
Resource	*Required?*	*Requirements*
Dynamic Shared Object (DSO) support	Optional	Instead of compiling modules in the Apache binary itself, you can create dynamic modules called DSO that can be loaded via the `httpd.conf` file at startup. DSO modules enable you to experiment with modules and configurations more freely than compiling everything in httpd. Currently, DSO support is available for Linux, FreeBSD; OpenBSD; NetBSD; BSDI; SunOS; Solaris; IRIX; HPUX, Digital Unix, UnixWare, AIX, SCO, ReliantUNIX, DGUX, Darwin/Mac OS, OpenStep/Mach, and DYNIX/ptx.
		Note that an Apache server using a DSO module may be approximately 20 percent slower at startup and approximately 5 percent slower during run time. On top of that, DSO is not always available in all platforms. Therefore, I do not recommend DSO for a production environment. It is great, however, for experimenting with modules in a development or staging environment.

Requirements for running an Apache Web server

Before displaying the Powered by Apache logo on your Web server, you want to make sure your Web server has enough "power" to run it.

Fortunately, Apache does not require massive computing resources to run. It runs fine on a Linux system with 5 to 12MB of hard disk space and 8MB of RAM. However, just being able to run Apache is probably not what you had in mind. Most likely, you want to run Apache to serve Web pages, launch CGI processes, and take advantage of all the wonderful stuff that the Web has to offer. In that case, you want disk space and RAM size figures that reflect your load requirements. You can go about this in two ways: you can ask someone who runs a similar site with Apache and find out what type of system resources they're using; or, you can try to figure out your realistic needs after you've installed Apache on your system.

In the latter case, you can use system utilities such as ps, top, and so on to display memory usage by a particular Apache process. You can then determine the total memory needed by multiplying a single process's memory usage by the total number of Apache processes that will be running at peak hours (see the `MaxSpareServers` directive in Chapter 4). This should give you a reasonable estimate of your site's RAM requirements for Apache. If you plan to run several CGI programs on your Apache server, you have to determine memory usage for these programs as well, and take this additional need into account. One of the ways you can determine your CGI program memory requirements is run the CGI program and use the `top` utility to watch how much memory it uses and then multiply that amount of memory by the number of CGI requests you need to be able to fulfill simultaneously.

The disk requirements for Apache source or binary files shouldn't be a concern with most systems because Apache binaries take no more than 1MB of space and the source file is about 5MB. You should really pay attention, however, to the log files that Apache creates, because each log entry takes up approximately 80 bytes of disk space. If you expect to get about 100,000 hits in a day, for example, your Apache access log file may be 8,000,000 bytes. In Chapter 8, you'll learn how to rotate the log files by emptying or archiving the log file and replacing it with a new one.

Finally, consider whether you have appropriate bandwidth for running a Web server. Estimating bandwidth requirement is not an easy task but you can come up with ballpark figures by doing a bit of math. Here is what you will need:

✦ **The average Web page size for your Web site:** If you don't know this already, you can run the following command in your document root directory to find out the average size of your Web pages:

```
find path_to_doc_root  -type f -name "*.html" -ls | \
awk 'BEGIN{ FILECNT = 0; T_SIZE = 0;} \
        { T_SIZE += $7; FILECNT++} \
     END{print "Total Files:", FILECNT, \
                "Total Size:", T_SIZE, \
                "Average Size:", T_SIZE  / FILECNT;}'
```

Note

Don't forget to replace `path_to_doc_root` with the actual document root directory of your Web site. For example, for a Web site with document root `/www/mysite/htdocs`, the above script returns the following output:

```
Total Files: 332 Total Size: 5409725 Average Size: 16294.4
```

✦ **The number of average size Web pages you can serve (assuming that Apache has no bottlenecks of its own and totally ignoring the bandwidth utilized by incoming requests):** For example, say you have an ISDN (128Kbits/sec) connection to the Internet and your average file size is 16K. Because 128 kilobits per second = 128/8 kilobytes per second = 16 kilobytes per second, you can send one average size file per second. If you include the other overhead, such as bandwidth needed for the inbound request traffic, you probably cannot service a request per second. In this case, network overhead becomes a big bottleneck if you wanted to allow N (where $N > 1$)

simultaneous users to connect to your Web site. For example, if you have an ISDN connection and want to service 12 simultaneous users per second when the average file size is 16K, you need 12 × ISDN (128 Kbps) connections, which is a T-1 (1.53 Mbps).

Downloading the Software

Before you download the Apache software for the first time, you should note a few things. There's a good chance that you will find two versions of Apache available: one is an official release version, and one is a beta release version that has the latest code and features. For example, if you see an Apache version 2.0.2 and a version called 2.3b3, then the first version is an official release and the second is a beta version. A third beta such as 2.3b3 (2.3b1 and 2.3b2 came before it) is likely to be stable, but using a beta version is not recommended for a production Web server. To download the version you want, go to `www.apache.org/dist/httpd/`.

Tip To find the geographically closest Apache mirror server, run the mirror Apache finder script at `www.apache.org/dyn/closer.cgi`.

This is the distribution directory of the Apache software. Here, you will find both the release and the beta versions of the software in multiple compression packages. For example:

```
httpd_2.0.4.tar.Z
httpd_2.0.4.tar.gz
httpd_2.0.4.zip

httpd_2.3b3.tar.gz
httpd_2.3b3_win32.exe
```

These are a few examples of the various types of compression formats that are used to distribute source code. You need to choose the compression format that your system can handle (in other words, make sure you have a utility to decompress the code). Typically with Linux, all you need are the `tar`, `gnuzip`, or `gzip` utilities to decompress the files. For example, to decompress the `httpd_version.tar.gz` file (where version is whatever version you have downloaded such as 2.0.4) on a Linux system, you use the `tar xvzf httpd_version.tar.gz` command. You could also use the `gzip -d httpd_version.tar.gz ; tar xvf httpd_version.tar` command, which will decompress and extract all the files in a subdirectory while keeping the relative path for each file intact.

Self-extracting compressed files are usually created for the Windows version of Apache. Any such file can be extracted by simply running the downloaded file. For Windows-specific installation and configuration details, you should skip the rest of this chapter and read Chapter 20.

The binaries are usually kept in a different directory where each operating system has a subdirectory of its own. Note that if your operating system does not appear in the binaries directory, this does not necessarily mean the operating system is not supported. All it means is that no one in the Apache development group or contribution groups have compiled a binary file for your system yet. You are likely to find binaries for the Linux, FreeBSD, Solaris, NetBSD, OS2, AIX, Ultrix, HPUX, and IRIX systems.

Installing Apache from Source Code

Installing Apache by compiling the code from the source distribution is the preferred installation method because it allows you to configure the server to fit your needs. Any binary installation that you download will have someone else's configuration, which you may not be able to alter to suit your needs.

For example, if you download and install a binary that has CGI support, you may have to live with the CGI support even if you never run CGI programs. If the CGI module is configured as a dynamically shared module, then you can disable it very easily; however, if the support is statically built into a binary, then you'll just have to live with CGI. If you compile a lean and mean Apache server from the source distribution, however, you get the components that you need with no wasted processes or disk space.

Note   Download the source distribution from the official Apache Web site or from a designated mirror site.

Configuring Apache source

The Apache source distribution comes with a script called `configure` that allows you to configure the source tree before you compile and install the binaries. From the Apache source distribution directory, you can run this script as follows:

```
./configure --prefix=apache_installation_dir
```

The `--prefix` option tells Apache to install the binaries and other necessary configuration and support files in *apache_installation_dir*. For example:

```
./configure --prefix=/usr/local/apache
```

Here Apache source will be configured so that all the binaries and supporting files will be installed in the `/usr/local/apache` directory.

There are many options that you can use with the `configure` script. Table 2-2 shows all the configuration options available.

Table 2-2
The Options for the Configure Script

Option	Meaning
`--cache-file=`*file*	Cache test results in *file*
`--help`	Print this message
`--no-create`	Do not create output files
`--quiet or --silent`	Do not print 'checking...' messages
`--version`	Print the version of `autoconf` that created configure Directory and filenames:
`--prefix=`*prefix*	Install architecture-independent files in *prefix* `[/usr/local/apache2]`
`--exec-prefix=`*eprefix*	Install architecture-dependent files in *eprefix* `[same as prefix]`
`--bindir=`*dir*	User executables in *dir* `[EPREFIX/bin]`
`--sbindir=`*dir*	System admin executables in *dir* `[EPREFIX/sbin]`
`--libexecdir=`*dir*	Program executables in *dir* `[`*eprefix*`/libexec]`
`--datadir=`*dir*	Read-only architecture-independent data in *dir*`[`*prefix*`/share]`
`--sysconfdir=`*dir*	Read-only single-machine data in *dir* `[`*prefix*`/etc]`
`--sharedstatedir=`*dir*	Modifiable architecture-independent data in dir `[`*prefix*`/com]`
`--localstatedir=`*dir*	Modifiable single-machine data in *dir*`[`*prefix*`/var]`
`--libdir=`*dir*	Object code libraries in *dir*`[`*eprefix*`/lib]`
`--includedir=`*dir*	C header files in *dir*`[`*prefix*`/include]`
`--oldincludedir=`*dir*	C header files for non-GCC in *dir* `[/usr/include]`
`--infodir=`*dir*	Info documentation in *dir*`[`*prefix*`/info]`
`--mandir=`*dir*	man documentation in *dir*`[prefix/man]`
`--srcdir=`*dir*	Find the sources in *dir*`[configure dir or ...]`
`--program-prefix=`*prefix*	Prepend *prefix* to installed program names

Option	Meaning
`--program-suffix=suffix`	Append *suffix* to installed program names
`--program-transform-name=program`	Run sed (stream editor) program on installed program names
`--build=build`	Configure for building on *build*
`--host=host`	Configure for *host*
`--target=target`	Configure for TARGET [TARGET=HOST]
`--disable-feature`	Do not include FEATURE (same as –enable-FEATURE=no)
`--enable- feature[=arg]`	Include *feature* [arg=yes]
`--with-package[=arg]`	Use *package* [arg=yes]
`--without-package`	Do not use *package* (same as –with-package=no)
`--x-includes=dir`	X include files are in *dir*
`--x-libraries=dir`	X library files are in *dir*
`--with-optim=flag`	Obsolete (use OPTIM environment variable)
`--with-port=port`	Port on which to listen (default is 80)
`--enable-debug`	Turn on debugging and compile-time warnings
`--enable-maintainer-mode`	Turn on debugging and compile-time warnings
`--enable-layout=layout`	Enable a directory layout
`--enable-modules=module-list`	Enable one or more named modules
`--enable-mods-shared=module-list`	Enable one or more named modules as shared modules
`--disable-access`	Disable host-based access control
`--disable-auth`	Disable user-based access control
`--enable-auth-anon`	Enable anonymous user access
`--enable-auth-dbm`	Enable DBM-based access databases
`--enable-auth-db`	Enable DB-based access databases
`--enable-auth-digest`	Enable RFC2617 Digest authentication
`--enable-file-cache`	Enable file cache

Continued

Table 2-2 (continued)	
Option	**Meaning**
--enable-dav-fs	Enable DAV provider for the filesystem
--enable-dav	Enable WebDAV protocol handling
--enable-echo	Enable ECHO server
--enable-charset-lite	Enable character set translation
--enable-cache	Enable dynamic file caching
--enable-disk-cache	Enable disk caching module
--enable-ext-filter	Enable external filter module
--enable-case-filter	Enable example uppercase conversion filter
--enable-generic-hook-export	Enable example of hook exporter
--enable-generic-hook-import	Enable example of hook importer
--enable-optional-fn-import	Enable example of optional function importer
--enable-optional-fn-export	Enable example of optional function exporter
--disable-include	Disable Server-Side Includes
--disable-http	Disable HTTP protocol handling
--disable-mime	Disable mapping of file-extension to MIME
--disable-log-config	Disable logging configuration
--enable-vhost-alias	Enable mass -hosting module
--disable-negotiation	Disable content negotiation
--disable-dir	Disable directory request handling
--disable-imap	Disable internal imagemaps
--disable-actions	Disable action triggering on requests
--enable-speling	Enable correct common URL misspellings
--disable-userdir	Disable mapping of user requests
--disable-alias	Disable translation of requests
--enable-rewrite	Enable URL rewriting rules
--disable-so	Disable DSO capability
--enable-so	Enable DSO capability
--disable-env	Clearing/setting of ENV vars
--enable-mime-magic	Automatically determine MIME type
--enable-cern-meta	Enable CERN-type meta files
--enable-expires	Enable Expires header control

Option	Meaning
`--enable-headers`	Enable HTTP header control
`--enable-usertrack`	Enable user-session tracking
`--enable-unique-id`	Enable per-request unique IDs
`--disable-setenvif`	Disable base ENV vars on headers
`--enable-tls`	Enable TLS/SSL support
`--with-ssl`	Use a specific SSL library installation
`--with-mpm=MPM`	Choose the process model for Apache to use: MPM={beos threaded prefork spmt_os2 perchild}
`--disable-status`	Process/thread monitoring
`--disable-autoindex`	Disable Directory listing
`--disable-asis`	Disable As-is filetypes
`--enable-info`	Enable Server information
`--enable-suexec`	Set UID and GID for spawned processes
`--disable-cgid`	Disable CGI daemon support
`--enable-cgid`	Enable CGI daemon support
`--disable-cgi`	Disable CGI scripts support
`--enable-cgid`	Enable CGI scripts support
`--enable-shared[=pkgs]`	Build shared libraries [default=no]
`--enable-static[=pkgs]`	Build static libraries [default=yes]
`--enable-fast-install[=pkgs]`	Optimize for fast installation [default=yes]
`--with-gnu-ld`	Assume the C compiler uses GNU ID [default=no]
`--disable-libtool-lock`	Avoid locking (might break parallel builds)
`--with-program-name`	Alternate executable name
`--with-suexec-caller`	User allowed to call SuExec
`--with-suexec-userdir`	User subdirectory
`--with-suexec-docroot`	SuExec root directory
`--with-suexec-uidmin`	Minimal allowed UID
`--with-suexec-gidmin`	Minimal allowed GID
`--with-suexec-logfile`	Set the logfile
`--with-suexec-safepath`	Set the safepath
`--with-suexec-umask`	Amask for process

Most of these options are not required for most sites. Typically, all you need is to specify the `--prefix` option and any options to enable or disable one or more modules. For example, say you do not want to install the CGI module on your system. You can run the `configure` script using the `--disable-cgi` `--disable-cgid` options to disable CGI support. Similarly, to disable the Server-Side Include (SSI) support you can use the `--disable-include` option.

After you have configured Apache using the `configure` script, you can use the `config.status` script instead of `configure` for any subsequent configuration needs. By using the `config.status` script, you can reuse your previous configuration and add or subtract new options. For example, say you configured Apache with the following command line:

```
./configure --prefix=/usr/local/apache --disable-cgi --disable-cgid
```

and a few days later decided to disable SSI. You can now use:

```
./config.status --disable-include
```

When you recompile Apache, the CGI modules will still not be included, because `./config.status` stores the options that you specified using the `configure` script earlier.

If you wish to start fresh, use `configure` every time.

Advanced configuration options for high-load Web sites

If you run Apache on a extremely busy server where hundreds of requests per second is a requirement, you might have to change the default hard limits set in the MPM module of your choice. See chapter 1 for details on various times of MPM modules. The hard limits that you want to consider changing are the default `HARD_SERVER_LIMIT` and `HARD_THREAD_LIMIT`. The `HARD_SERVER_LIMIT` sets the maximum number of child servers Apache can spawn. The `HARD_THREAD_LIMIT` sets the total number of threads Apache can create within all of its children. Table 2-3 shows the default limits and where to find them.

Note   The `%APACHE_SOURCE%` tag mentioned in the table refers to the Apache source distribution directory. For example, if you have extracted Apache source distribution in the `/usr/local/src/httpd_version` directory, then replace `%APACHE_SOURCE%` with `/usr/local/src/httpd_version` to locate the appropriate C header (include) file.

MPM	Limit Options	Default Value	Notes
threaded	HARD_SERVER_LIMIT for threaded mode	8	C header (include) filename: %APACHE_SOURCE%/server/mpm/ threaded/mpm_default.h #ifdef NO_THREADS #define HARD_SERVER_LIMIT 256 #endif #ifndef HARD_SERVER_LIMIT #define HARD_SERVER_LIMIT 8 #endif
threaded	HARD_THREAD_LIMIT for threaded mode	64	C header (include) filename: %APACHE_SOURCE%/server/mpm/ threaded/mpm_default.h
prefork	HARD_SERVER_LIMIT	256	C header (include) filename: %APACHE_SOURCE%/server/mpm/ prefork/mpm_default.h #ifndef HARD_SERVER_LIMIT #define HARD_SERVER_LIMIT 256 #endif
perchild	HARD_SERVER_LIMIT	8	C header (include) filename: %APACHE_SOURCE%/server/mpm/ perchild/mpm_default.h #ifndef HARD_SERVER_LIMIT #define HARD_SERVER_LIMIT 8 #endif
perchild	HARD_THREAD_LIMIT	64	C header (include) filename: %APACHE_SOURCE%/server/mpm/ perchild/mpm_default.h #ifndef HARD_SERVER_LIMIT #define HARD_SERVER_LIMIT 8 #endif

Table 2-3
Hard Limits for Various Apache MPM Modules

Continued

Table 2-3 *(continued)*			
MPM	Limit Options	Default Value	Notes
winnt	HARD_SERVER_LIMIT	1	C header (include) filename: `%APACHE_SOURCE%/server/mpm/winnt/mpm_default.h` `#define HARD_SERVER_LIMIT 1` **This setting should not be changed. Change the hard thread count instead.**

winnt	HARD_THREAD_LIMIT	4096	C header (include) filename: `APACHE_SOURCE/server/mpm/winnt/mpm_default.h`
			
			`#ifndef HARD_THREAD_LIMIT`
			
			`#define HARD_THREAD_LIMIT 4096`
			
			`#endif`

Caution

When changing `HARD_SERVER_LIMIT` or `HARD_THREAD_LIMIT` to higher than the default make sure you have the appropriate system resources. For example, changing the `HARD_SERVER_LIMIT` to 1024 for the `prefork` MPM will allow you to create 1024 Apache child processes by instructing Apache to create that many children by using the directives `StartServers`, `MinSpareServers`, and `MaxSpareServers`.

However, if your system does not have enough memory, then changing the hard limit to a higher value will not do much good. Remember that the higher the limits, the more resources you need. You also need to increase the number of file descriptors your system allows for a single user. On Linux and Unix systems you should find out what (and possibly set) the file descriptor limits are by using the `ulimit` command.

Also note that the `MaxClients` directive sets the limit on the number of child processes that will be created to serve requests. When the server is built without threading, no more than this number of clients can be served simultaneously. To configure more than 256 clients, you must edit the `HARD_SERVER_LIMIT` entry in `mpm_default.h` and recompile.

Compiling and installing Apache

After you have configured the Apache source using the `configure` script you need to follow these steps to compile and install Apache:

1. Run the `make` command to compile the source.

2. Run the `make install` command to install the httpd and support files in the directory you specified using the `--prefix` option.

3. Change to the installation directory and browse the directory. You should see subdirectories such `bin` `cgi-bin`, `conf`, `htdocs`, `icons`, `include`, `lib`, and `logs`. For example, if you use `--prefix=/usr/local/apache` with the configure script during source tree configuration, `make install` will create the following directory structure:

```
/usr/local/apache
|
+---include
+---lib
+---bin
+---conf
+---htdocs
|      |
|      +--manual
|           |
|           +--developer
|           +--howto
|           +--images
|           +--misc
|           +--mod
|           +--platform
|           +--programs
|           +--search
|           +--vhosts
|
+---icons
|      |
|      +---small
|
+---logs
+---cgi-bin
```

The following list gives a brief description of each of the directories in the Apache directory structure:

✦ `include` — Contains all the C header (include) files that are only needed if you develop Web applications that integrate with Apache or want to use use third-party software with Apache, which might require the header files. On a production server you can remove this directory.

✦ `lib` – Houses the Apache Portable Run-Time (APR) library files, the files that are required for running Apache, and other support utilities such as ab.

✦ `bin` — Contains the programs shown in Table 2-4.

✦ `conf` — Houses the configuration files for Apache. It contains the files listed in Table 2-5.

✦ htdocs — This is the default document root directory for the main Apache server. The httpd.conf file sets the DocumentRoot directive to this directory. You will learn how to set your own document root directory in Chapter 3. By default the htdocs directory also has the entire Apache manual installed in a subdirectory.

✦ icons — Used to store various Apache icons that are needed for displaying dynamically the build directory listing.

✦ logs — Used to store the Apache server logs, the CGI daemon socket (cgisock), and the PID file (httpd.pid). You will learn to change the log path in Chapter 3.

✦ cgi-bin — The default CGI script directory, which is set by using the ScriptAlias directive in httpd.conf. By default, Apache comes with two simple CGI scripts — printenv and test-cgi. Each of these scripts prints out CGI environment variables when requested via http://server_name/cgi-bin/script_name URL. These scripts are good for testing whether CGI configuration is working for you.

Caution   It is highly recommend that you remove the printenv and test-cgi scripts after you have your CGI configuration working. It is not a good idea to have a script that displays your system environment information to anyone in the world. The less you tell the world about how your system works or about what is available on your system, the more secure your system remains.

Table 2-4 provides a listing of the programs that you can find in the bin directory.

Table 2-4 Apache Programs in the bin Directory	
Apache Programs	*Purpose*
ab	This is the ApacheBench program. It enables you to benchmark Apache server. See Chapter 22 for more information on this program.
apachectl	This is a handy script that enables you to start, restart, and stop Apache server. See Chapter 3 for more information on this script.
apxs	This is a tool for building and installing extension modules for Apache. It allows you to build DSO modules that can be used in Apache by using the mod_so module. For more information on this program, see http://your_server_name/manual/programs/apxs.htm.
htdigest	This program creates and updates user authentication information when message digest (MD5) authentication is being used. For more information on this program, see http://your_server_name/manual/programs/htdigest.html.

Apache Programs	Purpose
htpasswd	This program is used to create and update user authentication information used in basic HTTP authentication. See Chapter 7 for details.
httpd	This is the Apache Web server program.
logresolve	This program converts (resolves) IP addresses from a log file to host names. See Chapter 8 for details.
rotatelogs	This program rotates Apache logs files when they reach a certain size. See Chapter 8 for details.

Table 2-5 lists the contents of the config directory.

Table 2-5
Apache config Directory Contents

Configuration File	Purpose
httpd.conf	This is the Apache configuration file.
httpd-std.conf	This is the sample copy of the httpd.conf file, which is not required by Apache. For new Apache users, this file can act as a means for recovering the default httpd.conf.
highperformance.conf	This is a sample configuration file that shows some pointers for configuring Apache for high performance.
highperformance-std.conf	This is a sample copy of the highperformance.conf file, which is not required by Apache.
magic	This file stores the magic data for mod_mime_magic Apache module.
mime.types	This file is used to decide which MIME-type headers are sent to the Web client for a given file.
	For more information about MIME types, please read RFC 2045, 2046, 2047, 2048, and 2077. The Internet media-type registry is at ftp://ftp.iana.org/in-notes/iana/assignments/media-types.

Installing Apache from RPM Binary Packages

You can download the Apache binaries appropriate for your system from `www.apache.org/dist/httpd/binaries` directory. Download the latest version and extract the compressed file into a temporary directory. To determine how to install the binaries in your specific platform, you must read the `INSTALL.bindist` file, which is included in each binary distribution.

If you wish to install the Apache RPM (Red Hat Package Management) package for your Linux system, then do the following:

1. Go to the `http://rpmfind.net` site and search for the string `Apache` to locate the Apache RPM packages. From the search result locate the latest version of the binary Apache RPM distribution and download it.

2. As root, run `rpm -ivh apache_rpm_package.rpm` command to install the package. For example, to install the `apache-2.0.4-i386.rpm` for a Red Hat Linux (Intel) system, run the `rpm -ivh apache-2.0.4-i386.rpm` command.

Keeping Up with Apache Development

Do you ever wonder whether, by the time you get around to installing the downloaded Apache source or binaries, a new version is out or perhaps a security patch is available? Software changes very quickly these days, and there's always one update after another—which is good, but not always easy to keep up with if you have a real job to do. There are two Apache resources that you should take advantage of immediately.

✦ **ApacheToday**—This is the best Apache news site in the world. You can get all the Apache news you want at `www.apachetoday.com`. By using its Your Apache Today feature, you can filter news contents and get just want interests you the most. You can also take advantage of triggers that pushes breaking news that you do not want to miss.

✦ **ApacheWeek**—Just subscribe (for free) to the great Apache resource called Apache Week, and all the Apache news will be e-mailed directly to you. The Apache Week Web site is at `www.apacheweek.com`. This is a great information resource for Apache administrators who want to be on top of Apache development news. You can also read many helpful articles on how to get the best out of your server. I highly recommend checking out this Web site.

✦   ✦   ✦

Getting Apache Up and Running

In This Chapter

Checking out the basics of Apache server configuration

Starting, stopping, and restarting Apache server

Testing a running Apache server

In the previous chapter, you learn how to compile and install the Apache Web server on your Unix system. Now you are ready to get it up and running! This chapter covers the basic configuration details to get your Apache server up and running.

Configuring Apache

By default, Apache reads a single configuration file called `httpd.conf`. Every Apache source distribution comes with a set of sample configuration files. In the standard Apache source distribution, you will find a directory called `conf`, which contains sample configuration files with the `-dist` extension.

The very first step you need to take before you modify this file is to create a backup copy of the original.

The `httpd.conf` file has two types of information: comments and server directives. Lines starting with a leading # character are treated as a comment line; these comments have no purpose for the server software, but they serve as a form of documentation for the server administrator. You can add as many comments as you want; the server simply ignores all comments when it parses the file.

Except for the comments and blank lines, the server treats all other lines as either complete or partial directives. A *directive* is like a command for the server. It tells the server to do a certain task in a particular fashion. While editing the `httpd.conf` file, you need to make certain decisions regarding how you want the server to behave. In the following sections, you learn what these directives mean and how you can use them to customize your server.

Cross-Reference You can find an in-depth explanation of all the core directives in Chapter 4.

Listing 3-1 shows the default `httpd.conf` created in the `conf` directory of your Apache installation. Most of the comments have been removed and code has been edited slightly for brevity.

Listing 3-1: **Default httpd.conf created from httpd.conf-dist**

```
### Section 1: Global Environment
ServerRoot "/usr/local/apache"

PidFile logs/httpd.pid

<IfModule !perchild.c>
    ScoreBoardFile logs/apache_runtime_status
</IfModule>

Timeout 300
KeepAlive On
MaxKeepAliveRequests 100
KeepAliveTimeout 15

<IfModule prefork.c>
    StartServers         5
    MinSpareServers      5
    MaxSpareServers      10
    MaxClients           20
    MaxRequestsPerChild  0
</IfModule>

<IfModule threaded.c>
    StartServers         3
    MaxClients           8
    MinSpareThreads      5
    MaxSpareThreads      10
    ThreadsPerChild      25
    MaxRequestsPerChild  0
</IfModule>

<IfModule perchild.c>
    NumServers           5
    StartThreads         5
    MinSpareThreads      5
    MaxSpareThreads      10
    MaxThreadsPerChild   20
    MaxRequestsPerChild  0
</IfModule>


### Section 2: 'Main' server configuration
Port 80
User nobody
Group #-1
```

```
ServerAdmin you@your.address

# Added
ServerName www.domain.com

DocumentRoot "/usr/local/apache/htdocs"

<Directory />
    Options FollowSymLinks
    AllowOverride None
</Directory>

<Directory "/usr/local/apache/htdocs">
    Options Indexes FollowSymLinks MultiViews
    AllowOverride None
    Order allow,deny
    Allow from all
</Directory>

UserDir public_html
DirectoryIndex index.html
AccessFileName .htaccess

<Files ~ "^\.ht">
    Order allow,deny
    Deny from all
</Files>

UseCanonicalName On
TypesConfig conf/mime.types
DefaultType text/plain

<IfModule mod_mime_magic.c>
    MIMEMagicFile conf/magic
</IfModule>

HostnameLookups Off
ErrorLog logs/error_log
LogLevel warn
LogFormat "%h %l %u %t \"%r\" %>s %b \"%{Referer}i\" \"%{User-
Agent}i\"" combined
LogFormat "%h %l %u %t \"%r\" %>s %b" common
LogFormat "%{Referer}i -> %U" referer
LogFormat "%{User-agent}i" agent
CustomLog logs/access_log common
ServerSignature On
Alias /icons/ "/usr/local/apache/icons/"

<Directory "/usr/local/apache/icons">
    Options Indexes MultiViews
    AllowOverride None
```

Continued

Listing 3-1 *(continued)*

```
        Order allow,deny
        Allow from all
</Directory>

ScriptAlias /cgi-bin/ "/usr/local/apache/cgi-bin/"

<Directory "/usr/local/apache/cgi-bin">
        AllowOverride None
        Options None
        Order allow,deny
        Allow from all
</Directory>

IndexOptions FancyIndexing VersionSort
AddIconByEncoding (CMP,/icons/compressed.gif) x-compress x-gzip

AddIconByType (TXT,/icons/text.gif) text/*
# Many more AddIconByType directives follow in the
# default httpd.conf but removed here to keep
# this simple.

AddIcon /icons/binary.gif .bin .exe
# Many more AddIcon directives follow in the
# default httpd.conf but removed here to keep
# this simple.

DefaultIcon /icons/unknown.gif
ReadmeName README
HeaderName HEADER
IndexIgnore .??* *~ *# HEADER* README* RCS CVS *,v *,t
AddEncoding x-compress Z
AddEncoding x-gzip gz tgz

AddLanguage da .dk
AddLanguage nl .nl
AddLanguage en .en
# Many more AddLanguage directives follow in the
# default httpd.conf but removed here to keep
# this simple.

LanguagePriority en da nl et fr de el it ja kr no pl pt pt-br
ltz ca es sv tw

AddDefaultCharset        ISO-8859-1
AddCharset ISO-8859-1    .iso8859-1  .latin1
AddCharset ISO-8859-2    .iso8859-2  .latin2 .cen
# Many more AddCharset directives follow in the
# default httpd.conf but removed here to keep
```

```
# this simple.

AddType application/x-tar .tgz
BrowserMatch "Mozilla/2" nokeepalive
BrowserMatch "MSIE 4\.0b2;" nokeepalive downgrade-1.0 force-
response-1.0
BrowserMatch "RealPlayer 4\.0" force-response-1.0
BrowserMatch "Java/1\.0" force-response-1.0
BrowserMatch "JDK/1\.0" force-response-1.0

### Section 3: Virtual Hosts
# No virtual server defined in this chapter.
```

Cross-Reference Because the goal of this chapter is to get your server up and running with minimal configuration, the chapter does not provide in-depth details of the configuration options here. You can learn all the details in the Chapter 4.

The `httpd.conf` file does not actually have any section delimiter. But it will help you understand the configuration file better if you think of it as shown in Figure 3-1.

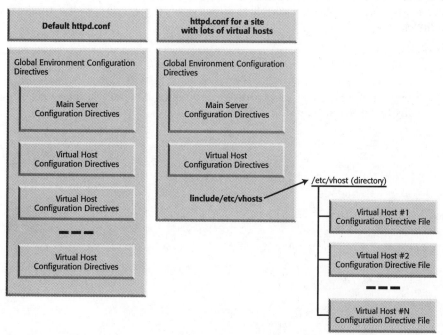

Figure 3-1: The `httpd.conf` configuration segments

The left side of the figure shows how the default httpd.conf can be visualized in your mind. There are configuration directives that create the global server environment that applies to everything; there are configuration options that apply to the main (default) Web site Apache servers, and there are configuration directives that only apply to optional virtual hosts. Because Apache uses a single configuration file, a site with lots of virtual hosts will have a very large file and management of the configuration becomes very cumbersome. This is why I also show another way to break down the httpd.conf file. But I discuss this approach (evident in the right side of the above figure) in Chapter 6. As I said before, here we are focused on getting up and running.

Note   Whenever I refer to %directive%, I am referring to the value of the directive set in the configuration file. For example, if a directive called ServerAdmin is set to kabir@domain.com, then a reference to %ServerAdmin% means "kabir@domain.com". So, if I tell you to change %ServerAdmin%, I am asking you to change the e-mail address in question.

Configuring the global environment for Apache

The directives discussed in this section create the global environment for the Apache Server. The directives are discussed in the same order in which they appear in the httpd.conf file. The very first directive is ServerRoot, which appears as follows:

```
ServerRoot "/usr/local/apache"
```

This directive specifies the top-level directory of the Web server. The specified directory is not where you keep your Web contents. It is really a directory, which normally has these subdirectories:

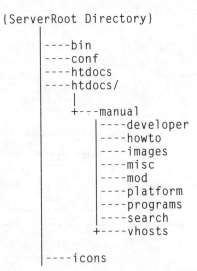

```
{ServerRoot Directory}
        |
        |----bin
        |----conf
        |----htdocs
        |----htdocs/
        |       |
        |       +---manual
        |           |----developer
        |           |----howto
        |           |----images
        |           |----misc
        |           |----mod
        |           |----platform
        |           |----programs
        |           |----search
        |           +----vhosts
        |
        |----icons
```

```
        |
        |    +---small
        |
        |----logs
        |----cgi-bin
        +----include
```

/usr/local/apache is the parent directory for all server-related files. The default value for ServerRoot is set to whatever you choose for --prefix option during source configuration using the configure script. By default, the make install command executed during server installation copies all the server binaries in %ServerRoot%/bin, server configuration files in %ServerRoot%/conf, and so on.

Note   You should only change the value of this directive if you have manually moved the entire directory from the place on installation to another location. For example, if you simply run cp -r /usr/local/apache /home/apache and want to configure the Apache server to work from the new location, you will change this directive to ServerRoot /home/apache. Note that in such a case you will also have to change other direct references to /usr/local/apache to /home/apache.

Also note that whenever you see a relative directory name in the configuration file, Apache will prefix %ServerRoot% to the path to construct the actual path. You will see an example of this in the directive in the following section.

PidFile

The PidFile directive sets the PID (process ID) file path. By default, it is set to logs/httpd.pid, which translates to %ServerRoot%/logs/httpd.pid (that is, /usr/local/apache/logs/httpd.pid). Whenever you want to find the PID of the main Apache process that runs as root and spawns child processes, you can run the cat %ServerRoot/logs/httpd.pid command. Don't forget to replace %ServerRoot% with an appropriate value.

Caution   If you change the %PidFile% value to point a different location, make sure the directory in which the httpd.pid file resides is not writable by anyone but the root user for security reasons

ScoreBoardFile

ScoreBoardFile is encapsulated within an if condition by using the <IfModule . . .> container as shown below:

```
<IfModule !perchild.c>
    ScoreBoardFile logs/apache_runtime_status
</IfModule>
```

This tells Apache to set the ScoreBoardFile to %ServerRoot%/logs/apache_runtime_status file only if you have chosen a multiprocessing module (MPM) other than perchild. Because the default MPM for most operating systems, including Linux, is threaded instead of `perchild`, the `if` condition will be true and Apache will set the `ScoreBoardFile` directive. This directive is used to point to a file, which is used to exchange run-time status information between Apache processes. If you have a RAM disk, you might consider putting this file in the RAM disk to increase performance a bit. In most cases, you should leave this directive alone.

Timeout, KeepAlive, MaxKeepAliveRequests, and KeepAliveTimeout

`Timeout` sets the server timeout in seconds. The default should be left alone. The next three directives `KeepAlive`, `MaxKeepAliveRequests`, and `KeepAliveTimeout` are used to control the keep-alive behavior of the server. You do not need to change them.

IfModule containers

Apache will use one of the next three `<IfModule . . .>` containers based on which MPM you chose. For example, if you configured Apache using the default MPM mode (threaded) on a Linux system, then the following `<IfModule . . .>` container will be used:

```
<IfModule threaded.c>
    StartServers         3
    MaxClients           8
    MinSpareThreads      5
    MaxSpareThreads      10
    ThreadsPerChild      25
    MaxRequestsPerChild  0
</IfModule>
```

On the other hand, if you chose `--with-mpm=prefork` during source configuration by using the configure script, then the following `<IfModule . . .>` container will be used:

```
<IfModule prefork.c>
StartServers         5
MinSpareServers      5
MaxSpareServers      10
MaxClients           20
MaxRequestsPerChild  0
</IfModule>
```

Similarly, the `--with-mpm=perchild` option forces Apache to use the last `<IfModule . . .>` container.

Directives for threaded (default) MPM behavior

If you followed my advice in the previous chapter, you did not change the default MPM behavior during source compilation and used the threaded behavior, so the directives that you need to consider are discussed below.

Note   If you did change the default MPM, you can find detailed information on the directives needed by your chosen MPM in Chapter 4.

StartServers

`StartServers` tells Apache to start three child servers as it starts. You can start more servers if you want, but Apache is pretty good at increasing number of child processes as needed based on load. So, changing this directive is not required.

MaxClients

In the default threaded MPM mode, the total number of simultaneous requests that Apache can process is `%MaxClients%` x `%ThreadsPerChild%`. So, because the default for MaxClients is 8 and the default for ThreadsPerChild is 25, the default maximum for simultaneous requests is 200 (that is, 8 times 5). If you use the pre-forking MPM mode, the maximum requests is limited to `%MaxClients%`. The default maximum of 200 simultaneous requests should work well for most sites, so leave the defaults.

MinSpareThreads

The `MinSpareThreads` directive specifies the minimum number of idle threads. These spare threads are used to service requests and new spare threads are created to maintain the minimum spare thread pool size. You can leave the default settings alone.

MaxSpareThreads

The `MaxSpareThreads` directive specifies the maximum number of idle threads; leave the default as is. In the default threaded mode, Apache kills child processes to control minimum and maximum thread count.

ThreadsPerChild

This directive defines how many threads are created per child process.

Note   If you are running Apache on a Windoiws system, set `ThreadsPerChild` to the maximum number of simultaneous requests that you want to handle, because on this platform there is only one child process, and it owns all the threads.

MaxRequestPerChild

The final directive for the global environment is `MaxRequestPerChild`, which sets the number of requests a child process can serve before getting killed. The default value of zero makes the child process serve requests forever. I do not like to the default value because it enables Apache processes to slowly consume large amounts of memory when a faulty `mod_perl` script, or even a faulty third-party Apache module, leaks memory. Thus, I prefer to set this to 30.

Tip   If you do not plan on running any third-party Apache modules or `mod_perl` scripts, you can keep the defaults or else set it to a reasonable number. A setting of 30 ensures that the child process is killed after processing 30 requests. Of course, a new child process is created as needed.

Configuring the main server

The main server configuration applies to the default Web site Apache serves. This is the site that will come up when you run Apache and use the server's IP address or host name on a Web browser.

Port

The very first directive in this section is the Port directive, which sets the TCP port that Apache listens to for connections. The default value of 80 is the standard HTTP port. If you change this to another number, such as 8080, you can only access the server using a URL such as http://hostname:8080/. You must specify the port number in the URL if the server runs on a nonstandard port.

There are many reasons for running Apache on nonstandard ports, but the only good one I can think of is that you do not have permission to run Apache on the standard HTTP port. As a nonroot user you can only run Apache on ports higher than 1024.

After you have decided to run Apache by using a port, you need to tell Apache what its user and group names are.

User and Group directives

The User and Group directives tell Apache the user (UID) and group (GID) names to use. These two directives are very important for security reasons. When the primary Web server process launches a child server process to fulfill a request, it changes the child's UID and GID according to the values set for these directives. Refer to Figure 3-1 to see how the primary Web server process that listens for the connection runs as a root user process, and how the child processes run as different user/group processes. If the child processes are run as root user processes, a potential security hole will be opened for attack by hackers. Enabling the capability to interact with a root user process maximizes a potential breach of security in the system; hence, this is not recommended. Rather, I highly recommend that you choose to run the child server processes as a very low-privileged user belonging to a very low-privileged group. In most Unix systems, the user named nobody (usually UID = -1) and the group named nogroup (usually GID = -1) are low-privileged. You should consult your /etc/group and /etc/passwd files to determine these settings.

If you plan to run the primary Web server as a nonroot (regular) user, it will not be able to change the UID and GID of child processes, because only root user processes can change the UID or GID of other processes. Therefore, if you run your primary server as the user named ironsheik, then all child processes will have the same privileges as ironsheik. Similarly, whatever group ID you have will also be the group ID for the child processes.

Note   If you plan on using the numeric format for user and/or group ID, you need to insert a # symbol before the numeric value, which can be found in /etc/passwd and in /etc/group files.

ServerAdmin

`ServerAdmin` defines the e-mail address that is shown when the server generates an error page. Set this to your e-mail address.ServerName.

Now you need to set the host name for the Server using the `ServerName` directive. This directive is commented out by default because Apache install cannot guess what host name to use for your system. So if the host name is called `www.domain.com`, set `ServerName` directive accordingly.

> **Note** Be sure, however, that the host name that you enter here has proper domain name server records that point it to your server machine.

DocumentRoot

Like all other Web servers, Apache needs to know the path of the top-level directory where Web pages will be kept. This directory is typically called the document root directory. Apache provides a directive called `DocumentRoot`, which can be used to specify the path of the top-level Web directory.

This directive instructs the server to treat the supplied directory as the root directory for all documents. This is a very important decision for you to make. For example, if the directive is set as:

```
DocumentRoot /
```

then every file on the system becomes accessible by the Web server. Of course, you can protect files by providing proper file permission settings, but setting the document root to the physical root directory of your system is definitely a major security risk. Instead, you should point the document root to a specific subdirectory of your file system. If you have used the `--prefix=/usr/local/apache` option in configuring the Apache source, this directive will be set as:

```
DocumentRoot "/usr/local/apache/htdocs"
```

A potentially better option, however, is to create a Web directory structure for your organization. Figure 3-2 shows the Web directory structure I prefer for a multiuser, multidomain system.

As the figure shows, I chose to create a partition called /www, and under it there are subdirectories for each Web site hosted by my system. /www/www.mycompany.com/ has three subdirectories: `public`, `stage`, and `development`. Each of these subdirectories has two subdirectories: `htdocs` and `cgi-bin`. The `htdocs` subdirectory is the document root directory, and the `cgi-bin` subdirectory is used for CGI scripts. So, the `DocumentRoot` setting for the `www.mycompany.com` Web site is:

```
DocumentRoot "/www/www.mycompany.com/public/htdocs"
```

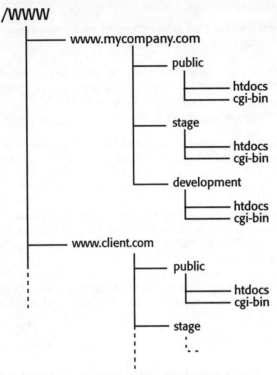

Figure 3-2: My preferred Web directory structure.

The advantage of this directory structure is that it keeps all Web documents and applications under one partition (/www). This enables easy backups, and the partition can be mounted on different systems via the Network File System (NFS) in case another machine in the network is given the task to provide Web services.

Cross-Reference   I discuss well-designed Web directory structures in more depth in Chapter 11.

Note that just because your document root points to a particular directory, this does not mean the Web server cannot access directories outside your document tree. You can easily enable it to do so by using symbolic links (with proper file permission) or by using aliases (aliases are discussed in the next chapter).

Caution   From an organization and security perspective, I don't recommend using a lot of symbolic links or aliases to access files and directories outside your document tree. Nonetheless, it is sometimes necessary to keep a certain type of information outside the document tree, even if you need to keep the contents of such a directory accessible to the server on a regular basis. If you have to add symbolic links to other directory locations outside the document tree, make sure that when you back up your files, your backup program can back up symbolic links properly.

Directory container directives

The next set of directives are enclosed in a ⟨Directory . . .⟩ container as shown here:

```
<Directory />
    Options FollowSymLinks
    AllowOverride None
</Directory>
```

The scope of the enclosed directives is limited to the named directory (with any subdirectories); however, you may only use directives that are allowed in a directory context (you learn about these directives in detail in the next chapter).

Here the Options and the AllowOverride directives apply to %DocumentRoot% that is root (/) or the top-level directory of the main Web site. Because directives enclosed within a directory container apply to all the subdirectories below the named directory, the directives apply to all directories within %DocumentRoot%.

The Options directive is set to FollowSymLinks, which tells Apache to allow itself to traverse any symbolic within %DocumentRoot%. Because the Options directive is only set to follow symbolic links, no other options are available to any of the directories within %DocumentRoot%. Effectively, the Options directive is:

```
Options FollowSymLinks  -ExecCGI -Includes -Indexes -MultiViews
```

The other options are explained in the Options directive section in the next chapter. However, be assured that the big idea here is to create a very closed server. Because only symbolic link traversal is allowed, you must explicitly enable other options as needed on a per directory basis. This is very good thing from a security prospective. The next directory container opens up the %DocumentRoot% directory as shown here:

```
<Directory "/usr/local/apache/htdocs">
    Options Indexes FollowSymLinks MultiViews
    AllowOverride None
    Order allow,deny
    Allow from all
</Directory>
```

If your %DocumentRoot% is different, change the named directory path. Here is what the above configuration means to Apache:

✦ The named directory and its subdirectories can be indexed. If there is an index file, it will be displayed; in the absence of an index file, the server will create a dynamic index for the directory. The Options directive specifies this.

✦ The named directory and all subdirectories under it can have symbolic links that the server can follow (that is, use as a path) to access information. The Options directive also specifies this.

✦ The named directory and all subdirectories under it can be part of content negotiations. The MultiViews option for the Options directive sets this. I am not a fan of this option but do not so dislike it as to remove it. For example, when the given Options directive is enabled within the %DocumentRoot% directory as shown above, a request for http://www.domain.com/ratecard.html can answered by a file called ratecard.html.bak, or ratecard.bak, ratecard.old, and the like if ratecard.html is missing. This may or may not be desirable.

✦ No options specified here can be overridden by a local access control file (specified by the AccessFileName directive in httpd.conf; the default is .htaccess). This is specified using the AllowOverride directive.

✦ The Allow directives are evaluated before the Deny directives. Access is denied by default. Any client that does not match an Allow directive or that does match a Deny directive is denied access to the server.

✦ Access is permitted for all.

The default setting should be sufficient.

Caution   If your server is going to be on the Internet, you may want to remove the FollowSymLinks option from the Options directive line. Leaving this option creates a potential security risk. For example, if a directory in your Web site does not have an index page, the server displays an automated index that shows any symbolic links you may have in that directory. This could cause sensitive information to be displayed, or may even allow anyone to run an executable that resides in a carelessly linked directory.

UserDir

The UserDir directive tells Apache to consider %UserDir% as document root (~username/%UserDir%) of each user Web site. This only makes sense if you have multiple users on the system and want to allow each user to have his or her own Web directory. The default setting is:

```
UserDir public_html
```

which means that if you set up your Web server's name to be www.yourcompany.com, and you have two users (joe and jenny), their personal Web site URLs would be:

```
http://www.yourcompany.com/~joe    Physical directory:
~joe/public_html
http://www.yourcompany.com/~jenny Physical directory:
~jenny/public_html
```

Note that on Unix systems, ~ (tilde) expands to a user's home directory. The directory specified by the UserDir directive resides in each user's home directory, and

Apache must have read and execute permissions to read files and directories within the public_html directory. This can be accomplished using the following commands on a Unix system:

```
chown -R <user>.<Apache server's group name>
  ~<user>/<directory assigned in UserDir>
chmod -R 770 ~<user>/<directory assigned in UserDir>
```

For example, if the username is joe and Apache's group is called httpd, and public_html is assigned in the UserDir directive, the preceding commands will look like this:

```
chown -R joe.httpd  ~joe/public_html
chmod -R 2770 ~joe/public_html
```

The first command, chown, changes ownership of the ~joe/public_html directory (and that of all files and subdirectories within it) to joe.httpd. In other words, it gives the user joe and the group httpd full ownership of all the files and directories in the public_html directory. The next command, chmod, sets the access rights to 2770 — in other words, only the user (joe) and the group (httpd) have full read, write, and execute privileges in public_html and all files and subdirectories under it. It also ensures that when a new file or subdirectory is created in the public_html directory, the newly created file has the group ID set. This enables the Web server to access the new file without the user's intervention.

Tip If you create user accounts on your system using a script (such as /usr/sbin/adduser script on Linux systems), you may want to incorporate the Web site creation process in this script. Just add a mkdir command to create a default public_html directory (if that's what you assign to the UserDir directive) to create the Web directory. Add the chmod and chown commands to give the Web server user permission to read and execute files and directories under this public directory.

DirectoryIndex

Next, you need to configure the DirectoryIndex directive, which has the following syntax:

```
DirectoryIndex [filename1, filename2, filename3, ... ]
```

This directive specifies which file the Apache server should consider as the index for the directory being requested. For example, when a URL such as www.yourcompany.com/ is requested, the Apache server determines that this is a request to access the / (document root) directory of the Web site. If the DocumentRoot directive is set as:

```
DocumentRoot "/www/www.yourcompany.com/public/htdocs"
```

then the Apache server looks for a file named `/www/www.yourcompany.com/public/htdocs/index.html`; if it finds the file, Apache services the request by returning the content of the file to the requesting Web browser. If the `DirectoryIndex` is assigned `welcome.html` instead of the `default index.html`, however, the Web server will look for `/www/www.yourcompany.com/public/htdocs/welcome.html` instead. If the file is absent, Apache returns the directory listing by creating a dynamic HTML page. Figure 3-3 shows what happens when `index.html` is missing in a directory and the server has generated a directory listing for the requesting browser.

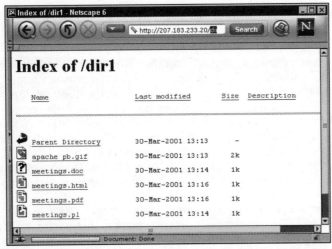

Figure 3-3: Dynamic directory listing in the absence of index.htm

You can specify multiple index filenames in the `DirectoryIndex` directive. For example:

```
DirectoryIndex index.html index.htm welcome.htm
```

tells the Web server that it should check for the existence of any of the three files, and if any one file is found, it should be returned to the requesting Web client.

Note   Listing many files as the index may create two problems. First, the server will now have to check for the existence of many files per directory request; this could make it slower than usual. Second, having multiple files as indexes could make your site difficult to manage from the organizational point of view. If your Web site content developers use various systems to create files, however, it might be a practical solution to keep both `index.html` and `index.htm` as index files. For example, an older Windows machine is unable to create filenames with extensions longer than three characters, so a user working on such a machine may need to manually update all of the user's `index.htm` files on the Web server. Using the recommended index filenames eliminates this hassle.

AccessFileName

The `AccessFileName` directive defines the name of the per-directory access control configuration file. The default name `.htaccess` has a leading period to hide the file from normal directory listing under Unix systems. The only reason to change the name to something else is to increase security by obscurity, which is not much of a reason. However, if you do change the filename to something else, make sure that you change the regular expression `"^\.ht"` to `"^\.whatever"` where `.whatever` is the first view character of what you set `AccessFileName` to. .

Files container

The following `<Files . . .>` container tells Apache to disallow access to any file that starts with a `.ht` (that is, the `.htaccess` or `.htpasswd`). This corresponds to the default `%AccessFileName%`.

```
<Files ~ "^\.ht">
    Order allow,deny
    Deny from all
</Files>
```

UseCanonicalName

Next directive is `UseCanonicalName`, which is set to `On`. It tells Apache to create all self-referencing URLs using `%ServerName%:%Port%` format. Leaving it on is a good idea.

TypesConfig

The `TypesConfig` directive points to the mime configuration file `mime.types` that resides in the default `conf` directory. You do not need to change it unless you have relocated this file.

DefaultType

The `DefaultType` directive sets the Content-Type header for any file whose MIME type cannot be determined from the file extension. For example if you have a file `%DocumentRoot%/myfile`, then Apache uses the `%DefaultType`, which is set to `text/plain`, as the content type for the file. This means that when the Web browser requests and receives such a file in response, it will display the contents in the same way it will display a plain-text file. Now, if you think most of your unknown file contents should be treated as HTML, then use `text/html` in place of `text/plain`.

IfModule container

The next `<IfModule . . .>` container tells Apache to enable the MIME magic module (`mod_mime_magic`) if it exists, and to use the `%MIMEMagicFile%` as the magic information (bytes patterns) needed to identify MIME-type files. The default should be left alone unless you want to change the path of the magic file.

```
<IfModule mod_mime_magic.c>
    MIMEMagicFile conf/magic
</IfModule>
```

HostnameLookups

The `HostnameLookups` directive tells Apache to enable DNS lookup per request if it is set to `On`. However, the default setting is `Off` and therefore no DNS lookup is performed to process a request, which speeds up response time. Performing a DNS lookup to resolve an IP address to the host name is a time-consuming step for a busy server and should only be done using the `logresolve` utility as discussed in Chapter 8. Leave the default as is.

ErrorLog

The `ErrorLog` directive is very important. It points to the log file dedicated to recording server errors. The default value of logs/errors translates to `%ServerRoot%/logs/error_log`, which should work for you, unless you want to write a log in a different place. Generally, it is a good idea to create a log partition for keeping your logs. It is also preferable that your log partition be on one or more dedicated log disks. If you have such a hardware configuration, you might want to change the directive to point to a new log path.

LogLevel

The `LogLevel` directive sets the level of logging that will be done. The default value of `warn` is sufficient for getting started. The `LogFormat` directives dictate what is logged and in what format it is logged. In most cases, you should be able to live with the defaults, so let's not make any changes before you read Chapter 8.

CustomLog

The `CustomLog` directive sets the path for the access log, which stores you server hits. By default it uses the common log format (CLF), which is defined in the preceding `LogFormat` directive. Consider the advice about keeping logs on their own disk and partition, and make changes to the path if necessary.

Tip   A good bit of advice for all logs, regardless of which directory you keep the logs in, is to make sure that only the primary server process has write access in that directory. This is a major security issue, because allowing other users or processes to write to the log directory can potentially mean someone unauthorized might be able to take over your primary Web server process UID, which is normally the root account.

ServerSignature

The next directive is `ServerSignature`, which displays server name and version number and is a server-generated page such as dynamic directory index pages, error pages, and the like. If you feel uncomfortable about displaying your server information so readily to everyone, set it to `Off`. I do.

Alias

The Alias directive defines a new directory alias called /icons/ to point to /usr/local/apache/icons/ (that is, %ServerRoot%/icons/). The icon images stored in this directory are used to display dynamic directory listings when no %DirectoryIndex%-specified files are found in that directory. You should leave the alias alone unless you changed the path of the icons directory. The directory container that follows the alias definition sets the permission for this icon directory. I do not like the idea that it enables directory browsing (that is, dynamic directory indexing) by setting Options to Indexes. You should change Options Indexes to Options -Indexes and not worry about the MultiViews option.

ScriptAlias

The ScriptAlias directive is used to set a widely used CGI script alias directory /cgi-bin/ to point to /usr/local/apache/cgi-bin/ (that is, %ServerRoot%/cgi-bin/). If you plan on using CGI scripts from the main server, keep it; otherwise, remove this directive. Or, if you want to change the CGI script directory another location, change the physical path given in the directive to match yours.

Caution

Never set CGI script path to a directory within in your document root, that is, %DocumentRoot%/somepath, because keeping CGI scripts in your document root directory opens it to various security issues. Set your CGI script path and DocumentRoot at the same level. In other words, if you set DocumentRoot to /a/b/c/htdocs, then set ScriptAlias to point to /a/b/c/cgi-bin not to /a/b/c/htdocs/cgi-bin or to /a/b/c/htdocs/d/cgi-bin.

Next, a directory container places restriction on the %ScriptAlias% directory to ensure that no directory level options are allowed. Here the Options directive is set to None, which means that the contents of %ScriptAlias% is not browsable, that symbolic links within the %ScriptAlias% directory are not followed.

The rest of the directives

The rest of the directives — IndexOptions; AddIconByEncoding; AddIconByType; AddIcon; DefaultIcon; ReadmeName; HeaderName; IndexIgnore; AddEncoding; AddLanguage; AddCharset; BrowserMatch; and AddType — are not important to get up and running, so they are ignored for now. You can learn about these directives in Chapter 4. However, there are two directives that you might want to consider changing if necessary: LanguagePriority and AddDefaultCharset.

LanguagePriority

By default, the LanguagePriority directive sets the default language to be en (English), which might not work for everyone in the world. So, you might want to change the default language to your native language, if it is supported.

AddDefaultCharset

AddDefaultCharset should be set to the character set that best suits your local needs. If you do not know which character set you should use, you can leave the default alone, find out which character set you should use, and change the default later.

Starting and Stopping Apache

After you have customized httpd.conf, you are ready to run the server. For this section, I assume that you took my advice (that is, setting --prefix to /usr/local/apache) in the previous chapter. If you did not take my advice, then make sure that you replace all references to /usr/local/apache to whatever is appropriate in the following discussion.

Starting Apache

Run the /usr/local/apache/bin/apachectl start command to start the Apache Web server. If apachectl complains about syntax errors, you should fix the errors in httpd.conf file and retry.

Also check the %ErrorLog% log file (that is, /usr/local/apache/logs/error_log) for error messages (if any). If you see errors in the log file, you need to fix them first. The most common errors are:

✦ **Not running the server as the root user.** You must start Apache as the root user. After Apache is started, it will spawn child processes that will use the User and Group directives-specified UID and GID. Most people are confused by this issue and try to start the server using the user account specified in the User directive.

✦ **Apache complains about being unable to "bind" to an address.** Either another process is already using the port that you have configured Apache to use, or you are running httpd as a normal user but trying to use a port below 1024 (such as the default port 80).

✦ **Missing log file paths.** Make sure that both %ErrorLog% and %CustomLog% paths exist and are not writable by anyone but the Apache server.

✦ **Configuration typo.** Anytime you change the httpd.conf configuration file, run /usr/local/apache/apachectl configtest to verify that you do not have a syntax error in the configuration file.

Tip   The quickest way to check whether the server is running is to try this command:

```
ps auxw | grep httpd
```

This command uses the ps utility to list all the processes that are in the process queue, and then pipes this output to the grep program. grep searches the output for lines that match the keyword `httpd`, and then displays each matching line. If you see one line with the word `root` in it, that's your primary Apache server process. Note that when the server starts, it creates a number of child processes to handle the requests. If you started Apache as the root user, the parent process continues to run as `root`, while the children change to the user as instructed in the `httpd.conf` file. If you are running Apache on Linux, you can create the script shown in Listing 3-2 and keep it in /etc/rc.d/init.d/ directory. This script allows you to automatically start and stop Apache when you reboot the system.

Listing 3-2: **The httpd script**

```
#!/bin/sh
#
# httpd    This shell script starts and stops the Apache server
# It takes an argument 'start' or 'stop' to receptively start
and
# stop the server process.
#
# Notes: You might have to change the path information used
# in the script to reflect your system's configuration.
#

APACHECTL=/usr/local/apache/bin/apachectl

[ -f $APACHECTL ] || exit 0

# See how the script was called.
case "$1" in
  start)
        # Start daemons.
        echo -n "Starting httpd: "
        $APACHECTL start
        touch /var/lock/subsys/httpd
        echo
        ;;
  stop)
        # Stop daemons.
        echo -n "Shutting down httpd: "
        $APACHECTL stop

        echo "done"
        rm -f /var/lock/subsys/httpd
        ;;
  *)
        echo "Usage: httpd {start|stop}"
        exit 1
esac
exit 0
```

Tip

To start Apache automatically when you boot up your system, simply run this command once:

```
ln -s /etc/rc.d/init.d/httpd /etc/rc.d/rc3.d/S99httpd
```

This command creates a special link called S99httpd in the /etc/rc.d/rc3.d (run-level 3) directory that links to /etc/rc.d/init.d/httpd script. When your system boots up, this script will be executed with the start argument and Apache will start automatically.

Restarting Apache

To restart the Apache server run /usr/local/apache/bin/apachectl restart command.

You can also use the kill command as follows:

```
kill -HUP 'cat /usr/local/apache/logs/httpd.pid'
```

When restarted with apachectl restart or by using the HUP signal with kill, the parent Apache process (run as root user) kills all its children, reads the configuration file, and restarts a new generation of children as needed.

Note

This type of restart is sudden to the Web clients that were promised service by the then-alive child processes. So, you might want to consider using graceful with apachectl instead of the restart option, and WINCH instead of HUP signal with the kill command. In both cases, the parent Apache process will advise its child processes to finish the current request and then to terminate so that it can reread the configuration file and restart a new batch of children. This might take some time on a busy site.

Stopping Apache

You can automatically stop Apache when the system reboots, or manually stop it at any time. These two methods of stopping Apache are discussed in the following sections.

Stopping Apache automatically

To terminate Apache automatically when the system is being rebooted, run this command once:

```
ln -s /etc/rc.d/init.d/httpd /etc/rc.d/rc3.d/K99httpd
```

This command ensures that the httpd script is run with the stop argument when the system shuts down.

Stopping Apache server manually

To stop the Apache server, run the `/usr/local/apache/bin/apachectl stop` command.

Apache server also makes it convenient for you to find the PID of the root Web server process. The PID is written to a file assigned to the `PidFile` directive. This PID is for the primary `httpd` process. Do not attempt to kill the child processes manually one by one because the parent process will recreate them as needed. Another way to stop the Apache server is to run:

```
kill -TERM 'cat /usr/local/apache/logs/httpd.pid'
```

This command runs the `kill` command with `-TERM` signal (that is, `-9`) for the process ID returned by the `cat /usr/local/apache/logs/httpd.pid` (that is, `cat %PidFile%`) command.

Testing Apache

After you have started the Apache server, access it via a Web browser using the appropriate host name. For example, if you are running the Web browser on the server itself, then use `http://localhost/` to access the server. However, if you want to access the server from a remote host, use the fully qualified host name of the server. For example, to access a server called `apache.pcnltd.com`, use `http://apache.pcnltd.com`. If you set the `Port` directive to a nonstandard port (that is, to a port other than 80), then remember to include the `:port` in the URL. For example, `http://localhost:8080` will access Apache server on port 8080.

If you have not made any changes to the default `htdocs` directory, you will see a page such as the one shown in Figure 3-4. This page is shipped with the Apache distribution and needs to be replaced with your own content.

Finally, you want to make sure the log files are updated properly. To check your log files, enter the `log` directory and run the following command:

```
tail -f path_to_access_log
```

The `tail` part of the command is a Unix utility that enables viewing of a growing file (when the `-f` option is specified). Make sure that you change the *path_to_access_log* to a fully qualified path name for the access log. Now, use a Web browser to access the site; if you are already at the site, simply reload the page you currently have on the browser. You should see an entry added to the listing on the screen. Press the reload button a few more times to ensure that the access file is updated appropriately. If you see the updated records, your access log file is working. Press Ctrl+C to exit from the `tail` command session. If you do not see any new records in the file, you should check the permission settings for the log files and the directory in which they are kept.

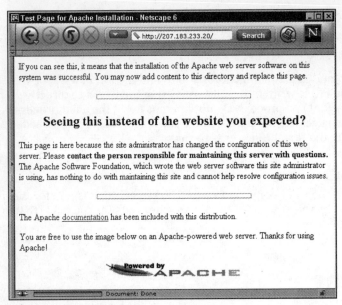

Figure 3-4: Default Apache home page

Another log to check is the error log file. Use:

```
tail -f path_to_error_log
```

to view the error log entries as they come in. Simply request nonexistent resources (such as a file you don't have) to view on your Web browser, and you will see entries being added. If you observe entries being added, then the error log file is properly configured.

If all of these tests were successful, then you have successfully configured your Apache server. Congratulations!

✦   ✦   ✦

Configuring Apache with Winnt MPM Directives

◆ ◆ ◆ ◆

In This Chapter

Understanding the Apache directive contexts

Becoming familiar with core directives

Configuring Apache with threaded MPM directives

Configuring Apache with prefork MPM directives

Configuring Apache with perchild MPM directives

◆ ◆ ◆ ◆

A directive is simply a command for Apache to act on. Apache reads directives from the configuration files I discussed in Chapter 3. By using directives, an Apache administrator can control the behavior of the Web server. Many directives are available for Apache, which makes it a highly configurable Web server. The directives that are part of the base Apache installation are called the *core directives*. These directives are always available.

Several other directives are also available from the standard modules that are part of the standard distribution of Apache. Those standard module-based directives are discussed in Chapter 5.

This chapter discusses the standard contexts in which directives (core and all others) apply, provides in-depth coverage of the core directives, and also the directives available in various Multi-processing Modules (or *MPMs*) that were introduced in Apache 2.0. Instead of providing an alphabetical listing of all the possible core directives, I've grouped them according to their usage; the categories include general configuration; performance and resource configuration; standard container; virtual host specific; logging; and authentication and security. Each directive description provides the following information:

Syntax: Shows the name of the directive and all possible arguments or values it takes.

Default setting: This line shows the default value for a directive. This is only shown where applicable.

Context: Specifies the context (or scope) at which a directive applies.

AllowOverride: Value needed to enable the directive in per-directory access configuration file (.htaccess by default). This is only shown where applicable.

First up in this chapter is a look at the contexts in which you can use directives.

Note Some directives are listed multiple times; all but one of these listings points to the main discussion of that directive elsewhere in the chapter. This is because some directives don't fit into just one category, and I want you to be able to see the various ways you can look at these types of directives.

Apache Directive Contexts

Before you use any of the core directives, it is important that you understand in which context a directive is usable; in other words, you need to know the *context* (or *scope*) of a directive. After discussing the terminology needed to discuss the core directives, I describe the core directives themselves.

There are three major contexts for using a directive, including:

✦ **Server config context:** A directive can appear anywhere in the primary server configuration files (this is called) outside any containers (which look very much like HTML tags).

✦ **Container context:** Directives are contained within containers that look like the following:

```
<Container_name>
    Directive
</Container_name>.
```

✦ **Per-directory context:** Directives are stored in a file (typically .htaccess) within a directory.

Server config context

Directives may appear anywhere in the primary server configuration files outside any containers. You can think of this context as the global context or scope; that is, treat a directive that is not enclosed in a container as a *global directive*. Directives that apply in this context affect all other contexts by default. These directives may be used anywhere in the server configuration files (such as httpd.conf, srm.conf, and access.conf), but not within any containers or a per-directory configuration file (.htaccess).

Container context

To limit the scope of a directive, you can use containers, which look just like HTML tag sets. A container tag pair encloses a set of directives, restricting the scope of the directives within itself. Apache offers these standard containers:

✦ `<VirtualHost ...> ... </VirtualHost>` is used to apply one or more directives to the virtual host specified in the opening tag of the container.

✦ `<Directory ...> ... </Directory>` is used to apply one or more directives to a certain directory. Note that if you specify one or more directives for a directory using this container tag, the directives automatically apply to all the subdirectories as well. If this is not a desirable side effect, however, you can create a separate directory container for each subdirectory and control the server's behavior differently in each sublevel of the directory.

✦ `<DirectoryMatch regex> ... <DirectoryMatch >` is exactly same as the `<Directory>` container; however, it takes a regular expression (*regex*) as an argument instead of a regular directory name. For example, `<DirectoryMatch "^/www/mydir[1-3]/">  ... </DirectoryMatch>` matches all the directories named `/www/mydir1`, `/www/mydir2`, and `/www/mydir3`.

Cross-Reference

A *regular expression* (regex) is typically composed of both normal and special characters to create a pattern. This pattern is used to match one or more substrings or an entire string. See Appendix B for more information about regular expressions.

✦ `<Files ...> ... </Files>` is used to apply one or more directives to a certain file or group of files.

✦ `<FilesMatch regex> ... </FilesMatch>` is exactly same as the `<Files>` container; however it takes a regular expression (*regex*) as an argument instead of one or more filenames. For example, `<FilesMatch "\.(doc|txt)$">  ... </FilesMatch>` will apply one or more directives to all files ending with `.doc` or `.txt` extensions.

✦ `<Location ...> ... </Location>` is used to apply one or more directives to a certain URI.

Note

URI (Uniform Resource Identifier) is the generic term for the family of Uniform Resource Identifiers, of which URL is but one member. The others are Uniform Resource Names (URN), Uniform Resource Characteristics (URC), and Location-Independent File Names (LIFN). Only URL is widely used, however.

✦ `<LocationMatch regex> ... </LocationMatch >` is exactly same as the `<Location>` container; however, it takes a regular expression (*regex*) as an argument instead of a URI.

✦ `<Limit ...> ... </Limit>` is used to apply one or more directives to control access to certain areas of a Web site or a particular HTTP request method. This container has the narrowest scope of all containers. Following is an example of container scope: a segment of an `httpd.conf` file:

```
<VirtualHost 206.171.50.50>

    ServerName www.nitec.com
    DocumentRoot "/www/nitec/public/htdocs"
    DirectoryIndex welcome.html

    <Location /secured/>
        DirectoryIndex login.html
    </Location>

</VirtualHost>
```

In this example, a virtual host called `www.nitec.com` is defined using the `<VirtualHost>` container. The three directives — `ServerName`, `DocumentRoot`, and `DirectoryIndex` — are in the virtual host context, and therefore apply to the entire virtual host. The `DirectoryIndex` directive specifies that if a request is made to access a directory in this virtual server, a file named `welcome.html` should be returned if available. However, the `<Location>` container specifies that a different file, `login.html`, should be returned when someone tries to access the `www.nitec.com/secured/` URL. Because the `<Location>` container defined a narrower scope (in the `/secured` subdirectory), it overrides the higher scope of the DirectoryIndex directive in the `<VirtualHost>` container.

Note   A container that defines a narrower scope always overrides the container with a higher scope.

You should keep a few rules in mind when using any of the containers to define a behavior for a section of your Web space:

✦ A `<VirtualHost>` container cannot be nested within another container of any kind.

✦ There can be no container within the narrowest context container, `<Limit>`.

✦ A `<Files>` container can have only the narrowest container, `<Limit>`, within itself.

✦ The `<Location>` and `<Directory>` containers do not mix, so do not use one inside another.

Per-directory context

You can also include directives in per-directory configuration files. A *per-directory configuration file* (default filename for the per-directory configuration is `.htaccess`) is a text file containing one or more directives that apply only to the current directory. These directives can also be enclosed in containers such as <Files ...> or <Limit ...>. Using per-directory configuration files, you can control how Apache behaves when a request is made for a file in a directory.

Note The AllowOverride directive allows you to disable all or part of what can be over-ridden in a per-directory configuration file in the server config or virtual host context. Therefore, all directives in this context may not be processed, depending on the overrides currently active.

General Configuration Directives

The directives discussed in this section are fundamental in nature and generally apply to both the primary server (*server config context*) and the virtual servers (*virtual host context*).

AccessFileName

The AccessFileName directive specifies the name of the per-directory access control file. The default setting (.htaccess) makes Apache look for the .htaccess file each time an access request is made by a client system.

> **Syntax:** AccessFileName *filename* [*filename* ...]
>
> **Default setting:** AccessFileName .htaccess
>
> **Context:** Server config, virtual host

For example, say that the DocumentRoot directive of an Apache-powered Web site called www.mycompany.com is set as DocumentRoot "/www/mycompany/public/htdocs" and a Web browser requests http://www.mycompany.com/feedback.html. This causes Apache to search for the following access control files:

✦ /.htaccess

✦ /www/.htaccess

✦ /www/mycompany/.htaccess

✦ /www/mycompany/public/.htaccess

✦ /www/mycompany/public/htdocs/.htaccess

Only after Apache has checked for all of these files does it look for the feedback.html file. If this seems like a lot of disk I/O, it is! You can avoid all that nonsense by specifying the access filename with this directive.

Tip

If you do not make use of the per-directory access control file and would like Apache to stop checking for it, simply use the `<Directory>` directive to disable privileges to override options as follows:

```
<Directory />
    AllowOverride None
</Directory>
```

See the sections on the `<Directory>` container and the `AllowOverride` directive in this chapter for more details.

AddDefaultCharset

The `AddDefaultCharset` directive sets the default character set for the Content-Type header sent to the browser by Apache.

> **Syntax:** AddDefaultCharset On | Off | *charset*
>
> **Default setting:** AddDefaultCharset Off
>
> **Context:** All

When this directive is turned on (using `On` option), Apache sends `iso-8859-1` (Western European) as the default character set unless you specify a character set as the second option to this directive. For example, `AddDefaultCharset On utf-8` will send `UTF-8` as the default character set. Commonly used character sets include:

✦ ISO-8859-1 — Western European

✦ ISO-8859-15 — Western European with Euro currency symbol support

✦ Windows-1252 — Western European

✦ CP850 — Western European

✦ UTF-8 — 8-bit Unicode

✦ UTF-7 — 7-bit Unicode

Note

If your HTML documents set the character set by using `<META http-equiv="Content-Type" content="`*content_type*`; charset=`*character_set_name*`">` tag, the `AddDefaultCharset` directive enables you to override it.

ContentDigest

When the `ContentDigest` directive is set, it generates a message digest (MD5) header for the entire content of the body, which enables the Web client to verify the integrity of the page. This is a major performance drag for the Web server because MD5 digests need to be computed on each static page served by the Web server.

Note that this digest is not generated for any output generated by any module other than the core. This means that Common Gateway Interface (CGI) output cannot use this feature. Because of the performance drain on the server, it is not a recommended feature unless you know your server has the power to spare.

> **Syntax:** ContentDigest On | Off
>
> **Default setting:** ContentDigest Off
>
> **Context:** All

DefaultType

The DefaultType directive is used to establish a default content type, so when Apache receives a request for a document whose file type is unknown (in other words, it cannot be determined from the MIME-type map available to the server), it uses the predetermined default type.

> **Syntax:** DefaultType *mime-type*
>
> **Default setting:** DefaultType text/html
>
> **Context:** All
>
> **Override:** FileInfo

For example, if you have a directory in which you keep a lot of text files with no extensions, you can use the DefaultType directive inside a <Directory> container that points to this directory. In this case, setting DefaultType to text/plain enables the server to tell the other side (the Web browser) that these are plain-text files. Here's an example:

```
<Directory /www/mycompany/public/htdocs/plaindata>
    DefaultType plain/text
</Directory>
```

Here, all the files in the /www/mycompany/public/htdocs/plaindata/ directory are treated as plain-text files.

DocumentRoot

The DocumentRoot directory specified by this directive becomes the top-level directory for all the documents serviced by Apache.

> **Syntax:** DocumentRoot "*directory_path*"
>
> **Default setting:** DocumentRoot "/usr/local/apache/htdocs"
>
> **Context:** Server config, virtual host

For example, if

```
DocumentRoot "/www/mycompany/public/htdocs"
```

is set for the server `www.mycompany.com`, then an access request for `www.mycompany.com/corporate.html` makes the server look for the following file:

```
/www/mycompany/public/htdocs/corporate.html
```

If the file is found, it is returned to the client (that is, the Web browser).

Note   A bug in the `mod_dir` module causes a problem when the `DocumentRoot` has a trailing slash (for example, `DocumentRoot /usr/web/`), so you should avoid entering a / character at the end of any path for any directive.

Tip   It is possible to have the server look for files in a directory outside the `DocumentRoot` directory. If you want to access some files outside the `DocumentRoot` tree, you can use the `Alias` directive to create a virtual directory name that can point to a physical directory anywhere in your server's file system.

ErrorDocument

When the server encounters a problem, it generates a standard error message with the error code in it. This is not very user-friendly for most people, however, so a more customized version of the error message, or possibly a recovery measure, is more desirable. If you need such customization, use the `ErrorDocument` directive to override standard error messages.

Syntax: `ErrorDocument error_code [filename | error_message | URL]`

Default setting: None

Context: All

Override: `FileInfo`

The directive requires two arguments. The first argument is the standard HTTP error code, which you can find in Appendix A; the second argument is the action item for the error. Depending on your needs, you can define what action you want the server to take for a particular error condition.

For example, if you want to provide a custom message for all requests that result in a standard "file not found" message, all you have to do is find the server status code for that error condition and use the `ErrorDocument` directive. Because the server status code for missing files is 404, the following directive setting enables Apache to display a custom message:

```
ErrorDocument 404 "Sorry, this is an invalid request because %s "
```

Notice that the entire message is quoted, and the server replaces %s with whatever information is available regarding the error. If you find this a bit limiting, however, you can use a file as your error message response. For example:

```
ErrorDocument 404 /errors/404.html
```

Whenever the missing file error occurs, the 404.html file found in the errors directory under the DocumentRoot directory is returned to the client (the Web browser).

Tip

If you want to do more than just return a static page, you can use a CGI script to perform some specific action. In such a case, you replace the filename with a call to your CGI script:

```
ErrorDocument 404 /cgi-bin/missingurl.cgi
```

This calls a CGI script called missingurl.cgi every time a 404 error occurs. You can also redirect the client to another site using a URL instead of a filename:

```
ErrorDocument 404 http://www.newsite.com/we.moved.html
```

This can be used when a page or an entire site has moved to another location.

Note

You cannot point the client to a remote server if an error 401 (unauthorized) occurs. The value of this directive must be a local file or a message.

<IfDefine>

The IfDefine container directive enables you to create a conditional configuration. The special_command_line_param option is specified by using the -D option with the httpd program.

Syntax: <IfDefine [!]special_command_line_param> ... </IfDefine>

Default setting: None

Context: All

For example, if you run the Apache server from the bin directory as ./httpd -D *something* then you can use:

```
<IfDefine something>
 #  #directives that should be executed only when
 #   -D something is specified
</IfDefine>
```

Note

Placing a ! character in front of the *special_command_line_param* tells Apache to process the directives within the IfDefine container only when a -D *something* was not found in the command-line. For example:

```
<IfDefine !something>
 #  directives that should be executed only when
 #   -D something is NOT specified
</IfDefine>
```

<IfModule>

Use the IfModule container directive if you have directives that are available from a custom module that may not always be present in your Apache installation.

> **Syntax:** <IfModule [!]module_name> ... </IfModule>
>
> **Default setting:** None
>
> **Context:** All

For example, if you want to use certain directives only if a module is available, then you can use the following conditional construct:

```
<IfModule module_name>
    # Assign the following directives their respective value
    # if the module is part of Apache.
    # Your directives go here.
</IfModule>
```

where the module_name argument is the filename of the module at the time it was compiled (for example, mod_rewrite.c).

If you need a conditional statement that is the exact opposite of the above, all you need to do is insert a ! (bang or exclamation point) before the module name. <IfModule> sections are nestable; this is a method that can be used to implement simple multiple-module condition tests. For example:

```
<IfModule module_A>

    # Process the directives here if module A is
    # part of Apache

    <IfModule module_B>

        # Come here only if module A and B both
        # are part of Apache


        <IfModule ! module_C>

            # Come here only if module A and B exists
            # but not module C as part of Apache
        </IfModule>

    </IfModule>

</IfModule>
```

Include

The Include directive enables you to include an external file as a configuration file.

> **Syntax:** Include *filename*
>
> **Default setting:** None
>
> **Context:** Server config

For example, if you want to load all your virtual host configurations using external files, you can have the following configuration in httpd.conf:

```
NameVirtualHost IP_Address
Include virtual_host_1.conf
Include virtual_host_2.conf
Include virtual_host_3.conf
...
Include virtual_host_N.conf
```

Tip
In each of these files you can define a <VirtualHost> container specific to the host. This is a good way of organizing the httpd.conf file if you have a lot of virtual hosts.

Options

The Options directive controls which server features are available in a particular directory.

> **Syntax:** Options [+|-]option [+|-]option ...
>
> **Default setting:** None
>
> **Context:** All
>
> **Override:** Options (see Table 4-1)

Note
When this directive is set to None, none of the extra features are enabled for the context in which the directive is used.

All the possible settings for this directive are listed in Table 4-1.

Table 4-1
Options directive settings

Setting	What It Means
None	No options.
All	All options except for MultiViews.
ExecCGI	Execution of CGI scripts is permitted.
FollowSymLinks	The server follows symbolic links in the directory. However, the server does not change the pathname used to match against <Directory> sections.
Includes	SSI commands are permitted.
IncludesNOEXEC	A restricted set of SSI commands can be embedded in the SSI pages. The SSI commands that are not allowed are #exec and #include.
Indexes	If a URL that maps to a directory is requested and there is no DirectoryIndex (for example, index.html) in that directory, then the server returns a formatted listing of the directory.
SymLinksIfOwnerMatch	The server only follows symbolic links for which the target file or directory is owned by the same user as the link.
MultiViews	Enables content negotiation based on a document's language.

Use the + and - signs to enable or disable an option in the Options directive. For example, the following configuration segment shows two directory containers in a single configuration file such as access.conf:

```
<Directory /www/myclient/public/htdocs >
    Options Indexes MultiViews
</Directory>

<Directory /www/myclient/public/htdocs>
    Options Includes
</Directory>
```

The /www/myclient/public/htdocs will only have the Includes option set. However, if the second <Directory> section uses the + and - signs as follows:

```
<Directory /www/myclient/public/htdocs>
    Options +Includes -Indexes
</Directory>
```

then the options MultiViews and Includes are set for the specified directory. When you apply multiple Options, be aware that the narrowest context always takes precedence over the broader context. For example:

```
ServerName www.domain.com

Options ExecCGI Includes

<VirtualHost 11.22.3311.22.33.1>

    ServerName www.myclient.com
    Options -ExecCGI -Includes

    <Directory /www/myclient/public/htdocs/ssi >

       Options Includes

    </Directory>

</VirtualHost>
```

In this example, the main server enables both CGI execution and SSIs by setting the `Options` directive to `ExecCGI` and `Includes`. The virtual host `www.myclient.com` disables both of these options, however, using the `-ExecCGI` and `-Includes` settings in its own `Options` directive. Finally, the virtual host has another `Options` directive for the `/www/myclient/public/htdocs/ssi` directory, that enables SSI execution. Note that `Includes` is the only option that is set for the `/www/myclient/public/htdocs/ssi` directory.

As you can see, if the `Options` directive uses the + or - signs, then the values are added or subtracted from the current `Options` list. On the other hand, if the `Options` directive does not use the relative + or - signs, then the values for that container will completely override any previous `Options` directives.

Port

The `Port` directive assigns a port number in the range of 0 to 65535 to a host. In the absence of any `Listen` or `BindAddress` directive specifying a port number, the `Port` directive sets the network port on which the server listens. If any `Listen` or `BindAddress` directive specifies a port number, then the `Port` directive has no effect on which address the server listens at. The `Port` directive sets the SERVER_PORT environment variable (for CGI and Server-Side Include (SSI)), and is used when the server must generate a URL that refers to itself.

> **Syntax:** `Port number`
>
> **Default setting:** `Port 80`
>
> **Context:** Server config

Although you can specify a port number between 0 and 65535, there is one restriction that you should keep in mind. All the port numbers below 1024 are reserved for standard services such as TELNET, SMTP, POP3, HTTP, and FTP. You can locate all the port number assignments to standard services in your `/etc/services` file.

Or, if you want to be safe, use any port number other than 80 for your Apache server (use a high address, such as 8000, for example).

Note If you are a nonroot user and want to run Apache for experimentation or some other noble cause, you need to use ports higher than 1024, because only root users can run services such as Apache on these restricted ports.

Tip The `<VirtualHost>` container can also be used to set up which port is used for a virtual host.

ServerAdmin

The `ServerAdmin` directive assigns an e-mail address that appears in conjunction with many error messages issued by the server. If you host a large number of virtual Web sites, you may want to use a different e-mail address for each virtual host so you can immediately determine which server a problem reporter is talking about.

> **Syntax:** `ServerAdmin` *e-mail_address*
>
> **Default setting:** None
>
> **Context:** Server config, virtual host

To give your virtual sites the professional look and feel they deserve, do not use an e-mail address that does not include the virtual site as the host part of the address. For example, if your company is an Internet Service Provider (ISP) named mycompany.net, and you have a client site called `www.myclient.com`, then set the `www.myclient.com` site's `ServerAdmin` to a `user@myclient.com` address such as `webmaster@myclient.com`, instead of `webmaster@mycompany.net`. This way, when the server displays an error message to someone visiting `www.myclient.com`, the visitor will see an e-mail address that belongs to `myclient.com`. This is considered to be more professional.

ServerName

The `ServerName` directive sets the host name of the server. When this directive is not used, Apache tries to determine the host name by doing a domain name server (DNS) request at startup. Depending on your DNS setup, however, this may not be desirable because the lookup done by Apache may choose an undesirable name for your server, for example, if you have canonical name records (CNAME) for your server. Therefore, it is best to just set this to whatever host name you prefer.

> **Syntax:** `ServerName` *fully_qualified_domain_name*
>
> **Default setting:** None
>
> **Context:** Server config, virtual host

Tip Make sure you enter a fully qualified domain name instead of just a shortcut. For example, if you have a host called `wormhole.mycompany.com`, you should not set the `ServerName` to `wormhole`. The valid choice is:

```
ServerName wormhole.mycompany.com
```

ServerRoot

The `ServerRoot` directive sets the directory in which the server files reside. Do not confuse this with `DocumentRoot` directive, which is used for pointing the server to your Web contents. The `ServerRoot` directory is used for locating all the server configuration files and log files. The standard distributions include `conf`, `bin`, `htdocs`, `icons`, `cgi-bin`, and `logs` directories under the `ServerRoot` directory. If you do not specify the `ServerRoot` directive, however, you can use the `-d` command-line option to tell Apache what your `ServerRoot` directory is.

> **Syntax:** ServerRoot *directory*
>
> **Default setting:** ServerRoot /usr/local/apache
>
> **Context:** Server config

ServerSignature

By using the `ServerSignature` directive you can create a simple footer for Apache-generated pages such as error messages and directory listings. This directive is not recommended unless you use Apache as a proxy server. On the other hand, when a user receives an error message, it is often difficult to determine which proxy server caused the error if there is a chain of proxies in the user's network path. This footer acts as an identifier in such cases. You can include an e-mail address that will appear in the footer so that others can e-mail you if there is a problem.

> **Syntax:** ServerSignature On | Off | *e-mail*
>
> **Default setting:** ServerSignature Off
>
> **Context:** All

ServerTokens

In response to a request, Apache can send a header that includes an identifier that tells the client what server you are running. The `ServerTokens` directive lets you control that identifier token. When `Minimal` option is used, Apache sends `"Apache/version"`; when `ProductOnly` option is used, only the string `"Apache"` is sent; when `OS` is used `"Apache/version (OS_Type)"` is sent; when `Full` is used, Apache sends `"Apache/version (OS_Type) Available_Module_Info"`.

Syntax: ServerTokens Minimal | ProductOnly | OS | Full

Default setting: ServerTokens Full

Context: Server config

Caution

I recommend using only the Minimal option if you want to avoid security issues from bug-based attacks; you don't want to advertise what type of server you use to the world.

SetInputFilter

The SetInputFilter directive sets the filters that will be used to process a request sent to the server. The filters are applied in the order that they appear in this directive.

Syntax: SetInputFilter *filter* [*filter* ...]

Default setting: None

Context: Directory

SetOutputFilter

The SetOutputFilter directive sets the filters that will be used to process a response before it is sent to the Web client. The filters are applied in the order they appear in this directive.

Syntax: SetOutputFilter *filter* [*filter*] ...

Default setting: None

Context: Directory

In the following example, all files in the /www/mysite/htdocs/parsed **directory** will be processed using the INCLUDES output filter, which is the SSI filter:

```
<Directory "/www/mysite/htdocs/parsed">
   Options +Includes
   SetOutputFilter INCLUDES
</Directory>
```

Performance and Resource Configuration Directives

These directives enable you to fine-tune Apache for higher performance and better control. You can fine-tune the Apache processes in many ways. Note that almost all of these directives require a clear understanding of how your system works in terms of the operating system, hardware, and so on; therefore, you should browse your operating system manuals and/or man pages to learn how your system limits system resources to processes, how it controls TCP/IP connectivity, and so on. The directives in this section are further divided into subfunctions.

Cross-Reference   See Chapter 22 for more info about how to speed up Apache.

Controlling Apache processes

The following directives are used to control how Apache executes in your system. Using these directives enables you to control how Apache uses resources on your system. For example, you can decide how many child server processes to run on your system, or how many threads you should allow Apache to use on a Windows platform. A few things to remember when configuring these directives:

✦ The more processes you run, the more load your CPU(s) experiences.

✦ The more processes you run, the more RAM you need.

✦ The more processes you run, the more operating system resources (such as file descriptors and shared buffers) are used.

Of course, more processes also could mean more requests serviced, and thus more hits for your site. So, setting these directives should be based on a combination of experimentation, requirements, and available resources.

ListenBacklog

See the ListenBacklog directive under the " MPM threaded-Specific Directives" section.

MaxClients

See MaxClients directive under the "MPM threaded-Specific Directives" section.

MaxRequestsPerChild

See MaxRequestsPerChild directive under the "MPM threaded-Specific Directives" section.

MaxSpareServers

See MaxSpareServers directive under the "MPM prefork Specific Directives" section.

MinSpareServers

See MinSpareServers directive under the "MPM prefork Specific Directives" section.

SendBufferSize

See `SendBufferSize` directive under the "MPM threaded Specific Directives" section.

StartServers

See `StartServers` directive under the "MPM threaded Specific Directives" section.

TimeOut

Apache server responds to requests. The requests and responses are transmitted via packets of data. Apache must know how long to wait for a certain packet. The `TimeOut` directive enables you to configure the time in seconds. The time you specify here is the maximum time Apache will wait before it breaks a connection. The default setting enables Apache to wait for 300 seconds before it disconnects itself from the client. If you are on a slow network, however, you may want to increase the time out value to decrease the number of disconnects.

> **Syntax:** `TimeOut` *number*
>
> **Default setting:** `TimeOut 300`
>
> **Context:** Server config

Currently, this `TimeOut` setting applies to:

✦ The total amount of time it takes to receive a GET request.

✦ The amount of time between receipt of TCP packets on a POST or PUT request.

✦ The amount of time between ACKs on transmissions of TCP packets in responses.

Making persistent connections

By using the `KeepAlive` directives discussed in this section, you can instruct Apache to use persistent connections so that a single TCP connection can be used for multiple transactions. Normally, every HTTP request and response uses a separate connection. This means that every time the server gets a request, it opens a connection to retrieve the request and then closes it. After the server has received the request, it opens another TCP connection to respond, and finally closes the connection after completing the service. This method increases the toll on high performance. Reuse of a single connection for multiple transactions reduces the overhead needed for setting up and closing a TCP connection repeatedly, and thereby increases performance.

To establish a persistent connection, however, both the server and the client need to have the persistent connection facility. Most popular browsers, such as Netscape Navigator and Microsoft Internet Explorer, have `KeepAlive` features built in.

Not all transactions can take advantage of the persistent connections. A requirement for a persistent connection is that the resources being transmitted must have a known size. Because many CGI scripts, SSI commands, and other dynamically generated contents do not have a known length before transmission, they are unable to take advantage of this feature.

KeepAlive

The KeepAlive directive enables you to activate/deactivate persistent use of TCP connections in Apache.

> **Syntax:** KeepAlive On | Off
>
> **Default setting:** KeepAlive On
>
> **Context:** Server config

Note   Older Apache servers (prior to version 1.2) may require a numeric value instead of On/Off when using KeepAlive This value corresponds to the maximum number of requests you want Apache to entertain per request. A limit is imposed to prevent a client from taking over all your server resources. To disable KeepAlive in the older Apache versions, use 0 (zero) as the value.

KeepAliveTimeout

If you have the KeepAlive directive set to on, you can use the KeepAliveTimeout directive to limit the number of seconds Apache will wait for a subsequent request before closing a connection. After a request is received, the timeout value specified by the Timeout directive applies.

> **Syntax:** KeepAliveTimeout seconds
>
> **Default setting:** KeepAliveTimeout 15
>
> **Context:** Server config

MaxKeepAliveRequests

The MaxKeepAliveRequests directive limits the number of requests allowed per connection when KeepAlive is on. If it is set to 0 (zero), unlimited requests will be allowed. I recommend that this setting be kept to a high value for maximum server performance.

> **Syntax:** MaxKeepAliveRequests *number*
>
> **Default setting:** MaxKeepAliveRequests 100
>
> **Context:** Server config

Controlling system resources

Apache is quite flexible in enabling you to control the amount of system resources (such as CPU time and memory) it consumes. These control features are handy for making your Web server system more reliable and responsive. Many typical hacking attempts try to make a Web server consume all system resources like a hog, and thus try to make the system nonresponsive and virtually halted. Apache provides a set of directives to combat such a situation. These directives are discussed in the following sections.

RLimitCPU

The `RLimitCPU` directive enables you to control the CPU usage of Apache children-spawned processes such as CGI scripts. The limit does not apply to Apache children themselves or to any process created by the parent Apache server.

> **Syntax:** `RLimitCPU` n | `'max'` [n | `'max'`]
>
> **Default setting:** Not set; uses operating system defaults
>
> **Context:** Server config, virtual host

The `RLimitCPU` directive takes the following two parameters: The first parameter sets a soft resource limit for all processes and the second parameter, which is optional, sets the maximum resource limit. Note that raising the maximum resource limit requires that the server be running as `root` or in the initial startup phase. For each of these parameters, there are two possible values:

✦ n is the number of seconds per process.

✦ and max is the maximum resource limit allowed by the operating system.

RLimitMEM

The `RLimitMEM` directive limits the memory (RAM) usage of Apache children-spawned processes such as CGI scripts. The limit does not apply to Apache chidren themselves or to any process created by the parent Apache server.

> **Syntax:** `RLimitMEM` n | `'max'` [n | `'max'`]
>
> **Default setting:** Not set; uses operating system defaults
>
> **Context:** Server config, virtual host

The `RLimitMEM` directive takes two parameters. The first parameter sets a soft resource limit for all processes, and the second parameter, which is optional, sets the maximum resource limit. Note that raising the maximum resource limit requires that the server be started by the root user. For each of these parameters, there are two possible values:

✦ n is the number of bytes per process

✦ `max` is the maximum resource limit allowed by the operating system

RLimitNPROC

The `RLimitNPROC` directive sets the maximum number of simultaneous Apache children-spawned processes per user ID.

Syntax: `RLimitNPROC  n | 'max' [ n | 'max']`

Default setting: Not set; uses operating system defaults

Context: Server config, virtual host

The `RLimitNPROC` directive takes two parameters. The first parameter sets the soft resource limit for all processes, and the second parameter, which is optional, sets the maximum resource limit. Raising the maximum resource limit requires that the server be running as `root` or in the initial startup phase. For each of these parameters, there are two possible values:

✦ `n` is the number of bytes per process

✦ `max` is the maximum resource limit allowed by the operating system

Note

If your CGI processes are run under the same user ID as the server process, use of `RLimitNPROC` limits the number of processes the server can launch (or "fork"). If the limit is too low, you will receive a "Cannot fork process" type of message in the error log file. In such a case, you should increase the limit or just leave it as the default.

UseCanonicalName

The `UseCanonicalName` directive sets how Apache constructs self-referencing URLS. When set to `on`, Apache uses `ServerName` and `Port` directive settings to create the self-referencing URL. If `UseCanonicalName` is set to `off`, then Apache uses the client-supplied host name and port number from the header information to construct the self-referencing URL. Finally, if `UseCanonicalName` is set to `dns`, Apache will perform a reverse DNS lookup on the server's IP address to determine the host name for the self-referencing URL. This option is not recommended because the reverse DNS lookup will slow down the request processing.

Syntax: `UseCanonicalName On | Off | dns`

Default setting: `UseCanonicalName On`

Context: Server config, virtual host, directory

Override: Options

Using dynamic modules

Apache loads all the precompiled modules when it starts up; however, it also provides a dynamic module loading and unloading feature that may be useful on certain occasions. When you use the following dynamic module directives, you can change the list of active modules without recompiling the server.

AddModule

The `AddModule` directive can be used to enable a precompiled module that is currently not active. The server can have modules compiled that are not actively in use. This directive can be used to enable these modules. The server comes with a preloaded list of active modules; this list can be cleared with the `ClearModuleList` directive. Then new modules can be added using the `AddModule` directive.

> **Syntax:** AddModule *module module ...*
>
> **Default setting:** None
>
> **Context:** Server config

ClearModuleList

You can use the `ClearModuleList` directive to clear the list of active modules and to enable the dynamic module-loading feature. Then use the `AddModule` directive to add modules that you want to activate.

> **Syntax:** ClearModuleList
>
> **Default setting:** None
>
> **Context:** Server config

Standard Container Directives

This section discusses the standard containers that are part of the base Apache server. These containers are widely used to apply a group of other directives to a certain directory, file, or location. You cannot randomly mix and match the containers.

The general guidelines for working with these directives are:

✦ Use the `<Directory>` or `<Files>` containers to specify directives for file system objects such as files and directories. You cannot use `<Directory>` inside an `.htaccess` file, because an `.htaccess` file applies only to the directory in which it is found.

✦ Use the `<Location>` container for matching URL objects. You cannot use this directive inside an `.htaccess` file.

✦ When using the regular expression version of a directive (for example, `<DirectoryMatch>`), follow the same guidelines as for the regular version. Use the regular expression version of the containers only if you are confident that your regular expressions are tightly expressed.

✦ Because of a mistake in the early stages of Apache development, the proxy control is still done with the `<Directory>` container, even though the `<Location>` container is more appropriate. This may be corrected in a future version. However, this really doesn't cause any harm, other than making things a bit more difficult to conceptualize.

Cross-Reference

The `<VirtualHost>` container is discussed in a separate section, later in this chapter.

`<Directory>`

The `<Directory>` and `</Directory>` container tags are used to enclose a group of directives that apply only to the named directory and its subdirectories. Any directive that is allowed in a directory context may be used. The argument can be a fully qualified pathname.

> **Syntax:** `<Directory directory> ... </Directory>`
>
> **Default setting:** None
>
> **Context:** Server config, virtual host

In the following example the directory `/www/mycompany/public/htdocs/download` is used as a fully qualified pathname. This example enables directory indexing in this directory.

```
<Directory /www/mycompany/public/htdocs/download>
    Options +Indexes
</Directory>
```

You can also use wildcard characters in specifying the path. In the following example, the ? will match any single character:

```
<Directory /www/mycompany/public/htdocs/downloa?>
    Options +Indexes
</Directory>
```

Therefore, directories such as `/www/mycompany/public/htdocs/download` and `/www/mycompany/public/htdocs/downloaD` will be matched. You can also use * (asterisk) to match any sequence of characters other than the / (slash) character. Extended regular expressions can also be used by adding the ~ (tilde) character. For example:

```
<Directory ~ "^/www/.*/">
```

would match any subdirectory under `/www/`. Note that regular expression-based `<Directory>` containers may not be applied until all normal (that is, without regular expression) `<Directory>` containers and `.htaccess` files have been applied.

Then, all the regular expressions are tested in the order in which they appeared in the configuration file.

Tip   For a detailed explanation of the regular expressions, see Appendix C.

If you specify more than one `<Directory>` container for the same directory space, the `<Directory>` container with the narrowest scope is applied first. For example:

```
<Directory /www>
    AllowOverride None
</Directory>

<Directory ~ "/www/mycompany/public/htdocs/*">
    AllowOverride FileInfo
</Directory>
```

According to this, when a request for `/www/mycompany/public/htdocs/somefile.cvs` arrives, Apache disables the per-directory access control file (`.htaccess`) for `/www` and then enables it for `/www/mycompany/public/htdocs`. It also accepts any `FileInfo` directive such as `DefaultType` from within the `/www/mycompany/public/htdocs/.htaccess` file.

\<DirectoryMatch>

The `DirectoryMatch` container is nearly identical to the `<Directory>` container except that it takes a regular expression as the argument and does not require the ~ (tilde) character. `<DirectoryMatch>` and `</DirectoryMatch>` are used to enclose a group of directives that apply only to the named directory and its subdirectories.

> **Syntax:** `<DirectoryMatch regex>` ... `</DirectoryMatch>`
>
> **Default setting:** None
>
> **Context:** Server config, virtual host

The following example would match all subdirectories of `/www/mycompany/public/htdocs` that have exactly eight uppercase letters as a name; therefore, `/www/mycompany/public/htdocs/AAAABBBB/` would match the preceding regular expression.

```
<DirectoryMatch "^/www/mycompany/pubic/htdocs/[A-Z]{8}/*">
```

Cross-Reference   For more details on regular expressions, see Appendix B.

\<Files>

To control access by filename, you need to use the Files container. `<Files>` sections are processed in the order in which they appear in the configuration file, after the `<Directory>` sections and `.htaccess` files are read, but before the `<Location>` sections are read.

> **Syntax:** `<Files filename> ... </Files>`
>
> **Default setting:** None
>
> **Context:** Server config, virtual host, per-directory

The `filename` argument should include a filename, or a wildcard string, where ? matches any single character, and * matches any sequence of characters except the / character. By using the ~ (tilde) character, you can enable extended regular expression checking on the argument. For example:

```
<Files ~ "\.(zip|tar|tgz|arj|zoo)$">
```

would match any file with the `.zip`, `.tar`, `.tgz`, `.arj`, or `.zoo` extension. Unlike `<Directory>` and `<Location>` sections, `<Files>` sections can be used inside `.htaccess` files. When using these from within an `.htaccess` file, you don't need to append the pathname, because an `.htaccess` file only applies to the directory where it is found.

`<FilesMatch>`

The `FilesMatch` container is exactly the same as the `<Files>` container, except that it takes a regular expression as its argument.

> **Syntax:** `<FilesMatch regex> ... </Files>`
>
> **Default setting:** None
>
> **Context:** Server config, virtual host, per-directory

For instance, the following example would match any file with the `.zip`, `.tar`, `.tgz`, `.arj`, and `.zoo` extensions. Notice that you do not need the ~ (tilde) character in this container to use a regular expression:

```
<FilesMatch "\.( zip|tar|tgz|arj|zoo)$">
```

`<Location>`

The `<Location>` container provides access control by URL. `<Location>` containers are processed in the order in which they appear in the configuration file, after the `<Directory>` containers and `.htaccess` files are read.

> **Syntax:** `<Location URL> ... </Location>`
>
> **Default setting:** None
>
> **Context:** Server, virtual host

The URL argument does not need the `http://servername`. It can use wildcard characters such as ? (matches any single character) or * (matches any sequence of characters except for the / character). You can also use an extended regular expression by using the ~ character before the expression. For example, `<Location ~ "/(my|your)/file">` would match URLs such as `/my/file` or `your/file`.

<LocationMatch>

The LocationMatch container is identical to the `<Location>` container, except that its argument (URL) is a regular expression and it does not require a ~ (tilde) before the expression. For example, `<LocationMatch "/(my|your)/file">` would match URLs such as `/my/file` or `your/file`.

> **Syntax:** <LocationMatch *regex*> ... </LocationMatch>
>
> **Default setting:** None
>
> **Context:** Server config, virtual host

Virtual Host-Specific Directives

These directives are used for creating virtual hosts. By default, Apache services only the Web site host specified by the `ServerName` directive. It is possible, however, to make Apache serve other Web sites using a virtual host container directive. Note that many of the directives that I discussed earlier in the General Configuration Directives section are also applicable to virtual hosts.

NameVirtualHost

If you plan to use name-based virtual hosts, you need to use the `NameVirtualHost` directive. Although `addr` can be the host name, I recommend that you always use an IP address.

> **Syntax:** NameVirtualHost *addr*[:*port*]
>
> **Default setting:** None
>
> **Context:** Server config

For example, for a virtual host named `www.mycompany.com` that uses the IP address `192.168.1.200`, the directive and virtual host definition would be:

```
NameVirtualHost 192.168.1.200

<VirtualHost 192.168.1.200>
    ServerName www.mycompany.com
    # Other directives go here
</VirtualHost>
```

If you have multiple name-based hosts on multiple addresses, repeat the directive for each address. In Listing 4-1, the first `NameVirtualHost` directive is used for the `www.mycompany.com` and `www.friendscomany.com` virtual hosts. The second container is used for the `www.myclient.com` and the `www.herclient.com` virtual hosts.

Listing 4-1: **NameVirtualHost directive**

```
NameVirtualHost 192.168.1.200

#
# First virtual host that corresponds to the above directive
#
<VirtualHost 192.168.1.200>
    ServerName www.mycompany.com
    # Other directives go here
</VirtualHost>


#
# Second virtual host that corresponds to the above directive
#
<VirtualHost 192.168.1.200>
    ServerName www.friendscompany.com
    # Other directives go here
</VirtualHost>

#   Another NameVirtualHost directive for a new set
#   of name-based virtual hosts that
#   use a different IP.

NameVirtualHost 192.168.1.100>

#
# First virtual host that corresponds to 192.168.1.100
#
<VirtualHost 192.168.1.100>
    ServerName www.myclient.com
    # Other directives go here
</VirtualHost>


#
# Second virtual host that corresponds to 192.168.1.100
#
<VirtualHost 192.168.1.100>
    ServerName www.herclient.com
    # Other directives go here
</VirtualHost>
```

Optionally, you can specify a port number on which the name-based virtual hosts should be used. For example:

```
NameVirtualHost 192.168.1.100:8080
```

ServerAlias

This directive lets you define an alias for your server's primary hostname. When you have a name-based virtual host with multiple IP names (CNAME records in the DNS database), you can use a single virtual host definition to service all of them.

> **Syntax:** `ServerAlias host1 [host2 ...]`
>
> **Default setting:** None
>
> **Context:** Virtual host

In the following example, `www.sac-state.edu` and `www.csu.sacramento.edu` are aliases for the `www.csus.edu` virtual host.

```
NameVirtualHost 192.168.1.100

<VirtualHost 192.168.1.100>
    ServerName www.csus.edu
    ServerAlias www.sac-state.edu   www.hornet.edu
</VirtualHost>
```

Tip   You can also use wildcard characters such as * in defining aliases.

ServerPath

The `ServerPath` directive sets the legacy URL path name for a host, for use with name-based virtual hosts. Typically, this is used to support browsers that are not HTTP 1.1-compliant.

> **Syntax:** `ServerPath pathname`
>
> **Default setting:** None
>
> **Context:** Virtual host

<VirtualHost>

The `VirtualHost` container directive specifies a virtual host configuration. All the enclosed directives found within the `<VirtualHost>` and the closing `</VirtualHost>` apply only to the named virtual host. Any directive that is allowed in a virtual host context may be used. When the server receives a request for a document on a particular virtual host, it uses the configuration directives enclosed in the `<VirtualHost>`.

Syntax: `<VirtualHost addr[:port] ...> ... </VirtualHost>`

Default setting: None

Context: Server config

To specify which IP address or IP name is to be used for a particular virtual host, you can use any of the following:

✦ **An IP address.** For example:

```
<VirtualHost 192.168.1.100>
    # directives go here
</VirtualHost>
```

✦ **An IP address with a port number.** For example:

```
<VirtualHost 192.168.1.100:8080>
    # directive go here
</VirtualHost>
```

✦ **Multiple IP addresses.** For example:

```
<VirtualHost 192.168.1.100 192.168.1.105>
    # directives go here
</VirtualHost>
```

✦ **Multiple IP addresses with port numbers.** For example:

```
<VirtualHost 192.168.1.100:8000 192.168.1.105:10000>
    # directives go here
</VirtualHost>
```

Caution   You can replace IP addresses with IP names, but this is not recommended; if the DNS lookup necessary to determine the address fails for some reason, the server may get confused and not service the virtual site at all.

The special name_default_ can be used, in which case, this virtual host will match any IP address that is not explicitly listed in another virtual host. In the absence of any _default_ virtual host, the primary server configuration, which consists of all the definitions outside any `VirtualHost` section, is used when no match occurs.

If a port is unspecified, then the port number defaults to the same port as the most recent `Port` directive of the primary server. You may also specify * to match all ports on that address.

Logging Directives

Logging server transactions is a must for any system running Apache. Server logs provide valuable information, such as who accesses your Web site(s), which pages are accessed, and which errors are generated by the server.

LogLevel

The LogLevel directive sets the verbosity of the log message stored in error log file. When you specify a log level, all the higher-level messages are written to a log. So, if you specify the level to be crit, then only emerg, alert, and crit errors are logged.

> **Syntax:** LogLevel *level*
>
> **Default setting:** LogLevel error
>
> **Context:** Server config, virtual host

Table 4-2 shows the available levels (in descending order) with their respective meanings.

Table 4-2
LogDirective Levels

Level	What It Means
Emerg	Extreme emergency situation
Alert	Immediate action required
Crit	Citical errors
Error	Error conditions
Warn	Warning messages
Notice	Notices of various kinds
Info	Informational messages
Debug	Debugging messages

The ErrorLog directive specifies the log filename used to log error messages that the server produces. If the filename does not begin with a slash (/), then it is assumed to be relative to the ServerRoot.

> **Syntax:** ErrorLog *filename*
>
> **Default setting:** ErrorLog logs/error_log
>
> **Context:** Server config, virtual host

If you need to disable error logging, you can use the following:

```
ErrorLog /dev/null
```

Note   It is very important that the permission settings for your server log directory indicate that only the Apache user (specified by the User directive) is allowed read/write access. Allowing anyone else to write in this directory could potentially create security holes.

PidFile

By using the PidFile directive, you can tell Apache to write the primary server (that is, the daemon process) process ID (or *PID*) in a file. If the filename does not begin with a slash (/), then it is assumed to be relative to the ServerRoot. The PidFile directive is used only in standalone mode.

> **Syntax:** PidFile *filename*
>
> **Default setting:** PidFile logs/httpd.pid
>
> **Context:** Server config

The PidFile directive's primary use is to make it convenient for the Apache administrator to find the primary Apache PID, which is needed to send signals to the server. For example, if the PID file is kept in the /usr/local/httpd/logs directory, and its name is httpd.pid, an administrator can force Apache server to reread its configuration by sending a SIGHUP signal from the shell prompt (as root) as follows:

```
kill -HUP 'cat /usr/local/httpd/logs/httpd.pid'
```

The same command makes Apache reopen the ErrorLog and TransferLog.

Caution   As with any other log files, make sure the PID file is not writeable or even readable by anyone other than the server process. For better security, you should make the log directory read/write-able only by the Apache server user.

ScoreBoardFile

The ScoreBoardFile directive sets the path to the file used for storing internal process data. If the filename does not begin with a slash (/), then it is assumed to be relative to the ServerRoot. This file is used by the primary server process to communicate with the child processes.

> **Syntax:** ScoreBoardFile *filename*
>
> **Default setting:** ScoreBoardFile logs/apache_status
>
> **Context:** Server config

If you want to find out if your system requires this file, just run the Apache server and see whether a file is created in the specified location. If your system architecture requires the file, then you must ensure that this file is not used at the same time by more than one invocation of Apache. Also, make sure that no other user has read or write access to this file, or even to the directory in which it is kept.

Note   Because the processes have to perform disk I/O to communicate, this could potentially cause a performance bottleneck; therefore, you should create a RAM disk for this file, if possible. Consult your operating system manuals for details.

Authentication and Security Directives

The authentication and security directives discussed in the following sections enable you to define authentication and access restrictions for your Web server. You can use username- and password-based authentication to restrict access to certain parts of your Web site. Also, you can use username-, IP address-, or hostname-based access control to ensure that only valid users or systems are allowed access to portions of your Web site.

AllowOverride

The `AllowOverride` directive tells the server which directives declared in an `.htaccess` file (as specified by `AccessFileName`) can override earlier directives found in configuration files. When `Override` is set to `None`, the server does not read the file specified by `AccessFileName` (default `.htaccess`). This could speed up the response time of the server, because the server does not have to look for an `AccessFileName` specified file for each request (see the `AccessFileName` section for details).

> **Syntax:** `AllowOverride` *option1 option2* `...`
>
> **Default setting:** `AllowOverride All`
>
> **Context:** directory

If you do want to allow `AccessFileName`-based control, you can specify one or more of the options. The override options are:

- ✦ `AuthConfig` — Enables use of the authorization directives (such as `AuthDBMGroupFile`, `AuthDBMUserFile`, `AuthGroupFile`, `AuthName`, `AuthType`, `AuthUserFile`, and `Require`).

- ✦ `FileInfo` — Enables use of the directives controlling document types (such as `AddEncoding`, `AddLanguage`, `AddType`, `DefaultType`, `ErrorDocument`, and `LanguagePriority`).

- ✦ `Indexes` — Enables use of the directives controlling directory indexing (such as `AddDescription`, `AddIcon`, `AddIconByEncoding`, `AddIconByType`, `DefaultIcon`, `DirectoryIndex`, `FancyIndexing`, `HeaderName`, `IndexIgnore`, `IndexOptions`, and `ReadmeName`).

- ✦ `Limit` — Enables use of the directives controlling host access (`Allow`, `Deny`, and `Order`).

- ✦ `Options` — Enables use of the directives controlling specific directory features (`Options` and `XBitHack`).

AuthName

The `AuthName` directive sets the authentication realm name for a resource (such as a directory) that requires authentication. The realm is usually displayed by a Web browser in a pop-up dialog window when prompting for a user name and password to access the requested (controlled) resource. There is no default realm name. The primary purpose of this label is to inform users on the client side about what resource they are trying to access.

> **Syntax:** `AuthName "`*`authentication_realm_name`*`"`
>
> **Default setting:** None
>
> **Context:** directory, .per-directory config
>
> **Override:** `AuthConfig`

For example, "`AuthName Secured Game Zone`" informs users that they are requesting to enter the Secured Game Zone area of a site. Note that for this directive to work, it must be accompanied by `AuthType`, `Require`, `AuthUserFile` and `AuthGroupFile directives`.

AuthType

The `AuthType` directive selects the user authentication type for a directory. Currently, only `Basic` HTTP authentication or `Digest` authentication types are implemented in Apache. The `Basic` authentication should not be used for serious needs; the password and username are transmitted in clear (plain) text. The password and username is retransmitted for each subsequent request that maps in the same restricted directory or its subdirectories. The `Digest` authentication is more secure than the `Basic` but it is not readily available for all Web browsers. See Chapter 7 for details. The `AuthType` directive must be accompanied by `AuthName` and requires other directives, such as `AuthUserFile` and `AuthGroupFile`, to work.

> **Syntax:** `AuthType Basic | Digest`
>
> **Default setting:** None
>
> **Context:** directory, .per-directory config
>
> **Override:** AuthConfig

HostNameLookups

The `HostNameLookups` directive instructs Apache to enable or disable a DNS lookup for each request. When enabled, Apache stores the host name of the client in the `REMOTE_HOST` environment variable of each CGI and SSI process it runs.

Syntax: `HostNameLookups on | off | double`

Default setting: `HostNameLookups off`

Context: Server, virtual host, directory, per-directory config

The `on` and `off` values do what their names imply. The `double` value refers to doing a double-reverse DNS lookup—that is, after a reverse lookup is performed, a forward lookup is then performed on that result. At least one of the IP addresses in the forward lookup must match the original address. However, the CGI and SSI processes do not get the results from the double DNS lookups.

Note No matter what you set this directive to, when `mod_access` (see Chapter 7) is used to control access by host name, a double-reverse lookup is performed, which is not fast but necessary for ensuring security

I recommend that you keep the default setting for this directive. This will remove a lot of unnecessary DNS traffic from the net. If you want to turn it on just so your log files contain IP names instead of IP addresses, you may want to consider another option, such as running the `logresolve` utility to resolve IP addresses to IP names.

IdentityCheck

The `IdentityCheck` directive tells Apache to log remote usernames by interacting with the remote user's `identd` (identification daemon) process, or an RFC1413-compliant server. This is rarely a useful directive because it will not work for all systems. Most systems do not run `identd` processes to provide user identifications to remote servers.

Syntax: IdentityCheck On | Off

Default setting: IdentityCheck Off

Context: server config, virtual host, directory, .per-directory config

Caution If you decide to use this directive in your configuration, be aware that the information you log is not to be trusted in any way except for usage tracking. This directive can also cause major performance problems because the server has to perform checking for each request. Also, when a remote user is either not providing an `identd` service or is behind a firewall or proxy, the checking process has to time out.

<Limit>

The <Limit> container directive is used to enclose a group of access control directives, which will then apply only to the specified HTTP methods. The method names listed can be one or more of the following: `GET`, `POST`, `PUT`, `DELETE`, `CONNECT`, and `OPTIONS`. If `GET` is used, it will also restrict `HEAD` requests. If you wish to limit all methods, do not include any method in the `<Limit>` directive at all. Note that this container cannot be nested, and neither can a `<Directory>` container appear within it. Method names are case-sensitive.

> **Syntax:** `<Limit method method ... > ... </Limit>`
>
> **Default setting:** None
>
> **Context:** All

<LimitExcept>

The `<LimitExcept>` container directive is used as the complete opposite of `<Limit>` directive (`<limit>` limits named (i.e. arguments) methods and `<LimitExcept>` limits everything *other* than the arguments). All the methods that are not listed as arguments are limited.

> **Syntax:** `<LimitExcept method method ... > ... </LimitExcept>`
>
> **Default setting:** None
>
> **Context:** All

In the following example, the limit applies to all HTTP methods except GET.

```
<LimitExcept GET>
    # directives
</LimitExcept>
```

LimitRequestBody

The `LimitRequestBody` directive enables you to set a limit on the size of the HTTP request that Apache will service. The default limit is 0, which means unlimited. You can set this limit from 0 to 2147483647 (2GB).

> **Syntax:** `LimitRequestBody bytes`
>
> **Default setting:** `LimitRequestBody 0`
>
> **Context:** Server config, virtual host, directory, per-directory

Setting a limit is recommended only if you have experienced HTTP-based denial of service attacks that try to overwhelm the server with large HTTP requests. This is a useful directive to enhance server security.

LimitRequestFields

The `LimitRequestFields` directive allows you to limit number of request header fields allowed in a single HTTP request. This limit can be 0 to 32767 (32K). This directive can help you implement a security measure against large request based denial of service attacks.

Syntax: `LimitRequestFields` *number*

Default setting: `LimitRequestFields 100`

Context: Server config

LimitRequestFieldsize

The `LimitRequestFieldsize` directive enables you to limit the size (in bytes) of a request header field. The default size of 8190 (8K) is more than enough for most situations. However, if you experience a large HTTP request-based denial of service attack, you can change this to a smaller number to deny requests that exceed the limit. A value of 0 sets the limit to unlimited.

Syntax: `LimitRequestFieldsize` *bytes*

Default setting: `LimitRequestFieldsize 8190`

Context: Server config

LimitRequestLine

The `LimitRequestLine` directive sets the limit on the size of the request line. This effectively limits the size of the URL that can be sent to the server. The default limit should be sufficient for most situations. If you experience a denial of service attack that uses long URLs designed to waste resources on your server, you can reduce the limit to reject such requests.

Syntax: `LimitRequestLine` *bytes*

Default setting: `LimitRequestLine 8190`

Context: Server config

Require

By using the `Require` directive, Apache determines which users or group can access a restricted directory. There are three types of entity names available: `user`, `group`, `valid-user`. For example, `require user joe jenny` tells Apache to allow only joe or jenny to enter the area after successful authentication. Only the named users can access the directory.

Syntax: `Require` *entity_name entity_name*...

Default setting: None

Context: directory, per-directory config

Override: `AuthConfig`

As an example of a group-based access requirement, only users in the named groups can access the directory in the following:

```
Require group my-group your-group his-group her-group
```

With the following line, all valid users can access the directory.

```
require valid-user
```

If the require directive appears in a `<Limit>` section, then it restricts access to the named methods; otherwise, it restricts access for all methods. For example:

```
AuthType Basic
AuthName "Game Zone Drop Box"
AuthUserFile  /www/netgames/.users
AuthGroupFile /www/ntgames/.groups

<Limit GET>
    require group coders
</Limit>
```

If the preceding configuration is found in an `.htaccess` file in a directory, only a group called coders is allowed access to the directory to retrieve files via the HTTP GET method. To work correctly, the `Require` directive must be accompanied by `AuthName` and `AuthType` directives, and by directives such as `AuthUserFile` and `AuthGroupFile`.

Cross-Reference   See Chapter 7 for details on authentication.

Satisfy

If you have created a basic HTTP authentication configuration in which both `Allow` and `Require` directives are used, you can use the `Satisfy` directive to tell Apache what authentication requirements will be sufficient.

> **Syntax:** `Satisfy Any | All`
>
> **Default setting:** `Satisfy all`
>
> **Context:** directory, per-directory

The value of the `Satisfy` directive can be either `all` or `any`. If the value is `all`, then the authentication succeeds only if both `Allow` and `Require` succeed. If the value is `any`, then the authentication succeeds if either `Allow` or `Require` succeeds.

The `Satisfy` directive is useful only if access to a particular area is being restricted by both the username/password and the client host address. In this case, the default behavior (all) requires that the client pass the address access restriction and enter a valid username and password. With the any option, the client is granted access if the user either passes the host restriction or enters a valid username and password. This directive can be used to restrict access to an area by using passwords, while simultaneously giving access to all clients from a particular IP address pool (that is, a set of IP addresses) without requiring them to enter passwords.

ScriptInterpreterSource

The ScriptInterpreterSource directive allows you to specify how Windows finds the interpreter for a script. Normally, the script interpreter is detected using the #! line found in a script. However, setting this directive to registry will force Windows to lookup the registry for the script's extension to find the associated program (that is, interpreter) for it.

> **Syntax:** ScriptInterpreterSource Registry | Script
>
> **Default setting:** ScriptInterpreterSource script
>
> **Context:** directory, .htaccess

MPM threaded-Specific Directives

This is like prefork MPM but instead of each child process having a single thread, each child process is allowed to have a specified number of threads. Because threads are more resource efficient than processes, this MPM is very scalable. Each thread within a child process can service a different request.

A process is added or removed by monitoring its spare thread count. For example, if a process has less than the minimum number of spare threads, a new process is added. Similarly, when a process has a maximum number of idle threads, it is killed.

Note   All processes run under the same user and group ID assigned to Apache server.

CoreDumpDirectory

The CoreDumpDirectory directive sets the directory that Apache tries to switch to before crashing and dumping the core (memory image of the server) file. The default location is the directory specified by the ServerRoot directive.

> **Syntax:** CoreDumpDirectory directory_path
>
> **Default setting:** Server's root directory
>
> **Context:** Server config

Group

The Group directive should be used in conjunction with the User directive. Group determines the group under which the standalone server answers requests. To use this directive, the standalone server must be run initially as root. The Group directive can be assigned a group number as well. Group looks up group names and their corresponding numeric values in your /etc/group file.

> **Syntax:** Group Unix-group
>
> **Default setting:** Group #-1
>
> **Context:** Server config, virtual host

Note All the warnings and recommendations I provide for the User directive (later) apply to this directive as well. Make sure that you read the User directive details later in this chapter.

Listen

By default, Apache responds to requests on all the IP addresses attached to the server machine, but only to the port address specified by the Port directive. The Listen directive can be used to make this situation more configurable. You can use the Listen directive to tell Apache to respond to a certain IP address, an IP address and port combination, or just a port by itself.

> **Syntax:** Listen [IP address:] *port_number*
>
> **Default setting:** None
>
> **Context:** Server config

Although Listen can be used instead of BindAddress and Port, you may have to use the Port directive if your Apache server generates URLs that point to itself.

Multiple Listen directives may be used to specify a number of addresses and ports to listen to. The server will respond to requests from any of the listed addresses and ports. For example, to make the server accept connections on both port 80 and port 8080, use:

```
Listen 80
Listen 8080
```

The following examples make Apache accept connections on two IP addresses and port numbers:

```
Listen 192.168.1.100:80
Listen 192.168.1.101:8080
```

ListenBacklog

The `ListenBacklog` directive enables you to take defensive action against a known security attack called Denial of Service (DOS) by enabling you to set the maximum length of the queue of pending connections. Increase this if you detect that you are under a TCP SYN flood (DOS) attack; otherwise, you can leave it alone.

> **Syntax:** `ListenBacklog` *backlog*
>
> **Default setting:** `ListenBacklog 511`
>
> **Context:** Server config

LockFile

If Apache is compiled with the `USE_FCNTL_SERIALIZED_ACCEPT` or `USE_FLOCK_SERIALIZED_ACCEPT` options, a lock file is used. You can use the `LockFile` directive to set the path to the filename of the lock file. Make sure that only the Apache server has read and write access to the file.

> **Syntax:** LockFile *filename*
>
> **Default setting:** `LockFile logs/accept.lock`
>
> **Context:** server config

Note   Storing the lock file on a Network File System (NFS) mounted partition is not a good idea because NFS is known to be problematic when it comes to file locking and security.

MaxClients

The `MaxClients` directive limits the number of simultaneous requests that Apache can service. Because Apache uses one child server for each request, this is also the effective limit for the number of child servers that can exist at the same time.

> **Syntax:** `MaxClients` *number*
>
> **Default setting:** `MaxClients 256`
>
> **Context:** Server config

The default limit is really the hard limit set in the `httpd.h` file in the Apache source distribution. This setting should be fine for most typical-to-moderate load sites. The Apache programmers put the hard limit there for two reasons: they do not want the server to crash the system by filling out some kernel table, and this maximum limit keeps the scoreboard file small enough to be easily readable. When the server reaches the maximum request count, it puts the incoming requests in a wait state until it is free to service them.

Tip   If you have a high-performance server system and have the necessary bandwidth, you can recompile the server with a higher hard limit by modifying appropriate MPM header file (mpmdefauls.h). See Table 2-3 in Chapter 2.

MaxRequestsPerChild

Apache launches a child server process to service a request; however, a child server can process multiple requests. The number of requests a child server can process is limited by the MaxRequestsPerChild directive.

> **Syntax:** MaxRequestsPerChild *number*
>
> **Default setting:** MaxRequestsPerChild 0
>
> **Context:** Server config

After servicing the maximum number of requests, the child process terminates. If the MaxRequestsPerChild is 0, then the process will never expire. If you suspect there are libraries on your operating system (for example, Solaris) that have memory-leaking code, you may want to set this directive to a nonzero value. This enables you to define a life cycle for a child process, reducing the chances of a process consuming leaked memory and slowly eating up all available memory. It also provides you with a small load-average number for your system, because the Apache-related load is reduced as your Web server becomes less busy.

MaxSpareThreads

The MaxSpareThreads directive sets the maximum number of idle threads. The threaded MPM deals with idle threads on a server-wide basis, which means that if there are too many idle threads in the server, it starts killing child processes until the number of idle threads is down to the number specified here.

> **Syntax:** MaxSpareThreads *number*
>
> **Default setting:** MaxSpareThreads 10 (for Perchild MPM) or 500 (for threaded MPM)
>
> **Context:** Server config

The perchild MPM counts idle threads on a per child basis, which means that if there are too many idle threads in a child the threads are destroyed until thread count per child is less than the number specified with MaxSpareThreads directive.

MinSpareThreads

The MinSpareThreads directive sets the minimum number of idle threads. The threaded MPM deals with the idle threads on a server-wide basis, which means that when there are fewer idle threads than the number specified here Apache creates new child processes to bring the total thread count to at least this number.

Syntax: MinSpareServers *number*

Default setting: MaxSpareThreads 5 (for Perchild MPM) or 250 (for threaded MPM)

Context: Server config

The perchild MPM handles idle thread count on a per child basis; thus, when a child has less than the number of minimum threads specified here, the server creates new threads within that child process.

SendBufferSize

The SendBufferSize directive sets the TCP send buffer size to the number of bytes specified. On a high-performance network, setting the directive to a higher value than the operating system defaults may increase server performance.

Syntax: SendBufferSize *bytes*

Default setting: None

Context: Server config

StartServers

The StartServers directive sets the number of child Apache server processes that are created on startup. The number of Apache child processes needed for a certain time period is dynamically controlled. The primary Apache server (the daemon process) launches new child processes as it encounters higher request loads. The actual number of child processes is controlled by the MinSpareServers, MaxSpareServers, and the MaxClients directives. Therefore, you have little to gain by adjusting this parameter.

Syntax: StartServers *number*

Default setting: StartServers 5

Context: Server config

Note   The StartServers directive is useful only when the Apache server is running as a standalone server. In other words, you need to have ServeType set to standalone for this directive to be effective.

Note   When running Microsoft Windows, this directive sets the total number of child processes running. Because the Windows version of Apache is multithreaded, one process handles all the requests. The rest of the processes are held in reserve until the primary process dies.

ThreadsPerChild

The Windows version of Apache is a multithreaded server. The ThreadsPerChild directive tells the server how many threads it should use. It also determines the maximum number of connections that the server can handle at any given time. Therefore, this value should be set reasonably high to allow the maximum number of possible hits.

> **Syntax:** ThreadsPerChild *number*
>
> **Default setting:** ThreadsPerChild 50
>
> **Context:** Server config (Windows)

User

The User directive sets the user ID that is used by the Apache children that services HTTP requests. Once the Apache server is started, it launches child processes to respond to requests. However, these child processes are not run as root. The parent Apache process (often called the daemon) changes the child process user ID to whatever is set in the User directive, as long as it is a valid user ID.

> **Syntax:** User *unix-userid*
>
> **Default setting:** User #-1
>
> **Context:** Server config, virtual host

If you start the server as a nonroot user, it fails to change to the user ID specified by the User directive, and instead continues to run as the original user. If you do start the server as root, then it is normal for the parent Apache process to remain running as root; however, it runs the child processes as the user specified by the User directive.

Caution Never set the User (or Group) directive to root unless you know exactly what you are doing and what the dangers are.

You can also use user ID numbers, which you can usually find in your /etc/password file. If you plan on using a numeric value instead of the actual username, the number should be preceded by a # sign.

Many Apache administrators use the default nobody user for their Web sites. This user is not available on all Unix systems, and is not always desirable. I highly recommend that you employ a unique user and group ID (see the Group directive) for your Apache server. Doing so will give you better control of what the server can or cannot access. The user ID you decide to use for Apache child processes should have very few access privileges. It should not be able to access files that are not intended to be visible to the outside world, and similarly, the user should not be able to execute applications that are not meant for HTTP requests.

Note Use of this directive in the `<VirtualHost>` container requires a properly configured `suEXEC` wrapper. When the wrapper is used inside a `<VirtualHost>` container in this manner, only the user that CGIs are run as is affected. Non-CGI requests are still processed with the user specified in the main `User` directive. So, the primary `User` directive cannot be completely overridden.

MPM perchild-Specific Directives

In this MPM model, a set number of child processes are started with a specified number of threads. As request load increases the processes add new threads as needed. When request count reduces, processes shrink their thread counts using a minimum and maximum thread count setting.

AssignUserID

The `AssignUserID` directive assigns a username and group name to a virtual host.

Syntax: `AssignUserID username groupname`

Default setting: None

Context: Virtual host

For example, in the following, the virtual host called `www.afactcat.com` is assigned to user `mrbert` and the group called `wheel`. You must use the `ChildPerUserID` to specify the number of child processes that can service this virtual host.

```
<VirtualHost 192.168.1.100>
    ServerName www.afatcat.com
    AssignUserID mrbert wheel

    #
    # Other directives go here
    #
</VirtualHost>
```

Note *username* and *groupname* must exist in your system. For example, on a Linux system *username* and *groupname* must exist in the `/etc/passwd` and `/etc/group` files, respectively.

ChildPerUserID

The `ChildPerUserID` directive assigns a number of child processes to a given username and group name for virtual hosts.

Syntax: ChildPerUserID *number_of_child username groupname*

Default setting: None

Context: Virtual host

For example, in the following, the virtual host www.afatcat.com will be serviced by 10 Apache children who run under the username mrbert and group wheel:

```
ChildPerUserID 10 mrbert wheel

<VirtualHost 192.168.1.100>
    ServerName www.afatcat.com
    AssignUserID mrbert wheel

    #
    # Other directives go here
    #
</VirtualHost>
```

Note   *username* and *groupname* must exist in your system for Apache to be able to use them. For example, on a Linux system the *username* and *groupname* must exist in the /etc/passwd and /etc/group files, respectively.

ConnectionStatus

The ConnectionStatus directive sets if status information is internally stored or not. When set to on, modules that use status information will function properly.

Syntax: ConnectionStatus On | Off

Default setting: ConnectionStatus On

Context: Server config

CoreDumpDirectory

See CoreDumpDirectory directive in the "MPM threaded-Specific Directives" section.

Group

See Group directive in the "MPM threaded-Specific Directives" section.

Listen

See Listen directive under the "MPM threaded-Specific Directives" section.

ListenBacklog

See `ListenBacklog` directive under the "MPM threaded-Specific Directives" section.

LockFile

See `LockFile` directive under the "MPM threaded-Specific Directives" section.

MaxRequestsPerChild

See `MaxRequestsPerChild` directive under the "MPM threaded-Specific Directives" section.

MaxSpareThreads

See `MaxSpareThreads` directive under the "MPM threaded-Specific Directives" section.

MaxThreadsPerChild

The `MaxThreadsPerChild` directive sets the maximum number of threads per child. The default number is a hard limit. If you wish to change this you have to change the appropriate header file. See Table 2-3 in Chapter 2 for details.

> **Syntax:** `MaxThreadsPerChild` *number*
>
> **Default setting:** `MaxThreadsPerChild 64`
>
> **Context:** Server config

MinSpareThreads

See `MinSpareThreads` directive under the "MPM threaded-Specific Directives" section.

NumServers

The `NumServers` directive sets the number of simultaneous child processes that are created by Apache.

> **Syntax:** `NumServers` *number*
>
> **Default setting:** `NumServers 2`
>
> **Context:** Server config

The per-child MPM uses the value set by this directive to determine the number of simultaneous children. The default value 2 might not be appropriate for most systems. You might want to set this to a higher limit such as 15 or 20. A higher number spawns more Apache processes, which means more simultaneous connections can be handled.

PidFile

See PidFile directive under the "MPM threaded-Specific Directives" section.

ScoreBoardFile

See ScoreBoardFile directive under the "MPM threaded-Specific Directives" section.

SendBufferSize

See SendBufferSize directive under the "MPM threaded-Specific Directives" section.

StartThreads

The StartThreads directive sets the initial thread count per child. Because thread counts are dynamically controlled, setting this to a higher number than the default is not necessary in most cases.

> **Syntax:** StartThreads *number*
>
> **Default setting:** StartThreads 5
>
> **Context:** Server config

User

See User directive under the "MPM threaded-Specific Directives" section.

MPM winnt-Specific Directives

This is the MPM for all versions of the Windows platform, including Windows NT/2000/XP and Windows 9*x*/ME. This module is multi-threaded; using this module Apache will create a parent process and a child process. The child process creates all the threads that service the request. This module now takes advantage of some Windows-only native function calls, which allows it to perform better than the earlier versions of Apache server on Windows platform.

CoreDumpDirectory

See `CoreDumpDirectory` directive under the "MPM threaded-Specific Directives" section.

Listen

See `Listen` directive under the "MPM threaded-Specific Directives" section.

ListenBacklog

See `ListenBacklog` directive under the "MPM threaded-Specific Directives" section.

MaxRequestsPerChild

See `MaxRequestsPerChild` directive under the "MPM threaded-Specific Directives" section.

PidFile

See `PidFile` directive under the "MPM threaded-Specific Directives" section.

SendBufferSize

See `SendBufferSize` directive under the "MPM threaded-Specific Directives" section.

ThreadsPerChild

See `ThreadsPerChild` directive under the "MPM threaded-Specific Directives" section.

MPM prefork Specific Directives

The prefork MPM creates a pool of child processes to service requests. Each child process has a single thread. For example, if Apache starts 30 child processes, it can service 30 requests simultaneously.

If something goes wrong and the child process dies, only a single request is lost. The number of child processes is controlled using a minimum and maximum setting. When the number of requests increases, new child processes are added until the maximum is reached. Similarly, when the requests fall, any extra child processes are killed.

CoreDumpDirectory

See `CoreDumpDirectory` directive under the "MPM threaded-Specific Directives" section.

Group

See `Group` directive under the "MPM threaded-Specific Directives" section.

Listen

See `Listen` directive under the "MPM threaded-Specific Directives" section.

ListenBacklog

See `ListenBacklog` directive under the "MPM threaded-Specific Directives" section.

LockFile

See `LockFile` directive under the "MPM threaded-Specific Directives" section.

MaxClients

See `MaxClients` directive under the "MPM threaded-Specific Directives" section.

MaxRequestsPerChild

See `MaxRequestsPerChild` directive under the "MPM threaded-Specific Directives" section.

MaxSpareServers

This directive lets you set the number of idle Apache child processes that you want on your server.

> **Syntax:** `MaxSpareServers` *number*
>
> **Default setting:** `MaxSpareServers 10`
>
> **Context:** Server config

If the number of idle Apache child processes exceeds the maximum number specified by the `MaxSpareServers` directive, then the parent process kills off the excess processes. Tuning of this parameter should only be necessary for very busy sites. Unless you know what you are doing, do not change the default.

MinSpareServers

The `MinSpareServers` directive sets the desired minimum number of idle child server processes. An idle process is one that is not handling a request. If there are fewer idle Apache processes than the number specified by the `MinSpareServers` directive, then the parent process creates new children at a maximum rate of 1 per second. Tuning of this parameter should only be necessary on very busy sites. Unless you know what you are doing, do not change the default.

Syntax: `MinSpareServers number`

Default setting: `MinSpareServers 5`

Context: Server config

PidFile

See `PidFile` directive under the "MPM threaded-Specific Directives" section.

ScoreBoardFile

See `ScoreBoardFile` directive under the "MPM threaded-Specific Directives" section.

SendBufferSize

See `SendBufferSize` directive under the "MPM threaded-Specific Directives" section.

StartServers

See `StartServers` directive under the "MPM threaded-Specific Directives" section.

User

See `User` directive under the "MPM threaded-Specific Directives" section.

✦   ✦   ✦

Apache Modules

In Chapter 4, I discuss core and multiprocessing module (MPM) directives. Apache offers many more directives, which are available from the modules distributed in the standard source distribution. These modules offer a great deal of functionality via the use of directives. This chapter discusses these modules and their directives.

An Overview of the Modules

Instead of listing all the modules in alphabetic order, I have grouped modules based on their similarities in functionality. The modules are divided into the following categories:

+ **Environment-related:** These directives allow you to set and reset environment variables.

+ **Authentication and access control:** These directives allow you to authenticate and authorize user access to restricted parts of your Web site.

+ **Dynamic contents generation:** These directives allow you to run external programs such as CGI scripts or Server Side Includes to create dynamic contents.

+ **Content-type configuration:** These directives allow you to control MIME types of files.

+ **Directory listing:** These directives allow you to control how directory listings are formatted.

+ **Response header:** These directives allow you to control HTTP response headers.

+ **Server information and logging:** These directives allow you to control server logs and status information.

+ **URL mapping:** These directives allow you to map, rewrite, and create aliases for a URL.

+ **Miscellaneous modules:** These directives allow you to control miscellaneous aspects of Apache such as proxy service, WEBDEV module, etc.

Environment-Related Modules

The modules listed in Table 5-1 enable you to manipulate the environment that is available to other modules or to external programs, such as CGI (Common Gateway Interface) scripts, SSI (Server-Side Include), mod_perl scripts, PHP scripts, Java servlets, and the like.

Table 5-1
Environment-Related Modules

Module	Purpose
mod_env	Passes environments to external programs such as CGI and SSI scripts.
mod_setenvif	Sets conditional environment variables using information from the client side.
mod_unique_id	This module generates a unique ID per request. It has no directives. This module is not compiled by default. You must configure the source by using --enable-unique-id option with the configure script and by compiling and installing Apache.

mod_env

mod_env is compiled by default. It enables you to pass environment variables to external programs such as CGI scripts, SSI, mod_perl scripts, PHP scripts, and the like. mod-env has the following directives.

PassEnv

The PassEnv directive tells the module to pass one or more environment variables from the server's own environment to the CGI and SSI scripts.

Syntax: PassEnv *variable [...]*

Context: Server config, virtual host

For example, the following directive passes the HOSTTYPE and PATH environment variables to programs.

```
PassEnv HOSTTYPE PATH
```

SetEnv

The SetEnv directive sets an environment variable to a given value, which is then passed on to CGI/SSI scripts. You can only define a single variable and value pair per SetEnv directive.

> **Syntax:** SetEnv *variable value*
>
> **Context:** Server config, virtual host

For example, the following SetEnv directive sets the CURRENT_CITY variable to SACRAMENTO:

```
SetEnv CURRENT_CITY SACRAMENTO
```

UnsetEnv

The UnsetEnv directive removes one or more environment variables from those that are passed to CGI/SSI scripts. This can be used to ensure that certain environment variables that are available to the Apache server are not available to your CGI scripts.

> **Syntax:** UnsetEnv *variable [...]*
>
> **Context:** Server config, virtual host

For example, the following UnsetEnv directive removes the CURRENT_STATE variable from the environment variable list:

```
UnsetEnv CURRENT_STATE
```

mod_setenvif

The mod_setenvif module is compiled in Apache by default. It enables you to create custom environment variables using information from an HTTP request. You can use such information in rewriting URLs or redirecting users to different pages.

BrowserMatch

The BrowserMatch directive sets and unsets custom environment variables when the regular expression matches a pattern found in the User-Agent header of a HTTP request. The User-Agent header is sent by Web clients such as Web browsers, Web robots, and the like.

> **Syntax:** BrowserMatch *regex variable[=value] [...]*
>
> **Context:** Server config

For example, the following sets a variable called vbscript to the value no if the User-Agent header field of the HTTP request contains the word Mozilla, and an environment variable called javascript is set to 1 because no value was specified for this variable:

```
BrowserMatch ^Mozilla vbscript=no javascript
```

Let's look at another example:

```
BrowserMatch IE vbscript !javascript
```

Here, the variable javascript is removed and the vbscript is set to 1 if the word IE is found in the User-Agent HTTP request header. The ! character removes the variable from the environment.

Note   A regular expression match is case sensitive.

BrowserMatchNoCase

The BrowserMatchNoCase directive is same as the BrowserMatch directive, except that it provides case-insensitive matching for regular expressions.

> **Syntax:** BrowserMatchNoCase *regex variable[=value] [...]*
>
> **Context:** Server config

For example, the following directive matches MSIE, msie, Msie, and so on:

```
BrowserMatchNoCase ^MSIE vbscript=yes
```

SetEnvIf

Like the BrowserMatch and BrowserMatchNoCase directives, the SetEnvIf directive enables you to set and unset custom environment variables. Actually, BrowserMatch and BrowserMatchNoCase are two special versions of SetEnvIf. These two directives can only perform the regular expression on the User-Agent HTTP request header field, whereas SetEnvIf can be used for all request header fields, as well as other request-related information, such as remote host name (Remote_Host), remote IP address (Remote_Addr), request method (Request_Method), requested URI (Request_URI), and referrer (Referer).

> **Syntax:** SetEnvIf *attribute regex envar[=value] [...]*
>
> **Context:** Server config

For example, the following SetEnvIf directive sets the local_user variable to true if the Remote_Host HTTP header is set to yourdomain.com.

```
SetEnvIf Remote_Host "yourdomain\.com" local_user=true
```

SetEnvIfNoCase

The SetEnvIfNoCase directive is the same as SetEnvIf, except that it offers case-insensitive regular expression matches.

> **Syntax:** SetEnvIfNoCase *attribute regex variable*[=*value*] [...]
>
> **Context:** Server config

mod_unique_id

The mod_unique_id module provides a magic token for each request that is guaranteed to be unique across "all" requests under very specific conditions. The unique identifier is even unique across multiple machines in a properly configured cluster of machines. The environment variable UNIQUE_ID is set to the identifier for each request. There are no directives for this module.

Authentication and Access Control Modules

Apache has a number of modules to perform authentication and authorization tasks. In most cases, the authentication modules use basic HTTP authentication, which uses plain text passwords. The authorization module allows you to control access to a directory of your Web site via a username or IP address. The modules shown in Table 5-2 enable you to perform authentication and access control tasks.

Table 5-2 Authentication and Access Control Modules	
Module	**Purpose**
mod_auth	This is the standard authentication module, which implements Basic HTTP authentication. See Chapter 7 for details.
mod_auth_anon	Gives anonymous user access to authenticated areas.
mod_auth_dbm	Provides user authentication using DBM files.
mod_auth_db	Provides User authentication using Berkeley DB files.
mod_auth_digest	This module implements Digest authentication using Message Digest 5 (MD5).
mod_access	This module allows you to authorize access by using host name or IP address. See Chapter 7 for details.

mod_auth_anon

The `mod_auth_anon` module enables anonymous access to authenticated areas. If you are familiar with anonymous FTP servers, this is very similar to such a setup. All users can use a user ID called "anonymous" and their e-mail addresses as the password to get access. The e-mail address entered is stored in log files and can be used to perform user tracking or to create a mailing list of prospective clients.

You have to enable this module by using the `--enable-auth-anon` option with the `configure` script in the source distribution, and by compiling and installing Apache.

Anonymous

By using the `Anonymous` directive you can specify one or more usernames that can be used to access the area. It is a good idea to keep the username "anonymous" in your chosen list, because it is widely associated with anonymous access. If the username you choose has a space character in it, make sure that the username is surrounded by quotation marks.

> **Syntax:** Anonymous *user user* ...
>
> **Context:** Directory, per-directory access control file (`.htaccess`)
>
> **Override:** AuthConfig

For example, the following directive allows users to enter **Unregistered User** or **anonymous** as the username to enter an anonymous area.

```
Anonymous "Unregistered User" anonymous
```

Note   The username strings are not case sensitive.

Anonymous_Authoritative

When set to `on`, the anonymous authentication becomes the authoritative authentication scheme for a directory. In other words, if you have multiple authentication requirements for a directory and it also has this directive set, then the other methods will be ignored.

> **Syntax:** Anonymous_Authoritative On | Off
>
> **Default setting:** Anonymous_Authoritative Off
>
> **Context:** Directory, per-directory access control file (`.htaccess`)
>
> **Override:** AuthConfig

Anonymous_LogEmail

When the `Anonymous_LogEmail` directive is set to `on`, whatever is entered in the password field of the browser's pop-up authentication window is logged in the Apache access log file.

> **Syntax:** `Anonymous_LogEmail On | Off`
>
> **Default setting:** `Anonymous_LogEmail On`
>
> **Context:** Directory, per-directory access control file (`.htaccess`)
>
> **Override:** `AuthConfig`

Anonymous_MustGiveEmail

When set to `On`, the `Anonymous_MustGiveEmail` directive enables the module to reject access requests that do not provide passwords in the form of e-mail addresses.

> **Syntax:** `Anonymous_MustGiveEmail On | Off`
>
> **Default setting:** `Anonymous_MustGiveEmail On`
>
> **Context:** Directory, per-directory access control file (`.htaccess`)
>
> **Override:** `AuthConfig`

Caution   You should not trust the e-mail addresses that people enter when this directive is set to `On`, because there is no way of checking who entered whose e-mail address.

Anonymous_NoUserID

If you want the users to leave the username field of the pop-up window empty, set the `Anonymous_NoUserID` directive to `On`; otherwise, a username that matches the values provided in the `Anonymous` directive is required.

> **Syntax:** `Anonymous_NoUserID On | Off`
>
> **Default setting:** `Anonymous_NoUserID Off`
>
> **Context:** Directory, per-directory access control file (`.htaccess`)
>
> **Override:** `AuthConfig`

Anonymous_VerifyEmail

When the `Anonymous_VerifyEmail` directive is set to `on`, it requires that the password be a valid e-mail address. However, the validity check is limited. The module only checks for an @ symbol and a period (.) in the password field. If the entered password has both of these symbols in it, it is accepted.

> **Syntax:** `Anonymous_VerifyEmail On | Off`
>
> **Default setting:** `Anonymous_VerifyEmail Off`

Context: Directory, per-directory access control file (.htaccess)

Override: AuthConfig

The following configuration shows how the preceding directives can be used to provide anonymous access to a directory.

```
Anonymous_NoUserId off
Anonymous_MustGiveEmail on
Anonymous_VerifyEmail on
Anonymous_LogEmail on
Anonymous anonymous guest "I do not know"
AuthName Use 'anonymous' & Email address for guest entry
AuthType basic
require valid-user
```

mod_auth_dbm

Text file-based authentication (using mod_auth) is inefficient for high-speed processing and could negatively affect a Web server's performance when a great number of users (more than 2000) need authenticated access to restricted Web sections. The mod_auth_dbm module is a better choice in such a case. The mod_auth_dbm module uses DBM files instead of text files to store data. A *DBM file* is a special type of data file that allows faster random access to stored data.

Note   Actually if you have a great many users, consider mod_auth_mysql-**based or** Apache::AuthDBI-**based authentication discussed in Chapter 7. DBM-based authentication is only recommended if you cannot use a database.**

A DBM file stores data records in a key=value pair and keeps a computed index table for the keys in the file. By using the index table in a DBM file, it is possible to retrieve the record associated with the key faster than the time needed to parse a large text file with tens of thousands of records. Many DBMs are available, the most common being GDBM, NDBM, SDBM, and Berkeley DB (BSD-DB). Table 5-3 shows a list of features for these DBMs.

Table 5-3 DBM Features				
Features	*NDBM*	*SDBM*	*GDBM*	*BSD-DB*
Licensing restrictions	Unknown	No	Yes	No
Byte-order independent	No	No	No	Yes
Default size limits	4K	1K	None	None

Features	NDBM	SDBM	GDBM	BSD-DB
Creates FTP-safe files	No	Yes	Yes	Yes
Speed	Unknown	Slow	Medium	Fast
Database size	Unknown	Small	Large	Medium
Code size	Unknown	Small	Large	Large
Source comes with Perl	No	Yes	No	No

This table is based on the information found in Perl 5 documentation. Before you can use any DBM with Apache, you have to make sure the DBM you choose is already installed in your system. Do this by confirming that the DBM library files are located in your system's default library directory. You are going to need Perl with DBM support. Make sure you have the latest version of Perl compiled with the chosen DBM support.

Note   You can download Perl from `www.perl.com`. Configuring Perl for DBM support is quite easy. Just run the configuration script, and it will prompt you for the DBM support. For example, if you choose NDBM or GDBM as your desired DBM, and if you have them installed on your system, the Perl configuration script should ask whether you want to compile Perl with `-lndbm`, `-lgdbm`, and library flags.

After you have installed the appropriate DBM libraries on your system, you then need to configure Apache for support of DBM files, because the standard Apache distribution does not enable DBM support. Configure Apache source by using `--enable-auth-dbm` option with `configure` script, and by compiling and installing Apache as usual.

Note   If you have trouble compiling Apache, try adding the `-lyour  dbmname` to `EXTRA_LIBS` in the `Configuration` file. For example, if you are using GDBM, you can add `-lgdbm` so that `EXTRA_LIBS=-lgdbm`. Make sure you rerun the `configure` script and run `make` again afterwards. In case of problems, it might be best to try GNU GDBM because it is heavily used by many different systems and you are likely to get help in USENET newsgroups.

After Apache is properly compiled for DBM files, you can use `dbmmanage` to create a DBM user file. Begin by using the `dbmmanage` Perl script found in the support directory of the standard Apache distribution (or the source distribution) for creating a DBM-based user file. The `dbmmanage` Perl script can create many popular DBM files such as NDBM, GDBM, and Berkley DB files. This script can be used to create a new DBM file, to add users and passwords, to change passwords, to delete users, or to view user information. Before using the script, you should modify the following line in the script so that the DBM you want to use is listed as the first item in the ISA array:

```
BEGIN { @AnyDBM_File::ISA = qw(DB_File, NDBM_File, GDBM_file) }
```

For example, if you plan to use GDBM files, change the line to:

```
BEGIN { @AnyDBM_File::ISA = qw(GDBM_file , DB_File, NDBM_File) }
```

To find out what options the script provides, run it as follows:

```
./dbmmanage
```

This shows you a syntax line with all the possible options. To create a new DBM file called /www/secrets/myuserdbm by adding a user named reader, enter the following command:

```
./dbmmanage /www/secrets/myuserdbm adduser reader
```

The script will ask you to enter (and reenter) a password for the user reader. After you have done so, it will add the username and encrypted password to the myuserdbm DBM file. Do not use the add option to add a user because it does not encrypt the password. To see a list of all users in a DBM file, use the following script:

```
./dbmmanage /path/to/your/dbmfile view
```

After you have recompiled Apache with DBM support, you can use the module mod_auth_dbm to provide DBM-based Basic HTTP authentication. Note that for Berkeley DB you have to use mod_auth_db instead of mod_auth_dbm.

The mod_auth_dbm module provides the directives AuthDBMUserFIle, AuthDBMGroupFile, and AuthDBMAuthoritative. Let's take a look at each of these directives and some examples that use the mod_auth_dbm module.

AuthDBMUserFile

The AuthDBMUserFile directive sets the fully qualified pathname of a DBM file to be used as the user file for DBM authentication. The file contains a key=value pair per record, in which the username is the key and the crypt()-encrypted password is the value. Note that each field in the record is separated by a colon, and arbitrary data can be appended after the initial username and password fields.

> **Syntax:** AuthDBMUserFile *filename*
>
> **Context:** Directory, per-directory access control file (.htaccess)
>
> **Override:** AuthConfig

Caution Never store user database files inside your Web document tree because someone might download the entire user database and abuse it.

AuthDbmGroupFile

The AuthDbmGroupFile directive sets the fully qualified pathname of the group file that contains the list of user groups. Each record in the file is a key=value pair, in which the key is the username and the value is a comma-separated list of group names to which the user belongs.

> **Syntax:** AuthDBMGroupFile *filename*
>
> **Context:** Directory, per-directory access control file (.htaccess)
>
> **Override:** AuthConfig

If you prefer not to use a separate group file, you can use a single DBM file to provide both password and group information. The format of the file is as follows:

DBM_Record_Key{*username*} = *encrypted_password*: *comma_separated_group_list*

Here, the username is the key, and the password and group lists are two fields of the value. Other data may be left in the DBM file after another colon, if desired; it is ignored by the authentication module. If you use a single DBM to provide both group and password information, you have to point both AuthDBMGroup and AuthDBMUserFile directives to the same file.

AuthDBMAuthoritative

When using multiple authentication schemes such as mod_dbm and standard mod_auth in the same directory, you can use the AuthDbmGroupFile directive to define whether mod_auth_dbm is the authoritative authentication scheme.

> **Syntax:** AuthDBMAuthoritative On | Off
>
> **Default setting:** AuthDBMAuthoritative On
>
> **Context:** Directory, per-directory access control file (.htaccess)
>
> **Override:** AuthConfig

The default value of the directive enables mod_auth_dbm to become the authoritative authentication for the directory. Thus, if the DBM-based authentication fails for a particular user, the user's credentials are not passed on to a lower-level authentication scheme. When set to the off value, the credentials of a failed authentication are passed on to the next authentication level.

Tip   A common use for this module is in conjunction with one of the basic auth modules, such as mod_auth.c. Whereas this DBM module supplies the bulk of the user credential checking, a few (administrator) related accesses fall through to a lower level with a well-protected .htpasswd file.

Now lets take a look at an example of how you can use a DBM based username and password.Assuming you have the user DBM file created, you are now capable of restricting access to any Web directory you want. In the following example, I assume that the user DBM file is /www/secrets/myuserdbm. You can add the authentication scheme to your global or virtual server using a <Directory> container, or you can use the .htaccess file — there is no difference. The example configuration looks like this:

```
AuthName "Apache Server Bible Readers Only"
AuthType Basic
AuthUserDBMFile /www/secrets/myuserdbm
require valid-user
```

Now Apache uses the `mod_auth_dbm` module for authentication in the directory where this configuration applies.

 Caution   Make sure that only Apache and the owner can read the DBM file. No one but the owner of the DBM file should be able to write to it.

mod_auth_db

If your system is not capable of using DBM, but Berkeley DB file support is available, you can use `mod_auth_db` to use DB files instead of the DBM modules for Apache. This module is not compiled in the standard Apache distribution.

Before configuring Apache with DB file based authentication module, make sure you know where the DB library files are stored on your system. For example, on a Linux system, the files are in the standard `/usr/lib` directory. If your system does not have the DB libraries, you will have to get the source code and compile DB support first. You can find DB library information at `www.sleepycat.com`.

After you have made sure that your system has DB libraries, you can proceed with reconfiguring and recompiling Apache. Use the `--enable-db` option with `configure` script to configure the Apache source for Berkeley DB support, and then compile and install Apache as usual.

At this point, you are ready to use the `mod_auth_db` module. This `mod_auth_db` module provides the `AuthDBUserFile`, `AuthDBGroupFile`, and `AuthDBAuthoritative` directives.

AuthDBUserFile

The `AuthDBUserFile` directive sets the fully qualified pathname of the user DB file that contains the list of users and encrypted passwords.

> **Syntax:** AuthDBUserFile *filename*
>
> **Context:** Directory, per-directory access control file (`.htaccess`)
>
> **Override:** AuthConfig

Like its DBM counterpart, the DB user file is also keyed using the username and the value is the `crypt()`-encrypted password.

 Caution   Always make sure your user files are kept outside the Web document tree and are only readable by Apache. No one but the owner (Apache) should have write access to these files.

AuthDBGroupFile

The `AuthDBGroupFile` directive sets the fully qualified pathname of the group DB file, which contains the list of user groups for user authentication. Like its DBM counterpart, the group file uses the username as the key and the comma-separated group list is treated as the value. There must be no whitespace within the value, and it must never contain any colons.

> **Syntax:** `AuthDBGroupFile` *filename*
>
> **Context:** Directory, per-directory access control file (`.htaccess`)
>
> **Override:** `AuthConfig`

If you do not prefer to use a separate group file, you can use a single DB file to provide both password and group information. The format of the file is:

```
DB_File_Key{username} = encrypted_password: comma_separated_group_list
```

where the username is the key, and the password and group lists are two fields of the value. Other data may be left in the DB file after another colon; it is ignored by the authentication module. If you use a single DB to provide both group and password information, you will have to point both `AuthDBGroup` and `AuthDBUserFile` directives to the same file.

AuthDBAuthoritative

When using multiple authentication schemes such as `mod_db`, `mod_dbm`, and `standard mod_auth` in the same directory, you can use the `AuthDBAuthoritative` directive to define whether `mod_auth_db` is the authoritative authentication scheme. The default value of the directive enables `mod_auth_db` to become the authoritative authentication for the directory. Thus, if the DB-based authentication fails for a particular user, the user's credentials are not passed on to a lower-level authentication scheme. When set to the `Off` value, the credentials of a failed authentication are passed on to the next authentication level.

> **Syntax:** `AuthDBAuthoritative On | Off`
>
> **Default setting:** `AuthDBAuthoritative On`
>
> **Context:** Directory, per-directory access control file (`.htaccess`)
>
> **Override:** `AuthConfig`

Dynamic Contents Generation Modules

The modules discussed here enable Apache to run CGI scripts, SSIs, filters, and the like. Table 5-4 lists these modules.

Table 5-4
Dynamic Contents Generation Module

Module	Purpose
mod_cgi	Runs CGI scripts. See Chapter 12 for details.
mod_include	SSI filter. See Chapter 13 for details.
mod_actions	Executing CGI scripts based on media type or request method.
mod_ext_filter	Filtering output with external programs.

mod_actions

The mod_actions module is compiled by default. mod_actions enables you to run a CGI script based on MIME-type or on the HTTP request method. It offers these directives.

Action

The Action directive enables you to associate an action for a specific MIME type. The action is usually a CGI script that processes the file being requested. This allows you to execute a CGI script for a given MIME type.

> **Syntax:** Action MIME_type cgi_script
>
> **Context:** Server config, virtual host, directory, per-directory access control file (.htaccess)
>
> **Override:** FileInfo

For example, the following directive makes Apache run the specified script whenever an HTML file is requested:

```
Action text/html /cgi-bin/somescript.pl
```

The script receives the URL and file path of the requested document via the standard CGI PATH_INFO and PATH_TRANSLATED environment variables. This can be useful in developing filter scripts. This section discusses one such filter script.

When a text file (.txt) is requested via the Web, it appears on the Web browser in a less-than-desirable format, because line breaks are not translated by most Web browsers in any manner. Usually, most text files appear as a large paragraph. By using the Action directive, you can develop a better solution.

For a more interesting example, let's say that you now want to develop a solution that not only displays the text files better on the Web browser, but also inserts a copyright message at the end of each text file. To accomplish this, you need to do two things. First, add the following directive in httpd.conf file:

```
Action plain/text /cgi-bin/textfilter.pl
```

Then, develop the Perl script textfilter which will display the text file the way you wish. Listing 5-1 shows one such script. You can find this script on the accompanying CD-ROM in the Scripts/Chapter 5 directory.

Listing 5-1: **textfilter.pl**

```
#!/usr/bin/perl
#
# Script: textfilter.pl
#
# Purpose: This filter script converts plain text files
#          into an HTML document but keeps the text layout
#          as is.
#
# Copyright (c) 2001 by Mohammed J. Kabir
#
# License: GPL
#

# The copyright message file is always stored in
# the server's document root
# directory and is called copyright.html.
#
my $copyright_file = $ENV{DOCUMENT_ROOT} . "/copyright.html";
# Get the requested document's path
my $path_translated = $ENV{PATH_TRANSLATED};

# Other variables needed for storing data
my $line;
my @text;
my @html;

# Store the path info and the file name of requested doc in an
array
@filename = split(/\//,$path_translated);

# Because HTML tags are used to display the text file,
# lets print the text/html content header.
print "Content-type: text/html\n\n";

# Read the document requested and store the data
# in @text array variable
```

Continued

Listing 5-1 *(continued)*

```perl
@text = &readFile($path_translated);

# Now print the following HTML document tags.
# These tags will be sent before the actual document content
#
print <<HEAD;
   <HTML>
   <HEAD> <TITLE>$filename[-1] </TITLE> </HEAD>
   <BODY BGCOLOR="white">
   <BLOCKQUOTE>
   <PRE>
HEAD

# Now print each line stored in the @text array
# (that is, the content of the document requested)
#
foreach $line (@text) { print $line; }
# Now read the copyright file and store the content
# in the @html array variable
#
@html = &readFile($copyright_file);
# Print each line stored in the @html array (that is,
# the content of the copyright message file)
#
foreach $line (@html){ print $line; }
# Exit the filter
exit 0;

sub readFile {
    #
    # Subroutine: readFile
    # Purpose: Reads a file if it exists or else prints
    # an error message and exits script
    #

    # Get the name of the passed file name and store
    # it in variable $file
     my $file = shift;

    # Local buffer variable
     my @buffer;

    # If the file exists, open it and read all the
    # lines into the @buffer array variable
     if(-e $file) {

         open(FP,$file) || die "Can not open $file.";
         while(<FP>){
```

```
        push(@buffer,$_);
    }

    close(FP);
} else {
    push(@buffer,"$file is missing.");
}

# Return the content of the buffer.
return (@buffer);
}
```

The preceding script reads the requested text file and prints out the content inside a few HTML tags that enable the content to be displayed as is. This is accomplished by using the HTML tag <PRE>. After the content is printed, the copyright message file content is inserted at the end of the output. This enables a copyright message to be printed with each requested text file. Figure 5-1 shows an example output where a text file is being displayed on the Web browser.

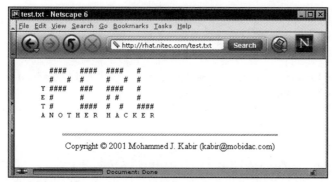

Figure 5-1: Output of `textfilter.pl`

As you can see, the requested filename appears as the title. The document is block quoted, and a custom copyright message is printed. The copyright message file is stored in the document's root directory. The file used in this example is:

```
</PRE>
<BLOCKQUOTE>
<CENTER>
<HR>
Copyright (c) 2001 Mohammed J. Kabir (kabir@mobidac.com})
</CENTER>
</BODY>
</HTML>
```

Script

The Script directive is like the Action directive, but instead of associating an action with a MIME-type, it associates the action with an HTTP request such as GET, POST, PUT, or DELETE. The CGI script receives the URL and file path of the requested document using the standard CGI PATH_INFO and PATH_TRANSLATED environment variables.

> **Syntax:** Script method *cgi-script*
>
> **Context:** Server config, virtual host, directory

This directive defines default action. In other words, if you have defined the following:

```
Script POST /cgi-bin/deafult_post.pl
```

in an Apache configuration file (such as srm.conf), then whenever a request is made via the HTTP POST method, it will be processed as usual, unless the default action specified by the directive needs to be used. For example, the following HTML form does not specify a CGI script as its action:

```
<FORM METHOD="POST">
Enter Name: <INPUT TYPE=TEXT NAME="name" SIZE=25>
<INPUT TYPE=SUBMIT VALUE="Click Here">
</FORM>
```

If a name is submitted by a user via this form, there is no specified CGI script to process the information, in which case, the default POST action /cgi-bin/default_post.pl script is run. However, if the <FORM . . .> tag is changed to:

```
<FORM ACTION="/cgi-bin/form_processor.pl" METHOD="POST">
```

then whenever the form is submitted, the /cgi-bin/form_processor.pl script is called as usual. What you do in the default action script is up to you. In an Internet service provider setup, I recommend making the default script print meaningful messages, so that the HTML form developer user can get a clue about what he or she is doing incorrectly.

In case of the GET request, the default action is used only if the request accompanies query data. For example, www.yoursite.com/somefile.html is processed as usual, but if a request such as http://www.yoursite.com/somefile.html?some=data is received, the default action for GET will be run.

mod_ext_filter

The mod_ext_filter module enables Apache to use an external program as an input and output filter. Any program that can read input from STDIN and write output to STDOUT can be used. Of course, running an external program to process input or output for each request is a time-consuming task and should be avoided in a production environment. Filters are better developed using Apache API (application programming interface) and run within the Apache server process.

ExtFilterDefine

The `ExtFilterDefine` directive lets you define a filter that can be later used by the filter name specified in this directive.

> **Syntax:** `ExtFilterDefine` *filter_name* `[mode=input | output]`
> `[intype=MIME-type] [outtype=MIME-type]`
> `[PreservesContentLength]`
>
> **Context:** Server config

In the following example, a filter called `gzfilter` is defined to be an output filter (`mode=output`), which runs the `/usr/bin/gzip` program when called:

```
ExtFilterDefine gzfilter mode=output cmd=/usr/bin/gzip
```

Here, mode can only be set to `output`. The `intype` and `outtype` settings are used to define the MIME type used for input and output. For example, if a filter receives `intype=text/plain` and `outtype=text/html`, then the filter is responsible for translating the data from plain text to HTML format. The `PreservesContentLength` parameter should be used when the filter does not change the size of the data in bytes.

Say you have a custom filter program called `/usr/local/bin/`*program* and want to use it as an output filter for all plain-text files in a Web directory called `/www/mysite/htdocs/mytxts`. Here is a sample configuration that allows you to do just that:

```
ExtFilterDefine my_test_filter \
                mode=output cmd=/usr/local/bin/program \
                intype=text/plain \
                outtype=text/html

<Directory "/www/mysite/htdocs/mytxts">

    SetOutputFilter my_test_filter
    AddType text/html

</Directory>
```

Here the `ExtFilterDefine` defines a filter called `my_filter` that runs `/usr/local/bin/`*program* when called and that takes text/plain data from `STDIN` and writes text/html data to `STDOUT`. Now the `<Directory>` container sets this filter as the output filter for this directory and also tells Apache that the output MIME type is text/html using the `AddType` directive. If you store text files in this directory and Web clients request them, the files will be translated into HTML using the `/usr/local/bin/`*program*.

ExtFilterOptions

The ExtFilterOptions directive sets debugging options for the module. When debugging needs to be set, use DebugLevel option. Setting this option to 0 disables debugging, which is the default. Setting it to 1 enables debugging log entries that show options. Setting it to 9 enables all the gory details of the filter processing.

Syntax: ExtFilterOptions DebugLevel=*n* LogStderr | NoLogStderr

Context: Server

Content-Type Configuration Modules

The modules in this section, shown in Table 5-5, enable you to configure, detect, and negotiate content types appropriate for serving requests.

Table 5-5
Content-Type Modules

Module	Purpose
mod_mime	Enables Apache to determine MIME type by using file extension.
mod_mime_magic	Enables Apache to determine MIME type by using magic numbers (bytes pattern).
mod_negotiation	Enables Apache to perform content negotiation to send out the best type of content that the client can accept.

mod_mime

The mod_mime module is compiled in Apache by default. It provides clients with meta information about documents. It also enables you to define a handler for a document to determine how the document is processed by Apache.

AddCharset

The AddCharset directive maps one or more file extensions to a MIME character set. This allows you to associate a character set to one or more file extensions.

Syntax: AddCharset *charset file_extension [file_extension ...]*

Context: Server config, virtual host, directory, per-directory configuration (.htaccess)

Override: FileInfo

The following example causes a file called `filename.utf8` to be mapped as a character set called UTF-8.

```
AddCharset UTF-8          .utf8
```

AddEncoding

The `AddEncoding` directive maps one or more file extensions to a `MIME-encoding` scheme. In other words, this directive associates an encoding scheme to one or more file extensions.

Syntax: `AddEncoding MIME file_extension [file_extension...]`

Context: Server config, virtual host, directory, per-directory configuration (.htaccess)

Override: `FileInfo`

For example, the following directives cause a file called `backup.gz` to be mapped as an `x-gzip`–encoded file, and a file called `tarball.tar` to be mapped as an x-tar–encoded file.

```
AddEncoding x-gzip gz
AddEncoding x-tar tar
```

AddHandler

The `AddHandler` directive defines a handler for one or more file extensions. Whenever Apache encounters a file with a defined handler it allows the handler to process the file.

Syntax: `AddHandler handler-name file-extension [file-extension ...]`

Context: Server config, virtual host, directory, per-directory access control file (`.htaccess`)

In the following example: the directive specifies that all `.cgi` files be processed by a handler called `cgi-script`.

```
AddHandler cgi-script .cgi
```

AddLanguage

The `AddLanguage` directive maps a list of file extensions to a MIME language. When Apache encounters a file with such extension it knows what language the file supports.

Syntax: `AddLanguage MIME_language file_extension [file_extension] [...]`

Context: Server config, virtual host, directory, per-directory access control file (.htaccess)

Override: FileInfo

The following example maps all files with extensions .en or .english to be mapped as English-language files. This is useful in content negotiation, where the server can return a document based on the client's language preference.

```
AddLanguage en .en .english
```

Or, in the following example, if the client prefers an English document, and both document.fr.html and document.en.html are available, the server should return document.en.html.

```
AddLanguage en .en
AddLanguage fr .fr
```

AddType

The AddType directive maps a list of file extensions to a MIME type so that when Apache encounters files with such extensions it knows what MIME type to use for them.

Syntax: AddType *MIME file_extension* [*file_extension ...*]

Context: Server config, virtual host, directory, per-directory access control file (.htaccess)

Override: FileInfo

For example, the following line associates the MIME type called text/html to htm, html, HTML, and HTML extensions.

```
AddType text/html htm html HTM HTML
```

DefaultLanguage

The DefaultLanguage directive sets the default language.

Syntax: DefaultLanguage *MIME_language*

Context: Server config, virtual host, directory, per-directory configuration (.htaccess)

Override: FileInfo

For example, in the following directive all the contents in the /www/mysite/Japanese directory are mapped to the default language, Japanese:

```
<Directory /www/mysite/japanese>
    DefaultLanguage .jp
</Directory>
```

ForceType

The `ForceType` directive forces a certain MIME type for all files in a directory. The directory can be specified by a `<Directory>` or `<Location>` container.

Syntax: `ForceType` *MIME_type*

Context: Directory, per-directory access control file (`.htaccess`)

For example, the following directive forces the `text/html` MIME-type for all files in the specified directory, regardless of their extensions:

```
<Directory /www/nitec/public/htdocs/files/with/no/extensions>
    ForceType text/html
</Directory>
```

SetHandler

The `SetHandler` directive defines a handler for a directory or a URL location.The handler is then used to process all files in the directory.

Syntax: `SetHandler` *handler_name*

Context: Directory, per-directory access control file (`.htaccess`)

For example, the following directive forces all files in the `/bin` location to be treated as CGI scripts, which are handled by the `cgi-bin` handler:

```
<Location /bin>
    Options ExecCGI
    SetHandler cgi-bin
</Location>
```

RemoveHandler

The `RemoveHandler` directive undoes a handler for a directory or a URL location. It is useful to limit `SetHandler`, which normally applies to all the files in a directory. Using `RemoveHandler` you can remove handlers for some files or even a subdirectory.

Syntax: `RemoveHandler` *handler_name*

Context: Directory, per-directory access control file (`.htaccess`)

For example, in the following directive, the handler `my-handler` is set to an `.mjk` extension outside the `/www/mysite/htdocs/special` directory, so it automatically applies to this directory as well. However, because `RemoveHandler` is applied to this directory to undo the `my-handler` association with `.mjk`, files with `.mjk` extensions in this directory are not handled with `my-handler`:

```
SetHandler my-handler .mjk

<Directory /www/mysite/htdocs/special>
    RemoveHandler .mjk
</Location>
```

TypesConfig

The TypesConfig directive specifies the default MIME configuration file. The default value should be fine for most Apache installations. If you want to add your own MIME types, use the AddType directive instead of modifying this file.

> **Syntax:** TypesConfig *filename*
>
> **Default setting:** TypesConfig conf/mime.types
>
> **Context:** Server config

Note If you need additional support for handling MIME-types, you may want to look at the mod_mime_magic module in the next section. For most Apache installations this is not necessary, so it is not discussed in this book.

mod_mime_magic

The mod_mime_magic module enables Apache to determine a file's MIME type by comparing a few bytes of the file with a magic value stored in a file. This module is only needed when mod_mime fails to guess a file's MIME type. In most cases, you do not need this module. This module has one directive called MimeMagicFile.

This directive enables the mod_mime_magic module and points to the magic file needed by the module. The Apache distribution comes with a magic file in the conf subdirectory, so if you wish to use this module, set this directive to conf/magic.

> **Syntax:** MimeMagicFile *magic_file_filename*
>
> **Context:** Server config, virtual host

mod_negotiation

The mod_negotiation module is compiled by default. It provides support for content negotiations. In a typical content-negotiation scenario, the client provides information about what type of content it can handle, and the server attempts to provide the most appropriate content. The server performs this with the help of type maps and the MultiViews search.

A *type map* provides a description of documents. Each document description contains one or more headers. It can also contain comment lines that start with a hash (#) character. Document descriptions are separated by blank lines. The document description headers are:

✦ **Content-Encoding** — This specifies the encoding type of the file. Only x-compress and x-gzip encoding are currently allowed.

✦ **Content-Language** — The language of the document.

✦ **Content-Length** — The length of the file in bytes.

✦ **Content-Type** — The MIME type of the document. Optional key-value parameters are allowed. The allowed parameters are level, which provides the version number (as an integer) of the MIME type, and qs, which indicates the quality (as a floating point number) of the document.

✦ **URI** — The path to the document relative to the map file.

A MultiViews search tries to determine the closest match for the missing document using the information it knows from the client, and returns the match if possible. When you enable the MultiViews option in the Options directive, the server is able to perform the MultiViews search when a requested document is not found. This module provides the following two directives.

CacheNegotiatedDocs

The CacheNegotiatedDocs directive enables content-negotiated documents to be cached by proxy servers. Note that the new HTTP 1.1 specification provides much better control for caching negotiated documents, and that CacheNegotiatedDocs has no effect in response to HTTP 1.1 requests. This directive is likely to disappear after HTTP 1.1 is widely used. Use of CacheNegotiatedDocs is not recommended.

> **Syntax:** CacheNegotiatedDocs
>
> **Context:** Server config

LanguagePriority

The LanguagePriority directive specifies what language preference the server should use in a MultiViews search scenario, when the client does not provide language preference information.

> **Syntax:** LanguagePriority MIME_language [MIME_language ...]
>
> **Context:** Server config, virtual host, directory, per-directory access control file (.htaccess)
>
> **Override:** FileInfo

In the following directive, for example, if the MultiViews option is turned on and the client does not provide language preference information for a file that is missing, the server first tries to serve the English version of the closest match, and then the French version, and so on. Like the CacheNegotiatedDocs directive, this directive is not effective in the HTTP 1.1 environment.

```
LanguagePriority en fr de
```

Directory Listing Modules

If you have a directory within your Web document tree that does not have a directory index file (set using DirectoryIndex directive) then Apache will automatically generate a directory listing if you have not disabled automatic directory listing using the Options -Indexes directive. Apache allows you to customize automatically generated directory listings. The modules in this section, as shown in Table 5-6, enable you to configure how directory listings are displayed.

Table 5-6 Directory-Listing Modules	
Module	**Purpose**
mod_dir	Basic directory handling
mod_autoindex	Automatic directory listings

mod_dir

The mod_dir module is compiled in Apache by default. By using this module, Apache can redirect any request for a directive that does not include a trailing forward slash character. For example, this module can redirect www.yoursite.com/somedirectory to www.yoursite.com/somedirectory/. It also provides the DirectoryIndex directive to help with indexing a directory's content.

The DirectoryIndex directive specifies the name(s) of files that Apache should look for before creating a dynamic directory index. The files can be anything from an HTML file to a CGI script. The default setting enables Apache to look for the index.html file for any request that ends with a directory name.

Syntax: DirectoryIndex *local_URL* [*local_URL* ...]

Default setting: DirectoryIndex index.html

Context: Server config, virtual host, directory, per-directory access control file (.htaccess)

Override: Indexes

For example, www.yoursite.com/some/directory/ causes Apache to look for a file called /some/directory/index.html. If the file exists, its content is delivered to the client. In the absence of this file, Apache creates a dynamic directory listing.

You can specify one or more files as the default directory index files. For example, the following tells Apache to look for all the named files for each directory request:

```
DirectoryIndex index.html index.htm welcome.html welcome.htm
```

Note that Apache will look for files in the same order (from left to right) as they appear in the preceding configuration. In other words, if Apache finds index.html, it will no longer look for index.htm, welcome.html, or welcome.htm. You can specify a CGI script name as the default index, as well. For example, the following directive makes Apache run the /cgi-bin/show_index.cgi script every time Apache gets a directory request:

```
DirectoryIndex /cgi-bin/show_index.cgi
```

mod_autoindex

The mod_autoindex module is compiledin Apache by default. When Apache receives a request for a directory, it looks for one or more of the directory index files specified by the DirectoryIndex directive. Typically, this file is index.html or index.htm. In the absence of such an index file, however, Apache can generate a dynamic directory listing. This module enables you to control how Apache creates the dynamic directory listing.

Apache generates two types of dynamic directory indices: simple and fancy. The fancy index and many other indexing options are available from this module. The directives for mod_authoindex are as follow.

AddAlt

When FancyIndexing is on, this directive sets the specified text as an alternative to the icon that is displayed for one or more files or file extensions specified as arguments. This is done for nongraphical browsers such as Lynx.

> **Syntax:** AddAlt "*text*" *filename* [*filename* ...]
>
> **Context:** Server config, virtual host, directory, per-directory access control file (.htaccess)
>
> **Override:** Indexes

For example, the following directive enables Apache to display the alternative text "Pictures" in place of the icon for each type of graphic file specified here. For graphical browsers such as Netscape Navigator or Internet Explorer, the alternative text is displayed as help text under popular Windows platforms. In such systems, users can get a tip or help about the file when they move their mouse cursor on top of the icon representing one of the file types.:

```
AddAlt "Pictures" gif jpeg jpg bmp
```

AddAltByEncoding

If you do not like to assign alternative text to filenames or file extensions via the AddAlt directive, you can use the AddAltByEncoding directive to assign such text for one or more MIME encodings. Like AddAlt, this directive is also only usable when FancyIndexing is turned on.

> **Syntax:** AddAltByEncoding "*text*" *MIME_encoding* [*MIME_encoding* ...]
>
> **Context:** Server config, virtual host, directory, per-directory access control file (.htaccess)
>
> **Override:** Indexes

For example, the following directive makes Apache display the "Compressed File" alternative text for all files of MIME type x-compress.

```
AddAltByEncoding "Compressed File" x-compress
```

AddAltByType

Like the AddAltByEncoding directive, the AddAltByType directive sets alternative text for a file, instead of an icon for FancyIndexing. However, it uses a MIME type instead of MIME encoding.

> **Syntax:** AddAltByType "*text*" *MIME-type* [*MIME_type* ...]
>
> **Context:** Server config, virtual host, directory, per-directory access control file (.htaccess)
>
> **Override:** Indexes

For example, the following directive shows the "HTML FILE" text in place of the icon for nongraphical browsers. In the case of graphical browsers, this text may appear as a tip or help:

```
AddAltByType "HTML FILE" text/html
```

AddDescription

The AddDescription directive sets the description text for a filename, for a partial filename, or for a wild-card filename when FancyIndexing is turned on.

> **Syntax:** AddDescription "*text*" *file* [*file* ...]
>
> **Context:** Server config, virtual host, directory, per-directory access control file (.htaccess)
>
> **Override:** Indexes

For example, the following directive displays the description for all GIF, JPEG, JPG, and BMP files in generated directory listing:

```
AddDescription "Graphics File" *.gif *.jpeg *.jpg *.bmp
```

AddIcon

The AddIcon directive enables you to assign icons to files and directory names that are displayed for FancyIndexing.

> **Syntax:** AddIcon *icon name file [filename ...]*
>
> **Context:** Server config, virtual host, directory, per-directory access control file (.htaccess)
>
> **Override:** Indexes

For example, the following directive tells Apache to show /icons/picture.gif next to files that have extensions such as .gif, .jpg, and .bmp:

```
AddIcon /icons/picture.gif .gif .jpg .bmp
```

If you also want to provide alternative text for the file extension listed, you can use a format such as the following, where IMG is the alternative text displayed for non-graphical browsers:

```
AddIcon (IMG, /icons/picture.gif) .gif .jpg .bmp
```

If you want to display an icon for a directory, you can use the directive as follows:

```
AddIcon /path/to/your/directory/icon    ^^DIRECTORY^^
```

Similarly, if you want to display an icon for each blank line displayed by the fancy indexing scheme, you can use:

```
AddIcon /path/to/your/blank/line/icon    ^^BLANKICON^^
```

AddIconByEncoding

The AddIconByEncoding directive lets you assign icons to MIME-encodings. In other words, you can assign an icon image to a MIME type.

> **Syntax:** AddIconByEncoding *icon_file MIME_encoding [MIME_encoding...]*
>
> **Context:** Server config, virtual host, directory, per-directory access control file (.htaccess)
>
> **Override:** Indexes

For example, the following AddIconByEncoding directive tells Apache to display /icons/zip.gif icon for all files that are x-gzip (i.e. .gz extension) MIME type files.

```
AddIconByEncoding  /icons/zip.gif       x-gzip
```

AddIconByType

The `AddIconByType` directive also enables you to assign icons to one or more MIME types.

> **Syntax:** `AddIconByType` *icon_file* *MIME_type* *[MIME_type...]*
>
> **Context:** Server config, virtual host, directory, per-directory access control file (`.htaccess`)
>
> **Override:** `Indexes`

For example, the following `AddIconByType` directive tells Apache to display the `/icons/html.gif` icon for all `text/html` files.

```
AddIconByType (HTML,/icons/html.gif) text/html
```

DefaultIcon

When no `AddIcon`, `AddIconByEncoding`, or `AddIconByType` is matched for a file, a default icon can be displayed. The `DefaultIcon` directive enables you to set that icon.

> **Syntax:** `DefaultIcon` *URL*
>
> **Context:** Server config, virtual host, directory, per-directory access control file (`.htaccess`)
>
> **Override:** `Indexes`

For example, the following directive shows `idontknow.gif` whenever a file's icon association is unknown:

```
DefaultIcon /icon/idontknow.gif
```

FancyIndexing

The `FancyIndexing` directive lets you enable and disable fancy indexing of directories. You can achieve the same effect with the `IndexOptions` directive.

> **Syntax:** `FancyIndexing On | Off`
>
> **Context:** Server config, virtual host, directory, per-directory configuration (.htaccess)
>
> **Override:** `Indexes`

HeaderName

If you use `FancyIndexing`, you can insert a file's content at the top of the index listing. The `HeaderName` directive lets you specify the name of the file for such an insertion.

>**Syntax:** `HeaderName` *filename*
>
>**Context:** Server config, virtual host, directory, per-directory access control file (`.htaccess`)
>
>**Override:** `Indexes`

For example, the following directive tells Apache to look for a file called `welcome` or `welcome.html` in the directory of the listing; if such a file is found, the content is inserted before the actual listing:

```
HeaderName welcome
```

IndexIgnore

If you need some files or file extensions to be invisible in the directory listing, you can use the `IndexIgnore` directive to accomplish this.

>**Syntax:** `IndexIgnore` *file* [*file...*]
>
>**Context:** Server config, virtual host, directory, per-directory access control file (`.htaccess`)
>
>**Override:** `Indexes`

For example, the following directive ensures that Apache does not list `welcome`, `welcome.html`, or per-directory configuration (`.htaccess`) files in directory listings:

```
IndexIgnore welcome welcome.html .htaccess
```

The `.` (dot) character is automatically in the `IndexIgnore` list; thus, files that start with this character are not listed. However, you may still prefer to add per-directory configuration (`.htaccess`) in the list, just so that you feel safer.

IndexOptions

The `IndexOptions` directive specifies the behavior of the automatically generated directory indexing.

>**Syntax:** `IndexOptions` *option* [*option*] [*...*]
>
>**Context:** Server config, virtual host, directory, per-directory access control file (`.htaccess`)
>
>**Override:** `Indexes`

Table 5-7 shows the options that you can use with IndexOptions.

Table 5-7
Options for IndexOptions

Option	What It Does
FancyIndexing	Turns on fancy indexing of directories. Note that the FancyIndexing and IndexOptions directives will override each other.
IconHeight[=pixels]	Enables Apache to include the HEIGHT=pixels attribute in the IMG tag of the icon, which makes the loading of the icon faster on most browsers. If you do not specify a pixel count, a standard default is used.
IconsAreLinks	Makes the icons part of the anchor for the filename, for fancy indexing.
IconWidth[=pixels]	Enables Apache to include the WIDTH=pixels attribute in the IMG tag of the icon, which makes the loading of the icon faster on most browsers. If you do not specify a pixel count, a standard default is used.
ScanHTMLTitles	If you want Apache to read the title (denoted by the <TITLE> and </TITLE> tag pair) of an HTML document for fancy indexing, use this option. If you have already specified a description using the AddDescription directive, however, this option is not used. Note that reading each file's content and searching for title information is a time-consuming task that may slow down the delivery of directory listings. I do not recommend this option.
SuppressColumnSorting	By default, Apache makes clickable column headings for a fancy directory index, which enables users to sort information in that column. This option disables this feature.
SuppressDescription	If you do not want to display file descriptions in the fancy directory listing, use this option.
SuppressHTMLPreamble	If the directory actually contains a file specified by the HeaderName directive, the module usually includes the contents of the file after a standard HTML preamble (<HTML>, <HEAD>, and so on). The SuppressHTMLPreamble option disables this behavior.
SuppressLastModified	Suppresses the display of the last modification date in fancy indexing listings.
SuppressSize	Suppresses the file size in fancy indexing listings.

IndexOrderDefault

The `IndexOrderDefault` directive enables you to change directory listing views by sorting various fields such as names, date, size, and description in directories that are displayed using the `FancyIndexing` feature.

> **Syntax:** `IndexOrderDefault Ascending | Descending Name | Date | Size | Description`
>
> **Context:** Server config, virtual host, directory, per-directory access control file (`.htaccess`)
>
> **Override:** `Indexes`

ReadmeName

If you want to insert a file at the end of the fancy directory listing, use the `ReadmeName` directive.

> **Syntax:** `ReadmeName` *`filename`*
>
> **Context:** Server config, virtual host, directory, per-directory access control file (`.htaccess`)
>
> **Override:** `Indexes`

For example, the following makes Apache look for a file called `readme.html` (extension is assumed) or `readme` to insert at the end of the listing:

```
ReadmeName readme
```

Response Header Modules

Apache allows you to send customer HTTP response header when sending data. The modules in this section, as shown in Table 5-8, enable you to configure various custom response headers.

Table 5-8
Response-Header Modules

Module	Purpose
`mod_asis`	Send files that contain their own HTTP headers.
`mod_headers`	Add arbitrary HTTP headers to resources.
`mod_expires`	Apply `Expires:` headers to resources.
`mod_cern_meta`	Support for HTTP header metafiles.

mod_asis

The mod_asis module is compiled by default. This module enables you to send a document as-is — in other words, the document is sent to the client without HTTP headers. This can be useful when redirecting clients without the help of any scripting. To send a file as is, you need to make sure that httpd.conf file contains an entry such as:

```
AddType httpd/send-as-is asis
```

This assigns the MIME type httpd/send-as-is to file extension .asis. If you create a file called foobar.asis and a client requests it, the file is sent to the client without any HTTP header. It is your job to include appropriate headers in the file. For example, if you want to provide a redirect mechanism via the .asis files, you can create files with headers such as:

```
Status: 301 Text Message
Location: new-URL
Content-type: text/html
```

Listing 5-2 shows a file called redirect.asis, which redirects the clients to a new location.

Listing 5-2: **redirect.asis**

```
Status: 301 We have moved.
Location: http://www.our-new-site/
Content-type: text/html
<H1>Notice to Visitors</H1>
Please update your bookmark to point to <A
HREF="http://www.our-new-site/ "> www.our-new-site/ </A><BR>
<BR>
Thanks.
```

When a client requests this file, the 301 status message tells the client to use the location information to redirect the request. You do not have to add the Date: and Server: headers, because the server automatically adds them. However, the server does not provide a Last-Modified header.

mod_headers

This module is not compiled by default. mod_headers enables you to manipulate HTTP response headers, and it offers a single directive called Header, which enables you to manipulate the HTTP response header.

Syntax: Header *action header value*

Context: Server config, virtual host, directory, per-directory access control file (.htaccess)

Override: FileInfo

The allowed actions are as follows:

Action	What It Does
Set	Sets a header. If an old header with the same name existed, its value is changed to the new value.
Add	Adds a header. This can cause multiple headers with the same name when one or more headers with the same name exist.
Append	Appends the value to an existing header value.
Unset	Removes a header.

For example, the following directive adds the Author header with the value "Mohammed J. Kabir":

```
Header add Author "Mohammed J. Kabir"
```

And the following line removes the same header:

```
Header unset Author
```

mod_expires

The mod_expires module is not compiled in Apache by default. It lets you determine how Apache deals with Expires HTTP headers in the server's response to requests. *Expires HTTP headers* provide you with means for telling the client about the time when the requested resource becomes invalid. This is useful when documents are cached by the client and need to be requested again. Most smart clients determine the validity of a rerequested document by investigating the cached document's expiration time provided by Expires HTTP headers. This module enables you to control the settings of the Expires HTTP headers.

ExpiresActive

The ExpiresActive directive enables or disables the generation of the Expires header. It does not guarantee that an Expires header will be generated. If the criteria are not met, no header is sent.

Syntax: `ExpiresActive On | Off`

Context: Server config, virtual host, directory, per-directory access control file (`.htaccess`)

Override: `Indexes`

ExpiresByType

The `ExpiresByType` directive specifies the value of the Expires HTTP header for documents of a specified `MIME-type`. The expiration time is specified in seconds. You can define the time in two ways. If you choose to use the `Mseconds` format to specify expiration time, then the file's last modification time is used as the base time. In other words, M3600 means that you want the file to expire one hour after it was last modified. On the other hand, if you use the `Aseconds` format, then client's access time is used as the base time. Following are some examples.

Syntax 1: `ExpiresByType MIME_type Mseconds | Aseconds`

Syntax 2: `ExpiresByType MIME-type "base_time [plus] num Years|Months|Weeks|Days|Hours|Minutes|Seconds"`

Context: Server config, virtual host, directory, per-directory access control file (`.htaccess`)

Override: `Indexes`

The following expires all plain-text files after one hour in the client's cache:

```
ExpiresByType text/plain A3600
```

And the following expires all GIF files after one week from the last modified time:

```
ExpiresByType image/gif M604800
```

If you want to use the second syntax for specifying expiration times, you need to determine the appropriate value of *base_time* by using the following options:

Value	What It Means
Access	Time when client accessed the file.
Now	Current time. This is the same as the access time.
Modification	Time when the file was last changed.

For example, the following directives tell Apache to send headers to tell the browser that HTML documents should be expired after seven days from the day of access and that the GIF images should be expired after any changes in file or three hours and ten minutes later.

```
ExpiresByType text/html "access plus 7 days"
ExpiresByType image/gif "modification plus 3 hours 10 minutes"
```

ExpiresDefault

The ExpiresDefault directive sets the default expiration time for all documents in the context in which it is specified. For example, if this directive is specified in the virtual host context, it will only apply to the documents accessible via the virtual host. Similarly, you can specify this directive in a per-directory context, which allows all documents in that directory to expire at a specified interval. See ExpiresByType for details on the syntax.

> **Syntax 1:** ExpiresDefault M*seconds* | A*seconds*
>
> **Syntax 2:** ExpiresDefault "*base_time* [plus] *num Years|Months|Weeks|Days|Hours|Minutes|Seconds*"
>
> **Context:** Server config, virtual host, directory, per-directory access control file (.htaccess)
>
> **Override:** Indexes

Following are two examples:

```
ExpiresDefault M3600
ExpiresDefault "access plus 2 days"
```

The first example sets the expiration time to one hour after the last modification time of the documents. The second one sets the expiration time to two days after access by the client.

mod_cern_meta

The mod_cern_meta module is not compiled by default. It provides support for metainformation. This information can either be additional HTTP headers such as:

```
Expires: Saturday, 19-May-01 12:00:00 GMT
```

or it can be any other information such as the following, where the meta information is stored in a file and appears along with the HTTP response header:

```
Foo=Bar
```

MetaFiles

The MetaFiles directive enables or disables metaheader file processing.

> **Syntax:** MetaFiles On | Off
>
> **Default setting:** MetaFiles Off
>
> **Context:** Per-directory access control file (.htaccess)

MetaDir

The `MetaDir` directive specifies the name of the directory that stores metaheader files. For example, if you have a directory called `/www/mycompany/public/htdocs` and want to store metainformation files for that directory, you need to create a sub-directory called `.web` if you use the default value for the `MetaDir` directive. The `.web` directory stores metaheader files.

> **Syntax:** `MetaDir directory`
>
> **Default setting:** `MetaDir .web`
>
> **Context:** Per-directory access control file (`.htaccess`)

MetaSuffix

The `MetaSuffix` directive specifies the filename extension for metainformation files. For example, if you have an HTML file called `mypage.html`, then you need to create `mypage.html.meta` (using the default value of this directive) to store your metaheaders. The `mypage.html.meta` file must reside in the directory specified by the `MetaDir` directive.

> **Syntax:** `MetaSuffix suffix`
>
> **Default setting:** `MetaSuffix .meta`
>
> **Context:** Per-directory access control file (`.htaccess`)

To enable Apache to send out metainformation for a directory called `/www/mycompany/public/htdocs`, you need to do the following:

1. Set the MetaFiles directive to `on` in the per-directory configuration file (`.htaccess`) for `/www/mycompany/public/htdocs`. You can also set the `MetaDir` and `MetaSuffix` directive in this file.

2. Create a subdirectory called `.web` (assuming you are using the default for `MetaDir` directive)

3. Create a text file with extension `.meta` (assuming you are using the default value for `MetaSuffix` directive).

4. Put all the HTTP headers that you want to supply in this file.

For example, to provide metaheaders for a file named `/www/mycompany/public/htdocs/mypage.html`, you need to create a file called `/www/mycompany/public/htdocs/.web/mypage.html.meta`. This file could include lines such as:

```
Expires: Saturday, 19-May-01 12:00:00 GMT
Anything=Whatever
```

Server Information and Logging Modules

The modules in this section, as shown in Table 5-9, enable you to log access, report server status and configuration information, and also to track users who are using cookies.

Table 5-9 Server Information and Logging Modules	
Module	**Purpose**
mod_log_config	Provides customizable access logging. See Chapter 8 for details.
mod_status	Displays status information. See Chapter 8 for details.
mod_info	Displays server configuration information. See Chapter 8 for details.
mod_usertrack	Provides user tracking by using HTTP Cookies. See Chapter 8 for details.

mod_log_config

This module is discussed in detail in Chapter 8. See the "Creating Log Files" section in this chapter to learn more about this module and its directives.

mod_status

This module is discussed in detail in Chapter 8. See the "Enabling status pages with mod_status" section in this chapter to learn more about this module and its directives.

mod_info

This module is discussed in detail in Chapter 8. See the "Accessing configuration information with mod_info" section in this chapter to learn more about this module and its directives.

mod_usertrack

This module is discussed in detail in Chapter 8. See the "Logging Cookies" section later in this chapter to learn more about this module and its directives.

URL Mapping Modules

The modules in this section, as shown in Table 5-10, enable you to map various URLs to specific physical directories, create complex rewriting rules, aliases, and automate virtual host URLs to physical directory mappings.

Table 5-10 URL Mapping Modules	
Module	**Purpose**
mod_userdir	Allows you to access personal Web sites stored in user home directories.
mod_rewrite	URL rewriting rules are created using this module. See Chapter 9 for details.
mod_alias	To map different parts of the host filesystem in the document tree and for URL redirection.
mod_speling	Automatic correction of minor typos in URLs.
mod_vhost_alias	Support for dynamically configured mass virtual hosting.

mod_userdir

The mod_userdir module enables Apache to enable user-specific Web directories that are accessible via http://your_server_name/~username. If you do not plan on supporting such Web sites, you do not need this module.

The UserDir directive (the only directive for this module) enables you to set the directory that Apache should consider as the document root for the user's Web site.

> **Syntax:** UserDir directory_filename
>
> **Default setting:** UserDir public_html
>
> **Context:** Server config, virtual host

For example, if you keep the default value, whenever Apache notices a ~username path after the server name in the requesting URL, it translates the ~username to user_home_directory/public_html. If user home directories are stored in /home, the translated path is /home/username/publich_html.

 Caution   You should add Userdir disabled root to disable the capability to set this directive to point to the root directory.

The directory name that you set with this directive must be accessible by the Web server. In other words, if /home/*username* is the home directory and you leave Userdir set to public_html, then /home/username/public_html must be accessible by the Web server. In fact, Apache will also require read and execute access to both the /home and the /home/username directories. Some security-conscious system administrators do not like the idea of creating a Web directory in a user's home directory, so you can set the UserDir to a different path such as:

```
UserDir /www/users
```

Now when http://your_server_name/~*username* is requested, Apache will translate this request to /www/users/*username*. This way you can keep a user's Web files outside the home directory (/home/*username*) by creating a new top directory in which you have to create a directory for each user. Remember to ensure that Apache has read and execute access to each of these directories.

mod_alias

The mod_alias module is compiled by default in Apache. It provides various directives that can be used to map one part of the server's file system to another, or even to perform URL redirection services.

Alias

The Alias directive enables you to map a path to anywhere in your system's file system.

Syntax: Alias URL-*path path*

Context: Server config, virtual host

For example, the following directive maps /data/ to /web/data; therefore, when a request such as http://www.yoursite.com/data/:

```
Alias /data/ "/web/data/"
```

http://data/datafile.cvs is received, the file called /web/data/datafile.cvs is returned.

Caution The aliased path does not have to reside inside your document root tree, so be careful when you create aliases — you might accidentally reveal some part of your file system to the entire world.

Note If you use a trailing / (slash) in defining an alias, the requests that are capable of accessing the aliased directory also need to contain a trailing /.

AliasMatch

The `AliasMatch` directive is similar to the `Alias` directive, except that it can make use of regular expressions.

> **Syntax:** AliasMatch *regex path*
>
> **Context:** Server config, virtual host

For example, the following directive matches `www.yoursite.com/data/index.html` to the `/web/data/index.html` file:

```
AliasMatch ^/data(.*)  /web/data$1
```

Redirect

The `Redirect` directive redirects a URL request to another URL. If you have moved a section of your Web site to a new directory or even a new Web site, you can use this directive to ensure that people who have bookmarked the old site are still able to find it.

> **Syntax:** Redirect [*status_code*] *old_URL new_URL*
>
> **Context:** Server config, virtual host, directory, per-directory access control file (`.htaccess`)

For example, the following directive redirects all URL requests containing the `/data` path to the new URL. Therefore, requests for `www.yoursite.com/data/some-file.txt` are redirected to `www.your-new-site.com/data/somefile.txt`:

```
Redirect /data www.your-new-site.com/data
```

The `Redirect` directive has precedence over the `Alias` and `ScriptAlias` directives. By default, the status code sent to the client is Temp (HTTP status code 302). If you want to specify a different status code, use the following:

Status Code	What It Does
Permanent	Tells the client that the redirect is permanent. The HTTP status code 301 is returned.
Temp	Returns a temporary redirect status (302). This is the default.
See other	Returns a See Other status (303), indicating that the resource has been replaced.
Gone	Returns a Gone status (410) indicating that the resource has been permanently removed. When this status is used, the URL argument should be omitted.

Note

You can provide valid HTTP status codes in numeric format as well. If the status you provide is between 300 and 399, the new-URL must be present; otherwise, it must be omitted. You may wonder about the use of different status codes. In the future, clients may be smart enough to recognize the status codes in a more meaningful manner. For example, if a proxy server receives a permanent redirect status code, it can store this information in a cache so that it can directly access the new resource in a later request.

RedirectMatch

The `RedirectMatch` directive is similar to the `Redirect` directive, but it accepts regular expressions instead of the simple old URL.

> **Syntax:** `RedirectMatch [`*`status_code`*`]` *`regex URL`*
>
> **Context:** Server config, virtual host

For example, the following directive redirects all requests that end with `.htm` to an `.html` version of the same request:

```
RedirectMatch (.*)\.htm$ www.yourserver.com$1.html
```

As an example of how this would work, the following request:

```
http://www.yoursite.com/some/old/dos/files/index.htm
```

is redirected to:

```
http://www.yoursite.com/some/old/dos/files/index.html
```

See the Redirect directive (last section) for information on status_code.

RedirectTemp

The `RedirectTemp` directive is similar to the `Redirect` directive. It lets the client know that the redirect is only temporary. Note that the `Redirect` directive also produces a temporary status by default.

> **Syntax:** `RedirectTemp` *`old_URL new_URL`*
>
> **Context:** Server config, virtual host, directory, per-directory access control file (`.htaccess`)

RedirectPermanent

The `RedirectPermanent` directive is similar to the `Redirect` directive. It lets the client know that the redirect is permanent. Note that the `Redirect` directive produces a temporary status by default, but you can use the status code 301 or the keyword `permanent`, as the status does, the same as this directive.

Syntax: `RedirectPermanent old_URL new_URL`

Context: Server config, virtual host, directory, per-directory access control file (`.htaccess`)

ScriptAlias

The `ScriptAlias` directive creates an alias for the physical directory path. Additionally, any filename supplied in the request is treated as a CGI script, and the server attempts to run the script.

Syntax: `ScriptAlias alias "physical_directory_path"`

Context: Server config, virtual host

For example, the following directive can be used to process a request such as `www.nitec.com/cgi-bin/somescript.pl`. The server tries to run `somescript.pl` if proper permission is verified. Note that the `ScriptAlias` directory is not browseable:

```
ScriptAlias /cgi-bin/ "/www/nitec/public/cgi-bin/"
```

ScriptAliasMatch

The `ScriptAliasMatch` directive is equivalent to the `ScriptAlias` directive except that it uses regular expression, which allows you to define a dynamic alias rule instead of a fixed alias.

Syntax: `ScriptAliasMatch regex directory`

Context: Server config, virtual host

For example, the following two directives do exactly the same thing:

```
ScriptAliasMatch ^/cgi-bin(.*)  "/www/nitec/public/cgi-bin$1"
ScriptAlias     /cgi-bin/      "/www/nitec/public/cgi-bin/"
```

mod_speling

The `mod_speling` module is not compiled in Apache by default. It enables you to handle misspelled or miscapitalized URL requests. It compares the requested (misspelled or miscapitalized) document name with all the document names in the requested directory for one or more close matches.

In the case of a misspelled document request, the module allows a single spelling error, such as an extra character insertion, a character omission, or a transposition. In the case of a miscapitalized document request, it performs a case-insensitive file-name comparison. Either way, if the module locates a single document that closely resembles the request, it sends a redirect request to the client. If there's more than one match, it sends the list to the client for selection. The single directive offered by this module is called `CheckSpeling`.

The CheckSpelling directive enables or disables the mod_speling module. Note that when the spelling correction is on, the server may experience performance loss due to extra searches that are needed for serving a misspelled document request.

> **Syntax:** CheckSpelling On | Off
>
> **Default setting:** CheckSpelling Off
>
> **Context:** Server config, virtual host

Note The mod_speling module only works with file and directory names.

mod_vhost_alias

The mod_vhost_alias module allows you to create dynamically configured virtual hosts. This module is only appropriate for Apache installations that require many virtual hosts. For example, an Internet Service Provider (ISP) using Apache can make use of this module to reduce the configuration work that would otherwise be needed for each new virtual host customer.

This module enables you to create dynamic virtual host configurations using the IP address or the hostname of a virtual Web site in creating the physical directory paths needed to service the site.

VirtualDocumentRoot

The VirtualDocumentRoot directive enables you to set the document root for the virtual hosts using an interpolated directory path.

> **Syntax:** VirtualDocumentRoot *interpolated_directory*
>
> **Context:** Server config, virtual host

In the following directive, for example, when a request for http://www.domain.com/somepage.html is received by Apache, it translates the request to /www/www.domain.com/htdocs/somepage.html:

```
UseCanonicalName        Off
VirtualDocumentRoot     /www/%0/htdocs
```

The UseCanonicalName is set to off so that Apache rely on the Host header for the hostname, which is supplied by all modern Web clients. The VirtualDocumentRoot is suitable for name-based virtual hosting scenario in which you have one IP address responsible for many virtual Web sites.

Note %0 is translated into the entire hostname (that is, www.domain.com). If you wish, you can use parts of the hostname. The hostname (or the IP address) is divided into parts separated by the dots. For example, use %1 (first part = www), %2 (second part = domain), or %-1 (last part = com) to create appropriate interpolated-directories for the directives provided by this module. You can also use %N.P convention where N represents a part (separated by the dot) and P represents a number of characters of that part. For example %1.2 will give you ww from www.domain.com.

VirtualDocumentRootIP

The VirtualDocumentRootIP directive enables you to set the document root for the virtual hosts by using an interpolated directory path that is constructed using the IP address of the Web site. This method is suitable if you use IP-based virtual hosting because you have unique IP addresses for each virtual Web site.

Syntax: VirtualDocumentRootIP *interpolated_directory*

Context: Server config, virtual host

In the following directive, for example, when a request for http://www.domain.com/somepage.html is received by Apache, it translates the request to /www/*IP_address_of_www.domain.com*/htdocs/somepage.html

```
VirtualDocumentRootIP    /www/%0/htdocs
```

VirtualScriptAlias

The VirtualScriptAlias directive enables to define a script alias (as done using ScriptAlias directive) that uses an interpolated directory path.

Syntax: VirtualScriptAlias *alias interpolated_directory*

Context: Server config, virtual host

In the following directive, for example, when a request for http://www.domain.com/cgi-bin/*script_name* is received by Apache, it translates the request to /www/www.domain.com/cgi-bin/*script_name*:

```
UseCanonicalName        Off
VirtualScriptAlias  /cgi-bin/    /www/%0/cgi-bin
```

The UseCanonicalName is set to off, requiring Apache to rely on the Host header for the hostname, which header is supplied by all modern Web clients. The VirtualDocumentRoot is suitable for name-based virtual hosting scenario in which you have one IP address responsible for many virtual Web sites.

VirtualScriptAliasIP

The `VirtualScriptAliasIP` directive enables you to define a script alias (as done using `ScriptAlias` directive) that uses an interpolated directory path.

Syntax: `VirtualScriptAliasIP alias interpolated_directory`

Context: Server config, virtual host

In the following directive, for example, when a request for `http://www.domain.com/cgi-bin/script_name` is received by Apache, it translates the request to `/www/IP_address/cgi-bin/script_name` `VirtualScriptAliasIP /cgi-bin/ /www/%0/cgi-bin`

Miscellaneous Modules

The modules in this section, as shown in Table 5-11, do not fall under any particular category.

Table 5-11
Miscellaneous Modules

Module	Purpose
`mod_so`	Support for loading modules at run-time.
`mod_imap`	The image map file handler.
`mod_proxy`	Turns Apache into a caching proxy server. See Chapter 10 for details.
`mod_isapi`	Windows ISAPI Extension support. See Chapter 21 for details.
`mod_file_cache`	Caches files in memory for faster serving.
`mod_dav`	Provides class 1 and 2 Web-based Distributed Authoring and Versioning (WebDAV) functionality.
`mod_example`	An example for module developer to learn about how to write an Apache module. Not useful to anyone but C programmers.

mod_so

The `mod_so` module enables Apache to load the executable code that is needed by other modules or to load other modules during Server startup. You can compile all the modules as DSO (Dynamic Shared Object) modules except this one.

LoadFile

The LoadFile directive loads the named file during startup. Typically, a dynamically linked library (DLL) file needed by another module is loaded using this directive (only in Windows).

Syntax: LoadFile *filename* [*filename...*]

Context: Server config

LoadModule

The LoadModule directive loads a module that has been compiled as a DSO.

Syntax: LoadModule *module_filename*

Context: Server config

mod_imap

The mod_imap module is compiled in Apache by default. It provides image map support, which had been provided by the CGI program imagemap. You can use the AddHandler directive to specify the imap-file handler (built into this module) for any file extension. For example, the following directive makes Apache treat all files with the .map extension as image maps, and Apache processes the files by using the mod_imap module:

```
AddHandler imap-file map
```

Note

The mod-imap module still supports the older format:

```
AddType application/x-httpd-imap map
```

However, the older format is not recommended because support for it may be dropped in the future.

The contents of an image map file can have any of the following syntax:

```
directive value [x,y ...]
directive value "Menu text" [x,y ...]
directive value x,y ... "Menu text"
```

The allowed directives in a image map file are:

✦ base—Relative URLs used in map files are considered relative to the value of this directive. Note that the Imapbase directive setting is overridden by this directive when found in a map file. It defaults to http://server_name/. base_uri, which is synonymous with base.

✦ default — Specifies the action to take when the coordinates do not fit into any poly, circle, or rect, and no point directives are given. The default value for this directive is nocontent, which tells the client to keep the same page displayed.

✦ poly — Defines a polygon using at least 3 points to a maximum of 100 points. If user-supplied coordinates fall within the polygon, this directive is activated.

✦ circle — Defines a circle using the center coordinates and a point on the circle. If user-supplied coordinates fall within the circle, this directive is activated.

✦ rect — Defines a rectangle using two opposing corner coordinates. If user-supplied coordinates fall within the rectangle, this directive is activated.

✦ point — Defines a single point coordinate. The point directive closest to the user-supplied coordinate is used when no other directives are satisfied.

The value is an absolute or relative URL, or one of the special values in the following list. The coordinates (*x,y*) are separated by whitespace characters. The double-quoted text (shown in the second syntax) is used as the text of the link if an image map menu is generated. Any line with a leading # character is considered a comment and is ignored by Apache.

The coordinates are written in x,y format, in which each coordinate is separated by a whitespace character. The quoted text string is used as the link when a menu is generated. In the absence of such a string, the URL is the link, as shown in the following image map file:

```
# Comments go here
#  Version 1.0.0
base http://www.yoursite.com/some/dir
rect thisfile.html "Customer info" 0,0 100,200
circle http://download.yoursite.com/index.html 295,0 100,22
```

If this image map file is called imagemap.map, it can be referenced as follows from another HTML file, such as:

```
<A HREF="/path/to/imagemap.map"><IMG ISMAP SRC="/path/to/imagemap.gif"></A>
```

ImapMenu

The ImapMenu directive determines the action for a request for an image map file without any valid coordinates.

Syntax: ImapMenu {None, Formatted, Semi-formatted, Unformatted}

Context: Server config, virtual host, directory, per-directory access control file (.htaccess)

Override: Indexes

`ImapMenu` allows the following actions:

Action	What It Does
None	No menu is generated, and the default action is performed.
Formatted	The simplest menu is generated. Comments are ignored. A level one header is printed, and then a horizontal rule, and then the links — each on a separate line.
Semi-formatted	In the semi-formatted menu, comments are printed, blank lines are converted into HTML breaks, and no header or horizontal rule is printed.
Unformatted	In the unformatted menu, comments are printed, and blank lines are ignored.

ImapDefault

The `ImapDefault` directive defines the default action for image maps. This default setting can be overridden in the image map file using the default directive.

Syntax: ImapDefault {Error, Nocontent, Map, Referer, URL}

Context: Server config, virtual host, directory, per-directory access control file (.htaccess)

Override: Indexes

The following table shows the meaning of each of the possible values for ImapDefault directive.

Value	What It Does
URL	A relative or absolute URL. Relative URLs resolve relative to the base.
Map	Same as the URL of the image map file itself. Unless `ImapMenu` is set to none, a menu will be created.
Menu	Same as Map.
Referer	Same as the URL of the referring document. Defaults to `http://servername/` if no `Referer:` header is present.
Nocontent	A status code of 204 is sent to tell the client to keep the same page displayed. This is not valid for base.
Error	A status code of 500 is sent to inform the client about a server error.

ImapBase

The ImapBase directive sets the default base used in the image map files. This base setting can be overridden by using the base directive within the image map file. If this directive is not present, the base defaults to http://servername/.

> **Syntax:** ImapBase {Map, Referer, URL}
>
> **Context:** Server config, virtual host, directory, per-directory access control file (.htaccess)
>
> **Override:** Indexes

mod_file_cache

The mod_file_cache module enables Apache to cache frequently used static files that do not change too often. By using this module, you can load a file in memory or preopen the file and reduce disk I/O for each request. This means that Apache does not have to read files from disk for each request. This module does not work on all platforms and should be used only if you are certain that frequently requested files are not going to change. If a cached file or preopened file changes, Apache server cannot deal with the change until you restart the server.

MMapFile

The MMapFile directive enables you to load a file into memory via mmap() system calls. After a file is loaded into memory, the server will not detect any changes in the physical file. So be careful when you use this directive. If you change a file that has been already loaded into memory, make sure you restart the Apache server.

> **Syntax:** MmapFile filename [filename] [...]
>
> **Context:** Server config

CacheFile

The CacheFile directive preopens a file and caches the file handle so that when a request comes, Apache does not have to perform system calls to open and read the file. After a file has been cached, any changes to the file require a restart of the Apache server.

> **Syntax:** CacheFile filename [filename] [...]
>
> **Context:** Server config

mod_dav

The mod_dav module enables you to use WebDAV extensions of the HTTP 1.1 protocol. To learn more about these extensions, visit www.webdav.org.

Dav

The `Dav` directive enables or disables the `mod_dav` module. It must be set to `On` if you wish to use the WebDAV feature within a directory container.

> **Syntax:** `Dav On | Off`
>
> **Context:** Directory

DavLockDB

The `DavLockDB` directive sets the fully qualified pathname of the lock database file.

> **Syntax:** `DavLockDB filename`
>
> **Context:** Server config, virtual host

DavMinTimeout

The `DavMinTimeout` directive sets the minimum resource lock timeout interval in seconds. The default value ensures that a WebDAV client is not locked out (due to any timeout) automatically by the server.

> **Syntax:** `DavMinTimeout seconds`
>
> **Default setting:** `DavMinTimeout 0`
>
> **Context:** Directory

DavDepthInfinity

The `DavDepthInfinity` directive enables a `PROPFIND` request with the `Depth` header set to infinity. The default is recommended.

> **Syntax:** `DavDepthInfinity On | Off`
>
> **Default setting:** `DavDepthInfinity Off`
>
> **Context:** Directory

✦　　✦　　✦

Web Site Administration

Administering Web sites involves chores such as managing virtual Web sites, controlling access to your Web sites, monitoring and analyzing access and error logs, redirecting traffic to different URLs when necessary, setting up proxy service, and generally just doing everything necessary to run perfect Web sites. This part is dedicated to all of these tasks.

P A R T

◆ ◆ ◆ ◆

In This Part

Chapter 6
Hosting Virtual
Web Sites

Chapter 7
Authenticating and
Authorizing Web Site
Visitors

Chapter 8
Monitoring Access to
Apache

Chapter 9
Rewriting your URLs

Chapter 10
Setting Up a Proxy
Server

Chapter 11
Running Perfect
Web Sites

◆ ◆ ◆ ◆

Hosting Virtual Web Sites

Apache can serve multiple Web sites from a single server. For example, a Web hosting company might have a single Web server machine running Apache, which is serving hundreds of client Web sites. Such a system has a primary hostname and many IP aliases or virtual hostnames. A Web site served via such a virtual host is called a Virtual Web site. Apache's support for virtual Web sites (called virtual hosts) is very impressive. This chapter discusses how to create various types of virtual hosts and how to manage them using various techniques.

Understanding Apache's Virtual Hosting Capabilities

When you set up Apache on an Internet host it can respond to an HTTP request for that host. For example, if you set up Apache on a host called server1.doman.com, Apache will serve HTTP requests for this host. However, if you set up your DNS records such that two other hostnames (say www.mycompany-domain.com and www.friendscompany-domain.com) point to the same machine, you can have Apache serve these two domains as virtual Web sites. In such a case www.mycompany-domain.com is considered the primary Web hostname (main server) and the rest of them will be considered as virtual Web site or virtual hosts.

Apache allows virtual hosts to inherit configuration from the main server, which makes the virtual host configuration quite manageable in large installations where some contents can be shared. For example, if you decided only to have a central CGI repository and to allow virtual hosts to use the scripts stored there, you do not need to create a ScriptAlias directive in each virtual host container. Simply use one in the main server configuration and you're done. Each virtual host can use the alias as if it was part of its own.

Apache's configuration file httpd.conf separates virtual host configuration from the main server configuration using the <VirtualHost> container. For example, look at the httpd.conf file in Listing 6-1.

Listing 6-1: **httpd.conf**

```
# httpd.conf file

ServerName main.server.com
Port 80
ServerAdmin mainguy@server.com
DocumentRoot "/www/main/htdocs"

ScriptAlias /cgi-bin/ "/www/main/cgi-bin/"
Alias /images/  "/www/main/htdocs/images/"

<VirtualHost 192.168.1.100>
    ServerName vhost1.server.com
    ServerAdmin vhost1_guy@vhost1.server.com
    DocumentRoot "/www/vhost1/htdocs"
    ScriptAlias /cgi-bin/ "/www/vhost1/cgi-bin/"
</VirtualHost>

<VirtualHost 192.168.1.110>
    ServerName vhost2.server.com
    ServerAdmin vhost2_guy@vhost2.server.com
    DocumentRoot "/www/vhost2/htdocs"
    ScriptAlias /cgi-bin/ "/www/vhost2/cgi-bin/"
    Alias /images/ "/www/vhost2/htdocs/images/"
</VirtualHost>
```

Listing 6-1 shows two virtual Web sites called vhost1.server.com and vhost2. server.com, which are defined in their own <VirtualHost> containers. All the directives included in each of the <VirtualHost> containers apply only to the virtual host it serves. So, when a Web browser requests http://vhost1.server. com/index.html, the Apache Web server looks for the index.html page in /www/ vhost1/htdocs directory. Similarly, when a Web browser requests http://vhost2. server.com/cgi-bin/hello.pl, the script is run from the /www/vhost2/ cgi-bin directory.

However, many directives in the main server configuration (that is, any directive outside of the <VirtualHost> container) still apply to virtual hosts that do not override them. For example, the vhost1.server.com in Listing 6-1 does not have an Alias directive for the /images/ directory alias. So, when a Web browser requests http://vhost1.server.com/images/pretty_pic.gif file the picture is served from /www/main/htdocs/images directory. Because the vhost2. server.com does override the /images/ alias with its own, a similar request is served from /www/vhost2/htdocs/images directory instead.

Setting Up a Virtual Host

There are three ways you can create virtual Web sites using Apache, as discussed in the following list:

✦ **Name-based:** Name-based virtual Web sites are very common. Such a configuration requires that you have multiple hostnames pointed to a single system. You can create multiple CNAME or A records in DNS to point to a single host. Because this method does not use IP addresses in Apache configuration, it is easy to port if you change your IP addresses for your Web server.

✦ **IP-based:** This method requires IP addersses in Apache configuration and thus makes it easy to port when IP addresses need to be changed.

✦ **Multiple main servers:** This method involves using multiple primary Web server configurations. This method is only recommended if you must keep separate configuration file per virtual hosts. This is the least recommended method and is hardly used.

Name-based virtual hosts

This method of creating a virtual host is the most recommended. It requires only a single IP address for hosting hundreds of virtual Web sites.

About the only issue you're likely to come up against with name-based virtual hosting is that this method will not work for Web browsers that do not support HTTP 1.1 protocol. Only the very early Web browsers, such as Microsoft IE 1.x or Netscape Navigator 1.x, don't support HTTP 1.1. So, this is really not a big issue any more. Most people are using 3.x or above versions of the Web browsers, which are compatible with name-based virtual hosting technique.

For example, say you have IP address `192.168.1.100` and want to host `vhost1.domain.com` and `vhost2.domain.com` on the same server. Here's how you can do that:

1. First create the appropriate DNS records on your DNS server to point to `vhost1.domain.com` and `vhost2.domain.com` to `192.168.1.100`. See the "Configuring DNS for a Virtual Host"section for details.

2. Create a configuration segment similar to the following in the `httpd.conf` file.

```
NameVirtualHost 192.168.1.100

<VirtualHost 192.168.1.100>
    ServerName vhost1.domain.com
    ServerAdmin someone@vhost1.domain.com
    DocumentRoot "/www/vhost1/htdocs"

    #
    # Any other directives you need can go here
```

```
</VirtualHost>

<VirtualHost 192.168.1.100>
    ServerName vhost2.domain.com
    ServerAdmin someone@vhost2.domain.com
    DocumentRoot "/www/vhost2/htdocs"

    #
    # Any other directives you need can go here
    #

</VirtualHost>
```

Don't forget to create the document root directories if you don't have them already. Also, if you need to add more directives in each of the virtual host configuration you can do so.

3. Restart Apache using the `/usr/local/apache/apachectl` **restart command** and access each of the virtual hosts using `http://vhost1.domain.com` and `http://vhost2.domain.com`.

As the above example configuration shows, both virtual host containers use the same IP address (`192.168.1.100`). So how does Apache know which virtual site is being requested when a request comes via the `192.168.1.100` IP address?

Well, it turns out that HTTP 1.1 requires that a header called `Host` be present in each request that the Web browser makes to a Web server. For example, following is a header dump of a HTTP request from a Web browser to a server running on `rhat.domain.com`.

```
GET / HTTP/1.1
Host: rhat.domain.com
Accept: text/html, text/plain
Accept: postscript-file, default, text/sgml, */*;q=0.01
Accept-Encoding: gzip, compress
Accept-Language: en
User-Agent: Lynx/3.0.0dev.9 libwww-FM/2.14
```

When Apache sees the `Host: rhat.domain.com` header, it can immediately service the request using the appropriate virtual host that has a matching `ServerName`.

IP-based virtual hosts

This method requires that you use IP addresses in creating virtual hosts. The IP addresses need to be hard-coded in the configuration file in each `<VirtualHost>` container tag. This can create maintenance headaches if you change IP addresses frequently. There is no benefit in using this method over name-based virtual hosting method described earlier. The following example shows three IP-based virtual hosts.

```
<VirtualHost 192.168.1.1>
    ServerName vhost1.server.com
    # Other directives go here
</VirtualHost>

<VirtualHost 192.168.1.2>
    ServerName vhost2.server.com
    # Other directives go here
</VirtualHost>

<VirtualHost 192.168.1.3>
    ServerName vhost3.server.com
    # Other directives go here
</VirtualHost>
```

Each of these IP addresses must be bound to the appropriate Ethernet interface on the server. For example, the above configuration requires a system hosting the above sites to have the following DNS records in its DNS server configuration file.

```
; Address Records
vhost1.server.com.    IN    A 192.168.1.1
vhost2.server.com.    IN    A 192.168.1.2
vhost3.server.com.    IN    A 192.168.1.3

; Reverse DNS records
1                     IN PTR   vhost1.server.com.
2                     IN PTR   vhost2.server.com.
3                     IN PTR   vhost3.server.com.
```

Each of these addresses must be bound to one or more Ethernet interfaces on the server. On a Linux system, multiple IP addresses usually can be bound by using the IP aliasing technique. For example:

```
/sbin/ifconfig eth0   192.168.1.1 up
/sbin/ifconfig eth0:0 192.168.1.2 up
/sbin/ifconfig eth0:1 192.168.1.3 up
```

In the above, all three IP addresses are bound to Ethernet interface eth0 and it's two aliases, eth0:0 and eth0:0. Consequently, the system will respond to each IP address.

Multiple main servers as virtual hosts

Using multiple main servers as virtual hosts is only recommended when you are required (typically, for nontechnical reasons) to maintain different httpd.conf files. For example, say you have 16 IP addresses and want to provide 16 different clients (or departments) with their own `httpd.conf` file so that each entity can manage everything on its own and even create virtual hosts using `<VirtualHost>` containers within their own `httpd.conf`.

Note   Before you actually proceed with this method, consider carefully whether you can avoid creating multiple main server instances by using `<virtualhost>` containers instead.

Listing 6-2 shows a simplified version of `httpd.conf` (called `httpd-100.conf`) that uses the `Listen` directive to tell Apache to only service the `192.168.1.100` IP address associated with the system it is running. This implements a single virtual host.

Listing 6-2: **httpd-100.conf**

```
ServerType standalone
ServerRoot "/usr/local/apache"
PidFile /usr/local/apache/logs/httpd-192.168.1.100.pid
ScoreBoardFile /usr/local/apache/logs/httpd-
192.168.1.100.scoreboard
Timeout 300
KeepAlive On
MaxKeepAliveRequests 100
KeepAliveTimeout 15
MinSpareServers 60
MaxSpareServers 100
StartServers 50
MaxClients 200
MaxRequestsPerChild 0
Port 80
Listen 192.168.1.100:80
User prod
Group prod
ServerName prod.domain.com
ServerAdmin kabir@prod.domain.com
DocumentRoot "/www/prod/htdocs"
```

Notice that the `Listen` directive also takes a port number as a parameter. In Listing 6-2, Apache is told to listen to the given IP address on port 80. The `Port` directive is still necessary because its value is used in Apache-generated self-referencing URLs.

Listing 6-3 shows another simplified `httpd.conf` file (called `httpd-101.conf`) that tells Apache to listen to the `192.168.1.101` address only. This implements another virtual host using the multiple main server method of creating virtual hosts.

Listing 6-3: **httpd-101.conf**

```
ServerType standalone
ServerRoot "/usr/local/apache"
PidFile /usr/local/apache/logs/httpd-192.168.1.101.pid
ScoreBoardFile /usr/local/apache/logs/httpd-
192.168.1.101.scoreboard
Timeout 300
KeepAlive On
MaxKeepAliveRequests 100
KeepAliveTimeout 15
MinSpareServers 5
MaxSpareServers 10
StartServers 5
MaxClients 10
MaxRequestsPerChild 0
Port 80
Listen 192.168.1.101:80
User stage
Group stage
ServerAdmin lance@stage.domain.com
DocumentRoot "/www/stage/htdocs"
```

A system that wants to run two main Apache servers using the configuration files in Listings 6-2 and 6-3 must have:

✦ One or more Ethernet interfaces responding to the named IP addresses. For example on a Linux system you can bind Ethernet interface eth0 to both 192.168.1.100 and 192.168.1.101 using IP aliasing command as shown here:

```
/sbin/ifconfig eth0 192.168.1.100 up
/sbin/ifconfig eth0:0 192.168.1.101 up
```

Of course, if a system has multiple Ethernet interfaces and you wanted to use a main server for each interface, you do not need to use IP aliases.

✦ The IP addresses must have host names associated with them. For the above configuration files, the 192.168.1.100 is associated with prod.domain.com and 192.168.101 is associated with stage.domain.com.

A system that has such IP addresses bound to its interface(s) can now run two main Apache daemons using the following commands:

```
/usr/local/apache/bin/httpd -f  conf/httpd-100.conf
/usr/local/apache/bin/httpd -f  conf/httpd-101.conf
```

If you run the ps auxww | grep httpd | grep root | grep conf command you will see two main Apache servers that run as the root user.

Configuring DNS for a Virtual Host

In most cases your ISP is responsible for providing DNS service for domains. If that is the case you can skip this section. However, if you do run BIND, the most widely used DNS server, on your own on a Linux or other Unix-like systems, I show you how to configure DNS for your virtual hosts here.

Windows users: Please read the Configuring Apache for Win32 chapter for details on how to configure your Windows DNS server.

Comprehending zone files

A zone file is necessary to set up DNS for a virtual host. A zone file is a textual description of your DNS records. This file is loaded by the DNS server to implement your DNS service for a single zone, which is often called an Internet domain.

Following is an example of a zone file. In it, I assume that the new virtual host that you want to setup is called www.newdomain.com, that the DNS server hostnames are ns1.domain.com (primary) and ns2.domain.com (secondary), and that your Web server host name is www.domain.com (192.168.1.100). Make sure you change the host names and IP addresses for your setup accordingly. The zone file for www.newdomain.com is called /var/named/newdomain.zone and it contains the following lines:

```
@ IN SOA newdomain.com.    hostmaster.newdomain.com.(
              20011201001  ; Serial YYYYMMDDXXX
              7200         ; refresh
              3600         ; (1 hour) retry
              1728000      ; (20 days) expire
              3600)        ; (1 hr) minimum ttl

; Name Servers
   IN NS    ns1.domain.com.
   IN NS    ns2.domain.com.

; A Records for IP-based virtual hosting
; www.newdomain.com.    IN    A    192.168.1.100

; CNAME for name-based virtual hosting
  www.newdomain.com.     IN    CNAME www.domain.com.
```

The above DNS configuration assumes that you will not be using IP-based virtual hosting and therefore does not create an A record for www.newdomain.com. The A record line is commented out. You can uncomment it if you use the IP-based virtual hosting method. Because name-based virtual hosting does not require a unique IP address, a CNAME record is created to point www.newdomain.com to www.domain.com (which is the primary Web server).

Here's what's going on in the preceding configuration:

✦ The first line starts a DNS record called the Start of Address (SOA), which specifies the serial number, refresh rate, retry rate, expiration time, and time-to-live (TTL) values.

✦ The serial number is used by DNS servers to determine whether or not they need to update their cached records. For example, the given example is set to 20011201001, which states that the last update was on 12/01/2001 and it is the first (001) change in that day. Now if the DNS administrator changed the DNS configuration on 12/02/2001 the serial number should be changed to reflect that, so that any remote DNS server that has cached the records can compare the serial numbers between the cached version and the new version and decide whether to upload new DNS data.

✦ The refresh rate says how often should the records be refreshed by the DNS server.

✦ The retry value states that in case of a failure the remote DNS server querying this DNS server retry again at the given interval.

✦ The expiration time tells remote DNS servers to forcefully expire any cached data they have on the given domain after specified number of days.

✦ The final entry in SOA states that records have a specified minimal time-to-live value. Note that anything following a semi-colon is treated as a comment line and ignored.

✦ The next two noncomment lines state that the DNS servers responsible for the newdomain.com are ns1.domain.com and ns2.domain.com. If you do not have a second DNS server, you should consider using a third-party secondary DNS service such as http://www.secondary.com.

Setting up DNS for new virtual hosts

You can set up DNS for each new virtual host on Linux as follows:

1. Create a zone file for the new domain. (See the preceding section for more on zone files.)

2. In the /etc/named.conf file, add the following lines to enable the newdomain zone.

```
zone "newdomain.com" IN {
        type master;
        file "newdomain.zone";
        allow-update { none; };
};
```

This tells the named (DNS daemon) that the zone file for newdomain.com is /var/named/newdomain.zone and that it is the primary (master) DNS server for this zone.

3. Run the `killall -HUP named` command to force the name server to reload the `/etc/named.conf` and the new zone file.

4. Try to ping `www.newdomain.com`. If you do not get a response, check the `/var/log/messages` file for any typos or other errors that name server (named_) might have reported in either `/etc/named.conf` or `/var/named/newdomain.zone` files. In such case, correct the typos or errors and restart the server as discussed in the previous step.

5. Once you can ping the `www.newdomain.com`, you are ready to create Apache configuration for this virtual host as described in earlier sections of this chapter.

Offering virtual mail services

To provide virtual mail service for the new virtual hosts you add, you have to modify the `newdomain.zone` file and add one or more appropriate MX record(s). For example, say that your mail server is `mail.domain.com` and it is configured to accept mail for `newdomain.com`. In such a case, you can modify the `/var/named/newdomain.zone` to be as follows:

```
@ IN SOA newdomain.com.    hostmaster.newdomain.com.(
            20011201002    ; Serial YYYYMMDDXXX
            7200           ; refresh
            3600           ; (1 hour) retry
            1728000        ; (20 days) expire
            3600)          ; (1 hr) minimum ttl

; Name Servers
    IN NS    ns1.domain.com.
    IN NS    ns2.domain.com.
    IN MX  10 mail.domain.com.

; CNAME for name-based virtual hosting
    www.newdomain.com.    IN   CNAME  www.domain.com.
```

Note that if you have multiple mail servers you can add them using a simple priority scheme. For example, say that you want all mail for `newdomain.com` to go to `mail.domain.com` and if this mail server is unavailable, you want to use `bkupmail.domain.com`. You can simply add a second MX record as shown here:

```
IN MX  10 mail.domain.com.
IN MX  20 bkupmail.domain.com.
```

The lower number in front of `mail.domain.com` makes it a higher priority mail server than `bkupmail.domain.com`. Make sure you have configured your mail server software to support virtual mail domains.

Setting User and Group per Virtual Host

If you have compiled Apache using the Perchild MPM module, you can set user and group per virtual host, which is discussed here. But the biggest benefit of using this method instead of a multiple httpd.conf-based mail server setup is simplicity of configuration.

Caution   This approach is slower than running multiple main Apache servers with different IP addresses and different User and Group directives. The speed is lost because of the increased complexity in internal request processing. The concept behind this method is as follows: you instruct Apache to run a cluster of child processes with a given user ID and group ID. When a request for a virtual host comes in and a child process is given the request, the child process first determines whether it can handle the request. If the child is not responsible for the requested virtual host it must pass the request to the appropriate child process via socket calls, which slows the request processing. Because this is a new concept, the speed issue might be resolved or reduced in the future versions of Apache.

The material that follows assumes that you want to set up two virtual hosts called vhost1.domain.com and vhost2.domain.com. Make sure to replace them with whatever hostnames you need to use. Table 6-1 shows the user IDs and group IDs to be used for these virtual domains.

Table 6-1		
User and Group Ids for the Virtual Hosts		
Virtual Host	**User ID**	**Group ID**
vhost1.domain.com	vh1user	vh1group
vhost2.domain.com	vh2user	vh2group

Apache can be configured to support different user and group ID per virtual host as follows:

1. Add the following lines to httpd.conf:

```
ChildPerUserID 10 vh1user vh1group
ChildPerUserID 10 vh2user vh2group
```

The ChildPerUser directive tells Apache to associate ten child processes (each being multiple threads that service requests) to user and group ID for the vhost1.domain.com site. Similarly, the second line associates another ten child processes to user and group ID for the vhost2.domain.com site.

2. Create a `<VirtualHost>` container for each site:

```
NameVirtualHost 192.168.1.100

<VirtualHost 192.168.1.100>
    ServerName vhost1.domain.com
    AssignUserID vh1user vh1group

    #
    # Other directives go here
    #
</VirtualHost>

<VirtualHost 192.168.1.100>
    ServerName vhost2.domain.com
    AssignUserID vh2user vh2group

    #
    # Other directives go here
    #
</VirtualHost>
```

The `AssignUserID` directive used in each of the virtual host configuration tells Apache to associate each of the virtual hosts to appropriate user and group ID. Don't forget to change the IP address as necessary.

3. Restart the Apache server using the `/usr/local/apache/bin/apachectl restart` command and you are done.

Managing a Large Number of Virtual Hosts

If you maintain a lot of virtual hosts, the `httpd.conf` file could become very long and cumbersome to manage. An easy solution is to put each virtual host configuration in a file by itself and to include each file by using the `Include` directive. For example, Listing 6-4 shows a `httpd.conf` file with two virtual host configurations that are external to main configuration file.

Listing 6-4: **httpd.conf with two external virtual host configurations**

```
ServerType standalone
ServerRoot "/usr/local/apache"
PidFile /usr/local/apache/logs/httpd.pid
ScoreBoardFile /usr/local/apache/logs/httpd.scoreboard
Timeout 300
KeepAlive On
MaxKeepAliveRequests 100
```

```
KeepAliveTimeout 15
MinSpareServers 5
MaxSpareServers 10
StartServers 5
MaxClients 10
MaxRequestsPerChild 0
Port 80
User httpd
Group httpd
ServerName www.domain.com
ServerAdmin webmaster@domain.com
DocumentRoot "/www/mysite/htdocs"

# Name Virtual Hosts
NameVirtualHost 192.168.1.100
Include vhost1.domain.com.conf
Include vhost2.domain.com.conf
```

Notice that the `NameVirtualHost` directive is followed by the `Include` directive, which tells Apache to read the `vhosts1.domain.com.conf` and `vhost2.domain.com.conf` files to load virtual host configuration. These files can simply contain the `<VirtualHost>` containers that you would normally put in `httpd.conf`. The benefit of this approach is that you can create a very elaborate configuration for each virtual host without cluttering up `httpd.conf`.

Automating Virtual Host Configuration using mod_perl

Although using the `Include` directive (as discussed in the previous section) helps to make `httpd.conf` manageable, it is still not good enough solution for sites that use many Web servers, which, in turn, run many virtual Web sites. Ideally, you want to write Apache configuration with a program or script, if possible, so that many common configuration options are automatically created.

If you use the `mod_perl` module with Apache (discussed in Chapter 16), you can write Perl code to generate your Apache configuration. Because `mod_perl` compilation and installation is covered in Chapter 16 I will not repeat it here. I discuss how you can use Perl code to generate Apache configuration next.

Cross-Reference See Chapter 16 if you still need to compile and installed `mod_perl` support in Apache. Just remember when compiling `mod_perl` by following the instructions in Chapter 16 that you have to use either the EVERYTHING=1 option or PERL_SECTIONS=1 option with the configure script.

To use Perl code to generate Apache configuration, you need to use the `<Perl>` container in `httpd.conf`. For example:

```
<Perl>

 #
 # Your Perl code goes here
 #

 1;
</Perl>
```

The above Perl container is the absolute bare minimum you must have in `httpd.conf` to be able to use Perl-based configuration. The last line within the container returns a 1 (true value), which is necessary to satisfy `mod_perl`. Your code can be any Perl script. The code in a `<Perl>` container is compiled in a special package and `mod_perl` communicates the configuration information to the Apache core configuration module. The syntax that describes the configuration is discussed next.

The directives that take a single value are represented as scalar variables (scalar variables are a Perl concept). For example:

```
User httpd
```

This `User` directive takes a single string value and therefore can be written as:

```
<Perl>
 $User = "httpd";
 1;
</Perl>
```

Here is an example configuration:

```
<Perl>
  $User = "httpd";
  $Group = "httpd";
  $ServerAdmin    = 'kabir@mobidac.com';
  $MinSpareServers = 5;
  $MaxSpareServers = 5;
  $MaxClients = 40;
  1;
</Perl>
```

The directives that require multiple values can be represented as lists. For example, `PerlModule Apache::TestOne Apache::TestTwo` can be represented as:

```
@PerlModule = qw(Apache::TestOne Apache::TestTwo );
```

Containers are represented using hash (hash is a computer programming construct that is very commonly used in Perl and other modern languages such as C), for example:

```
<VirtualHost 206.171.50.50>
    ServerName www.nitec.com
    ServerAdmin kabir@nitec.com
</VirtualHost>
```

this can be represented as the following:

```
$VirtualHost{"206.171.60.60"} = {
    ServerName => 'www.nitec.com',
    ServerAdmin => 'kabir@nitec.com'
  }
```

A slightly more involved example is:

```
$Location{"/some_dir_alias/"} = {
    AuthUserFile => '/www/nitec/secret/htpasswd',
    AuthType => 'Basic',
    AuthName => 'Subscribers Only Access',
    DirectoryIndex => [qw(welcome.html welcome.htm)],
    Limit => {
        METHODS => POST GET',
        require => 'user reader'
    }
  };
```

In the preceding, the configuration segment is used to create a restricted area using basic HTTP authentication method for an alias called /some dir alias/. A set of filenames are also defined as directory indexes for this alias.

You can define other containers such as <Directory>, <Files>, and so on in a similar manner. Some example configurations follow.

Assume that you have three Web server systems — host_a, host_b, and host_c — and that host_a is more powerful than host_b, and host_b is more powerful than host_c. To define a <Perl> container that enables you to create a single configuration for all three hosts, follow this example of such an httpd.conf file:

```
<Perl>
# Get the host name using the Unix hostname utility and store
it
# in the $thisHost variable.
my $thisHost = '/bin/hostname';
if ($thisHost =~ /host_a/) {
    # configuration for host_a goes here
    $MinSpareServers = 10;
    $MaxSpareServers = 20;
    $StartServers     = 30;
    $MaxClients = 256;
    }
elsif ($thisHost =~ /host_b/) {
    # configuration for host_b goes here
```

```
        $MinSpareServers = 5;
        $MaxSpareServers = 10;
        $StartServers      = 10;
        $MaxClients  = 50;
        }
    else {
        # configuration for host_c goes here
        $MinSpareServers = 3;
        $MaxSpareServers = 5;
        $StartServers       = 5;
        $MaxClients  = 30;
            }
    1;
    </Perl>
```

To make this scenario more interesting, assume that you have different virtual hosts for each of the three hosts and would like to configure them in an elegant manner. For example:

```
<Perl>
    # Get the host name using the UNIX hostname utility
    # and store it in the $thisHost variable.

    my $thisHost = '/bin/hostname';
    my $thisDomain = 'mydomain.com';
    my @vHosts = ();

    my $anyHost;

    if ($thisHost =~ /(host_a)/) {

        # configuration for host_a goes here
        @vHosts = qw(gaia, athena, romeo, juliet, shazam);

    } elsif ($thisHost =~ /host_b/) {

        # configuration for host_b goes here
        @vHosts = qw(catbart, ratbart, dilbert);

    } else {

        # configuration for host_c goes here
        @vHosts = qw(lonelyhost);

    }

    for $anyHost (@vHosts) {
        %{$VirtualHost{"$anyHost.$domainName"}} = {
                "ServerName"  => "$anyHost.$domainName",
                "ServerAdmin" => "webmaster\@$anyHost.$domainName"
```

```
        }
    }
    1;
</Perl>
```

After you have created a suitable Perl-based configuration for your Apache servers, you can check your code syntax to make sure that the code is syntactically correct by running the `/usr/local/apache/bin/apachectl configtest` command. If there is a syntax error you will see the error message on screen. Correct the error(s) and reissue this command to make sure Apache accepts the code.

Generating Virtual Host Configuration By Using the makesite Script

If adding virtual hosts becomes a daily or weekly matter for you because you work for an ISP or a large organization that has a marketing department that likes creating new product Web sites frequently, you need `makesite`. It is a simple Perl script that I wrote years ago and that I still use to create new virtual hosts. This script is provided in the CD-ROM and it can also be downloaded from `http://sourceforge.net/projects/mkweb/`.

For example, to create a new virtual host called `newsite.com`, you can simply run `makesite newsite.com` and the script creates and appends the necessary `httpd.conf` configuration. It will also create the necessary DNS configuration files by using two templates. To use `makesite`, follow these steps.

1. Copy the `makesite` script, `named.template`, and `httpd.template` files to suitable locations on your server. I usually keep `makesite` in the `/usr/bin` directory so that it is in my normal path. I recommend creating `/var/makesite` directory and moving the `named.template` and `httpd.template` files there. In the following steps, I assume that you will do the same.

2. Using your favorite text editor, modify the `makesite` script. You need to modify one or more of the following lines:

```
my $MAKESITE_DIR      = '/var/makesite';
my $USER              = 'httpd';
my $GROUP             = 'httpd';
my $PERMISSION        = '2770';
my $BASE_DIR          = '/www';
my $HTDOCS            = 'htdocs';
my $CGIBIN            = 'cgi-bin';
my $NAMED_PATH        = '/var/named';
my $NAMED_FILE_EXT    = '.zone';
```

```
my $NAMED_TEMPLATE    = "$MAKESITE_DIR/named.template";
my $NAMED_CONF        = '/etc/named.conf';
my $HTTPD_CONF        = '/usr/local/apache/conf/httpd.conf';
my $VHOST_TEMPLATE    = "$MAKESITE_DIR/httpd.template";
my $LOG_FILE          = "$BASE_DIR/makesite.log";
```

You may need to make changes as follows:

- If you followed my recommendation and created /var/makesite where you kept named.template and httpd.template files, you do not need to make any changes to $MAKESITE_DIR.

- If you run Apache using a different user/group than httpd, then change the $USER and $GROUP values. If you wish the default Web directory permissions to be something other than 2770 then change the $PERMISSION value.

- The $BASE_DIR is set to /www, which is where virtual host site directory is created. The virtual host site directory will be /www/ virtual_hostname and there will be htdocs (set by $HTDOCS) and cgi-bin (set by $CGIBIN) subdirectories under it. Change the values as needed.

- If you want document root directories to be something other than htdocs, change $HTDOCS.

- Similarly, if you do not use the traditional /cgi-bin/ alias for ScriptAlias, change $CGIBIN accordingly.

- On Linux systems, the default DNS records directory is /var/named; if you have changed it to some other path, make sure you change $NAMED_PATH.

- If you keep the httpd.conf in a different path than /usr/local/apache, then change $HTTPD_CONF value.

3. Modify the /var/makesite/named.template so that it reflects the name server, and Web server host names for your system. The default named. template file assumes that your primary and secondary name servers are ns1.domain.com and ns2.domain.com; that your mail server is mail. domain.com; and that your Web server is www.domain.com. Make sure you change these host names accordingly.

4. Make sure that the /var/makesite/httpd.template has all the directives that you want to add to each new virtual host you create using this script.

Now you are ready to run the script to create a new virtual host. As a precaution, back up your /etc/named.conf and /usr/local/apache/httpd.conf files. To create a new virtual host called vhost1.com run the makesite vhost1.com command. Review the /usr/local/httpd.conf file; you should see:

```
#
# Domain Configuration for www.vhost1.com
#

<VirtualHost www.vhost1.com>
  ServerName www.vhost1.com
  ServerAdmin webmaster@vhost1.com

  DocumentRoot /tmp/vhost1/htdocs
  ScriptAlias /cgi-bin/ /tmp/vhost1/cgi-bin/

  ErrorLog logs/www.vhost1.com.error.log
  TransferLog logs/www.vhost1.com.access.log

</VirtualHost>

#
# End of Domain Configuration for www.vhost1.com
#
```

This is the <VirtualHost> configuration that the makesite script creates.

Tip

If you are creating a name-virtual host for the first time, make sure you add NameVirtualHost IP_Address **as the last line in the** httpd.conf **file before running** makesite **script for the first time.**

Also check the /etc/named.conf file; you should see the following:

```
// vhost1.com was created on 2001-04-25-17-25
zone "vhost1.com" {
        type master;
        file "vhost1.zone";
};
```

As you can see, the script created the appropriate zone configuration information for the virtual host. You can find the DNS zone information in /var/named/vhost1.zone file, which shows:

```
@   IN SOA vhost1.com.  hostmaster.vhost1.com. (
                   20010425000   ; serial YYYYMMDDXXX
                   7200          ; refresh
                   3600          ; (1 hour) retry
                   1728000       ; (20 days) expire
                   3600)            ; (1 hour) minimal TTL

; Name Servers
     IN   NS   ns1.domain.com.
     IN   NS   ns2.domain.com.
     IN   MX   10 mail.domain.com.

; CNAME records
www  IN   CNAME  www.domain.com.
```

Look under /www (or whatever $BASE_DIR is pointing to); you should see vhost1 directory with the following files and subdirectories:

```
./vhost1
./vhost1/htdocs
./vhost1/htdocs/index.html
./vhost1/cgi-bin
```

Restart the name server by using the killall -HUP named command. Also restart the Apache server by using the /usr/local/apache/bin/apachectl restart command. You should be able to access the new virtual Web site by using www. vhost1.com/. The default index.html page is there to help you identify the domain via Web.

Managing Virtual Hosts By Using MySQL with mod_v2h Module

The mod_v2h module is a mass virtual-hosting module with support for performing URL translation paths from MySQL database. This module can cache URL translation paths into memory for faster performance. You will need to have MySQL installed on a server. To learn about MySQL visit www.mysql.com.

With MySQL already installed, follow these steps to compile and install mod_v2h:

1. Download the latest version of mod_v2h from www.fractal.net/mod_v2h.tm.

2. As root, extract the source distribution using the tar xvzf mod_v2h.tar.gz command in the modules subdirectory of your Apache source tree. For example, if you keep the Apache source in /usr/local/src/httpd_2_0_16 directory, than extract the mod_v2h.tar.gz file in the /usr/local/src/ httpd_2_0_16/modules directory. A new subdirectory called mod_v2h will be created.

3. Change your current directory to /usr/local/src/httpd_2_0_16/ modules/v2h and edit the config.m4 file.

Note   You only need to edit this file if you notice that the include and lib directory path for MySQL files are incorrect. For example, on my Linux system, the MySQL include files are installed in /usr/include/mysql directory and the library files are in /usr/lib/mysql directory. The default config.m4 points to /usr/ local/include/mysql and /usr/local/lib/mysql for the include and library files, respectively; thus, I had to correct the path. Simply edit the paths if needed. I also needed to add -lz in the LDFLAGS line so that it looked like LDFLAGS="$LDFLAGS -L/usr/lib/mysql -lz -Wl,-R,/usr/lib/mysql".

4. Change directory to `/usr/local/src/httpd_2_0_16` and run the `autoconf` command to create necessary configuration file.

5. Run `./configure` with whatever options you need as shown in Chapter 2 and then run `make && make` install commands to compile and install Apache with `mod_v2h` support. For example, I ran `./configure --prefix=/usr/local/httpd --disable-module=cgi` to configure Apache source and then ran the `make && make` install commands to install Apache in `/usr/local/httpd` with `mod_v2h` support and without `mod_cgi` support. You can use whatever options you used earlier by not running `./configure` and by running `./config.status` instead.

After you have compiled Apache with `mod_v2h`, you need to use the new `mod_v2h` directives, which are shown in Table 6-2, in `httpd.conf`.

Table 6-2
The mod_v2h directives

Directive	Purpose
v2h	Set to On to turn on this module. Otherwise set it to Off.
v2h_Mysql_Db	Set to the name of the MySQL database
v2h_Mysql_Tbl	Set to the name of the MySQL database table
v2h_Mysql_Serv_Fld	Set to the table field name where server name (for example, `www.domain.com`) is stored
v2h_Mysql_Path_Fld	Specifies the physical path the URI which should be translated to (that is, `/htdocs/www.fractal.net/`).
v2h_Mysql_Host	Set to the host name of the MySQL server.
v2h_Mysql_Port	Set to the MySQL server port number which is used to connect to it.
v2h_Mysql_Pass	Set to the password (if any) for the database access.
v2h_Mysql_User	Set to the username (if any) for the database access.
v2h_Mysql_Env_Fld	Set to the value of additional database field which is used to set the an environment variable called VHE_EXTRA.
v2h_PathHead	Set to the extra path that can be prefixed to the path pointed by `v2h_Mysql_Path_Fld`
v2h_UseImage	Set to On or Off to enable or disable caching in memory
v2h_ImagePath	Set to the path to store the memory image.
v2h_DeclineURI	Set to URI that would be declined.

✦   ✦   ✦

Authenticating and Authorizing Web Site Visitors

Support for basic HTTP authentication in Apache has been around for quite a while. Many modules have been written to provide basic HTTP authentication in Apache. In this chapter you will learn about various ways of authenticating and authorizing access to the Web server, how you can authenticate users using password files, database servers, etc., and how to control access by restricting access via IP address or usernames.

Authentication vs. Authorization

Many people confuse authentication and authorization, and some even think they are the same thing, which they aren't. To understand the differences consider the following example. When you want to visit a foreign country what do you need? A passport and a visa. The passport is a document that authenticates you to the foreign country. It tells them that you are really who you claim to be. So, when you present your passport, you are authenticating yourself to the foreign officials. Next, you must show proof that you are allowed (that is, authorized) to enter the foreign country. This is the visa document.

Now, in computer terms, the *authentication* typically involves submitting a username and password. A successful submission and acceptance of a username and password states that you are who you claim to be. In other words, you have *authenticated* yourself.

A given resource that you are trying to access may require authorization in addition to authentication. For example, if you are accessing a computer at 4 a.m., the computer might refuse to let you in at that time because the system administrator has decided that you are not authorized to access it at

4 a.m. Similarly, you might be authorized to view a restricted Web site from the office but not from home because the company policy dictates to the network administrator that all restricted access be performed on premises.

Understanding How Authentication Works

Basic HTTP authentication is really quite simple. A challenge and response mechanism is used to authenticate users. The steps are shown in Figure 7-1 and discussed below:

1. Authentication begins when a Web browser requests a URL that is protected by the HTTP authentication scheme. This is shown as (1) in the figure.

2. The Web server then returns a 401 status header along with a WWW-Authenticate response header, which implies that authentication is required to access the URL. The header contains the authentication scheme being used (currently only basic HTTP authentication is supported) and the realm name. This is (2) in the figure.

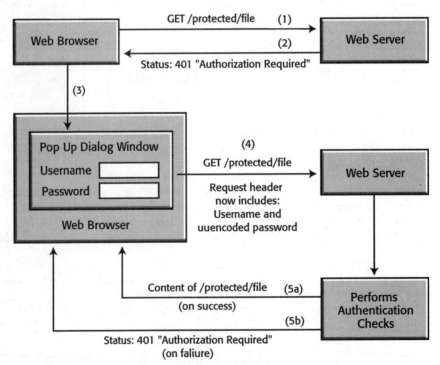

Figure 7-1: The basic HTTP authentication process.

3. At this point, a Web browser dialog box appears, asking the user to enter a username and a password. This is (3) in the figure.

4. The user enters the required username and password and clicks OK. The browser then sends the username and password along with the previous URL request to the server. The server checks whether the username and password are valid. This is (4) in the figure.

Caution

When the password is sent from the client system (the host running the Web browser), it is neither sent in clear text nor encrypted. Instead, it is uuencoded and transmitted over the Internet. This is disadvantageous for this method of authentication, because anyone armed with network traffic sniffer hardware and software might be able to retrieve the IP packet carrying the uuencoded password. Because uuencode is a widely used data-encoding scheme, the decoder, uudecode, is also widely available, thus enabling practically anyone to decode a uuencoded password and to possibly abuse it. It is true that the packet sniffer has to be able to find the right packet to be able to do the decoding, but technically it is possible. This is why you should never use Basic HTTP authentication for any critical application. Do not, for example, protect your nation's secrets using this scheme. However, if you are already allowing Telnet or ftp access to your system, then you are already using authentication methods (in these services) that are very similar to Basic HTTP authentication. If you trust your server to be connected to the Internet, open to attempts to Telnet in by anyone who wants to try, then you have no reason not to trust this method.

5. If the username and password are valid (that is, authentic), the server returns the requested page. This is (5a) in the figure. If the username and password are invalid, the server responds with a 401 status and sends the same WWW-Authenticate response header to the browser. This is (5b) in the figure.

6. In each subsequent request during the browser session to the same server, the browser will send the username and password pair so that the server does not have to generate a 401 status header for calls that fall in the same area of the site. For example, if the URL http://apache.nitec.com/protected/ requires Basic HTTP authentication, subsequent calls to http://apache.nitec.com/protected/a_page.html and http://apache.nitec.com/protected/b_page also require the username and password. This is why the browser sends both before another authentication challenge — that is, the 401 status header and the WWW-Authenticate response header — is issued by the server. This is faster and more practical than generating a challenge for each request and having the user enter the username and password repeatedly.

Authenticating Users Via the mod_auth Module

The `mod_auth` module is Apache's default authentication module. This module enables you to authenticate users whose credentials are stored in text files. Typically a text file containing a username and encrypted password is used. You can also use a text file to create user groups, which can be used to create authorization rules (discussed later in this chapter). It is recommended that you use `mod_auth`-based authentication for small numbers of users. Often when a text file reaches even just a few thousand usernames, lookup performance drops dramatically. So, if you have a very large user base, using this module is not recommended. However, this module is perfect for a few hundred users or so.

You can use `/usr/local/apache/bin/httpd -l` to verify whether this module is already compiled into your Apache binary. If not, you have to use the `--enable-module=auth` option with the `configure` script, and recompile and reinstall your Apache distribution.

Understanding the mod_auth directives

The `mod_auth` module offers the Apache directives `AuthUserFile`, `AuthGroupFile`, and `AuthAuthoritative`. Let's look at these directives and some examples that use this module.

AuthUserFile directive

This directive sets the name of the text file that contains the usernames and passwords used in the basic HTTP authentication. This directive requires that you provide a fully qualified path to the file to be used.

> **Syntax:** `AuthUserFile` *filename*
>
> **Context:** Directory, per-directory access control file (`.htaccess`)
>
> **Override:** `AuthConfig`

For example, the following directive sets `/www/mobidac/secrets/.htpasswd` as the username and password file:

```
AuthUserFile /www/mobidac/secrets/.htpasswd
```

The username and password file is usually created using a utility called `htpasswd`, which is available as a support program in the standard Apache distribution. The format of this file is very simple. Each line contains a single username and an encrypted password. The password is encrypted using the standard `crypt()` function.

Caution It is important that the `AuthUserFile`-specified file resides outside the document tree of the Web site. Putting it inside a Web-accessible directory might enable someone to download it.

AuthGroupFile directive

This directive specifies a text file to be used as the list of user groups for Basic HTTP authentication. The filename is the absolute path to the group file. You can create this file using any text editor.

Syntax: `AuthGroupFile filename`

Context: Directory, per-directory access control file (`.htaccess`)

Override: `AuthConfig`

The format of this file is:

```
groupname: username username username [...]
```

For example:

```
startrek: kirk spock picard data
```

This creates a group called `startrek`, which has four users: `kirk`, `spock`, `picard`, and `data`. The Caution icon in the previous section also applies to this directive.

AuthAuthoritative directive

If you are using more than one authentication scheme for the same directory, you can set this directive to `off` so that when a username/password pair fails with the first scheme, it is passed on to the next (lower) level.

Syntax: `AuthAuthoritative On | Off`

Default: `AuthAuthoritative On`

Context: Directory, per-directory access control file (`.htaccess`)

Override: `AuthConfig`

For example, if you are using `mod_auth_mysql` (discussed later in this chapter) and the standard `mod_auth` module to provide authentication services, and a username/password pair fails for one of them, the next module is used to authenticate the user, if possible. When a user name/password pair fails all modules, the server reissues a 401 status header and sends the WWW-Authenticate response header for reauthentication. However, if a particular module successfully authenticates a username/password pair, the lower-level modules never receive the username/password pair.

It is recommended that you leave the default value as-is because you should not design a trickle-down authentication scheme in which a user may fail one and pass another.

Creating a members-only section in your Web site

By using the mod_auth directives you can create a members-only section on your Web site that requires username/password-based authentication. For example, let's say that you want to create a members-only section called http:// your_server_name/memberonly. Here is how to do it.

1. Determine which physical directory you want to restrict access to. Most people use a directory within the DocumentRoot-specified directory but you can use whatever directory you want as long as the Apache user (set by User directive) is allowed to read the contents of the directory. Here, I assume that your DocumentRoot is set to /www/mysite/htdocs and that you want to restrict access to a directory named /www/mysite/htdocs/memberonly.

2. Modify the httpd.conf file to create a new alias called /memberonly/ as shown below:

   ```
   Alias /memberonly/ "/www/mysite/htdocs/memberonly/"
   ```

3. Next add the following directives to the httpd.conf file to setup /memberonly/ as a restricted section that requires user authentication.

   ```
   <Location /memberonly/>
       AuthName "Member-Only Access"
       AuthType  Basic
       AuthUserFile /www/secrets/.members
       require valid-user
   </Location>
   ```

   Here the AuthName directive simply creates a label that is displayed by the Web browsers to the users. This label should be something meaningful so that the user knows what is being requested. Make sure you use double-quotes as shown above. The AuthType is always set to Basic because HTTP only supports Basic authentication by default. The AuthUserFile points to a password file called .members. The Require directive states that only valid users are allowed access.

4. Now, use the htpasswd utility to create a password file. Assuming you have installed Apache in /usr/local/apache, the htpasswd command should be run as follows only for the first time:

   ```
   /usr/local/apache/bin/htpasswd -c path_to_password_file
   username
   ```

   The -c option is only needed to create the file and should be used just once. For example, to create the first user called mrbert for the above /memberonly/ configuration, run:

   ```
   /usr/local/apache/bin/htpasswd -c /www/secrets/.members mrbert
   ```

5. To ensure that the user is created in the password file, view its contents using a text editor. Also make sure that only the Apache user (set using the User directive) can access this file. For example, if you run Apache as httpd user,

you can run `chown httpd:httpd /www/secrets/.members && chmod 750 /www/secrets/.members` commands to ensure that only httpd user (and group) can read this file.

6. Restart the Apache server using the `/usr/local/apache/bin/apachectl restart` command.

7. Now, use `http://your_server_name/memberonly/` to access the member-only section; you should be prompted for a username and password. You should see the value of the `AuthName` (`"Member-Only Access"`) in the displayed dialog box.

8. Enter an invalid username and password and you should see a rejection message.

9. Finally, try and access the site again and then enter a valid username and password as created by the `htpasswd` utility. You should have access to the restricted section.

Note   If you are using the default common log format to log access, you can see logged-in usernames in your log files.

Creating a members-only section using a .htaccess file

For organizations such as Internet Service Providers (ISPs) and large companies with many departments running virtual Web sites on the same Web server, adding member-only configuration in `httpd.conf` (which was discussed in the last section) may not be a manageable solution, because you will have to add or remove configurations as quickly as various users (in case of an ISP setup) request such changes. By using a `.htaccess`-based authentication, however, you can allow a user or department to create as many member-only sections as they want without your involvement — a blessing for a busy system administrator.

To use `.htaccess`-based authentication for member-only authentication, follow these steps.

1. Add the following directive in your `httpd.conf` file:

```
AccessFileName .htaccess
```
Note   If you wish to enable the `.htaccess`-based authentication only for a virtual host, add this directive within the appropriate `<VirtualHost>` container.

2. Change the following default configuration:

```
<Directory />
    Options FollowSymLinks
    AllowOverride None
</Directory>
```

to:

```
<Directory />
    Options FollowSymLinks
    AllowOverride AuthConfig
</Directory>
```

This enables use of the authorization directives (`AuthDBMGroupFile`, `AuthDBMUserFile`, `AuthGroupFile`, `AuthName`, `AuthType`, `AuthUserFile`, `Require`, and so on) in an `.htaccess` file.

3. Restart the Apache server using `/usr/local/apache/bin/apachectl restart` command.

4. Now you can create an `.htaccess` file in any Web accessible directory and control access to it. You need to have these directives in the `.htaccess` file:

```
AuthName "Enter Appropriate Label Here"
AuthType  Basic
AuthUserFile  path_to_user_password_file
Require valid-user
```

For example, say you have a directory called `/www/mysite/htdocs/asb` and want to restrict access to this directory to users listed in `/www/mysite/secrets/users.pwd`. To do so, you would use the following configuration:

```
AuthName "ASB Member Only Access"
AuthType  Basic
AuthUserFile  /www/mysite/secrets/users.pwd
Require valid-user
```

Note   Make sure that the `.htaccess` file is readable only by the Apache user (set using User directive). For example, if you run Apache as httpd, then you would run `chown httpd:httpd .htaccess && chmod 750 .htaccess` commands from the directory where you keep the file. Also note that creation or modification of an `.htaccess` file does not require restarting Apache server, so you can try out the restricted section of your Web site to determine whether the authentication process is working properly.

Grouping users for restricted access to different Web sections

If you different users need access to different parts of your Web site, you have several choices. Instead of just requiring a valid-user configuration, which opens up the restricted section for all valid users, you can use specific usernames. For example:

```
<Location /financial>
AuthName "Members Only"
AuthType  Basic
AuthUserFile /www/mysite/secrets/.users.pwd
require cgodsave jolson
```

```
  </Location>

<Location /sales>
AuthName "Members Only"
AuthType  Basic
AuthUserFile /www/mysite/secrets/.users.pwd
require  esmith jkirk
  </Location>
```

Here only `cgodsave` and `jolson` have access to the `/financial` section and `esmith` and `jkirk` have access to `/sales` section. However, naming all users in the configuration is a cumbersome and often unmanageable undertaking. One approach is to create either separate password files, which would make the above configuration segments look as follows:

```
<Location /financial>
AuthName "Members Only"
AuthType  Basic
AuthUserFile /www/mysite/secrets/.financial-team.pwd
require valid-user
  </Location>

<Location /sales>
AuthName "Members Only"
AuthType  Basic
AuthUserFile /www/mysite/secrets/.sales-team.pwd
require valid-user
  </Location>
```

Now, add only the users who should be added to `/www/mysite/secrets/` `.financial-team.pwd`, in this case, `cgodsave` and `jolson`, and add only the users who should be added to `/www/mysite/secrets/.sales-team.pwd`, in this case, `esmith` and `jkirk`.

However, if maintaining multiple password files is not appealing to you, there is another approach. For example, take a look at the following configuration segments:

```
<Location /financial>
AuthName "Members Only"
AuthType  Basic
AuthUserFile /www/mysite/secrets/.members.pwd
AuthGroupFile /www/mysite/secrets/.groups
require group financial
  </Location>

<Location /sales>
AuthName "Members Only"
AuthType  Basic
AuthUserFile /www/mysite/secrets/.members.pwd
AuthGroupFile /www/mysite/secrets/.groups
require group sales
  </Location>
```

Here the same password file .members.pwd is used for both locations but each location uses a different group. The group file is common because a group file can contain multiple groups. The group file /www/mysite/secrets/.groups is a simple text file, which for the above example looks like:

```
financial: cgodsave jolson
sales: esmith jkirk
```

Now, to add new users to a group does not require changing the httpd.conf file (or if you are using .htaccess files, the <Location> containers). You can simply add the user to the appropriate group in the group file after you have created the user account using htpasswd command.

Authorizing Access via Host Name or IP Addresses

In this authorization scheme, the host name or the host's IP address controls access. When a request is made for a certain resource, the Web server checks whether the requesting host is allowed access to the resource and takes action based on its findings.

The standard Apache distribution includes a module called mod_access, which enables access control based on the Internet host name of a Web client. The host name can be either a fully qualified domain name (FQDN), such as blackhole. mobidac.com, or an IP address, such as 192.168.1.100. The module provides this access control support by using these Apache directives: allow, deny, order, allow from env=variable, and deny from env=variable.

allow directive

This directive enables you to define a list of hosts (containing one or more hosts or IP addresses) that are allowed access to a certain directory. When more than one host or IP address is specified, they should be separated with space characters. Table 7-1 shows the possible values for the directive.

Syntax: Allow from host1 host2 host3 ...

Context: Directory, location, per-directory access control file (.htaccess)

Override: Limit

Table 7-1
Possible Values for the allow Directive

Value	Example	Description
All	`allow from all`	This reserved word allows access for all hosts. The example shows how to use this option.
A FQDN of a host	`allow from wormhole.mobidac.com`	Only the host that has the specified domain name (FQDN) is allowed access. The `allow` directive in the example only allows access to `wormhole.mobidac.com`. **Note that this compares whole components;** `toys.com` would not match `etoys.com`.
A partial domain name of a host	`allow from .mainoffice.mobidac.com`	Only the hosts that match the partial host name are allowed access. The example permits all the hosts in `.mainoffice.mobidac.com` network to access the site. For example, `developer1.mainoffice.mobidac.com` and `developer2.mainoffice.mobidac.com` have access to the site. However, `developer3.baoffice.mobidac.com` is not allowed access.
A full IP address of a host	`allow from 192.168.1.100`	Only the specified IP address is allowed access. The example shows the full IP address (all four octets of IP are present), `192.168.1.100` that is allowed access.
A partial IP address	Example 1: `allow from 192.168.1` Example 2: `allow from 130.86`	When less than four octets of an IP address are present in the `allow` directive, the partial IP address is matched from left to right, and hosts that have the matching IP address pattern (that is, it is part of the same subnet) are allowed access. In the first example, all hosts with IP addresses in the range of 192.168.1.1 to 192.168.1.255 have access. In the second example, all hosts from the network are allowed access.

Continued

Table 7-1 *(continued)*

Value	Example	Description
A network/ netmask pair	`allow from 192.168.1.0/ 255.255.255.0`	This enables you to specify a range of IP addresses using the network and the netmask address. The example allows only the hosts with IP addresses in the range of 192.168.1.1 to 192.168.1.255 to have access.
A network/nnn CIDR specification	`allow 206.171.50.0/24`	Similar to the previous entry, except that the netmask consists of nnn high-order 1 bits. The example is equivalent to allowing access to hosts with IP addresses from 206.171.50.0/255.255.255.0.

deny directive

This directive is the exact opposite of the `allow` directive. It enables you to define a list of hosts that are denied access to a specified directory. Like the `allow` directive, it can accept all the values shown in Table 7-1.

> **Syntax:** `deny from host1 host2 host3 [...]`
>
> **Context:** Directory, location, per-directory access control file (`.htaccess`)
>
> **Override:** `Limit`

order directive

This directive controls how Apache evaluates both `allow` and `deny` directives.

> **Syntax:** `order deny, allow | allow, deny | mutual-failure`
>
> **Default:** `order deny, allow`
>
> **Context:** Directory, location, per-directory access control file
>
> **Override:** `Limit`

For example, the following directive denies the host `myboss.mycompany.com` access, while allowing all other hosts to access the directory. The value for the `order` directive is a comma-separated list, which indicates which directive takes precedence:

```
<Directory /mysite/myboss/rants>
    order deny, allow
    deny from myboss.mycompany.com
    allow from all
</Directory>
```

Typically, the one that affects all hosts is given lowest priority. In the preceding example, because the allow directive affects all hosts, it is given the lower priority.

Although allow, deny and deny, allow are the most widely used values for the order directive, you can use another value, mutual-failure, to indicate that only those hosts appearing on the allow list but not on the deny list are granted access. In all cases, every allow and deny directive is evaluated.

allow from env=variable directive

This directive, a variation of the allow directive, allows access when the named environment variable is set.

> **Syntax:** allow from env=variable
>
> **Context:** Directory, location, per-directory access control file (.htaccess)
>
> **Override:** Limit

This is only useful if you are using other directives such as BrowserMatch to set an environment variable. For example, say you want to allow Microsoft Internet Explorer 6, the latest version of Internet Explorer, to access a directory where you stored some HTML files with embedded VBScript. Because the other leading Web browser, Netscape Navigator, does not support VBScript directly, you'd rather not have Navigator users go into the directory. In such a case, you can use the BrowserMatch directive to set an environment variable when Internet Explorer 5.5 is detected. The directive would be:

```
BrowserMatch "MSIE 5.5" ms_browser
Now you can use a <Directory> container to specify the allow
directive, as follows:
<Directory /path/to/Vbscript_directory >
    order deny,allow
    deny from all
    allow from env=ms_browser
</Directory>
```

Here the Apache server will set the ms_browser environment variable for all browsers that provide the "MSIE 6" string as part of the user-agent identifier. The allow directive will allow access only to browsers for which the ms_browser variable is set.

deny from env=variable

This directive, a variation of the deny directive, denies access capability for all hosts for which the specified environment is set.

Syntax: deny from env=variable

Context: Directory, location, per-directory access control file (.htaccess)

Override: Limit

For example, if you want to deny all hosts using Microsoft Internet Explorer access, you can use the BrowserMatch directive to set a variable called ms_browser whenever a browser identified itself to the server with the string "MSIE".

```
BrowserMatch "MSIE" ms_browser
```

Now you can use a <Directory> container to specify the deny directive, as follows:

```
<Directory /path/to/vbscript_directory >
    order deny,allow
    allow from all
    deny from env=ms_browser
</Directory>
```

If you are interested in blocking access to a specific HTTP request method, such as GET, POST, or PUT, you can use the <Limit> container to do so. For example:

```
<Location /cgi-bin>
    <Limit POST>
        order deny,allow
        deny from all
        allow from yourdomain.com
    </Limit>
</Location>
```

This example allows POST requests to the cgi-bin directory only if hosts in the yourdomain.com domain make the request. In other words, if this site has some HTML forms that send user input data via the HTTP POST method, only the users in yourdomain.com will be able to use these forms effectively. Typically, CGI applications are stored in the cgi-bin directory, and many sites feature HTML forms that use the POST method to dump data to CGI applications. Using the preceding host-based access-control configuration, a site can allow anyone to run a CGI script but only allow a certain site (in this case, yourdomain.com) to actually post data to one or more CGI scripts. This gives the CGI access in such a site a bit of read-only character. Everyone can run applications that generate output without taking any user input, but only users of a certain domain can provide input.

Combining Authentication and Authorization

The basic HTTP user authentication support in `mod_auth` and access authorization support in `mod_access` can be combined to implement practical access control problems. For example, lets say that you want to allow a group of users access to a the `/aolbuddies/` sections of your Web site only if they are browsing the Web site via an AOL connection. Here is the configuration that you can add to `httpd.conf` after replacing the path and filenames as appropriate:

```
Alias /aolbuddies/    "/path/to/web/directory/for/aolbuddies/"

<Location /aolbuddies/>
    Deny from all
    Allow from .aol.com

    AuthName "AOL Buddies Only"
    AuthType  Basic
    AuthUserFile /path/to/.myusers.pwd
    AuthGroupFile /path/to/.mygroups
    require group aolbuddies

    Satisfy all
</Location>
```

The `Satisfy all` directive tells Apache to only allow access to those who pass both authentication and authorization tests. When an AOL user connects to `http://your_server/aolbuddies/` via AOL, the user is prompted for a username and password. If the user enters a username that belongs to the `aolbuddies` group and the user's password is correct, the user will be allowed access.

Note   You must add all your AOL buddies as users in `/path/to/.myusers.pwd` and also create a group called `aolbuddies` in `/path/to/.mygroupsm` which lists all the AOL buddies (users in `/path/to/.aol` that you added earlier) in it.

Authenticating with a Relational Database

If you run a relational database server on your network (or even on the Web server) and have a lot of users (that is, more than 1,000 users) to authenticate via the Web, you can use the database server to replace the text file-based (`mod_auth`) authentication discussed earlier. There are several advantages to using a database server for large number of users; the primary advantages are:

✦ The `mod_auth` authentication becomes really slow when a large number of users are stored in a text file.

✦ If you allow users to change their passwords via the Web by using a custom application, text files are not safe because you must ensure that write access to the file is locked and unlocked properly. Storing data in database servers removes such additional burden from your scripts and provides a much better degree of overall data integrity.

✦ In a relational database you can store a great deal of information about a user that can be used by your Web applications. So, centralizing your user database using a database server such as MySQL makes good sense for the long-term.

Note You can use most modern relational database servers such as MySQL, Postgres, DB2, Oracle, and Microsoft SQL as the user database. Installation of any of these database servers is beyond the scope of this book. I assume that you have installed one of these database servers on your network or on the Web server.

Tip For a site that has many users, you may want to create a dedicated database server that is accessible on your Web network. Ideally the database server should be accessible via a back-end network instead of the Internet. Most of the time, it is better to have a second Ethernet interface on each server system and to create a LAN that is only accessible to the servers in the LAN. (See Chapter 23 for details on how to create such network.)

Using MySQL database server for authentication

MySQL is the most widely used free database server in the open source community; it is available under the GNU Public License. It is easy to install and set up your server as a user-authentication database server. With the Linux platform, you can simply download and install the server, client, and development RPM packages and can be ready in a matter of minutes! MySQL server is available for download at `www.mysql.com`.

Creating the user-authentication database in MySQL server

To use MySQL server as an authentication database you need to have at least username and password information in a table in a database. If you already have an existing database table with such information you do not need to follow the steps given here.

1. Log on to the MySQL server using the `mysql -u root -p` command. You will be asked to enter the root password for the database.

Caution The root password for the MySQL server should always be different than the root password on your Unix system. They serve different purposes and therefore should be kept apart.

2. After you are logged into MySQL, run the `create database auth;` command, which creates a database called `auth`.

3. Change your current database to the newly created `auth` database using the following command:

```
use auth;
```

4. Now create a table called `wwwusers` by entering the following lines in the MySQL command prompt.

```
create table wwwusers (
   username varchar(40)    not null primary key,
   passwd   varchar(20)    not null
);
```

Each row in this table consists of three fields: `username`, `passwd`, and `groups`. The `username` field is the primary key, which means that MySQL uses this field to index the table, making lookups that use the username very fast. This field is limited to 40 characters. The use of varchar (variable character) instead of fixed char type saves space if usernames are not always 40 characters. The `username` field cannot be null (that is, empty) because it is also the primary key. The password field is called `passwd`, which is a maximum of 20 characters long and of the varchar type. It cannot be null.

5. Now enter `describe wwwusers;` command, which should show the following output:

```
mysql> describe wwwusers;
+----------+-------------+------+-----+---------+-------+
| Field    | Type        | Null | Key | Default | Extra |
+----------+-------------+------+-----+---------+-------+
| username | varchar(40) |      | PRI |         |       |
| passwd   | varchar(20) |      |     |         |       |
+----------+-------------+------+-----+---------+-------+
2 rows in set (0.00 sec)
```

This is a verification of the fact the table `wwwusers` was created as desired.

6. Now you need to add user(s) to the table. To add users manually, you need to run the following SQL statement:

```
insert into wwwusers (username , passwd)
          values ('user_name',
                  'user_password'
                  );
```

For example:

```
insert into wwwusers (username , passwd)
          values ('esmith','sale007');
```

Here a user called `esmith` is added with `sale007` as the password in the `sales` group. Add as many users as you would like. See " Managing Users and Groups in Any RDBM " for details on how to manage users using utility scripts.

7. If you plan to use user groups for authentication, then create the following table.

```
create table wwwgroups (
    username      varchar(40),
    groupname     varchar(40)
);
```

8. Now enter the `describe wwwgroups;` command, which should show the following output:

```
+-------------+--------------+------+-----+---------+-------+
| Field       | Type         | Null | Key | Default | Extra |
+-------------+--------------+------+-----+---------+-------+
| username    | varchar(40)  | YES  |     | NULL    |       |
| groupname   | varchar(40)  | YES  |     | NULL    |       |
+-------------+--------------+------+-----+---------+-------+
2 rows in set (0.00 sec)
```

This is a verification that the table wwwgroups was created as desired.

9. You can add existing users to new groups by using the following SQL statement:

```
insert into wwwgroups (username , groupname)
         values ('user_name',
                 'name_of_the_group'
                 );
```

For example:

```
insert into wwwgroups (username , groupname)
         values ('kabir',
                 'www_wheel'
                 );
```

adds user Kabir to a new group called www_wheel. Note that you can add the same user to multiple groups.

Granting Apache server access to the user-authentication database in MySQL

Like most modern RDBM servers, MySQL uses username- and password-based authentication itself to allow access to the databases it stores. So, before you can use Apache with MySQL, you should create a MySQL user called httpd, which should have access to whichever database you plan on using with Apache. Here is how to create a MySQL user for Apache:

1. Log on to the MySQL server using the `mysql -u root -p` command. You will be asked to enter the root password for the database.

2. After you are logged into MySQL, you can issue a grant statement as follows:

```
grant all privileges on name_of_database
      to username@hostname identified by 'user_password'
      with GRANT option;
```

For example, to grant a user called httpd (that is, the username specified in the User directive in httpd.conf file) all privileges to a database called auth when using the 2manysecrets password from localhost run:

```
grant all privileges on auth
        to httpd@localhost identified by '2manysecrets'
        with GRANT option;
```

This allows the httpd user to access the auth database from localhost. This assumes that the MySQL server and the Apache server run on the same machine. If the database is on a different machine, you should use the appropriate host name as the replacement of localhost.

Caution

If you do not plan to add Web applications that need to write to the user authentication database, then do not grant all privileges to the Web server user. For example, if you simply want to authenticate the user but never update or remove the user via the Web server (that is, using a CGI script or other Web application), then replace all privileges with select. This ensures that the Web server user is only allowed to perform select queries on the database, which is equivalent to read-only access.

3. Enter the flush privileges command to instruct the MySQL server to reload the grant table.

4. You should now exit MySQL monitor program by entering exit at the mysql> prompt.

   Now log in to MySQL by entering the mysql -u httpd -p command and by supplying the appropriate password (2manysecrets in this case). You should be able to access the database auth by entering use auth; after you are at the mysql> prompt. If you cannot access the database, make sure you are on the host that you specified in the grant statement issued earlier.

Compiling and installing mod_auth_mysql module

MySQL database server's favorable status in the open source community has led to the development of an Apache module called mod_auth_mysql. This module can be used to interface with a MySQL server for authentication. You can download the latest version of this module from www.mysql.com/Downloads/Contrib/. Here is how you can compile and install mod_auth_mysql.

1. As root extract the mod_auth_mysql source distribution in /usr/local/src directory. A new subdirectory called mod_auth_mysql-version. Change to this directory and run:

   ```
   ./configure --with-apache=/usr/local/src/apache_version
   --with-mysql=/usr
   ```

   Make sure you change the /usr/local/src/apache_version with the Apache source distribution path and the /usr with the path where MySQL header files are installed. If you have installed MySQL using the default configuration, the headers file are installed in `/usr/local/mysql` and supplying `--with-mysql=/usr` is the right value for such setup because the `mod_auth_mysql` script generates `/usr/local/mysql` by appending `/local/mysql` to `/usr`.

2. Run make and then change directory to the apache source distribution and run either `./config.status --activate-module=src/modules/auth_mysql/libauth_mysql.a` (if you have compiled Apache already) or `./configure --activate-module=src/modules/auth_mysql/libauth_mysql.a --prefix=/usr/local/apache` (if you are compiling Apache for the first time).

3. Finally, run `make && make install` to compile and install Apache with `mod_auth_mysql` support.

4. Now restart the Apache server using the `/usr/local/apache/bin/apachectl restart` command.

Authenticating users using mod_auth_mysql module

After you have compiled and installed `mod_auth_mysql`, created the database containing user and group tables, and also created a database-level user for Apache to access these tables, you can configure Apache as follows:

1. In `httpd.conf` add the following lines outside any `<VirtualHost>` or any other type of containers such as `<Directory>`, `<Location>`, and the like.

```
Auth_MySQL_Info db_hostname db_username db_password
Auth_MySQL_General_DB database_name
```

The first directive tells Apache which database server to connect to by using which database username and password. The database username and password are created in MySQL. This username-password pair must not match any interactive user account on your system.

The second directive states which database to connect to. If you use a single database for all your user authentication needs, you can simply set the database name here. Doing so will save you from typing in a database name for each authentication configuration segment.

2. To require authentication for a subdirectory under document root called `protected_dir` you can either create a `<Directory>` or a `<Location>` container in `httpd.conf`, or you can use a `.htaccess` file (assuming you have `AllowOverride AuthConf` set in `httpd.conf` to the main server or to an appropriate virtual host) to have the following configuration segment:

```
AuthName "Members Only"
AuthType Basic
require valid-user

Auth_MYSQL on
```

```
Auth_MySQL_DB database_name
Auth_MySQL_Password_Table password_table_name
Auth_MySQL_Username_Field username_field_name
Auth_MySQL_Password_Field password_field_name

Auth_MySQL_Group_Table group_table_name
Auth_MySQL_Group_Field group_field_name

Auth_MySQL_Empty_Passwords off
Auth_MySQL_Encrypted_Passwords on
Auth_MySQL_Encryption_Types Crypt_DES
Auth_MySQL_Scrambled_Passwords off
Auth_MySQL_Authoritative on
Auth_MySQL_Non_Persistent off
```

Note

Don't forget to replace the database_name, password_table_name, user-name_field_name, password_field_name, group_table_name, and group_field_name with appropriate information.

- The Auth_MYSQL directive turns mod_auth_mysql on or off.

- The Auth_MySQL_DB directive specifies the database name, which holds the Auth_MySQL_Password_Table-specified password table and the Auth_MySQL_Group_Table-specified group table.

- The Auth_MySQL_Username_Field and Auth_MySQL_Password_Field directives specify the field names used to store the username and password in the password table.

- The Auth_MySQL_Group_Field directive specifies the group name field.

- The Auth_MySQL_Empty_Passwords is set to off because empty passwords are not appropriate for most authentication needs.

- Encrypted password support is turned on using Auth_MySQL_Encrypted_Passwords and encryption type is set to the traditional Unix style Crypt_DES by using Auth_MySQL_Encryption_Types.

Note

Although you can choose from Plaintext, Crypt_DES, and MySQL encryption types, I never recommend the plaintext password. Support for Auth_MySQL_Scrambled_Passwords is turned off because it is inappropriate in most scenarios.

- Because it is not a good idea to allow a trickle-down authentication scheme (that is, if one scheme fails to allow a user access another might be used to allow access), the Auth_MySQL_Authoritative directive is turned on. This tells Apache to ignore all other authentication schemes used for the same directory. If the mod_auth_mysql cannot allow a user to access a restricted directory, Apache will simply reissue request for authentication.

- The final directive, Auth_MySQL_Non_Persistent, tells Apache to not disconnect from the database server per authentication request. Disconnecting per request would mean Apache would have to connect for every new request for authentication, which is not good for performance. So the default value (off) is recommended.

3. If you added the above to a <Directory> or <Location> container in httpd.conf you need to restart the Apache server using the /usr/local/apache/bin/apachectl restart command. On the other hand, if you used the above configuration in a .htaccess file, you can use it without restarting the server.

Using other databases for user authentication

You use Postgres, IBM DB2, Oracle, or another server as your database instead of MySQL server for user authentication with Apache. Although you might not find an Apache module such as mod_auth_mysql for your flavor of the RDBM, you can use Apache::AuthDBI module for mod_perl (see Chapter 16, which discusses using mod_perl, for details on how to install mod_perl) to communicate with your database server and to perform user authentication. Follow these steps to do so:

1. Make sure that you all the necessary libraries and include files that came with your database server package are installed. Typically, this means that you need to install the Software Development Kit (SDK) for your RDBM.

2. Install the latest version of the DBI module using perl -MCPAN -e 'install DBI' command.

3. Install the latest version of the appropriate database driver for Perl (DBD) using perl -MCPAN -e 'install DBD::database' command. For example, to install the database driver for IBM DB2 you will run perl -MCPAN -e 'install DBD::db2'.

4. Install the latest version of Apache::AuthDBI using perl -MCPAN -e 'install Apache::AuthDBI' command.

5. Create a database user account for Apache to use to connect to the database server. This is not an account to access your system such as the Linux server itself. It is an account on the database engine that grants permission to access the user database and its tables to Apache.

6. Next you need to create the auth database and the wwwuser table discussed in the "Creating the user-authentication database in mysql server" section earlier in this chapter. Also, be sure to create one or more test users using the manage_users.pl script discussed in "Managing users and groups in any RDBM" section later in this chapter.

7. In httpd.conf add the following line:

```
PerlModule Apache::AuthenDBI
```

This tells Apache that you want to use the Apache::AuthenDBI module.

8. Create an alias called `/memberonly/` to point to the directory you want to restrict access to using the following `Alias` directive:

```
Alias /memberonly/  "path_to_restricted_access_directory"
```

For example:

```
Alias /memberonly/ "/usr/local/apache/htdocs/protected/"
```

Here `/memberonly/` alias points to `/usr/local/apache/htdocs/protected/` directory.

9. Now create the following configuration segment in `httpd.conf`:

```
<Location /memberonly/>
    AuthName "Home"
    AuthType Basic
    PerlAuthenHandler Apache::AuthenDBI
    PerlSetVar Auth_DBI_data_source dbi:mysql:database=auth
    PerlSetVar Auth_DBI_username       httpd
    PerlSetVar Auth_DBI_password       2manysecrets
    PerlSetVar Auth_DBI_pwd_table      wwwusers
    PerlSetVar Auth_DBI_uid_field      user
    PerlSetVar Auth_DBI_pwd_field      passwd
    PerlSetVar Auth_DBI_encrypted      on
    require valid-user
</Location>\
```

The following list gets you up to speed with what's going on in the above listing:

- The above configuration tells Apache to use the `Apache::AuthenDBI` as the handler for the `/memberonly/` alias.

- The `PerlSetVar` directives are used to set key=value pairs needed by this module.

  The `Auth_DBI_data_source` key sets the database DSN that tells the module which database to connect by using which Perl DBD. Here, the value is set to connect to a MySQL database called `auth`. You should set the driver to whatever RDBM you are using. For example, if you are using IBM DB2, your database source name (DSN) might say `dbi:db2:database=auth`.

- The `Auth_DBI_username` and `Auth_DBI_password` keys set the database username and password to be used to connect to the named user database (that is, `auth`).

  The name of the password table is specified by the `Auth_DBI_pwd_table` key; similarly, the username and password fields are specified by `Auth_DBI_uid_field` and `Auth_DBI_pwd_field` keys respectively.

  The `Auth_DBI_encrypted` key is set to `on` so that passwords stored in the database are assumed to be encrypted using the traditional Unix style one-way hash encryption function called `crypt`.

- Finally, the `require valid-user` directive tells Apache to only allow access for those users who pass the authentication test.

10. You can restart the Apache server by using the `/usr/local/apache/bin/apachectl restart` command and can try accessing the `http://your_server_name/memberonly` directory to see if you can access the directory with invalid usernames and passwords. If you enter a valid username and password, you should be authenticated.

Managing Users and Groups in Any RDBM

Managing users and groups in a database by hand is very cumbersome. Thankfully, you don't have to deal with such tasks. You can use a set of Perl scripts to handle these chores quite efficiently. Here is how.

1. You will need to install the DBI package and the appropriate `DBD::database` modules from the Comprehensive Perl Archive Network (CPAN). For example, if you installed MySQL database, as the root user you can install the DBI and DBD modules from the command-line as follows:

```
perl -MCPAN -e 'install DBI'
perl -MCPAN -e 'install DBD::mysql'
```

2. Check whether you have two CPAN modules called `HTTPD::UserAdmin` and `HTTPD::GroupAdmin` in your installed Perl distribution. You can run the `locate UserAdmin.pm` and `locate GroupAdmin.pm` commands to determine whether you have them. Typically, these two modules are installed as part of the standard distribution. For example, on my system these modules appear as follows:

```
/usr/lib/perl5/site_perl/5.6.0/HTTPD/UserAdmin.pm
/usr/lib/perl5/site_perl/5.6.0/HTTPD/GroupAdmin.pm
```

If you don't have one or both of the modules, install them as follows: as root download the `HTTPD::UserAdmin` and `HTTPD::GroupAdmin` CPAN modules from CPAN. On a Linux system you can simply run the following commands to install them:

```
perl -MCPAN -e 'install HTTPD::UserAdmin'
perl -MCPAN -e 'install HTTPD::GroupAdmin'
```

Tip You might want to install the `HTTPD::Tools` package because it includes the two modules as well as other modules that are useful for Web servers in general.

3. Copy the `manage-users.pl` script from the companion CD-ROM to `/usr/bin` directory (see the CD Appendix for information on where to find `/usr/bin`). Change the file permission to allow you to run it. Set the permission using `chmod 750 /usr/bin/manage_users.pl` command.

4. Use your favorite text editor to modify the following lines of the script.

```
my $DB_HOST        = 'localhost';
my $DB_PORT        = '';
my $DATABASE       = 'auth';
my $DB_DRIVER      = 'mysql';
```

```
my $DB_USER              = 'kabir';
my $DB_PASSWORD          = $dbpwd;
my $ENCRYPTION           = 'crypt';
my $USER_TABLE           = 'wwwusers';
my $USERNAME_FIELD       = 'username',
my $PASSWORD_FIELD       = 'passwd',
my $GROUP_TABLE          = 'wwwgroups';
my $GROUP_FIELD          = 'groupname';
my $MAXSZ_USER           = 40;
my $MAXSZ_PWD            = 20;
my $MAXSZ_GRP            = 40;
```

In the above code, you need to set the following variables:

- The $DB_HOST variable should be set to the database server you want to connect to. If the database server is on the same machine as the Web server, the default value 'localhost' can be left alone.

- The $DB_PORT variable should be set to the database server port. By default, the port is automatically selected unless you have used an untraditional port on the database server for client connection.

- The $DATABASE variable should be set to the database name. The default database name is 'auth' and will only work if you have followed instructions in earlier sections.

- The $DB_DRIVER variable should be set to the database driver you need to connect to the database server. For MySQL database server this driver is called mysql and therefore the default will only work if you are using a MySQL database.

- The $DB_USER variable should be set to the user who has been granted access to create, modify, or delete records in the $DATABASE-specified tables. See Granting Apache Server Access to the User-Authentication Database in MySQL earlier in this chapter, to know about how you can grant a user access to a MySQL database.

- The $DB_PASSWORD is intentionally not stored in the script to enhance security. You must provide the password needed to access the database using the command-line option -dbpwd=*database_password* whenever you run the manage_users.pl script. You can hard code a password, but I recommend removing the hard coded password after you are done with the script.

- The $ENCRYPTION variable can be set to none, crypt (default), or MD5. When set to none, passwords are stored in plain-text; when crypt is used, passwords are encrypted with the one-way hashing algorithm used in traditional Unix environment; when MD5 is used, password is stored as a message digest (MD5) value.

- The $USER_TABLE variable should be set to the user table in your database. This table must have $USERNAME_FIELD-specified username field and also the $PASSWORD_FIELD-specified password field.

- The $GROUP_TABLE variable should be set to the group table in your database. This table must have the $USERNAME_FIELD-specified user name field and also the $GROUP_FIELD-specified group name field.
- The maximum size of the $USERNAME_FIELD is set using $MAXSZ_USER field, which should correspond to what you have used in the $USER_TABLE creation process. The $PASSWORD_FIELD size is controlled in a similar manner by using the $MAXSZ_PWD field. Finally, the $GROUP_FIELD size is controlled using $MAXSZ_GRP field.

5. Save the changes.

Adding a new user to the user table

To add a new user to the user table run the following command:

```
manage_user.pl -db=user \
               -action=add \
               -user=user_name \
               -password=user_password \
               -dbpwd=database_password
```

For example, to add a user named kabir with user password go#forward you can run the following command

```
manage_user.pl -db=user \
               -action=add \
               -user=kabir \
               -password=go#forward \
               -dbpwd=mydbpwd
```

Note that here the mydbpwd is the database password needed to write to the database.

Removing an existing user from the user table

To remove a user from the user and group table run the following command:

```
manage_user.pl -db=user \
               -action=del \
               -user=user_name \
               -dbpwd=database_password \
               -auto=on
```

For example, to delete a user named kabir from the user and group tables using a database access password mydbpwd you can run the following command:

```
manage_user.pl -db=user \
               -action=del \
               -user=kabir \
               -dbpwd=mydbpwd \
               -auto=on
```

Tip   Setting the `-auto` option ensures that user is removed from all the groups in the group table.

Updating an existing user's password in the user table

To update a user's password in the user table, run the following command:

```
manage_user.pl -db=user \
               -action=update \
               -user=user_name \
               -dbpwd=database_password
```

For example, to update user `kabir`'s password to `mksecret` by using the `mydbpwd` database password, run the following command:

```
manage_user.pl -db=user \
               -action=update \
               -user=kabir \
               -dbpwd=mydbpwd
```

Adding a user to a group

To add an existing user to a new or existing group, run the following command:

```
manage_user.pl -db=group \
               -action=add \
               -user=user_name \
               -group=group_name \
               -dbpwd=database_password
```

For example, to add a user named `kabir` to a group called administrators, run the following command:

```
manage_user.pl -db=group \
               -action=add \
               -user=kabir \
               -group=administrators \
               -dbpwd=mydbpwd
```

Here `mydbpwd` is the database password needed to write to group table.

Deleting a user from a group

To delete a user from a group, run the following command :

```
manage_user.pl -db=group \
               -action=del \
               -user=user_name \
               -group=group_name \
               -dbpwd=database_password
```

For example, to delete a user named kabir from a group called administrators, run:

```
manage_user.pl  -db=group \
                -action=del \
                -user=kabir \
                -group=administrators \
                -dbpwd=mydbpwd
```

Here mydbpwd is the database password needed to update the group table.

Secure Authenticated Sessions Using Cookies

As mentioned earlier in the this chapter, Basic HTTP authentication requires that the Web browser always pass the username and the encoded (not encrypted) password each time a page under a restricted section is requested. This makes the *man-in-the-middle attack* too easy. This attack involves a cracker intercepting packets between a Web server and a Web browser by using Basic HTTP authentication to determine passwords.

The solution to the man-in-middle attack is to use a secure socket layer (SSL) connection and a session-based authentication scheme in which the user is authenticated once using the Basic HTTP authentication and all subsequent requests to the restricted resource are authorized using a secure (encrypted) session cookie instead of the encoded password.

This section discusses a solution that uses MySQL database (however, you can use any other RDBM as well) and mod_perl modules from CPAN. Here is how you can implement such solution.

1. If they aren't installed already, install the mod_perl module as discussed in Chapter 16.

2. Install two CPAN modules for Apache using the following command as root:

   ```
   perl -MCPAN -e 'install Apache::AuthCookie'
   perl -MCPAN -e 'install Apache::AuthTicket'
   ```

3. Once you have installed the above modules, you will need to create the auth database and the wwwuser table discussed in the "Creating the user authentication database in mysql server" section earlier in this chapter. You will also need to add the following two tables.

   ```
   CREATE TABLE tickets (
       ticket_hash CHAR(32) NOT NULL,
       ts          INT NOT NULL,
       PRIMARY KEY (ticket_hash)
   ```

```
);

CREATE TABLE ticketsecrets (
    sec_version  BIGINT,
    sec_data     TEXT NOT NULL
);
```

Follow the instructions given in the "Creating the user-authentication database in mysql server" section earlier in this chapter to add these tables in the auth database.

4. After you have created the above tables, you must add a secret in the ticketsecrets table. The simplest way to add a secret is to login onto your database server and connect to the auth database and issue an insert statement as follows:

```
insert into ticketsecrets (sec_version, sec_data) values
('number', 'random_data');
```

5. Determine which Web directory location you want to restrict access and issue session cookies for. In this example, I call this location /protected. Add the following configuration to your httpd.conf file:

```
PerlModule Apache::AuthTicket
PerlSetVar ProtectedTicketDB
DBI:mysql:database=auth;host=localhost
PerlSetVar ProtectedTicketDBUser httpd
PerlSetVar ProtectedTicketDBPassword secret1
PerlSetVar ProtectedTicketTable tickets:ticket_hash:ts
PerlSetVar ProtectedTicketUserTable wwwusers:username:passwd
PerlSetVar ProtectedTicketSecretTable
ticketsecrets:sec_data:sec_version
PerlSetVar ProtectedTicketPasswordStyle crypt
```

The following list tells you what's going on in the above configuration:

- Here the PerlModule directive tells Apache that you want to use the Apache::AuthTicket module.

- The PerlSetVar directives are used to set various key=value pairs that are needed by that module.

- The ProtectedTicketDB key sets the data source name (DSN) for the database.

- The sample value DBI:mysql:database=auth;host=localhost tells the AuthTicket module that we want to use MySQL database driver (mysql) and connect to database called auth, which resides on the localhost (same machine as the Web server). Make sure you change this to appropriate host name if you are not running the MySQL database server on the same machine as the Apache Web server.

- The ProtectedTicketDBUser and ProtectedTicketDBPassword directives tell the AuthTicket module which database username and password are needed to access the database server.

- The `ProtectedTicketTable`, `ProtectedTicketUserTable`, and `ProtectedTicketSecretTable` keys tell the module which ticket and user tables to use in the database and what fields are needed.

- The `ProtectedTicketPasswordStyle` sets the encryption type. You have three choices: traditional Unix style one-way hash encryption (a.k.a crypt), or plaintext (not recommended), or MD5.

6. Next add the following configuration lines:

```
PerlSetVar ProtectedTicketExpires 30
PerlSetVar ProtectedTicketLogoutURI /protected/index.html
PerlSetVar ProtectedTicketLoginHandler /protectedlogin
PerlSetVar ProtectedTicketIdleTimeout 15
PerlSetVar ProtectedPath /
PerlSetVar ProtectedDomain .domain_name
PerlSetVar ProtectedSecure 1
PerlSetVar ProtectedLoginScript /protectedloginform
```

The following list tells you what's happening in the above configuration:

- The `ProtectedTicketExpires` key sets the session (ticket) expiration time in minutes.

- The `ProtectedTicketLogoutURI` key sets the URL that is displayed after a user logs out.

- The `ProtectedTicketLoginHandler` sets the path to the login handler, which must correspond to a `<Location>` container, as discussed later.

- The `ProtectedTicketIdleTimeout` sets number of minutes a session is allowed to be idle.

- The `ProtectedPath` sets the cookie path. The default value of / ensures that the cookie is returned with all requests. You can restrict the cookie to the protected area only by changing / to /protected (or whatever location you are protecting).

- The `ProtectedDomain` sets the domain name of the cookie. The leading dot ensures that the cookie is sent to all Web hosts in the same domain. For example, setting this to `.mobidac.com` would allow the cookie to be seen in `web1.Mobidac.com` or `web2.Mobidac.com`. You can also restrict the cookie to a single host by specifying the fully qualified host name here.

- The `ProtectedSecure` setting of 1 ensures that the cookie is secure.

- The `ProtectedLoginScript` sets the location for the login form, which is generated by the module.

7. Now you need to create a `<Location>` container for the /protected directory as follows:

```
<Location /protected>
    AuthType Apache::AuthTicket
    AuthName Protected
    PerlAuthenHandler Apache::AuthTicket->authenticate
```

```
        PerlAuthzHandler Apache::AuthTicket->authorize
        require valid-user
</Location>
```

Here Apache is told to require valid user credentials, which are to be authenticated by the `Apache::AuthTicket` module.

8. Now you need to setup the handlers for the login screen, login script, and logout functions of the module as follows:

```
<Location /protectedloginform>
    AuthType Apache::AuthTicket
    AuthName Protected
    SetHandler perl-script
    Perlhandler Apache::AuthTicket->login_screen
</Location>

<Location /protectedlogin>
    AuthType Apache::AuthTicket
    AuthName Protected
    SetHandler perl-script
    PerlHandler Apache::AuthTicket->login
</Location>

<Location /protected/logout>
    AuthType Apache::AuthTicket
    AuthName Protected
    SetHandler perl-script
    PerlHandler Apache::AuthTicket->logout
</Location> </Location>
```

9. After you have created the above configuration, make sure you have added at least one user to the `wwwusers` table. See "Managing users and groups in any RDBM" section earlier in this chapter for details on how to manage users in a database.

10. Restart the Apache Web server by using `/usr/local/apache/bin/apachectl restart` command.

11. To make sure that you see the cookie, set your Web browser to prompt for cookie. For Netscape Navigator, you can check the Warn me before storing a cookie option using Edit ⇨ Preference ⇨ Advanced ⇨ Cookies option. For Microsoft IE, you must use Tools ⇨ Internet Options ⇨ Security ⇨ Custom Levels ⇨ Cookies ⇨ Prompt options.

12. Now access the `http://your_server_name/protected/` directory and you should see a Web form requesting your username and password. Enter the a valid username and an invalid password and the Web form should simply redisplay itself. Now enter a valid username/password pair and your Web browser will ask your permission to store a cookie. A sample session (ticket) cookie is shown below

```
Cookie Name: Apache::AuthTicket_Protected
Cookie Domain: nitec.com
Path: /
```

```
Expires: End of session
Secure: Yes
Data:
expires:988390493:version::user:kabir2:hash:bf5ac94173071cde9
4489ef79f24b158:time:988389593
```

13. Allow the Web browser to store the cookie and you should have access to the restricted Web section.

14. Next, you should verify that there is a new ticket in the tickets table. You can log onto your database server and view the contents of the tickets table. For example, on Linux system running a MySQL server, I can run the `select *` `from tickets` command after I am logged onto MySQL via the `mysql -u` `httpd -p auth` command. A sample output is shown below:

```
mysql> select * from tickets;
+---------------------------------+-----------+
| ticket_hash                     | ts        |
+---------------------------------+-----------+
| 145e12ad47da87791ace99036e35357d | 988393278 |
| 6e115d1679b8a78f9b0a6f92898e1cd6 | 988393401 |
+---------------------------------+-----------+
2 rows in set (0.00 sec)
```

Here MySQL reports that there are two sessions currently connected to the Web server.

15. You can force Web browsers to log in again by removing the tickets stored in this table. For example, issuing the `delete from tickets` command on your database server removes all records in the tickets table and forces everyone to login again.

✦   ✦   ✦

Monitoring Access to Apache

Have you ever wondered who is accessing your Web site? Or how your Apache server is performing on your system? Monitoring, logging, and analyzing Apache server can provide you with a great deal of information that is vital to the smooth system administration of the Web servers, and it can also help with the marketing aspects of your site. In this chapter, I show you how to monitor and log information on an Apache server to satisfy your need to know.

Among other things, in this chapter I show you how to:

✦ Quickly access Apache server configurations

✦ Monitor the status of a running Apache server

✦ Create log files in both CLF and custom formats

✦ Analyze log files using third-party applications

Monitoring Apache

Apache enables you to monitor these two types of very valuable information via the Web:

✦ **Server configuration information:** This information is static, but being able to quickly access a running server's configuration information can be very useful when you want to find out what modules are installed on the server.

✦ **Server status:** This information changes constantly. Using Apache's Web-based server-status monitoring capabilities, you can monitor information such as the server's uptime, total requests served, total data transfer, status of child processes, and system resource usage.

I discuss both types of information in the following sections.

Accessing configuration information with mod_info

System configuration information can be accessed via the mod_info module. This module provides a comprehensive overview of the server configuration, including all installed modules and directives in the configuration files. This module is contained in the mod_info.c file. It is not compiled into the server by default. You have to compile it using the --enable-info option with the configure script. For example:

```
./configure   --prefix=/usr/local/apache \
              --with-mpm=prefork \
              --enable-info
```

This command configures Apache to be installed on /usr/local/apache directory, configures the source to run as a preforking server, and enables the mod_info module. Run make and make install to compile and install the newly built Apache server.

After you have installed this module in the server, you can view server configuration information via the Web by adding the following configuration to the httpd.conf file:

```
<Location /server-info>
    SetHandler server-info
    Order deny,allow
    Deny from all
    Allow from 127.0.0.1 .domain.com
</Location>
```

This allows the localhost (127.0.0.1) and every host on your domain to access the server information. Do not forget to replace the .domain.com with your top-level domain name. For example, if your Web site is www.nitec.com, you need to add:

```
Allow from 127.0.0.1 .nitec.com
```

The dot in front of the domain name enables any host in the domain to access the server information. However, if you wish to limit this to a single host called sysadmin.domain.com, then change the Allow from line to:

```
Allow from 127.0.0.1 sysadmin.domain.com
```

After the server is configured and restarted, the server information is obtained from the localhost (that is, running a Web browser such as lynx on the server itself) by accessing http://localhost/server-info.

This returns a full configuration page for the server and all modules. If you wish to access it from a different location, use the fully qualified server name in place of localhost. For example, if your Web server is called www.nitec.com, you access the server information by using http://www.nitec.com/server-info.

The mod_info module also provides a directive called AddModuleInfo, which enables you to add descriptive text in the module listing provided by the mod_info module. The descriptive text could be anything including HTML text. AddModuleInfo has this syntax:

```
AddModuleInfo module_name descriptive_text
```

For example:

```
AddModuleInfo mod_info.c 'See <a
href="http://localhost/manual/mod/mod_info.html">man mod_info</a>'
```

This shows an HTML link next to the listing of mod_info.c, providing a quick way to get more information on the module from the Apache online manual, as shown below.

```
Module Name: mod_info.c
Content handlers: (code broken)
Configuration Phase Participation: Create Server Config, Merge Server Configs
Module Directives:
AddModuleInfo - a module name and additional information on that module
Current Configuration:
AddModuleInfo mod_info.c 'man mod_info'

Additional Information:
man mod_info
```

You can also limit the information displayed on the screen as follows:

✦ **Server configuration only.** Use http://server/server-info?server, which shows the following information:

```
Server Version: Apache/2.0.14 (Unix)
Server Built: Mar 14 2001 12:12:28
API Version: 20010224:1
Hostname/port: rhat.nitec.com:80
Timeouts: connection: 300    keep-alive: 15
MPM Information: Max Daemons: 20 Threaded: no Forked: yes
Server Root: /usr/local/apache
Config File: conf/httpd.conf
```

✦ **Configuration for a single module.** Use http://server/server-info?module_name.c. For example, to view information on only the mod_cgi module, run http://server/server-info?mod_cgi.c, which shows the following information:

```
Module Name: mod_cgi.c
Content handlers: (code broken)
Configuration Phase Participation: Create Server Config,
Merge Server Configs
Module Directives:
ScriptLog - the name of a log for script debugging info
ScriptLogLength - the maximum length (in bytes) of the script
debug log
ScriptLogBuffer - the maximum size (in bytes) to record of a
POST request
Current Configuration:
```

✦ **A list of currently compiled modules.** Use `http://server/server-info?list`, which shows the following information:

```
mod_cgi.c
mod_info.c
mod_asis.c
mod_autoindex.c
mod_status.c
prefork.c
mod_setenvif.c
mod_env.c
mod_alias.c
mod_userdir.c
mod_actions.c
mod_imap.c
mod_dir.c
mod_negotiation.c
mod_log_config.c
mod_mime.c
http_core.c
mod_include.c
mod_auth.c
mod_access.c
core.c
```

Of course, your listing will vary based on which modules you have enabled during source configuration. Now, let's look at how you can monitor the status of a running Apache server.

Enabling status pages with mod_status

The `mod_status` module enables Apache administrators to monitor the server via the Web. An HTML page is created with server statistics. It also produces another page that is program friendly. The information displayed on both pages includes:

✦ The current time on the server system

✦ The time when the server was last restarted

✦ Time elapsed since the server was up and running

✦ The total number of accesses served so far

✦ The total bytes transferred so far

✦ The number of children serving requests

✦ The number of idle children

✦ The status of each child, the number of requests that child has performed, and the total number of bytes served by the child

✦ Averages giving the number of requests per second, the number of bytes served per second, and the average number of bytes per request

✦ The current percentage CPU used by each child and used in total by Apache

✦ The current hosts and requests being processed

Note   Some of the above information is only available when you enable displaying of such informatino using the ExtendedStatus directive, which is discussed later in this section.

Like the `mod_info` module, this module is also not compiled by default in the standard Apache distribution, so you need use the `--enable-status` option with the `configure` script and compile and install Apache.

Viewing status pages

After you have the `mod_status` module compiled and built into your Apache server, you need to define the URL location that Apache should use to display the information. In other words, you need to tell Apache which URL will bring up the server statistics on your Web browser.

Let's say that your domain name is `domain.com`, and you want to use the following URL:

```
http://www.domain.com/server-status
```

Using the `<Location . . .>` container, you can tell the server that you want it to handle this URL using the server-status handler found in the `mod_status` module. The following will do the job:

```
<Location /server-status>
    SetHandler server-status
    Order deny,allow
    Deny from all
    Allow from 127.0.0.1 .domain.com
</Location>
```

Here, the `SetHandler` directive sets the handler (`server-status`) for the previously mentioned URL. After you have added the configuration in `httpd.conf`, restart the server and access the URL from a browser. The `<Location . . .>` container enables you to access the status information from any host in your domain, or from the server itself. Don't forget to change `.domain.com` to your real domain name, and also don't forget to include the leading dot.

Tip You can also have the status page update itself automatically using the `http://server/server-status?refresh=N` URL to refresh the page every *N* seconds.

To view extended status information, add the `ExtendedStatus On` directive in the server configuration context. For example, your entire server status-related configuration in `httpd.conf` could look as follows:

```
ExtendedStatus On
<Location /server-status>
    SetHandler server-status
    Order deny,allow
    Deny from all
    Allow from 127.0.0.1 .domain.com
</Location>
```

An example of the extended status information is shown here:

```
Apache Server Status for rhat.nitec.com
Server Version: Apache/2.0.14 (Unix)
Server Built: Mar 14 2001 12:12:28


--------------------------------------------------------------------------------
Current Time: Thursday, 15-Mar-2001 11:05:08 PST
Restart Time: Thursday, 15-Mar-2001 11:02:40 PST
Parent Server Generation: 0
Server uptime: 2 minutes 28 seconds
Total accesses: 17807 - Total Traffic: 529 kB
CPU Usage: u173.4 s.03 cu0 cs0 - 117% CPU load
120 requests/sec - 3660 B/second - 30 B/request
4 requests currently being processed, 8 idle servers
_WKKK...........................................................................
_...............................................................................
_...............................................................................
_...............................................................................
_...............................................................................
_...............................................................................
_...............................................................................
_...............................................................................

Scoreboard Key:
"_" Waiting for Connection, "S" Starting up, "R" Reading Request,
"W" Sending Reply, "K" Keepalive (read), "D" DNS Lookup,
"L" Logging, "G" Gracefully finishing, "." Open slot with no current process
```

```
Srv PID Acc M CPU  SS Req Conn Child Slot Client VHost Request
0-0 0 0/87/87 _  0.07 1726072572 0 0.0 0.10 0.10   (unavailable)
0-0 0 105/105/105 W  0.00 1726072572 0 50.5 0.05 0.05   (unavailable)
0-0 0 166/166/166 K  0.02 1726072572 0 233.5 0.23 0.23   (unavailable)
0-0 0 49/49/49 K  0.01 1726072572 0 25.2 0.02 0.02   (unavailable)
0-0 0 77/77/77 K  0.08 1726072572 0 116.6 0.11 0.11   (unavailable)
4-0 0 0/0/17323 _  173.25 1726072572 0 0.0 0.00 0.00   (unavailable)


-----------------------------------------------------------------

Srv Child Server number - generation
PID OS process ID
Acc Number of accesses this connection / this child / this slot
M Mode of operation
CPU CPU usage, number of seconds
SS Seconds since beginning of most recent request
Req Milliseconds required to process most recent request
Conn Kilobytes transferred this connection
Child Megabytes transferred this child
Slot Total megabytes transferred this slot


-----------------------------------------------------------------

Apache/2.0.14 Server at rhat.nitec.com Port 80
```

Simplifying the status display

The status page displayed by the `mod_status` module provides extra information that makes it unsuitable for using as a data file for any data analysis program. For example, if you want to create a graph from your server status data using a spreadsheet program, you need to clean up the data manually. However, the module provides a way for you to create machine-readable output from the same URL by modifying it using `?auto` as in `http://server/server-status?auto`. An example status output is shown here:

```
Total Accesses: 17855
Total kBytes: 687
CPULoad: 14.1982
Uptime: 1221
ReqPerSec: 14.6233
BytesPerSec: 576.157
BytesPerReq: 39.4001
BusyServers: 8
IdleServers: 8
Scoreboard:
_KKWKKKKK................................................_..........
.........................................................._..........
..........................................._.......................
......................_.............................................
_.........................................................._........
..............................................._...................
.............................
```

Storing server status information

Apache comes with a Perl script (found in the support directory of the source distribution) called `log_server_status` that can be used to periodically store server status information (using the `auto` option) in a plain-text file.

You can run this script as a `cron` job to grab the status information on a desired time frequency. Before you can use the script, however, you may have to edit the script source to modify the value of the `$wherelog`, `$port`, `$server`, and `$request` variables. The default values are:

```
$wherelog = "/var/log/graph/";  # Logs will be like "/var/log/graph/19960312"
$server = "localhost";          # Name of server, could be "www.foo.com"
$port = "80";                   # Port on server
$request = "/status/?auto";     # Request to send
```

For most sites the following should work:

```
$wherelog = "/var/log/apache";
$server   = "localhost";
$port     = "80";
$request  = "/server-status?auto"
```

You might need to make the following changes:

✦ Change the value of `$wherelog` to the path where you would like to store the file created by the script. Make sure the path already exists or else create it using `mkdir -p` *pathname*. For example, `mkdir -p /var/log/apache` will make sure all the directories (`/var`, `/var/log`, `/var/log/apache`) are created as needed.

✦ The `$port` variable value should be the port number of the server that you want to monitor. The default value of 80 is fine if your server is running on a standard HTTP port.

✦ The `$server` variable should be assigned the host name of your server. The default value `localhost` is fine if the script and the server run on the same system. If the server is on another machine, however, specify the fully qualified host name (for example, `www.mydomain.com`) as the value.

✦ The `$request` variable should be set to whatever you used in the `<Location . . .>` directive plus the `?auto` query string.

If you do not like the record format the script uses, you can modify the following line to fit your needs:

```
print OUT "$time:$requests:$idle:$number:$cpu\n";
```

The script uses a socket connection to the Apache server to send the URL request; therefore, you need to make sure that you have socket support for Perl. For example, on a Linux system the Perl socket code is found in `socket.ph`. You can use the `locate socket.ph` to determine whether this file exists in your system.

Creating Log Files

Knowing the status and the configuration information of your server is helpful in managing the server, but knowing who or what is accessing your Web site(s) is also very important, as well as exciting. You can learn this information by using the logging features of Apache server. The following sections discuss how logging works and how to get the best out of Apache logging modules.

As Web-server software started appearing in the market, many Web server log-analysis programs started appearing as well. These programs became part of the everyday work life of many Web administrators. Along with all these came the era of log file incompatibilities, which made log analysis difficult and cumbersome; a single analysis program didn't work on all log files. Then came the Common Log Format (CLF) specification. This enabled all Web servers to write logs in a reasonably similar manner, making log analysis easier from one server to another.

By default, the standard Apache distribution includes a module called `mod_log_config`, which is responsible for the basic logging, and it writes CLF log files by default. You can alter this behavior using the `LogFormat` directive. However, CLF covers logging requirements in most environments. The contents of each line in a CLF log file are explained in the paragraphs that follow.

The CLF log file contains a separate line for each request. A line is composed of several tokens separated by spaces:

```
host ident authuser date request status bytes
```

If a token does not have a value, then it is represented by a hyphen (-). Tokens have these meanings:

✦ `authuser`: If the requested URL required a successful Basic HTTP authentication, then the user name is the value of this token.

✦ `bytes`: The number of bytes in the object returned to the client, excluding all HTTP headers.

✦ `date`: The date and time of the request.

✦ `host`: The fully qualified domain name of the client, or its IP address.

✦ `ident`: If the `IdentityCheck` directive is enabled and the client machine runs identd, then this is the identity information reported by the client.

✦ `request`: The request line from the client, enclosed in double quotes (").

✦ `status`: The three-digit HTTP status code returned to the client.

Cross-Reference   See Appendix A for a list of all HTTP/1.1 status codes.

The date field can have this format:

```
date = [day/month/year:hour:minute:second zone]
```

The date field sizes are given in Table 8-1.

Table 8-1 Date Field Sizes	
Fields	*Value*
Day	2 digits
Month	3 letters
Year	4 digits
Hour	2 digits
Minute	2 digits
Second	2 digits
Zone	(`+` | `-`) 4*digit

The following sections give you a look at the directives that can be used with mod_log_config. There are four directives available in this module.

TransferLog directive

TransferLog sets the name of the log file or program where the log information is to be sent. By default, the log information is in the CLF format. This format can be customized using the LogFormat directive. Note that when the TransferLog directive is found within a virtual host container, the log information is formatted using the last LogFormat directive found within the context. If a LogFormat directive is not found in the same context, however, the server's log format is used.

Syntax: TransferLog *filename* | "| path_to_external/program"

Default setting: none

Context: server config, virtual host

The TransferLog directive takes either a log file path or a pipe to an external program as the argument. The log filename is assumed to be relative to the ServerRoot setting if no leading / character is found. For example, if the ServerRoot is set to /etc/httpd, then the following tells Apache to send log information to the /etc/httpd/logs/access.log file:

```
TransferLog logs/access.log
```

When the argument is a pipe to an external program, the log information is sent to the external program's standard input (STDIN).

<table>
<tr><td>Note</td><td>A new program is not started for a VirtualHost if it inherits the TransferLog from the main server. If a program is used, then it is run under the user who started httpd. This will be the root if the server was started by the root. Be sure that the program is secure.</td></tr>
</table>

LogFormat directive

LogFormat sets the format of the default log file named by the TransferLog directive. If you include a nickname for the format on the directive line, you can use it in other LogFormat and CustomLog directives rather than repeating the entire format string. A LogFormat directive that defines a nickname does nothing else; that is, it only defines the nickname, and it doesn't actually apply the format.

Syntax: LogFormat *format* [*nickname*]

Default setting: LogFormat "%h %l %u %t \"%r\" %>s %b"

Context: Server config, virtual host

See the "Customizing Your Log Files" section later in this chapter for details on the formatting options available.

CustomLog directive

Like the TransferLog directive, this directive enables you to send logging information to a log file or to an external program. Unlike the TransferLog directive, however, it enables you to use a custom log format that can be specified as an argument.

Syntax: CustomLog *file* | *pipe* [*format* | *nickname*] [env=[!]*environment_variable*]

Default setting: None

Context: Server config, virtual host

For example, in the following, each line in the access.log file will be written using the given format specifiers. The format specifies a format for each line of the log file:

```
CustomLog logs/access.log "%h %l %u %t \"%r\" %>s %b"
```

The options available for the format are exactly the same as for the argument of the LogFormat directive. If the format includes any spaces (which it will in almost all cases), it should be enclosed in double quotes. Instead of an actual format string, you can use a format nickname defined with the LogFormat directive. For example:

```
LogFormat "%h %t \"%r\" %>s" myrecfmt
CustomLog logs/access.log myrecfmt
```

Here the `access.log` will have lines in the `myrecfmt` format.

> **Note**   The `TransferLog` and `CustomLog` directives can be used multiple times in each
> server to cause each request to be logged to multiple files. For example:
>
> ```
> CustomLog logs/access1.log common
> CustomLog logs/access2.log common
> ```
>
> Here the server will create two log entries per request and store each entry in
> `access1.log` and `access2.log`. This is really not useful unless you use different
> format per log and need each format for a different reason.

Finally, if you use the `mod_setenvif` (installed by default) or the URL rewrite
module (`mod_rewrite`, which is not installed by default) to set environment variables based on a requesting URL, you can create conditional logging using the
`env=[!]environment_variable` option with the `CustomLog` directive. For example, say that you allow people to download a PDF white paper and want to log all
downloads in a log file called `whitepaper.log` in your usual log directory. Here is
the necessary configuration:

```
SetEnvIf Request_URI \.pdf$ whitepaper
CustomLog logs/whitepaper.log common env=whitepaper
CustomLog logs/access.log common env=!whitepaper
```

The first line sets the environment variable `whitepaper` whenever a requesting
URL ends in the `.pdf` extension. Then when the entry is to be logged, Apache uses
the `env=whitepaper` settings for the first `CommonLog` directive to determine
whether it is set. If it is set, a log entry using the common format is made to the
`logs/whitepaper.log` file. When the `whitepaper` environment variable is not
set, the log entry is made to the `logs/access.log` file as usual.

CookieLog directive

`CookieLog` enables you to log cookie information in a file relative to the path
pointed to by the `ServerRoot` directive. This directive is not recommended,
because it's not likely to be supported in Apache for long. To log cookie data, use
the user-tracking module (`mod_usertrack`) instead. The user-tracking module is
discussed later in this chapter.

> **Syntax:** `CookieLog` *filename*
>
> **Default setting:** None
>
> **Context:** Server config, virtual host

Customizing Your Log Files

Although the default CLF format meets most log requirements, sometimes it is useful
to be able to customize logging data. For example, you may want to log the type of

browsers that are accessing your site, so your Web design team can determine which type of browser-specific HTML to avoid or use. Or, perhaps you want to know which Web sites are sending (that is, referring) visitors to your sites. All this is accomplished quite easily in Apache. The default logging module, mod_log_config, supports custom logging.

Custom formats are set with the LogFormat and CustomLog directives of the module. A string is the format argument to LogFormat and CustomLog. This format string can have both literal characters and special % format specifiers. When literal values are used in this string, they are copied into the log file for each request. The % specifiers, however, are replaced with corresponding values. The special % specifiers are shown in Table 8-2.

Table 8-2
Special % Specifiers for Log Entries

% Specifier	Description
%a	Client IP address
%A	Server IP address
%B	Bytes sent, excluding HTTP headers; 0 for no byte sent
%b	Bytes sent, excluding HTTP headers; – for no byte sent
%c	Connection status when response is done. The "X" character is written if connection was aborted by the client before response could be completed. If client uses keep-alive protocol, a "+" is written to show that connection was kept alive after the response until timeout. A "–" is written to signify that connection was closed after the response
%{mycookie}C	The contents of a cookie called mycookie
%D	The amount of time (in microseconds) taken to complete the response
%{myenv}e	The contents of an environment variable called myenv
%f	The filename of the request
%h	The remote host that made the request
%H	The request protocol (for example, HTTP 1/1)
%{ IncomingHeader }i	The contents of IncomingHeader; that is, the header line(s) in the request sent to the server. The i character at the end denotes that this is a client (incoming) header
%l	If the IdentityCheck directive is enabled and the client machine runs identd, then this is the identity information reported by the client

Continued

Table 8-2 *(continued)*

% Specifier	Description
%m	The request method (GET, POST, PUT, and so on)
%{ ModuleNote }n	The contents of the note ModuleNote from another module
%{ OutgoingHeader }o	The contents of OutgoingHeader; that is, the header line(s) in the reply. The o character at the end denotes that this is a server (outgoing) header
%p	The port to which the request was served
%P	The process ID of the child that serviced the request
%q	The query string
%r	The first line of the request
%s	Status returned by the server in response to the request. Note that when the request gets redirected, the value of this format specifier is still the original request status. If you want to store the redirected request status, use %>s instead
%t	Time of the request. The format of time is the same as in CLF format
%{format}t	The time, in the form given by format. (You can also look at the man page of strftime on Unix systems.)
%T	The time taken to serve the request, in seconds
%u	If the requested URL required a successful Basic HTTP authentication, then the username is the value of this format specifier. The value may be bogus if the server returned a 401 status (Authentication Required) after the authentication attempt
%U	The URL path requested
%v	The name of the server or the virtual host to which the request came
%V	The server name per the UseCanonicalName directive

It is possible to include conditional information in each of the preceding specifiers. The conditions can be presence (or absence) of certain HTTP status code(s). For example, let's say you want to log all referring URLs that pointed a user to a nonexistent page. In such a case, the server produces a 404 status (Not Found) header. So, to log the referring URLs you can use the format specifier:

```
'%404{Referer}i'
```

Similarly, to log referring URLs that resulted in an unusual status, you can use:

```
'%!200,304,302{Referer}i'
```

Notice the use of the ! character to denote the absence of the server status list.

Similarly, to include additional information at the end of the CLF format specifier, you can extend the CLF format, which is defined by the format string:

```
"%h %l %u %t \"%r\" %s %b"
```

For example:

```
"%h %l %u %t \"%r\" %s %b \"%{Referer}i\" \"%{User-agent}i\"".
```

This format specification logs CLF format data and adds the Referer and User-agent information found in client-provided headers in each log entry.

You learned about adding custom fields to the log file, but what if you need to store this data in more than one log file? The next section discusses how to use multiple log files.

Creating Multiple Log Files

Sometimes, it is necessary to create multiple log files. For example, if you are using a log analysis program that cannot handle non-CLF data, you may want to write the non-CLF data to a different file. You can create multiple log files very easily using the TransferLog and/or the CustomLog directive of the mod_log_config module. Simply repeat these directives to create more than one log file.

If, for example, you want to create a standard CLF access log and a custom log of all referring URLs, then you can use something similar to this:

```
TransferLog logs/access_log
CustomLog   logs/referrer_log      "%{Referer}i"
```

When you have either TransferLog or CustomLog defined in the primary server configuration, and you have a virtual host defined, the virtual host-related logging is also performed in those logs. For example:

```
TransferLog logs/access_log
CustomLog   logs/agents_log        "%{User-agent}i"

<Virtual Host 206.171.50.51>
```

```
ServerName reboot.nitec.com
DocumentRoot  "/www/reboot/public/htdocs"
ScriptAlias /cgi-bin/ "/www/reboot/public/cgi-bin/"

</VirtualHost>
```

Here, the virtual host `reboot.nitec.com` does not have a `TransferLog` or `CustomLog` directive defined within the virtual host container tags. All logging information will be stored in the `logs/access_log` and the `logs/agents_log`. Now, if the following line is added inside the virtual host container:

```
TransferLog vhost_logs/reboot_access_log
```

then all logging for the virtual host `reboot.nitec.com` is done in the `vhost_logs/reboot_access_log` file. None of the `logs/access_log` and `logs/agents_log` files will be used for the virtual host called `reboot.nitec.com`.

Logging Cookies

So far, the discussed logging options do not enable you to uniquely identify visitors. Uniquely identifying visitors is important, because if you know which requests which visitor makes, you will have a better idea of how your content is being used. For example, say that you have a really cool page on your Web site somewhere, and you have a way to identify the visitors in your logs. If you look at your log and see that many visitors have to go from one page to another to find the cool page at the end, you might reconsider your site design and make that cool page available sooner in the click stream. Apache has a module called `mod_usertrack` that enables you to track your Web site visitor by logging HTTP cookies.

HTTP Cookies . . . minus chocolate chips

An HTTP cookie is not made with cookie dough. It is simply a piece of information that the server gives to the Web browser. This information is usually stored in a key=value pair and can be associated with an entire Web site or with a particular URL on a Web site. After a cookie is issued by the server and accepted by the Web browser, the cookie resides in the Web browser system. Each time the Web browser requests the same URL, or any URL that falls under the realm of the cookie URL, the cookie information is returned to the server. When setting the cookie, the server can tell the Web browser to expire the cookie after a certain time. The time can be specified so that the cookie is never used in a later session, or it can be used for a long period of time.

There has been much controversy over the use of cookies. Many consider cookies as an intrusion of privacy. Using cookies to track user behavior is very popular. In fact, several advertisement companies on the Internet make heavy use of cookies to track users. It should be stressed that cookies themselves cannot cause any harm.

Cookie data is usually written in a text file in a directory of your browser software. For example, using the `CustomLog` directive in the standard logging module, you can store the cookies in a separate file:

```
CustomLog logs/clickstream "%{cookie}C %r %t"
```

Now, let's take a look at the new `mod_usertrack` module.

Remember that `mod_usertrack` does not save a log of cookies; it just generates unique cookies for each visitor. You can use `CustomLog` (as discussed earlier) to store these cookies in a log file for analysis.

The `mod_usertrack` directive is not compiled into the standard distribution version of Apache, so you need to compile it using the `--enable-usertrack` option before you can use it. The module provides the directives discussed in the following sections.

CookieExpires directive

This directive is used to set the expiration period of the cookies that are generated by the module. The expiration period can be defined in terms of number of seconds, or in a format such as "1 month 2 days 3 hours."

> **Syntax:** `CookieExpires expiry-period`
>
> **Context:** Server config, virtual host

In the following example, the first directive defines the expiration period in seconds, and the second directive defines the expiration period using the special format. Note that when the expiration period is not defined in a numeric form, the special form is assumed. However, the special format requires that you put double quotes around the format string. If this directive is not used, cookies last only for the current browser session.

```
CookieExpires 3600
CookieExpires "2 days 3 hours"
```

CookieTracking directive

This directive enables or disables the generation of automatic cookies. When it is set to on, Apache starts sending a user-tracking cookie for all new requests. This directive can be used to turn this behavior on or off on a per-server or per-directory basis. By default, compiling `mod_usertrack` does not activate cookies.

> **Syntax:** `CookieTracking On | Off`
>
> **Context:** Server config, virtual host, directory, per-directory access control file (`.htaccess`)
>
> **Override:** `FileInfo`

Using Error Logs

This chapter has discussed several ways of logging various interesting data from the request and response phases of each Web transaction. The more data you collect about your visitors, the happier your marketing department will be. As a system administrator, however, you are happy if everything is going smooth. Apache lets you know what's broken by writing error logs. Without logging errors, you are unable to determine what's wrong and where the error occurs. It is no surprise that error logging is supported in the core Apache and not in a module such as mod_log_config.

The ErrorLog directive enables you to log all of the errors that Apache encounters. This section explores how you can incorporate your Apache error logs into the widely used syslog facility found on almost all Unix platforms.

Syslog is the traditional way of logging messages sent out by daemon (server) processes. You may ask, "Apache is a daemon, so why can't it write to syslog?" It can, actually. All you need to do is replace your existing ErrorLog directive in the configuration file with:

```
ErrorLog syslog
```

and then restart Apache. Using a Web browser, access a nonexistent page on your Web server and watch the syslog log file to see if it shows an httpd entry. You should take a look at your /etc/syslog.conf file for clues about where the httpd messages will appear.

For example, Listing 8-1 shows /etc/syslog.conf for a Linux system.

Listing 8-1: /etc/syslog.conf

```
# Log all kernel messages to the console.
# Logging much else clutters up the screen.
#kern.*                      /dev/console

# Log anything (except mail) of level info or higher.
# Don't log private authentication messages!
*.info;mail.none;authpriv.none     /var/log/messages

# The authpriv file has restricted access.
authpriv.*              /var/log/secure

# Log all the mail messages in one place.
mail.*                  /var/log/maillog

# Everybody gets emergency messages, plus log
# them on another machine.
*.emerg                     *
```

```
# Save mail and news errors of level err and higher in a
# special file.
uucp,news.crit          /var/log/spooler

# Save boot messages also to boot.log
local7.*                /var/log/boot.log
```

There are two important lines (as far as Apache is concerned) in this listing, which I've set off in bold above.

The first line (which starts with `*.info;mail.none;`) tells `syslog` to write all messages of the info type (except for mail and private authentication) to the `/var/log/messages` file, and the second line (which starts with `*.emerg`) states that all emergency messages should be written to all log files. Using the `LogLevel` directive, you can specify what type of messages Apache should send to `syslog`. For example:

```
ErrorLog syslog
LogLevel debug
```

Here, Apache is instructed to send debug messages to `syslog`. If you want to store debug messages in a different file via `syslog`, then you need to modify `/etc/syslog.conf`. For example:

```
*.debug             /var/log/debug
```

Adding this line in `/etc/syslog.conf` and restarting `syslogd (kill -HUP syslogd_PID)` and Apache will enable you to store all Apache debug messages to the `/var/log/debug` file. There are several log-level settings:

✦ **Alert:** Alert messages

✦ **Crit:** Critical messages

✦ **Debug:** Messages logged at debug level will also include the source file and line number where the message is generated, to help debugging and code development

✦ **Emerg:** Emergency messages

✦ **Error:** Error messages

✦ **Info:** Information messages

✦ **Notice:** Notification messages

✦ **Warn:** Warnings

Tip   If you want to see updates to your `syslog` or any other log files as they happen, you can use the `tail` utility found on most Unix systems. For example, if you want to see updates for a log called `/var/log/messages` as they occur, use:

```
tail -f /var/log/messages
```

Analyzing Your Log Files

So far, you have learned to create standard CLF-based logs and custom logs. Now, you need a way to analyze these logs to make use of the recorded data. Your log analysis needs may vary. Sometimes you may need to produce extensive reports, or maybe you just want to do a simple checking on the logs. For simple tasks, it is best to use whatever is available at hand. Most Unix systems have enough utilities and scripting tools available to do the job.

Using Unix utilities, you can quickly grab needed information; however, this method requires some Unix know-how, and is not always convenient because your boss may want a "pretty" report instead of some dry textual listing. In such a case, you can either develop your own analysis programs or use third-party analysis tools.

Let's use a Unix utility to get a list of all the hosts. If you use the default logging facility or a custom log with CLF support, you can find a list of all the hosts quite easily. For example:

```
cat /path/to/httpd/access_log | awk '{print $1}'
```

prints out all the host IP addresses (if you have DNS [domain name server] lookup enabled, then host aliases are shown). The `cat` utility lists the `access_log` file, and the resulting output is piped to the `awk` interpreter, which prints out only the first field in each line using the `print` statement. This prints all the hosts; but what if you wanted to exclude the hosts on your network? In that case, you would use:

```
cat /path/to/httpd/access_log | awk '{print $1}'   | egrep -v '(^206.171.50)'
```

where `206.171.50` should be replaced with your network address. Here I am assuming that you have a class C network. If you have a class B network, you only need to use the first two octets of your IP address. This version enables you to exclude your own hosts using the egrep utility, which is told to display (via `-v`) only the hosts that do not start with the `206.171.50` network address. This still may not be satisfactory, however, because there are likely to be repeats. Therefore, the final version is:

```
cat /path/to/httpd/access_log | awk '{print $1}'   | uniq | egrep -v
'(^206.171.50)'
```

Here, the `uniq` utility filters out repeats and shows you only one listing per host. Of course, if you want to see the total number of unique hosts that have accessed your Web site, you can pipe the final result to the `wc` utility with a `-l` option as follows:

```
cat /path/to/httpd/access_log | awk '{print $1}' | \
uniq | egrep -v '(^206.171.50)' | wc -l
```

This gives you the total line count (that is, the number of unique host accesses).

Many third-party Web server log-analysis tools are available. Most of these tools expect the log files to be in CLF format, so make sure you have CLF formatting in your logs. Table 8-3 lists some of these tools and where to find them.

Table 8-3 Third-Party Log Analysis Tools	
Product Name	**Product URL**
WebTrends	`www.webtrends.com/`
Wusage	`www.boutell.com/wusage/`
wwwstat	`www.ics.uci.edu/pub/websoft/wwwstat/`
Analog	`www.statslab.cam.ac.uk/~sret1/analog/`
http-analyze	`www.netstore.de/Supply/http-analyze/`
Pwebstats	`www.unimelb.edu.au/pwebstats.html`
WebStat Explorer	`www.webstat.com/`
AccessWatch	`http://netpressence.com/accesswatch/`

The best way to learn which tool will work for you is to try all the tools, or at least visit their Web sites so that you can compare their features. Two utilities that I find very useful are Wusage and wwwstat.

Wusage is my favorite commercial log-analysis application. It is highly configurable and produces great graphical reports using the company's well-known GD graphics library. Wusage is distributed in a binary format. Evaluation copies of wusage are provided free for many Unix and Windows platforms.

`wwwstat` is one of the freeware analysis programs that I prefer. It is written in Perl, so you need to have Perl installed on the system on which you want to run this application. `wwwstat` output summaries can be read by `gwstat` to produce fancy graphs of the summarized statistics.

Creating logs in Apache is easy and useful. Creating logs enables you to learn more about what's going on with your Apache server. Logs can help you detect and identify your site's problems, find out about your site's best features, and much more. Can something so beneficial come without a catch? If you said no, you guessed right. Log files take up a lot of valuable disk space, so they must be maintained regularly.

Log Maintenance

By enabling logging, you may be able to save a lot of work, but the logs themselves do add some extra work for you: they need to be maintained. On Apache sites with high hit rates or many virtual domains, the log files can become huge in a very short time, which could easily cause a disk crisis. When log files become very large, you should rotate them.

You have two options for rotating your logs: you can use a utility that comes with Apache called rotatelog, or you can use logrotate, a facility that is available on most Linux systems.

Using rotatelog

Apache comes with a support utility called rotatelog. You can use this program as follows:

```
TransferLog "| /path/to/rotatelogs logfile rotation_time_in_seconds>"
```

For example, if you want to rotate the access log every 86,400 seconds (that is, 24 hours), use the following line:

```
TransferLog "| /path/to/rotatelogs /var/logs/httpd 86400"
```

Each day's access log information will be stored in a file called /var/logs/httpd.nnnn, where nnnn represents a long number.

Using logrotate

The logrotate utility rotates, compresses, and mails log files. It is designed to ease the system administration of log files. It enables the automatic rotation, compression, removal, and mailing of log files on a daily, weekly, or monthly, or size basis. Normally, logrotate is run as a daily cron job. Read the man pages for logrotate to learn more about it.

If your system supports the logrotate facility, you should create a script called /etc/logrotate.d/apache as shown in Listing 8-2.

Listing 8-2: **/etc/logrotate.d/apache**

```
# Note that this script assumes the following:
#
# a. You have installed Apache in /usr/local/apache
# b. Your log path is /usr/local/apache/logs
# c. Your access log is called access_log (default in Apache)
# d. Your error log is called error_log (default in Apache)
# e. The PID file, httpd.pid, for Apache is stored in the log
#    directory (default in Apache)
#
# If any of the above assumptions are wrong, please change
# the path or filename accordingly.
#
/usr/local/apache/logs/access_log {
    missingok

    compress
    rotate 5
    mail webmaster@yourdomain.com
    errors webmaster@yourdomain.com
    size=10240K

    postrotate
        /bin/kill -HUP `cat /usr/local/apache/logs/httpd.pid 2>/dev/null` 2>
/dev/null || true
    endscript
}

/usr/local/apache/logs/error_log {
    missingok

    compress
    rotate 5
    mail webmaster@yourdomain.com
    errors webmaster@yourdomain.com
    size=10240K


    postrotate
        /bin/kill -HUP `cat /usr/local/apache/logs/httpd.pid 2>/dev/null` 2>
/dev/null || true
    endscript
}
```

This configuration specifies that the both Apache access and error log files be rotated whenever each grows over 10MB (10,240K) in size, and that the old log files

be compressed and mailed to webmaster@yourdomain.com after going through
five rotations, rather than being removed. Any errors that occur during processing
of the log file are mailed to root@yourdomain.com.

Using logresolve

For performance reasons you should have disabled hostname lookups using the
HostNameLookups directive set to off. This means that your log entries shows IP
addresses instead of hostnames for remote clients. When analyzing the logs, it
helps to have the hostnames so that you can determine who came where easily.
For example, here are a few sample log entries from my
/usr/local/apache/logs/access_log file.

```
207.183.233.19 - - [15/Mar/2001:13:05:01 -0800] "GET /book/images/back.gif
HTTP/1.1" 304 0
207.183.233.20 - - [15/Mar/2001:14:45:02 -0800] "GET /book/images/forward.gif
HTTP/1.1" 304 0
207.183.233.21 - - [15/Mar/2001:15:30:03 -0800] "GET /book/images/top.gif
HTTP/1.1" 304 0
```

If you had HostNameLookups turned on, Apache will resolve the client IP addresses
207.183.233.19, 207.183.233.20, and 207.183.233.21 into appropriate hostnames; and if you left the default LogFormat as shown below:

```
LogFormat "%h %l %u %t \"%r\" %>s %b" common
```

and used the common format in logging using CustomLog logs/access_log
common, these the sample log entries will look as follows:

```
nano.nitec.com - - [15/Mar/2001:13:05:01 -0800] "GET /book/images/back.gif
HTTP/1.1" 304 0
rhat.nitec.com - - [15/Mar/2001:14:45:02 -0800] "GET /book/images/forward.gif
HTTP/1.1" 304 0
r2d2.nitec.com - - [15/Mar/2001:15:30:03 -0800] "GET /book/images/top.gif
HTTP/1.1" 304 0
```

Because turning on DNS lookups causes Apache server to take more time to complete
a response, it is widely recommended that hostname lookups be done separately by
using the logresolve utility, which can be found in your Apache bin directory
(/usr/local/apache/bin). The log_resolver.sh script shown in Listing 8-3
can run this utility.

Listing 8-3: log_resolver.sh

```
#!/bin/sh

#
# Make sure you change the pathnames according to
```

```
# your Apache installation
#

# Fully qualified path name (FQPN) of the
# log-resolver utility
LOGRESOLVER=/usr/local/apache/bin/logresolve

# Statistic file generated by the utility
STATFILE=/tmp/log_stats.txt

# Your Apache Log file
LOGFILE=/usr/local/apache/logs/access_log

# New log file that has IP addressed resolved
OUTFILE=/usr/local/apache/logs/access_log.resolved

# Run the command
$LOGRESOLVER -s $STATFILE < $LOGFILE > $OUTFILE

exit 0;
```

When this script is run from the command line or as a `cron` job, it creates a file called `/usr/local/apache/logs/access_log.resolved`, which has all the IP addresses resolved to their respective hostnames. Also, the script generates a statistics file called `/tmp/log_stats.txt` that shows your cache usage information, total resolved IP addresses, and other information that resolver utility reports. An example of such a statistics file is shown here:

```
logresolve Statistics:
Entries: 3
    With name   : 0
    Resolves    : 3
Cache hits      : 0
Cache size      : 3
Cache buckets   :       IP number * hostname
   130    207.183.233.19 - nano.nitec.com
   131    207.183.233.20 - rhat.nitec.com
   132    207.183.233.21 - r2d2.nitec.com
```

Notice that the utility could not utilize the cache because all three IP addresses that it resolved (for the sample log entries shown above) are unique. However, if your log file has IP addresses from the same host, the cache will be used to resolve them instead of blindly making DNS requests.

If you think you can use this script, I recommend that you run it as a `cron` job. For example, on my Apache Web server running on Linux, I simply add the script to `/etc/cron.daily` to create a resolved version of the log every day.

✦   ✦   ✦

Rewriting Your URLs

URLs bring visitors to your Web site. As an Apache administrator, you need to ensure that all possible URLs to your Web site are functional. How do you do that? You keep monitoring the server error logs for broken URL requests. If you see requests that are being returned with a 404 Not Found status code, it is time to investigate these URLs. Often, when HTML document authors upgrade a Web site, they forget that renaming an existing directory could cause a lot of visitors' bookmarked URLs to break.

As an administrator, how do you solve such a problem? The good news is that there is a module called mod_rewrite that enables you to solve these problems and also lets you create very interesting solutions using URL rewrite rules. This chapter discusses this module and provides practical examples of URL rewriting.

The URL-Rewriting Engine for Apache

When Apache receives a URL request, it processes the request by serving the file to the client (the Web browser). What if you wanted to intervene in this process to map the URL to a different file or even to a different URL? That's where mod_rewrite shows its value. It provides you with a flexible mechanism for rewriting the requested URL to a new one using custom URL rewrite rules. A URL rewrite rule has the form:

```
regex_pattern_to_be_matched
regex_substitution_pattern
```

However, it is also possible to add conditions (such as more *regex_patterns_to_be_matched*) to a rule such that the substitution is only applied if the conditions are met. Apache can handle the substituted URL as an internal subrequest, or it can be sent back to the Web browser as an external redirect. Figure 9-1 shows an example request and the result of a mod_rewrite rule.

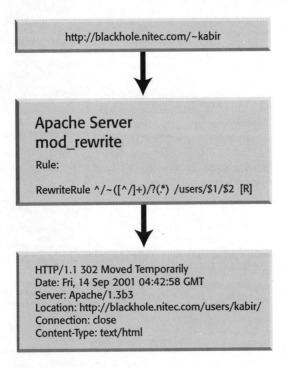

Figure 9-1: Example of a rule-based rewrite URL operation

The figure shows a request for http://blackhole.nitec.com/~kabir being made to the Apache server. The server receives the request and passes it to the mod_rewrite module at the URL translation stage of the processing of the request. The mod_rewrite module applies the rewrite rule defined by a directive called RewriteRule. In this particular example, the rule states that if a pattern such as /~([^/]+)/?(.*) is found, it should be replaced with /users/$1/$2. Because there is a redirect [R] flag in the rule, an external URL redirect response should also be sent back to the Web browser. The output shows the redirect location to be http://blackhole.nitec.com/users/kabir/.

As you can see, this sort of redirect can come in handy in many situations. Let's take a look at the directives that give you the power to rewrite URLs. You should also familiarize yourself with the server variables shown in Table 9-1, which can be used in many rewrite rules and conditions.

Table 9-1
Server Variables Available for URL Rewrite Rules

Server Variable	Explanation
SERVER_NAME	Host name of the Web server
SERVER_ADMIN	Web server administrator's e-mail address
SERVER_PORT	Port address of the Web server
SERVER_PROTOCOL	Version of HTTP protocol being used by the Web server
SERVER_SOFTWARE	Name of the Web server vendor
SERVER_VERSION	Version of the Web server software
DOCUMENT_ROOT	Top-level document directory of the Web site
HTTP_ACCEPT	MIME types that are acceptable by the Web client
HTTP_COOKIE	Cookie received from the Web client
HTTP_FORWARDED	Forwarding URL
HTTP_HOST	Web server's host name
HTTP_PROXY_CONNECTION	The HTTP proxy connection information
HTTP_REFERER	The URL that referred to the current URL
HTTP_USER_AGENT	Information about the Web client
REMOTE_ADDR	IP address of the Web client
REMOTE_HOST	Host name of the Web client
REMOTE_USER	Username of the authenticated user
REMOTE_IDENT	Information about remote user's identification
REQUEST_METHOD	HTTP request method used to request the current URL
SCRIPT_FILENAME	Physical path of the requested script file
PATH_INFO	Path of the requested URL
QUERY_STRING	Query data sent along with the requested URL
AUTH_TYPE	Type of authentication used
REQUEST_URI	Requested URI
REQUEST_FILENAME	Same as `SCRIPT_FILENAME`
THE_REQUEST	Requested URL
TIME_YEAR	Current year
TIME_MON	Current month
TIME_DAY	Current day

Continued

Table 9-1: *(continued)*	
Server Variable	**Explanation**
TIME_HOUR	Current hour
TIME_MIN	Current minute
TIME_SEC	Current second
TIME_WDAY	Current weekday
TIME	Current time
API_VERSION	Version of API used
IS_SUBREQ	Set if request is a subrequest

RewriteEngine

This directive provides you with the on/off switch for the URL rewrite engine in the mod_rewrite module. By default, all rewriting is turned off. To use the rewrite engine, you must turn the engine on by setting this directive to on.

Syntax: RewriteEngine On | Off

Default: RewriteEngine Off

Context: Server config, virtual host, per-directory access control file (.htaccess)

When enabling URL rewriting per-directory configuration (.htaccess) files, you must enable (that is, set to On) this directive inside the per-directory configuration file and make sure that you have enabled the following directive in the appropriate context for the directory:

```
Options FollowSymLinks
```

In other words, if the directory belongs to a virtual host site, make sure that this option is enabled inside the appropriate virtual host container. Similarly, if the directory in question is part of the main server's Web document space, make sure that this option is enabled in the main server configuration.

Note   Enabling rewrite rules in per-directory configurations could degrade the performance of your Apache server. This is because mod_rewrite employs a trick to support per-directory rewrite rules, and this trick involves increasing the server's processing load. Therefore, you should avoid using rewrite rules in per-directory configuration files whenever possible.

RewriteOptions

This directive enables you to specify options to change the rewrite engine's behavior. Currently, the only available option is `inherit`. By setting this directive to the `inherit` option, you can force a higher-level configuration to be inherited by a lower-level configuration.

> **Syntax:** RewriteOptions *option1 option2* [...]
>
> **Default:** None
>
> **Context:** Server config, virtual host, per-directory access control file (.htaccess)

For example, if you set this directive in your main server configuration area, a virtual host defined in the configuration file will inherit all the rewrite configurations, such as the rewrite rules, conditions, maps, and so on.

Similarly, when this directive is set in a per-directory configuration file (.htaccess), it will inherit the parent directory's rewrite rules, conditions, and maps. By default, the rewrite engine does not permit inheritance of rewrite configuration, but this directive permits you to alter the default.

RewriteRule

This directive enables you to define a rewrite rule. The rule must have two arguments. The first argument is the search pattern that must be met to apply the substitution string. The search pattern is written using regular expression (see Appendix B for basics of regular expression). The substitution string can be constructed with plain text, back-references to substrings in the search pattern, values from server variables, or even map functions. The flag list can contain one or more flag strings, separated by commas, to inform the rewrite engine about what to do next with the substitution.

> **Syntax:** RewriteRule *search_pattern substitution_string* [*flag_list*]
>
> **Default:** None
>
> **Context:** Server config, virtual host, per-directory access control file (.htaccess)

Let's take a look at an example:

```
RewriteRule /~([^/]+)/?(.*)  /users/$1/$2 [R]
```

Here, the search pattern is /~([^/]+)/?(.*) and the substitution string is /users/$1/$2. Notice the use of back-references in the substitution string. The first back-reference string $1 corresponds to the string found in the first set of parentheses (from the left). So $1 is set to whatever is matched in ([^/]+) and $2 is set to the next string found in (.*). When a URL request is as follows:

```
http://blackhole.evoknow.com/~kabir/welcome.html
```

The value of $1 is `kabir`, and $2 is `welcome.html`; so the substitution string looks like:

```
/users/kabir/welcome.html
```

When you have more than one `RewriteRule` specified, the first `RewriteRule` operates on the original URL and if a match occurs, the second rule no longer operates on the original URL. Instead, it gets the URL substituted by first rule as the URL on which to apply rules. In a scenario in which a match occurs at every step, a set of three rewrite rules will function as follows:

```
RewriteRule   search-pattern-for-original-URL      substitution1
[flags]
RewriteRule   search-pattern-for-substitution1     substitution2
[flags]
RewriteRule   search-pattern-for-substitution2     substitution3
[flags]
```

It is possible to apply more than one rule to the original URL by using the `C` flag to instruct the rewrite engine to chain multiple rules. In such a case, you may not want to substitute until all rules are matched so that you can use a special substitution string to disable a substitution in a rule.

Table 9-2 lists the details of the possible flags.

Table 9-2 RewriteRule Flags	
Flag	**Meaning**
C	chain	This flag specifies that the current rule be chained with the next rule. When chained by a `C` flag, a rule is looked at if and only if the previous rule in the chain results in a match. Each rule in the chain must contain the flag, and if the first rule does not match, the entire chain of rules is ignored.
E=var:value | env=var:value	You can set an environment variable using this directive. The variable is accessible from rewrite conditions, Server Side Includes, CGI scripts, and so on.
F | forbidden	When a rule using this flag is matched, an HTTP response header called FORBIDDEN (status code 403) is sent back to the browser. This effectively disallows the requested URL.

Flag	Meaning
G | gone	When a rule using this flag is matched, an HTTP response header called GONE (status code 410) is sent back to the browser. This informs the browser that the requested URL is no longer available on this server.
L | last	This tells the rewrite engine to end rule processing immediately so that no other rules are applied to the last substituted URL.
N | next	This tells the rewrite engine to restart from the first rule. However, the first rule no longer tries to match the original URL, because it now operates on the last substituted URL. This effectively creates a loop. You must have terminating conditions in the loop to avoid an infinite loop.
NC | nocase	This tells the rewrite engine to become case insensitive for the pattern match
NS | nosubreq	Use this flag to avoid applying a rule on an internally generated URL request.
P | proxy	Using this flag will convert a URL request to a proxy request internally. This will only work if you have compiled Apache with the mod_proxy module and configured it to use the proxy module.
QSA | qsappend	This flag allows you to append data (such as key=value pairs) to the query string part of the substituted URL.
R [= HTTP code] | redirect	Forces external redirects to client while prefixing the substitution with http://server[:port]/. If no HTTP response code is given, the default redirect response code 302 (MOVED TEMPORARILY) is used. This rule should be used with the L or last flag.
S=n | skip=n	Skips next n rules.
T=MIME-type | file type=MIME-type	Forces the specified MIME-type to be the MIME-type of the target of the request.

Note You can add conditions to your rules by preceding them with one or more RewriteCond directives, which are discussed in the following section.

RewriteCond

The RewriteCond directive is useful when you want to add an extra condition for a rewrite rule specified by the RewriteRule directive. You can have several RewriteCond directives per RewriteRule. All rewrite conditions must be defined before the rule itself.

Syntax: RewriteCond *test_string condition_pattern [flag_list]*

Default: None

Context: Server config, virtual host, perl-directory config (.htaccess)

The test string may be constructed with plain text, server variables, or back-references from both the current rewrite rule and the last rewrite condition. To access the *n*th back-reference from the last RewriteRule directive, use $*n*; to access the *n*th back-reference from the last RewriteCond directive, use %*n*.

To access a server variable, use the %{variable name} format. For example, to access the REMOTE_USER variable, specify %{REMOTE_USER} in the test string.

Table 9-3 lists several special data access formats.

Table 9-3
Data Access Formats for RewriteCond Directive

Format Specifier	Meaning
%{ENV:*variable*}	Use this to access any environment variable that is available to the Apache process.
%{HTTP:*header*}	Use this to access the HTTP header used in the request.
%{LA-U:*variable*}	Use this to access the value of a variable that is not available in the current stage of processing. For example, if you need to make use of the REMOTE_USER server variable in a rewrite condition stored in the server's configuration file (httpd.conf), you cannot use %{REMOTE_USER} because this variable is only defined after the server has performed the authentication phase, which comes after mod_rewrite's URL processing phase. To look ahead at what the username of the successfully authenticated user is, you can use %{LA-U:REMOTE_USER} instead. However, if you are accessing the REMOTE_USER data from a RewriteCond in a per-directory configuration file, you can use %{REMOTE_USER} because the authorization phase has already finished and the server variable has become available as usual. The lookup is performed by generating a URL-based internal subrequest.
%{LA-F:*variable*}	Same as the %{LA-U:*variable*} in most cases, but lookup is performed using a filename-based internal subrequest.

The condition pattern can also use some special notations in addition to being a regular expression. For example, you can perform lexical comparisons between the test string and the condition pattern by prefixing the condition pattern with a <, >, or = character. In such a case, the condition pattern is compared with the test string as a plain-text string.

There may be times when you want to check whether the test-string is a file, directory, or symbolic link. In such a case, you can replace the condition pattern with the special strings shown in Table 9-4.

Table 9-4
Conditional Options for Test-String in RewriteCond Directive

Conditional Options	Meaning
-d	Tests whether the test-string specified directory exists
-f	Tests whether the test-string specified file exists
-s	Tests whether the test-string–specified nonzero-size file exists
-l	Tests whether the test-string–specified symbolic link exists
-F	Tests the existence and accessibility of the test-string–specified file
-U	Tests the validity and accessibility of the test-string–specified URL

You can use ! in front of the above conditions to negate their meanings. The optional flag list can consist of one or more comma-separated strings as shown in Table 9-5.

Table 9-5
Flag Options for RewriteCond Directive

Flag	Meaning
NC | nocase	Performs a case-insensitive condition test.
OR | ornext	Normally, when you have more than one RewriteCond for a RewriteRule directive, these conditions are ANDed together for the final substitution to occur. However, if you need to create an OR relationship between two conditions, use this flag.

RewriteMap

The RewriteMap directive facilitates a key-to-value lookup through the use of a map. Think of a map as a table of data in which each row has a key and a value. Typically, a map is stored in a file. However, the map can be a text file, a DBM file, an internal Apache function, or an external program. The type of the map corresponds to the source of the map. Table 9-6 lists the applicable map types.

Syntax: RewriteMap *name_of_map type_of_map:source_of_map*

Default: None

Context: Server config, virtual host

Table 9-6
Flag Options for RewriteMap Directive

Map Type	Description
txt	Plain text file that has key value lines such that each key and value pair are on a single line and are separated by at least one whitespace character. The file can contain comment lines starting with # characters or can have blank lines. Both comments and blank lines are ignored. For example: Key1 value1 Key2 value2 defines two key value pairs. Note that text file-based maps are read during Apache startup and only reread if the file has been updated after the server is already up and running. The files are also reread during server restarts.
rnd	A special plain-text file, which has all the restrictions of txt type but allows flexibility in defining the value. The value for each key can be defined as a set of ORed values using the | (vertical bar) character. For example: Key1 first_value_for_key1 | second_value_for_key1 Key2 first_value_for_key2 | second_value_for_key2 this defines two key value pairs where each key has multiple values. The value selected is decided randomly.
Int	The internal Apache functions toupper(key) or tolower(key) can be used as a map source. The first function converts the key into all uppercase characters, and the second function converts the key to all lowercase characters.

Map Type	Description
dbm	A DBM file can be used as a map source. This can be very useful and fast (compared to text files) when you have a large number of key-value pairs. Note that DBM-file–based maps are read during Apache startup and only reread if the file has been updated after the server is already up and running. The files are also reread during server restarts.
prg	An external program can generate the value. When a program is used, it is started at the Apache startup and data (key, value) is transferred between Apache and the program via standard input (stdin) and standard output (stdout). Make sure you use the RewriteLock directive to define a lock file when using an external program. When constructing such a program, also make sure that you read the input from the stdin and write it on stdout in a nonbuffered I/O mode.

RewriteBase

This directive is only useful if you are using rewrite rules in per-directory configuration files. It is also only required for URL paths that do not map to the physical directory of the target file. Set this directive to whatever alias you used for the directory. This will ensure that mod_rewrite will use the alias instead of the physical path in the final (substituted) URL.

>**Syntax:** RewriteBase *base_URL*
>
>**Default:** Current directory path of per-directory config (.htaccess)
>
>**Context:** Per-directory access control file (.htaccess)

For example, when an alias is set as follows:

```
Alias /icons/   "/www/nitec/htdocs/icons/"
```

and rewrite rules are enabled in the /www/nitec/htdocs/icons/.htaccess file, the RewriteBase directive should be set as follows:

```
RewriteBase /icons/
```

RewriteLog

If you want to log the applications of your rewrite rules, use this directive to set a log filename. Like all other log directives, it assumes that a path without a leading slash (/) means that you want to write the log file in the server's root directory.

Syntax: RewriteLog *path_to_logfile*

Default: None

Context: Server config, virtual host

For example, the following directive writes a log file in the logs subdirectory under your server's root directory:

```
RewriteLog logs/rewrite.log
```

As mentioned earlier, a log written by server should be only writable by the server user.

RewriteLogLevel

This directive enables you to specify what gets logged in the log file. A default value of 0 means that nothing will be logged. In fact, a log level of 0 means no log-related processing is done inside the module. Therefore, if you wanted to disable logging, keep it set to 0.

Syntax: RewriteLogLevel *level*

Default setting: RewriteLogLevel 0

Context: Server config, virtual host

Note If you set the RewriteLog directive to /dev/null and the RewriteLogLevel to a nonzero value, the internal log-related processing will still be done, but no log will be produced. This is a waste of your system's computing resources, so if you don't want logging, keep this directive set to its default value. You have a choice of 10 log levels, ranging from 0 to 9. The higher the level, the more logging data is written.

RewriteLock

RewriteLock directive allows you to specify an external mapping program for creating rewrite maps. You need to specify a filename when using the RewriteLock directive. This file is used as a lock file for synchronizing communication with external mapping programs.

Syntax: RewriteLock *filename*

Default: None

Context: Server config, virtual host

URL Layout

This section provides examples of URL rewrites that deal with the layout of URLs. Often, you will need to redirect or expand a URL request to another URL. The following examples show you how `mod_rewrite` can help in such cases.

Expanding a requested URL to a canonical URL

Web sites that offer user home pages usually support a URL scheme such as:

```
http://hostname/~username
```

This is a shortcut URL and needs to be mapped to a canonical URL. You may also have other shortcuts or internal URLs that need to be expended to their canonical URLs. This example shows you how `~username` is translated to `/u/username`. Figure 9-2 illustrates what needs to happen.

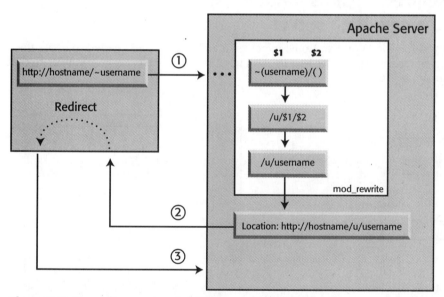

Figure 9-2: Expanding a requested URL to a canonical URL

When a request for `http://hostname/~username` is received in (1), the rewrite rule will translate that into `/u/username` and redirect the new URL to the browser (2). The browser then rerequests the `http://hostname/u/username` URL in (3) and the usual Apache request processing completes the request.

The external HTTP redirect is necessary because any subsequent requests must also use the translated canonical URL instead of ~*username*. The rule needed to do this is:

```
RewriteRule    ^/~([^/]+)/?(.*) /u/$1/$2   [R,L]
```

Note   Note that the R flag is used to redirect and the L flag is used to indicate that no other rewrite rule can be applied to the substituted URL.

Many ISP sites with thousands of users use a structured home directory layout; that is, each home directory is in a subdirectory that begins, for instance, with the first character of the username. So, /~foo/*anypath* is /home/f/foo/www/*anypath*, while /~bar/*anypath* is /home/b/bar/www/*anypath*. To implement a translation scheme from shortcut URLs to canonical URLs in this case, the following rule can be used:

```
RewriteRule    ^/~(([a-z])[a-z0?9]+)(.*) /home/$2/$1/www$3 [R,L]
```

Redirecting a user home directory to a new Web server

If you have a lot of user home pages on a Web server and needed to move them to a new machine for some reason, you need to have a redirect rule similar to that shown in Figure 9-3.

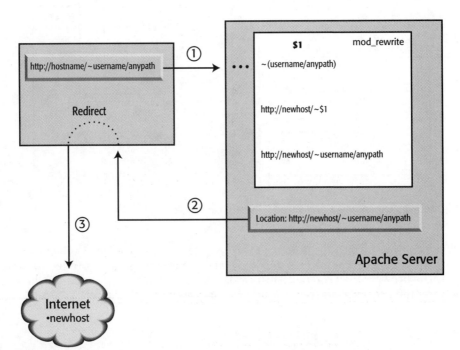

Figure 9-3: Redirecting user home directories to a new Web server

The solution is simple with `mod_rewrite`. When the browser requests `http://hostname/~username/anypath` as shown in (1) in the figure, the Web server translates it to `http://newhost/~username/anypath` as shown in (2) and redirects the browser to this new location. On the old Web server (i.e. the one redirected the URL) just redirect all `/~user/anypath` URLs to `http://new~host/~user/anypath` as follows:

```
RewriteRule   ^/~(.+)  http://newhost/~$1   [R,L]
```

Searching for a page in multiple directories

Sometimes it is necessary to let the Web server search for pages in more than one directory. Here, `MultiViews` or other techniques cannot help. For example, say that you want to handle a request for `http://hostname/filename.html` so that if `filename.html` is not present in the `dir1` directory of your Web server, the server tries a subdirectory called `dir2`. Figure 9-4 illustrates what needs to happen.

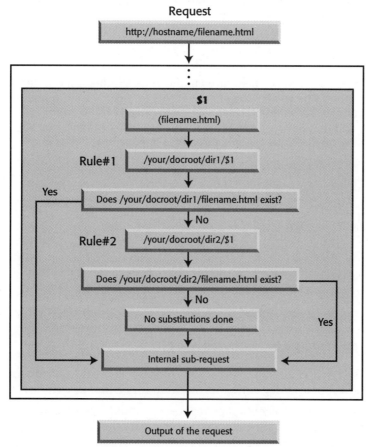

Figure 9-4: Searching for a page in multiple directories

The rules needed to implement this are:

```
RewriteCond       /your/docroot/dir1%{REQUEST_FILENAME}  -f
RewriteRule  ^(.+)  /your/docroot/dir1$1  [L]

RewriteCond       /your/docroot/dir2%{REQUEST_FILENAME}  -f
RewriteRule  ^(.+)  /your/docroot/dir2$1  [L]

RewriteRule   ^(.+)  -  [PT]
```

The first rule substitutes the requested URL with /your/docroot/dir1/$1
(where $1 is the target file in the request) only if the requested file exists in
your/docroot/dir1/ subdirectory. If the condition is met, this is the last rule
applied to this URL. However, if no match is found, then the next rule applies. This
rule does the same thing as the first one but this time subdirectory dir2 is used
for the path. This rule is also final if a match is found. In the event that none of the
rules match, the request is not substituted and is passed on for regular processing.

To verify the rule using the log, first, turn on rewrite logging by adding the following
directives before the above rules.

```
RewriteLog logs/rewrite.log
RewriteLogLevel 5
```

The rewrite log rewrite.log will be written in the logs subdirectory under the
ServerRoot directory. The level of logging is set to 5 to include a fair amount of
information. Assuming that your DocumentRoot directive is set to /usr/local/
apache/htdocs and that ServerRoot is set to /usr/local/apache, you will need
to use the following rewrite-rule–specific directives in your httpd.conf.

```
RewriteLog logs/rewrite.log
RewriteLogLevel 5

RewriteCond
/usr/local/apache/htdocs/dir1%{REQUEST_FILENAME}  -f
RewriteRule  ^(.+)  /usr/local/apache/htdocs/dir1$1  [L]

RewriteCond
/usr/local/apache/htdocs/dir2%{REQUEST_FILENAME}  -f
RewriteRule  ^(.+)  /usr/local/apache/htdocs/dir2$1  [L]

RewriteRule    ^(.+)  -  [PT]
```

After you have restarted Apache, do the following:

1. As root, run tail -f /usr/local/apache/logs/rewrite.log. This command enables you to see log entries as there are added to the rewrite.log file.

2. Run mkdir -p /usr/local/apache/htdocs/dir1 and chmod -R httpd:
   httpd /usr/local/apache/htdocs/dir1 to create the dir1 directory under

your document and to change its ownership to httpd user and group. Here I also assume that you are running Apache as the httpd user. Do the same for `dir2`.

3. Run the `lynx -dump -head http://localhost/kabir.html` command. This launches the Lynx Web browser and tells it to show only the response headers returned by the Web server. Now, assuming that you do not have a file named `Kabir.html` in the `/usr/local/apache/dir1`, or the `/usr/local/apache/dir2`, or the `/usr/local/apache` directory, you should see a response similar to the following:

```
HTTP/1.1 404 Not Found
Date: Fri, 16 Mar 2001 06:06:51 GMT
Server: Apache/2.0.14 (Unix)
Connection: close
Content-Type: text/html; charset=iso-8859-1
```

4. Now look at the `rewrite.log` entries as shown below. I have removed the IP address, timestamp, and a few other fields for brevity.

```
(2) init rewrite engine with requested uri /kabir.html
(3) applying pattern '^(.+)' to uri '/kabir.html'
(4) RewriteCond:
input='/usr/local/apache/htdocs/dir1/kabir.html' pattern='-f'
=> not-matched
(3) applying pattern '^(.+)' to uri '/kabir.html'
(4) RewriteCond:
input='/usr/local/apache/htdocs/dir2/kabir.html' pattern='-f'
=> not-matched
(3) applying pattern '^(.+)' to uri '/kabir.html'
(2) forcing '/kabir.html' to get passed through to next API
URI-to-filename handler
```

Note   Notice how mod_rewrite attempted to locate the `kabir.html` file in `dir1` and `dir2` and then gave up, which resulted in Apache lookup for the same file in the document root because the request was `http://localhost/kabir.html`.

5. Now create this test file, `kabir.html`, in either the `dir1` or the `dir2` subdirectory, and change the ownership of the file so that Apache (httpd user) can read it. Then run the same `lynx -dump -head http://localhost/kabir.html` command again and look at the contents of the `rewrite.log`. You will see that one of the rules has succeeded based on where (`dir1` or `dir2`) you place the file.

6. If you have the test file in all three directories — `/usr/local/apache/htdocs/dir1`, `/usr/local/apache/htdocs/dir2`, and `/usr/local/apache/htdocs` — the rewrite rule chooses the file in the `dir1` subdirectory because the first matching condition wins as a consequence of the `[L]` (last) flag.

Setting an environment variable based on a URL

You may want to keep status information between requests and use the URL to encode it. But you may not want to use a CGI wrapper script for all pages just to strip out this information. You can use a rewrite rule to strip out the status information and store it via an environment variable that can be later dereferenced from within XSSI or CGI. This way a URL /foo/S=java/bar/ is translated to /foo/bar/ and the environment variable named STATUS is set to the value java. Figure 9-5 illustrates what happens.

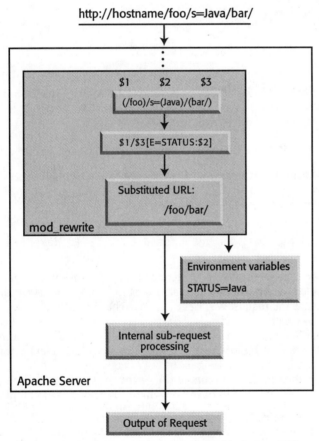

Figure 9-5: Setting an environment variable from a URL.

When request for http://hostname/foo/s=java/bar/ is detected the Apache server assigns $1 to foo, $2 to java, and $3 to bar as shown in the Figure 9-5. The value for $2 is used to set environment variable STATUS and the Web server performs an internal redirect to the /foo/bar location. The URL rewriting steps shown in Figure 9-5 can be implemented using this rewrite rule:

```
RewriteRule   ^(.*)/S=([^/]+)/(.*) $1/$3 [E=STATUS:$2]
```

Here the value of $2 is stored in the environment variable called STATUS using the E
flag. When this rule is in place and a request such as `lynx -dump -head http://
localhost/dir1/S=value/kabir.html` is made, the rewrite log (if enabled)
will show:

```
(2) init rewrite engine with requested uri /dir1/S=value/kabir.html
(3) applying pattern '^(.*)/S=([^/]+)/(.*)' to uri '/dir1/S=value/kabir.html'
(2) rewrite /dir1/S=value/kabir.html -> /dir1/kabir.html
(5) setting env variable 'STATUS' to 'value'
(2) local path result: /dir1/kabir.html
(2) prefixed with document_root to /usr/local/apache/htdocs/dir1/kabir.html
(1) go-ahead with /usr/local/apache/htdocs/dir1/kabir.html [OK]
```

I have shortened the rewrite log output for brevity. Notice that mod_rewrite has set
the STATUS variable to 'value', so now if a Perl-based CGI script wanted to access
the value of the STATUS environment variable, it can use $ENV{STATUS}. Similarly, a
Server-Side Include (SSI) directive can also access this environment variable.

Creating www.username.domain.com sites

Let's say that you have a few friends who want Web sites on your server. Instead of
giving them the `http://www.domain.com/~username`-type site, you decide to create
`http://www.username.domain.com`-type sites for each of them. Naturally, you add
each username-based host name (for example, `www.kabir.domain.com`) in your DNS
using a simple CNAME record that points to your Web server. For example, in your
DNS you might have:

```
www.domain.com.              IN      A      192.168.1.100.
```

To create Web site for two friends named Joe and Jennifer you need the following
DNS records for `domain.com`:

```
www.domain.com.              IN      A      192.168.1.100.
www.joe.domain.com.          IN      CNAME  www.domain.com.
www.jennifer.domain.com.     IN      CNAME  www.domain.com.
```

After the DNS is ready and tested, you want to configure Apache to service these
sites using /home/*username*/www directories, where each username is the user
account name of your friend.

The following rewrite rule set can be used to rewrite
`http://www.username.domain.com/anypath` internally to /home/
username/www/anypath:

```
RewriteCond   %{HTTP_HOST}   ^www\.[^.]+\.domain\.com$
RewriteRule   ^(.+)          %{HTTP_HOST}$1            [C]
RewriteRule   ^www\.([^.]+)\.domain\.com(.*) /home/$1/www/$2
```

Figure 9-6 illustrates how this works.

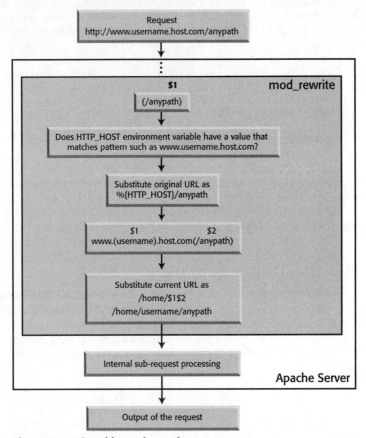

Figure 9-6: Virtual hosts for each username

This is an example of a chained-rule set. The first rule has a condition that checks whether the environment variable HTTP_HOST matches a pattern such as www.*username*.domain.com. If it does, the rule is applied. In other words, www.*username*.*domain*.com/*anypath* is substituted for a request such as http://www.username.domain.com/anypath. This could be a bit confusing because the substitution is not quite obvious. This substitution is needed so that the username can be extracted using the second rule. The second rule extracts the username part from the substituted request and creates a new URL /home/ *username*/www/*anypath* for an internal subrequest.

Redirecting a failing URL to another Web server

If you have a multiserver Web network and often move contents from one server to another, you may face the problem of needing to redirect failing URL requests from Web server A to Web server B. There are many ways to do this: you can use the ErrorDocument directive, write a CGI script, or use mod_rewrite to rewrite the failing URLs to the other server. Using the mod_rewrite-based solution is less preferable than using an ErrorDocument directive or a CGI script. The mod_rewrite solution has the best performance, but is less flexible and less error-safe:

```
RewriteCond /your/docroot/%{REQUEST_FILENAME} !-f
RewriteRule ^(.+) http://Web serverB.dom/$1
```

The problem is that this solution will only work for pages inside the DocumentRoot directive. Although you can add more conditions (to handle home directories, for example), there is a better variant:

```
RewriteCond    %{REQUEST_URI} !-U
RewriteRule    ^(.+)              http://Web serverB.dom/$1
```

This variant uses the URL look-ahead feature of mod_rewrite, and will work for all types of URLs. This does have a performance impact on the Web server, however, because for every request made there is an additional internal subrequest. If your Web server runs on a powerful CPU, use this solution; if it is a slow machine, use the first approach, or, better yet, an ErrorDocument directive or a CGI script.

Creating an access multiplexer

This example shows you how to create a rule set to redirect requests based on a domain type, such as .com, .net, .edu, .org, .uk, .de, and so on. The idea is to redirect the visitor to the geographically nearest Web site. This technique is employed by many large corporations to redirect international customers to an appropriate Web site or FTP server.

The first step in creating such a solution is to create a map file. For example, the following shows a text-based map file called site-redirect.map:

```
com        http://www.mydomain.com/download/
net        http://www.mydomain.com/download/
edu        http://www.mydomain.com/download/
org        http://www.mydomain.com/download/
uk         http://www.mydomain.uk/download/
de         http://www.mydomain.de/download/
ch         http://www.mydomain.ch/download/
```

When a request is received for `http://www.mydomain.com/downlod/anypath` from a host called `dialup001.demon.uk`, the request needs to be redirected to the Web site `www.mydomain.uk/download/`; similarly, any requests from hosts that belong to the top-level domains `.com`, `.net`, `.edu`, and `.org` are routed to the `www.mycompany.com/download/` site.

Here are the rules that are needed for the above setup:

```
RewriteMap   sitemap          txt:/path/to/site-redirect.map
RewriteRule  ^/download/(.*)  %{REMOTE_HOST}::$1  [C]
RewriteRule  ^.+\.([a-zA-Z]+)::(.*)$ %{sitemap:$1|www.mydomain.com/download/}$2
[R,L]
```

Figure 9-7 illustrates the use of this rule.

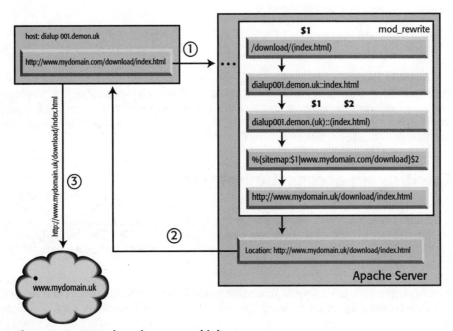

Figure 9-7: A URL-based access multiplexer

As Figure 9-7 shows, when a host such as `dialup001.demon.uk` requests the `www.mydomain.com/download/index.html` page (1), the first rule rewrites the request by using the hostname of the requesting host as follows:

```
dialup001.demon.uk::index.html
```

Then the next rule in the chain is applied. This rule gets applied when the search pattern matches and the substitution URL is created by looking up the map file for the top-level domain. If no matches are found, the default `www.mydomain.com` is used. This is done by the | (or) operator in the substitution URL string. Perhaps it is easier to understand the second rule using the algorithm shown in Listing 9-1.

Listing 9-1: Algorithm for the second rewrite rule

```
if(current URL matches a fully-qualified-hostname::anything)
then

# substitute the current URL using the domain type information
# stored in $1 perform a lookup in the map file.

If  (map file has a key that matches the domain type) then
#use the key's value as follows:

        Substituted URL = value-of-the-key$2
        #where $2 is anything after
        #fully-qualified-hostname::  pattern

Else
        # Use default value www.mydomain.com/download/$2

        Substituted URL = www.mydomain.com/download/$2
endif

Endif
```

The R flag makes this an external URL redirect and the L flag makes this the last rule for the substituted URL. The new location created by rule #2 is sent to the Web browser in (2) and the browser gets the page in (3) as shown in Figure 9-7.

Creating time-sensitive URLs

Ever wonder whether it would be possible to have a URL that would point to different files based on time? Well, mod_rewrite makes it easy to create such a URL. There are a lot of variables named TIME_xxx for rewrite conditions. Using the special lexicographic comparison patterns <STRING, >STRING, and =STRING you can do time-dependent redirects, for example:

```
RewriteCond    %{TIME_HOUR}%{TIME_MIN} >0700
RewriteCond    %{TIME_HOUR}%{TIME_MIN} <1900
RewriteRule    ^foo\.html$              foo.day.html
RewriteRule    ^foo\.html$              foo.night.html
```

This provides the content of foo.day.html under the URL foo.html from 07:00 to 19:00, and the remaining time provides the contents of foo.night.html.

Content Handling

The examples in this section deal with content-specific rewriting rules. I show you how to create backward-compatible URLs, browser-based content rewriting, end-user transparent HTML to CGI redirects, and more.

Adding backward compatibility in URLs

Say that you have recently renamed the page `bar.html` to `foo.html` and now you want to provide the old URL for backward compatibility. Additionally, you do not want the users of the old URL to recognize that the page was renamed. How can this be done? Here is how:

```
RewriteRule    ^foo\.html$  bar.html
```

If you want to let the browser know about the change, you can do an external rewrite so that the browser will display the new URL. All you need to do is add the R flag as follows:

```
RewriteRule    ^foo\.html$  bar.html [R]
```

Creating browser-matched content URLs

You can use rewrite rules to dish out different contents (using internal subrequests) to different browsers. You cannot use content negotiation for this because browsers do not provide their types in that form. Instead, you have to act on the HTTP header User-Agent. For example, if a browser's User-Agent header matched Mozilla/5 then you can send out a Netscape Navigator 5 (or above) features-friendly page, or you can send out a different page if the browser is either an older version of Navigator or another type of browser.

If the HTTP header User-Agent begins with Mozilla/5, the page foo.html is rewritten to foo.NS.html and the rewriting stops. If the browser is Lynx or Mozilla versions 1 to 4, the URL becomes foo.dull.html. All other browsers receive the page foo.cool.html. This is done by the following rules:

```
RewriteCond %{HTTP_USER_AGENT}   ^Mozilla/5.*
RewriteRule ^foo\.html$          foo.cool.html  [L]

RewriteCond %{HTTP_USER_AGENT}   ^Lynx/.*  [OR]
RewriteCond %{HTTP_USER_AGENT}   ^Mozilla/[1234].*
RewriteRule ^foo\.html$          foo.dull.html  [L]
```

When a request for an URL such as http://hostname/foo.html is received, the first condition tests whether the environment variable HTTP_USER_AGENT has a value that contains the string Mozilla/5. or not. If it does contain the string, then the first rule is applied. This rule substitutes foo.cool.html for the original URL and all rewriting is complete; however, when the first rule is not applied, the second rule is invoked. There are two OR conditions. In other words, one of these conditions must match before this rule can be applied.

The first condition tests the same environment variable for the substring Lynx/, and the second condition tests the same environment variable for the substring Mozilla/1 through Mozilla/4. If any of these conditions are met, the rule is applied. The rule substitutes foo.dull.html, the original URL. The substituted URL is turned into a subrequest and is processed by Apache as usual.

Creating an HTML to CGI gateway

If you want to seamlessly transform a static page foo.html into a dynamic variant foo.cgi — that is, without informing the browser or user — here's how:

```
RewriteRule    ^foo\.html$  foo.cgi  [T=application/x-httpd-cgi]
```

The rule rewrites a request for foo.html to a request for foo.cgi. It also forces the correct MIME-type, so that it is run as a CGI script. A request such as http://hostname/foo.html is internally translated into a request for the CGI script. The browser does not know that its request was redirected.

Access Restriction

These examples deal with access control issues. In this section I show you how to control access to certain areas of your Web site using the URL rewrite module.

Blocking robots

It's easy to block an annoying Web spider program (also called *robots*) from retrieving pages of a specific Web site. You might try a /robots.txt file containing entries of the Robot Exclusion Protocol, but that is typically not enough to get rid of such a robot. A sample solution is:

```
RewriteCond %{HTTP_USER_AGENT}    ^NameOfBadRobot.*
RewriteCond %{REMOTE_ADDR}        ^123\.45\.67\.[8?9]$
RewriteRule ^/not/to/be/indexed/by/robots/.+    -    [F]
```

This rule has two conditions:

```
If  (HTTP_USER_AGENT of the robot matches a pattern "NameOfBadRobot" ) and
    (REMOTE_ADDR of the requesting host is 123.45.67.8 to 123.45.67.9) then
       No substitution but send a HTTP "Forbidden" header (status code 403)
endif
```

As you can see, the robot's User-Agent header is matched, along with the IP address of the host it uses. The above conditions allow for multiple IP addresses (123.45.67.8 and 123.45.67.9) to be checked.

Creating an HTTP referer-based URL deflector

You can program a flexible URL deflector that acts on the Referer HTTP header and configure it with as many referring pages as you like. Here's how:

```
RewriteMap  deflector txt:/path/to/deflector.map
RewriteRule ^/(.*)
${deflector:%{HTTP_REFERER}|/$1}
RewriteRule ^/DEFLECTED   %{HTTP_REFERER} [R,L]
RewriteRule .* - [PT]
```

This is used in conjunction with a corresponding rewrite map such as the following:

```
http://www.badguys.com/bad/index.html    DEFLECTED
http://www.badguys.com/bad/index2.html   DEFLECTED
http://www.badguys.com/bad/index3.html   http://somewhere.com/
```

This automatically redirects the request back to the referring page if the URL matches the DEFLECTED value in the map file. In all other cases, the requests are redirected to specified URLs.

✦   ✦   ✦

Setting up a Proxy Server

A *proxy server* is a system that sits between the client hosts and the servers that they need access to. When a client host requests a certain remote resource using a URL, the proxy server receives this request and fetches the resource to fulfill the client's request. In a general sense, a proxy server acts like a server to the client hosts and a client to the remote servers.

In typical proxy scenarios, this process enables the proxy server to store the requested content in a cache. Any new request that asks for information already in the cache no longer needs to be serviced by fetching it from the remote server. Instead, the new request is serviced from the cached data. This allows proxy servers to ease network bottlenecks. However, this is not all that a proxy server does.

This chapter teaches you to turn Apache into a proxy server that can perform a multitude of services. You learn how to turn Apache into a caching (forward) proxy server. Deploying such a server at the network bottleneck can reduce delays in response times, conserve bandwidth, and help reduce your overall communications expense. Because proxy is usually used for networks with large user communities, I also cover various aspects of client configuration including automatic proxy configuration.

Who Should Use a Proxy Server?

The purpose of this proxy server is to fetch the requested resource from the remote server, return it to the requesting user, and cache it in local drives. Proxy service is ideal for scenarios in which more than one user is accessing the network. Many organizations have several host computers that access the Internet via a single Internet connection such as an ISDN router or other dedicated or on-demand connection. A proxy can be very helpful in such a network.

You can gain the following benefits by using a proxy for both Internet and intranet resources:

✦ **Proxying:** If the internal network uses nonroutable IP addresses for either security or cost reasons, you can use a proxy server to provide Internet resources to hosts that normally cannot access the Internet. This chapter teaches you how to do this.

✦ **Caching:** Using a caching proxy such as Apache (with mod_perl), you can provide seemingly faster access to Internet resources to the local users. This will not only enhance the user's perception of network performance but also cut down on bandwidth usage costs.

✦ **Logging and Access Control:** By using a proxy server, you can monitor Internet (or even intranet) usage by employees or students. You can block access to certain Web sites to protect your company from potential lawsuits, and you can stop abuse of company time. By analyzing your proxy server's access and error logs, you can identify usage patterns and make better network usage policy in future.

Understanding Types of Proxy Servers

Before talking about using Apache as a proxy server, let's discuss the types of proxy servers and how they work. There are two types of proxy servers:

✦ **Forward proxy server:** When this type of proxy server is used, users pass their requests to the proxy server and the proxy server gets the intended response from the target host of the request. Forward proxies are typically explicitly defined in user's programs (such as the Web browser).

✦ **Reverse proxy server:** When this type of proxy server is used, users are usually unaware of them because they think they are accessing the intended resource. All requests made by the users are sent to the reverse proxy, which serves the response from its cache or by requesting information from another host.

Forward proxy

A *forward proxy server* usually sits between the user hosts and the remote resources that they want to access. A resource can be an Internet resource, as shown in Figure 10-1, or it can be an intranet resource. The next request for the same resource will be serviced from the cached data if the data has not expired.

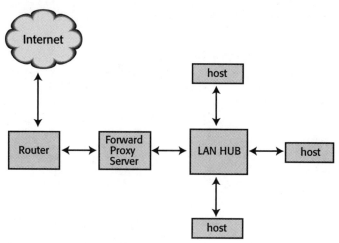

Figure 10-1: A forward proxy server

The user hosts know that they are using a proxy server because each host must be configured to use the proxy server. For example, you must tell a Web browser to use a proxy server before the browser can use it. All remote requests are channeled via the forward proxy server as shown in Figure 10-1, providing a manageable and cost-effective solution for reducing bandwidth usage and implementing user access policy.

This type of proxy server is also referred to as a *caching proxy server.* The reverse proxy server also caches data but it acts in the reverse of the forward proxy server.

Reverse proxy

A *reverse proxy server* sits in front of an Internet resource, as shown in Figure 10-2, or in front of an intranet resource. In such a setup the reverse proxy retrieves the requested resource from the original server and returns it to the user host.

The user hosts that connect to the proxy server are unaware that they are connecting to a proxy server instead of directly to the resource's server, unlike when a forward proxy server is used. As far as the end user is concerned, the requested resource is being accessed directly.

Figure 10-2 shows that users from Internet cannot connect to the Web server without going through the reverse proxy. Because this is a reverse proxy, the users are unaware of it and they think they are connecting to the Web server instead. The LAN users can directly connect to the Web server from the internal network, as shown in the figure.

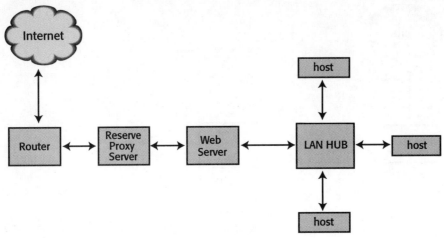

Figure 10-2: A reverse proxy server.

For example, if a reverse proxy server is used for a Web site called www.csus.edu, then all a CSUS (California State University, Sacramento) student has to do is point his or her browser to www.csus.edu and not tell the browser anything about any proxy configuration. The browser places a request to the server known as www.csus.edu. Little does the browser know that the www.csus.edu server is really a reverse proxy server that internally translates the request to a Web server called internal-www.csus.edu to get the content for the request. What does such a setup gain? Because the data is cached from each request, the proxy server can provide some load-balancing support for the real servers behind the scene.

Note   Apache currently does not support reverse proxy service; however, this will be implemented in the next version of the mod_proxy module.

mod_proxy Directives

The proxy support in Apache comes from the mod_proxy module. This module is not compiled by default. You have to reconfigure Apache using ./config.status --enable-module=proxy from the Apache source distribution directory and run make && make install to recompile and reinstall updated Apache server. Currently, it only implements a caching proxy server in Apache. It is capable of supporting HTTP 1.1, HTTPS (via CONNECT for SSL), and FTP protocols. The module can also be configured to connect to other proxy modules for these and other protocols. It provides the directives discussed in the following sections.

ProxyRequests

`ProxyRequests` allows you to enable or disable the caching proxy service. However, it does not affect the functionality of the `ProxyPass` directive.

> **Syntax:** `ProxyRequests On | Off`
>
> **Default setting:** `ProxyRequests Off`
>
> **Context:** Server config, virtual host

ProxyRemote

`ProxyRemote` enables you to interface your proxy server with another proxy server.

> **Syntax:** `ProxyRemote` *`match remote_proxy_server_URL`*
>
> **Default setting:** None
>
> **Context:** Server config, virtual host

The value of match can be one of the following:

✦ The name of an URL scheme that the remote server supports

✦ A partial URL for which the remote server should be used

✦ To indicate the server should be contacted for all requests

The *`remote_proxy_server_URL`* can be specified as `http://hostname-:port`. Note that, currently, only the HTTP protocol is supported. In other words, you can only specify a proxy server that deals with the HTTP protocol; however, you can forward FTP requests from your proxy server to one that supports both HTTP and FTP protocols as follows:

```
ProxyRemote ftp http://ftp.proxy.evoknow.com:8000
```

This sends all FTP requests that come to the local proxy server to `ftp://ftp.proxy.evoknow.com`. The requests are sent via HTTP, so the actual FTP transaction occurs at the remote proxy server.

If you just want to forward all proxy requests for a certain Web site to its proxy server directly, you can do that with this directive. For example:

```
ProxyRemote http://www.bigisp.com/  http://web-proxy.bigisp.com:8000
```

This sends all requests that match `www.bigisp.com` to `web-proxy.bigisp.com`. If you want to forward all of your proxy requests to another proxy, however, you can use the asterisk as the match phrase. For example:

```
ProxyRemote * http://proxy.domain.com
```

sends all local proxy requests to the proxy server at `proxy.domain.com`.

ProxyPass

`ProxyPass` enables you to map a Web server's document tree onto your proxy server's document space.

> **Syntax:** `ProxyPass relative_URL destination_URL`
>
> **Context:** Server config, virtual host

For example:

```
ProxyPass /internet/microsoft      www.microsoft.com/
```

If `ProxyPass` is found in the `httpd.conf` file of a proxy server called `proxy.evoknow`, it will permit users of the proxy server to access the Microsoft Web site by using the URL:

```
http://proxy.evoknow.com/internet/microsoft
```

This acts like a mirror of the remote Web site. Any request that uses the `<relative-URL>` will be converted internally into a proxy request for the `<destination-URL>`.

If the remote site includes absolute references, images may not appear and links may not work. Also you cannot use this directive with SSL destination servers.

ProxyBlock

The `ProxyBlock` directive enables you block access to a named host or domain.

> **Syntax:** `ProxyBlock partial_or_full_hostname [. . .]`
>
> **Context:** Server config, virtual host

For example:

```
ProxyBlock gates
```

blocks access to any host that has the word `gates` in its name. This way, access to `http://gates.ms.com` or `http://gates.friendsofbill.com` is blocked. You can also specify multiple hosts. For example:

```
ProxyBlock apple orange.com bannana.com
```

blocks all access to any host that matches any of the above words or domain names. The mod_proxy module attempts to determine the IP addresses for these hosts during server start-up, and caches them for matching later.

To block access to all hosts, use:

```
ProxyBlock *
```

This effectively disables your proxy server.

NoProxy

NoProxy gives you some control over the ProxyRemote directive in an intranet environment.

> **Syntax:** NoProxy *Domain_name| Subnet | IP_Address | Hostname*
>
> **Default setting:** None
>
> **Context:** Server config, virtual host

You can specify a domain name, or a subnet, or an IP address, or a host name not to be served by the proxy server specified in the ProxyRemote directive. For example:

```
ProxyRemote    *  http://firewall.yourcompany.com:8080
NoProxy           .yourcompany.com
```

Here all requests for <anything>.yourcompany.com (such as www.yourcompany.com) are served by the local proxy server and everything else goes to the firewall.yourcompany.com proxy server.

ProxyDomain

ProxyDomain specifies the default domain name for the proxy server.

> **Syntax:** ProxyDomain *Domain*
>
> **Default setting:** None
>
> **Context:** Server config, virtual host

When this directive is set to the local domain name on an intranet, any request that does not include a domain name will have this domain name appended to it; for example:

```
ProxyDomain      .evoknow.com
```

When a user of the `evoknow.com` domain sends a request for an URL such as `http://marketing/us.html`, the request is regenerated as the following URL:

```
http://marketing.evoknow.com/us.html
```

Note that the domain name you specify in the `ProxyDomain` directive must have a leading period.

CacheRoot

`CacheRoot` allows you to enable disk caching. You can specify a directory name where the proxy server can write cached files.

> **Syntax:** `CacheRoot directory`
>
> **Default setting:** None
>
> **Context:** Server config, virtual host

The Apache server running the proxy module must have write permission for the directory, for example:

```
CacheRoot /www/proxy/cache
```

This tells Apache to write proxy cache data to the `/www/proxy/cache` directory. Note that you will need to specify the size of the cache using the `CacheSize` directory before the proxy server can start using this directory for caching. You may also need to use other cache directives (discussed later) to create a usable disk-caching proxy solution.

CacheSize

`CacheSize` specifies the amount of disk space (in kilobytes) that should be used for disk caching. The cached files are written in the directory specified by the `CacheRoot` directive.

> **Syntax:** `CacheSize kilobytes`
>
> **Default setting:** `CacheSize 5`
>
> **Context:** Server config, virtual host

Note
Although it is possible for the proxy server to write more data than the specified limit, the proxy server's garbage collection scheme will delete files until the usage is at or below this setting. The default setting (5K) is unrealistic; I recommend anywhere from 10MB to 1GB depending on your user load.

CacheGcInterval

`CacheGcInterval` specifies the time (in hours) when Apache should check the cache directories for deleting expired files. This is also when Apache will enforce the disk space usage limit specified by the `CacheSize` directive.

> **Syntax:** `CacheGcInterval` *hours*
>
> **Default setting:** None
>
> **Context:** Server config, virtual host

CacheMaxExpire

`CacheMaxExpire` specifies the time (in hours) when all cached documents expire. This directive overrides any expiration date specified in the document itself; so, if a document has an expiration date that is later than the maximum specified by this directive, the document is still removed.

> **Syntax:** `CacheMaxExpire` *hours*
>
> **Default setting:** `CacheMaxExpire 24`
>
> **Context:** Server config, virtual host

The default value allows the cached documents to expire in 24 hours. If you wish to expire the documents later change this value.

CacheLastModifiedFactor

`CacheLastModifiedFactor` specifies a factor used to calculate expiration time when the original Web server does not supply an expiration date for a document.

> **Syntax:** `CacheLastModifiedFactor` *floating_point_number*
>
> **Default setting:** `CacheLastModifiedFactor 0.1`
>
> **Context:** Server config, virtual host

The calculation is done using this formula:

```
expiry-period =  (last modification time for the document ) *
(floating point number)
```

So, if a document was last modified 24 hours ago, then the default factor of 0.1 makes Apache calculate the expiration time for this document to be 2.4 hours. If the calculated expiration period is longer than that set by `CacheMaxExpire`, the expiration period `CacheMaxExpire` takes precedence.

CacheDirLength

When disk caching is on, Apache creates subdirectories in the directory specified by the `CacheRoot` directive. This directive specifies the number of characters used in creating the subdirectory names. You really do not need to change the default for this directive. For curious users who want to know how or why these subdirectories are created, a simplified answer follows.

> **Syntax:** `CacheDirLength length`
>
> **Default setting:** `CacheDirLength 1`
>
> **Context:** Server config, virtual host

Apache uses a hashing scheme when creating the path and filename for a URL's data to be cached. For example, when you have caching turned on and access a URL (such as `www.microsoft.com`) via your proxy Apache server, the server hashes this URL so that it can later retrieve the data quickly. This hash could look like `1YSRxSmB2OQ_HkqkTuXeqvw`. If the defaults are used for both the `CacheDirLength` and `CacheDirLevels` directives, Apache stores the data found on `www.microsoft.com` in a file called:

```
%CacheRoot%/1/Y/S/RRxSmB2OQ_HkqkTuXeqvw
```

Here `%CacheRoot%` is the directory specified by the `CacheRoot` directive. The `1/Y/S` directories are created because of the default value of the `CacheDirLevels` directive. When this document is requested again using the same URL, Apache need only recalculate the hash to retrieve the page from the specified path.

CacheDirLevels

`CacheDirLevels` specifies the number of subdirectories that Apache will create to store cache data files. See the previous section for related information.

> **Syntax:** `CacheDirLevels levels`
>
> **Default setting:** `CacheDirLevels 3`
>
> **Context:** Server config, virtual host

CacheDefaultExpire

`CacheDefaultExpire` provides a default time (in hours) that is used to expire a cached file when the last modification time of the file is unknown. `CacheMaxExpire` does not override this setting.

> **Syntax:** `CacheDefaultExpire hours`
>
> **Default setting:** `CacheDefaultExpire 1`
>
> **Context:** Server config, virtual host

NoCache

Syntax: NoCache *Domain_name* | *Subnet* | *IP_Address* | *Hostname* . . .]

Default setting: None

Context: Server config, virtual host

The NoCache directive specifies a list of hosts, domain names, and IP addresses, separated by spaces, for which no caching is performed. This directive should be used to disable caching of local Web servers on an intranet. Note that the proxy server also matches partial names of a host. If you want to disable caching altogether, use the following:

```
NoCache *
```

Configuring an Apache Proxy Server

In this section I show you how you can configure Apache (with mod_proxy) as a forward proxy server. After you have the mod_proxy module compiled into Apache (as discussed earlier), setting up a proxy server is quiet easy.

To enable the proxy server, you need to set the ProxyRequests to On in an httpd.conf file. Any additional configuration depends on what you want to do with your proxy server. Regardless of what you decide to do with the proxy server, any directives that you want to use to control the proxy server's behavior should go inside a special <Directory . . .> container that looks like the following:

```
<Directory proxy:*>
. . .
</Directory>
```

The asterisk is a wild card for the requested URL. In other words, when a request for www.evoknow.com is processed by the Apache server, it looks like:

```
<Directory proxy:http://www.evoknow.com/>
. . .
</Directory>
```

You can also use the <Directory ~ /RE/> container, which uses regular expressions that allows you greater flexibility in defining the proxy configuration. For example:

```
<Directory ~ proxy:http://[^:/]+/.*>
. . .
</Directory>
```

Now let's look at a few commonly used proxy configurations.

Scenario 1: Connecting a private IP network to the Internet

In this scenario, only one computer on this network has an Internet-routable IP address assigned to it, as shown in Figure 10-3. This computer runs the Apache proxy server with the ProxyRequest set to On, and no additional proxy configuration is needed. The proxy server services all requests.

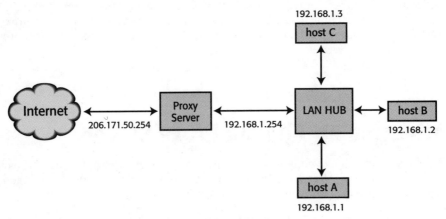

Figure 10-3: Proxy for private IP network to Internet.

In such a configuration, the proxy server needs to be multihomed; in other words, it needs to have access to both the nonroutable private network (192.168.1.0) and the routable IP network (206.171.50.0). In a way, this proxy acts as a firewall for the private network although the chosen nonroutable IP pool does that already. The proxy permits the hosts to get access to Internet services, such as the Web, FTP, and so on.

Scenario 2: Caching remote Web sites

Because a great deal of Web content on both the Internet and intranets is likely to be static, caching them on a local proxy server could save valuable network bandwidth. A cache-enabled proxy server fetches requested documents only when the cache contains an expired document or when the requested document is not present in the cache. To enable caching on your proxy server, you need to specify caching directives inside the special directory container. For example:

```
<Directory proxy:*>
    CacheRoot /www/cache
    CacheSize 1024
    CacheMaxExpire 24
</Directory>
```

This configuration defines a caching proxy server that writes cache files to the /www/cache directory. It is permitted to write 1024K of data (1MB) and the cache must expire after each day (24 hours).

If you do not want to permit outsiders to abuse your proxy server, you can restrict proxy server access either by host or by username/password authentication.

To control which hosts have access to the proxy server, you can create a configuration, such as the following:

```
<Directory proxy:*>

    AuthType Basic
    AuthName Proxy
    order deny,allow
    deny from all
    allow from myhost.evoknow.com

</Directory>
```

This configuration denies access to all but myhost.evoknow.com. If you want to use username/password authentication, you can use something similar to the following:

```
<Directory proxy:*>

    AuthType Basic
    AuthName Proxy
    AuthUserFile /path/to/proxy/.htpasswd
    AuthName Proxy
    require valid-user
</Directory>
```

Cross-Reference If you are not sure how to create the necessary password files, see Chapter 7.

It is also possible to restrict access for a protocol. For example:

```
<Directory proxy:http:*>
. . .
</Directory>
```

enables you to control how HTTP requests are processed by your proxy server. Similarly, you can use the following to control how the proxy server handles each protocol:

```
<Directory proxy:ftp:*>
. . .
</Directory>
```

or

```
<Directory proxy:https:*>
. . .
</Directory>
```

You can also create a virtual host exclusively for proxy server. In that case, the directives should go inside the proxy host's `<VirtualHost>` container:

```
<VirtualHost proxy.host.com:*>
. . .
</VirtualHost>
```

Scenario 3: Mirroring a Web site

A mirror Web site is a local copy of a remote Web site. For example, if you wanted to mirror the `www.apache.org` Web site so that your users can connect to your mirror site for quick access to Apache information, you can use the proxy server to create such a mirror, as follows:

```
ProxyPass /   www.apache.org/
CacheRoot /www/cache
CacheDefaultExpire 24
```

This makes a proxy server a mirror of the `www.apache.org` Web site. For example, this configuration turns my proxy server `blackhole.evoknow.com` into an Apache mirror. When a user enters `http://blackhole.evoknow.com` as the URL, the user receives the Apache mirror's index page as if she had gone to `www.apache.org`.

Before you mirror someone else's Web site, it is important that you get permission, as there may be copyright issues involved.

Setting Up Web Browsers to use a Proxy

After your proxy server is configured, you are ready to set up Web browsers on your client hosts. The popular Web browsers make it quite easy to use proxy servers. In the following sections, I show you how to configure Netscape Navigator 6 and Microsoft Internet Explorer (IE) 5.5 for proxy. There are two ways to set up a proxy server for these browsers: manual or automatic proxy configuration.

Manually configuring Web browsers for proxy is not difficult. However, if you have a lot of user computers that need to be configured, this could become a big hassle every time you needed to change your proxy configuration. This is where automatic proxy configuration for browsers comes in handy.

Manual proxy configuration

You want to do manual proxy configuration in situations in which you have only a few client machines and your proxy configurations do not change often. If your needs are different, i.e. you have a hundreds of client machines, you should skip to the section on "Automatic Proxy Configuration."

Configuring Netscape manually

The following steps guide you through the manual proxy configuration of Netscape:

1. Choose Edit ⇨ Preferences from Navigator's menu bar. You should see a dialog window as shown in Figure 10-4.

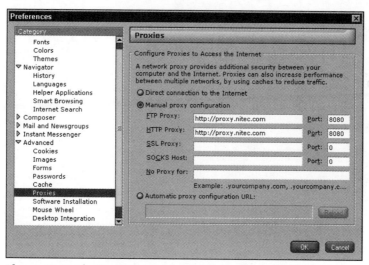

Figure 10-4: The Netscape Navigator proxy setup window.

2. Click on the Advanced category.

3. Click on the Proxies category.

4. Click on the Manual proxy configuration option.

5. Enter the proxy server URLs for the HTTP, FTP, and Security (HTTPS) data entry fields, along with the port information. Because I am using a single proxy server for all of these protocols, the URL (`http://proxy.evoknow.com /`) and the port (8080) are all same. If you have different proxy servers for each of these services, you should specify them accordingly.

6. After you have entered the information, make a request for a remote document to determine whether your proxy is working as it should. A good way to determine what's going on is to monitor the proxy server's access and error logs. On most Unix systems you can use a command such as the following to view log entries as they get written to the file:

```
tail -f /path/to/access/log
```

Configuring Internet Explorer manually

Now let's configure Microsoft Internet Explorer for the Windows platform. To manu-ally configure Internet Explorer for proxy, follow these steps:

1. Choose Tools ➪ Internet Options. This brings up the dialog window shown in Figure 10-5.

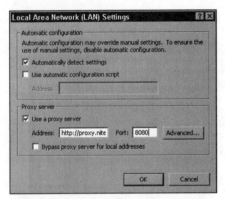

Figure 10-5: Microsoft Internet Explorer manual proxy setup window

2. Click on the Connection tab and then click the LAN Settings button. I assume that you are using a LAN gateway/router connection to the Internet.

3. Select the Use a proxy server option.

4. Enter the proxy server URL and port number in the fields provided.

5. Click OK to complete configuration.

Tip

If you want to specify different proxy server information for different protocols, then you can use the Advanced button to bring up the window shown in Figure 10-6.

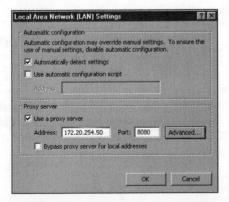

Figure 10-6: The Internet Explorer advanced proxy setup window.

Here, as in Netscape Navigator, you can specify different proxy server settings. After you click OK and click the Apply button to apply the new settings, your browser is configured to use the proxy server.

Automatic proxy configuration

The good folks at Netscape Communications thought about the problems involved with manually configuring proxy for several client computers and came up with a way to get around this hassle. When the Web browser starts, it loads the function from the JavaScript file (how the file is made available to the Web browser is discussed later) and calls FindProxyForURL for each URL request. The browser supplies the host and URL arguments to the function so that it can return the most appropriate proxy configuration.

Note   Microsoft has also caught up with autoconfiguring options for Internet Explorer. Unfortunately, Microsoft has made autoconfiguring a bit harder to incorporate into the browser. You must obtain the Internet Explorer Administrator Kit (IEAK) to create autoconfiguration files. Because getting IEAK requires a licensing agreement that asks each IEAK licensee to report quarterly to Microsoft regarding IEAK-related use, this author didn't get one. However, I have confirmation from a good source that the IEAK documentation discusses a Netscape-like automatic proxy configuration scenario and can even use the same scripts. This section applies to both IE and Navigator. The only difference is that if you want this to work with IE, you must figure out how to create the appropriate files by using IEAK.

The proxy autoconfiguration is done using a special JavaScript. This is true for both Netscape Navigator and IE. The special JavaScript has these requirements:

The proxy autoconfiguration JavaScript must implement a function called FindProxyForURL. This function has the following skeleton:

```
function FindProxyForURL(url, host) {

    // java script code goes here

    return "proxy to use for servicing the URL";

}
```

The arguments that this function receives are url and host. The url is the full URL being requested and the host is the host name extracted from the URL. For example, when a request for a Web page is detected by the Web browser, it calls the function:

```
ret = FindProxyForURL(", )
```

Note   The host argument in the function call is really the substring between the :// and the first : or /. The port number is not included in this parameter.

The function must return a string containing the necessary proxy configuration for a particular URL request. The acceptable string values that represent a proxy configuration are shown in Table 10-1.

Table 10-1 Acceptable String Values for Proxy Configuration	
String	**Meaning**
NULL	When a NULL value (not the string NULL) is returned, it tells the browser not to use any proxy for this request.
DIRECT	Connections should be made directly, without any proxies.
PROXY *host:port;*	The specified proxy should be used.
SOCKS *host:port;*	The specified SOCKS server should be used.

Setting return values for FindProxyForURL

As discussed in the Table 10-1, there are four potential return values. Obviously, the real interesting return values are DIRECT and PROXY. When you have multiple proxy or SOCKS servers, you can return a list instead of a single *host:port* pair. For example, the following proxy configuration:

```
PROXY best-proxy.evoknow.com:8080; PROXY good-proxy.evoknow.com:8081; PROXY
soso-proxy.evoknow.com:8082
```

tells the browser to try best-proxy.evoknow.com first, and if it fails, to then try the next one (good-proxy.evoknow.com), and so on. Note that each *host:port* pair is separated by a semicolon and the keyword PROXY is repeated for each pair. If all the proxy servers fail, the user will be asked before attempting a direct connection.

When all proxies fail and there is no DIRECT option specified, the browser asks the user whether the proxies should be temporarily ignored and direct connections attempted.

To avoid user interaction, the configuration can be replaced with the following:

```
PROXY best-proxy.evoknow.com:8080; PROXY good-proxy.evoknow.com:8081; PROXY
soso-proxy.evoknow.com:8082; DIRECT
```

Because direct connection is already specified as the last resort, the user will not be asked before making such a connection in case of total proxy failure. You can also mix PROXY and SOCKS. For example:

```
PROXY best-proxy.evoknow.com:8080; SOCKS socks4.evoknow.com:1080; DIRECT
```

Here the SOCKS-based proxy will be used when the primary proxy server best-proxy.evoknow.com fails to respond.

When a proxy fails to respond, Web browser retries the proxy after 30 minutes. Each subsequent time it fails, the interval is lengthened by another 30 minutes.

Using pre-defined functions in FindProxyForURL

To help Web administrators (who must also know JavaScript programming), a set of predefined functions are available. These functions and their descriptions are listed in Table 10-2.

Table 10-2
Predefined Functions for Programming Automatic Proxy Configuration Script

Function Name	Explanation	Examples
isPlainHostName (host)	Returns true if there is no dot in host. In other words, if the domain name is not included.	isPlainHostName ("blackhole") returns true. isPlainHostName ("blackhole.evoknow.com") returns false.evoknow.com
DnsDomainIs (host, domain)	Returns true if host belongs to the domain. Note that the domain name must contain a leading period.	dnsDomainIs("www.evoknow.com", ".evoknow.com") returns true. dnsDomainIs("www.apache.org", ".evoknow.com") returns false.evoknow.com
localHostOrDomainIs (host, fqdnhost)	Returns true if host part of fqdnhost (fully qualified host name) matches with host.	localHostOrDomainIs ("a.b.com", "a.b.com") returns true. localHostOrDomainIs ("a.b", "a.b.com") returns true. localHostOrDomainIs ("a.b.org", "a.c.com") returns false.

Continued

Table 10-2 *(continued)*

Function Name	Explanation	Examples
`isResolvable(host)`	If DNS server can resolve the host name to an IP, returns true; otherwise, it returns false. Use of this function can slow down browsers because a DNS query is required to perform the test.	`isResolvable ("{hyperlink}")` returns true (because {hyperlink} has DNS records).
`isInNet(host, IP address pattern, netmask)`	Returns true if the IP address of the host matches the pattern specified in the second argument. The match is done using the netmask as follows: if one of the octets of the mask is a 255, the same octet of the IP address of the host must match. If an octet of the mask is 0, the same octet of the IP address of the host is ignored. Use of this function can slow down browsers because a DNS query will be required to perform the test.	If the host has an IP address of 206.171.50.51, `isInNet (host, "206.171.50.50", "255.255.255.0")` returns true because, according to the netmask, only the first three octets must match and the last one should be ignored.
`dnsResolve(host)`	Returns the IP address of the host if successful. Note that use of this function can slow down browsers because a DNS query will be required to perform the test.	`dnsResolve("proxy. evoknow.com")` returns "206.171.50.50".
`myIpAddress()`	Returns the IP address of the host the Web browser is running. Use of this function can slow down e browsers because a DNS query will be required to perform the test.	`var hostIP = myIpAddress ()` returns the IP of the Web browser host and stores it in a variable called hostIP.
`dnsDomainLevels (host)`	Returns number of domain levels in the host name.	`dnsDomainLevels("www. nitec. com")` returns 2.

Function Name	Explanation	Examples
shExpMatch(string, shellExpression)	Returns true if string matches the shell expression.	shExpMatch("path/to/dir","*/to/*") returns true. shExpMatch("abcdef", "123") returns false.
WeekdayRange (weekday1, weekday2, gmt)	Only the first argument weekday1 is required. Returns true if the day this function is executed is equal to weekday1 or in the range of weekday1 to weekday2. If the third parameter, gmt, is GMT then GMT time is used instead of local time. Acceptable weekday values for weekday1 or weekday2 are SUN, MON, TUE, WED, THU, FRI, or SAT.	weekdayRange("FRI") returns true if day is Friday in local time. weekdayRange("MON", "FRI", "GMT") returns true if day is in the Monday-Friday range in GMT time.
dateRange(day) dateRange(day1, day2) dateRange(month) dateRange(month1, month2) dateRange(year) dateRange(year1, year2) dateRange(day1, month1, day2, month2) dateRange(month1, year1, month2, year2) dateRange(day1, month1, year1, day2, month2, year2) dateRange(day1, month1,year1, day2, month2, year2, gmt)	Returns true if current day, month, year, or all three are in the range. The value of day can be 1-31; month can be JAN, FEB, MAR, APR, MAY, JUN, JUL, AUG, SEP, OCT, NOV, or DEC; year is a four-digit number; gmt is "GMT" or nothing (local time).	dateRange(31) returns true if current day is the 31st. dateRange("JAN", "APR") returns true if current month is in the January to April range. dateRange(1995) returns true if current year is 1995.

Continued

Table 10-2 *(continued)*

Function Name	Explanation	Examples
timeRange(hour) timeRange(hour1, hour2) timeRange(hour1, min1, hour2, min2) timeRange(hour1, min1, sec1, hour2, min2, sec2) timeRange(hour1, min1, sec1, hour2, min2, sec2, gmt)	Returns true if the hour, min, or sec specified is current. If a range is specified, then returns true when the current corresponding unit of time is in the range specified. The value of hour can be 0-23; min can be 0-59; second can be 0?59; and gmt is "GMT" or nothing (local time).	timeRange(9, 17) returns true if current hour is between 9 a.m. and 5 p.m.

With the help of the predefined functions and your custom functions, you can write FindProxyForURL so that it returns an appropriate proxy configuration string for each request.

Following are some example scenarios in which the FindProxyForURL function can be written in different ways.

Scenario 1: Using proxy only for remote URL requests

In this scenario, the idea is to tell the Web browser that proxy should be only for remote URL requests, as shown in Figure 10-7. Here a request for http://www.microsoft.com, from host A, is evaluated by the FindProxyForURL() method, which returns proxy.nitec.com:8080 as the proxy server and then also instructs it to try direct access if proxy is down. Similarly, a Web browser on host B uses FindProxyForURL() method to evaluate how to access http://www.nitec.com. The figure shows that the FindProxyForURL() method instructs the browser to directly access the site.

Listing 10-1 is a simple example of such a FindProxyForURL function.

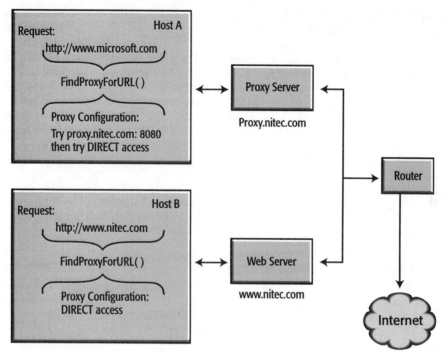

Figure 10-7: Using proxy only for remote URL requests

Listing 10-1: **Using proxy only for remote URL requests**

```
function FindProxyForURL(url, host) {

    // Check whether the host is a local host.
    // If it is a local
    // host specify DIRECT connection (that is, no proxy)
    // or else use the proxy.

if (isPlainHostName(host) || dnsDomainIs(host, ".nitec.com"))

        return "DIRECT";

else

        return "PROXY proxy.nitec.com:8081; DIRECT";

}
```

When a request for a URL `http://www.domain.com` is made by the Web browser user, the browser calls `FindProxyForURL` with the `url` argument set to http://www. *domain*.com and the host set to www.*domain*.com. The function first calls the `isPlainHostName` function to see whether or not the request is for a plain host (just `www`). Because it is not, `isPlainHostName` returns `false`. Now the `dnsDomainIs` function is called to test whether is in the `.nitec.com` domain. This also returns `false`. Because both of these tests return `false`, the `else` part of the conditional statement is executed. In other words, the URL request for `http://www.domain.com` returns the following proxy configuration to the Web browser:

```
PROXY proxy.nitec.com:8081; DIRECT
```

This tells the Web browser to use proxy server named `proxy.nitec.com` on port 8081 if it is not down. If it is down, the request should be serviced by a direct HTTP request to `http://www.domain.com`. For most proxy server installations, this configuration is sufficient. Let's take a look at more complex scenario.

Scenario 2: Using multiple proxy severs

In this scenario, there are multiple proxy servers. Figure 10-8 illustrates a network where there are three proxy servers: `http-proxy.nitec.com` is used for all remote HTTP URL requests; `ftp-proxy.nitec.com` is used for all remote FTP URL requests; and `ssl-proxy.nitec.com` is used for all remote HTTPS URL requests. All other remote URL requests that use other protocols such as GOPHER, NEWS, and so on, are directly connected. All types of local requests are serviced directly as well.

To implement this configuration, `FindProxyForURL` becomes a bit complex and looks similar to Listing 10-2.

This function first checks whether the URL request is a local one. If it is local, then it is serviced directly. If the request is for a remote server, the URL protocol is matched to locate the appropriate proxy server. However, only HTTP, FTP, and HTTPS protocols are recognized and URLs that request remote resources by using such protocols are directed to proxy servers. When a remote URL request does not match any of the stated protocols, it is connected directly.

Scenario 3: Dynamically generating FindProxyForURL using CGI script

It is also possible to customize your proxy server configuration based on the host that is accessing the proxy server. This can be done using a CGI script that outputs the `FindProxyForURL` differently depending on the `REMOTE_HOST` (the browser host). Listing 10-3 shows one such script, `proxy.pl`, written in Perl.

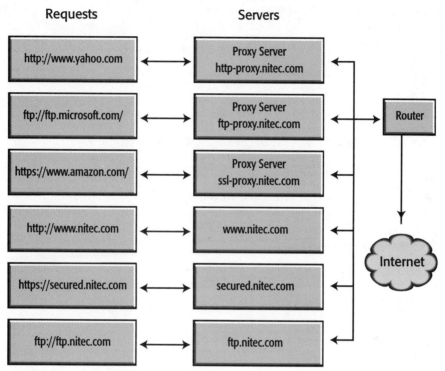

Figure 10-8: Using multiple proxy servers

Listing 10-2: FindProxyForURL for multiproxy server configuration

```
function FindProxyForURL(url, host) {

   //
   // Is the URL local? If it is, then use a
   // DIRECT connection
   //
   if (isPlainHostName(host) ||
       dnsDomainIs(host, ".nitec.com")) {

      return "DIRECT";
```

```
    } else {

        // OK, the URL is remote so check which
        // proxy to use.

        if (url.substring(0, 5) == "http:") {

            return "PROXY http-proxy.nitec.com:8080";

        } else if (url.substring(0, 4) == "ftp:") {

            return "PROXY ftp-proxy.nitec.com:8080";

        } else if (url.substring(0, 6) == "https:") {

            return "PROXY ssl-proxy.nitec.com:8080";

        } else{

            return "DIRECT";

        }
    }
}
```

Listing 10-3: **proxy.pl**

```perl
#!/usr/bin/perl
#
# A Perl script that outputs proxy server configuration.
# $Author$
# $Revision$
# $Id$

# Get the remote host IP from the CGI environment variable
# REMOTE_HOST
my $client = $ENV{REMOTE_HOST};

# Print out the necessary content-type to let the browser
# know that this is a proxy configuration.
print "Content-type: application/x-ns-proxy-autoconfig\n\n";

# If the request came from a host with IP address
# 206.171.50.51 then output proxy configuration
# from subroutine &specialClient
#
if ($client =~ /206\.171\.50\.51/){

    &specialClient;
```

```perl
    } else {

        # If the request came from any other clients, then
        # send proxy configuration for all other clients

        &otherClients;
    }

exit 0;

sub specialClient{
#
# This subroutine outputs a proxy server configuration
#

    print <<FUNC;

        function FindProxyForURL(url, host)
        {
            if (isPlainHostName(host) ||
                dnsDomainIs(host, ".nitec.com"))
                return "DIRECT";
            else if (shExpMatch(host, "*.com"))
                return "PROXY com-proxy.nitec.com:8080; "

            else if (shExpMatch(host, "*.edu"))
                return "PROXY edu-proxy.nitec.com:8080; "

            else
                return "DIRECT";
        }
FUNC

}

sub otherClients{
#
# This subroutine outputs a proxy server configuration
#

    print <<FUNC;

        function FindProxyForURL(url, host)
        {
            return "DIRECT";
        }

FUNC

}
```

This script outputs a special proxy server configuration for a host with the IP address 206.171.50.51; all other hosts get a different configuration. To access this proxy configuration, I can set up the Netscape Navigator or IE to point to this script at http://www.nitec.com/cgi-bin/proxy.pl. For example, in IE you can specify a URL such as the above as the automatic proxy configuration script address in Tools ➪ Internet Options ➪ Connections ➪ LAN Settings ➪ Use automatic configuration script option, except that you are asking the browser to request a CGI script instead of a .pac file. But because the script sends out the content-type of a .pac file, the browser has no quarrel about why it got the proxy configuration from a CGI script and not a .pac file. Although the example script does not do much, you can use similar scripts for complex proxy configurations.

✦   ✦   ✦

Running Perfect Web Sites

By now, you probably have one or more Web sites up and running on your new Apache Web server. Everyone in your organization is crediting you for a wonderful job. You are in Web heaven, right? Wrong! Pretty soon many of your fellow colleagues may ask you how to update their pages on the Web site. For example, the marketing department may call and ask how to update the pricing information, or the legal department may ask how they can add more legal content in one of the Web sites.

This is what happens to Web administrators of medium-to-large organizations. Such administrators soon find themselves in the midst of a mass of update requests and wish lists. So, how do you manage your Web now? In this chapter, you learn how to create a professional Web management environment that will keep you and your Web developers sane and in sync with the Web.

This chapter deals with various issues relating to developing a perfect Web site. A perfect Web site exhibits these characteristics:

   ✦ High-quality content — Of course! If you do not have useful or entertaining content why should people visit your Web site? However, what content works for you depends on the purpose of the Web site.

   ✦ A consistent look and feel — Web sites that have a consistent theme throughout all the pages are more appealing and often indicate a thought process. Creating a consistent look and feel requires tools and a systematic process. This chapter introduces you to a process called the *Web cycle*, which requires that you use three phases (development, staging, and production) to manage your Web sites.

✦ Automated publishing — My experience is that constantly developing new and exiting contents is a big challenge itself. If you add manual content-presentation tasks to the process, things soon get out of control. For example, if you have three content authors writing actual HTML pages for a site, you might start with an understanding of common look and feel, but drift away from it as time passes. To enforce strict presentation rules, you must use HTML templates and integrate contents using an automated process. A few such processes are discussed in this chapter.

✦ Aderence to standard practices — To keep the Web site user-friendly there are many guidelines that need to be followed. I discuss some of the more important ones in this chapter.

What Is a Web Development Cycle?

Unfortunately, typical Web development projects do not start with the design of a manageable Web. In most projects, much of the time is spent getting the servers running and the content developed; it is rarely spent worrying about the long-term management aspects of the Web. Ironically, as soon as everything seems to be working, things start falling apart because of the lack of a clear, maintainable cycle. In this section, you learn about the Web cycle, which enables you to create a highly manageable Web solution.

A Web cycle consists of three phases: development, staging, and production. By implementing each of these phases, you can create a maintainable, manageable Web. Figure 11-1 shows a high-level diagram of a Web cycle.

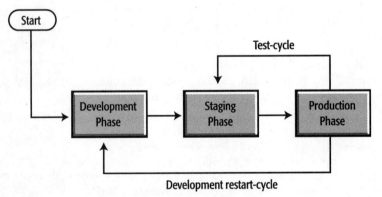

Figure 11-1: A high-level diagram of a Web cycle.

As this figure shows, a Web cycle starts at the development phase, continues to the staging phase, and ends in the production phase. When the cycle restarts, however, it starts from the production phase and repeats the previous cycle path. The phases in the cycle are:

✦ **Development phase** — In this phase, you start developing your Web content. The content, be it HTML documents or CGI scripts or something else, is completely developed and tested in this phase. After the developers are absolutely sure that their work is ready for integration with the Web site(s), the newly developed content moves to the next phase.

✦ **Staging phase** — The staging phase enables integration of the newly developed content with the existing content, and enables performance of testing cycles. Once in the staging phase, developers no longer participate in the staging process. In this process, you introduce testers who are not developers, in order to remove developer bias — in other words, developers might not test the content completely because of overconfidence that the content is correctly written. At this point, you either see problems or you end up with a successful set of tests. In the latter case, you are ready to move the newly developed, staged, and tested content to the production phase. If problems are created by the new content, you will need to restart from the development phase after the developers have fixed the problem in the development area. Do not allow the developer(s) to fix problems in the staging area.

✦ **Production phase** — This phase consists of content backup and content deployment tasks. First, you back up your existing (functional) content, and then you move the staging content to your production Web space. The switchover has to happen as quickly as possible so as to reduce disconnects from visitors and to prevent loss of Web-collected data.

When you are ready to begin another development cycle (to restart the entire process), copy the content from the production phase and make it available in the development phase, so that developers can work on it. The cycle continues in the same manner whenever needed.

What does all this buy you? It buys you reliability and management options. For example, if you are currently developing content and dumping it directly on your production system before a full suite of tests, you are living dangerously. In most cases, content developers claim to have tested their new content in their local environment, and are quick to apply the seal of completion. Because a developer's local environment typically lacks the integration of current content with the new content, the tests are not always realistic. Only by integrating existing and new content together can you detect possible incompatibilities. For example, without the staging phase, a direct dump on the production system from the development phase is can cause any of these errors:

✦ Files in the production system could be overridden by the new contents. This typically happens with image files, because of the lack of a standard file naming convention or because of the use of common directories for image files.

✦ Data files on the live (production) system could be overridden, because the CGI developers used old data files when developing the content.

✦ When multiple developers are involved, some old files may reappear on the production server, because each developer may have started working with a copy at a different time. One developer dumps his copy, and then another developer dumps hers, and the result is a mess.

Many other problems can appear if several developers are involved and their projects are interconnected. If you cannot risk having such problems on your production server, you need the staging phase. Apache can help you implement these phases.

After you get used to the cycle, you'll find that it makes it easy to track development and integration problems, and it also ensures that all your production sites are functional at all times.

Putting the Web Cycle into Action

You are ready to put your Web cycle into action. Ideally, you do not want to perform any development work on the production server system. If your budget does not permit deployment of multiple machines for your Web, however, you should use your lone server to implement the cycle.

First, you need to set up your server(s) for the Web cycle. Although there are many ways to do this, I discuss only three. A brief description of each of the three methods follows.

✦ **A single computer with two virtual hosts for development and staging.** The production server is the main Apache server. Be careful when modifying any Apache configuration in this setup, because changes could affect how your production server behaves.

✦ **A single computer with three main Apache servers for development, staging, and production.** With this method, you create separate configurations for each (main) Apache server so that you can experiment with Apache configurations in the development site without disturbing the production configuration.

✦ **At least three different computers as development, staging, and production Apache servers.** All three computers run Apache servers on port 80.

Setting up for the Web cycle

You can set up for the Web cycle in two ways: you can either use two new virtual hosts to implement the development and staging sites on your production server, or you can create three separate Apache configurations for the production server, the development server, and the staging server.

If your development work includes tweaking Apache configuration files or testing a newly released Apache server, you should use separate configuration files for the production Apache server and the other two Apache servers. If your normal Web development does not include Apache-related changes, however, you can use the virtual host approach.

A good Web cycle requires a well-planned Web directory structure. Figure 11-2 shows one such directory structure for a Web cycle.

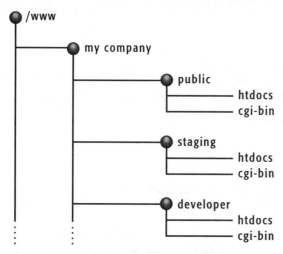

Figure 11-2: The directory structure used for public, staging, and developer sites for "my company"

This figure shows a good example of a directory structure because it enables you to keep the public, staging, and developer sites for each Web site under a single top-level directory (in this case, mycompany). Adding a new Web site means creating a similar directory structure for it.

In the example configurations discussed in the following sections, I assume that you have the preceding directory structure in place. I also assume that your Web server host is called `www.mycompany.com`, and that it has the IP address `206.171.50.50`. Make sure you replace these values with whatever is appropriate for your own configuration.

Creating a virtual host for each phase

If you plan to modify Apache configuration files as part of your development process, do not use this scheme; you only need one set of Apache configuration files in this setup, and changing the files for experimentation can affect your production server. In such a case, you can still use a single machine, but you need to run multiple Apache (main) servers. This approach is described in the next section.

If you decide that you do not need to make Apache-related changes to your configuration files, you can use this scheme to create a virtual host for each phase. To do so, you should create two virtual hosts that have the same ServerName but run on different port addresses. Table 11-1 shows a sample port assignment for such a setup.

Table 11-1	
Port Assignments for Apache Servers for the Web Cycle	
Port	**Server Type**
80	Production server (main server)
1080	Staging server (virtual host)
8080	Development server (virtual host)

You can choose any other port assignments that you wish, as long as you don't use a port address that is already being used or that is greater than 65535. The production server port should not be changed from 80, because default HTTP requests are sent to this port address.

To create these virtual hosts per the port assignment shown in Table 11-1, you need to edit the Apache server's `httpd.conf` file as follows.

1. To make the Apache server listen to these ports, use the `Listen` directive:

```
Listen 80
Listen 1080
Listen 8080
```

2. Create two virtual hosts as follows:

```
# Do not forget to change the IP address, ServerName,
# DocumentRoot, ScriptAlias,
# TransferLog, and ErrorLog directive values with whatever is
# appropriate for your
# actual configuration setup.
#
<VirtualHost 206.171.50.50:1080>
    ServerName  www.mycompany.com
    DocumentRoot  "/www/mycompany/staging/htdocs"
    ScriptAlias   /cgi-bin/ "/www/mycompany/staging/cgi-bin/"
    TransferLog  logs/staging-server.access.log
    ErrorLog     logs/staging-server.error.log
</VirtualHost>

<VirtualHost 206.171.50.50:8080>
    ServerName  www.mycompany.com
    DocumentRoot  "/www/mycompany/developer/htdocs"
    ScriptAlias   /cgi-bin/ "/www/mycompany/developer/cgi-
bin/"
    TransferLog  logs/developer-server.access.log
    ErrorLog     logs/developer-server.error.log
</VirtualHost>
```

Note   In the preceding example, the same IP address is used in both virtual hosts, but different ports are specified in the `<VirtualHost . . .>` container. The IP address is the same as the main server, `www.mycompany.com`. The `ServerName` directive is set to the main server name as well. Your main server configuration will be as usual.

The `http://www.`*`mycompany`*`.com:1080` URL can be used to access the staging site; to access the developer site, this URL can be used: `http://www.`*`mycompany`*`. com:8080`.

Using multiple Apache (main) server processes

You should use more than one (main) server process if you plan to experiment with Apache itself as part of your Web development phase. Create three sets of configuration files, with each set pointing to a different `DocumentRoot` and `ScriptAlias`. After you have done that, you can start up the three Apache (main) server processes as follows from the main directory where you installed Apache (e.g. `/usr/local/apache`):

```
httpd -f conf/httpd.conf
httpd -f conf/staging/httpd.conf
httpd -f conf/developer/httpd.conf
```

When you decide to compile a new version of Apache and run it under the developer server, you can simply feed it the configuration file for the developer server. For example, if you've decided to add a new module and want to see the effect of the module on your content, you can simply run the developer and staging servers using that executable instead of your production server executable (httpd). After compiling a new executable, you may want to rename it to something like httpd-xx80 to ensure that you do not accidentally overwrite the production server executable with it.

To implement the cycle, follow these instructions.

1. Create two subdirectories in your Apache configuration directory called staging and developer, as follows:

```
mkdir /path/to/Apache/server/root/conf/staging
mkdir /path/to/Apache/server/root/conf/developer
```

Note Don't forget to replace /path/to/Apache/server/root/conf with the actual path of your server configuration directory.

2. Copy all *.conf files to both the staging and developer subdirectories, as follows:

```
cp /path/to/Apache/server/root/conf/*.conf
/path/to/Apache/server/root/conf/staging/*
cp /path/to/Apache/server/root/conf/*.conf
/path/to/Apache/server/root/conf/developer/*
```

3. Modify the httpd.conf file in the staging subdirectory to listen to port 1080 instead of the default 80. You can either use the Port or the Listen directive to do this. Similarly, you need to modify the httpd.conf in the developer subdirectory so that the Port or the Listen directive is set to 8080.

4. Modify the srm.conf (or httpd.conf) files in the staging and developer subdirectories so that they point their DocumentRoot and ScriptAlias directives to the appropriate path. For example, the changes needed here for the directory structure shown in Figure 11-2 is:

```
DocumentRoot    "/www/mycompany/staging/htdocs"
ScriptAlias    /cgi-bin/   "/www/mycompany/staging /cgi-bin/"
```

for the staging site configuration. For the developer site configuration file, it is:

```
DocumentRoot    "/www/mycompany/developer/htdocs"
ScriptAlias    /cgi-bin/   "/www/mycompany/developer/cgi-bin/"
```

Note If you use a special configuration for your production server that uses absolute path information, you may have to edit the new configuration files further, for the staging and developer subdirectories.

Using multiple Apache server computers for the Web cycle

If you can afford to have multiple Apache server computers (that is, one for development, one for staging, and one for production) to create the Web cycle environment, you don't need to create special Apache configurations. You can simply install Apache on all your involved hosts, and treat one host as the developer site host, a second host as the staging site host, and the third host as the production site. Because you now have Apache servers running on three different hosts, you can also run each server on port 80. That's all you need to do for a multihost Web-cycle environment.

Implementing the Web cycle

To initiate your Web cycle, copy your production content from the production server's document root directory to your development site. For example, if your configuration is one of the first two in the above list, you can easily copy your entire Web content to the development site using the following Unix commands:

```
cd  /path/to/production/docroot/dir
tar cvf  -  .  | (cd /path/to/development/site/docroot/dir ;
tar xvf - )
```

This copies all the files and directories in your production server to the development site's document root. Just make sure you change the path information to whatever is appropriate on your system.

For a multicomputer Web-cycle environment, you can create a tar archive of your production server and copy it to your development site via FTP.

Set the file permissions so that Apache can read all files and execute the CGI scripts. If you have directories in which Apache should have write access (for CGI scripts that write data), you should also set those permissions. After you are done, start or restart Apache to service the development site.

Now, make sure the development site appears (via the Web browser) exactly the same as the production site. Perform some manual comparisons and spot checks. Make sure the scripts are also working.

If any of your CGI scripts produce hard-coded URLs for your production server, they will keep doing the same for your development site. You can either ignore these URLs or get them fixed so they use the SERVER_NAME environment variable and SERVER_PORT port address.

Testing the Web cycle

When everything is working as it should, you have successfully created a Web-cycle environment. Now you can ask your developers to put new content and scripts in the development site and test them. Whenever a new content development is completed, you should first test it in the development area. The testing should focus on these issues:

✦ Does it serve its purpose? In other words, does the functionality provided by the new content meet your specification?

✦ Does the new content have any side effects? For example, if the new content is really a new CGI script, you should use Apache's script debugging support to monitor how the script works.

Moving the new site to the production server

After you are satisfied with the test results, avoid having to perform another set of functionality tests by ceasing any further development on the new content. When it's time for a production site update, make a copy of your production site and place it on your staging site. Here's some tips for doing so:

✦ Make sure the staging site is exactly the same as the production site. After you've done some manual checking to ensure that everything looks and feels the same, you can move new contents and scripts to the staging site and integrate them.

✦ Move one project at a time so that you can find and resolve problems in stages. For example, if you added three new CGI scripts to your development system, move one script at a time to the staging area. Perform both functional and site-integration testing. If the script passes the tests, move the next new script to the staging area. After you have moved over all the new content, you can perform site-level integration tests. Monitor your staging site logs carefully. Do you notice anything odd in the error logs? If not, then you are ready to perform an update to your production site. You have to be very careful in doing so, however. For example, if you have any CGI scripts on the production server that create data files in the production area, you do not want to override any of these data files with what you have in the staging area.

✦ The best time to update your production site is when you expect the production server to be the least busy. At this time, you can grab the data files from your production server and apply them to the appropriate directories in the staging version of the site. This gets your staging site in sync with the production site. At this point, you have to quickly dump your staging site into the production area. This could be very tricky because the production site is live, and you never know when a visitor may be accessing a page or using a CGI script that needs to read or write data files.

To minimize the switchover time (at least on a single-server setup) you can create a shell script that does the following:

1. Copies all live data files to appropriate areas of your staging site.

2. Renames your top-level production directory (such as the public directory in Figure 11-2) to something like `public.old`.

3. Renames your top-level staging directory (such as the `staging` directory in Figure 11-2) to what you used to call your top-level production directory — for example, `public`.

4. Renames the old production directory (such as public.old) to what you used to call your staging top-level directory — for example, staging.

This way, the staging site becomes the production site in only a few steps, without a great number of file copy operations. A sample of such a script that corresponds to the environment shown in Figure 11-2 is provided in Listing 11-1.

Listing 11-1: **stage2production.sh script**

```sh
#!/bin/sh
# Purpose: a simple shell script to copy live data files
# to staging area and to rename the staging area into a live
# production site. It also renames the old production
# area into a staging area.
#
# Copyright (c) 2001 Mohammed J. Kabir
# License: GNU Public License

# You will need to change these variables to use this script.
DATA_FILES="/www/mycompany/public/htdocs/cgi-data/*.dat";
TEMP_DIR="/www/mycompany/public.old";
PRODUCTION_DIR="/www/mycompany/public";
STAGE_DIR="/www/mycompany/staging";

# Copy the live data to the staging directory.
/bin/cp $DATA_FILES $STAGE_DIR

# Temporarily rename current production directory to TEMP_DIR
/bin/mv PRODUCTION_DIR    TEMP_DIR

# Rename the current staging site to
# production directory
/bin/mv STAGE_DIR    PRODUCTION_DIR

# Rename the temporary (old) production directory
# to staging directory
/bin/mv TEMP_DIR   STAGE_SITE

# To be safe, change the current production directory's
# permission setting so that the Apache user (httpd)
# and Apache group (httpd) can read all files.
# If you use some other user and group for Apache, you
# have to modify this command according to
# your setup.

/bin/chown -R httpd.httpd  $PRODUCTION_DIR

# Change the  file permission so that the owner
# (httpd in this case) has  read, write, and
# executepermission, the group (httpd in this case)
# has read and execute permission, and everyone no
# one else has permission to see the production
# directory files

/bin/chmod - R 750  $PRODUCTION_DIR
```

After running this script, you should perform a quick check to make sure everything is as it should be. In case of a problem, you can rename the current production directory to something else, and change the staging directory name back to your production directory name to restore your last production site.

Building a Web Site by Using Templates and makepage

Maintaining a strict Web cycle provides you with a repeatable process for publishing great Web sites. However, you still need a content presentation process that is highly automated and requires very little human interaction.

Many expensive software programs claim to help in the process. Some people use Microsoft Front Page to manage content development; some use Dreamweaver; some use other products. Some people use more robust methods from Web development companies that cost hundreds of thousands of dollars. What follows is a solution that works for me (and has for years) in maintaining Web sites ranging from a few pages to few hundred pages in size. The requirements for this solution are:

✦ Create a simple mechanism for content authors to publish Web pages with consistent look and feel.

✦ Require the least amount of work on the content author's part so that most of the work is automated.

✦ Assume that the content developer knows very little HTML and prefers to submit contents in text format.

To implement such a solution, I wrote makepage, a script that is included on this book's CD-ROM. This script uses a set of HTML templates and a body text (contents) page to build each page on the Web site. When I started this project, I wanted to generate each page on-the-fly by using CGI or mod_perl, but I later decided to generate the contents once a day because my sites were being updated only once or twice a day. However, it is extremely easy to increase the frequency of the update, as you learn in this section. The makepage script assumes that each page consists of:

✦ A left navigation bar

✦ A right navigation bar

✦ A bottom navigation menu

✦ A body area that houses the contents of a page

Whenever the makepage script is run on a given directory, it looks for all the files ending with .txt extension and creates corresponding .html pages. For example, if you run the makepage script in a directory with a text file called index.txt, the script will run and produce output similar to this:

```
Processing ./index.txt
RSB template ./.-rsb.html chosen: /home/mjkabir/www/default-
rsb.html
LSB template ./.-lsb.html chosen: /home/mjkabir/www/default-
lsb.html
Backed up ./index.html as ./index.html.bak
        Template: /home/mjkabir/www/default-tmpl.html
        BODY file: ./index.txt
         LSB file: /home/mjkabir/www/default-lsb.html
         RSB file: /home/mjkabir/www/default-rsb.html
 Bottom Nav file: /home/mjkabir/www/default-bottom.html
    Top Nav file: /home/mjkabir/www/default-top.html
        HTML file: ./index.html
```

The script's output shows that it is processing the `index.txt` file in the current directory (denoted by the dot character). It then shows which RSB (Right Side Navigation Bar) template file it is using for the `index.html`. The script looks for the RSB template file called `index-rsb.html` first and if it cannot find a RSB file specific to the text file, it uses the default RSB file for the entire directory, which happens to be `default-rsb.html`. It repeats the same process for selecting the LSB (Left Side Navigation Bar) template. Then it backs up the `current index.html` (the output of last run) to `index.html.bak` and uses the default body template `default-tmpl.html` for creating the `index.html` page. If it finds a body template called `index-tmpl.html`, it uses that template instead of the directory's default body template. This gives you flexibility in designing each Web page. You can simply create a directory-wide template set and have all the pages in the directory look the same. Or you can customize a single page in the directory with its own RSB, LSB, and BODY templates.

If you run the script in your document root directory by using the command `makepage path_to_document_root`, the script automatically creates pages in all the subdirectories in the document root. Thus, you can set up this script as a `cron` job to be run every hour, or day, or week, or even minute as your update needs require. The content authors simply drop their text files and pages get created automatically. When a new text file is dropped and you do not supply the page-specific RSB, LSB, or BODY template, the page is created with the directory's default template, which makes it extremely easy to add a new page. Simply type up a page in your favorite text editor and FTP the file to the correct directory at your Web site and it should get published in the next `makepage` run via `cron`.

The `makepage` package supplied on the companion CD-ROM includes default templates that you can study to build your own.

Using HTTP PUT for Intranet Web Publishing

Apache supports the `PUT` method, which enables you to publish a Web page. However, this feature has major security risks associated with if it is not implemented carefully.

After all you do not want to allow just anyone to change your Web site. I only recommend using this feature for intranets which are not accessible from the Internet.

You need the `mod_put` module, which implements the PUT and DELETE methods found in HTTP 1.1. The PUT method allows you to upload contents to the server and the DELETE method allows you to delete resources from the server. You can download this module from `http://hpwww.ec-lyon.fr/~vincent/apache/mod_put.html`.

Understanding the directives in mod_put module

The `mod_put` module provides the three directives to control PUT- and DELETE-based publishing.

EnablePut

`EnablePut` enables or disables the PUT method. To use the PUT method, you must enable it by setting this directive to On.

> **Syntax:** `EnablePut On|Off`
>
> **Default setting:** `EnablePut Off`
>
> **Context:** Directory, location

EnableDelete

`EnableDelete On | Off` enables or disables the DELETE method, which allows you to delete a Web page via HTTP. To use the DELETE method, you must enable it by setting this directive to On.

> **Syntax:** `EnableDelete On | Off`
>
> **Default value:** `EnableDelete Off`
>
> **Context:** Directory, location

umask

`umask octal_` sets the default permission mask (that is, `umask`) for a directory. The default value of 007 ensures that each file within a directory is created with 770 permission, which only permits the file owner and group to read, write, and execute the file.

> **Syntax:** `umask octal_value`
>
> **Default value:** `umask octal_007`
>
> **Context:** Directory, location

Compiling and installing mod_put

After you have downloaded mod_put, you need to perform these steps to compile and install it:

1. Extract the mod_put.tar.gz source and move the directory it creates to within the modules subdirectory of your Apache source distribution.

2. Add the mod_put module to Apache using the configure script (or config.status if you have already compiled Apache before). Run either script with add --enable-module=put option.

3. Compile and install Apache by using the make && make install command.

4. Restart Apache by using the /usr/local/apache/bin/apachectl restart command.

Setting up a PUT-enabled Web directory

Web clients such as Netscape, AOLPress, and Amaya, can publish Web pages via the PUT method. This section teaches you how to set up httpd.conf to enable PUT-based publishing for a single Web directory under your document root tree.

Caution

Be very careful with the PUT method if you plan to use it beyond your intranet. Using PUT in a world-accessible Web site on the Internet might increase your security risks greatly because someone can deface your Web site if the Web-based authentication process that is described here is compromised. I only recommend the PUT method for internal use.

1. Create the following configuration in httpd.conf:

```
Alias location_alias
"physical_directory_under_document_root"

<Location location_alias>
    EnablePut On
    AuthType Basic
    AuthName "Name_of_the_Web_section"
    AuthUserFile path_to_user_password_file

    <Limit PUT>
        require valid-user
    </Limit>

</Location>
```

Here's what's going on in the above code (to learn more about these authentication-related directives, read Chapter 7):

- An alias called *loc_alias* is associated with a physical path called *physical_directory_under_document_root*.

- The <Location> directory sets directives for this alias.

- The EnablePut directive enables the mod_put module.

- The AuthType directive sets the authentication type to Basic HTTP authentication.

- The AuthName directive sets a label for the section. This label is displayed on the authentication dialog box shown to the user by Web browsers, so be sure that this label is meaningful.

- The AuthUserFile specifies the user password file that is used to authenticate the user.

- The <Limit> container sets limits for the PUT method. It tells Apache to require valid users when a PUT request is submitted by a Web client.

Here is an example of the above configuation:

```
Alias /publish/ "/www/mysite/htdocs/publish/"

<Location /publish>
    EnablePut On
    AuthType Basic
    AuthName "Web Publishing Section"
    AuthUserFile /www/mysite/secrets/.users

    <Limit PUT>
        require valid-user
    </Limit>

</Location>
```

In the preceding example, the physical directory /www/mysite/htdocs/publish has PUT method enabled for all the users in /www/mysite/secrets/.users file.

2. Restart Apache server by using the /usr/local/apache/bin/apachectl restart command and use your Web browser with PUT support to publish a document in the http://your_web_server/loc_alias directory. For the sample configuration, this URL is http://server/publish.

When a file is published by using the PUT method, it will have the permission setting that has been set using the umask directive for the mod_put module. The file will be owned by the user under which Apache is running. For example, if you set the User and the Group directives in httpd.conf to be httpd, then the file is owned by the user httpd, and the group ownership is also owned by httpd.

Setting up a virtual host to use mod_put module

The user set in the `User` directive in `httpd.conf` owns files created by `mod_put`. This is a problem for a site with many different users because now everyone can override everyone else's file by using the `PUT` method. You can easily solve this problem by using a separate virtual host for each user, as shown below.

1. Add the following lines to `httpd.conf`:

   ```
   ChildPerUserID number_of_chid_servers username1 groupname1
   ```

   Where the *username1 groupname1* pair is the user and group to be used for a virtual host. Change these names to the actual user and group name you use. Create as many `ChildPerUserID` lines as you need. The `num_of_chid_servers` is a number that Apache uses to launch child processes associated with this virtual host. For example, if you have two users called `carol` and `john` and want to allocate 10 Apache children per virtual host, then add the following lines in `httpd.conf`:

   ```
   ChildPerUserID 10 carol carol_group
   ChildPerUserID 10 john john_group
   ```

   Make sure that the users and the groups actually exist in `/etc/passwd` and `/etc/group`, respectively.

2. Create a `VirtualHost` for each user that requires `PUT` publishing as follows:

   ```
   NameVirtualHost IP_Address

   <VirtualHost IP_Address>

       ServerName vhost_domain_name
       AssignUserID user_name group_name

       Alias location_alias
   "physical_directory_under_document_root"

       <Location location_alias>
           EnablePut On
           AuthType Basic
           AuthName "Name_of_the_Web_section"
           AuthUserFile path_to_user_password_file

           <Limit PUT>
               require username
           </Limit>

       </Location>
   ```

```
    # Other directives that you need for the site

</VirtualHost>
Example:
NameVirtualHost 192.168.1.100

<VirtualHost 192.168.1.100>
    ServerName carol.domain.com
    AssignUserID carol carol_group
    DocumentRoot /www/intranet/htdocs/carol

    Alias /publish/ "/www/intranet/htdocs/carol/publish/"

    <Location /publish>
        EnablePut On
        AuthType Basic
        AuthName "Carol's Publishing Site"
        AuthUserFile /www/intranet/secrets/.users

        <Limit PUT>
            require carol
        </Limit>

    </Location>

</VirutalHost>
```

User `carol` can publish in the `http://carol.domain.com/publish` **directory** by using her own user account. The files created by the Web server are also accessible to her via FTP, as well as by other means, because the files are owned by user `carol`.

3. After you create a virtual host for each user, restart the Apache server by using the `/usr/local/apache/bin/apachectl restart` command and test each user's setup by publishing a test page using the appropriate URL.

Maintaining Your Web Site

After you've implemented the Web cycle and have a content-generation process in place, it is important to maintain your Web. Typical Web maintenance tasks include server monitoring, logging, and data backup. The server monitoring and logging aspects of Web site maintenance are discussed in Chapter 8. This section discusses data backup. You should have two types of backup, if possible — online and offline — which I describe in the following sections.

Online backup

Online backup is useful in the event of an emergency. You can access the backup data fairly quickly and, in most cases, perform necessary restoration tasks in a few minutes. To obtain an online backup solution, you can either look for a commercial online backup vendor or talk to your ISP. If you are hosting your Web server(s) on your own network, however, you can keep backups on another host on your network. On most Unix systems, you can run a program called rdist to create mirror directories of your Web sites on other Unix hosts (Chapter 23 has an example of an rdist-based site-mirroring application).

It may even be a good idea to keep a compressed version of the Web data on the Web server itself. On Unix systems, you can set up a cron job to create a compressed tar file of the Web data on a desired frequency. For example:

```
# for system V-ish Unix, weekday range is  0-6 where 0=Sunday
# For BSD-ish system use weekday range 1-7 where 1=Monday
# This example is for a Linux system (System V-ish cornd)
30 2 * * 0,1, 3, 5,   root  /bin/tar czf /backup/M-W-F-Sun.tgz
/www/*
30 2 * * 2, 4, 6      root  /bin/tar czf /backup/T-TH-Sat.tgz
/www/*
```

If these two cron entries are kept in /etc/crontab, then two files will be created. Every Monday, Wednesday, Friday, and Sunday, the first cron job will run at 2:30 a.m. to create a backup of everything in /www, and it will store the compressed backup file in the /backup/M-W-F-Sun.tgz file. Similarly, on Tuesday, Thursday, and Saturday mornings (at 2:30 a.m.), the second cron entry will create a file called T-TH-Sat.tgz in the same backup directory for the same data. Having two backups ensures that you have at least last two days' backup in two compressed files.

Offline backup

You should also perform backups on removable media and keep them in safe locations. Restoring from this type of backup is usually a time-consuming operation. You can use tape drives, removable hard drives (such as Jaz disks) to perform this backup. I prefer an 8-mm tape-based backup because it provides 8GB of data storage capacity; also, 8-mm tape drives have been on the market much longer than the new compact removable media.

As your Web sites grow richer in content, the available Web space is rapidly filling. This is often a consequence of files that are unused but that are never removed for fear that something (such as a link) will break somewhere. If you think this is true for your Web site, and you are on a Unix platform, you may want to consider running the find utility to locate files that have not been accessed for a long time. For example:

```
find /www -name "*.bak" -type f -atime +10 -exec ls -l {} \;
```

This lists all files in /www directories that end with the .bak extension and have not been accessed for the last 10 days. If you want to remove these files, you can replace the ls -l command and do a find such as:

```
find /www -name "*.bak" -type f -atime +10 -exec rm -f {} \;
```

If this helps, perhaps you can create a `cron` entry that runs this command on a regular schedule.

Standardizing Standards

With a Web cycle in place, you have an environment that can accommodate many developers; however, just creating the Web cycle does not ensure high-quality Web production. A high-quality Web requires high-quality content, and there are guidelines that you should follow regarding content development. The theme here is to standardize your standards.

Each Web site should offer unique content to make it attractive to potential visitors. All types of Web content can be categorized as either static or dynamic. *Static content* is typically created with HTML files, and *dynamic content* is usually the output of CGI or other server-side or client-side applications. Most sites use a mix of both static and dynamic content to publish their information; therefore, standards are needed for both static and dynamic content development.

HTML document development policy

Although you can provide static content in a number of ways, such as a plain-text or PDF file, most Web sites use HTML documents as the primary information repository. To help guide your HTML authors, you should create an HTML development policy. Following are some guidelines that you can adapt for your organization.

Always use standard HTML tags

HTML developers should always use the latest standard HTML. Use of browser-dependent HTML may make a page look great on one type of browser, but terrible on another.

For example, the following shows a skeleton HTML document that meets the minimal HTML document standard.

```
<HTML>
<HEAD><TITLE> Document title goes here </TITLE> </HEAD>
<BODY>
   Document body goes here
</BODY>
</HTML>
```

Each of your documents should contain at least these HTML tags.

Keep in-line images along with the documents

The in-line images of a document should reside in a subdirectory of the document's directory. The source references to these images should be relative, so if the document is moved from one location to another along with the image directory, the image is still rendered exactly the same way it was before.

Note There is one exception to this rule: If some of your images are reusable, you should consider putting them in a central image directory. An example of such a case is a standard navigation bar implemented using image files. The navigation bar can be reused in multiple documents, so you may want to store these images in a central directory instead of keeping them with each document. This provides better control and saves disk space.

The following example shows you how to create a portable HTML document that has multiple graphic files linked to it. Say you want to publish two HTML documents (`mydoc1.html` and `mydoc2.html`) that contain three images (`image1.gif`, `image2.gif`, and `image3.gif`). You can first create a meaningful subdirectory under your document root directory or under any other appropriate subdirectory. Let's assume that you create this directory under the server's document root directory (`/www/mycompany/htdocs`) and you called it `mydir`.

Now, create a subdirectory called `images` under the `mydir` directory and store your three images in this directory. Edit your HTML documents so that all links to the images use the `SRC` attribute as follows:

```
SRC="images/image1.gif"
SRC="images/image2.gif"
SRC="images/image3.gif"
```

An example of an in-line image link for image3 might look like this:

```
<IMG SRC="images/images3.gif" HEIGHT="20" WIDTH="30" ALT="Image
3 Description">
```

The `SRC` attributes in the preceding lines do not contain any absolute path information. If the documents were to be moved from `mydir` to `otherdir` along with the images subdirectory, there would be no broken images. However, if the links contained path information such as:

```
<IMG SRC="mydir/images/images3.gif" HEIGHT="20" WIDTH="30"
ALT="Image 3 Description">
```

or

```
<IMG SRC="/mydir/images/images3.gif" HEIGHT="20" WIDTH="30"
ALT="Image 3 Description">
```

then these documents would need to be fixed after the move. Many sites keep their images in a central image directory (such as `images`) under document root and link documents by using `IMG` tags such as:

```
<IMG SRC="/images/images3.gif" HEIGHT="20" WIDTH="30"
ALT="Image 3 Description">
```

This is fine, but when you want to delete the HTML document, you need to make sure you also delete the appropriate image in the central image directory. If you fail to do this, eventually a lot of disk space will disappear in your image pit. Therefore, it is not a good idea to keep images in a central directory. You should keep images in a subdirectory with their links.

Display clear copyright messages on each document

Each document should contain an embedded (commented) copyright message that clearly names the owner of the document and all its images. A similar copyright message should also appear on each page. To make it easy to update the copyright message, you may want to consider using an SSI directive as follows:

```
<!-#include file=/copyright.html" -->
```

Now, all you need to do is to create an HTML page called copyright.html, and place it under your server's document root directory. Because the content of this HTML page is inserted in the SSI-enabled document that makes this call, you should not use the <HTML>, <HEAD>, <TITLE>, or <BODY> tags in this document. Using this SSI call will make your life easier when you need to update the year in the copyright message, or need to make another change.

Dynamic application development policy

Dynamic content is usually produced by CGI scripts or other applications that implement CGI or some server-side interface. A vast majority of dynamic content is produced using Perl-based CGI scripts. Because CGI scripts and applications usually have a very short life span, many CGI developers do not devote the time to producing a high-quality application.

If you plan to use FastCGI or mod_perl-based scripts and applications, it is important that they be developed in a proper manner. You should consider the following policies when implementing scripts and applications for your dynamic content.

Always use version control

CGI developers must use version control, which enables you to go back to an older version of an application in case the newly developed and deployed version contains a bug. On most Unix systems, you can use the Concurrent Versions System (CVS) software to implement a version-controlled environment. You can find the latest version of the CVS software at ftp://prep.ai.mit.edu.

Do not use absolute pathnames in CGI scripts or applications

No absolute pathnames should be used in CGI scripts. This ensures that the scripts can be used on multiple Web sites without modification. If absolute pathnames are required for a special purpose, a configuration file should be supplied for the script; this way, the paths can be updated by modifying the textual configuration file.

Provide both user- and code-level documentation

Source code needs to be well-documented so future developers can update the scripts without spending a lot of time trying to figure out how it works.

Avoid embedding HTML tags in scripts or applications

The output of CGI scripts should be template-driven. In other words, a CGI script reads an output page template and replaces dynamic data fields (which can be represented using custom tags). This makes output page updating easy for HTML developers, because the HTML is not within the CGI script. In fact, CGI scripts should contain as little HTML as possible.

Do not trust user input data

To reduce security risks, make sure that user input data is checked before it is used. You can learn more about checking user input in Chapter 18, which discusses input-related security risks and solutions in detail.

Avoid global variables in Perl-based CGI scripts

When developing CGI scripts in Perl, you should avoid global variables. Limiting the scope of a variable is one way to eliminate unpredictable script behavior. Perl programmers should use the following for variable declarations:

```
my $variable;
```

instead of :

```
local $variable;
```

because the former creates a variable that is only available in the scope it is created. The latter definition simply creates a local instance of a global variable, which creates a great deal of confusion. Perl 6 will most likely rename the keyword 'local' to 'temp' to make this concept clearer for programmers.

Giving Your Web Site a User-Friendly Interface

Using standard HTML and well-written CGI scripts/applications can certainly make your Web site better than many of the sites that exist out there. However, there's another aspect of Web site design that you need to consider — the user interface.

Think of a Web site as an interactive application with a Graphical User Interface (GUI) that is visible in a Web browser. The GUI needs to be user-friendly for people to have a pleasant Web experience while they are visiting your Web site.

The key issues in developing a user-friendly GUI are discussed in this section. Along with making your GUI user-friendly, you need to watch out for broken links or requests for deleted files. Use your server error logs to detect these kinds of problems. You should also have a way for visitors to give you feedback. Most sites use a simple HTML form-based feedback CGI script. You can develop one that suits your needs. Gathering feedback is a good way to learn what your visitors think about your Web site.

Make your site easy to navigate

Users must be able to go from one page to another without pulling their hair out. They should be able to locate buttons or menu bars that enable them to move back and forth or jump to related information.

Many Web page designers argue that popular Web browsers already include a Back and Next button, so having a Back or Next button on a page is redundant. Wrong! Imagine that a user lands on one of your pages (other than the home page) from a search engine's output. The user simply searched for one or more keywords, and the search engine provided a URL to a page on your site. The user is very interested in knowing more about the topic on your site, so the user wants to start from the beginning of the document — but there's no way the user can do that, because the browser's Back button returns the user to the search engine output page!

Alas, if only this page had a link (or a button) to a previous page, the user could have gone back to the last page easily. The Web page designers who don't like the extra buttons insist that the user should have simply manipulated the URL a bit to go back to the home page and start from there. Well, this assumes that there is a clear link to this page (that matched the search keyword) from the home page, which is not always true.

It's a good idea to implement a menu bar that enables the user to go back and forth, and that also enables the user to jump to a related location, or even to a home page.

Create an appealing design

Think of Web sites as colorful and interactive presentations that are active 24 hours a day. If the look and feel of this presentation is not just right, your visitors will click away from your site(s). Consider the following guidelines for developing an appealing site design.

Appropriate foreground and background colors

Make sure you don't go overboard with your color choices. Use of extreme colors makes your Web site appear unprofessional and dull. Be color-conscious and use an appropriate coloring scheme. For example, If your Web site is about kids' toys, it should probably be a very colorful site. If your site is about Digital Signal Processor benchmarks, however, you probably don't need many bright colors or flashy backgrounds.

Appropriate text size

Try to make your primary content appear in normal font. Use of a special font through `<FONT FACE="myVerySpecialFont">` may make the page look good on your Web browser (because you happen to have the font), but on someone else's browser, the page may look completely different and may be difficult to read. Also, be careful with the size of the text; do not make it too large or too small. Remember that if your visitors can't read what you have to say on your Web page, they won't be able to like what you have to say.

Less use of images and animations

Beware unnecessary images. Images make your Web pages download more slowly. Remember that not everyone is connecting to your site via an ADSL or ISDN line; most people still use 56K or 28.8K modems for their Internet connection. A slow page download could make a potential client click away from your pages.

Also, be cautious about using animations. Even the cutest animations become boring after the first few visits, so make sure you are not overcrowding your pages with them.

Remove cryptic error messages

Configure Apache with the `ErrorDocument` directive, so that users do not receive server error messages that are difficult to understand (at least to the average user). For example, when a requested URL is not found on the server, the server may display a cryptic error message. To make this error message friendlier, you can add an `ErrorDocument` directive such as:

```
ErrorDocument  404  /sorry.html
```

in the `httpd.conf` file, so that the error message is easily understood by average Web visitors.

Test your Web GUI

One of the best ways to test your Web interface is to use a system that resembles the average Internet user's computer, or perhaps your potential client's computer. If you think your clients will all have high-performance computers with fast connections, you may not need to worry about using fewer graphics or client-side applications such as Java applets and Shockwave animations.

In most cases, you do not know the potential client's computer and network specifications, so you should go with the average user's setup. Use a low-end Pentium computer with 16MB of RAM and a 28.8K modem connection to test your Web site from an ISP account. Try low monitor resolutions such as 640×480 or 800×600 pixels; if your target visitors use Web-TV systems, try a resolution of 550×400 pixels.

If you enjoyed looking through your Web site, others will probably enjoy it, too. On the other hand, if you didn't like what you saw, others probably won't like it either!

Tip

If you prefer, you can have a third party test your Web site. For example, Netscape.com provides a Web-based, free tune-up service at `http:// websitegarage.netscape.com`. Netscape's back-end application can examine any Web site for page download time, quality of the HTML, dead links, spelling errors, HTML design quality, and link popularity. To try it out, just go to the preceding Web site and enter your own Web site address and e-mail address and wait a few seconds to a few minutes. You will get a free diagnosis of your Web site.

Promoting Your Web Site

What good is a perfect Web site if nobody knows about it? You should think about promoting your Web site on the Web. You can hire advertising agencies to help you in this regard, although advertising on the Web can be expensive. If your budget gets in the way, you can do some promoting yourself. The following list gives you some pointers to properly promote your site.

✦ **Search engines:** Before you do anything to promote your Web site, ask yourself, "How do I find information on the Web?" The answer is: through search engines. Is your company listed in the search engines? If not, this is the first step in promoting your site.

Almost all search engines enable you to submit your URL to their search robot's database so that it can traverse your Web in the future. You should make a list of search engines that you consider important, and submit your Web site's URL to these engines. This process can take days or weeks.

✦ **META tags:** You can add META information in your content to help your URL appear in a decent position when a potential customer does a search. For example, you can add META information such as:

```
<META NAME="KEYWORD" CONTENT="keyword1 keyword2 keyword3
..."> 
<META NAME="DESCRIPTION" CONTENT="Description of your
company">
```

✦ **Link exchanges:** To increase traffic, you can also participate in link exchanges such as `www.linkexchange.com`. Link exchanges require that you put a special set of HTML tags in your Web pages; these tags pull advertisement graphic (banner ad) files into your pages. In return, your banner advertisement graphics are also displayed in Web sites operated by others who agreed to show someone else's banner on their pages. This type of advertisement sharing is quite popular among personal and small business sites.

Whether you buy advertisement space on high-profile Web sites such as Yahoo, AltaVista, or Netscape, or you use the link exchange method, you should periodically check your site's standing in the search engines output by generating search queries yourself.

✦   ✦   ✦

Running Web Applications

The practice of serving static HTML pages is almost a thing of the past. These days, most popular Web sites have a great deal of dynamic content. People do not visit Web sites that do not change frequently. Therefore, it is important to know how to enable dynamic contents using CGI scripts, Server Side Includes, FastCGI applications, PHP, mod_perl scripts, and Java servlets. This part shows you how to use all of these technologies with Apache.

Running CGI Scripts

Dynamic contents drive the Web. Without dynamic, personalizable contents the Web would be a "been there, done that" type of place. After all, why would people come again and again to see and experience the same old contents over and over? The dynamic contents moved from concept to reality with a lot of help from a specification called the Common Gateway Interface (CGI). The CGI specification tells a Web server how to interact with external application. A Web server that runs CGI applications practically enables anyone to run a selected list of programs on the server on demand. This chapter discusses the basics of CGI to give you a clear understanding of it, and the details of setting up Apache to support CGI executions.

What Is CGI?

To provide dynamic, interactive contents on the Web, a lot of popular Web sites use CGI applications. Chances are that you have already used one or more CGI applications on the Web. For example, when you fill out a Web form it is likely to be processed by a CGI script written in Perl or some other language.

Of course, as more and more Web technologies emerge, new means of delivering dynamic contents over the Web are becoming available. Most of these solutions are either language specific, or operating system or commercial software dependent. CGI, on the other hand, is a language-independent gateway interface specification that can be implemented using virtually any widely popular application development language, including C, C++, Perl, shell scripting languages, and Java.

This section gives you a look at how a CGI program works (see Figure 12-1). The basic idea is that the Web server gets a certain URL that magically — at least for now — tells the Web server that it must run an external application called

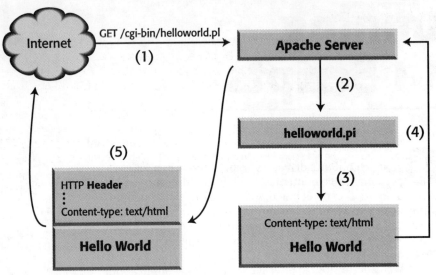

Figure 12-1: How a CGI program works.

helloworld.cgi. The Web server launches the application, waits for it to complete, and returns output. Then, it transmits the application's output to the Web client on the other side.

What happens when you want the client to be capable of interacting with the application? Well, input data from the client must be supplied to the application. Similarly, when an application produces output, how does the server or client know what type of output to return? A program can produce a text message, an HTML form for further inputs, an image, and so on. As you can see, the output can vary a lot from application to application, so there must be a way for applications to inform the Web server and the client about the output type.

CGI defines a set of standard means for the server to pass client input to the external applications, and it also defines how an external application can return output. Any application that adheres to these defined standards can be labeled as a CGI application/program/script. For simplicity, I use the term *CGI program* to mean anything (such as a Perl script or a C program) that is CGI-specification compliant. In the following section, I discuss how the CGI input/output process works.

CGI Input and Output

There are many ways a Web server can receive information from a client (such as a Web browser). The HTTP protocol defines the way in which a Web server and a client can exchange information. The most common methods of transmitting request data to a Web server are GET requests and POST requests, which I describe in the following sections.

GET requests

The GET request is the simplest method for sending HTTP request. Whenever you enter a Web site address in your Web browser, it generates a GET request and sends it to the intended Web server. For example, if you enter `http://www.hungryminds.com` in your Web browser, it sends an HTTP request such as the following:

```
GET /
```

to the `www.hungryminds.com` Web server. This GET request asks the Hungry Minds Web server to return the top-level document of the Web document tree. This document is often called the *home page,* and usually refers to the `index.html` page in the top-level Web directory. Furthermore, HTTP enables you to encode additional information in a GET request. For example:

```
http://www.mycompany.com/cgi-bin/search.cgi?books=cgi&author=kabir
```

Here, the GET request is:

```
GET www.mycompany.com/cgi-bin/search.cgi?books=cgi&author=kabir
```

This tells the server to execute the `/cgi-bin/search.cgi` CGI program and pass to it the `books=cgi` and `author=kabir` input data.

When a CGI-compliant Web server such as Apache receives this type of request, it follows the CGI specifications and passes the input data to the application (in this case, the `search.cgi` in the `cgi-bin` directory). When a CGI resource is requested via an HTTP GET request method, Apache:

1. Sets the environment variables for the CGI program, which includes storing the HTTP request method name in an environment variable called REQUEST_METHOD, and the data received from the client in an environment variable called QUERY_STRING.

2. Executes the requested CGI program.

3. Waits for the program to complete and return output.

4. Parses the output of the CGI program if it is not a nonparsed header program. (A *nonparsed header* CGI program creates its own HTTP headers so that the server does not need to parse the headers.)

5. Creates necessary HTTP header(s).

6. Sends the headers and the output of the program to the requesting client.

   Figure 12-2 illustrates this process.

Now let's look at what a CGI program has to do to retrieve the input to use it for its internal purposes.

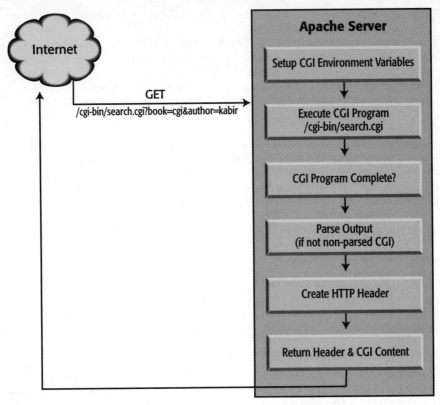

Figure 12-2: CGI server processing.

As Figure 12-3 shows, a CGI program

1. Reads the REQUEST_METHOD environment variable.

2. Determines whether the GET method is used or not by using the value stored in the REQUEST_METHOD variable.

3. Retrieves the data stored in the QUERY_STRING environment variable, if the GET method is used.

4. Decodes the data.

5. Processes the decoded data as it pleases.

6. Writes the Content-Type of the output to its standard output device (STDOUT) after processing is complete.

7. Writes the output data to the STDOUT and exits.

The Web server reads the STDOUT of the application and parses it to locate the Content-Type of the output. It then transmits appropriate HTTP headers and the Content-Type before transmitting the output to the client. The CGI program is exited and the entire CGI transaction is completed.

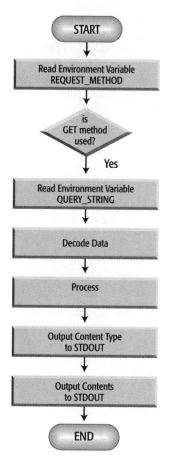

Figure 12-3: CGI program processing.

 Note If a CGI program is to provide all of the necessary HTTP headers and Content-Type information itself, its name has to be prefixed by nph (which stands for nonparsed header). An nph CGI program's output is not parsed by the server and transmitted to the client directly; most CGI programs let the server write the HTTP header and are, therefore, parsed header programs.

Using the GET request method to pass input data to a CGI program is limiting in many ways, including these ways:

✦ The total size of data that can be transmitted as part of a URL is limited by the client's URL-length limit. Many popular Web browsers have hard limits for the length of a URL, and therefore, the total data that can be sent via an encoded URL is quite limited. However, on occasion it might be a good idea to pass data to CGI programs via a URL. For example, if you have an HTML form that uses the GET method to send data to a CGI program, the submitted URL can be bookmarked for later use without going through the data-entry form again. This can be a user-friendly feature for database-query applications.

✦ The length of the value of a single environment variable (QUERY_STRING) is limiting. Many, if not all, operating systems have limits on the number of bytes that an environment variable's value can contain. This effectively limits the total bytes that can be stored as input data.

These limits are probably not of concern for CGI programs that require little or no user input. For programs that require a large amount of user input data, however, another HTTP request method — POST — is more applicable. The POST request method is discussed in the following section.

POST requests

The HTTP POST request method is widely used for passing data to CGI programs. Typical use of this method can be found in the many HTML forms you fill out on the Web. For example, Listing 12-1 shows one such form.

Listing 12-1: An HTML Form Using HTTP POST Request Method

```
<HTML>
  <HEAD>
        <TITLE> Apache Server 2.0 - Chapter 12 Listing 12-1
</TITLE>
  </HEAD>

<BODY>
<H1>Listing 12-1</H1>
<H2>An Example HTML Form Using the HTTP POST Request
Method</H2>
<HR>
<FORM ACTION="/cgi-bin/search.cgi" METHOD="POST">

<PRE>
 Type of Book <INPUT TYPE="TEXT" NAME="book" SIZE="10"
MAXSIZE="20">
Author's Name <INPUT TYPE="TEXT" NAME="author" SIZE="10"
MAXSIZE="20">
</PRE>
<INPUT TYPE=SUBMIT VALUE="Search Now">

</FORM>

</BODY>
</HTML>
```

Notice that there is a <FORM> </FORM> section in the listing. An HTML form usually has a starting <FORM> tag that defines the ACTION and the request METHOD for the form. In the example above, the action is the `/cgi-bin/search.cgi` CGI program and the method is `POST`.

Following the starting `<FORM>` tag, there is usually one or more `INPUT` entity; `INPUT` entities might include text input boxes, drop-down menus, and lists. In our example, there are three input entities. The first one enables the user to enter a value for the book variable. The next one is similar, enabling the user to enter a value for the author variable. The third one is a bit special; it enables the user to submit the form. When the user submits the form, the client software transmits a `POST` request to the server for the `ACTION` (that is, `/c/s.dll/search.cgi`) resource, and also transmits the `book=<user entered value>` and `author=<user entered value>` in an encoded format.

Comparing GET and POST

What is the difference between the `GET` and the `POST` requests? The `POST`ed data does not get stored in the `QUERY_STRING` environment variable of a CGI program. Instead, it is stored in the standard input (`STDIN`) of the CGI program. The `REQUEST_METHOD` variable is set to `POST`, while the encoded data is stored in the `STDIN` of the CGI program, and a new environment variable called `CONTENT_LENGTH` is set to the number of bytes stored in the `STDIN`.

The CGI program must now check the value of the `REQUEST_METHOD` environment variable. If it is set to `POST` for HTTP POST requests, the program should first determine the size of input data from the value of the `CONTENT_LENGTH` environment variable and then read the data from the `STDIN`. Note that the Web server is not responsible for inserting an End-of-File (`EOF`) marker in the `STDIN`, which is why the `CONTENT_LENGTH` variable is set to the length of data, in bytes, making it easier for the CGI program to determine the data's total byte count.

It is possible to use `GET` and `POST` at the same time. Here is a sample HTML form that officially uses the `POST` method, but also sneaks in a query string, `username=joe`, as part of the CGI `ACTION`.

```
<FORM ACTION="/cgi-bin/edit.cgi?username=joe" METHOD=POST>
<INPUT TYPE=TEXT NAME="PhoneNumber">
</FORM>
```

In this sample, the `username=joe` query would be part of the URL, but the other field (`PhoneNumber`) would be part of the `POST` data. The effect: The end-user can bookmark the URL and always run the `edit.cgi` script as `joe` without setting values for any of the other fields. This is great for online database applications and search engines.

Whether you use `GET`, or `POST`, or both, the data is encoded and it is up to the CGI program to decode it. The following section discusses what is involved in decoding the encoded data.

Decoding input data

The original HTTP protocol designers planned for easy implementation of the protocol on any system. In addition, they made the data-encoding scheme simple.

The scheme defines certain characters as special characters. For example, the equals sign (=) facilitates the making of key=value pairs; the plus sign (+) replaces the space character, and the ampersand character (&) separates two key=value pairs.

If the data itself contains characters with special meaning, you might wonder what is transmitted. In this case, a three-character encoding scheme is used, which can encode any character. A percent sign (%) indicates the beginning of an encoded character sequence that consists of two hex digits.

Hex is a base 16 number system in which 0 to 9 represents the same value as the decimal 0 to 9, but it also has an extra set of digits. Those are A (=10), B (=11), C (=12), D (=14), and F (=15). For example, 20 in hex is equal to 32 in a decimal system. The conversion scheme is:

```
20 = 2 x (16^1 ) + 0 x (16^0)
```

These two hex digits consist of the value that can be mapped into the ASCII (for English language) table to get the character. For example, %20 (hex) is 32 (decimal) and maps to the space character in the ASCII table.

Apache CGI Variables

There are two ways in which Apache can implement support for CGI. The standard Apache distribution includes a CGI module that implements the traditional CGI support; however, there is a new module (FastCGI) that implements support for high-performance CGI applications. This section discusses the standard CGI support issues.

In the previous sections, you learned that a CGI-compliant Web server uses environment variables, standard input (STDIN) and standard output (STDOUT) to transfer information to and from CGI programs. Apache provides a flexible set of environment variables for the CGI program developers. Using these environment variables, a CGI program not only retrieves input data, but also recognizes the type of client and server it is dealing with.

In the following sections, I discuss the environment variables that are available from the standard CGI module compiled into Apache.

Note   The source distribution Apache 2.x.x version support --enable-cgid option for the configure script. This option forces Apache to use a script server (called the CGI daemon) to manage CGI script processes, which enhances Apache's overall performance.

Server variables

These variables are set by Apache to inform the CGI program about Apache. Using server variables, a CGI program can determine various server-specific information, such as a version of the Apache software, an administrator's e-mail address, and so on.

SERVER_SOFTWARE

SERVER_SOFTWARE is set by Apache, and the value is usually in the following form:

```
Apache/Version (OS Info)
```

Here, Apache is the name of the server software running the CGI program, and the version is the version number of the Apache. A sample value is:

```
Apache/2.0.14 (Unix)
```

This is useful when a CGI program is to take advantage of a new feature found in a newer version of Apache, and still be capable of performing in older versions.

GATEWAY_INTERFACE tells the CGI program what version of CGI specification the server currently supports. A sample value is:

```
CGI/1.1
```

A CGI program can determine the value of this variable and conditionally make use of different features available in different versions of CGI specifications. For example, if the value is CGI/1.0, the program may not use any CGI/1.1 features, or vice versa.

The first integer before the decimal point is called the major number, and the integer after the decimal point is called the minor number. Because these two integers are treated as separate numbers, CGI/2.2 is an older version than CGI/2.15.

SERVER_ADMIN

If you use the ServerAdmin directive in the httpd.conf file to set the e-mail address of the site administrator, this variable will be set up to reflect that. Also, note that if you have a ServerAdmin directive in a virtual host configuration container, the SERVER_ADMIN variable is set to that address if the CGI program being accessed is part of the virtual host.

DOCUMENT_ROOT

This variable is set to the value of the DocumentRoot directive of the Web site being accessed.

Client request variables

Apache creates a set of environment variables from the HTTP request header it receives from a client requesting a CGI program. It provides this information to the CGI program by creating the following set of environment variables.

SERVER_NAME

This variable tells a CGI program which host is being accessed. The value is either an IP address or a fully qualified host name, as follows:

```
SERVER_NAME = 192.168.1.100
SERVER_NAME = www.domain.com
```

HTTP_HOST

See `SERVER_NAME` variable.

HTTP_ACCEPT

This variable is set to the list of MIME types that the client is capable of accepting, including these:

```
HTTP_ACCEPT = image/gif, image/x-xbitmap, image/jpeg, image/pjpeg, image/png, */*
```

Here, the client claims to be capable of handling GIF, JPEG, PNG, and other images. This enables the CGI program to determine what output will be ideal for the client. For example, a CGI program could produce either GIF or JPEG and receive an `HTTP_ACCEPT` as follows:

```
HTTP_ACCEPT = image/gif,  */*
```

Then, it can send GIF output instead of JPEG because the client does not prefer it.

HTTP_ACCEPT_CHARSET

This variable specifies which character set is acceptable to the client, for example:

```
HTTP_ACCEPT_CHARSET = iso-8859-1,*,utf-8
```

HTTP_ACCEPT_ENCODING

This variable specifies which encoding schemas are acceptable to the client, for example:

```
HTTP_ACCEPT_ENCOMDING = gzip
```

In this case, the client accepts gzip (compressed) files. Thus, a CGI script can compress a large page by using gzip compression and send it, and the Web client will be able to decompress it.

HTTP_ACCEPT_LANGUAGE

This variable specifies which language is acceptable to the client, for example:

```
HTTP_ACCEPT_LANGUAGE = en
```

In this case, the client accepts en (English) language contents.

HTTP_USER_AGENT

This variable specifies what client software the requesting system is running and what operating system it is running on, for example:

```
HTTP_USER_AGENT = Mozilla/4.04 [en] (WinNT; I)
```

The preceding is equivalent to the following:

```
Client Software = Netscape Navigator ()
Client Software Version = 4.04 (English version)
Operating System = Windows NT (Intel)
```

Notice that Mozilla is a keyword used by Netscape for the Navigator code base. Although exclusively only Netscape browsers used the word Mozilla, many other vendors have started using Mozilla as part of the HTTP header. For example, Microsoft Internet Explorer (IE) 5.5 produces the following HTTP_USER_AGENT data when run from the same machine:

```
HTTP_USER_AGENT = Mozilla/5.5 (compatible; MSIE 5.5; Windows NT)
```

This user agent information is used heavily by many Web sites. A site that is optimized for Netscape Navigator (that is, it uses a feature of HTML, or JavaScript, or a plug-in, that works well in Netscape Navigator) might use the HTTP_USER_AGENT information to return a different page for users surfing to the site with IE, or any of the other less popular browsers. However, I recommend that you stick to standard HTML (HTML specification for the current standard is available at www.w3.org), and that you not implement browser-specific features at all. Although optimizing your pages for a single browser might make them look cool on that browser, not everybody is using that particular browser. This means that your browser-specific HTML tags or plug-ins may make it harder for others (who do not use your preferred browser) to visit your Web site.

HTTP_REFERER

This variable is set to the Uniform Resource Identifier (URI) that forwarded the request to the CGI program being called. By using this variable, you can tell whether a request is coming from a link on one of your Web pages or from a remote URI. Note that the misspelling of the variable name is unfortunate and often confuses CGI developers who spell it correctly in their applications and scripts just to discover that they do not work. So, if you plan to use this variable, spell it as it is stated here.

HTTP_CONNECTION

The HTTP_CONNECTION variable is set to the type of connection being used by the client and the server. For example:

```
HTTP_CONNECTION = Keep-Alive
```

This states that the client is capable of handling persistent connections using Keep-Alive and currently using it.

SERVER_PORT

The value of the SERVER_PORT variable tells a CGI program which server port is currently being used to access the program. A sample of this is:

```
SERVER_PORT = 80
```

If a CGI program creates URLs that point back to the server, it might be useful to include the port address, which is found as the value of this variable in the URL.

REMOTE_HOST

The REMOTE_HOST variable tells a CGI program about the IP address or IP name of the client, as follows:

```
REMOTE_HOST = dsl-666.isp24by7.net
```

Note that if the Apache server is compiled with the MINIMAL_DNS option, this variable is not set.

REMOTE_PORT

This port number is used in the client-side of the socket connection:

```
REMOTE_PORT = 1163
```

I have not yet seen any use for this variable.

REMOTE_ADDR

The REMOTE_ADDR variable is the IP address of the client system:

```
REMOTE_ADDR = 192.168.1.100
```

Note that if the client is behind a firewall or a proxy server, the IP address stored in this variable may not be the IP address of the client system.

REMOTE_USER

The REMOTE_USER variable will be set only when access to the CGI program requires HTTP basic authentication. The username used in the basic authentication is stored in this variable for the CGI program. The CGI program, however, will have no way of identifying the password used to access it. If this variable is set to a username, the CGI program can safely assume that the user supplied the appropriate password to access it.

SERVER_PROTOCOL

SERVER_PROTOCOL is the protocol and version number the client used to send the request for the CGI program:

```
SERVER_PROTOCOL = HTTP/1.1
```

REQUEST_METHOD

The REQUEST_METHOD variable is set to the HTTP request method used by the client to request the CGI program. The typical values are: GET, POST, and HEAD.

```
REQUEST_METHOD=GET
```

The input is stored in the QUERY_STRING variable when the request method is GET. When the method is POST, the input is stored in the STDIN of the CGI program.

REQUEST_URI

The REQUEST_URI variable is set to the URI of the request.

```
REQUEST_URI = /cgi-bin/printenv2
```

REMOTE_IDENT

REMOTE_IDENT will only be set if the IdentityCheck directive is set. This variable stores the user identification information returned by the remote identd (identification daemon).Because many systems do not run this type of daemon process, REMOTE_IDENT should not be considered a reliable means for identifying users. I recommend using this variable in an intranet or an extranet environment in which you or your organization is running an identd server.

AUTH_TYPE

If a CGI program is stored in a section of the Web site where authentication is required to gain access, this variable is set to specify the authentication method used.

CONTENT_TYPE

This variable specifies the MIME type of any data attached to the request header. For example:

```
CONTENT_TYPE = application/x-www-form-urlencoded
```

When using HTML form and the POST request method, you can specify the content type in the HTML form using the TYPE attribute of the <FORM> tag, as follows:

```
<FORM ACTION="/cgi-bin/search.cgi"
      METHOD="POST"
      TYPE= "application/x-www-form-urlencoded">
```

CONTENT_LENGTH

When HTTP POST request method is used, Apache stores input data (attached to the request) in the STDIN of the CGI program. The server does not, however, insert an End-of-File (EOF) marker in the STDIN. Instead, it sets the total byte count as the value of this variable. For example, if

```
CONTENT_LENGTH = 21
```

then the CGI program in question should read 21 bytes of data from its STDIN.

SCRIPT_NAME

SCRIPT_NAME is the URI of the requested CGI program:

```
SCRIPT_NAME = /cgi-bin/search.cgi
```

SCRIPT_FILENAME

SCRIPT_FILENAME is the physical, fully qualified pathname of the requested CGI program:

```
SCRIPT_FILENAME = /www/kabir/public/cgi-bin/search.cgi
```

QUERY_STRING

If a Web client such as a Web browser uses the HTTP GET request method and provides input data after a question mark (?), the data is stored as the value of this variable. For example, a request for the following CGI program:

```
http://apache.domain.com/cgi-bin/search.cgi?key1=value1&key2=value2
```

will make Apache set:

```
QUERY_STRING = key1=value1&key2=value2
```

which the CGI program /cgi-bin/search.cgi can read and decode before use.

PATH_INFO

If input data for a CGI program is part of the URI, the extra path (which is really some data for the program being called) is stored as the value of the variable. For example:

```
http://apache.domain.com/cgi-bin/search.cgi/argument1/argument2
```

will have Apache set:

```
PATH_INFO = /argument1/argument2
```

> **Note**   `PATH_INFO` **will not have anything that is part of the query string. In other words, if the URI includes a query string after a ?, this part of the data will be stored in the** `QUERY_STRING` **variable. For example:**
>
> ```
> http://apache.domain.com/cgi-
> bin/search.cgi/CA/95825?book=apache&author=kabir
> ```
>
> **will have Apache set the following variables:**
>
> ```
> PATH_INFO = /CA/95825
> QUERY_STRING= book=apache&author=kabir
> ```

PATH_TRANSLATED

This is the absolute path of the requested file. For example, when a Web client such as a Web browser requests `http://server/cgi-bin/script.cgi` the actual path of the script can be `path_to_cgi_alias/script.cgi`.

Configuring Apache for CGI

This section discusses how to configure Apache to process CGI requests. The configuration process includes telling Apache where you store your CGI programs, setting up CGI handlers for specific file extensions, and indicating which file extensions should be considered CGI programs. It is a good idea to keep your CGI programs in one central directory. This permits better control of your CGI programs. Keeping CGI programs scattered all over the Web space might make such a Web site unmanageable, and it could also create security holes that would be hard to track.

Aliasing your CGI program directory

Making a central CGI program directory is the first step in setting up a secured CGI environment. It is best to keep this central CGI program directory outside of your `DocumentRoot` directory so that CGI programs cannot be accessed directly by a Web client such as a Web browser. Why? Well, when it comes to CGI programs, you want to provide as little information as possible to the outside world. This will ensure better security for your site(s). The less a hacker knows about where your CGI programs are physically located, the less harm that person can do.

First you need to create a directory outside of your `DocumentRoot` directory. For example, if `/www/mycompany/public/htdocs` is the `DocumentRoot` directory of a Web site, then `/www/mycompany/public/cgi-bin` is a good candidate for the CGI program directory. To create the alias for your CGI program directory, you can use the `ScriptAlias` directive.

If you are setting up CGI support for the primary Web server, edit the `httpd.conf` file and insert a `ScriptAlias` line with the following syntax:

```
ScriptAlias  /alias/  "/fully/qualified/path/to/cgi/scripts/dir/"
```

For example:

```
ScriptAlias /cgi-bin/ "/www/mycompany/public/cgi-bin/"
```

If you are setting up CGI support for a virtual site, add a `ScriptAlias` line in the `<VirtualHost . . . >` container that defines the virtual host. For example:

```
NameVirtualHost 192.168.1.100

<VirtualHost 192.168.1.100>

    ServerName blackhole.domain.com
    DocumentRoot "/www/blackhole/public/htdocs"
    ScriptAlias /apps/ "/www/blackhole/public/cgi-bin/"

</VirtualHost>
```

Here the `/apps/` alias is used to create a CGI program directory alias. If there is a CGI program called `feedback.cgi` in the `/www/blackhole/public/cgi-bin` directory, it can only be accessed via the following URL:

```
http://blackhole.domain.com/apps/feedback.cgi
```

After you set up the `ScriptAlias` directive, make sure that the directory permission permits Apache to read and execute files found in the directory.

The directory pointed to by `ScriptAlias` should have very strict permission settings. No one but the CGI program developer or the server administrator should have full (read, write, and execute) permission for the directory. You can define multiple CGI program directory aliases so that the `ScriptAlias` specified directory is not browseable (by default) for security reasons.

When requested, Apache will attempt to run any executable (file permission-wise) file found in the `ScriptAlias`ed directory. For example:

```
http://blackhole.domain.com/apps/foo.cgi
http://blackhole.domain.com/apps/foo.pl
http://blackhole.domain.com/apps/foo.bak
http://blackhole.domain.com/apps/foo.dat
```

All of the above URL requests will prompt Apache to attempt running the various `foo` files.

Choosing specific CGI file extensions

I am not particularly fond of the idea that any file in the ScriptAlias-specified directory can be run as a CGI program. I prefer a solution that enables me to restrict the CGI program names such that only files with certain extensions are treated like CGI programs. The following section discusses how you can implement this using an Apache Handler found in mod_cgi module and contains a sample configuration where I enable a select set of file extensions to be treated as CGI programs by using the AddHandler handler.

For this example, assume that the Apache server name is www.domain.com, and that it's DocumentRoot directory is set to /www/mysite/public/htdocs; the CGI program directory is /www/nitec/public/cgi-bin. Notice that the CGI program directory is kept outside of the DocumentRoot-specified directory intentionally. This ensures that the directory cannot be browsed by anyone, as Apache can only see it via the alias.

Follow these steps to set up Apache to run CGI scripts with given extension(s) to run from a directory:

1. Disable any existing ScriptAlias directive by either removing it completely from the httpd.conf, or turning it into a comment line by inserting a number sign (#) as the first character in that line.

2. Create an alias for CGI program directory. There is no way to access the CGI program directory without an alias (or a symbolic link), as it resides outside the document tree. You can define an alias using the Alias directive, which has the following syntax:

   ```
   Alias /alias/ "/path/to/cgi/dir/outside/doc/root/"
   ```

   Following this syntax, the needed Alias directive looks like the following:

   ```
   Alias /cgi-bin/ "/www/mysite/public/cgi-bin/"
   ```

3. Instruct Apache to execute CGI programs from this directory by defining a <Directory > container for this special directory. The directory container definition that is needed to make it all happen (that is, to turn the directory into a CGI program directory) is:

   ```
   <Directory "/path/to/cgi/dir/outside/doc/root">
       Options ExecCGI -Indexes
       AddHandler cgi-script extension-list
   </Directory>
   ```

   The Options directive sets two options for the /path/to/cgi/dir/outside/doc/root directory. First, the ExecCGI option is set, which tells Apache to permit CGI program execution from within this directory. Second, the -Indexes option tells Apache to disallow directory listing since because it is not a good idea to allow visitors to see the contents of your CGI script directory. Next the AddHandler directive sets the cgi-script handler for a list of file extensions found in this directory. Any file with the named extensions in the list is treated as a CGI program. When a Web client makes a request for such a file, the program is run and output is returned to the Web client. The actual directives for our current example look as follows:

```
<Directory "/www/mysite/public/cgi-bin">
    Options ExecCGI -Indexes
    AddHandler cgi-script .cgi .pl
</Directory>
```

Here, you have enabled .cgi and .pl as CGI program extensions and, therefore, when requests, such as these

```
http://www.domain.com/cgi-bin/anything.cgi
http://www.domain.com/cgi-bin/anything.pl
```

are made, Apache will attempt to execute these files as CGI programs. Of course, if these files are not really executables or non-existent, Apache will display and log error messages.

The CGI program directory permission settings mentioned earlier still apply to this configuration. The same configuration also applies to virtual host sites. For example, in the following example the /cgi-bin/ alias for www.client01.com is set up to execute CGI programs in /www/client01/public/cgi-bin directory:

```
<VirtualHost 192.168.2.100>

    ServerName www.client01.com
    DocumentRoot "/www/client01/public/htdocs"

    CustomLog logs/www.client01.com.access.log
    ErrorLog  logs/www.client01.com.errors.log

    Alias /cgi-bin/ "/www/client01/public/cgi-bin/"

    <Directory "/www/client01/public/cgi-bin">
        Options ExecCGI -Indexes
        AddHandler cgi-script .cgi .pl
    </Directory>

</VirtualHost>
```

Here the /cgi-bin/ alias for www.client01.com is set up to execute CGI programs in /www/client01/public/cgi-bin directory.

Enabling cgi-bin access for your users

Many Internet Service Providers (ISP) offer Web site space with user accounts. These Web sites usually have URLs, such as:

```
http://www.isp.net/~username
```

These sites often get requests for cgi-bin access from the users via their clients (browsers). The term *cgi-bin access* is a general one that is used to indicate CGI facility on a Web server. Traditionally, the CGI program directory has been aliased as /cgi-bin/, hence, this term was created. The other common term that became very popular is *home page,* which refers to the top-level index page of a Web directory of a user.

The following sections discuss two ways to providing cgi-bin access for users on an Apache Web server. You only need to implement any one of these methods.

Directory or DirectoryMatch containers

When the UserDir directive is set to a directory name, Apache considers it as the top-level directory for a user Web site, for example:

```
ServerName www.domain.com
UserDir public_html
```

Now when a request for http://www.*domain*.com/~*username* comes, Apache locates the named user's home directory (usually by checking the /etc/passwd file on Unix systems), and then appends the UserDir-specified directory to create the pathname for the top-level user Web directory. For example, the URL

```
http://www.domain.com/~joe
```

makes Apache look for /home/joe/public_html (assuming /home/joe is joe's home directory). If the directory exists, the index page for that directory will be sent to the requesting client.

One way to add CGI support for each user is to add the following configuration in the httpd.conf file:

```
<Directory ~ "/home/[a-z]+/public_html/cgi-bin">
    Options ExecCGI
    AddHandler cgi-script .cgi .pl
</Directory>
```

Or you can use this configuration:

```
<DirectoryMatch "/home/[a-z]+/public_html/cgi-bin">
    Options ExecCGI
    AddHandler cgi-script .cgi .pl
</DirectoryMatch>
```

In both methods, Apache translates http://www.*yourcompany*.com/~*username*/cgi-bin/ requests to /home/*username*/public_html/cgi-bin/ and permits any CGI program with the proper extension (.cgi or .pl) to execute.

Note   All usernames must be comprised of all lowercase characters for this to work. If you have usernames that are alphanumeric, you have to use a different regular expression. For example, if you have user names such as steve01 or steve02, you need to change the [a-z]+ character set to include numbers using [a-z0-9]+, or if you also allow upper case user names, than you use [a-zA-Z0-9]+ as the regular expression.

ScriptAliasMatch

By using ScriptAliasMatch directive, you can support CGI program directories for each user. For example:

```
ScriptAliasMatch ^~([a-z]+)/cgi-bin/(.*)
/home/$1/public_html/cgi-bin/$2
```

matches *username* to back reference variable $1, where $1 is equal to *~username* and where *username* is a lower case string, such as joe or steven, and then Apache matches everything followed by /cgi-bin/ to back reference variable $2. Then, Apache uses $1 and $2 variables to create the actual CGI program path. For example:

```
http://www.domain.com/~joe/cgi-bin/search.cgi?author=kabir
```

Here ([a-z]+) will map one or more lowercase characters following the tilde mark (~) to $1. In other words, this regular expression enables us to capture everything between the tilde (~) and the trailing forward slash (/) after the username. So, $1 is set to joe for the above example. Note that the ^ ensures that the directive is only applied to URLSs that starts with ~, as shown in the above example.

The next regular expression in the directive is (.*), which maps everything following the /cgi-bin/ to $2. So, $2 is set to search.cgi?author=kabir.

Now Apache can create the physical path of the CGI program directory by using:

```
/home/$1/public_html/cgi-bin/$2
```

This regular expression results in the following path for the previous example:

```
/home/joe/public_html/cgi-bin/search.cgi?author=kabir
```

Because this is where the CGI program search.cgi is kept, it executes and returns output to the Web client.

If you are not fond of having the CGI program directory under public_html (that is, the UserDir-specified directory), you can keep it outside of that directory by removing the public_html part of the expression as follows:

```
ScriptAliasMatch ^~([a-z]+)/cgi-bin/(.*)  /home/$1/cgi-bin/$2
```

This will map the following example URL request:

```
http://www.domain.com/~joe/cgi-bin/search.cgi?author=kabir
```

to the following physical file:

```
/home/joe/cgi-bin/search.cgi?author=kabir
```

Of course, if you are not fond of keeping a user subdirectory world-readable (that is, `public_html`), you can remedy this by creating a Web partition (or a directory) for your users and giving them individual directories to host their home pages. Here is an example:

```
ScriptAliasMatch ^~([a-z]+)/cgi-bin/(.*)   /www/$1/cgi-bin/$2
```

This matches requests to /www/*username*/cgi-bin/*scriptname* and since because this directory is not in the user's home directory (/home/*username*), you might be able to exercise better control over it as a system administrator.

Creating new CGI extensions by using AddType

If you want to create new CGI program extensions in a particular directory, you can also use the `.htaccess` (or the file specified by the `AccessFileName` directive).

Before you can add new extensions using the per-directory access control file (`.htaccess`), you have to create a `<Directory>` container as follows:

```
<Directory "/path/to/your/directory">
    Options ExecCGI -Indexes
    AllowOverride FileInfo
</Directory>
```

The first directive inside the directory container tells Apache that you want to enable CGI program execution in this directory and disables the directory-listing feature for security. The second directive tells Apache to enable the `FileInfo` feature in the per-directory access control file (`.htaccess`). This feature enables you to use the `AddType` directive in the per-directory access control file.

To add a new CGI program extension (`.wizard`), all you need to do is create an `.htaccess` (or whatever you specified in `AccessFileName` directive) file in the directory with the following:

```
AddType application/x-httpd-cgi .wizard
```

Then, rename an existing CGI program in that directory to have the `.wizard` extension, and request it via your browser. Make sure all of the file permission settings for the directory and the CGI programs are set to read and execute by Apache.

Running CGI Programs

Chances are that if you are an Apache administrator, you will have to set up CGI programs, or you may even know how to write them. In this section, I discuss the basics for creating very simple CGI programs. Because this is a not a CGI programming book, I do not provide in-depth coverage of CGI programming. My focus is on revealing things about CGI programs that will help an Apache administrator manage his or her CGI-capable Web sites better.

Many of the examples in this section use Perl. If you do not have Perl on your system, you can obtain the source, or possibly the binaries, from `www.perl.com`. Whenever possible, it is good to compile binaries for a system rather than trusting binaries that have been created by someone else.

Writing CGI Scripts in Perl

CGI scripting is synonymous to Perl scripting; in my humble opinion, Perl is the king of all scripting languages, and it was Perl that popularized CGI scripting became widely popular due to Perl. As a yet another Perl hacker, I have written Perl-based CGI scripts since 1995, and I still continue to use Perl for small- to mid -range Web solutions. Because this is a not a Perl programming book, I do not cover how to write Perl scripts in general. Instead, I will discuss how you can write CGI scripts in Perl. If you are not familiar with Perl, I recommend that you read a Perl programming book as soon as possible.

When writing CGI scripts in Perl, the following set of guidelines or programming style should be followed. They are as follows:

✦ **Separate contents and logic — keep contents out of scripts.** Use HTML or XML templates to ensure that the interface aspect of your CGI script is not in the scripts themselves. This will make ensure that a nonprogrammer user, such as a graphics or HTML expert, can change the interface easily.

✦ **Use configuration files — never hardcode customizable information in a script.** Use a configuration file to read in the information. This will allow your scripts to be more flexible.

✦ **Normalize user data — when collecting data from users for future use, make sure you normalize the data before storing in files or database.** For example, if you collect e-mail addresses from your visitors, it would be a good idea to normalize each e-mail address in a preferred case (upper or lower) and fix user omissions and data entry errors. I have seen make instances of where AOL users writing their e-mail addresses in Web forms without the .com or putting extra spaces between the @ and the name or the host name. I have also seen thousands of instances where users enter their name in either upper case or lower case. Just think of the impression it will leave on them when you customize a newsletter using an un-normalized name (which the user himself entered in your Web form) or how many bounces you will get when your mailing list system finds thousands of "@AOL" or "user @ aol" type of data errors.

✦ **Sanity check user data — CGI scripts are often the target of many security attacks.** If your CGI script accepts user input make sure you validate user data before making use of it.

Before you start reinventing the wheel, check the Comprehensive Perl Archive Network (CPAN) site at `http://cpan.perl.com` for existing Perl modules that you can use to solve your current problem or to reduce your development efforts by reusing existing CPAN modules. In this section, I use many CPAN modules for building CGI scripts. Whenever you see a module listed in any of the scripts discussed here, you can add the module to your system using the CPAN module that is shipped with standard Perl.

Apache for Windows users should consult Perl documentation for how to use CPAN modules because it differs from the standard approach discussed here. See also the Windows-specific section of this book for details.

For example, say that you see a script list a module called `HTML::Template` and would like to install this module so that you can run the script that uses it. To install the CPAN module, run `perl -MCPAN -e shell` from the command prompt as root.

If you are running the `perl -MCPAN -e` shell command for the first time you will be asked to configure the current CPAN.pm module, which is used to install other CPAN modules. Simply follow the instructions and prompts to configure the CPAN.pm module and then proceed to the discussion below.

After you are at the CPAN prompt, run the `install HTML::Template` command to install the module. The CPAN module will install this module for you. If it complains about a dependency, you might have to install some other modules before you can install a module that depends on other CPAN modules. After you're done, run `quit` from the CPAN prompt to return to shell.

If you do not want to run the interactive CPAN shell using `perl -MCPAN -e` **shell** to install a module, you can run `perl -MCPAN -e 'CPAN::Shell->install (modulename)'` **instead. For example,** `perl -MCPAN -e shell 'CPAN:: Shell->install(HTML::Template)'` **will install the HTML::Template module. You can also run this command from a shell script.**

Analyzing a simple CGI script

CGI scripts are typically used to take user input and perform one or more operations based on the input and return results in a HTML page. In this section I show you how to create a simple script to get started and to understand CGI scripting concepts. The script that we will develop here will perform a single task: it will take a user's full name, format it properly, and return a personalized greeting message. Listing 12-2 shows `greetings.pl` script that does exactly that.

Listing 12-2: **greetings.pl**

```perl
#!/usr/bin/perl
#
#
#    Name: greetings.pl
#
#    Purpose:
#
#    Show a greeting message
#
################################################################

use strict;
use CGI;


#
# Get user data
#
my $query = new CGI;
my $name = $query->param('name');


#
# Process data
#
$name       = lc($name);
my @strArray = ();

foreach my $str (split(/ /,$name)) {
   push(@strArray, ucfirst($str));
}

my $formattedName = join(' ', @strArray);

#
# Display results
#
print $query->header;
print $query->start_html('Greetings');
print $query->p( 'Hello ' . $formattedName . ',');
print $query->p( 'Thanks for coming to our Web site.');
print $query->end_html;

#
# Terminate
#
exit 0;
```

Now, lets take a close look at this script. The very first line is a special line:

```
#!/usr/bin/perl
```

This line tells the system to run Perl whenever executing this script. If you have installed Perl in a non-standard directory, then you must modify this line accordingly. For example, if you installed Perl in /usr/local/bin/perl, then you must change this line to reflect that. All the lines (other than the very first one) that start with a '#' sign are a commented out and ignored by Perl.

The next code segment is:

```
use strict;
use CGI;
```

The use strict is a Perl pragma (think of pragma as a directive), which tells Perl to evaluate the script for unsafe programming habits. The next line tells Perl to load a popular module that is now part of the standard Perl distribution, module called CGI.pm, which makes writing CGI programs very easy. This modules handles all the underlying details of getting input data that are passed onto the script via STDIN by the Apache server, parsing and decoding input fields, providing methods for displaying content headers, creating HTML contents, and so on. It is simply the super -CGI module available to you. No one should write CGI scripts in Perl without the CGI.pm module. The only exception to that rule is if you have a resource constraint and don't want to load a large module each time a script is called. But in most cases, this is not an issue, especially since because I do not recommend CGI solutions for high -volume Web sites.

The next code segment is:

```
my $query = new CGI;
my $name = $query->param('name');
```

Here a new CGI object called $query is created and the param() method of the $query CGI object is called to get the value for the user input 'name'. The value for this input is stored in $name variable. For example, if the greetings.pl script is called as follows:

```
http://www.domain.com/cgi-bin/greetings.pl?name=kabir
```

Then the CGI object will receive the name=kabir as a user input from the Apache server and the script will be able to access the value ('kabir') via $query-> param('name') method call, as it does in this script.

The next code segment is the meat of the script; it is the processing block as shown below:

```
$name      = lc($name);
my @strArray = ();

foreach my $str (split(/ /,$name)) {
```

```
        push(@strArray, ucfirst($str));
    }

    my $formattedName = join(' ', @strArray);
```

Here the $name variable is processed. The first line uses Perl's built-in lc() function, which lowercases a given string. Because lc() is given the $name string as the parameter, it returns a lowercase value of the name, which we store back in the name variable $name. We lowercase the name so that we can uppercase only the first letter of each name. Now a user named Carol Godsave might enter many different combinations of her name. For example:

```
Carol Godsave
CAROL GODSAVE
carol godsave
carol GODSAVE
cAROL godSave
carol GoDsAvE
```

As you can see the user can enter one of these or many other combinations of letters to represent her name. However, we would want to display "Carol Godsave" since because that's the proper formatting for her name. So our processing code block uses the following algorithm:

1. Lower case the name. This effectively turns whatever Carol entered for her name into 'carol godsave'.

2. Split each word separated by a space character. This gives us are 'carol' and 'godsave'.

3. Uppercase only the first letter of each part. This gives us 'Carol' and 'Godsave'.

4. Put together the parts by separating them with a space character. This returns 'Carol Godsave', which is exactly what we want.

In this code segment we use an array called @strArray, which we initialize to empty the list. Then a foreach loop is used to cycle through the each part of the name that is split using the split() function found in Perl. The split() is called with two parameters: separator, which in this case is a white space character written in regular expression format / /, and the string that needs to be separated, which in this case is $name. The split() function returns the separated parts in an array. So, effectively, in Carol's case the foreach loop looks like:

```
foreach my $str ('carol' 'godsave') {
    push(@strArray, ucfirst($str));
}
```

The loop cycles through each part and uppercases only the first character of each part using the built-in ucfirst() function call. When ucfirst() is given a string parameter, it uppercases only the first character and returns the modified string. For example ucfirst('carol') will return 'Carol'; similarly, ucfirst('godsave') returns 'Godsave'. Each of the modified name parts is stored in an array called @strArray. For example, after processing Carol's name, the @strArray is array = ('Carol', 'Godsave'). Finally, we join each part of the name in a new variable called $formattedName to form the complete name. The built-in join() function is used to join each element of the @strArray by a white space character in the join(' ', @strArray) call. Now we have a formatted name in $formattedName variable and simply need to display it.

The display code segment is:

```
print $query->header;
print $query->start_html('Greetings');
print $query->p( 'Hello ' . $formattedName . ',');
print $query->p( 'Thanks for coming to our Web site.');
print $query->end_html;
```

The very first line in this segment sets the content header. A Content-Type header is required. To determine how to display the contents sent by the server, the client uses this header. Because a CGI script generates the contents, it must tell the server what type of contents it is passing to the server for delivery to the client. The CGI module provides a method called header(), which creates the appropriate Content-Type header. For example, $query->header; returns Content-Type: text/html; charset=ISO-8859-1. When the header() is called without a specific type parameter, it defaults to text/html Content-Type. However, if your script needed to output a different type, say text/plain, you can use the header(-type => 'text/plain') parameter instead. For example:

```
#!/usr/bin/perl

use CGI;

my $query = new CGI;

print $query->header(-type=>'image/gif');

open(GIF, "/tmp/weather.gif");
while(<GIF>){   print; }
close(GIF);
```

This little script displays a GIF file called /tmp/weather.gif using the Content-Type: image/gif header. Now back to the greetings.pl script. After displaying the default content header, the script users CGI module's HTML methods, such as start_html(), p(), and end_html(), to create the HTML content. For example, say that Carol enters the following URL:

```
http://server/cgi-bin/greetings.pl?name=carol godsave
```

Her Web browser will automatically encode the space between carol and godsave into %20 (a hex number 20, which is equivalent to decimal 32, which is the ASCII space character). A good thing about a CGI module is that it takes cares of decoding this and gives the script 'carol godsave' as the name. The script displays a page as shown in Figure 12-4.

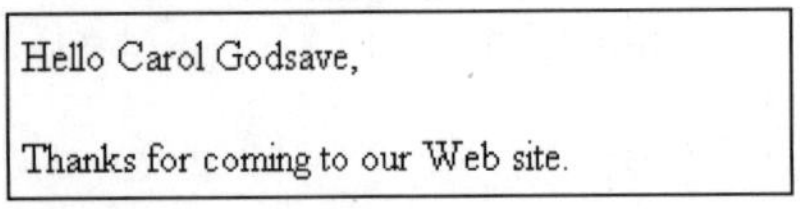

```
Hello Carol Godsave,

Thanks for coming to our Web site.
```

Figure 12-4: Output of greetings.pl script.

The p() method creates an HTML paragraph tag pair, which is used to sandwich the parameter it receives. For example, the first p() call:

```
print $query->p( 'Hello ' . $formattedName . ',');
```

translates into:

```
<p>Hello Carol Godsave,</p>
```

The entire output document that is sent to the Web browser looks like this:

```
<?xml version="1.0" encoding="utf-8"?>
<!DOCTYPE html
         PUBLIC "-//W3C//DTD XHTML Basic 1.0//EN"
         "http://www.w3.org/TR/xhtml-basic/xhtml-basic10.dtd">

<html xmlns="http://www.w3.org/1999/xhtml"
      lang="en-US">

<head>
  <title>Greetings</title>
</head>
<body>

<p>Hello Carol Godsave,</p>
<p>Thanks for coming to our Web site.</p>

</body></html>
```

The start_html() method produces the following contents:

```
<?xml version="1.0" encoding="utf-8"?>
<!DOCTYPE html
         PUBLIC "-//W3C//DTD XHTML Basic 1.0//EN"
         "http://www.w3.org/TR/xhtml-basic/xhtml-basic10.dtd">

<html xmlns="http://www.w3.org/1999/xhtml"
      lang="en-US">

<head>
```

```
    <title>Greetings</title>
  </head>
  <body>
```

Notice the title 'Greetings' that was passed onto the method. The two p()
methods produces the following:

```
  <p>Hello Carol Godsave,</p>
  <p>Thanks for coming to our Web site.</p>
```

And finally, the end_html() method produces the following:

```
  </body></html>
```

which ends the HTML document.

Careful readers will notice that we have violated the first CGI programming style
guide, which states that we should separate contents and logic. This little script
has HTML inside the script, which makes it harder to modify for a non-programmer.
But this script was meant as a mere exercise. In the following section, I look at a
useful, production-grade script that conforms to the style guidelines.

Creating a basic Web form processor

Most common CGI scripts are used as the back-end of a Web form. Virtually, every
Web site has a Web form that takes user input and stores it in a file or database. In
the following section, I present a very customizable CGI script that can work with
virtually any single-page Web form.

Features of a basic Web form processing CGI script

Say that your Web site will have one or more Web forms that need to collect data
from Web visitors to store in files or databases. One CGI script-based solution,
which has the following features:

✦ **Supports multiple Web forms:** A single script will work for multiple, single -
  page Web forms. A single -page Web form asks all its questions in a page.
  There are times when you will be asked to build a multi-page Web form,
  which falls into the category of custom form -processing applications.
  Such form-processing applications usually use custom business logic to
  display multiple forms and are beyond the scope of this book. My personal
  recommendation, based on years of Web development, is to avoid multipage
  Web forms because people often become discouraged when asked to answer
  a long series of questions. Also, when designing a single-page Web form, do
  not ask too many questions. Keeping the data collection to a minimum is good
  practice when generating new leads. Experience tells me that new prospects
  and leads are turned off by a huge form or by a multi-page form session, and
  often decide to forget about doing business with the site all together.

✦ **Centralized configuration for all Web forms:** The script uses a configuration file, which supports multiple Web forms. Each Web form configuration can be separately stored in this standard configuration file, which means you can centralize your form configuration information—a very good thing for a busy system administrator.

✦ **Comma Separated Value (CSV) files for data storage:** The script allows you to save data in CSV files. Each form can have its own CSV file. You can also specify the order of fields and which fields you want to store.

To make learning about this CGI script simpler and more realistic, I will assume that you have a User Registration Web form called `register.html` as shown in Listing 12-3.

Listing 12-3: register.html

```
<html>

<body bgcolor="white">

<font face="Arial" size=+1>User Registration Form</font><br>

<p>
<form action="/cgi-bin/formwizard.pl" method="POST">

<table border=0
        cellpadding=3
        cellspacing=0
        bgcolor="#000000">
<tr>
<td>

<table border=0
        cellpadding=5
        cellspacing=5
        bgcolor="#abcdef">

<tr>
<td> Name </td>
<td> <input name="name" type=text size=30 maxsize=50> </td>
</tr>

<tr>
<td> Email </td>
<td> <input name="email" type=text size=30 maxsize=50> </td>
</tr>


<tr>
<td> Zipcode</td>
<td> <input name="zipcode" type=text size=30 maxsize=50> </td>
```

```
</tr>

<tr>
<td> Can we send you junk mail?</td>
<td>
<input type=radio name="opt-in" value="yes">Yes, Please!
<input type=radio name="opt-in" value="no">No, Never!
</td>
</tr>

<tr>
<td align=center> <input type=submit value="Register Me"</td>
<td align=center> <input type=reset> </td>
</tr>

</table>

</td>
</tr>
</table>
</form>
<p>

</html>
```

This Web form looks as shown in Figure 12-5.

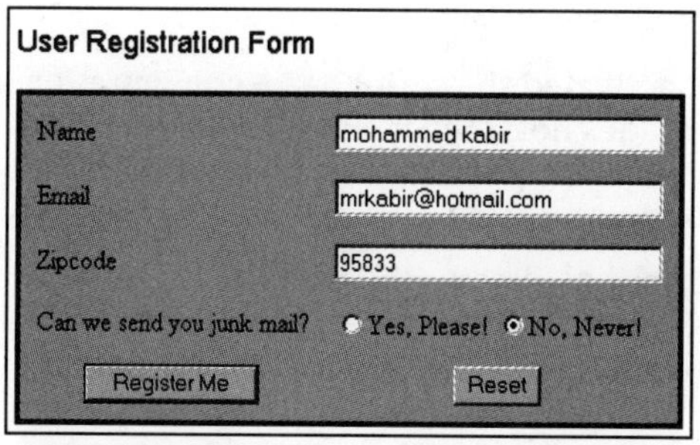

User Registration Form

Name	mohammed kabir
Email	mrkabir@hotmail.com
Zipcode	95833
Can we send you junk mail?	○ Yes, Please! ● No, Never!
Register Me	Reset

Figure 12-5: The `register.html` form in a Web browser.

This example Web form has four data fields: name, email, zipcode and an opt-in question. This is a typical user registration form except that most sites will not ask the opt-in question as (honestly) posed in this form. When a user fills out this form, the data has to be stored in a file, and the user is displayed a thank you message or taken to a new page. For example, when the above form is filled out, it can show a thank you message as shown in Figure 12-6.

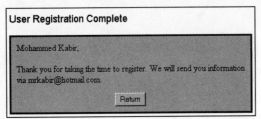

Figure 12-6: Thank you message for filling out `register.html`.

Developing a Web form processor CGI script in Perl

Now let's develop a CGI script in Perl that enables you to create a Web form-processing solution as shown in the example in the last section. Figure 12-7 shows the flow diagram of such a CGI solution.

When this script is called as the form action in `register.html`, as shown here:

```
<form action="/cgi-bin/formwizard.pl" method="POST">
```

This script performs the following tasks:

1. Loads all external standard (i.e. part of standard Perl distribution) and other CPAN modules

2. Loads the central configuration file, which should have a configuration specific to the Web form that posted data to it.

3. Creates a CGI object that enables it to retrieve posted data and to access other information supplied by the Web server.

4. Determines if the Web form that activated the script has a configuration in the central configuration file. If it does not, then it simply displays an error message stating that this form cannot be processed by this script. If it does have a configuration, it starts form processing.

5. As the first processing step, the script validates the user data. This step involves checking data validity based on the requirements stated in the configuration file and performing sanity checks on data fields supplied by the user.

6. If the validation step returns no errors, the data is stored in a data file. On the other hand, if the data validation step fails because of user error(s), then an error message specific to the type of error(s) is displayed and processing is aborted.

7. If the previous step is successful, the script displays a thank you message or redirects the user to another URL and terminates.

On the CD-ROM   The formwizard.pl script is included in the CDROM.

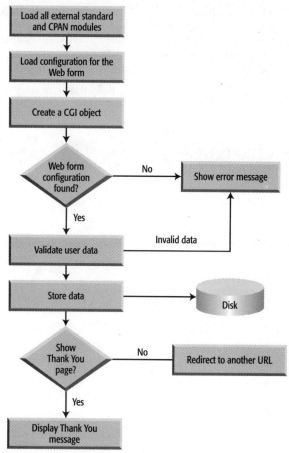

Figure 12-7: CGI Web form-processing diagram.

Looking at formwizard.pl

The formwizard.pl script implements this flow diagram. In the formwizard.ini configuration file, the register.html fields have these restrictions:

✦ The name field is required and set to be from 3 to 50 characters in length. The field value must be composed of characters ranging from a- to z and the period. If the field value passes the length and pattern tests, it is stored as a string in which each word starts with a capital letter.

✦ The email field is also required and it must be between 6 and 100 characters. Acceptable characters for an e-mail address are a to z, 0 to 9, dash (-), underscore (_), period. and the AT (@) symbol. The email pattern test is applied to the value of this field and if all (length, character set, and pattern) tests are passed by the value, it is stored in lowercase format.

✦ The `zipcode` field is treated as an optional number field, which must pass the `us_zipcode` pattern test if the user enters a value. The `us_zipcode` pattern test simply checks whether the entered number is either a five-digit number or a five-digit number with a four-digit number to form zip codes such as 95825-1234. The only characters allowed are 0 to 9 and the dash.

✦ Finally, the `opt-in` field is considered a required text field that can only have a value of `'yes'` or `'no'`.

Listing 12-4: **formwizard.ini Configuration File**

```
# -----------------------------------------------------------------
#
# Web Form Configuration for *** register.html *** form
#
# -----------------------------------------------------------------


[register.html]
template_dir = /www/asb2/ch12/forms/register


# -----------------------------------------------------------------
# After the form is processed, the script must acknowledge to
# the user that the system received the data. This is done
# using a "Thank You" (called thankyou hereafter)
# message.
#
# Set the name of the thank you template here
# -----------------------------------------------------------------
thankyou_template = thanks.html


# -----------------------------------------------------------------
# If you wish to redirect the user to another URL,
# set the URL here. Do not set this to any URL
# if you wish to show the thankyou message instead
#
# If the URL is set, it is always used instead of
# showing the thankyou message.
# -----------------------------------------------------------------
thankyou_redirect_url = /asb2/ch12/forms/feedback.html


# -----------------------------------------------------------------
# The script will either show the thankyou message or
# redirect the user to another URL.
# If you wish to send data to the redirect URL via GET method
# set this to 'yes'; otherwise, set it to 'no'.
# -----------------------------------------------------------------
send_data_on_redirect = no


# -----------------------------------------------------------------
# Having a specific list of form fields
# ensures that we only use what we need.
# We will ignore any additional field(s)
```

```
# a bad guy might submit.
# ----------------------------------------------------------------
form_field_info=<<FORM_FIELDS
name,text,required,max_chars=50,min_chars=3,case=ucfirst,exclude_regex=[^a-z
.],pattern=none
email,text,required,max=100,min=6,case=lowerall,exclude_regex=[^a-z0-9-
_.\@],pattern=email
zipcode,number,optional,pattern=us_zipcode,exclude_regex=[^0-9-]
opt-in,text,required,case=lower,pattern=none,valid_data=yes|no
FORM_FIELDS

# ----------------------------------------------------------------
# When data entry error(s) occur, a pop-up message is displayed.
# The message lists the field(s) that are missing or invalid.
#
# You can personalize the ACTION of the message. In other words,
# enter text tells the user to
# make corrections and resubmit.
# ----------------------------------------------------------------
data_error_msg = Please enter missing data and resubmit.

# ----------------------------------------------------------------
#
# Specify the
data_directory=/tmp
data_filename=registration.csv
data_field_separator=,
data_field_order=email,name,zipcode,opt-in
```

Analyzing formwizard.ini

Now, let's look more closely at this script so that you can configure it for your specific needs.

The very first line is a special line:

```
#!/usr/bin/perl
```

This line tells the system to run Perl whenever the system executes this script. If you have installed Perl in a nonstandard directory, then you must change this accordingly. For example, if you installed Perl in /usr/local/bin/perl, then change this line to reflect that.

The next block of code segment is:

```
use strict;
use Config::IniFiles;
use File::Basename;
use HTML::Template;
use Fcntl qw(:DEFAULT :flock);
use CGI;
```

This loads all the necessary standard and CPAN modules. The CPAN modules used by this script are `Config::IniFiles`, `HTML::Template`, and `CGI`. The `CGI` module is actually now shipped as a standard Perl module, but you must install the other two using the `CPAN` module. Here are two quick commands that will install these modules for you from a root shell:

```
perl -MCPAN -e 'CPAN::Shell->install('Config::IniFiles')
perl -MCPAN -e 'CPAN::Shell->install('HTML::Template')
```

You can also run

```
perl -MCPAN -e 'CPAN::Shell->install('CGI')
```

to make sure your `CGI.pm` module is the latest version from the CPAN network.

The next code segment is

```
my $cfg      = new Config::IniFiles -file => "formwizard.ini";
my $query    = new CGI;
my $formName = get_form_name($ENV{HTTP_REFERER});
```

This segment creates a configuration object called `$cfg`, which loads the `formwizard.ini` file. The `formwizard.ini` file is the central configuration file for this script and it must reside in the same directory as the CGI script, `formwizard.pl`, does. If you wish to keep it in a different directory than the CGI script itself, you need to change the path. For example, to store the configuration file in a directory called `/www/myscripts/conf`, modify the script as follows:

```
my $cfg      = new Config::IniFiles
               -file => "/www/myscripts/conf/formwizard.ini";
```

Ensure that Apache user (that is, the user used for the `User` directive in the `httpd.conf` file) can read the configuration file. The CGI object the script creates is called `$query`. Next, the script calls a subroutine called `get_form_name()` to get the name of the Web form that called it. The subroutine is:

```
sub get_form_name {
    my $referrer = shift;

    # If the HTTP referrer has a query string in it
    # return only the non-query string part of it
    #
    if ($referrer =~ /\?/) {

        ($referrer, undef) = split(/\?/,$referrer);

    }

    return basename($referrer);
}
```

This subroutine is passed from the CGI environment variable HTTP_REFERER when called. This variable is set to the URL, which called the script. For example, if the register.html form can is accessed from an URL such as http://rhat.nitec.com/asb2/ch12/forms/register.html, then when it is submitted to the /c/s.dll/formwizard.pl script, the CGI object $query sets up HTTP_REFERER to be http://rhat.nitec.com/asb2/ch12/forms/register.html. The get_form_name() code returns the 'register.html' portion of the URL.

The script then stores the Web form name in a global variable called $formName.

The next code segment is:

```
my $templateDir = $cfg->val($formName, 'template_dir');
my @fieldInfo   = $cfg->val($formName, 'form_field_info');
```

This segment passes the Web form name to the configuration object as a section name and retrieves configuration information for the current Web form's template directory and form field information. The information is stored in $templateDir and @fieldInfo arrays, respectively. The configuration file example, formwizard.ini, is shown in Listing 12-4, which shows a sample configuration for a Web form called register.html. The configuration file format is quite simple:

```
[section1]
key1 = value
key2 = value
key3 = value

key4 = <<MULTIPLE_VALUES
value1
value2
value3
...
valueN
MULTIPLE_VALUES
...
keyN = value
[section2]
```

This type of configuration file is common in the Windows world and is typically referred as the "ini" file. Hence, the module we used here is called Config:IniFiles. In our example formwizard.ini file, the section name is really the name of the Web form register.html. The $templateDir variable and the @fieldInfo array are set from these configuration lines:

```
[register.html]

template_dir = /www/asb2/ch12/forms/register

form_field_info=<<FORM_FIELDS
name,text,required,max_chars=50,min_chars=3,case=ucfirst,exclude_
regex=[^a-z .],pattern=none
```

```
email,text,required,max=100,min=6,case=lowerall,exclude_regex=
[^a-z0-9-_.\@],pattern=email
zipcode,number,optional,pattern=us_zipcode,exclude_regex=[^0-9-]
opt-in,text,required,case=lower,pattern=none,valid_data=yes|no
FORM_FIELDS
```

The `template_dir` line in the configuration file is set to a directory in which the HTML template(s) for this Web form (`register.html`) are kept. In the current version of the script, the only template we use is the HTML template for the thank you page, so it is kept in this directory.

The `form_field_info` configuration is an extended version of the key=value pair concept. Here a single key, `form_field_info`, has many values. The values are the lines between the `FORM_FIELDS` strings. Each value line has multiple fields. For example:

```
name,text,required,max_chars=50,min_chars=3,case=ucfirst,exclude_regex=[^a-z .],
pattern=none
```

Here the form field `name` is found in `register.html` as shown here:

```
<input name="name" type=text size=30 maxsize=50>
```

To control user input, the script uses a set of parameters per input field. The parameters are discussed in Table 12-1. Each parameter is separated with comma and stored in the configuration file as follows:

```
form_field_info=<<FORM_FIELDS
fieldname1,parameter1,parameter2,parameter3,...,parameterN
fieldname2,parameter1,parameter2,parameter3,...,parameterN
fieldname3,parameter1,parameter2,parameter3,...,parameterN
...
fieldnameN,parameter1,parameter2,parameter3,...,parameterN
FORM_FIELDS
```

Table 12-1
User Input Control Parameters in Configuration Files

Parameter	Example	Explanation
Text,	name,text	This parameter states that the named field is a string of character.
Number	zipcode,number	This parameter states that the named field is a number.
required,	name,required	This parameter states that the named field is a required input field. If this field is missing a value, or if the value is invalid, an error message needs to be displayed and form processing must abort.

Parameter	Example	Explanation
Optional	zipcode,optional	This parameter states that the named field is an optional input field. If this field is missing, form processing still continues.
Max_chars=n	name,max_chars=50	Maximum number of characters allowed for the named input field. If the user enters more than the specified number of characters, an error message is displayed.
Min_chars=n,	name,min_chars=3,	Minimum number of characters allowed for the named input field. If the user enters less than the specified number of characters, an error message is displayed.
case=ucfirst | upper | lower | lcfirst	name,case=ucfirst	Before storing the named input field the script formats the field using the specified function. For example: ucfirst: Formats the value of the form field to have only the first character in upper case. This is useful when storing name. upper: Formats the value of the form field to be all upper case. lower: Formats the value of the form field to be all lower case. lcfirst: Formats the value of the form field to have only the first character in lowercase.
exclude_regex= [character set]	name,exclude_ regex=[^a-z .] The name field value must be composed of the characters a to z or the period. No other characters are allowed.	The only characters that are allowed to be the value of the named form field. Everything else is excluded. An error message is generated when the value contains excluded characters.

Continued

Table 12-1 *(Continued)*

Parameter	Example	Explanation
`pattern=none`	`email,pattern= email` **The e-mail pattern specifies that the value of the named field (**`email`**) is checked for a valid e-mail address.**	The pattern parameter specifies a special pattern to be considered for the named form field. If the field value does not correspond to the specified pattern, it is rejected and an error message is generated. Supported patterns are: `none`, `email`, `us_zipcode`, **and** `large_plain_ text`. You can add a new pattern-checking subroutine called `sub check_newpattern { # your checking code }` **to the script to support new patterns for other types of form fields.**
`valid_data= value1|value2`	`opt-in,valid_ data=yes|no` **Here the** `opt-in` **field can only have a value of** `'yes'` **or** `'no'`.	This parameter is used for text fields that can only have one of the specified values, which are separated by a | character.

After the form field information is loaded in `@fieldInfo` array, the next code segment, as shown below, checks whether the configuration file has a template directory (that is, value for `$templateDir` variable), or whether the `@fieldInfo` array is empty.

```
if ($templateDir eq '' || $#fieldInfo < 1 ) {
    print $query->header;
    print alert("Sorry, $formName is not managed by this script.");
    exit 0;
}
```

These tests are done to determine whether the current form is configured in the `formwizard.ini` file. If it is not configured, the script returns an error message stating that the named form is not managed by the script and terminates the program. If the Web form is configured properly in `formwizard.ini` file, then the script continues to the next code segment:

```
my @errors = validate_data(\@fieldInfo);
if ($#errors >= 0) {
    print $query->header;
    print alert(join('\\n',@errors) . '\\n\\n' .
```

```
                              $cfg->val($formName,'data_error_msg'));
        exit 0;
}
```

Here the script calls the `validate_data()` subroutine, which is passed the `@fieldInfo` array reference to verify that the entered user data has no errors. This subroutine does the following:

1. It loops through each form field specific information found in the `@fieldInfo` array (which is passed to the subroutine as a reference) and retrieves the field name, field type, field requirements, and so on.

2. For each form field it retrieves the value from the `$query` object using the `$query->param($fieldname)` method. The value is stored in `$value` variable.

3. If the field is required and the value is empty, an error message is stored in the `@errors` array, and the loop continues with the next field. If the field is optional and the user has entered no value, the loop continues to the next field.

4. When there is a value (for a required or an optional field), the `check_data_field()` subroutine is called to verify that the value meets the field requirements stated in the configuration file.

5. If the field value passes the validation checks performed by the `check_data_field()` subroutine, the case of the value is changed per configuration requirements. In other words, the value is either uppercased, lowercased, or mixed case and stored in the CGI object using the `$query->param()` method. The `check_data_field()` routine returns a list of errors (if any).

6. If errors are returned by the `check_data_field()` subroutine, the script displays an error message using the `alert()` subroutine and aborts. On the other hand, if there is no error to report, the script continues to write data to disk using the `write_data()` subroutine. The `write_data()` uses the data filename from the configuration file. The fully qualified data file path is based on the configuration parameters `data_directory` and `data_filename`. This routine writes user-entered, case-modified data in the order given in the `data_field_order` configuration parameter using the field separator named in `data_field_separator` parameter. Note that the data file is opened for append mode only and that it is exclusively locked during the write operation so that no other copies of `formwizard.pl` have access to it during this critical period.

7. Then the script uses the `thankyou_redirect_url` configuration option found in `formwizard.ini` to determine whether the user should be redirected to another URL or a thank you message should be displayed to the user. If the `thankyou_redirect_url` is not empty in the configuration file, the script uses the `redirect_data()` subroutine to redirect the user to the named URL. The `redirect_data()` subroutine packs all the form fields as key=value pairs in the URL and redirects the user's Web browser to the URL. For example, if the `register.html` is filled out with name=mohammed kabir, zipcode=95833, email=MRKABIR@hotmail.com, and opt-in=yes, and if the `thankyou_redirect_url` is set to http://www.domain.com/friends.pl, then the `redirect_data()` subroutine redirects the Web browser to:

```
http://www.domain.com/friends.pl?name=Mohammed%20Kabir&zipcode=
95833&email=mrkabir@hotmail.com&opt-in=yes
```

This allows the remote site to receive the cleaned-up user data via the HTTP GET method. Note that if you simply want to redirect the user to another page and not submit the data via GET, set the send_data_on_redirect parameter in the configuration file to no.

8. If the thankyou_redirect_url is not set, the script loads the thank you template filename from the configuration file using the thankyou_template configuration parameter. This template is assumed to be in the template directory pointed to by the template_dir configuration parameter. The script uses the show_thanks() subroutine to display the thank you page. The show_thanks() subroutine personalizes the thank you by replacing special tags with user-entered (yet cleaned-up) data field values. This is done by creating an instance of the HTML::Template object, which is initialized with the template page pointed to by the thankyou_template parameter. The HTML::Template object called $template uses its $template->param() method to replace special tags with a $query->Vars() method created hash.

Finally, the output of the script is displayed and script terminates.

The thank you template used in this example is shown in Listing 12-5.

Listing 12-5: **thankyou.html Page**

```
<html>

<body bgcolor="white">

<font face="Arial" size=+1>User Registration Complete</font><br>

<p>
<form action="<TMPL_VAR name=REFERRER>" method="GET">

<table border=0
       cellpadding=3
       cellspacing=0
       bgcolor="#000000">
<tr>
<td>

<table border=0
       cellpadding=5
       cellspacing=5
       bgcolor="#abcdef">

<tr>
<td>

<TMPL_VAR NAME=name>, <p>
```

```
Thank you for taking the time to register. We will send you information via
<TMPL_VAR NAME=email>.

</td>

</tr>


<tr>
<td align=center> <input type=submit value="Return"</td>
</tr>

</table>

</td>
</tr>
</table>
</form>
<p>

</html>
```

Notice the `<TMPL_VAR NAME=name>` and the `<TMPL_VAR NAME=email>` tags in this HTML template. These two tags are replaced with the user-entered `name` and `email` field values. Remember that during the data validation, the script updates the case for the user-entered fields so that the actual value displayed is well formatted, which is great when displaying information back to the user. Thus, the user can enter `carol godsave` in the name field but the thank you page will show `Carol Godsave`, which should make the user happier than if it were to show data as is. Here is an example data file after four `register.html` form submissions.

```
kabir@domain.com,Mohammed J. Kabir,12345,no
carol@domain.com,Carol Godsave,95833,yes
joegunchy007@aol.com,Joe Gunchy,07024,yes
jennygunchy007@aol.com,Jennifer Gunchy,07024,no
```

Managing a Web form with formwizard.ini

As you can see in the previous section, the `formwizard.pl` script, which uses the `formwizard.ini` configuration file, is very configurable and enables you to manage many single-page Web forms by using a single script and a single central configuration file. To manage new Web forms, simply copy the configuration file for `register.html` and create a new section in the `formwizard.ini` file. Here are the steps you need to take to manage a Web form called `feedback.html` by using this script.

1. Create a new section called `[feedback.html]` in the `formwizard.ini` file as follows:

```
[register.html]
template_dir              = /path/to/feedback/template/dir
```

```
thankyou_template       = thanks.html
send_data_on_redirect = no

form_field_info=<<FORM_FIELDS
#
# insert field info here
#
FORM_FIELDS

data_error_msg = Please enter missing data and resubmit.

data_directory=/feedback/data/directory
data_filename=feedback.csv
data_field_separator=,
data_field_order=comma separated field list goes here
```

Make necessary changes by looking at the [register.html] section.

2. Change the feedback form's action line to

```
<form action="/c/s.dll/formwizard.pl" method="POST">
```

3. Create the thanks.html template in the directory specified by template_dir parameter in the [feedback.html] section. This template file should use <TMPL_VAR name=fieldname> tags to personalize the thank you message.

That's all there is to managing a new Web form with formwizard.pl. Web form management is a big part of the CGI workload for most Web sites, and the formwizard.pl script helps you to centralize the Web form management, making it easy for you to support the forms.

Tip

While I was developing the script, I gave it to many people to try. They constantly found new features and cool tweaks for this script. I have created a SourceForge project site for all the CGI scripts that I have released under GNU Public License (GPL), so you should be able to obtain the latest version of this script at any time at https://sourceforge.net/projects/mkweb/.[MJK1]

Creating a send-page-by-e-mail script

Many popular Web sites have a feature that enables a visitor to send the Web page to a friend or colleague via e-mail. This type of feature allows the Web site to increase traffic to the site and is often labeled as a great viral marketing tool by the marketing department. In this section, I show you how you can add a CGI script to your Web site that will enable your visitors to send any of your Web pages to someone else via e-mail. First, let's look at how this works.

A user can enter a friend or colleague's e-mail address and click on the send button to send this Web page to someone who might be interested in looking at it. The actual HTML contents of the page are unimportant; what is important is the little embedded HTML form shown here:

```
<form action="/cgi-bin/mime-mail.pl" method="POST">
<input type=text name="name"   value="your-name" size=12
maxsize=50> <br>
<input type=text name="email"  value="friend-email" size=12
maxsize=100> 
<input type=submit value="Send">
</form>
```

When the user enters his or her name and a friend or colleague's e-mail address
and clicks Send, the `/c/s.dll/mime-mail.pl` script is called, which is shown in
Listing 12-6.

Listing 12-6: /cgi-bin/mime-mail.pl

```perl
#!/usr/bin/perl -w
#
#
#   Name: mime-mail.pl
#
#   Purpose:
#
#   Sends the referrer page via email
#
################################################################

use strict;

use CGI;
use MIME::Lite;
use MIME::Lite::HTML;
use Config::IniFiles;
use File::Basename;

#
# Create a CGI object
#
my $query = new CGI;

#
# Create a configuration object by loading the mime-mail.ini
# file from the physical directory pointed by /cgi-bin/
#
my $cfg       = new Config::IniFiles -file => "mime-mail.ini";


#
# Get the referrer URL
#
```

Continued

Listing 12-6 *(Continued)*

```perl
my $referrerURL = $ENV{HTTP_REFERER};

#
# Get the referrer page name from the referrer
# information
my $pageName = get_form_name($referrerURL);

#
# Print content type header to be text/html
#
print $query->header;

#
# If the referrer page does not have a [section] in
# the mime-mail.ini file, then use default section
$pageName = 'defaults' if ($cfg->val($pageName, 'from') eq '');

#
# Get the e-mail address. If no e-mail address is supplied,
# show error message
#
my $to = ( $query->param('email') eq '' ||
    ! check_email($query->param('email'), 'email')) ?
    abort('Email address is missing.') : $query->param('email');

my $senderName = ( $query->param('name') eq '') ?
    abort('Your name is missing.') : $query->param('name');

$senderName = format_name($senderName);


#
# Create a MIME::Lite::HTML object and initialize
# it with referrer, an
my $mailHTML = new MIME::Lite::HTML
                From => $senderName . '<' .
                        $cfg->val($pageName, 'from') . '>',
                To   => $to,
                Subject => $cfg->val($pageName, 'subject');


#
# Parse the referrer URL and create a MIME mail object
#
my $MIMEmail = $mailHTML->parse($referrerURL);

#
# Send the MIME mail
#
$MIMEmail->send;
```

```perl
#
# Check error string for errors
#
my @errors = $mailHTML->errstr;


#
# If no error found, tell the user that page was
# sent to her friend; otherwise, show error message
#
if ($#errors > -1 ) {
    print abort('Error(s) found: ' . join('\\n', @errors));
} else {
    print abort("Page sent to $to.\\nThank you.");
}


#
# Terminate
#
exit 0;

sub abort {

   # Print javascript abort message
   print sprintf("<script>alert('%s');history.go(-1);
</script>",shift);
   exit 0;
}

sub get_form_name {
   my $referrer = shift;

   # If the HTTP referrer has a query string in it
   # return only the nonquery string part of it
   #
   if ($referrer =~ /\?/) {

       ($referrer, undef) = split(/\?/,$referrer);

   }

   return basename($referrer);
}

sub format_name {

   my @str = ();
   foreach my $part (split(/\s/,shift)) {
       push(@str, ucfirst(lc($part)));
   }
```

Continued

Listing 12-6 *(Continued)*

```perl
        return join(' ',@str);
}

sub check_email {
    my $email = shift;
    my $fieldName = shift;

    # Special note
    # This e-mail checker routine might return false (0)
    # for some rarely used RFC-compliant e-mail addresses
    # that are not common. For example, bob&sandra@domain.com
    # will fail. If you wish to allow such "technically" valid
    # e-mails, you must modify the regular expressions used
    # in this routine.

    # Untaint e-mail address
    $email =~ /(\S+)\@([\w.-]+)/;
    $email =  $1 . '@' . $2;

    # Store untainted value in query object
    $query->param($fieldName, $email);

    # Split the user@host e-mail into user and host
    my ($user, $host) = split(/@/, $email);

    # Return false if host part does not have
    # hostname.domain.tld or domain.tld format
    #
    return ($host !~ /(^[a-z0-9._-]+\.[a-z]{2,3})$/i) ? 0 : 1;
}
```

Here's what's going on in this script:

✦ The script creates a CGI object called $query and loads the mime-mail.ini configuration file in another object called $cfg. It then stores the HTTP referrer information in a variable called $referrerURL and uses the get_form_name() subroutine to determine the name of the page that called this script. The name of the page is stored in $pageName variable.

✦ The default content header (text/html) is printed using the $query->header method. It then checks whether there is a configuration section for the named page. It uses $cfg->val($pageName, 'from') method to locate a parameter called 'from' in the mime-mail.ini configuration file. This parameter must be set in the appropriate section for the page. Following is a sample mime-mail.ini configuration file.

```
[default]
subject  = A Web page forwarded by a friend
from     = webmaster@domain.com

[mybooks.html]
subject  = Check out Kabir's linux books!
From     = webmaster@domain.com
```

For example, if the CGI script was called from a URL such as `http://www.domain.com/mybooks.html`, then the script will set the `$pageName` to `'mybooks.html'` and look for the `'from'` parameter in the `[mybooks.html]` section using the `$cfg->val($pageName, 'from')` method call. If the parameter is missing because it is not set or because the section is missing, than it sets the `$pageName` to `'default'`, which allows it to use the parameters from the `[default]` section. Thus, having a `[default]` section is a good idea if you do not wish to define a separate section for each page on which you show the send-page-by-e-mail form.

✦ Next the script determines whether the user has entered an e-mail address, and if the user has, whether the e-mail address is in the user@host format. If the e-mail is missing or invalid, an error message is displayed and the script terminates using the `abort()` subroutine. If the e-mail address is accepted, it checks whether the user has entered his or her name in the `name` field of the Web form. If the name is missing, it aborts.

✦ If both e-mail address and name are accepted, the script formats the user's name using the `format_name()` subroutine and creates the `MIME::Lite::HTML` object. This object is initialized with From, To, and Subject information. The From address is composed of the user's name and an e-mail address read from the configuration file. For example, if a user named John Olson fills out the send-page-by-e-mail form on the `http://www.domain.com/mybooks.html` page, the script will create the From header as `John Olson <webmaster@domain.com>`. The user's e-mail address is used in the name to tell the friend or colleague who is receiving the e-mail about the person who initiated the e-mail. Had we collected the user's e-mail address as well, we could have used it to set the From header. But collecting both the user's e-mail and the friend's e-mail address in two small text boxes might become too confusing without appropriate labels, which would take away from your page's real estate; thus, such a scheme is avoided.

✦ The `$mailHTML` object is then used to parse the referrer URL. At this stage, the CGI script actually acts an embedded Web client and retrieves the referrer Web page and creates the necessary MIME contents needed to send the e-mail. The `$mailHTML->send` method is used to send the e-mail. The `$mailHTML->errstr` method is used to detect errors and to store them in `@errors`. If there are no errors, the script displays a page sent message and terminates; if there are errors, it shows an error message and terminates.

Enabling CGI Debugging Support in Apache

To help CGI developers, Apache has logs for CGI output. For each CGI program error, the log file contains a few lines of log entries. The first two lines contain the time of the request, the request URI, the HTTP status, the CGI program name, and so on. If the CGI program cannot be run, two additional lines contain information about the error. Alternatively, if the error is the result of the script returning incorrect header information, the information is logged in as: all HTTP request headers, all headers outputted by CGI program, and STDOUT and STDIN of the CGI program. If the script failed to output anything, the STDOUT will not be included.

To log CGI output in Apache, use the directives described in the following sections in the mod_cgi module, which is part of standard distribution. With these directives you can set up the logging of CGI programs that you are developing or attempting to install on your system.

ScriptLog

The ScriptLog directive sets the log filename for CGI program errors. If the log filename is relative (that is, it does not start with a leading /), it is taken to be relative to the server root directory set by ServerRoot directive.

> **Syntax:** ScriptLog *filename*
>
> **Context:** Resource config

When you use this directive, make sure that the log directory is writeable by the user specified by UserDir directive. Using this directive on a daily basis might not be a good idea as far as efficiency or performance goes. I recommend using it when needed and turning it off when the debugging is completed.

ScriptLogLength

The ScriptLogLength directive limits the size of the log file specified by the ScriptLog directive. The script log file can log a lot of information per CGI error and, therefore, can grow rapidly. By using this directive, you can limit the log size so that when the file is at the maximum length, no more information will be logged.

> **Syntax:** ScriptLogLength *size*
>
> **Default:** ScriptLogLength 10385760
>
> **Context:** Resource config

ScriptLogBuffer

The `ScriptLogBuffer` directive limits the size of `POST` or `PUT` data that is logged.

> **Syntax:** `ScriptLogBuffer size`
>
> **Default:** `ScriptLogBuffer size 1024`
>
> **Context:** Resource config

Debugging Your Perl-Based CGI Scripts

If you use Perl-based CGI scripts, as discussed earlier in this chapter, you have lot more help in troubleshooting your CGI scripts than just what Apache offers as CGI logs. You can debug a Perl-based CGI script from the command line by using the famous `CGI.pm` module. Or, you can write debug messages to the standard error log (STDERR) file, which Apache automatically redirects to the Apache error log. I will discuss these techniques in the following sections.

Debugging from the command line

If you use the famous CGI module, as I did in all of the practical CGI scripts discussed in this chapter, you are in luck. The CGI module enables you to troubleshoot your CGI script from the command line, which makes it really convenient to debug a script. Let's look at an example CGI script called `badcalc.pl`, which is shown Listing 12-7.

Listing 12-7: badcalc.pl

```perl
#!/usr/bin/perl -w

use CGI;

my $query = new CGI;

my $num1 = $query->param('num1');
my $num2 = $query->param('num2');

my $sum = $num1 + num2;

#print $query->header;

print "$num1 + $num2 = $sum";

exit 0;
```

When this script is accessed via a URL such as `http://www.domain.com/cgi-bin/notready.pl`, it returns an internal server error message and logs an error message in the server's error log file. You want to know why this small script does not work. Here is a typical debugging session.

1. Enable command-line debugging for the CGI module by changing the `use CGI` line to:

   ```
   Use CGI qw(-debug);
   ```

   This enables the command-line debugging for the module.

2. As `root`, `su` to the Apache user (that is, the user you set the `User` directive to) and run the script from the command line. You will see this message:

   ```
   (offline mode: enter name=value pairs on standard input)
   ```

   and the script will wait for your input.

3. In command-line mode, enter key=value pairs in each line to simulate input from the Web. For example, to feed the above script, an example command-line session would look similar to this:

   ```
   (offline mode: enter name=value pairs on standard input)
   num1=100
   num2=200
   ```

   The preceding sets the `num1` input field to `100` and the `num2` input field to `200`. Each field is set to a value in its own line.

4. When you are done entering all input, press Ctrl+D to terminate the input part of the debugging and watch what the script does. The complete debugging session for the above input is shown here:

   ```
   (offline mode: enter name=value pairs on standard input)
   num1=100
   num2=200
   [control+d]
   100 + 200 = 100
   ```

   As you can see, the script added the two numbers and printed the data as expected. So why did this script bomb when run from the Web? Well, do you see any Content-Type header before the output? No. If you look at the script you will notice that the print `$query->header;` line is commented out. If you remove the comment and rerun the script in command-line mode, you will see the following:

   ```
   (offline mode: enter name=value pairs on standard input)
   num1=100
   num2=200
   Content-Type: text/html; charset=ISO-8859-1

   100 + 200 = 100
   ```

Debugging by using logging and debug printing

This type of command-line debugging is very useful for small, less-complex scripts, but if you have a fairly large script, such as the `formwizard.pl`, command-line debugging is too cumbersome. In such a case, you need to use a combination of logging and debug printing. Here is an example script, called `calc.pl`, that uses logging and debug printing:

```perl
!/usr/bin/perl -w

use CGI qw(-debug);

use constant DEBUG => 1;

my $query = new CGI;

my $num1 = $query->param('num1');
my $num2 = $query->param('num2');

print $query->header;

if ($num1 == $num2) {

    # do something useful
    DEBUG and print STDERR "num1 and num2 are same.\n";

} elsif ($num1 > $num2 ) {

    # do something useful
    DEBUG and print STDERR "num1 is greater than num2.\n";

} elsif ($num1 < $num2 ) {

    # do something useful
    DEBUG and print STDERR "num1 is less than num2\n";

}

print $query->start_html('Calculator');
print $query->h1("Calculator");
print $query->p("Number 1: $num1");
print $query->p("Number 2: $num2");
print $query->end_html;

exit 0;
```

When this script is called from a URL such as `http://www.domain.com/cgi-bin/calc.pl?num1=100&num2=300`, it prints information in the standard error log for that site. For the above-mentioned URL, the entry in the error log will similar to this:

```
[Tue Mar 20 20:04:26 2001] [error] [client 207.183.233.19] num1 is less than
num2
```

The following statement prints this error message:

```
DEBUG and print STDERR "num1 is less than num2\n";
```

The interesting thing about this line is that it uses a constant called DEBUG, which is set in the beginning of the script with this line:

```
use constant DEBUG => 1;
```

The logic in the DEBUG and print statement follows:

✦ When DEBUG is set to 1 or to any nonzero number it is the equivalent of the 'true' value obtained when DEBUG is used in a logical operation.

✦ The built-in print function always returns a nonzero value when it is successful in printing.

✦ So, when Perl evaluates DEBUG and print, it executes the print statement.

✦ When DEBUG is set to 0, the DEBUG and print statement does not execute.

This enables you to insert print statements that can be part of your code but that can be turned off when you are done debugging. Notice that the print statement writes to STDERR, which always writes the data to the error logs for the Web site.

To turn off these statements, you simply set the DEBUG constant to 0. Now, some might argue that you should completely remove these statements from your script when you are ready to hand the script to production. The reasoning behind such an argument is that Perl still evaluates these DEBUG statements even though they do not print anything, thereby slowing down the script. The truth is that in a CGI solution, the speed difference might not matter because CGI scripts already have a heavier overhead than does a mod_perl or other persistent solution. But if you are concerned, then remove the DEBUG statements before sending the script to production.

Debugging with CGI::Debug

Now let's take a look at another debugging solution. You can get a great deal of help in debugging your CGI script using the CGI::Debug module. Simply add this module right after the use CGI; statement in your script, and you will be able to catch all types of errors. For example:

```
!/usr/bin/perl -w

use CGI;
use CGI::Debug;


my $query = new CGI;
```

```
    my $num1 = $query->param('num1');
    my $num2 = $query->param('num2');


    #print $query->header;

    print $query->start_html('Calculator');
    print $query->h1("Calculator");
    print $query->p("Number 1: $num1");
    print $query->p("Number 2: $num2");
    print $query->end_html;

    exit 0;
```

I intentionally commented out the $query->header line, which would normally generate an internal server error message on the Web browser. But because I added the use CGI::Debug; statement in this script, the script will show the following when it is accessed as http://www.domain.com/c/s.dll/cgidebug. pl?num1=1&num2=200:

```
/cgi-bin/cgidebug.pl

Malformed header!

--- Program output below  ----------------------
<?xml version="1.0" encoding="utf-8"?>
<!DOCTYPE html
    PUBLIC "-//W3C//DTD XHTML Basic 1.0//EN"
      "http://www.w3.org/TR/xhtml-basic/xhtml-basic10.dtd">
<html xmlns="http://www.w3.org/1999/xhtml" lang="en-
US"><head><title>Calculator</title>
</head><body><h1>Calculator</h1><p>Number 1: 1</p><p>Number 2:
200</p></body></html>
-------------------------------------------------


This program finished in 0.078 seconds.

Parameters
----------
num1 =    1[1]
num2 =    3[200]


Cookies
-------


Environment
-----------
DOCUMENT_ROOT           = 15[/home/kabir/www]
```

```
GATEWAY_INTERFACE      =    7[CGI/1.1]
HTTP_ACCEPT            = 133[image/gif, image/x-xbitmap, image/jpeg, image/pjpeg,
applica]...
HTTP_ACCEPT_ENCODING = 13[gzip, deflate]
HTTP_ACCEPT_LANGUAGE =    5[en-us]
HTTP_CONNECTION       =   10[Keep-Alive]
HTTP_HOST             =   14[rhat.nitec.com]
HTTP_USER_AGENT       =   50[Mozilla/4.0 (compatible; MSIE 5.5; Windows NT 5.0)]
PATH                  =
60[/usr/bin:/bin:/usr/sbin:/sbin:/usr/X11R6/bin:/home/kabir/bin]
QUERY_STRING          =   15[num1=1&num2=200]
REMOTE_ADDR           =   14[207.183.233.19]
REMOTE_PORT           =    4[2841]
REQUEST_METHOD        =    3[GET]
REQUEST_URI           =   36[/cgi-bin/cgidebug.pl?num1=1&num2=200]
SCRIPT_FILENAME       =   37[/home/kabir/www/asb2/ch12/cgidebug.pl]
SCRIPT_NAME           =   20[/cgi-bin/cgidebug.pl]
SERVER_ADDR           =   14[207.183.233.20]
SERVER_ADMIN          =   16[you@your.address]
SERVER_NAME           =   14[rhat.nitec.com]
SERVER_PORT           =    2[80]
SERVER_PROTOCOL       =    8[HTTP/1.1]
SERVER_SIGNATURE      =   66[<ADDRESS>Apache/2.0.14 Server at rhat.nitec.com Port
80</ADD]...
SERVER_SOFTWARE       =   20[Apache/2.0.14 (Unix)]


<EOF>
```

As you can see, there is a ton of information that will help you to troubleshoot the
problem and to fix the script quickly. For example, one line in the preceding program
output states that the header is malformed.

✦   ✦   ✦

Server Side Includes (SSI)

In Chapter 12, I discuss how dynamic Web content can be created using CGI programs; however, there are tasks that might not call for the development of full-blown CGI programs but that still require some dynamic intervention.

For example, say you want to add a standard copyright message to all your HTML pages; how would you implement this? Well, you have two solutions:

+ Add the content of the copyright message to each HTML page.
+ Write a CGI program that adds the message to each HTML page.

Neither of these options is elegant. The first option requires that anytime that you make a change to the copyright message, you manually update all your files. The second option requires that you have some way to get your CGI program running before each page is sent to the Web browser. This also means that every link on each page has to call this CGI program so that it can append the message to the next page. Situations like these demand a simpler solution. Server Side Include (SSI), the topic of this chapter, is that simpler solution.

What Is a Server Side Include?

Typically, an SSI page is an HTML page with embedded command(s) for the Apache Web server. Web servers normally do not parse HTML pages before delivery to the Web browser (or to any other Web client). However, before delivery the Web server always parses an SSI-enabled HTML page, and if any special SSI command is found in the page, it is executed. Figure 13-1 shows the simplified delivery cycle of an HTML page and an SSI-enabled HTML (SHTML) page from a Web server.

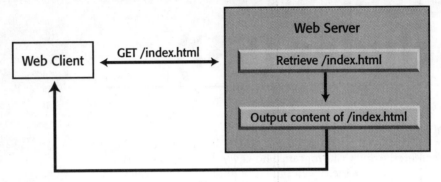

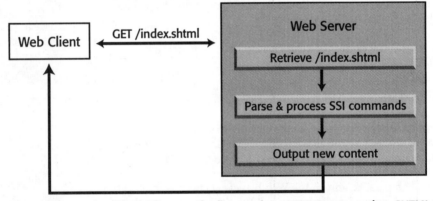

Figure 13-1: A simplified delivery cycle diagram for an HTML page and an SHTML page

As you can see, the SSI version of the HTML page is first parsed for SSI commands. These commands are executed, and the new output is delivered to the Web browser (that is, the Web client.)

Apache implements SSI as an INCLUDES filter. Before you can configure Apache for SSI, you need to check your current Apache executable (httpd) to ensure that the mod_include module is included in it. I show you how in the next section.

Configuring Apache for SSI

Before you use SSI with Apache, you need to make sure SSI support is enabled. To find out if you have mod_include built into your current Apache binary, run the httpd -l | grep include command from the /usr/local/apache/bin directory or from wherever you have installed the Apache binaries. This enables you to see the list of all modules used in building your Apache executable. By default, you should have this module compiled; if not, you need to configure Apache source using the `--enable-include` option and then recompile and reinstall Apache.

Although the `mod_include` module is compiled by default in the standard Apache distribution, the parsing of HTML pages is not enabled by default. You can enable SSI for an entire directory or a single file type as discussed in the next section.

Enabling SSI for an entire directory

To enable SSI for a directory called `/www/mysite/htdocs/parsed` add the following configuration to `httpd.conf`:

```
<Directory "/www/mysite/htdocs/parsed">
    Options +Includes
    SetOutputFilter INCLUDES
</Directory>
```

Here the Options directive is set to `+Includes`, which enables SSI parsing in this directory. The `SetOutputFilter` directive tells Apache to parse all pages from this directory for SSI commands. This means that files with any extension in this directory will be server-parsed.

For example, say that you have the following virtual host configuration:

```
<VirtualHost 192.168.1.100>

    ServerName vh1.domain.com
    DocumentRoot "/www/mysite/htdocs"
    ScriptAlias /cgi-bin/ "/www/mysite/htdocs/cgi-bin/"

    <Directory "/www/mysite/htdocs/parsed">
        Options +Includes
        SetOutputFilter INCLUDES
    </Directory>

</VirtualHost>
```

Now, if the `/www/mysite/htdocs/parsed` directory has any `any.txt`, `any.html`, or `any.shtml` files in it, these URL requests will be parsed:

```
http://vh1.domain.com/parsed/any.txt
http://vh1.domain.com/parsed/any.html
http://vh1.domain.com/parsed/any.shtml
```

In most cases, parsing a text file (`.txt`) or an html file (`.html`) is not needed because these files are not typically used for SSI commands. So, the above configuration will make Apache do extra work unless you intentionally want the parsing of all types of files. Now let's see how you can limit SSI parsing to a specific file type.

Enabling SSI for a specific file type

To limit the scope of the SSI parsing in a directory, simply use `AddType` directive to set the desired Content-Type header for the SSI-enabled file type and then wrap the `INCLUDES` filter in a `FilesMatch` container. For example:

```
Options +Include
AddType text/html .shtml

<FilesMatch "\.shtml[.$]">
   SetOutputFilter INCLUDES
   </FilesMatch>
```

Here the `Options` directive is set to `+Includes`, which enables SSI parsing. The `AddType` directive is used to set Content-Type header for a file type called `.shtml` to `text/html`. Then the `SetOutputFilter` directive is set to `INCLUDES` for `.shtml` files using the `FilesMatch` directive and a regular expression `"\.shtml[.$]"`.

Now look again at the virtual host example from the previous section. This time let's add the `FilesMatch` container as shown here:

```
<VirtualHost 192.168.1.100>

   ServerName vh1.domain.com
   DocumentRoot "/www/mysite/htdocs"
   ScriptAlias /cgi-bin/ "/www/mysite/htdocs/cgi-bin/"

   <Directory "/www/mysite/htdocs/parsed">
      Options +Includes

      AddType text/html .shtml

      <FilesMatch "\.shtml[.$]">
         SetOutputFilter INCLUDES
      </FilesMatch>

   </Directory>

</VirtualHost>
```

Now, if there are `any.txt`, `any.html`, or `any.shtml` files in the parsed subdirectory, only the following URL request will tell Apache to parse the output of the `.shtml` file.

```
http://vh1.domain.com/parsed/any.shtml
```

The server will not parse the other two URLS, `http://vh1.domain.com/parsed/any.txt` and `http://vh1.domain.com/parsed/any.html`, for SSI commands. This is the preferred configuration for most sites because you want to limit server parsing to a specific type of file for both performance and site organizational purposes.

Caution   If you plan to disable execution of external programs via SSI commands, you can use the `IncludesNOEXEC` option with the Options directive. This disables execution of external programs. However, it also disables loading of external files via the SSI command `Include`.

Using XBitHack for .htm or .html files

As mentioned before, enabling SSI parsing for the entire directory degrades server performance. You should try hard to avoid using the `.html` or `.htm` extensions for SSI; if you must use them, then use the `XBitHack` directive found in the `mod_include` module. The `XBitHack` directive controls server parsing of files associated with the MIME-type `text/html`:

> **Syntax:** `XBitHack On | Off | Full`
>
> **Default:** `XBitHack Off`
>
> **Context:** Server config, virtual host, directory, per-directory access control file (`.htaccess`)
>
> **Override:** `Options`

Typically, only `.html` and `.htm` files are associated with `text/html`. The default value `off` tells the server not to parse these files. When this is set to `on`, any HTML file that has execute permission for the file owner is considered an SSI file and is parsed. When the directive is set to `full`, it makes the server check the owner and the group executable bits of the file permission settings. If the group executable bit is set, then Apache sets the last-modified date of the returned file to be the last modified time of the file. If it is not set, then no last-modified date is sent. Setting this bit enables clients and proxies to cache the result of the request. Use of the value `full` is not advisable for SSI pages that produce a different output when parsed and processed.

Note   You will still have to use `Options +Includes` when using the `XBitHack` directive to enable SSI support.

If you use per-directory access control file (`.htaccess`) to enable SSI support, make sure that the `AllowOverride` directive for the site owning that directory allows such an operation. The `AllowOverride` directive for such a site must allow the `Includes` option to be overridden. For example, if the `AllowOverride` is set to `None` for a site, no SSI parsing will occur.

Note   If you do not use the + sign in the `Options` line in the preceding example, all the options except `Includes` are disabled.

Now that you know how to enable SSI support in Apache, the next section discusses the SSI commands in detail.

Using SSI Commands

SSI commands are embedded in HTML pages in the form of comments. The base command structure looks like this:

```
<!--#command argument1=value argument2=value argument3=value -->
```

The value is often enclosed in double quotes; many commands only allow a single attribute-value pair. Note that the comment terminator `-->` should be preceded by white space to ensure that it isn't considered part of the SSI command.

The following sections examine all the available SSI commands.

config

The `config` command enables you to configure the parse error message that appear, as well as the formatting that is used for displaying time and file size information. This is accomplished with the following lines of code:

```
config errmsg="error message"
config sizefmt=["bytes" | "abbrev"]
config timefmt=format string
```

`config errmsg="error message"` shows you how to create a custom error message, which is displayed when a parsing error occurs. For example, Listing 13-1 shows a file called `config_errmsg.shtml`.

Listing 13-1: **config_errmsg.shtml**

```
<HTML>
<BODY>
   <TITLE> Apache Server 2 - Chapter 13 </TITLE>
</HEAD>

<BODY BGCOLOR="white">

<FONT SIZE=+1 FACE="Arial"> Simple SSI Example #1</FONT>
<HR SIZE=1>

<P> Example of the SSI <STRONG>config errmsg</STRONG> command:
</P>
<P> Embedded commands: <BR><BR>

<CODE>
  &lt;!-#config errmsg="SSI error! Please notify the
webmaster." -&gt; <BR>
  &lt;!-#config badcommand="whatever" -&gt;
```

```
</CODE>

</P>

<P> Result: <BR>

<!--#config errmsg="SSI error! Please notify the Web master." -
->
<BR>
<!--#config badcommand="whatever" -->

</P>

</BODY>
</HTML>
```

In this example file, there are two SSI commands:

```
<!--#config errmsg="SSI error! Please notify the webmaster." -->
```

and

```
<!--#config badcommand="whatever" -->
```

The first is a valid SSI config errmsg command that sets the error message to the string "SSI error! Please notify the Web master.". The second command is an invalid SSI command, which I intentionally entered into this file so that you would see what happens when Apache parses it. Figure 13-2 shows what is returned to the browser when this page is parsed by the server.

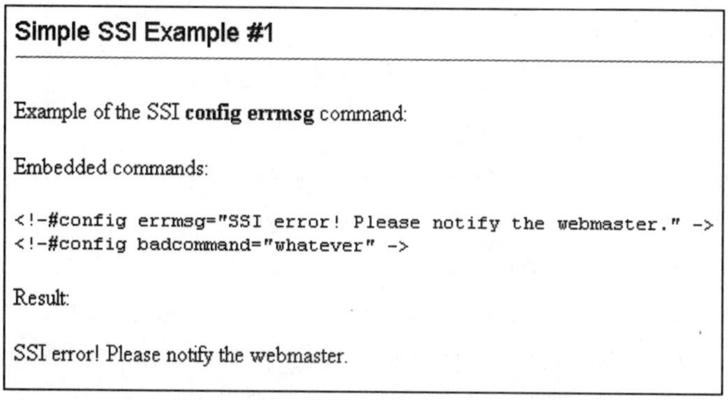

Simple SSI Example #1

Example of the SSI **config errmsg** command:

Embedded commands:

```
<!-#config errmsg="SSI error! Please notify the webmaster." ->
<!-#config badcommand="whatever" ->
```

Result:

SSI error! Please notify the webmaster.

Figure 13-2: Example of the `config errmsg` **command**

As you can see from the figure, the second command caused a parse error, and the error message is displayed as a result. The message appears where the command is found.

Note You can enter HTML tags or even to insert client-side script in the string of the error message. For example, the following displays a pop-up JavaScript alert window with an error message:

```
<!-#config errmsg="<SCRIPT LANGUAGE=JavaScript>
alert('An error occurred. \n Please report to
webmaster@domain.com');</SCRIPT>" -->
```

`config sizefmt=["bytes" | "abbrev"]` enables you to choose the output format for the file size. Acceptable format specifiers are `"bytes"` or `"abbrev"`. For example:

```
<!-#config sizefmt="bytes" -->
```

shows file sizes in bytes. To show files in kilobytes or megabytes, use:

```
<!-#config sizefmt="abbrev" -->
```

`config timefmt=format string` lets you to choose the display format for time:

```
config timefmt=format string
```

The commonly used value of the format string can consist of the identifiers shown in Table 13-1.

Table 13-1
Format Identifiers for config timefmt

Identifier	Meaning
%a	The abbreviated weekday name according to the current locale
%A	The full weekday name according to the current locale
%b	The abbreviated month name according to the current locale
%B	The full month name according to the current locale
%c	The preferred date and time representation for the current locale
%d	The day of the month as a decimal number (range 01 to 31)
%H	The hour as a decimal number using a 24-hour clock (range 00 to 23)
%I	The hour as a decimal number using a 12-hour clock (range 01 to 12)
%j	The day of the year as a decimal number (range 001 to 366)
%m	The month as a decimal number (range 01 to 12)
%M	The minute as a decimal number
%p	Either a.m. or p.m., according to the given time value or locale
%S	The second as a decimal number

Identifier	Meaning
%w	The day of the week as a decimal, Sunday being 0
%x	The preferred date representation for the current locale without the time
%X	The preferred time representation for the current locale without the date
%y	The year as a decimal number without a century (range 00 to 99)
%Y	The year as a decimal number including the century
%Z	The time zone name or abbreviation
%%	A literal % character

For example, the following sets the time format such that time is displayed in the format such as Sat Mar 17 00:31:58 2001:

```
<!--#config timefmt="%c" -->
```

And the following sets the time format such that time that is shown in a format such as 03/17/2001:

```
<!--#config timefmt="%m/%d/%Y" -->
```

echo

The echo command prints one of the Include variables (defined later) or any of the CGI environment variables. The syntax is:

```
echo var="variable_name"
```

If the value of the variable is not available, it prints (none) as the value. Any dates printed are subject to the currently configured timefmt. For example:

```
<!--#config timefmt="%m/%d/%Y" -->
<!--#echo var="DATE_LOCAL" -->
```

which prints a date such as 03/17/2001, in conformity with the specified timefmt string.

exec

The exec command enables you to execute an external program. The external program can be a CGI program or any other type of executable such as shell scripts or native binary files. The syntax for CGI programs is:

```
exec cgi="path_to_cgi_program"
```

The syntax for other programs is:

```
exec cmd="path_to_other_programs"
```

Note   If you used the `IncludesNOEXEC` value for the `Options` directive, this command is disabled.

Let's look at how to use each of these options.

cgi

The `cgi` value specifies a (%-encoded) URL relative path to the CGI script. If the path does not begin with a slash (/),it is taken to be relative to the current document. The document referenced by this path is invoked as a CGI script, even if the server would not normally recognize it as such. However, the directory containing the script must be enabled for CGI scripts (with `ScriptAlias` or the `ExecCGI` Option).

The CGI script is given the `PATH_INFO` and query string (`QUERY_STRING`) of the original request from the client; these cannot be specified in the URL path. The `Include` variables are available to the script, in addition to the standard CGI environment.

Listing 13-2 shows a simple CGI script called `colors.pl`, which displays a list of common colors in an HTML table.

Listing 13-2: **colors.pl**

```perl
#!/usr/bin/perl -w

use strict;

my @COLOR_LIST = qw(red blue brown yellow green gray white black);

print "Content-type: text/html\n\n";

print '<table border=1 cellpadding=3 cellspacing=0>';

foreach my $color (sort @COLOR_LIST) {

    print <<TABLE_ROW;

    <tr><td>$color</td>
        <td bgcolor="$color">         </td>
```

```
        </tr>

TABLE_ROW

}

print '</table>';

exit 0;
```

Now notice how this script is being called from the `exec_cgi1.shtml` file, which is shown in Listing 13-3.

Listing 13-3: **exec_cgi1.shtml**

```
<HTML>
<HEAD> <TITLE> Apache Server 2 - Chapter 13 </TITLE></HEAD>

<BODY BGCOLOR="white">
<FONT SIZE=+1 FACE="Arial">SSI Example #2</FONT>
<HR SIZE=1>

<P> Example of the SSI <STRONG>exec cgi</STRONG> command: </P>
<P> Embedded commands: <BR><BR>

<CODE> &lt;!-#exec cgi="/cgi-bin/colors.pl" -&gt; <BR> </CODE>
</P>
<P> Result: <BR>  <!--#exec cgi="/cgi-bin/colors.pl" --> </P>

</BODY>
</HTML>
```

By using the `<!--#exec cgi="/cgi-bin/colors.pl" -->` command, `exec_cgi1.shtml` produces the output shown in Figure 13-3.

The beauty of embedding a CGI script using a SSI call such as the above is that from the client prospective there is no way to tell that a page was assembled using both static and dynamic (that is, CGI script contents) data.

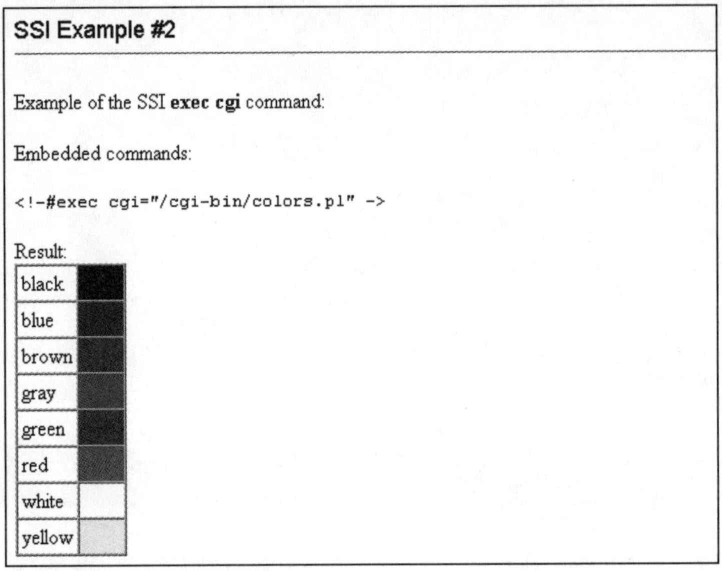

SSI Example #2

Example of the SSI **exec cgi** command:

Embedded commands:

```
<!-#exec cgi="/cgi-bin/colors.pl" ->
```

Result:

black	
blue	
brown	
gray	
green	
red	
white	
yellow	

Figure 13-3: Output of the `exec_cgi1.shtml` file

Note that if a CGI script returns a `Location` header instead of output, the header is translated into an HTML anchor. For example, the Listing 13-4 shows a simple Perl CGI script called `relocate.pl` that prints out a `Location:` header as the output.

Listing 13-4: **relocate.pl**

```
#!/usr/bin/perl -w

print 'Location: http://apache.nitec.com' . "\n\n";

exit 0;
```

When a Web browser requests the `exec_cgi2.shtml` file, shown in Listing 13-5, the server turns the `Location:` header into an HTML anchor instead of redirecting the browser to the `http://apache.nitec.com` site.

Listing 13-5: **exec_cgi2.shtml**

```
<HTML>
<HEAD> <TITLE> Apache Server 2 - Chapter 13 </TITLE></HEAD>

<BODY BGCOLOR="white">
<FONT SIZE=+1 FACE="Arial">SSI Example #3</FONT>
```

```
<HR SIZE=1>

<P> Example of the SSI <STRONG>exec cgi</STRONG> command: </P>
<P> Embedded commands: <BR><BR>

<CODE> &lt;!-#exec cgi="/cgi-bin/relocate.pl" -&gt; <BR>
</CODE>
</P>

<P> Result: <BR>   <!--#exec cgi="/cgi-bin/relocate.pl" --> </P>

</BODY>
</HTML>
```

In the listing, the only SSI call in the file is:

```
<!--#exec cgi="/cgi-bin/relocate.pl" ->
```

The output of this is an HTML anchor, as shown in Figure 13-4.

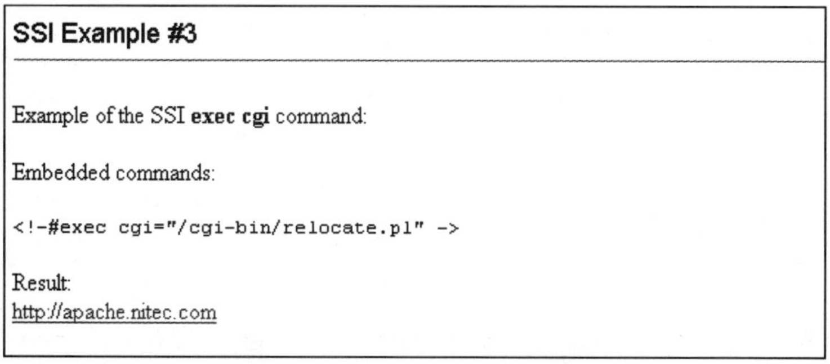

SSI Example #3

Example of the SSI **exec cgi** command:

Embedded commands:

`<!-#exec cgi="/cgi-bin/relocate.pl" ->`

Result:
http://apache.nitec.com

Figure 13-4: Output of the `exec_cgi2.shtml` file

cmd

When calling a program other than a CGI program, you can use the cmd version of
the `exec` call. The server executes the given string using the sh shell (`/bin/sh`) on
most Unix systems. The `Include` variables are available to this command. For
example, Listing 13-6 shows a file called `exec_cmd.shtml`.

Listing 13-6: **exec_cmd.shtml**

```
<HTML>
<HEAD> <TITLE> Apache Server 2 - Chapter 13 </TITLE></HEAD>
<BODY BGCOLOR="white">
```

```
<FONT SIZE=+1 FACE="Arial"> Simple SSI Example #4</FONT>
<HR SIZE=1>

<P> Example of the SSI <STRONG>exec cmd</STRONG> command: </P>
<P> Embedded commands: <BR><BR>

<CODE>
&lt;!-#exec cmd="/bin/date +%m/%d/%y" -&gt; <BR>
&lt;!-#exec cmd="/bin/ls -l ./" -&gt; <BR>
</CODE>

</P>
<P> Result: <BR>

<!--#exec cmd="/bin/date +%m/%d/%y" --> <BR>

<PRE>

<!--#exec cmd="/bin/ls -l ./*.html" --> <BR>

</PRE>

</P>
</BODY>
</HTML>
```

This file has two cmd calls:

```
<!--#exec cmd="/bin/date +%m/%d/%y" -->
<!--#exec cmd="/bin/ls -l ./*.html" -->
```

The first calls the Unix /bin/date utility with the argument +%m/%d/%y; the second calls the Unix ls utility with ./*.html as the argument. The output of this file is shown in Figure 13-5.

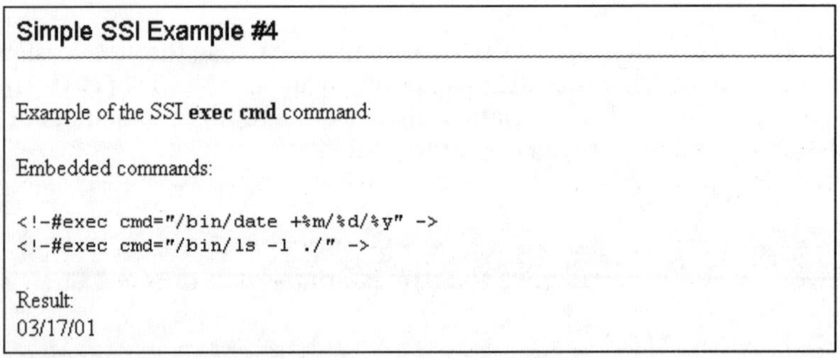

```
Simple SSI Example #4
─────────────────────────────────────────────

Example of the SSI exec cmd command:

Embedded commands:

<!-#exec cmd="/bin/date +%m/%d/%y" ->
<!-#exec cmd="/bin/ls -l ./" ->

Result:
03/17/01
```

Figure 13-5: Output of the exec_cmd.shtml file

Notice that the `ls` output is nicely formatted using the `<PRE>` and `</PRE>` pair. If you want to output something that uses new lines, you may have to use `<PRE>` tags to keep the output readable, as shown in Figure 13-5.

fsize

This command prints the size of the specified file. The syntax you use for this command depends on whether the path to the directory is relative or virtual:

```
fsize file="path"
fsize virtual="URL"
```

When the first syntax is used, the path is assumed to be relative to the directory containing the current SSI document being parsed. You cannot use `../` in the path, nor can absolute paths be used. You cannot access a CGI script in this fashion. You can, however, access another parsed document. For example:

```
<!--#fsize file="download.zip" -->
```

If the second syntax is used, the virtual path is assumed to be a (%-encoded) URL path. If the path does not begin with a slash (/), then it is taken to be relative to the current document. You must access a normal file this way, but you cannot access a CGI script in this fashion. Again, however, you can access another parsed document. For example:

```
<!--#fsize virtual="/download/free_software.zip" -->
```

The output format is subject to the `sizefmt` format specification. See the `config` command for details.

flastmod

The `flastmod` command prints the last modification date of the specified file. Again, there are two syntax options, depending on the path to the directory:

```
flastmod file="path"
flastmod virtual="URL"
```

The output is subject to the `timefmt` format specification. For example:

```
<!--#flastmod file="free_software.zip" -->
<!--#flastmod virtual="/download/free_software.zip" -->
```

If you are unclear about the syntax difference, see the `fsize` command as an example. To control how the modification date is printed, see the `config` command.

include

The include directive inserts the text of a document into the SSI document being processed. The syntax depends on the path to the directory:

Syntax 1: include file="*path*"

Syntax 2: include virtual="*URL*"

See the fsize command a couple sections back for the difference between file and virtual mode.

Any included file is subject to the usual access control. If the directory containing the parsed file has the Option IncludesNOEXEC set, and including the document would cause a program to be executed, then it is not included. This prevents the execution of CGI scripts. Otherwise, CGI scripts are invoked as they normally are, using the complete URL given in the command, including any query string. For example:

```
<!--#include file="copyrights.html" -->
```

includes the copyrights.html file in the current document. This command is useful for adding repeatable HTML code in files. Many sites use a standard menu bar on each page; if this menu bar is put in an HTML file called menu.html, it can be called from all SSI pages using a similar include file call, as in the preceding example. In the future, when changes need to be made to the menu, the site administrator only needs to update the menu.html page. This will save a lot of work if there are many files in the site.

Recursive inclusions are detected and an error message is generated after the first pass. For example, if a.shtml has an SSI call such as:

```
<!--#include file="b.shtml" -->
```

and b.shtml has a call such as:

```
<!--#include file="a.shtml" -->
```

then Apache logs and displays an error stating that a recursive include has been detected.

printenv

The printenv command prints a listing of all existing variables and their values. The syntax is:

```
printenv
```

For example:

```
<!--#printenv -->
```

prints all the Include and CGI environment variables available. To make the output more readable, use of the <PRE> tag pair is recommended.

set

The set command sets the value of a user-defined variable. The syntax is:

```
set var="variable name" value="value of the variable"
```

For example:

```
<!--#set var="home" value="index.shtml" -->
```

SSI Variables

The SSI module makes a set of variables, in addition to the CGI environment variables (see Chapter 12), available to all SSI files. These variables are called the include variables. These can be used by SSI commands (echo, if, elif, and so on) and by any program invoked by an SSL command. The include variables are listed in Table 13-2.

Table 13-2
Include Variables

Variable	Meaning
DATE_GMT	The current date in Greenwich Mean Time.
DATE_LOCAL	The current date in the local time zone.
DOCUMENT_NAME	The current SSI filename.
DOCUMENT_URI	The (%-decoded) URL path of the document.
LAST_MODIFIED	The last modification date of the current file. The date is subject to the config command's timefmt format.

The include variables and the CGI variables are preset and available for use. Any of the variables that are preset can be used as arguments for other commands. The syntax for using defined variables is:

```
<!--#command argument1="$variable1" argument2="$variable2" ...-->
```

As you can see, the variable name is prefixed by a $ sign. Here's another example:

```
<!--#config errmsg="An error occurred in $DOCUMENT_NAME
page." -->
```

When using variables in a var="*variable*" field, the $ sign is not necessary.
For example:

```
<!--#echo var="DOCUMENT_NAME" -->
```

Note   If you need to insert a literal dollar sign into the value of a variable, you can insert the dollar sign using backslash quoting. For example:

```
<!--#set var="password" value="\$cheese" -->
<!--#echo var="password" -->
```

This prints $cheese as the value of the variable "password".

Also, if you need to reference a variable name in the middle of a character sequence that might otherwise be considered a valid identifier on its own, use a pair of braces around the variable name. For example:

```
<!--#set var="uniqueid" value="${DATE_LOCAL}_${REMOTE_HOST}" -->
```

This sets uniqueid to something similar to Saturday, 17-Mar-2001 13:02:47 PST_207.183.233.19, depending on the timefmt setting and the IP address of the Web client.

Flow Control Commands

Like many programming languages, program flow control is also available in the SSI module. By using flow control commands, you can conditionally create different output. The simplest flow control (that is, conditional) statement is:

```
<!--#if expr="test_expression" -->
<!--#endif -->
```

Here, the "test_expression" is evaluated, and if the result is true, then all the text up to the endif command is included in the output. The "test_expression" can be a string, which is true if the string is not empty, or an expression comparing values of two strings.

The comparison operators allowed are =, !=, <, >, <=, or >=. A generic form of such an SSI statement looks as follows:

```
<!--#if expr="string1 operator string2" -->
<!--#endif -->
```

Note that `string2` can be a regular expression in the `/regular expression patterns/` form. See Appendix B for details on regular expressions.

Let's look at an example of a string by itself:

```
<!--#if expr="foobar" -->
This test is always successful.
<!--#endif -->
```

This syntax always prints `This test is successful.` because the expression is true when the `test_expression` is not an empty string. If `expr="foobar"` is changed to `expr=""` or to `expr="''"`, however, then the text within the `if-endif` block will never be part of the output.

Now let's look at an example of a string equality test:

```
<!--#set var="quicksearch" value="yes" -->

<!--#if expr="$quicksearch = yes" -->

    Quick search is requested.

<!--#endif -->
```

Here, the variable called `quicksearch` is being set with the value `yes`, and is later being compared with `yes`. Because the set value and the comparison value are equal, the `Quick search is requested` line will be the output.

Using logical operators such as `!`, `&&`, and `||`, you can create more complex `test_expressions`. For example:

```
<!--#if expr="${REMOTE_ADDR} = /207\.183\.233/
        && ${DOCUMENT_NAME} = /timesheet/" -->

    <!--#include virtual="/cgi-bin/timecard.pl">

<!--#endif -->
```

Here, the `test_expression` is composed of two smaller expressions. The first subexpression, `${REMOTE_ADDR} = /207\.183\.233/`, is evaluated to determine whether the server-defined variable `REMOTE_ADDR` matches the `207.183.233` network address. Note that the address is written using the simple regular expression `/207\.183\.233/`, where each `.` (period) is escaped using a `\` (backslash) character. This was necessary to undo the `.` character's special meaning in regular expressions. See Appendix C for more details on regular expressions.

The second subexpression, `${DOCUMENT_NAME} = /timesheet/`, is evaluated to determine whether the current SSI file being processed has a name that matches the string `timesheet`. And, finally, the && (logical AND) requires that both subexpressions be true for the entire expression to be true. If the final expression is true, then the `/cgi-bin/timecard.pl` script is run using the `include virtual` command.

Other logical operations that you can perform on the `test_expression` are:

```
<!--#if expr="! test_expression" -->
This is printed only when the test_expression is false.
<!--#endif -->
```

and

```
<!--#if expr="test_expression1 || test_expression2" -->
This is printed when at least one of the test_expressions is
true.
<!--#endif -->
```

The = (equal) and != (not equal) operators have higher precedence than the && (and) and the || (or) operators. The ! (not) operator has the highest priority. You can use a pair of parentheses to increase priority. For example:

```
<!--#if expr="($win = yes && $loss = false) != ($profit =
yes)" -->
```

Here, the (`$win = yes && $loss = false`) is evaluated before the != operator is evaluated.

Anything that is not recognized as a variable or as an operator is treated as a string. Strings can also be quoted, like this: `'string'`. Unquoted strings cannot contain white space (blanks and tabs) because they are used to separate tokens such as variables. If multiple strings are found in a row, they are concatenated using blanks.

If you require more complex flow control constructs, you can use the following:

```
<!--#if expr="test_condition1" -->

    Do something specific to the first test condition.

<!--#elif expr="test_condition2" -->

    Do something specific to the first second condition.

<!--#else -->

    Do something as default.

<!--#endif -->
```

The `elif` enables you to create an `else-if` condition. For example:

```
<!--#if expr="${HTTP_USER_AGENT} = /MSIE/" -->

    <!--#set var="browser" value="MicrosoftIE" -->
    <!--#include flie="mypage.asp" -->

<!--#else -->

    <!--#set var="browser" value="Others" -->
    <!--#include flie="mypage.html" -->

<!--#endif -->
```

Here, the `HTTP_USER_AGENT` variable is checked to determine whether it contains the string `MSIE` (a string used by Microsoft Internet Explorer browser). If it does contain this string, then the browser variable is set to `MicrosoftIE`, and a file named `mypage.asp` is inserted in the current document. On the other hand, if the `HTTP_USER_AGENT` does not contain the `MSIE` string, it is assumed to be the another browser (such as Netscape Navigator, Lynx), and thus the browser variable is set to `Others` and the `mypage.html` file is inserted in the current document. By using the `if-then-else` construct, this example sets a different value to the same variable and loads different files.

✦   ✦   ✦

Configuring Apache for FastCGI

This chapter discusses FastCGI and how it solves the performance problems inherent in CGI, without introducing the overhead and complexity of proprietary APIs. FastCGI is fast, open, and maintainable. It offers features such as in-memory caching, persistent connections, and distributed architecture. The migration path from CGI to FastCGI is also reasonably simple.

What is FastCGI?

Simply speaking, a FastCGI application acts like a server application, which is often called a daemon in the Unix world. Unlike a CGI script, a FastCGI application is persistent and services all incoming requests by using a single instance, eliminating the overhead of starting a new process per request as in the CGI version. For example, if you need to generate a set of dynamic pages by using contents from a database, a CGI script has to connect to the database every time it is run per request. On the other hand, a FastCGI application can connect once and keep the connection alive for all the subsequent requests, and this time-saving results in higher performance. Hence, FastCGI is considered a high-performance alternative to CGI for writing Web-server applications in a variety of languages, including Perl, C, C++, Java, and Python.

The existence of CGI, FastCGI, and the Server API creates a great deal of confusion for developers and server administrators. To shed some light on this murky subject, Table 14-1 provides some key feature comparisons among these technologies.

Table 14-1
Comparing CGI, Server API, and FastCGI

Feature	CGI	Server API	FastCGI
Programming language dependency	Language independent. CGI applications can be written in almost any programming language (usually C/C++).	Applications have to be written in a language supported by the vendor API programming language.	Language independent. Like CGI, FastCGI applications can be written in any programming language.
Process isolation	Applications separate processes; buggy applications cannot crash the Web server or access the server's private internal state and compromise security. Bugs in the core server can corrupt applications.	Feature not supported. Because the FastCGI applications run in the server's address space, buggy applications can corrupt the core server.	A buggy application cannot crash or corrupt the core server or other applications.
Type of standard	Open standard. Some form of CGI has been implemented on every Web server.	Proprietary. Coding your application to a particular API locks you into a particular vendor's server.	Nonproprietary, proposed open standard. Support is under development for other Web servers, including commercial servers from Microsoft and Netscape. Apache currently supports FastCGI as a third-party module.
Platform dependency	Platform independent. CGI is not tied to any particular server architecture (single-threaded, multithreaded, threaded, and so on).	Tie-in to server architecture. API applications have to share the same architecture as the server. If the Web server is multi-threaded, the application has to be thread safe. If the Web server has single-threaded processes, multithreaded applications don't gain any performance advantage.	Platform independent. The FastCGI is not tied to any particular server architecture. Any Web server can implement the FastCGI interface.

Feature	CGI	Server API	FastCGI
Performance	A new process is created for each request and thrown away whether request is done; efficiency is poor.	Applications run in the server process and are persistent across requests. The CGI startup/initialization problem is absent.	FastCGI processes are persistent; they are reused to handle multiple requests. The CGI startup/initialization problem is absent.
Complexity	Easy to understand.	Very complex. Vendor APIs introduce a steep learning curve, with increased implementation and maintenance costs.	Simple, with easy migration from CGI.
Distributed architecture	Not supported. To run CGI applications on a remote system, a Web server is needed on that system, because CGI applications are run by Web servers.	Depends on vendor.	Supported. FastCGI applications can be run on any host that supports TCP/IP.

Achieving high performance by using caching

How fast is FastCGI? The answer depends on the application. If an application reads data from files and the data can be cached into memory, the FastCGI version of this application provides better performance than either CGI or an API-based Web-server application. A CGI application by specification cannot make use of in-memory cache because a new instance of the application runs per request and exists after request processing is complete. Similarly, most widely used API-based Web-server applications run on child processes that do not share memory, and therefore no caching can be applied. Even if in-memory caching is implemented per child process in this model, it works very poorly because each child process has to have a copy of the cache in memory, which wastes a great deal of memory.

FastCGI is designed to enable effective in-memory caching. Requests are routed from any child process to a FastCGI application server. The FastCGI application process maintains an in-memory cache. Note that in some cases a single FastCGI application server would not provide enough performance. With multithreading you run an application process designed to handle several requests at the same time. The threads handling concurrent requests share process memory, so they all have access to the same cache.

Scalability through distributed applications

Unlike CGI applications, FastCGI applications do not get the CGI environment variables from their process environment table. Instead, a full-duplex connection between the application and the Web server is used to communicate the environment information, standard input and output, and errors. This enables FastCGI applications to run on remote machines using TCP/IP connections to the Web server, as shown in Figure 14-1. This figure shows that requests from the Internet are handled by www.nitec.com (the Web server), which connects remotely via TCP connection to fcgi.nitec.com where requests are then handled by Fast CGI scripts.

Putting FastCGI through its paces

The developers of FastCGI performed tests that used three versions of an application (based on CGI, FastCGI, and a popular Web server-based API specification) that interacted with a database server. What the developers learned was that when the FastCGI version of the application used in-memory caching and persistent connection to the database server, it outperformed both CGI and the API-based versions of the application by a large margin.

When the in-memory cache was disabled for the FastCGI application, and persistent connection was used for the API-based application, the API-based application performed slightly better than the FastCGI version. This means that only when a level playing field is used (that is, FastCGI advantages such as the in-memory caching feature are disabled) the API version wins. But why would you disable caching? In other words, as long as you do not write a crippled FastCGI application, it is likely to outperform both CGI and API versions.

The tests demonstrated that the FastCGI-based application's architectural advantage resulted in a performance that was three times faster than the API counterpart. This factor is likely to be more dramatic if the applications have to connect to remote resources such as a remote database server. However, they also point out that a multithreaded Web server capable of maintaining cache and persistent connections for its API application threads is likely to outperform FastCGI applications. This is caused by the absence of interprocess communication overhead in a threaded environment. Developing multithreaded applications requires very careful design and programming, as a single faulty thread can shut down the entire Web server system.

On the other hand, FastCGI processes take advantage of the process isolation model, where they run as external processes. This provides a safety net for the Web server system. In case of a faulty FastCGI application, the Web server will still function. If you just love multithreading and can't live without it, you can always write your FastCGI applications in a multithreaded model, which still takes advantage of the process isolation model.

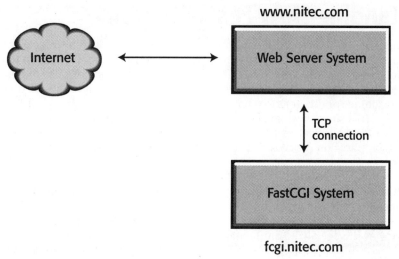

Figure 14-1: FastCGI on a remote machine

When CGI- and API-based applications become performance bottlenecks because of heavy load; the typical solution is to get either a more powerful Web server or more Web servers to run them. By using FastCGI, FastCGI applications can be run on dedicated application servers on the network, thus freeing the Web server for what it does the best — service Web requests. The Web server(s) can be tailored to perform Web service better and at the same time the FastCGI application server can be tailored to run applications efficiently. The Web administrator never has to worry about how to balance the resource requirements of the Web server and the applications on the same machine. This provides for a more flexible configuration on the Web server side as well as the application side.

Many organizations want to provide database access on their Web sites. Because of the limitations of CGI and vendor APIs, however, they must replicate a limited version of the database on the Web server to provide this service. This creates considerable work for the administrator. With remote FastCGI, the applications can run on the internal network, simplifying the administrator's job. When used with appropriate firewall configuration and auditing, this approach provides a secure, high-performance, scalable way to bring internal applications and data to the Internet.

Remote FastCGI connections have two security issues: authentication and privacy. FastCGI applications should only accept connections from Web servers that they trust (the application library includes support for IP address validation). Future versions of the protocol might include support for applications authenticating Web servers, as well as support for running remote connections over secure protocols such as Secured Socket Layer (SSL).

Understanding How FastCGI Works

FastCGI applications use a single connection to communicate with a Web server. The connection is used to deliver the environment variables and STDIN data to the applications and the STDOUT and the STDERR data to the Web server. Use of this simple communication protocol also permits FastCGI applications to reside on a different machine (or different machines) from the Web server, enabling applications to scale beyond a single system and providing easier integration with existing systems. For local applications, the server uses a full-duplex pipe to connect to the FastCGI application process. For remote applications, the server uses a TCP/IP connection.

The FastCGI Protocol used to communicate between the Web server and the applications employs a simple packet record format. Most application developers will use the FastCGI application library and won't have to worry about the protocol details. However, specialized applications can implement the FastCGI protocol directly.

Because CGI is very similar to FastCGI, let's review the CGI request process. Figure 14-2 shows the simplified CGI request-processing model.

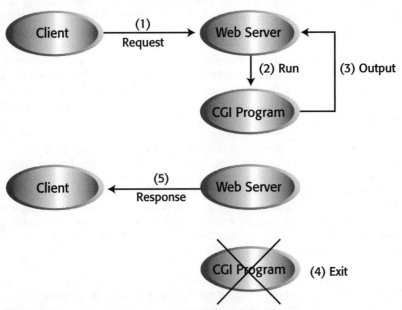

Figure 14-2: The CGI request-processing model

For each CGI request, the following happens (refer to the figure above):

1. Client system sends a request to the Web server. The Web server determines if the request needs to be serviced by a CGI program or not.

2. The Web server creates a new CGI process and the process initializes itself. The Web server passes various request-related information to the program via environment variables. Depending on the request method (GET or POST), the user data is stored in either an environment variable called QUERY_STRING or put in the process's standard input.

3. The CGI application performs its tasks and sends all its output to the standard output, which the Web server reads and parses (with the exception of nonparsed header applications).

4. The CGI program exits and the server returns the CGI output to the client.

5. The output of the CGI program is sent to the client system.

FastCGI processes are persistent. After finishing a request, they wait for a new request instead of exiting, as shown in Figure 14-3.

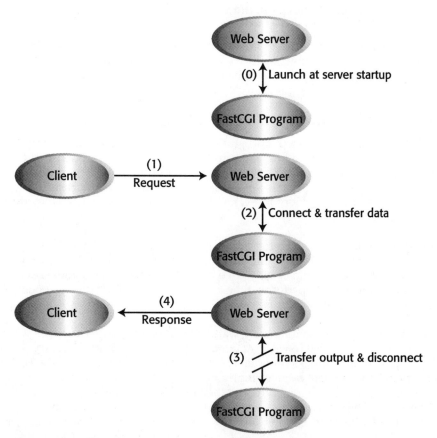

Figure 14-3: The FastCGI request-processing model

In the case of nonparsed header applications, the CGI application is responsible for producing appropriate HTTP headers, and in all other cases the Web server produces appropriate HTTP headers based on the content type found in the STDOUT of the program. The Web server logs any error information that is written to the CGI program's standard error.

The Web server creates FastCGI application processes to handle requests. The processes may be created at startup or on demand. The FastCGI program initializes itself and waits for a new connection from the Web server. Client request processing in a single-threaded FastCGI application proceeds as follows:

1. When a client request comes in, the Web server decides if the connection needs to be handled by a FastCGi program or not.

2. If the request needs to be serviced by a FastCGI program, the Web server then opens a connection to the FastCGI process, which is already running.

3. The server sends the CGI environment variable information and standard input over the connection. The FastCGI process sends the standard output and error information back to the server over the same connection and then the FastCGI process closes the connection.

4. The Web server responds to the client with the data that has been sent by the FastCGI process, completing the request. The FastCGI process then waits for another connection from the Web server.

Basic architecture of a FastCGI application

As you already know, unlike a CGI program, a FastCGI program keeps running after it processes a request. This allows it to process future requests as soon as they come, and also makes the architecture of the FastCGI program different from a CGI program. A CGI program executes sequentially and exits, whereas a FastCGI program executes sequentially and loops forever. Figure 14-4 shows the basic architecture of a FastCGI application.

As the figure shows, a FastCGI program typically has an initialization code segment and a response loop segment that encapsulates the body of the program. The initialization code is run exactly once, when the application is initialized. Initialization code usually performs time-consuming operations such as opening databases or calculating values for tables.

The response loop runs continuously, waiting for client requests to arrive. The loop starts with a call to FCGI_Accept, a routine in the FastCGI library. The FCGI_Accept routine blocks program execution until a client requests the FastCGI application. When a client request comes in, FCGI_Accept unblocks, runs one iteration of the response loop body, and then blocks again, waiting for another client request. The loop terminates only when the system administrator or the Web server kills the FastCGI application.

Basic Architecture of FastCGI Application

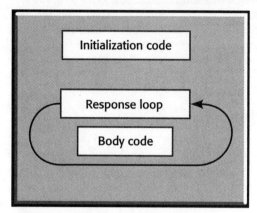

Figure 14-4: The basic architecture of a
FastCGI application

The body of the program is executed in each iteration of the response loop. In other words, for each request, the body is executed once. FastCGI sets up the request information, such as environment variables and input data, before each iteration of the body code. When the body code is executed, a subsequent call to FCGI_Accept informs the server that the program has completed a request and is ready for another. At this point FCGI_Accept blocks the execution until a new request is received.

FastCGI applications can be single-threaded or multithreaded. For single-threaded applications, the Web server maintains a pool of FastCGI processes (if the application is running locally) to handle client requests. The size of the pool is user configurable. Multithreaded FastCGI applications can accept multiple connections from the Web server and can handle them simultaneously in a single process.

Different types of FastCGI applications

Another important aspect of FastCGI is that it supports *roles* (types) of applications. Unlike a CGI application, a FastCGI application is persistent, and therefore it can be used for purposes that are not practical in CGI-based applications. The following paragraphs discuss two new types of applications that FastCGI supports.

A FastCGI application can do all that a CGI application can do, so the typical FastCGI applications are the same as their CGI counterparts. The following list shows you the new roles of applications available with FastCGI support:

✦ **Filters:** You can create a FastCGI filter application to process a requested file before it is returned to the client. For example, say you want to apply a standard set of headers and footers for each HTML (.html) page returned by the Web server. This is possible using a FastCGI filter application. When a request for an .html file comes to the server, it sends the file request to the FastCGI filter responsible for adding the header and footer. The FastCGI application returns the resulting HTML page to the server, which, in turn, is transmitted to the client.

FastCGI filter applications can significantly improve performance by caching filter results (the server provides the modification time in the request information so that applications can flush the cache when the server file has been modified). Filter applications are useful in developing parsers for HTML pages with embedded SQL statements, on-the-fly file format converters, and so on.

✦ **External authentication applications:** Other new types of applications that can be developed using FastCGI support include external authentication programs and gateways to third-party authentication applications. For example, if you use an external database server to store authentication information such as username, passwords, or other permission-specific data, you can create a FastCGI application to keep a persistent connection to the database server and to perform queries to authenticate access requests. Can this be done with a CGI application? Yes, except that a CGI application has to open the connection to the database server each time it is run. This could become expensive in terms of resource (CPU, network) utilization.

On the other hand, the FastCGI version of the same application maintains a single connection to the database server, performs queries, and returns appropriate HTTP status code based on the results of the queries. For example, when an access request is accompanied with a valid username/password pair, the FastCGI application queries the database server to determine whether the pair is allowed access to the requested resource. If the database server returns a specific value indicating that access should be allowed, the FastCGI application returns a 200 OK HTTP status code; when authorization fails, it can send a different HTTP status code, such as 401 Unauthorized.

Migrating from CGI to FastCGI

One of the main advantages of FastCGI is that the migration path from CGI to FastCGI is reasonably simple. Special Perl-based CGI scripts that use CGI.pm module can easily be turned into FastCGI applications. Any CGI program written in other languages such as C, C++, Tcl, or Java can also be converted using the FastCGI Software Development Kit (SDK).

The developers of FastCGI specifications provides a freely available software development kit (SDK) to help ease the process of FastCGI application development. The SDK is also included on the CD-ROM. This kit, provided as a compressed tar file, helps you to write FastCGI applications in C, C++, Perl, Tcl, and Java. When you uncompress and extract the tar file, it creates a `fcgi-devel-kit` directory. An `index.html` file provides information on what is available in the kit. The kit can also be obtained from the FastCGI Web site at `www.fastcgi.com/applibs`.

Things to keep in mind about migrating

The following list gives you a few tips to keep in mind when migrating CGI applications:

✦ Another issue to be aware of is this: If the CGI application being migrated has code that might interfere with a second run of the body code, it has to be fixed. The solution to this problem could be as simple as adding code to reinitialize some variables, arrays, and so on. The application must ensure that any state it creates in processing one request has no unintended effect on later requests.

✦ It's a common practice among CGI developers to subdivide a large application into smaller CGI applets, as a way to compensate for the initialization penalty associated with CGI applications. With FastCGI, it's better to have related functionality in a single executable so that there are fewer processes to manage and applications can take advantage of sharing cached information across functions.

✦ To ease migration to FastCGI, executables built with the FCGI module can run as either CGI or FastCGI programs, depending on how they are invoked. The module detects the execution environment and automatically selects FastCGI or regular I/O routines, as appropriate.

✦ Many CGI applications are written so that they do not attempt to perform any memory management operations. This is a consequence of CGI applications exiting after execution, and in most cases, the operating system is able to restore memory for other use. On top of that, many CGI applications do not even attempt to close files, as the responsibility is handed over to the operating system at exit.

In such a case, it is very important that these types of applications be fixed while migrating to the FastCGI version. Remember that FastCGI applications reside in memory as long as the Web server or the administrator does not kill them. If a CGI application that leaked memory is converted to FastCGI without anyone dealing with the memory issue, the FastCGI version might leak memory over time, eventually causing a resource fault. Avoid long weekends in the office by looking at this issue beforehand. If the CGI application is very complex, and fixing it to behave nicely (memory usage-wise) is too expensive in terms of time and effort, another solution is available to you.

You can keep a count of how many times this memory-leaking application has serviced requests and kill it by programming around it. Listing 14-1 shows a simple example of how request-processing count is kept in a simple C-based FastCGI application. As the listing shows, when the maximum number of requests have been processed the FastCGI application exits.

Listing 14-1: **memory_hog.c**

```
#include <fcgi_stdio.h>
void main(void){
    int maxRequests = 100;        // maximum num of request
before
    exiting.
    int requestCount = 0;          // used to keep count of
requests processed so far.

    while(FCGI_Accept() >= 0) {    // start of response loop
        /* body code */

        printf("Content-type: text/html\r\n");
        printf("\r\n");
        printf("Number of requests processed so far is %d.",
requestCount++);

        /* some memory leaking code could go here */


        /* end of application code */

        if(requestCount >= maxRequests) {
            /* clean-up code goes here */
            exit 0;
        }

        /* end of body code */

    }

    / * termination or clean-up code (if any) */
    exit(0);
}
```

Migrating a sample script

This section demonstrates how to migrate `fontsize.cgi`, a simple CGI script (written in Perl), which is listed in Listing 14-2.

Listing 14-2: **fontsize.cgi**

```perl
#!/usr/bin/perl -w

# Variables
my $MAX = 10;
my $i;

# Content Header
print "Content-type: text/html\n\n";

# Main loop
for ($i=0; $i < $MAX; $i++){

    print "<FONT SIZE=$i>Font Size = $i</FONT><BR>";

}

exit 0;
```

This CGI application produces the output shown in Figure 14-5.

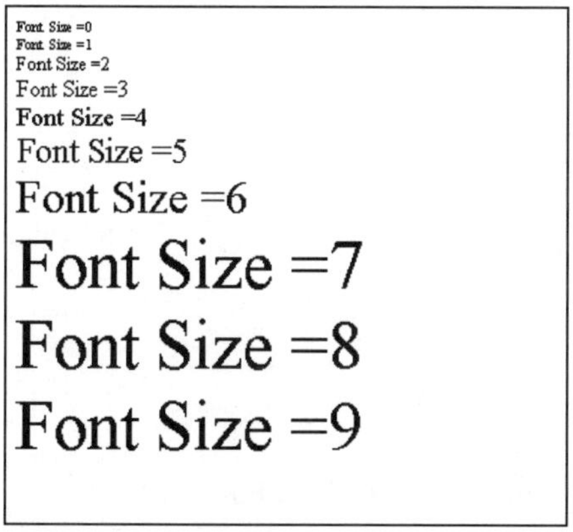

Figure 14-5: Output of the `fontsize.cgi` script

Now let's convert this to a FastCGI application. First you need to make sure you have installed the FCGI module from a Comprehensive Perl Archive Network (CPAN) site by following these steps:

1. As root, from the command-line run the following command:

```
perl -MCPAN -e shell
```

2. At the cpan> prompt enter the install FCGI command, which will install the latest version of this CPAN module if you do not already have the latest.

3. As the second line in the above script, add the following line:

```
use FCGI;
```

This tells Perl to load the FCGI module when running the script.

4. Identify the initialization block of the CGI application. For this script the initialization block consists of the following two variable declarations:

```
my $MAX = 10;
my $i;
```

5. Identify the response loop and body blocks of the CGI application. Because every request must be responded to with an appropriate Content-Type header, the body of the main code begins with this line:

```
print "Content-type: text/html\n\n";
```

The for loop responsible for the actual processing is the rest of the body.

6. Now that the body code is identified, you need to put the response loop around it. This is done using the following code:

```
while(FCGIaccept() >= 0) {

    # body code goes here

}
```

Now the body looks like this:

```
while(FCGI::accept() >= 0) {
    print "Content-type: text/html\n\n";

    for ($i=0; $i < $MAX; $i++){
        print "<FONT SIZE=$i>Font Size = $i</FONT><BR>";
    }
}
```

FastCGI applications act like server applications, so the following line is only executed if by the Web server or by the administrator sends the application a signal to terminate:

```
exit 0;
```

The FastCGI version of the entire application is listed in Listing 14-3.

Listing 14-3: **fontsize.fcgi**

```perl
#!/usr/bin/perl

# Load the FCGI module
use FCGI;

# Global variables
my $MAX = 10;
my $i;

# FastCGI Loop
while(FCGI::accept() >= 0) {

    # Content Header
    print "Content-type: text/html\n\n";

    # Main Loop
    for ($i=0; $i < $MAX; $i++){
        print "<FONT SIZE=$i>Font Size = $i</FONT><BR>";
    }
}

exit 0;
```

Setting Up FastCGI for Apache

To install `mod_fastcgi` with Apache, follow these steps:

1. Download the latest mod_fastcgi module for Apache from www.fastcgi.com for Apache.

2. Extract the source in the /usr/local/src directory. A new directory called mod_fastcgi_version is created. Read the INSTALL file in this new directory for details on how to install the module, as the installation changes from time to time.

3. Copy the new directory to a subdirectory called fastcgi under the modules directory within your Apache source tree.

4. From the Apache source distribution directory, run the following `configure --enable-module=fastcgi` and any other options that you want to specify with the `configure` script. (See Chapter 3 for details on other options available for the configure script.) If you have already compiled Apache you can replace configure with `config.status` in the preceding command to ensure that all of the options you specified when you ran configure last time are applied again.

5. Run `make` and `make install` to compile and install Apache with `mod_fastcgi` support.

6. Restart Apache using the `/usr/local/apache/bin/apachectl restart` command.

FastCGI directives for Apache

The `mod_fastcgi.c` module provides set of directives to control how you can use FastCGI applications. These directives are discussed below:

AppClass directive

This directive enables you to start FastCGI applications.

> **Syntax:** `AppClass` `path_to_FastCGI_application` `[-processes N]` `[-listen-queue-depth N]` `[-restart-delay N]` `[-priority N]` `[-port N]` `[-socket sock-name]` `[-initial-env key=value]` `[-restart-delay N]` `[-priority N]` `[-port N]` `[-socket sock-name]` `[-initial-env key=value]`
>
> **Context:** Server config

For example, the following directive enables `mod_fastcgi` to load the `/www/development/fcgi-devel-kit/echo.fcg` FastCGI application\:

```
AppClass /www/development/fcgi-devel-kit/echo.fcg -port 9000
```

The application listens on port 9000. When a FastCGI application loaded by this directive dies, `mod_fastcgi` restarts the application and writes a log entry in the error log file. The optional parameters to the AppClass directive are:

✦ `processes` — This option specifies how many FastCGI processes to create. In a high-load scenario, loading multiple instances of the same FastCGI application can provide better performance. The default value is 1.

✦ `listen-queue-depth` — This option specifies how deep the listen queue is for the FastCGI application(s) loaded with the directive. The default value is sufficient in most cases, but in a high-load scenario, you can increase the depth of the queue. This decreases chances of a request being rejected because of application(s) being busy. However, if you expect a high load, and your server is capable of running a few extra FastCGI processes, increase the number of processes instead of the depth of the listen queue. The default value is 5.

✦ `restart-delay` — This option specifies the number of seconds that will be used to delay a restart of a dead FastCGI process. This is only useful when you are using multiple instances of the same FastCGI application. In the case of a single FastCGI application, it is restarted immediately, and this option has no effect. The default value is 5. You might wonder why this delay is needed. Normally, a FastCGI application should not die; if it is dying, there is a chance that something is wrong with it. In such a case, this delay allows your server to do other useful tasks besides repeatedly restarting a faulty application.

✦ `Priority` — This option sets the process priority of a FastCGI application. The default value enables a FastCGI application to have the same priority as the Apache server itself. Other appropriate values are defined by your operating system's `setpriority` system call. In a Red Hat Linux system, the `setpriority` system call permits a value in the range of –20 to 20. The lower the number, the more favorable the scheduling used for the process. However, `mod_fastcgi` does not allow a negative value, which means that you cannot set a FastCGI process to have a higher priority than the Apache server itself. So, all you can do is use a positive integer number to lower the priority of the application. The default value is 0.

✦ `Port` — This option specifies the TCP port that the FastCGI application will listen on. Because ports lower than 1024 are used for standard services, you have to use a higher port number. Use of this option enables you to access the application from another system. No environment variable is provided by default.

✦ `Socket` — This option specifies the path name of the Unix domain socket that the application listens on. The module creates this socket within the directory specified by the `FastCgiIpcDir` directive. The default value is `Default Socket`. If you do not provide either the port or socket option, the module creates a Unix domain socket for the application by itself.

✦ `initial-env` — This option can be used to insert an environment variable (with value) in the FastCGI application's environment table. You can use this option multiple times to insert more than one key=value pair in the environment of the application. No environment variable is provided by default.

Note that the `-socket` and `-port` options are mutually exclusive. Pathname must not equal the pathname supplied to an earlier `AppClass` or `ExternalAppClass` directive.

ExternalAppClass directive

Use this directive when you have a FastCGI application running on another system.

> **Syntax:** `ExternalAppClass` *FastCGI_application_name* [*-host host:port*] [*-socket sock_name*]
>
> **Context:** Server config

In the following example, the `echo.fcg` application is running on a host called `fcgi.nitec.com` and listening to port 9090. The `<FastCGI-application-name>` is just an identifier that can be used to describe the application running on the remote host, so it can be any name you want. Make sure the name you choose is not already used in another `AppClass` or `ExternalAppClasss` directive.

```
ExternalAppClass echo.fcg  -host fcgi.nitec.com:9090
```

The optional parameters to the ExternalAppClass directive are:

✦ host — This option enables you to specify the host and the TCP port number of the FastCGI application running on another system. Use host:port format to specify the host and port. You can use either a hostname or an IP address.

✦ socket — This option enables you to specify the pathname of the Unix domain socket being used by a FastCGI application.

FastCgiIpcDir directive

This directive specifies the default path for Unix domain sockets created by the module. The default /tmp location is fine as long as you do not have cron jobs set up to clean up your /tmp directory from time to time.

Syntax: FastCgiIpcDir path_to_UNIX_domain_socket

Default: FastCgiIpcDir /tmp

Context: Server config

The socket name has the following format:

OM_WS_n.pid

n is a number and pid is the process ID of the main Apache process. If you do set this directive to a path, make sure only Apache has read and write access to the directory.

Configuring httpd.conf for FastCGI

To configure FastCGI applications, you need a combination of mod_fastcgi directives and directives provided by the Apache server.

Use the AppClass directive to start the FastCGI applications that you want to be managed by this Web server. The applications are managed in the sense that the server logs an error message when a managed process dies and attempts to restart managed processes that die.

Use one or both of the AppClass and ExternalAppClass directives to define an association between a pathname and the connection information for a FastCGI application. Connection information is either the pathname of a Unix domain socket or the IP address and port number of a TCP port. The difference between the two directives is this: A single AppClass directive both starts an application and sets up the association for communicating with it, whereas ExternalAppClass only defines the association. In the case of AppClass, the pathname used in the association is always the pathname of the application's executable; with ExternalAppClass, the pathname is arbitrary.

For an HTTP request to be processed by `mod_fastcgi`, the request's handler must be `fastcgi-script` or the request's MIME type must be `application/x-httpd-fcgi`. Apache provides several ways to set the handler and MIME type of a request:

✦ `SetHandler` (in the context of a Location or Directory section or per-directory access control file) can associate the handler `fastcgi-script` with a specific file or all the files in a directory.

✦ `AddHandler` can associate the handler `fastcgi-script` with files based on file extension.

✦ `ForceType` (in the context of a Location or Directory section or `.htaccess` file) can associate the MIME type `application/x-httpd-fcgi` with a specific file or all the files in a directory.

✦ `AddType` can associate the MIME type `application/x-httpd-fcgi` with files based on file extension.

After the `mod_fastcgi` module is configured, it handles requests as follows:

1. The connection information associated with the requested pathname is retrieved. If no connection information is associated with the pathname, the server returns the error code `404 Not Found`.

2. The `mod_fastcgi` module connects to the FastCGI application process. If the connection attempt fails, the server returns `500 Server Error`.

3. The request is transmitted to the FastCGI application process, which generates a response.

4. The application's response is received and transformed into an HTTP response. The server sends this response back to the client.

You should back up your existing `httpd.conf` file but do not use the example configuration file in Listing 14-4 right away. It is a minimal configuration that only uses the `httpd.conf` file for testing purposes. Use this configuration for initial testing with FastCGI, and when you've verified that this configuration works, merge the FastCGI-specific aspects of this configuration with your own configuration.

Listing 14-4: **Example httpd.conf Configuration File**

```
# httpd.conf-minimal for mod_fastcgi

Port 80

# You should replace the User/Group directive with appropriate
# user/group name
User $HTTP_USER
```

Continued

Listing 14-4 *(continued)*

```
Group $HTTP_GROUP

# Configure just one idle httpd child process, to simplify
# debugging
StartServers 1
MinSpareServers 1
MaxSpareServers 1

# Tell httpd where it should live, turn on access and error
# logging
ServerRoot      $APACHE
ErrorLog        logs/error.log
TransferLog     logs/access.log
ScoreBoardFile  logs/httpd.scoreboard

# Tell httpd where to get documents
#
DocumentRoot $FASTCGI

# This is how you'd place the Unix-domain socket files in the
# logs directory (you'd probably want to create a subdirectory
# for them.)
# Don't do this until you've verified that everything works
# with the socket files stored locally, in /tmp!
# FastCgiIpcDir $APACHE/logs
# Start the echo app
#
AppClass $FASTCGI/examples/echo -initial-env SOMETHING=NOTHING

# Have mod_fastcgi handle requests for the echo app #
# (otherwise the server will return the app's binary as a
file!)
#
<Location /examples/echo>
    SetHandler fastcgi-script
</Location>

# Start a FastCGI application that's accessible from other
# machines
AppClass $FastCGI/examples/echo.fcg -port 8978

<Location /examples/echo.fcg>
    SetHandler fastcgi-script
</Location>

# Connect to "remote" app started above. Because the app is
# actually local, communication will take place using TCP
# loopback.
# To test true remote operation, start one copy of this # Web
# server on one machine, and then start another copy with
```

```
# "localhost" in the line below changed to the host name of the
# first machine.
#
#ExternalAppClass remote-echo -host localhost:8978

<Location /examples/remote-echo>
    SetHandler fastcgi-script
</Location>

# This is how you'd have mod_fastcgi handle any request
# for a file with extension .fcg:
AddHandler fastcgi-script fcg

# End of httpd.conf
```

Make sure you have built the new httpd with the mod_fastcgi module and that
the FastCGI Developer's Kit is built properly. I make use of the echo program that
comes with FastCGI Developer's Kit in the example directory. Do not forget to
restart Apache after you have placed the new httpd.conf file from Listing 14-4 in
the $APACHE/conf directory. Use a browser to access http://$YOUR_HOST/
examples/echo.

$YOUR_HOST is the IP address of the host running httpd. Look for
SOMETHING=NOTHING in the initial environment that echo displays. The request
counter should increment each time you reload the page. Before you can use this
configuration, you have to make some substitutions, as shown in Table 14-2.

Table 14-2
Substitution for Example Configuration

Keyword	Replace With
$APACHE	Fully qualified pathname of the directory containing Apache
$FASTCGI	Fully qualified pathname of the directory containing your FastCGI Developer's Kit
$HTTP_USER	Username you use for the User directive
$HTTP_GROUP	Group name you use for the Group directive

✦　　✦　　✦

PHP and Apache

Only a few years ago, PHP, the PHP Hypertext Preprocessor, started out to be a macro language for HTML. Today it is deployed in six percent or more of the world's Web sites and is the de facto method of doing server-side scripting with database connectivity. PHP is a full-blown programming language that focuses on dynamic Web applications. It can run as a stand-alone script to do system administration tasks, similar to Perl and other shell programming languages, but its primary target is dynamic Web pages that render data from relational databases such as MySQL, Postgres, Oracle, DB2, and MS SQL Server.

Although PHP competes with Microsoft's ASP, Allaire's Cold Fusion, Sun's JSP, and even an open-source cousin called mod_perl, it actually predates almost all of its competitors by at least a year! Because PHP is easy to deploy, easy to use, has cross-platform support, and has native database connectivity, it has an impressive track record for being easy to learn and implement.

In this chapter, you learn how to compile, install, and configure Apache to use mod_php, the PHP module for Apache. You also learn to secure PHP and to use many of PHP's applications.

Cross-Reference If you are using Apache on Windows, I show you how to run PHP scripts on Apache for Windows in Chapter 21.

Understanding How PHP Works

PHP is an interpreted language that is traditionally used for server-side scripting. An HTML page is embedded with PHP code, which is parsed by either a server module or a CGI script to produce desired output, which is sent to the Web client; the Web client never sees any PHP code. Here is an example of a simple PHP-embedded page.

```
<HTML>
<HEAD><TITLE> Simple PHP Example </TITLE></HEAD>
<BODY>

    <?php echo "Welcome to PHP"; ?>

</BODY>
</HTML>
```

This PHP page prints out a string "Welcome to PHP" in the Web browser after the PHP engine on the server side parses it.

This method of embedding code within an HTML page is not without controversy. Many traditional software developers dislike this practice because it mixes code with presentation. If you consider HTML as a presentation vehicle for the data, then intermixing code in presentation seems very shortsighted. However, millions of users of PHP don't seem to care. Opponents of PHP and its like often argue that mixing code in presentation makes the job of the presentation expert harder. In the Web arena, the presentation expert is actually an HTML or graphics designer who is not likely to have programming knowledge. So embedding scripts in HTML pages might make life hard for the HTML designer. However, PHP offers a variety of libraries that work with page templates to solve this problem, offering an efficient development methodology and a simpler maintenance process. This way, developers focus on the business logic, and page designers can change the layout of a dynamic page without involving the developer or interfering with the PHP code. More than three million Web sites have found this to be worthwhile, making PHP a Rapid Application Development (RAD) platform.

PHP need not be used exclusively for Web development. It can also be compiled as standalone script interpreter, and it can handle simple system administration tasks as well. The latest version of PHP (version 4) has the core language engine, the Zend parser, abstracted sufficiently to be considered for other technologies where PHP can be the embedded language platform like VBA is for Microsoft Office suite.

Bringing PHP to Your Company

Although open-source software such as Linux, MySQL, and Perl are becoming more commonplace in the corporate environment, it is still often necessary to sell such technology to upper-level management. Here is what worked for me on many occasions, when PHP fit the bill, but management needed a laundry list of reasons why PHP is the right solution:

✦ **Rapid Web development** — Getting up and running with PHP scripting is very fast. Writing a Web and database integration application in PHP is a matter of hours to days, whereas programming languages such as C/C++ and Java can take months. Unlike most of the general-purpose languages, PHP is a scripting language, with a particular affinity for and emphasis on dynamic Web-page development.

✦ **Portable across major OS platforms** — PHP runs on all major platforms including Unix, Linux, Windows, OS/2, and Mac OS.

✦ **Portable across major Web server platforms** — In PHP 4.0, the Web server interface (Server API, or SAPI) is abstracted, which allows it to integrate well with different Web servers including Apache, IIS, iPlanet/Netscape Enterprise Server, and Zeus.

✦ **Built-in support for major databases** — PHP implements native interfaces for all major databases, including MySQL, Postgres, Oracle, DB2, and MS SQL Server, which makes it a good candidate for database-driven Web development.

✦ **High performance** — PHP 4 was revamped for high performance; it is is many times faster than PHP 3. A free add-on module called the Zend Optimizer from Zend Technologies can optimize an application to be 40 to 100 times faster than one that is not optimized. Many large Web sites are using PHP; you can learn about them at the PHP Web site at www.php.net.

✦ **Easy to learn for new developers** — PHP is a C-like language with automatic memory management (that is, no pointers to worry about). PHP also has elements of Perl, Java, and C++. Someone who knows any of these major languages can learn PHP in a matter of hours to days.

✦ **Supports Internet standards** — Internet standards, including IMAP, FTP, POP, XML, WDDX, LDAP, NIS, and SNMP, are supported. This means that PHP can interface with different standards and technologies with ease — all from one common tool set, without the need for expensive third-party modules.

✦ **Enterprise friendly** — Many large enterprises have bought into the Java platform already and many Java evangelists in such companies often find ways of making Java the "ideal" platform for even the smallest project, which often results in lengthy development cycles. Such companies are often ready to say no to everything else by stating that other core business logic has been already implemented in Java and therefore there is no room for PHP or its kind. Now you can say, not so fast! PHP 4 supports direct access to Java objects on any system that has Java Virtual Machines. It even supports Distributed COM (DCOM) on a Windows platform. PHP is becoming aggressive about integrating with Java and other enterprise technologies so that it can become hard to say no to PHP.

✦ **Open source community** — Open-source has proven to be a very effective software development approach. As an open-source project of the Apache Group, PHP enjoys the benefits of this approach. The PHP core developers participate in many open-source support forums such as Usenet news groups and IRC channels. Commercial support is also available from many Web-software consulting companies.

Prerequisites for PHP

Most sites using PHP also use MySQL as the database. If you plan to use MySQL, you should download the MySQL source or binary distribution from www.mysql.com/downloads/index.html. Read the installation documentation to learn how to install

MySQL on your system. You also need the MySQL development packages. Covering MySQL installation for all the platforms is beyond the scope of this book.

On my Linux system running Apache, I have installed:

✦ The server RPM for i386 systems

✦ Client programs RPM for i386 systems

✦ Include files and libraries RPM for development for i386 systems

✦ Client shared libraries RPM for i386 systems

The include files and libraries are needed for PHP if you want to compile it with MySQL support.

Compiling and Installing PHP

The current version of PHP is 4.0. You can download PHP source or binary distributions from www.php.net. This section assumes that you have downloaded the latest source distribution of PHP, php-4.1.0.tar.gz.

 Note   If you are on Windows platform, read the Running PHP Scripts in Chapter 21 to install PHP for Apache.

After downloading the source distribution, extract the source in a directory by using the tar xvzf php-4.1.0.tar.gz command. I recommend that you install it in the same directory as you installed the Apache source. For example, if you installed Apache source in /usr/local/src/httpd-2.0.16 directory, then extract PHP into the /usr/local/src directory. A new subdirectory, called php-4.1.0, will be created.

At this point, you have to decide how you plan to run PHP. PHP can be run as an Apache module (embedded in the server itself or as a DSO module) or as a CGI solution. The CGI solution means that you will not have any performance advantage over regular CGI scripts with PHP scripts because a PHP interpreter will be loaded each time to process a CGI-mode PHP script.

Building PHP as a CGI solution

Like Perl, PHP can be used in standalone scripts as well as embedded in Web pages. To build the PHP interpreter for CGI-mode operations, do the following:

1. As root change to the PHP source distribution directory and run:

    ./configure --enable-discard-path

2. Now run make && make install to compile and install the PHP interpreter on your system.

Building PHP as an Apache module

You can either store the PHP module within the Apache binary or install it as a DSO module for Apache. An advantage of a DSO module is that it can be unloaded by just commenting out a configuration line in `httpd.conf`, thus saving some memory.

Building PHP as a static Apache module

I assume that you have installed Apache source in `/usr/local/src/httpd-version` and PHP source in `/usr/local/src/php-version` directories. Here is how to compile and install PHP as a static Apache module:

1. If you have not yet installed Apache, run the following command as root from the Apache source distribution directory:

   ```
   ./configure --prefix=/usr/local/web/apache
   ```

   You can add other options if you wish to use them. Run `./configure --help` to determine whether any other option is suitable for your needs.

2. Now from the PHP source distribution directory run:

   ```
   ./configure --with-apache=../httpd-version \
               --with-mysql=/usr
   ```

   Here the `--with-mysql` option is set to `/usr` because MySQL RPM packages install the include files in `/usr/include/mysql` directory. If your system has MySQL includes in a different location, you should use a different directory name. You can discover where MySQL includes are kept by using the `locate mysql.h` command, which is available on most Unix systems with the locate database feature.

Note   You do not need the `--with-mysql` option if you do not plan on using MySQL with PHP or want to use PHP's built-in support for MySQL, which is only recommended if you do not plan on using MySQL with mod_perl or other Apache modules.

3. Run the `cp php.ini-dist /usr/local/lib/php.ini` command to copy the `php.ini-dist` file to `/usr/local/lib` as `php.ini`. This is the PHP configuration file that is discussed later in the "Configuring PHP By Using php.ini" section.

4. Run `make && make install` to compile and install the PHP side of the source code.

5. Now change directory to the Apache source distribution and run:

   ```
   /configure --prefix=/usr/local/apache\
              --activate-module= modules/php4/libphp4.a
   ```

   You can add any other options in the above command-line. Run the `./configure --help` command for information about other options.

6. Run `make && make install` to compile and install Apache with PHP support.

7. Run the `/usr/local/apache/bin/apachectl restart` command to restart (or start) Apache.

Building PHP as a Dynamic Shared Object (DSO) module

You must have DSO support enabled in Apache before you can use PHP as a DSO module. To recompile Apache with DSO support, do the following:

1. From the Apache source distribution directory run the following command as root:

```
./configure --prefix=/usr/local/apache --enable-so
```

   You can also add other options as necessary.

2. You can compile and install Apache using `make && make install` command.

After you have a DSO support-enabled Apache server, you can do the following to create a DSO module for PHP:

1. From the PHP source distribution directory run the following command as root:

```
./configure --with-apxs2=/usr/local/apache/bin/apxs \
            --with-mysql=/usr
```

   Here the `--with-mysql` option is set to `/usr` because MySQL RPM packages install the include files in `/usr/include/mysql` directory. If your system has MySQL includes in a different location, you should use a different directory name. You can find out where MySQL includes are kept by using the `locate mysql.h` command, which is available on most Unix systems with the locate database feature.

2. Now run `make && make install` to compile and install the DSO version of PHP module for Apache.

3. Run the `/usr/local/apache/bin/apachectl restart` command to restart (or start) Apache.

Configuring Apache for PHP

After you have installed the `mod_php` module for Apache and configured `php.ini` as discussed earlier, you are ready to configure Apache for PHP as follows:

1. If you have compiled and installed PHP as a DSO module for Apache, add the following line to httpd.conf file:

```
LoadModule php4_module  modules/libphp4.so
```

2. Add the following lines to the `httpd.conf` file

```
<Files *.php>
    SetOutputFilter PHP
    SetInputFilter PHP
</Files>
```

   This tells Apache that any file with `.php` extension must be treated as PHP scripts and should be processed using PHP input and output filters.

Tip

There is no reason to use a different extension for PHP scripts. For example, you can set the above AddType directive to AddType application/x-httpd-php .html and have all your HTML pages treated as PHP script. I don't recommend using the .html extension because chances are that many of your HTML pages are not PHP scripts and you simply do not want to slow down your Web server by having it parse each page for PHP scripts.

3. Save the httpd.conf file and restart the Apache Web server as usual.

Now you are ready to create PHP scripts for your Web site. You can create PHP scripts and store them anywhere in your Web site's document tree and Apache will automatically process them as PHP scripts.

Configuring PHP by Using php.ini

The PHP configuration file is called php.ini, and it is stored in the /usr/local/lib directory. When a PHP module is loaded it reads the php.ini file. The module looks for php.ini in the current working directory, the path designated by the environmental variable PHPRC, and in /usr/local/lib.

Note

If you use PHP as a CGI solution, the php.ini is read every time a PHP CGI is run. On the other hand, when PHP is loaded as an Apache module, it is read once. You must restart the Apache server by using the /usr/local/apache/bin/ apachectl restart command to reload any changes that you make in php.ini file.

PHP directives in httpd.conf

With version PHP 4 only four mod_php-specific directives, as shown in the following sections, are allowed in httpd.conf. All other PHP directives must be in php.ini file.

php_admin_flag

The php_flag directive allows you to set a boolean value (On or Off) for a configuration parameter. This directive cannot appear in directory containers or per-directory .htaccess files.

Syntax: php_admin_flag *name* On | Off

Context: Server config, virtual host

php_admin_value

The php_admin_value directive allows you to set a value for a configuration parameter. This directive cannot appear in directory containers or per-directory .htaccess files.

Syntax: `php_admin_value` *name value*

Context: Server config, virtual host

php_flag

The `php_flag` directive allows you to set a boolean value (On or Off) for a configuratio parameter.

Syntax: `php_flag name On | Off`

Context: Server config, virtual host, directory, per-directory (`.htaccess`)

For example:

```
php_flag display_errors On
```

php_value

The `php_value` directive allows you to set value for a configuration parameter.

Syntax: `php_value` *name value*

Context: Server config, virtual host, directory, per-directory (`.htaccess`)

For example:

```
php_value error_reporting 15
```

PHP Directives directives in php.ini

The `php.ini` file has a simple *directive = value* structure syntax. Lines consisting of leading semicolons or lines with only whitespaces are ignored. Section names are enclosed in brackets. You can learn about all the directives that go in `php.ini` at `www.php.net/manual/en/configuration.php`. The following sections discuss the most useful directives.

auto_append_file

The `auto_prepend_file` directive enables you to set a footer document with each PHP-parsed page.

Syntax: `auto_prepend_file` *filename*

auto_prepend_file

The `auto_prepend_file` directive enables you to set a header document with each PHP-parsed page.

Syntax: `auto_prepend_file filename`

The following example `preload.php` page will be loaded before each PHP page is processed. This page is a good place to establish database connections.

```
auto_prepend_file preload.php
```

default_charset

The `default_charset` directive sets the default character set.

> **Syntax:** `default_charset char_set`

The following example sets the default character set to 8-bit UTF:

```
default_charset = "UTF-8"
```

disable_functions

The `disable_functions` directive enables you to disable one or more functions for security reasons.

> **Syntax:** `disable_functions function_name [function_name]`

You can specify a comma-delimited list of PHP functions as shown below:

```
disable_functions = fopen, fwrite, popen
```

In the above, the functions responsible for opening, writing file or pipes are disabled.

Note   This directive is not affected by the `safe_mode` directive.

display_errors

The `display_errors` directive enables or disables printing of error message on screen. This is recommended only for use on development systems and not for use on production servers. For production systems, you should use `log_errors` along with `error_log` directives to log error messages to files or to a syslog server.

> **Syntax:** `display_errors On | Off`

enable_dl

The `enable_dl` directive enables or disables the capability to dynamically load a PHP extension.

> **Syntax:** `enable_dl On | Off`
>
> **Default setting:** `enable_dl On`

error_append_string

The `error_append_string` directive sets the string that is appended to the error message. See `error_prepend_string` directive above.

> **Syntax:** `error_append_string` *string*

error_log

The `error_log` directive sets the PHP error log path. You can specify a fully qualified pathname of the log file, or you can specify the keyword `syslog` on Unix systems to log using the syslog facility. On Windows systems, setting this directive to `syslog` writes log entries in the Windows Event log.

> **Syntax:** `error_log` *fqpn*

error_prepend_string

The `error_prepend_string` directive sets the string that is prepended to an error message. This directive is used with the `error_append_string`.

> **Syntax:** `error_prepend_string` *string*

If you do not log errors, then error messages are shown on screen. For example, by using these two directives, you can print error messages in red font color:

```
error_prepend_string = "<font color=red>"
error_append_string = "</font>"
```

error_reporting

The `error_reporting` directive enables you to specify a bit field to specify an error reporting level. The bit field can be constructed using the predefined constants shown in Table 15-1.

> **Syntax:** `error_reporting` [bit field] [*predefined_ constant*]

Table 15-1
Constants for error_reporting Directive

Constant	Meaning
E_ALL	Displays all errors, warnings, and notices
E_ERROR	Displays only fatal run-time errors
E_WARNING	Displays run-time warnings
E_PARSE	Displays parse errors

Constant	Meaning
E_NOTICE	Displays notices of likely problems in code.
E_CORE_ERROR	Displays fatal errors that occur during PHP's initial startup
E_CORE_WARNING	Displays warnings that occur during PHP's initial startup
E_COMPILE_ERROR	Displays fatal compile-time errors
E_COMPILE_WARNING	Displays compile-time warnings (nonfatal errors)
E_USER_ERROR	User-generated error message
E_USER_WARNING	User-generated warning message
E_USER_NOTICE	User-generated notice message

You can use bit field operators such as ~ (inverts), & (bitwise meaning "AND"), and | (bitwise meaning "OR") to create a custom error-reporting level. For example:

```
Error_reporting = E_ALL & ~E_WARNING & ~E_NOTICE
```

This tells the PHP engine to display all errors except warnings and notices. Displaying error messages on a production server is not recommended. You should display errors only on your development system or during the development phase of your production server. On production servers, use `log_errors` and `error_log` directives to write logs to files or to a syslog facility.

extension

The `extension` directive enables you to load a dynamic extension module for PHP itself.

> **Syntax:** extension *module_name*

For example, the following directive loads the graphics library GD extension for PHP for Windows via the extension directive. The PHP engine loads such dynamic modules at server startup.

```
extension=php_gd.dll
```

Similarly, the following directive loads the MySQL DSO module for Apache on the Unix platform with DSO support:

```
extension=mysql.so
```

You can repeat `extension` as many times as needed to load different modules.

extension_dir

The extension_dir directive defines the directory where dynamically loadable PHP modules are stored. The default value is appropriate for most PHP installations.

> **Syntax:** extension_dir *directory*
>
> **Default setting:** extension_dir ./

implicit_flush

The implicit_flush directive enables or disables implicit flushing of script output as it uses print, echo, and HTML blocks for output. When turned on, this directive will issue the flush() call after every print(), echo, or HTML block output. This is really useful for debugging purposes, but a major performance drain on the production environment. It is only recommended for development systems.

> **Syntax:** implicit_flush On | Off
>
> **Default setting:** implicit_flush Off

include_path

The include_path directive sets the path for include() and require() functions. You can list multiple directories.

> **Unix Syntax:** include_path *path*[:*path*]
>
> **Windows Syntax:** include_path *path*[;*path*]

For example, the following specifies that PHP should first look for include files in the /usr/local/lib/php directory and then in the current directory:

```
include_path = /usr/local/lib/php:.
```

On Windows, this directive is set as follows:

```
include_path = /usr/local/lib/php;.
```

log_errors

The log_errors directive enables or disables logging of PHP errors. You must use the error_log directive to specify a log path or a syslog file.

> **Syntax:** log_errors On | Off

magic_quotes_gpc

The magic_quotes_gpc directive enables or disables escaping of quotes (single quotes, double quotes, null, and backslash characters) for GET, POST, and cookie data.

Syntax: `magic_quotes_gpc On | Off`

Default setting: `magic_quotes_gpc On`

magic_quotes_runtime

The `magic_quotes_runtime` directive enables or disables automatic quoting of internally generated text. In other words, if you retrieve a record from database that has the `<?php anything goes here ?>` type of tag embedded in it, the contents within the tags (which is part of the data) will be escaped (i.e. not processed) and not treated as PHP code.

Syntax: `magic_quotes_runtime On | Off`

Default setting: `magic_quotes_runtime = Off`

max_execution_time

The `max_execution_time` directive sets the maximum time that a script can run to produce output. After a script goes past specified amount of seconds, PHP times out the script. Unless you plan on running PHP scripts that take a lot of time, the default value should be acceptable for most situations.

Syntax: `max_execution_time seconds`

Default setting: `max_execution_time 30`

memory_limit

The `memory_limit` directive sets the maximum RAM a PHP script can consume. The default, 8MB, should be plenty for small-to-modest PHP scripts. You can specify memory in bytes as well.

Syntax: `memory_limit bytes [nM]`

Default setting: `memory_limit 8M`

For example, the following are equivalent:

```
memory_limit 8M
memory_limit 8388608
```

output_buffering

The `output_buffering` directive allows you to enable or disable output buffering. When it is set to On, you can print HTTP headers anywhere in a PHP script. Being able to output a header in the middle of a script even after printing other contents means that a script can display an error page even if it was partially successful earlier.

Syntax: `output_buffering On | Off`

Default setting: `output_buffering On`

You can also use the built-in `ob_start()` and `ob_end_flush()` directives to start and end flushing of the contents directly. For example:

```
<?php

ob_start();  // Buffer all output

echo "Buffered contents \n";

ob_end_flush(); // Page rendered, flush the output buffer.

?>
```

Here the output is buffered.

safe_mode

The `safe_mode` directive sets the safe mode for PHP when it is used as a CGI solution. When set to `On`, this directive ensures that PHP scripts run by the PHP interpreter in CGI mode are not allowed any access beyond the document root directory of the Web site.

> **Syntax:** `safe_mode On | Off`
>
> **Default setting:** `safe_mode Off`

safe_mode_allowed_env_vars

The `safe_mode_allowed_env_vars` directive enables you to set a prefix for all the environment variables that a user can change by using the `putenv()` function. The default value enables users to change any environment variable that starts with `PHP_` prefix.

> **Syntax:** `safe_mode_allowed_env_vars` *prefix*
>
> **Default setting:** `safe_mode_allowed_env_vars PHP_`

safe_mode_protected_env_vars

The `safe_mode_protected_env_vars` directive allows you to set a comma-delimited list of environment variables that cannot be changed by any PHP script that uses the `putenv()` function.

> **Syntax:** `safe_mode_protected_env_vars` *environment_variable* [*environment_variable* ...]
>
> **Default setting:** `safe_mode_protected_env_vars = LD_LIBRARY_PATH`

If you wish to protect all the environment variable that starts with HTTP_ prefix, you can use:

```
safe_mode_protected_env_vars = HTTP_
```

track_errors

The `track_errors` directive enables or disables storing of error message in a PHP variable called $php_errormsg.

>**Syntax:** `track_errors On | Off`

upload_max_filesize

The `upload_max_filesize` directive sets the maximum size of a file that can be uploaded via PHP. The default limit is 2MB (2M). Alternatively, you can specify just the kilobyte number.

>**Syntax:** `upload_max_filesize kilobytes`
>
>**Default setting:** `upload_max_filesize 2M`

For example, the following are equivalent:

```
upload_max_filesize = 2M
upload_max_filesize = 2097152
```

upload_tmp_dir

The `load_tmp_dir` directive defines the temporary directory location for files uploaded via PHP. It is customary to set this to `/tmp` on Unix systems; on Windows systems, this is typically set to `/temp` or left alone, in which case, PHP uses the system default.

>**Syntax:** `load_tmp_dir directory`

Working with PHP

This section shows you a few examples of how you can use PHP scripts to generate dynamic Web contents.

Creating a simple command-line PHP script

After you have configured PHP, you can run a PHP script from the command-line just like you can run a Perl script. By default the PHP interpreter is installed in the `/usr/local/bin` directory on Unix systems; on Windows systems, it is installed in the directory where you extracted the distribution. You can create a simple PHP script called `test.php` as shown in Listing 15-1.

Listing 15-1: test.php

```
#!/usr/local/bin/php -q
# For Windows change the above line to:
#!Drive:/path/to/php -q
#
#

<?php

    echo "Welcome to the PHP World\n";

?>
```

You can run this script from the command line by using /usr/local/bin/php test.php, or you can change the file permission for the script by using chmod +x test.php and execute it using ./test.php from the script directory. The -q option used here tells PHP to suppress HTTP content-type headers, which it prints to make output Web compliant.

Creating simple PHP Web pages

Creating a PHP script for your Web site is as simple as the example in the last section. Listing 15-2 shows a simple script called hello.php.

Listing 15-2: hello.php

```
<html>
    <head><title>Hello World Script</title>
<body>

<?php echo "Hello World from PHP"; ?>

</body>
</html>
```

When you save this script in a directory within your Web server's document tree, you can access it via http://your_web_server/path/to/hello.php. If you have used a directive such as AddType application/x-httpd-php.php as instructed in the "Configuring Apache for PHP" section earlier in this chapter, then the PHP module will parse and execute the one-line PHP script that prints out "Hello World from PHP" sentence. Note that PHP automatically prints the appropriate Content-Type header (text/html).

Now lets make a little more useful script, as shown in Listing 15-3, which shows information about PHP as it is installed on your Web server.

Listing 15-3: **info.php**

```
<html>
    <head><title>Hello World Script</title>
<body>

<?php
  phpinfo();
?>

</body>
</html>
```

This page calls a PHP function called phpinfo() to display a great deal of PHP options as they are currently configured using php.ini.

Using a PHP script as a Server-Side Include

If you wish to use PHP scripts in Server-Side Include (SSI) calls, you can call your PHP script using the following SSI tag:

```
<!--#include virtual="/path/script_name.php"-->
```

For example:

```
<!--#include virtual="/phpssi/test.php"-->
```

Here the PHP script called /phpsssi/test.php script will be loaded from the page that uses the above SSI calls. For the PHP scripts to work with SSI, you must do the following:

1. Enable the ExecCGI option in the directory containing the PHP scripts that need to be run via SSI calls.

2. Make sure the IncludesNoExec option is disabled for the same directory. For example:

    ```
    DocumentRoot "/www/mysite/htdocs"

    <Directory "/www/mysite/htdocs/parsed">
    ```

```
        Options +Includes

        AddType text/html .shtml

        <FilesMatch "\.shtml[.$]">
            SetOutputFilter INCLUDES
        </FilesMatch>

    </Directory>

    <Directory "/www/mysite/htdocs/php">
        Options +ExecCGI

        <Files *.php>
            SetOutputFilter PHP
            SetInputFilter PHP
        </Files>

    </Directory>
```

In the above configuration segment, all files ending with the .shtml extension in the /www/mysite/htdocs/parsed directory are treated as SSI pages and all files in the /www/mysite/htdocs/php directory are treated as PHP scripts that can also be run via SSI calls. Now, a SSI page in /www/mysite/htdocs/parsed directory can call a script in /www/mysite/htdocs/php via the following SSI call:

```
<!--#include virtual="/php/script_name.php"-->
```

Using a PHP page for a directory index

If you have enabled PHP support in httpd.conf as discussed earlier in "Configuring Apache for PHP," you can also use PHP scripts as a directory index page. For example:

```
DirectoryIndex index.html index.php
```

Here the directive sets index.html as the preferred index page for a directory, but if index.html is missing, index.php is used instead.

However, if you wish to use PHP scripts as the default index, then reverse the order of the filenames so that index.php is before others. For example:

```
DirectoryIndex index.php index.html
```

Now Apache will look for the index.php script first.

Using include files

PHP lets you include an external PHP code library file or an ordinary HTML file in a script. For example:

```
<html>
<head>
   <title> PHP Resource Site </title>
</head>

<body>
<h1>PHP Resource</h1>
<hr>

<p>Welcome to PHP Resource Site. </p>

<?php

   include('/www/mysite/htdocs/global/copyright.html');

?>

</body>
</html>
```

Here the simple PHP script is a single function call `include('/www/mysite/htdocs/global/copyright.html');`, which tells PHP to include a file called `/www/mysite/htdocs/global/copyright.html`. This `copyright.html` page is included in the current page, like the `<!--#include virtual="/path/filename"-->` Server Side Include (SSI) tag. However, the included file can be a PHP script itself. For example:

```
include('/www/mysite/htdocs/global/copyright.php');
```

loads a PHP script called `copyright.php` from the given directory. The script in the included file will be executed. Any code in the included file has access to variables in the parent script. For example, the `copyright.php` script has access to $year variable.

```
<?php

  $year = '2001';

  include('/www/mysite/htdocs/global/copyright.php');

?>
```

So, the `copyright.php` script can contain statement such as `echo "The current year is: $year \n";`. You can include multiple files, or you can include the same file multiple times. Each time the included script will be executed. For example:

```php
<?php

  $year = '2001';

  include('/www/mysite/htdocs/global/copyright.php');

  $year = '2002'

  include('/www/mysite/htdocs/global/copyright.php');


?>
```

If the copyright.php script consists of a simple PHP script such as `<?php echo "The current year is: $year\n"; ?>`, then above script will display:

```
The current year is: 2001
The current year is: 2002
```

You can also use `include_once()` to include a PHP script or a static HTML file. However, if you use `include_once()` instead of `include()`, the code in the included script is executed just once. For example:

```php
<?php

  $year = '2001';

  include_once('/www/mysite/htdocs/global/copyright.php');

  $year = '2002'

  include_once('/www/mysite/htdocs/global/copyright.php');

?>
```

Here the output for the same `copyright.php` is:

```
The current year is: 2001
```

The second `include_once()` will not execute `copyright.php` again. You can use `include()` or `include_once()` functions to centralize common code or HTML files that are needed for many PHP pages.

You can also use the require() and require_once() functions similarly. The require() function replaces itself with the contents of the named file. This replacement happens during code compilation by the PHP engine, not during the execution of the calling script. The require_once() function only inserts the contents of the required script once.

Note The include(), include_once(), require(), **and** require_once() functions can access any file anywhere in the file system as long as the user ID that is used to run the Web server has read access to the file.

Enhancing error handling with PHP

Apache provides a directive called ErrorDocument that enables you to display a custom error page for a server error. For example:

```
ErrorDocument 404 /missing.html
```

Whenever the server encounters a request for a missing file or directory it sends a Status: 404 Not Found response and then displays the /missing.html page. You can change this to:

```
ErrorDocument 404 /missing.php
```

which causes the PHP script called missing.php to be executed whenever Apache encounters the same error. However, Microsoft IE detects a 40x response and displays a custom error message that it generates. To bypass such a page, you can make the missing.php page return a Status: 200 OK response instead. For example, with this code:

```
<?php

header("Status: 200 OK\n");
header("Location: /missing.html");

?>
```

the missing.php script displays the HTTP success header and then instructs Apache to redirect the Web client to /missing.html.

Processing Web forms with PHP

PHP makes Web form processing simple. You can access Web form data fields as variables within a PHP script. Listing 15-4 shows a simple Web form that has a single input field called keywords.

Listing 15-4: **simple_form.html**

```html
<html>
<head><title>Simple HTML Form</title>
</head>

<body>

<form action="form.php">
<input type="text" name="keywords" size=30>
<input type=submit>

</form>
</body>
</html>
```

When a user submits this form via a Web browser, the browser sends a GET request such as `http://server/form.php?keywords=value_entered_in_the_form`.

For example, if you enter the keyword `makesite` and submit the above form to `www.domain.com`, the Web server will receive a request for `http://www.domain.com/form.php?keywords=makesite`.

The `form.php` script responsible for processing this Web form is shown in Listing 15-5.

Listing 15-5: **form.php**

```php
<?php

    echo "You have entered $keywords keyword(s).\n";

?>
```

This simple PHP script prints out the keywords entered in the keywords field in the HTML form called `form.html`.

For the following request:

```
http://www.domain.com/form.php?keywords=makesite
```

the script prints:

```
You have entered makesite as keyword(s).
```

Here the variable $keywords is assigned the value makesite' because keywords=makesite is the query string passed to the server via the GET method. If the Web form's <form action="form.php"> line is changed to <form action="form.php" method="POST">, then the HTTP POST method will be used and the keywords=makesite data will be read by the PHP module and automatically made available to the script as the value of the script variable $keywords.

If the Web form has multiple fields, all the fields are turned into script variables that are named accordingly. For example, a modified version of simple_form.html is shown in Listing 15-6.

Listing 15-6: **modifed_simple_form.html**

```html
<html>
<head>
    <title>Simple HTML Form</title>
</head>

<body>
<form action="modified_form.php" method="POST">

<input type="text" name="keywords" size=30>
<select name="case">
<option value="lower">Lower case</option>
<option value="upper">Upper case</option>
<option value="dontcare">Don't Care</option>
</select>

<input type=submit>

</form>
</body>
</html>
```

Here the form has two input fields (keywords and case).

When this Web form is submitted via the POST method, the modified_form.php shown in Listing 15-7 receives all the data.

Listing 15-7: **modified_form.php**

```php
<?php

print "You entered:<br>Keywords: $keywords <br>Case: $case\n";

?>
```

For example, when a user enters `makesite` as the `keywords` field value and chooses the `dontcare` case option from the drop-down list, the script (`modified_form.php`) displays the following:

```
You entered:
Keywords: makesite
Case: upper
```

Creating sessions with PHP

PHP 4 introduced native session management, which makes creating user sessions simple. This means that you can track a user as the user moves from one page to another. There are two ways to maintain sessions with PHP.

Using HTTP cookies to create user sessions

This is the default method. To create a session you need to call the `session_start()` function in your PHP page. For example, look at simple PHP page called `start.php`, which is shown in Listing 15-8.

Listing 15-8: **start.php**

```php
<?php
  session_start();
  session_register('count');
  $count++;
?>
<html>
<head><title>Start Session</title>
</head>
<body bgcolor="Red">

<?php echo "You have visited this page $count time(s)."; ?>

<p>
<a href="/next_page.php">Next</a>
</body>
</html>
```

In the listing you can see two PHP scripts. The first script creates a session by calling the `session_start()` function. It also registers a session variable called count by using the `session_register()` function and increments the variable by one. Notice that this script is kept outside the `<html>` tag. This is required because the script sets the session cookie, which is an HTTP header that must come before any contents. The above PHP page assumes that you have `output_buffering` set to Off in php.ini. This is the default setting because output buffering causes PHP pages to be slower. If you turn on output buffering by setting output_buffering = On in php.ini, you can place the PHP scripts anywhere in the page.

The second script simply prints the value of $count. Now if you load this page using a Web browser for the first time, the session_start() function will create a new HTTP cookie-based session. The cookie sent to your Web browser will have attributes similar to the following:

```
Cookie Name: PHPSESSID
Domain     : 192.168.1.100
Path       : /
Expires    : End of session
Secure     : No
Data       : 3de4aa1f73e33dd8f2c8b8d9f69e442e
```

The name of the cookie that is sent to the Web browser is PHPSESSID. This is the default name set in php.ini by using the following line:

```
session.name = PHPSESSID
```

You can change this to another name if you wish. By default the cookie is valid for only the Web server itself. The sample cookie above shows the domain field of the cookie is set to the IP address of the Web server. If you wish to allow a session cookie to be valid throughout multiple Web servers within your domain, you can set the session.cookie_domain directive in the php.ini file to the top-level domain name of your Web sites. For example, if you have three Web sites — corp.domain.com, www.domain.com, and extranet.domain.com—and would like the session cookie to be valid in all three of these sites, you can set the session.cookie_domain as follows:

```
session.cookie_domain = .domain.com
```

Notice the leading period before the top-level domain name (domain.com); it enables the cookie to be valid over all hosts under this domain.

The default session cookie expires at the end of a session. In other words, when a Web browser is closed, the session cookie is expired. This default behavior is set using the session.cookie_lifetime directive in the php.ini file. By default it is set to 0, which makes the cookie expire at the end of a session (that is, when the user closes the browser):

```
session.cookie_lifetime = 0
```

Note

PHP does not store any user data within the cookie. The cookie is simply an identifier that points to user data on the server side.

After the first script in Listing 15-8 creates the session, you can easily access the session variable(s) in other pages. For example, Listing 15-9 shows next_page.php, which uses the session variable called $count created in start.php.

Listing 15-9: next_page.php

```
<html>
<head><title>Using Session Variables</title>
</head>
<body bgcolor="Red">

<?php
    session_start();
    $count++;
    echo "You have visited this page $count time(s).";
?>

</body>
</html>
```

Any time you want to make use of a current session in a new page you must use the session_start() method. This is a bit confusing because it might cause you to think that you are creating a new session. Actually, session_start()detects the existing session and uses it. The session variables become available after you have issued the session_start() function call. Notice that in this page, we do not place the script before the contents. In other words, we have not placed the script before <html> tag because we are no longer issuing a new session, so no new cookie needs to be set. However, this assumes that you have an existing session. To be able to create a new session if one does not exist, move the script outside the content such as the start.php page or enable output_buffering in php.ini. Also, if you plan to allow session creation on any page, you have to use the session_register() method to register variables as shown in start.php.

In any page in which you use session_start() to select the current session, you can also use session_register() to add new variables to the user session.

Using URL encoding to create user sessions

If you do not want to rely on cookies for maintaining a session, you can use *URL-encoded sessions*. Setting the session.use_cookies directive to 0 in php.ini enables this mode. However, unlike the cookie mode, this mode requires that you pass session ID (set via session.name in php.ini) by using <?=SID?> as part of URLs in a page. For example, Listing 15-10 shows a page called start_url_encoded_session.php.

Listing 15-10: start_url_encoded_session.php

```
<?php
  session_start();
  session_register('count');
```

```
   $count++;
?>

<html>
<head><title>Session Management</title>
</head>
<body bgcolor="Red">


<p>
<?php echo "You have visited this page $count time(s)."; ?>

<p>
<a href="/next_page.php?<?=SID?>">Next Page</a>
</body>
</html>
```

Notice the link titled Next Page. When the user clicks on this link, the browser requests /next_page.php and a query string called PHPSESSID=*session_ identifier* is passed to the Web server. Here's a sample URL request:

```
http://207.183.233.21/next_page.php?PHPSESSID=6b2cee31528316080ff88fe81f800bf8
```

This enables the PHP script (next_page.php) to know which session the user belongs to and to avoid the use of HTTP cookies. If you wish to maintain the session by using this method, all the links in the PHP page have to have the <?=SID?> tag appended to them; otherwise, the session will not be available on every PHP page.

Terminating a user session

Ending a session is as simple as creating one. For example, the following PHP script will terminate the current user session:

```
<?php
   session_start();
   $sessionArray=$HTTP_SESSION_VARS;
   session_destroy();

   foreach ($sessionArray as $session_name => $session_value) {
      unset($$session_name);
   }
   unset($sessionArray);
?>
```

Here the session_start() is needed to connect the script page to the current session. Then $sessionArray is assigned the session variables stored in global variable $HTTP_SESSION_VARS. The session_destroy() function is called to remove session data from the server. The foreach loop explicitly unsets each session variable. Finally, the $sessionArray variable is also unset to completely remove the session.

Note By default, session data are stored in files (because `session.save_handler = files` in `php.ini`) and also by default the data is stored in session files (prefix `sess_identifier`) in the `/tmp` directory. If you wish to change the session file directory, set the `session.save_path` directive in `php.ini` to point to a different directory. Make sure session files are not readable by anyone other than the Web server user.

Using MySQL with PHP

PHP works very well with MySQL, Postgres, Oracle, and other popular databases. MySQL is the most widely used database platform for PHP. If you have not yet installed MySQL on your system, you can learn how to install it at `www.mysql.com`.

Creating a simple PHP page to access a MySQL database

To access a MySQL database you need a username and password that MySQL accepts for access to the desired database. For example, Listing 15-11 shows a PHP script called `simple_query.php`, which accesses a MySQL database called `www` as user `httpd` with password `no1secret` from the local host.

Listing 15-11: **simple_query.php**

```php
<?php

    $host = 'localhost';
    $user = 'httpd';
    $passwd = 'no1secret';
    $database_name = 'www;
    $table = 'users';

    $dbh = mysql_connect($host, $user, $passwd);

    mysql_select_db($database_name, $dbh);

?>
<html>
<head><title>Simple Query Script</title></head>
<body>

<table border=1>
<tr><th>Name</th> <th>Password</th></tr>

<?php

    $result = mysql_query("SELECT * from $table", $dbh);
```

```
    while ($myRow = mysql_fetch_row($result)) {
        printf("<tr><td>%s</td><td>%s</td></tr>", $myRow[0],
$myRow[1]);
    }
?>

</table>
</body>
</html>
```

Here's what's going on in the above listing:

1. This script defines the $host, $user, $passwd, $database, and $table
   variables that can be set to the appropriate MySQL server host name,
   username, password, database name, and table name.

2. The script then uses the mysql_connect() function to create a connection to
   the database server every time the page is requested. The connection handle
   is stored in another variable called $dbh.

3. The mysql_select_db() function selects the $database-specified database
   to use. At this point, the $dbh handle is connected to the database server and
   it operates on the named database.

4. The script prints out a regular HTML document, which has another tiny PHP
   script embedded in it, which performs a SQL query to the connected database
   by using the mysql_query() function. The query is supplied as the argument
   for this function along with the database handle ($dbh).

5. After the query is done, the script uses mysql_fetch_row() method to
   extract rows of data from the resulting data set. This function returns an array
   of columns for each row of data returned.

6. A printf() function is used to print two elements of the $myRow array. Notice
   that the very first element of the $myRow array is indexed with 0.

7. The while loop continues until there are no more rows left for
   mysql_fetch_row to fetch, at which time the script completes and rest
   of the HTML document is printed. The resulting page looks as follows on
   some sample data:

```
<html>
<head><title>Simple Query Script</title></head>
<body>

<table border=1>
<tr><th>Name</th> <th>Password</th></tr>

<tr><td>kabir</td><td>mysecret1</td></tr><tr><td>esmith</td><
td>sale007</td></tr>
```

```
</table>
</body>
</html>
```

8. As you can see, the embedded PHP script is parsed out and the end user on the browser side does not even know which database or which user/password was used to produce this page.

If you have a lot of pages where you use the same MySQL database to display data elements using various queries, you should use the `include()` function to simplify your code management tasks. For example, Listing 15-12 shows a modified version of `simple_query.php` script that includes the `include()` function.

Listing 15-12: **simple_query2.php**

```php
<?php include('/usr/local/apache/secrets/mysql/header.inc'); ?>

<html>
<head><title>Simple Query Script</title></head>
<body>

<table border=1>
<tr><th>Name</th> <th>Password</th></tr>

<?php

    $sth = mysql_query("SELECT * from $table", $dbh);
    while ($myRow = mysql_fetch_row($sth)) {
        printf("<tr><td>%s</td><td>%s</td></tr>", $myRow[0],
$myRow[1]);
    }
?>

</table>
</body>
</html>
```

When the above script is accessed via the Web the resulting page is same as the one produced by `simple_query.php`. However, here the script users a header file that contains the database connection script as shown below:

```php
<?php

    $host = 'localhost';
    $user = 'httpd';
    $passwd = 'no1secret';
    $database_name = 'www;
```

```
    $table = 'users';

    $dbh = mysql_connect($host, $user, $passwd);

    mysql_select_db($database_name, $dbh);

?>
```

By removing this script from each page that uses it, you make it very easy to change the host name, username, password, database name, and table name. If you have 20 pages that use the same database and table, you can now update the password once in the header.inc file and be done!

Securing PHP include files

If you use include files, as shown in the last section, to store username, password, and other information, such as database host name, database name, and table names, that are not to be seen by users, make sure you keep the include files in a safe directory where Web browsers cannot browse them. The best place is outside the document tree of the Web site. If the document root is /www/mysite/htdocs, then create a directory called /www/mysite/secrets/mysql and keep the include files there.

If you must create the include files inside the document root, disallow Web browsing by using the following configuration in httpd.conf:

```
<Directory /path/to/include_files>
    <Limit>
      order deny,allow
      deny from all
    </Limit>
</Directory>
```

Don't forget to replace /path/to/include_files with the path to the real directory of the include files. If you keep your include files all over the Web site, you can still disable Web access to them by using the following configuration segment in httpd.conf:

```
<Files ~ "\.inc$">
    Order allow,deny
    Deny from all
</Files>
```

Note   This will only work if you always make sure all your PHP include files are named with the extension .inc.

Authenticating users with PHP and MySQL

You can use a PHP script to authenticate users via MySQL database. Listing 15-13 shows a simple script that uses a MySQL database to authenticate users.

Listing 15-13: auth.php

```php
<?php

ob_start();
include('/usr/local/apache/htdocs/mysql/header.inc');

function show_dialog($realm = "Restricted Section") {

    header("WWW-Authenticate: Basic realm='$realm'");
    header('HTTP/1.0 401 Unauthorized');
    echo 'Authorization Required.';
    exit;

}


if ((!isset($PHP_AUTH_USER)) || (!isset($PHP_AUTH_PW))) {

    show_challenge();

} else if ((isset($PHP_AUTH_USER)) && (isset($PHP_AUTH_PW))){

    $sth = mysql_query("SELECT 1 from $table WHERE
                                username = '$PHP_AUTH_USER'
                                and
                                passwd = '$PHP_AUTH_PW'",
                                $dbh);

    $success = mysql_fetch_row($sth);

    if ($success[0] == '') {

        show_challenge();

    } else {

        echo "<P>You're authorized!</p>";

        # Do something here
    }
}

ob_end_flush();
?>
```

When this script is requested, it uses the isset() function checks whether two variables called $PHP_AUTH_USER and $PHP_AUTH_PW are set. These two variables are set by PHP if a user has entered a username and password in response to a basic authentication challenge.

Because the first-time user has not yet seen the authentication challenge dialog box, these two variables are empty and the show_challenge() function is called. This function simply prints out the Basic HTTP authentication headers, which forces the Web browser to display a dialog box asking the user to enter a username and a password.

When the user enters a username and password pair, the pair is sent via the authentication response header to the Apache server, which is seen by PHP. PHP then sets the $PHP_AUTH_USER and $PHP_AUTH_PW variables accordingly. After the script is called again automatically in the authentication response request, the script uses the MySQL database to verify whether or not the username/password pair exists. If the user credentials (username/password pair) are valid, the script displays the message "You're authorized!" and terminates. On the other hand, if the credentials are invalid, the authentication challenge is reissued.

Notice that the include('/usr/local/apache/htdocs/mysql/header.inc') call hides all the database connectivity code. The header.inc file is shown below:

```php
<?php

    $host = 'localhost';
    $user = 'httpd';
    $passwd = 'no1secret';
    $database_name = 'www;
    $table = 'users';

    $dbh = mysql_connect($host, $user, $passwd);

    mysql_select_db($database_name, $dbh);
?>
```

Here the MySQL database called www is on localhost and can be accessed by a user called httpd using no1secret as the password. The www database has a table called users. You can change these parameters as desired to connect to the appropriate database on the local host or a remote MySQL database server. This include file opens a connection to the named database on the appropriate host and returns a connection handle called $dbh, which is available to auth.php.

In the auth.php script, notice this line:

```php
$sth = mysql_query("SELECT 1 from $table
                  WHERE username = '$PHP_AUTH_USER' and
                        passwd = '$PHP_AUTH_PW'",
                  $dbh);
```

This line performs an SQL query that returns 1 if user-supplied credentials (stored in $PHP_AUTH_USER and $PHP_AUTH_PW automatically by PHP) matches a username and passwd field, respectively, in the (users) table.

Note   If your users table has a different field name for `username` or `passwd`, make sure you change the query statement to reflect those names.

The `$success` = `mysql_fetch_row($sth)` statement returns an array called `$success`, which should have returned the value 1 as the first element in `$success[0]` if the query is successful. Or else the element is undefined.

By using the first element `$success[0]`, the decision to display (or not to display) the authentication challenge by using `show_challenge()` is made.

After a user is authenticated, this simple `auth.php` script does not do anything other than print a message stating that the user was successfully authenticated. You can, of course, have the script do much more than that. For example, you can redirect the user to a protected subdirectory by using the `Header("Location: /path/to/subdirectory");`.

✦   ✦   ✦

Using Perl with Apache

A primary goal of the Apache/Perl integration project was to bring the full power of the Perl programming language into the Apache server. This resulted in the development of mod_perl, which you can compile and link together with Apache and Perl to provide an object-oriented Perl interface to the server's C language API. This enables Perl programmers to write Apache modules in Perl. An Apache-Perl module may step in during the handler, header parser, URI translation, authentication, authorization, access, type check, fix-up, logger, and cleanup stages of a request.

The mod_perl module is widely used with Apache to create dynamic contents. mod_perl is a very efficient way to use Perl with Apache; you no longer have to run Perl-based CGI scripts, which are slow, resource consuming, and often not suitable for sites that receive a large number of simultaneous requests per second. This chapter discusses how to compile, install, and configure Apache for mod_perl, how to run your old CGI scripts by using mod_perl, and how to develop mod_perl modules to take advantage of the Apache API.

Compiling and Installing mod_perl

Here is how you can download, compile and install mod_perl on your system:

1. Download the latest version of the mod_perl source into the /usr/local/src directory from the http://perl.apache.org/dist site or from an official mirror site.

Caution   Please make sure you read the installation notes and README files in the source distribution before proceeding with the compilation. The steps discussed below might change with newer version of mod_perl and/or newer Apache.

2. As `root`, **extract the** `mod_perl` **source distribution by using the** `tar xvzf mod_perl-version.tar.gz` **command. This section assumes that you extracted the Apache source distribution into** `/usr/local/src`.

3. **Change to the** `/usr/local/src/mod_perl-version` **directory and run:**

```
Perl Makefile.PL APACHE_SRC=../apache-version \
DO_HTTPD=1 \
USE_APACHE=1 \
PERL_MARK_WHERE=1 \
EVERYTHING=1
```

Don't forget to change `../apache-version` **with the appropriate pathname.**

4. **Run the** `make && make test && make install` **command to compile, test, and install the mod_perl library into the Apache source distribution.**

5. **Change to the Apache source distribution directory and run** `make install` **to compile and install Apache with mod_perl support.**

6. **Start the newly compiled Apache server by using the** `/usr/local/apache/bin/apachectl start` **command. If you are already running a previous version of Apache server, use the** `/usr/local/apache/bin/apachectl stop` **command to stop it and then run the start command to relaunch the new server with** `mod_perl` **capabilities. If you're on a Unix system, you can run the** `lynx -dump -head http://localhost/` **command to dump the headers that the server displays. If** `mod_perl` **is installed properly, you will see** `mod_perl/version` **information in the header information.**

Running CGI Scripts by Using mod_perl

Because CGI scripts are slow and take up more resources under heavy load, in an ideal world you will not run CGI scripts when `mod_perl` is working on your system. However, the reality is that system administrators are busy people and porting something that is working already is often ignored because other, more serious, work is awaiting elsewhere. Fortunately, `mod_perl` enables you to run your CGI scripts by using a default `mod_perl` module called `Apache::Registry.pm`. So, you can run your CGI scripts under `mod_perl` immediately. Here is how.

1. In `httpd.conf` file, create an alias called `/apps/` to point to your CGI script directory by adding the following line:

```
Alias /apps/  "/www/mysite/cgi-bin"
```

Make sure you change the `/www/mysite/cgi-bin` to whatever is the appropriate CGI script directory on your system.

2. Tell Apache to load the `Apache::Registry` module during startup by adding the following line in `httpd.conf`:

```
PerlModule Apache::Registry
```

3. Tell Apache to run all scripts via `Apache::Registry` for the `/apps/` directory by adding the following configuration segment in `httpd.conf`:

```
<Location /apps>
    SetHandler perl-script
    PerlHandler Apache::Registry
    Options ExecCGI
</Location>
```

4. Restart the Apache server by using the `/usr/local/apache/bin/apachectl restart` command.

5. Access a CGI script using a Web browser by using `http://your_server_name/apps/script_name`. If you have a ScriptAlias directive setup to point `/cgi-bin/` to `/www/mysite/cgi-bin` (or whatever the CGI script directory on your system is called), then you can access the CGI scripts as "CGI" script by using `http://your_server_name/cgi-bin/script_name`, or you can access the same script with `mod_perl` by using `http://your_server_name/apps/script_name`. The latter has the advantage of not spawning a new CGI process for each request, enabling it to perform faster. Note that the `mod_perl` environment variable can distinguish how a script is being run (CGI or `mod_perl`). Consider, for example, the following code segment:

```
if ($ENV{MOD_PERL} ne '') {

    # Run as mod_perl script as a native mod_perl
    # module or Apache::Registry run script

} else {

    # CGI Script being run via mod_cgi as a
    # separate process
}
```

The above conditional statement detects how a script is being run. The scripts in the apps directory will be run via the `Apache::Registry` module. This means that you can remove the `mod_cgi` module from your system completely by recompiling Apache with `--disable-module=cgi` option.

Don't Reinvent the Wheel

Before you go about writing a cool `mod_perl` module for your Web server, consider looking around on CPAN for existing modules that might solve your problem. As of this writing, there are about 500 `mod_perl`-specific Perl modules on CPAN. You can view the available modules on CPAN as follows:

1. Run the `perl -MCPAN -e shell` command.

2. At the `cpan>` prompt, enter `i /Apache/`. You should receive a list of all the available Apache-related modules.

Creating mod_perl Module By Using the Perl API for Apache

When you installed mod_perl on your system you also installed a very powerful Perl Application Programming Interface (API) for Apache. By using this API, you can develop mod_perl scripts that take advantage of mod_perl in a "native" way. Although you can run CGI scripts by using mod_perl, they are not designed for mod_perl that uses the Perl API and therefore cannot take full advantage of power of mod_perl. The following material shows how you can develop scripts that are written using the Perl API for Apache to take full advantage of the mod_perl module.

A native mod_perl script is written as a Perl module with the following architecture:

```
package MODULE_NAME;

sub handler {

    # use the Apache API provided request
    # object to do something useful
}

sub module_method_1 { # do something useful }
sub module_method_2 { # do something useful }
sub module_method_3 { # do something useful }
...
sub module_method_N { # do something useful }

1;
```

Here, the module file starts with a package name. The name of the package must match the name of the module file. For example, if you name your package (that is, module) as:

```
Package MyModule;
```

then you must name the file that contains this module as MyModule.pm. Typically, Perl module files are kept in a subdirectory within the list of directories pointed to by the @INC array. You can find out which directories are pointed to by @INC by running the following command from the command-line:

```
perl -le 'print join("\n", @INC)'
```

You might see output similar to the following:

```
/usr/lib/perl5/5.6.0/i386-linux
/usr/lib/perl5/5.6.0
/usr/lib/perl5/site_perl/5.6.0/i386-linux
/usr/lib/perl5/site_perl/5.6.0
/usr/lib/perl5/site_perl
```

If you use a Perl version other than 5.6.0, then the paths should reflect that. When mod_perl encounters the first request for a module, it looks at the directories to locate the module. Because it is not a good idea to mix your custom module(s) with the standard modules provided with Perl and mod_perl, you should create a new directory called Development in /usr/lib/perl5/site_perl and keep your custom modules in that directory. This enables mod_perl to find your custom modules in the /usr/lib/perl5/site_perl/Development directory when they are needed. Also, make sure you set the file permissions for this new directory so that Apache user (set via User directive in httpd.conf) can read this directory and the files within it. You can use the following commands to create the new directory and to set the file permissions:

```
mkdir -p /usr/lib/perl5/site_perl/Development
chown -R Apache_User:Apache_Group /usr/lib/perl5/site_perl/Development
chmod -R 750 /usr/lib/perl5/site_perl/Develpoment
```

Don't forget to change Apache_User and Apache_Group to the appropriate user and group names as set in httpd.conf, by using User and Group directives, respectively.

After you have created a directory, you can create a simple module as shown in Listing 16-1. Save this module as /usr/lib/perl5/site_perl/ Develpoment/SimpleAPI.pm.

Listing 16-1: **A Simple Example of a Perl API for Apache**

```
package Development::SimpleAPI;

use strict;

use Apache::Constants qw(:common);

my $callCounter = 0;

sub handler {

    my $r = shift;

    $r->send_http_header('text/html');

    print <<HTML_DOC;

<html>
<head><title>Simple Perl API Example Script</title> </head>
<body>
    <h1>Simple Perl API Example Script</h1>
    <hr>
```

Continued

Listing 16-1 *(continued)*

```
      <p>Process ID: $$ </p>
      <p>Request count: $callCounter </p>
      <hr>
   </body>
   </html>

HTML_DOC

   $callCounter++;

   return OK;

}


1;
```

The module name is `Development::SimpleAPI`. This tells `mod_perl` to load the module from a subdirectory called `Development` under any of the directories pointed to by `@INC`. Because you created the `Development` subdirectory in the `/usr/lib/perl5/site_perl` directory, `mod_perl` will load the `SimpleAPI.pm` module from this directory. This module's purpose is to demonstrate `mod_perl` features.

This module works as follows:

✦ The `use strict;` line tells Perl to enforce checking of unsafe constructs. This is a very important line for `mod_perl` modules. For example, if a variable is used in the script without properly declaring it by using a `my` statement, then Perl will complain about it and force you to declare it before using it.

Note   This type of checking is very important because `mod_perl` modules are loaded in memory once and run until the server is stopped. If one or more unnecessary variables are used, the chance of a memory leak occurring might increase.

✦ The `use Apache::Constants qw(:common);` line simply loads the `Constants.pm` module, which defines a set of constants, such as `OK`, `REDIRECT`, and `DONE`, that can be used readily in the script.

✦ The next line defines the `$callCounter` variable and sets it to zero. This variable is global to the entire script and its value is available to all invocations of the script from within the Apache child process. Also, note that the variable is set to zero after when the module is initially loaded.

✦ Next, a `handler()` method is defined. This method is given the Apache request object (`$r`) as a parameter, which it uses to write a Content-Type header by using the built-in `send_http_header()` method.

✦ The handler() method then prints a minimal HTML document, which displays the Process ID ($$) of the Apache child process and requests a count by using the $callCounter variable. The $callCounter variable is incremented afterwards. The method returns with an OK status and the request processing terminates.

✦ The final line 1; is necessary for Perl modules, which must return a non-zero number to qualify as a module.

The following steps show how you can run the SimpleAPI.pm module.

1. First, add the following configuration segment to the httpd.conf file:

```
# Configuration for running mod_perl modules
PerlModule Development::SimpleAPI

<Location /firstone>
  SetHandler perl-script
  PerlHandler Development::SimpleAPI
</Location>
```

Here's what's going on in the above segment:

- The PerlModule directive loads the Development::SimpleAPI module at Apache server startup.

- The <Location> directive is sets a handler of type perl-script for location /firstone.

- The PerlHandler directive tells Apache that the perl-script (that is, mod_perl) handler for the /firstone location is the Development::SimpleAPI module, which can be found in Development/SimpleAPI.pm file under a directory pointed to by the @INC array.

2. Restart the Apache server by using the /usr/local/apache/bin/apachectl restart command.

3. Run the SimpleAPI.pm module for the first time by using the http://*your_server_name*/firstone URL.

The request count starts from 0 and goes up if you keep refreshing the page. Also, the PID of the Apache child process changes very infrequently. To make sure that you know how mod_perl modules work, you must understand that:

✦ During server startup each child process gets shared access to a copy of the SimpleAPI.pm code. This removes the CGI cost (that is, the cost of invoking a CGI script every time it is requested) because the module is already loaded in memory and is available to each child process and to each child processes' threads (if any).

✦ The first time you access http://*your_server_name*/firstone, the module is run for the first time and the $callCounter variable is incremented. Subsequent calls (via your browser's refresh button) increase the request count. The count is only increasing for the child process that is servicing your request, however. Another child process starts the counter from zero; the $callCounter is really not shared among the child processes. In other words, although the module code is shared among the Apache children, the data is not shared.

✦ Whenever the SimpleAPI.pm module is called, Apache passes a request object called $r to the handler() method. The handler() method acts as the point-of-entry for the module. Code outside the method is only executed if the hander() method directly or indirectly requires it. For example, in the following code, method_one() and method_two() are called because handler() requires them:

```
sub handler {

    my $r = shift;

    method_one();
    method_two();


    return OK;
}

sub method_one {
    # something useful
}

sub method_two {
    # something useful
}
```

✦ The handler() method must return an Apache status code such as OK, DECLINED, DONE, NOT_FOUND, FORBIDDEN, AUTH_REQUIRED, or SERVER_ERROR. You can find a complete list of Apache status constants in the Constants.pm file supplied with mod_perl. Use the locate Constants.pm command to locate the file, or use your system's file finder utility to locate it. On Linux systems running Perl 5.6.0, the file path is /usr/lib/perl5/site_perl/5.6.0/i386-linux/Apache/Constants.pm.

Using CGI.pm to Write mod_perl Modules

Most people who use Perl with Apache know how to use the CGI.pm module for writing CGI scripts in Perl. Thankfully, the CGI.pm author realized that people who are used to using this module might want to still use it in a non-CGI environment such as mod_perl, so the module's author made sure that this module is very usable under mod_perl. For example, Listing 16-2 shows a CGI.pm version of the SimpleAPI.pm module, which is now called SimpleAPIUsingCGI.pm.

Listing 16-2: A Simple Example that Uses a CGI.pm Module in a mod_perl Module

```
package Development::SimpleAPIUsingCGI;

use strict;

use Apache::Constants qw(:common);

use CGI (-compile: all);

my $callCounter = 0;

sub handler {

  my $query = new CGI;

  print $query->header;
  print $query->start_html('Simple Perl API Example Using
CGI.pm'),
        $query->h1('Simple Perl API Example Using CGI.pm
Module'),
        $query->hr,
        $query->p("Process ID: $$"),
        $query->p("Request count: $callCounter"),
        $query->hr,
        $query->end_html;

  $callCounter++;

  return OK;

}

1;
```

Avid CGI.pm developers will notice that I used the -compile: all option when telling Perl that I want to use the CGI.pm module. Here Perl is told to compile all CGI.pm code once during the initial loading of the module during server startup. This ensures that all CGI.pm features are readily available to the SimpleAPIUsingCGI.pm module. No more time will be necessary to compile any CGI.pm-specific code during a request cycle. Of course, if you do not use a lot of features of CGI.pm, you can use

CGI qw(-compile :standard), or CGI qw(-compile :standard :html3), and so on, to reduce memory usage by CGI.pm itself. Remember that keeping a lot of unused code in memory wastes your system resources.

Also notice that the CGI object, $query, is created within the handler() method. This is necessary because if you create a CGI object outside the handler() method in the global section of the module, such as the $callCounter, the object will be created once for the first request and it will only have that request's information. For example, if you move the my $query = new CGI; line outside of the handler() method and place it right after the my $callCounter = 0; line, the script will treat each subsequent request after the initial request as the same request. Thus, if you need to access the query string information using the $query->param() method, you will only get the data for the first request because the $query object is not created for each request. This is why it is very important that you create the request-specific $query object within the handler() method as shown in Listing 16-2.

The SimpleAPIUsingCGI.pm module provides the same functionality as the SimpleAPI.pm and can be run via the http://*your_server_name*/*cgipm_example* URL after you add the following lines to httpd.conf and restart the server:

```
# Configuration for running mod_perl modules
PerlModule Development::SimpleAPIUsingCGI

<Location /cgipm_example>
  SetHandler perl-script
  PerlHandler Development::SimpleAPIUsingCGI
</Location>
```

Preloading Perl Modules to Save Memory

If you use a lot of CPAN modules such as CGI or DBI, or have a lot of custom-developed modules for your Apache server, you might want to use the PerlModule directive to preload them during server startup. Doing so saves time during the first request for such modules and also increases the chances of sharing the code pages (memory) among the Apache child processes. For example, if you use the standard CGI, DBI, and Digest::MD5 modules in one or more of your mod_perl modules, you can simply preload these modules by placing the following directives in httpd.conf:

```
PerlModule CGI
PerlModule DBI
PerlModue Digest::MD5
```

Another approach is to use the PerlRequire directive. This directive can be set to an external Perl script that loads all the modules that you want to preload and possibly share among the Apache child processes. For example:

```
PerlRequire /usr/local/apache/apps/startup.pl
```

This tells Apache require the `/usr/local/apache/apps/startup.pl` script during startup. This script is loaded into memory, which, in turn, should load the necessary modules. For example, this script can be as follows:

```perl
#!/usr/bin/perl

use CGI ();
use DBI ();
use Digest::MD5 ();
1;
```

Each of the use *module_name* () lines loads a specific module. The empty parentheses ensure that default importing of symbols from these modules is not performed, which saves some memory.

 Note   If you use all the features of the `CGI.pm` module you can add `CGI->compile(':all')` to the `startup.pl` script to compile them, which saves time during request processing.

Also, make sure that the `startup.pl script` is accessible and executable by the Apache user (set using `User` directive in `httpd.conf` file).

Keeping Track of mod_perl Modules in Memory

Being able to keep track of which `mod_perl` modules your Web server is using is a great help in system administration. By using the `Apache::Status` module that comes with mod_perl, you can keep track of loaded modules and get lots of information about them. To do so, follow these steps:

1. As root, you must install the prerequisite `Devel::Symdump` module from a CPAN mirror site by using this command:

   ```
   perl -MCPAN -e 'install Devel:Symdump'
   ```

2. Add the following configuration segment to the `httpd.conf` before any other `PerlModule` directive.

   ```
   PerlModule Apache::Status

   <Location /perl-status>
       SetHandler  perl-script
       PerlHandler Apache::Status
   </Location>
   ```

   This code ensures that the `Apache::Status` module is loaded before any other modules. If you use the `PerlRequire` directive to load modules via an external startup script, you do not need the `PerlModule Apache::Status` line. Instead, load the `Apache::Status` module in the startup script before any other module.

3. Restart the Apache server and access information on loaded mod_perl modules by using `http://your_server_name/perl-status`. This page displays a list of options (links), as shown here:

```
Perl Configuration
Loaded Modules
Inheritance Tree
Enabled mod_perl Hooks
Environment
PerlRequired Files
Signal Handlers
Symbol Table Dump
ISA Tree
Compiled Registry Scripts
```

4. Click on the `Loaded Modules` link to view all the loaded `mod_perl` modules. The other links also provide valuable status information on the `mod_perl` specifics.

Implementing ASP by Using the Apache::ASP Module

Active Server Page (ASP) is a common scripting platform in the Windows world. However, it is no longer a Windows-only scripting platform. By using `mod_perl` with the `Apache::ASP` CPAN module you can create ASP pages that have embedded Perl-based ASP scripts. Here is how:

1. As `root`, run the following command:

```
perl -MCPAN -e 'install Apache::ASP'
```

The CPAN module installs the `Apache::ASP` module from a local CPAN mirror site. If it fails for some reason, investigate why and resolve the issues. Usually installation is successful unless you are missing a prerequisite module. In such event, install the missing prerequisite module in the same manner, and then install `Apache::ASP`.

2. After the `Apache::ASP` module is installed, create a subdirectory called `asp` in your document root directory. I assume that your `DocumentRoot` directive is set to `/www/mysite/htdocs` and that you created the `/www/mysite/htdocs/asp` directory.

3. Create a test script called `test.asp` as shown below and store it in `/www/mysite/htdocs/asp` directory.

```
<html>
<head><title>ASP Example</title></head>
<body>

<%
        $Application->Lock();
```

```
        $Application->{Count}+=1;
        $Application->UnLock();

%>

<h1> ASP Page </h1>
<hr>
<p>
This page has been called <%=$Application->{Count}%> times.

</body>
</html>
```

This simple `test.asp` ASP page simply increments the ASP Application object by one each time this page is called.

4. Add the following lines to the `httpd.conf` file:

```
Alias /asp/ "/www/mysite/htdocs/asp"

<Location /asp/>
  SetHandler perl-script
  PerlHandler Apache::ASP
  PerlSetVar Global /tmp
</Location>
```

Here's what's going on in the preceding lines:

- The `/asp/` alias points to the `/www/mysite/htdocs/asp` directory. Make sure you change this so that it points to appropriate directory in your system.

- The `<Location>` container tells Apache to use the `Apache::ASP` module to handle all the files in this directory; it also sets the `Global` variable to the `/tmp` directory.

- The `Apache::ASP` module creates a directory called `/tmp/.state` in which it stores state information so that even if you shutdown and restart the server, the state information is not lost.

5. Change the file permissions for the `asp` directory and its contents to enable Apache user (i.e. whatever you set the User directive to in `httpd.conf`) to access the files. For example, use the `chown -R httpd:httpd /www/mysite/htdocs/asp && chmod -R 750 /www/mysite/htdocs/asp` commands to ensure that Apache user (`httpd`) and Apache group (`httpd`) can access the directory and files stored in it.

6. Restart the Apache server by using the `/usr/local/apache/bin/apachectl restart` command and access the `test.asp` page by using `http://your_server_name/asp/test.asp`.

Note   To learn more about how to write ASP scripts in Perl visit the ASP Web site at www.apache-asp.org.

◆   ◆   ◆

Running Java Servlets and JSP Pages with Tomcat

Over the last few years, Java has become the leading Web-application platform for enterprise-grade Web development needs. Many large companies refuse to consider using any platform but Java for Web development. Fortunately, Apache deals with Java quite well. Using an Apache adapter (module) it can interact with Tomcat, the official reference implementation of both Java servlet 2.2 and JSP 1.1 specification.

A *servlet* is a Java program that runs within the Java Virtual Machine (JVM) on the Web-server system. When a request for a servlet is received, a new thread is created from an already-loaded servlet. Thus, a servlet has a much smaller startup requirement than does a CGI script. Like a CGI program, a servlet can interact with HTTP requests from Web browsers, and with relational databases such as Oracle, Postgres, and MySQL, or with other external applications, and then write results in HTTP response. A servlet has access to user-supplied data, HTTP headers such as cookies, browser information, host information, and so on, just as a CGI program does.

Tomcat, an open -source Java run-time environment (called a *container*), for Java servlets, is pretty good at handling servlet requests, but there is a compromise you can establish between Tomcat and Apache. You can use an Apache module called mod_jk (it was previously called mod_jserv) to interact with Tomcat so that Tomcat can be responsible for serving the servlet requests and Apache can handle everything else.

Tomcat also implements Java Server Page (JSP) support that allows you to place Java code in HTML pages with .jsp extensions. Pages with such extensions are parsed by the servlet very similarly to how PHP or ASP pages are parsed. This makes JSP very similar to PHP or Active Server Pages (ASP) — with the added advantages of having the portability of Java and the robustness of the JSP Application Programming Interface (API). Actually, JSP has all the capabilities of Java servlets, but it is easier to write Java code for small programming tasks. JSP scripts are actually converted automatically into servlets by Tomcat when they are first referenced, and compiled and instantiated in the servlet container.

This chapter discusses how to make Tomcat and mod_jk work with Apache so that you can use servlets and JSP.

Note   If you are not familiar with Java servlets or JSP consider reading a book on these before proceeding with this chapter. A detailed discussion of servlet or JSP is beyond the scope of this book.

Why Use Servlets?

The advantages of running servlets versus CGI scripts, or even mod_perl or FastCGI applications, are:

✦ Servlets are truly platform-independent and therefore highly portable. All modern server platforms support Java. Therefore, deploying servlets in a hybrid network is much easier than any other Web application platform.

✦ Fewer overheads than a CGI program because of a smaller startup footprint. No new processes need to be spawned to service a request. Simply a new thread is created to service the new request, which has a much smaller resource cost than starting a new process.

✦ Database connectivity via Java Database Connectivity (JDBC) is preferable to connectivity via the Perl DBI, which has major performance issues in high-load environments. CGI scripts connect to the database every time they start up; mod_perl scripts can cache database connection but have no good way of managing connections. An Apache server running 50 children can potentially open 50 database connections. Because high-performance sites have many Web servers such database connection requirement alone will be impossible to manage for most RDBM available today. The best approach is connection pooling which can be done in a mod_perl environment with a great deal of custom coding but it is quite simple in a servlet environment.

✦ Java servlets run in the Java "send box" (JVM), which makes them more secure option over other Web application platforms — no more buffer overrun to worry about.

Installing Tomcat

To install Tomcat on your server you need to have a Java Run-time Environment (JRE), and if you plan on developing servlets then you will also need Java Development Kit (JDK). Also, to use Tomcat with Apache you need the mod_jk module. In this section I discuss how to install these components to create a Tomcat server environment.

Installing the latest JDK for Tomcat

Before you install Tomcat, you need an appropriate Java Runtime Environment (JRE). A full software development kit (SDK) is necessary if you'll be writing and compiling your own Java servlets. The Java Development Kit (JDK), available for free from Sun Microsystems (http://java.sun.com/), includes both JRE and development packages. You can install JDK for a Linux system by following these steps:

1. Download the latest release version of JDK (that is, SDK) from the official Java Web site. As of this writing the latest version is 1.3 and it is offered as a self-extracting shell script that creates a binary RPM package. You can download the j2sdk-1_3_0_02-linux-rpm.bin (or a later version if available) in a directory.

2. As root, run

   ```
   sh j2sdk-version-linux-rpm.bin
   ```

   For example, for the 1.3 version you can run:

   ```
   sh j2sdk-1_3_0_02-linux-rpm.bin
   ```

   When this script runs it displays a license, which you should say yes to. The script unpacks and creates an RPM package called j2sdk-version-linux.rpm (for JDK 1.3 it is j2sdk-1_3_0_02-linux.rpm).

3. Run the rpm -ivh j2sdk-version-linux.rpm to install the JDK. For example, to install the JDK 1.3, run the rpm -ivh j2sdk-1_3_0_02-linux.rpm command.

4. The JDK is installed in the /usr/java/jdkversion directory. For example, the 1.3 JDK is installed in the /usr/java/jdk1.3.0_02 directory. This directory is the JAVA_HOME directory. You should set up an environment variable called $JAVA_HOME to point to this directory. If you use the bash shell, you can set this in your ~/.bashrc file as follows:

   ```
   export JAVA_HOME=/usr/java/jdkversion
   ```

   For example:

   ```
   export JAVA_HOME=/usr/java/jdk1.3.0_02
   ```

   Enter echo $JAVA_HOME in your shell prompt to determine whether this environment variable is set. If you just added it to the .bashrc file, then you must run source ~/.bashrc to export the variable.

Note
If you use a different shell, such as `tcsh` or `csh`, use the `setenv JAVA_HOME /usr/java/jdkversion` command instead of the preceding `export` command.

5. Add the `$JAVA_HOME` directory in your `$PATH` environment variable using the following line in your `~/.bashrc` file.

```
export PATH=${PATH}:${JAVA_HOME}/bin
```

This line must follow the `JAVA_HOME` line discussed in the last step.

6. Test the JDK installation by running the `java -version` command. You should see output similar to the following:

```
java version "1.3.0_02"
Java(TM) 2 Runtime Environment, Standard Edition (build
1.3.0_02)
Java HotSpot(TM) Client VM (build 1.3.0_02, mixed mode)
```

Installing Tomcat and the mod_jk module

After you have installed the latest release version of JDK from the official Java Web site (as described in the last section), you're ready to install Tomcat and the `mod_jk` module as follows:

Download the latest Tomcat binary packages from the official Tomcat Web site at `http://jakarta.apache.org`. As of this writing the latest release version of Tomcat is 3.2, which will change to 4.0 by the time this book is in the stores. So make sure you change the version numbers mentioned in the instructions given below.

For Linux, the latest binary RPM packages can be downloaded from `http://jakarta.apache.org/builds/jakarta-tomcat/release/v3.2.1/rpms` directory. The packages you should download for Linux are:

✦ `tomcat-version.noarch.rpm` (current version: `tomcat-3.2.1-1.noarch.rpm`). This is the binary distribution of Tomcat.

✦ `tomcat-mod-version.i386.rpm` (current version: `tomcat-mod-3.2.1-1.i386.rpm`). This contains the binary distribution of `mod_jk` and the older `mod_jserv` modules for Apache. This will install the `mod_jk.so` module in `/usr/lib/apache` directory. Because this is an Apache Dynamic Shared Object (DSO) module, you must have Apache compiled with shared object support. You can quickly check whether the Apache binary you are running has `mod_so` support. Run the `/usr/local/apache/bin/httpd -l` command to list all the modules currently compiled into Apache binary. If `mod_so.c` is not listed, you need to recompile Apache by using `--enable-module=so` option in the configure script found in Apache source distribution, and then run the `make && make install` command to reinstall Apache with DSO support.

✦ `tomcat-manual-version.noarch.rpm` (current version: `tomcat-manual-3.2.1-1.noarch.rpm`). This is the Tomcat document package.

Download all of the foregoing files into a temporary new directory and run `rpm -ivh tomcat*.rpm` command from that directory as root to install all the software.

By default, Tomcat is installed in `/var/tomcat` directory. You need to add the following environment variable in your `~/.bashrc` file:

```
export TOMCAT_HOME=/var/tomcat
```

Load the variable in your current shell by running the `source ~/.bashrc` command.

Configuring Tomcat

In this section I discuss how to configure Tomcat for Apache and how to manage security for Tomcat using the Java Security Manager tool.

Configuring Tomcat for Apache

The primary configuration file for Tomcat is `/var/tomcat/server.xml`. As you can tell from the extension, it is an XML file.

Tomcat can use two types of connection handlers, the Ajp13 and Ajp12 protocols. The Ajp13 protocol is the newer protocol, and provides better performance, and which also supports Secure Socket Layer (SSL) connectivity.

To activate the Ajp13 protocol-based connection handler in Tomcat, you should make sure that that the following connector configuration is not commented out in `server.xml` file:

```
<Connector
className="org.apache.tomcat.service.PoolTcpConnector">

<Parameter name="handler"

value="org.apache.tomcat.service.connector.Ajp13ConnectionHandl
er"/>

    <Parameter name="port" value="8009"/>
</Connector>
```

Caution The `servlet.xml` file should already have a block of code similar to the preceding for Ajp12 connections on port 8007. Even if you plain to use the Ajp13-based connector, you should not delete this connector. It is required to shut down Tomcat.

The properties of a Tomcat instance, called *worker,* are defined in `/var/tomcat/conf/workers.properties` file. The default file (without comments) contains the properties shown in Listing 17-1.

Listing 17-1: **Default Tomcat (worker) properties**

```
workers.tomcat_home=c:\jakarta-tomcat
workers.java_home=c:\jdk1.2.2
ps=\
worker.list=ajp12, ajp13

worker.ajp12.port=8007
worker.ajp12.host=localhost
worker.ajp12.type=ajp12
worker.ajp12.lbfactor=1

worker.ajp13.port=8009
worker.ajp13.host=localhost
worker.ajp13.type=ajp13
worker.ajp13.lbfactor=1

worker.loadbalancer.type=lb
worker.loadbalancer.balanced_workers=ajp12, ajp13

worker.inprocess.type=jni
worker.inprocess.class_path=$(workers.tomcat_home)$(ps)classes

worker.inprocess.class_path=$(workers.tomcat_home)$(ps)lib$(ps)jaxp.jar
worker.inprocess.class_path=$(workers.tomcat_home)$(ps)lib$(ps)parser.jar


worker.inprocess.class_path=$(workers.tomcat_home)$(ps)lib$(ps)jasper.jar
worker.inprocess.class_path=$(workers.tomcat_home)$(ps)lib$(ps)servlet.jar
worker.inprocess.class_path=$(workers.tomcat_home)$(ps)lib$(ps)webserver.jar

worker.inprocess.class_path=$(workers.java_home)$(ps)lib$(ps)tools.jar

worker.inprocess.cmd_line=-config
worker.inprocess.cmd_line=$(workers.tomcat_home)/conf/jni_server.xml
worker.inprocess.cmd_line=-home
worker.inprocess.cmd_line=$(workers.tomcat_home)

worker.inprocess.jvm_lib=$(workers.java_home)$(ps)jre$(ps)bin$(ps)classic$(ps)jv
m.dll

worker.inprocess.stdout=$(workers.tomcat_home)$(ps)inprocess.stdout
worker.inprocess.stderr=$(workers.tomcat_home)$(ps)inprocess.stderr
worker.inprocess.sysprops=tomcat.home=$(workers.tomcat_home)
```

This default properties file defines an ajp12 worker, ajp13 worker, a jni worker, and a lb worker. The differences among these worker types are shown in Table 17-1.

Table 17-1
Differences Among Types of Workers

Worker Type	Description
ajp12	This worker uses the ajpv12 protocol to forward requests to out-of-process Tomcat workers that are using the ajpv12 protocol.
ajp13	This worker uses the ajpv13 protocol to forward requests to out-of-process Tomcat workers that are using the ajpv12 protocol. Because ajpv13 is a newer protocol than ajpv12, the ajp13 type of worker can achieve better performance than can an ajp12 type worker. Also, ajp13 offers SSL support.
jni	By using the Java Network Interface (JNI) this type of worker can forward requests to in-process Tomcat workers. An in-process worker runs within a JVM opened in Apache's own memory space.
lb	By using a simple round-robin load-balancing scheme, this worker can forward requests.

The workers.properties file has a few settings that are "global" to all types of workers. For example:

```
workers.tomcat_home=c:\jakarta-tomcat
workers.java_home=c:\jdk1.2.2
ps=\
worker.list=ajp12, ajp13
```

These settings are global. The first one sets the home directory for Tomcat. This should be set to the value of the $TOMCAT_HOME environment variable. Because the default installation of Tomcat creates /var/tomcat as the directory under Linux system, you should change the default value (c:\Jakarta-tomcat) as follows:

```
workers.tomcat_home=/var/tomcat
```

Similarly, the workers.java_home sets the top-level path for the JDK installation directory, which under Linux is /usr/java/jdkversion (for example, for JDK 1.3, this is /usr/java/jdk1.3.0_02). So, this should be set as follows:

```
workers.java_home=/usr/java/jdk1.3.0_02
```

The next line tells Tomcat what separator to use for separating directory elements. The default value \ works for Windows system because on Windows platforms directory names are separated by using \. On UNIX systems, it should be /. So, set this line as shown here:

```
ps=/
```

The `worker.list` tells Tomcat the number of works you want to define. The default list defines ajp12 and ajp13 as two workers.

Each of these workers can have its own properties set using `worker.<worker_name>.properties = value` lines. For example, in default file, the ajp13 worker has these attributes set:

```
worker.ajp12.port=8007
worker.ajp12.host=localhost
worker.ajp12.type=ajp12
worker.ajp12.lbfactor=1
```

The first line sets the port number, which is used by the ajp12 worker to listen for requests. The second line defines the hostname where this worker is listening for connections. The third line defines the type of the worker. I think it was a poor choice to name the worker ajp12 when it is also type ajp12. You can name a worker anything you want as long as the name consists of letters and numbers. The forth line gives the worker a weight rating for load-balancing purposes. A high number indicates a powerful machine and when there are multiple machines involved in a load-balanced scenario, the load-balancer worker will choose the worker, which has the highest lbfactor first.

The same properties for the ajp13 worker are defined in the next four lines in the `workers.properties` file.

The next two lines define a worker called `loadbalancer`, which is of type lb and which balances workers ajp12 and ajp13 using a round-robin schema. These two lines are:

```
worker.loadbalancer.type=lb
worker.loadbalancer.balanced_workers=ajp12, ajp13
```

The next two lines define a worker called `inprocess` of type jni. This worker's `class_path` is defined by setting the second line to `/var/tomcat/classes` for a Linux system:

```
worker.inprocess.type=jni
worker.inprocess.class_path=$(workers.tomcat_home)$(ps)classes
```

The next six lines add six library files to the class path:

```
worker.inprocess.class_path=$(workers.tomcat_home)$(ps)lib$(ps)jaxp.jar
worker.inprocess.class_path=$(workers.tomcat_home)$(ps)lib$(ps)parser.jar
worker.inprocess.class_path=$(workers.tomcat_home)$(ps)lib$(ps)jasper.jar
worker.inprocess.class_path=$(workers.tomcat_home)$(ps)lib$(ps)servlet.jar
worker.inprocess.class_path=$(workers.tomcat_home)$(ps)lib$(ps)webserver.jar
worker.inprocess.class_path=$(workers.java_home)$(ps)lib$(ps)tools.jar
```

The final class path (on Linux) for the inprocess worker looks as shown here:

```
/var/tomcat/classes:/var/tomcat/lib/jaxp.jar:/var/tomcat/lib/parser.jar:/var/tom
cat/lib/jasper.jar:/var/tomcat/lib/servlet.jar:/var/tomcat/lib/webserver.jar:/us
r/java/jdk1.3.0_02/lib/tools.jar
```

The next four lines, as shown below, define a set of command-line options for the inprocess worker:

```
worker.inprocess.cmd_line=-config
worker.inprocess.cmd_line=$(workers.tomcat_home)/conf/jni_server.xml
worker.inprocess.cmd_line=-home
worker.inprocess.cmd_line=$(workers.tomcat_home)
```

The next line defines the JVM library path:

```
worker.inprocess.jvm_lib=$(workers.java_home)$(ps)jre$(ps)bin$(
ps)classic$(ps)jvm.dll
```

The JVM library path (on Linux) is /usr/java/jdk1.3.0_02/jre/lib/i386/classic/libjvm.so. So you must change the above jvm_lib line to be:

```
worker.inprocess.jvm_lib=$(workers.java_home)$(ps)jre$(ps)lib$(
ps)i386$(ps)classic$(ps)libjvm.so
```

The next two lines define the filenames that are used to write the STDOUT and STDERR for the inprocess worker:

```
worker.inprocess.stdout=$(workers.tomcat_home)$(ps)inprocess.
stdout
worker.inprocess.stderr=$(workers.tomcat_home)$(ps)inprocess.
stderr
```

The STDOUT is written to /var/tomcat/inprocess.stdout and STDERR is written to /var/tomcat/inprocess.stderr on a Linux system.

The final line defines a system property for the inprocess worker. The default property set by the following line is tomcat.home with the value /var/tomcat on Linux:

```
worker.inprocess.sysprops=tomcat.home=$(workers.tomcat_home)
```

Configuring Tomcat to use the Java Security Manager

The Java Security Manager enforces security restrictions on everything Java, which includes applets, servlets, JSP, and even Tomcat itself. By using the Java Security Manager, you can control what each application can or cannot do. Table 17-2 shows the types of permissions you can set.

Table 17-2	
Java Security Manager Permission Types	
Permission Type	**Meaning**
`java.util.PropertyPermission`	Controls read/write access to JVM properties such as `java.home`.
`java.lang.RuntimePermission`	Controls use of some system or run-time functions such as `exit()` and `exec()`.
`java.io.FilePermission`	Controls files and directories permissions
`java.net.SocketPermission`	Controls use of network sockets.
`java.net.NetPermission`	Controls use of multicast network connections.
`java.lang.reflect.ReflectPermission`	Controls use of reflection to do class introspection.
`java.security.SecurityPermission`	Controls access to security methods.
`java.security.AllPermission`	Allows everything, which is effectively same thing as not using the Java Security Manager.

The security policies for Tomcat are defined in `/var/tomcat/conf/tomcat.policy` file. This file typically grants permissions using the following syntax:

```
grant codeBase code_source {
    permission_type class [name [, action_list]];
};
```

For example, the default `/var/tomcat/conf/tomcat.policy` file grants the following permissions:

```
// Example webapp policy
// By default we grant read access to webapp dir and
// write to workdir
grant codeBase "file:${tomcat.home}/webapps/examples" {
        permission java.net.SocketPermission "localhost:1024-",
"listen";
        permission java.util.PropertyPermission "*", "read";
};
```

The files in `${tomcat.home}/webapps/examples` (that is, `/var/tomcat/webapps/examples`) are granted permission to use network sockets to listen on localhost using 1024 or higher ports and to allow only read access to all JVM properties.

If you want an application called /var/tomcat/webapps/*your_app_name* to connect to the Lightweight Directory Access Protocol (LDAP) server using TCP port 389, the grant permission that you need is:

```
grant codeBase "file:${tomcat.home}/webapps/ app_name" {
     permission java.net.SocketPermission "localhost:389",
"connect";
     permission java.util.PropertyPermission "*", "read";
};
```

By default, the Java Security Manager is disabled for Tomcat. You must enable it as follows:

1. In /var/tomcat/conf/server.xml file you should find the following:

   ```
   <!-- Uncomment out if you have JDK1.2 and want to use policy

   <ContextInterceptor
   className="org.apache.tomcat.context.PolicyInterceptor" />

   -->
   ```

   This default setting disables the Security Manager, so you must remove the comments so that you have the following instead:

   ```
   <ContextInterceptor
   className="org.apache.tomcat.context.PolicyInterceptor" />
   ```

2. Restart Tomcat using the -security option. For example, /usr/bin/tomcat -security restarts Tomcat with Java Security Manager.

   The JVM will throw an AccessControlException or a SecurityException when the Java Security Manager intercepts a security policy violation.

Configuring Apache for Servlets and JSP

When you start Tomcat, it creates a configuration file called /var/tomcat/conf/mod_jk.conf-auto. You need this file to be loaded by Apache to interact with Tomcat. To do so, modify httpd.conf to add the following line:

```
Include /var/tomcat/conf/mod_jk.conf-auto
```

The automatically generated mod_jk.conf-auto file has one problem. It instructs Apache to load the mod_jk.so module from a subdirectory called libexec under the server's root directory (pointed to by ServerRoot directive in httpd.conf). Unfortunately, this directory does not exist and mod_jk.so is installed in /usr/lib/apache directory. So, you have two choices:

✦ Instead of pointing to `/var/tomcat/conf/mod_jk.conf-auto` file by using the `Include` directive, you can copy this file with another name (for example, `mod_jk.conf`) and use:

```
Include /var/tomcat/conf/mod_jk.conf
```

You then modify the `mod_jk.conf` file to have the `LoadModule jk_module libexec/mod_jk.so` line changed to `LoadModule jk_module /usr/lib/apache/mod_jk.so`.

✦ Or, you can simply create a subdirectory called `libexec` within your Apache server root directory and put `mod_jk.so` in it. In this case, you must start Apache after starting Tomcat because the `/var/tomcat/conf/mod_jk.conf-auto` is generated by Tomcat every time it starts.

I assume that you made the first choice, which is more manageable. The very first configuration line is:

```
LoadModule jk_module /usr/lib/apache/mod_jk.so
```

The `LoadModule` directive loads the `mod_jk.so` DSO module that enables Apache to interact with Tomcat.

```
JkWorkersFile /var/tomcat/conf/workers.properties
```

This line sets the `JkWorkersFile` directive to point to `/var/tomcat/conf/workers.properties`, which provides `mod_jk` with the needed information to connect to the different tomcat instances, which are also called workers. Leave this directive alone.

```
JkLogFile /var/tomcat/logs/mod_jk.log
```

Here the log file path is defined using the `JkLogFile` directive.

```
JkLogLevel error
```

The above line sets the log level for recording errors in log files. Possible log levels are `debug`, `warn`, `error`, and `emerg`, but `warn` should be your default selection.

```
JkMount /*.jsp ajp12
JkMount /servlet/* ajp12
```

The two lines shown above assign `/*.jsp` and `/servlet/*` URL prefixes to the Tomcat worker called `asp12`. This means that any URL request that has `/<anything>.jps` (for example, `/foo.jsp`, `/bar.jsp`) or `/servlet/<anything>` (for example, `/servlet/foo`, `/servlet/bar`) will be assigned to the asp12 worker. It is recommended that you change these two lines so that the worker is asp13 (faster) instead, as shown here:

```
JkMount /*.jsp ajp13
JkMount /servlet/* ajp13
```

The directives shown here are typical Apache directives:

```
Alias /examples "/var/tomcat/webapps/examples"
<Directory "/var/tomcat/webapps/examples">
    Options Indexes FollowSymLinks
</Directory>
```

An alias called /examples is created, which points to a physical directory called /var/tomcat/webapps/examples. The directory container enables directory listing and symbolic links in the aliased directory.

The next two directives, as shown below, assign /examples/servlet/* and /examples/* to Tomcat worker asp12:

```
JkMount /examples/servlet/* ajp12
JkMount /examples/*.jsp ajp12
```

You can change them to asp13 if you wish. It is not critical because these are simply examples.

The next group of directives, as shown below, disables access to the WEB-INF and META-INFO directories under the examples tree. These two directories should not be browseable, so this measure is appropriate:

```
<Location "/examples/WEB-INF/">
    AllowOverride None
    deny from all
</Location>

<Location "/examples/META-INF/">
    AllowOverride None
    deny from all
</Location>
```

The next group of directives, as shown below, creates exactly the same configuration as was created for /examples.

```
Alias /admin "/var/tomcat/webapps/admin"
<Directory "/var/tomcat/webapps/admin">
    Options Indexes FollowSymLinks
</Directory>

JkMount /admin/servlet/* ajp12
JkMount /admin/*.jsp ajp12

<Location "/admin/WEB-INF/">
    AllowOverride None
    deny from all
</Location>

<Location "/admin/META-INF/">
```

```
        AllowOverride None
        deny from all
</Location>
```

Feel free to change the worker for /admin/servlet/* and /admin/*.jsp to ajp13 to take advantage of this new, faster protocol. Finally, the same configuration is repeated for /test:

```
Alias /test "/var/tomcat/webapps/test"
<Directory "/var/tomcat/webapps/test">
    Options Indexes FollowSymLinks
</Directory>

JkMount /test/servlet/* ajp12
JkMount /test/*.jsp ajp12

<Location "/test/WEB-INF/">
    AllowOverride None
    deny from all
</Location>

<Location "/test/META-INF/">
    AllowOverride None
    deny from all
</Location>
```

After you have finished modifying the previous configuration and have saved the httpd.conf file, restart the Apache server. You can access the servlet and JSP examples by using http://your_web_server/examples/. You can also access the admin tool by using http://your_web_server/admin/. However, if you to view contexts (that is, virtual directory) information using the Web-based admin tool, you must create a user called admin in /var/tomcat/conf/tomcat-users.xml file. This file looks like this:

```
<tomcat-users>
  <user name="tomcat" password="tomcat" roles="tomcat" />
  <user name="role1"  password="tomcat" roles="role1"  />
  <user name="both"   password="tomcat" roles="tomcat,role1" />
</tomcat-users>
```

In the following example, I have added a user called admin with a password mypwd.

```
<tomcat-users>
  <user name="tomcat" password="tomcat" roles="tomcat" />
  <user name="role1"  password="tomcat" roles="role1"  />
  <user name="both"   password="tomcat" roles="tomcat,role1" />
  <user name="admin"  password="mypwd"  roles="admin" />
</tomcat-users>
```

With this user, you can view the contexts via the Web interface if you enable the `trusted = true` for the admin context as shown below:

```
<Context path="/admin"
    docBase="webapps/admin"
    crossContext="true"
    debug="0"
    reloadable="true"
    trusted="true" >
    </Context>
```

The default admin context configuration has the trusted attribute set to false. If you set it to true so that you can create, delete, or view contexts via the Web interface, you must restart Tomcat for the change to take effect. Also note that you should never leave the trusted attribute set to true after you have used it. Leaving this set to trusted at all time opens your server to serious security risks. For example, when the admin context is trusted (by setting `trusted="true"`) you can create a context via `http://your_server_hostname/admin` that exposes your entire filesystem to the Web. To exploit this, a cracker needs a Tomcat system with admin context set to trusted and the plain-text XML file `/var/tomcat/conf/tomcat-users.xml` with an admin username and password. The best way to deal with this is to remove the admin context completely, or at least to make sure that you have this set to untrusted (that is, `trusted="false"`).

Working with Tomcat

After you have configured Tomcat you can start working with it. In this section I show you how to disable Tomcat's default Web service (on port 80) that is meant to serve static pages because Apache does a better job of serving static pages. I then show you how to start and stop the Tomcat server and lastly I discuss a shell script that can be used to automate Tomcat startup process.

Disabling Tomcat's default HTTP service

By default, Tomcat services HTTP requests on port 8080. However, after you have Apache and Tomcat integrated using the `mod_jk.so` module, it is unnecessary to have Tomcat service HTTP requests on port 8080. You can fix this in the following section of the `/var/tomcat/conf/server.xml` file:

```
<!-- Normal HTTP -->
<Connector
className="org.apache.tomcat.service.PoolTcpConnector">
    <Parameter name="handler"

value="org.apache.tomcat.service.http.HttpConnectionHandler"/>
```

```
        <Parameter name="port"
            value="8080"/>
</Connector>
```

 Note   You must make sure Apache is not listening to 8007 or 8080 ports. Check the `Listen` and `Port` directives in `httpd.conf` to ensure this.

You can disable this service by either removing the above configuration or by commenting it out, as shown here:

```
<!-- *** DISABLED Normal HTTP on Port 8080

<Connector
className="org.apache.tomcat.service.PoolTcpConnector">
    <Parameter name="handler"

value="org.apache.tomcat.service.http.HttpConnectionHand
ler"/>
    <Parameter name="port"
        value="8080"/>
    </Connector>

*** DISABLED Normal HTTP Service on Port 8080 -->
```

Starting and stopping Tomcat

Before you can start or stop Tomcat, you must make sure that environment variables such as `$JAVA_HOME` and `$TOMCAT_HOME` are set and that the `$PATH` variable has the `$JAVA_HOME/bin` path in it. You can use the `echo` command to check whether these variables are set already in your shell. If you have followed the installation sections above you should have these variables set in your `~/.bashrc` file.

If you have these environment variables set, you can simply run the `/usr/bin/tomcat start` command or the `tomcatclt start` command to start Tomcat. You can use the `/usr/bin/tomcat stop` command to stop it. You can also run the `/usr/bin/tomcat run` command to run it in the foreground. Running it in the foreground is only recommended for troubleshooting when you need to see Tomcat error messages on the console.

Starting Tomcat with a shell wrapper script

It very useful to create the necessary environment in a shell script and run these commands using a shell wrapper script called `/usr/bin/tomcatctl`, which is shown in Listing 17-2. This saves a lot of typing and helps avoid mistyping errors.

Listing 17-2: **/usr/bin/tomcatctl**

```
#!/bin/sh

# Change the version number below if your
# JDK is not 1.3.0_02
#
VERSION=1.3.0_02

export JAVA_HOME=/usr/java/jdk$VERSION
export PATH=${PATH}:${JAVA_HOME}/bin
export TOMCAT_HOME=/var/tomcat

/usr/bin/tomcat $1

# end
```

After this script is stored in /usr/bin and you have enabled execute permission by running the chmod 755 /usr/bin/tomcatctl command, you can start or stop Tomcat without worrying about the environment variables. For example, to start Tomcat you can run the tomcatctl start command; to stop run the tomcatctl stop command; and to run it in the foreground, run the tomcatctl run command.

The binary RPM package also installs the /etc/rc.d/init.d/tomcat script. This script is symbolically linked to the appropriate run-level so that Tomcat automatically starts and stops every time you reboot the system. However, the default value for JAVA_HOME and for the JDK path in /etc/rc.d/init.d/tomcat might not be appropriate for everyone. For example, the default values set in this script for these two variables are shown below:

```
export PATH=$PATH:/opt/IBMJava2-13/bin:/opt/IBMJava2-13/jre/bin
export JAVA_HOME=/opt/IBMJava2-13
```

These appear to be the RPM developer's own settings. If you followed my earlier instructions to download the JDK from Sun Microsystems's Web site, your installation path for the JDK will differ. So, be sure to modify these two settings in /etc/rc.d/init.d/tomcat script. For example, the correct values are:

```
export PATH=$PATH:/usr/java/jdk1.3.0_02/bin:/usr/java/jdk1.3.0_02/jre/bin
export JAVA_HOME=/usr/java/jdk1.3.0_02
```

Running Java servlets

In this section I discuss how you can set up Tomcat to run the example servlets that are shipped with it, and I show you how you to run your own servlets or JSP pages that you have developed or downloaded from the Internet.

Caution   Never run Tomcat as root. Create a new user and group called `tomcat` and change
the file and directory permissions for `/var/tomcat` by using the `chmod -R 755`
`/var/tomcat` command.

Running Java example servlets via Tomcat

To run Java servlets, you do not need Apache. You can use Tomcat, which is an
open-source Java run-time environment called a *container,* for Java servlets.
Tomcat can be installed in parallel to your Web server and it can service both static
and servlet requests. However, Tomcat is much less versatile when it comes to
configuration and serving static requests. It is simply not a replacement for the
highly configurable Apache Web server. If you want to use Tomcat, though, this
section's for you.

By default, when Tomcat is started it services servlet requests from port 8080.
After you've started Tomcat, you should be able to access example servlets and
JSP pages using `http://localhost:8080` if you are running the Web browser
on the Tomcat server. Or, you can access it from another machine using the
`http://your_web_server_hostname:8080/`. When you access the default
Tomcat server, the page looks similar to Figure 17-1.

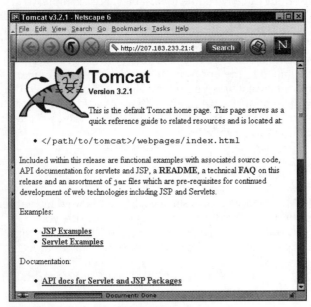

Figure 17-1: The default Tomcat server page.

Click on the JSP Examples link and you will see a page as shown in Figure 17-2.

Figure 17-2: A sample JSP listing.

There are a number of JSP example pages that you can try out to test your installation. For example, click on the Execute link for the Date JSP page. You should see an output page similar to the one shown in Figure 17-3.

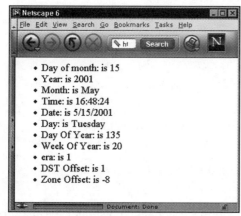

Figure 17-3: Output of the /examples/jsp/ dates/date.jsp file.

The JSP code for this JSP page is stored in /var/tomcat/webapps/examples/ jsp/dates/date.jsp, which is shown in Listing 17-3.

Listing 17-3: **date.jsp**

```
<html>
<!--
  Copyright (c) 1999 The Apache Software Foundation.  All rights
  reserved.
-->

<%@ page session="false"%>

<body bgcolor="white">
<jsp:useBean id='clock' scope='page' class='dates.JspCalendar'
type="dates.JspCalendar" />

<font size=4>
<ul>
<li>    Day of month: is  <jsp:getProperty name="clock" property="dayOfMonth"/>
<li>    Year: is  <jsp:getProperty name="clock" property="year"/>
<li>    Month: is  <jsp:getProperty name="clock" property="month"/>
<li>    Time: is  <jsp:getProperty name="clock" property="time"/>
<li>    Date: is  <jsp:getProperty name="clock" property="date"/>
<li>    Day: is  <jsp:getProperty name="clock" property="day"/>
<li>    Day Of Year: is  <jsp:getProperty name="clock" property="dayOfYear"/>
<li>    Week Of Year: is  <jsp:getProperty name="clock" property="weekOfYear"/>
<li>    era: is  <jsp:getProperty name="clock" property="era"/>
<li>    DST Offset: is  <jsp:getProperty name="clock" property="DSTOffset"/>
<li>    Zone Offset: is  <jsp:getProperty name="clock" property="zoneOffset"/>
</ul>
</font>

</body>
</html>
```

You can see that the JSP code is embedded in the HTML using the
`<jsp:getProperty name="`*name*`" property="`*property_name*`""/>` **tags.**

If you return to the top page and click on the Servlet Examples link you will see a
page as shown in Figure 17-4.

Click on the Execute link for the Hello World servlet and you should see an output
page as shown in Figure 17-5.

Return to the previous page using the Web browser's back button and click on
the Source link for Hello World to view the simplified source code for this servlet.
The source code is shown in Figure 17-6.

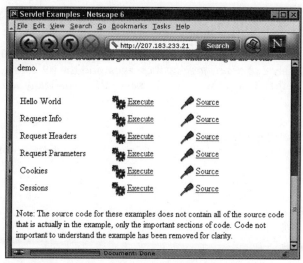

Figure 17-4: Example servlet listings.

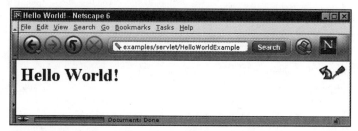

Figure 17-5: Output of /examples/servlet/HelloWorldExample.

As you can see, this is a fairly simple servlet — it simply prints out a bunch of HTML tags to create the output.

Running your own servlets or JSP

This section teaches you to configure your own servlets to run via mod_jk. Say that your servlet is called myapp. Here is what you need to do to get it working with Apache and Tomcat:

1. Create the following configuration in /var/tomcat/conf/server.xml:

```
<Context path="/myapp"
         docBase="/var/tomcat/webapps/myapps"
         debug="0"
         reloadable="true" >
</Context>
```

The path attribute specifies the path in the URL that will refer to your servlet called `myapp`. The `docBase` attribute specifies the path where this servlet is found. This can be either an absolute path or a path relative to the Tomcat Context Manager (which by default is `$TOMCAT_HOME/webapps`). The debug attribute specifies the level of debug logging messages, and the reloadable attribute specifies whether Tomcat will reload a servlet automatically when it is changed.

2. Stop and restart Tomcat using `/usr/bin/tomcat stop ; /usr/bin/tomcat start` command. This will generate a new `/var/tomcat/conf/mod_jk.conf-auto` file, which should have this configuration segment:

```
Alias /myapp "/var/tomcat/webapps/myapp"

<Directory "/var/tomcat/webapps/myapp">
    Options Indexes FollowSymLinks
</Directory>

JkMount /myapp/servlet/* ajp12
JkMount /myapp/*.jsp ajp12

<Location "/myapp/WEB-INF/">
    AllowOverride None
    deny from all
</Location>

<Location "/myapp/META-INF/">
    AllowOverride None
    deny from all
</Location>
```

3. Create the `/var/tomcat/webapps/myapp`, `/var/tomcat/webapps/myapp/WEB-INF`, `/var/tomcat/webapps/myapp/WEB-INF/classes`, and `/var/tomcat/webapps/myapp/META-INF` directories.

4. Store the `web.xml` configuration file for the `myapp` servlet in `/var/tomcat/webapps/myapps/WEB-INF` directory.

5. Copy the servlet classes for `myapps` to the `/var/tomcat/webapps/myapps/WEB-INF/classes` directory.

6. Make sure the Tomcat user (that is, the user ID used to run Tomcat) can access the new `/var/tomcat/webapps/myapps` (including all subdirectories and files) directory.

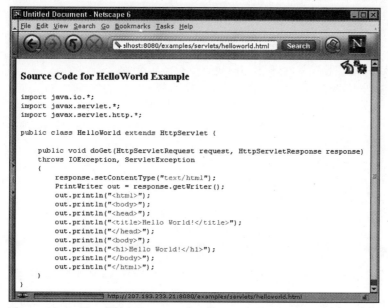

Figure 17-6: Simplified source code of `/examples/servlet/HelloWorldExample`.

That's it! You should be able to access the servlet using `http://your_web_server/myapps`.

Securing Your
Web Site

Ensuring Web site security is a critical part of a Web administrator's job. In this part, I discuss the various security issues that can arise with Apache, and how to resolve these issues by using various tools, techniques, and policies or guidelines. I also show you how to turn your Apache server into a Secure Socket Layer (SSL)-capable Web server using either the mod_ssl or Apache-SSL modules.

Web Security

The need for security is often unclear to novice administrators. Many administrators think about security only after a breach of security has occurred — too late! This chapter provides an idea of the hidden risks that make security so important.

Understanding Web Security

The moment you get your Web server up and running and available to the rest of the world, you open a window for others to get into your network. You intended to do this, right? Most people will use the information available on your Web site, but some may look for holes in this window so that they can get to information that they are not supposed to access. Some of these people are vandals who want to create embarrassing situations, and some are information thieves. Either way, if anyone succeeds in finding that hole, you may find your Web sites mutilated with obscene materials, or you might even lose confidential data. Sometimes the attacks do not affect your site directly. The infiltrators may use your server and other resources to get to another network, putting you at legal risk. None of these scenarios is desirable.

To avoid such risk and embarrassment, this chapter shows you how to secure your Web sites. I assume that the following security requirements are applicable for your Web site:

+ Maintaining the integrity of the information you publish on the Web.

+ Preventing the use of your Web server host as a point for break-ins into your organization's network (which could result in breaches of confidentiality, integrity, or availability of information resources).

+ Preventing the use of your Web server host as a staging area for intrusions into other networks (which could result in your organization being liable for damages).

Most Web security incidents occur because confidential information is made vulnerable by improperly configured software. The software could be the Web server itself, or applications (such as CGI programs, Server-Side Includes, and Server API applications) that are run by the Web server. This can result in the inadvertent disclosure of confidential information. Subsequent attacks can be launched by exploiting the confidential information.

If your Web server configuration is tight and the applications run by the Web server are fairly secured, are you done? No, because the attacks could be targeted to the Web server via different routes. Your Web server might become compromised by way of totally unrelated applications, or by a bug in the operating system, or by poor network architecture.

To be secure, you have to look at each and every detail. This can be a daunting task; but remember that it is impossible to have a completely secured environment. There is never a foolproof solution to all security issues, because all issues are not known. Your goal is to improve your security as much as possible.

The Security Checkpoints

The very first step in protecting your Web server from vandals is to understand and identify the risks involved. Not too long ago, Web sites only served static HTML pages, which made them less prone to security risks. The only way a vandal could hack into such Web sites was to break into the server by gaining illegal access. This was typically done by using a weak password or by fooling another daemon (server) software. However, most Web sites no longer serve static HTML pages; they serve dynamic contents that are often personalized to provide a rich user experience. Many Web sites tie in applications to provide valuable customer service or to perform e-commerce activities. This is when the risks start to weigh more and more. Yes, Web applications are the heart of the Web security problem. Most Web sites that have been hacked by vandals were not vandalized because of the Web server software. They were hacked because of one or more holes in the application or script that the Web server software ran.

There are several security checkpoints that you need to review to improve the security of your public Web server. Figure 18-1 shows the overall security checkpoint diagram. This diagram identifies the security checkpoints that must be examined thoroughly before considering an Internet-connected network secure.

There are three primary checkpoints:

✦ **Your network:** This is the outter most checkpoint, which needs to be very strong. Your network connects to the Internet via either a router, firewall system, or a gateway server. Therefore your nework is a primary security checkpoint. Securing your network should be your primary security concern.

✦ **Your operating system:** The operating system you use for your Web server is very important If you run Apache on a version of the operating system (whether it be Linux, Windows, or Solaris) that is known to be a security risk then your server can be attacked. Running an up-to-date opearating system is a must.

✦ **Your Web server software:** This is your third security checkpoint. Make sure that you're running a version of Apache that has no known security risks.

I discuss these checkpoints in the following sections.

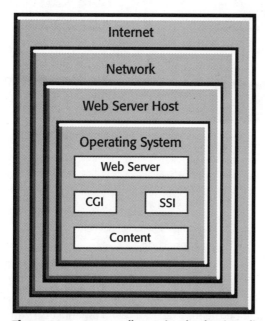

Figure 18-1: An overall security checkpoints diagram.

Checkpoint 1: Your network

The first checkpoint to consider is your network, and how it is connected to the Internet. The real issue is where you place your Web server. The general idea is to isolate your internal network, keeping it away from prying eyes as much as possible. Definitely consider installing a firewall in your Internet-to-LAN router. If a firewall is not an option, you can consider the proxy-server option. A proxy server takes one network's request to another network without ever connecting the two. This might be a good solution because it also provides an excellent logging facility.

As you can see, you should be more concerned about your internal network than the Web server, itself. Because networks introduce Internet-accessible Web server(s) within the network, they are likely to get broken into by way of exploiting a security hole in the Web server software, or by a hole in an application (such as a CGI program) that is running on the Web server. The chances of this occurring are reduced by choosing a network architecture that isolates the LAN from the Web server.

If you have a network configuration, such as the one shown in Figure 18-2, your network is virtually unprotected.

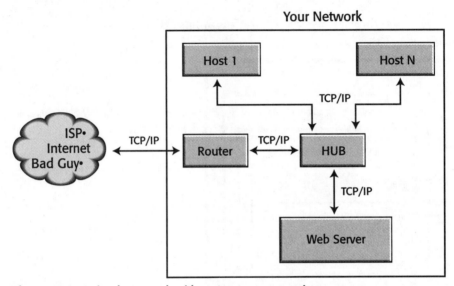

Figure 18-2: A simple network with an Internet connection.

To keep things simple, the discussion assumes that you only have a single connection to the Internet. In this network model, all Internet traffic can be routed to and from your network. In other words, anyone on the Internet can reach any host on your network and vice versa. This also means that a hacker on the Internet can find a weak point in one of the many hosts that you have on your network. Of course, not all of these hosts are servers with services enabled for others to use; but, even if you have a Windows machine with file sharing enabled, it is a potential target. Because the entire network uses TCP/IP, a simple file-sharing option on a Windows workstation machine can lead to a break-in. This network almost invites criminals who want to break in.

If you have this configuration, check your router documentation to determine whether you can enable IP-based restrictions. I recommend this configuration be avoided at all costs.

Cross-
Reference   See the Choosing a Security Configuration section later in this chapter for some network configurations you can use.

Checkpoint 2: The operating system

Apache runs on virtually all Unix platforms, and it is already starting to run on Windows 2000, Windows 95, and even on the new Macintosh operating system, Mac OS X. But just because Apache runs on virtually any platform does not mean that you should use just any operating system to run Apache. Choosing the right operating system (OS) can be a significant factor in system security. Well-known Unix and Unix-like operating systems include Mac OS X, BSDI, FreeBSD, SunOS, Solaris, HP-UX, Digital Unix, and Linux. Internet server administrators favor these operating systems. Although the quality and reliability may vary among these operating systems, all are deigned for use as server operating systems.

If you do not like Unix, look into the Windows 2000 server platform. Windows 2000 is a very powerful Unix competitor, likely to give Unix a run for its money in the future; however, Windows 2000 is new to the Internet game. Most Unix and Unix-like operating systems have been around long enough to suffer numerous hacks and attacks. They stand as the survivors and — though never completely hack-proof — remain tall.

Tip   After you have chosen an operating system, you should disable any extra features that you don't intend to use on the Web server machine running that OS. For example, if you do not need SMTP/POP mail or FTP services, disable them or completely remove the mail server programs from the system. If you don't need a lot of powerful system utilities, delete them. Make certain that your Web server is just a Web server and has only the services it needs.

Cross-Reference   You can learn about vulnerabilities that exist in your operating platform by browsing www.cert.org. CERT (Computer Emergency Response Team) works with the Internet community to facilitate awareness of, and response to, security issues. The organization also conducts research targeted at improving the security of computer systems.

Checkpoint 3: Web server software

Obviously, you use Apache as the Web server software or you would not be reading this book. Make sure, however, that you use the latest, stable version of Apache 2 server for your system. It is a good idea to compile your own Apache binaries instead of using those of a binary distribution.

Apache is freely available software, so it is important that you obtain it from a reliable source. Do not ever download Apache binaries or source code from just any Web or FTP site. Always check with the official site, www.apache.org, first. Apache source is PGP (Pretty Good Privacy) signed. Also note that the current Apache distribution includes a PGP key-ring file containing the PGP keys of most active Apache developers.

The Apache group PGP signatures are in the file KEYS in the top-level distribution of Apache. If you trust the site from which you obtained your distribution, you can add these keys to your own key ring. If you do not how to use PGP on your system, learn about it at www.pgp.com.

Each Apache source distribution is PGP signed and these signatures are stored in files with an .asc extension (for example, the signature for apache_2.0.tar.gz is stored in apache_2.0.tar.gz.asc). These can be used to check the validity of the distribution if you have added the KEYS file contents to your key ring.

The latest stable version of Apache does not have any known bugs; however, its capability to incorporate external third-party modules gives rise to a security issue: Can you trust a third-party module? People all over the world write many of the Apache modules. Make sure that you only use modules that are available on the official Apache Web site or registered in the Apache module registry located at http://modules.apache.org/.

 Tip Never use experimental modules in your production sites. In fact, it is a good idea to determine which modules you really need, and then to configure and compile Apache accordingly. This way you have a smaller, faster server with potentially better security.

When configuring Apache, pay a great deal of attention to security configuration issues. The basic idea is to disable anything you do not use. This way, you are taking preventive security measures and are likely to reduce risks.

Choosing a Security Configuration

There are many ways you can configure Apache while enhancing your overall Web security. Before you can choose a configuration suitable for you, you need to develop a security policy and then choose a configuration suitable to meet your policy requirements. When it comes to security there is always a chance that you can overestimate the risks and become too paranoid or underestimate your security needs and keep things too open. In the sections below I discuss a few configurations that suit different environments.

Security policy considerations

An administrative security policy identifies practices that are vital to achieving robust network security. If you do not yet have one, consider adding some of the following items to an administrative security policy as a start.

✦ **Log everything:** I cannot emphasize this enough. The server log files record information on the server's behavior in response to each request. Analysis of the log can provide both business information (for instance, which Web pages are most popular) and security information. Make sure you set up Apache to log both access and errors. With the help of log files you can track who is accessing what. Get in the habit of browsing logs whenever you can — if you notice anything unusual, take a closer look. Your error log is probably the most important log to monitor closely.

For more information on logging, see "Logging and Security" section later in this chapter and Chapter 8 where I describe logging with Apache.

✦ **Maintain an authoritative copy of your Web site(s):** Keep the authoritative copy of your Web site on a more secure host. If the integrity of the public information on your Web server is ever compromised, you need an authoritative copy from which to restore it. Typically, the authoritative copy is kept on a host that is accessible to the Web site administrator (and, perhaps, to the people in your organization who are responsible for the creation and maintenance of Web content). It is often kept on the organization's internal network.

To ensure security, use robust cryptographic-checksum technologies to generate a checksum for each file. Keep authoritative copies of files and checksums on write-protected or read-only media stored in a physically secure location. You can use MD5 encryption to generate cryptographic checksums for your files.

✦ **Administer your site from the Web host console:** You should administer your Web site from the Web host's console. Doing this eliminates the need for network traffic between the Web server and the administrator's workstation. There are, however, many situations when this is not feasible (such as in organizations in which the Web server is not easily accessed by the administrator). When you must do remote administration, be sure to use a strong authentication scheme to login to the Web server. If you use a Web-based administrative tool, make sure it does not use Basic HTTP authentication. In other words, you want to make sure the passwords are not traveling from your workstation to the Web server in a nonencrypted format. Also, you should configure the Web server system to accept connection from a single host within your internal network.

✦ **Be aware of public domain CGI applications:** Whenever using a public domain CGI, make sure you or someone in your organization (or an outside consultant) has complete understanding of the code. Never get a copy of an application from a nonauthentic source. Search USENET newsgroups to see if anyone has discovered problems with the application that you intend to install on your Web server. If possible, install the application in a staging server and test it yourself. Keep monitoring your log files during the test period and look for errors and warnings produced by the applications. If the application uses mail services, monitor the mail log as well.

✦ **Compare contents:** Vandals often substitute, modify, and damage files on the systems to which they gain access. In order to regain illegal access to the system, they often modify system programs so that the programs appear to function normally, but include back doors for the vandals. Vandals also modify system log files to remove traces of their activities. Vandals may even create new files on your systems.

To avoid this, therefore, it's a good idea to compare the attributes and contents of files and directories to the authoritative copy. If you have created cryptographic checksums for files, you can compare the checksums of the current and authentic copy to determine if any difference exists. You should look into Tripwire at `www.tripwire.com` for details on how to keep contents safe using checksums.

✦ **Use MD5 to verify the integrity of file contents:** The MD5 program generates a unique, 128-bit cryptographic message-digest value derived from the contents of a file. This value is considered a highly reliable fingerprint that can be used to verify the integrity of the file's contents. If even a single bit value in the file is modified, the MD5 checksum for the file will change. Forgery of a file in a way that causes MD5 to generate the same result as that for the original file, is considered difficult.

A set of MD5 checksums for critical system, application, and data files provides a compact way of storing information for use in periodic integrity checks of those files. If any changes cannot be attributed to authorized activity, you should consider your system compromised and take prompt actions. In case the change is found to be valid, re-create your authoritative copy and checksum.

Cross-Reference Details for the MD5 cryptographic-checksum program are provided in RFC 1321. Source code and additional information are available at `www.faqs.org/rfcs/rfc1321.html`.

A sensible security configuration for Apache

Sensible (that is, less paranoid) security configurations for Apache use a dedicated non-privileged user and group for Apache, a well-defined directory structure of the Web documents and log files, and appropriate file and directory permissions that only allow the Web server to read and/or write to files and directories. This configuration also disables access to everything by default and enables access to resources (such as directories) only by explicit rules. The details of this configuration are discussed in the following sections.

Use a dedicated user and group for Apache

Apache can be run as a standalone, or as an inetd daemon-run service. If you choose to run Apache as an inetd service, you do not have to worry about the User and Group directives. If you run Apache as a standalone server, however, make sure that you create a dedicated user and group for Apache. Do not use the nobody user or the nogroup group, especially if your system has already defined these. It is likely that there are other services or other places where your system is using them. This might lead to administrative headaches. Instead, create a fresh new user and group for Apache, and use them with the directives mentioned.

When you use a dedicated user and group for Apache, permission-specific administration of your Web content becomes simple. All you need to do is ensure that only the Apache user has read access to the Web content. If you need to create a directory to which some CGI scripts might write data, you need only enable write permissions for only the Apache user.

Use a safe directory structure

In most Apache installations, there are four main directories:

1. ServerRoot-specified directory where server configuration (conf subdirectory) and binary files (bin subdirectory) and other server-specific files are stored.

2. DocumentRoot-specified directory where your Web site contents, such as HTML pages, Java Scripts, and images, are stored.

3. ScriptAlias-specified directory where your CGI scripts are stored.

4. CustomLog- or ErrorLog-specified directory where access and error log files are stored. You can specify a different directory for each of these directives but keeping a single log directory for all the log files is likely to be more manageable in the long run.

I recommend that you use a directory structure in which each of the four primary directories is independent of the others. In other words, none of the above directories are subdirectories of another directory. ServerRoot should point to a directory that can only be accessed by the root user. The DocumentRoot directory needs to be accessible to user(s) who maintain your Web site and to the Apache user or group (specified by using the User and Group directives in httpd.conf file). The ScriptAlias-specified script directory should only be accessible to script developer(s) and Apache user or group. The CustomLog- or ErrorLog-specified directory should only be accessible by the root user. Not even the Apache user or group should have access to the log directory. An example of such a directory structure is shown below.

```
/
|
|
|
+---home
|    |
|    +---httpd     (ServerRoot)
|
+---www
|    |
|    +---htdocs    (DocumentRoot)
```

```
|
+---cgi-bin   (ScriptAlias)
|
+---logs          (CustomLog and ErrorLog)
```

The above directory structure is safe in many ways. To understand why, first look at the following Apache configuration in `httpd.conf` for the above directory structure.

```
ServerRoot      "/home/httpd"
DocumentRoot    "/www/htdocs"
ScriptAlias     /cgi-bin/        "/www/cgi-bin/"
CustomLog       /www/logs/access.log common
ErrorLog        /www/logs/error.log
```

Because each of these major directories is independent (that is, none is a subdirectory of another) they are safe from one another. A permission mistake in one directory will not affect another directory. If you do not think this is a big deal, count the number of years you have been involved with users and Linux and then read all of Murphy's laws.

The appropriate permission settings for the above directory structure need to be set.

Appropriate file and directory permissions

The `ServerRoot`-specified directory should be only accessible by the root user because no one but the root needs to configure or run Apache. The `DocumentRoot` should be accessible to one or more users who manage the contents of your Web site and the Apache user (specified by using `User` directive) or the Apache group (specified by using `Group` directive). For example, if you want a user called `htmlguru` to publish contents in your Web site, and you run Apache as `httpd` user, you can give both Apache and the named user access to the `DocumentRoot` directory by following these steps:

1. Create a new group called `webteam`:

   `groupadd webteam`

2. Add `htmlguru` user to the `webteam` group:

   `usermod -G webteam htmlguru`

3. Change the ownership of the `DocumentRoot` directory (and all the subdirectories below it):

   `chown -R httpd.webteam /www/htdocs`

This command sets the directory ownership to Apache (that is, the `httpd` user) and the group ownership to `webteam`, which includes the `htmlguru` user. In other words, both Apache and htmlguru will both have access to the document tree.

4. Change the permission of the `DocumentRoot` directory (and all the subdirectories below it) as follows:

```
chmod -R 2570 /www/htdocs
```

This command ensures that the files and subdirectories under the `DocumentRoot` are readable and executable by the Apache user and that the `webteam` group can read, write, and execute everything. It also ensures that whenever a new file or directory is created in the document tree, the `webteam` group will have access to it.

A great advantage of this method is that adding new users to the webteam is as simple as running the following command:

```
usermod -G webteam new_username
```

Similarly, if you wish to remove an existing user from the `webteam` group, simply run:

```
usermod -G username [group1,group2,group3,...]
```

where *group1, group2, group3,* and so on are groups (excluding `webteam` group) that this user belongs to.

Tip You can find out which group(s) a user belongs to by running the `group username` command.

The `ScriptAlias`-specified directory should be only accessible to the CGI developers and the Apache user specified using the `User` directive in `httpd.conf`. I recommend that you create a new group called `webdev` for the developer(s.) Although the developer group (such as `webdev`) needs read, write, and execute access for the directory, the Apache user only requires read and execute access. Do not allow Apache user to write files in this directory. For example, say you have the following `ScriptAlias` in your `httpd.conf`:

```
ScriptAlias    /cgi-bin/       "/www/cgi-bin/"
```

If `httpd` is your Apache user and `webdev` is your developer group, you should set permission for `/www/cgi-bin` as follows:

```
chown -R httpd.webdev /www/cgi-bin
chmod -R 2570 /www/cgi-bin
```

Alternatively, if you only wish to allow only a single user (say `cgiguru`) to develop CGI scripts, you can set the file and directory permission as follows:

```
chown -R cgiguru.httpd /www/cgi-bin
chmod -R 750 /www/cgi-bin
```

Here the user `cgiguru` owns the directory and the group (specified by `Group` directive) used for Apache server is the group owner of the directory and its files.

Finally, the log directory used in the `CustomLog` and `ErrorLog` directives should only be writable by the `root` user. Recommended permission setting for such directory (say `/www/logs`) is as follows:

```
chown -R root.root /www/logs
chmod -R 700 /www/logs
```

Caution   Do not allow anyone (including the Apache user or group) to read, write, or execute files in the log directory specified in `CustomLog` and `ErrorLog` directives.

Always make sure that you take a minimalist approach to allowing access to new directories that are accessible via the Web. Also ensure that you do not allow Web visitors to view any directory listings. You can hide your directory listings using the methods discussed later.

Directory index file

Whenever a user requests access to a directory via the Web, Apache does one of the following:

1. Checks whether the directory is accessible. If it is, it continues; otherwise, it displays an error message.

2. After it has determined that the directory is accessible, it looks for the directory index file specified by using the `DirectoryIndex` directive. By default, this file is `index.html`. If it can read this file in the requested directory, the contents of the file are displayed. In the event that such a file does not exist, Apache checks whether it can create a dynamic listing for the directory. If it is allowed to create a dynamic listing, it creates it and displays the contents of the directory to the user.

Because an Apache-created dynamically generated directory listing provides potential bad guys with clues about your directory structure, you should not allow such listings. The simplest way to avoid creating a dynamic directory listing is to create a file with the filename specified in `DirectoryIndex` directive. For example, if you set `DirectoryIndex` as follows:

```
DirectoryIndex index.html index.htm
```

Apache will first look for `index.html` in the requested directory of the URL, and then it will look for `index.htm` if `index.html` is missing.

However, a common reasons why many Web sites have exposed directories is that when the new directory is created, the creator forgets to create the index file or uploads an index file with the wrong case, such as `INDEX.HTML` or `INDEX.HTM`.

If this happens frequently, you can use a CGI script to automatically redirect users to your home page or to an internal search engine interface. Simply modify the DirectoryIndex directive to be:

```
DirectoryIndex index.html index.htm /cgi-bin/index.pl
```

Now add a CGI script such as the one shown in Listing 18-1 in the ScriptAlias-specified directory.

Listing 18-1: **index.pl**

```perl
#!/usr/bin/perl
#
# Purpose: this script is used to redirect
#          users who enter a URL that points to
#          directories without index.html page.
#

use CGI qw(:standard);

# Set the automatically redirect URL
my $AUTO_REDIRECT_URL = '/';

# Get the current URL path
my $curDir = $ENV{REQUEST_URI};

# If the current URL path is not home page (/) then
# redirect user to home page
if ($curDir ne '/'){
    print redirect($AUTO_REDIRECT_URL);

# If the home page is also missing the index page,
# we can't redirect back to home page (to avoid
# recursive redirection), so display an error message.
} else {
    print header;
    print "HOME PAGE NOT FOUND!";
}

exit 0;
```

This script runs after Apache fails to find the directory index files (index.html or index.htm). The script simply redirects a user whose URL points to a directory with no index file to the Web site's home page.

Make sure to change /cgi-bin/ from the path of the above directive if you use a different alias name. If you do not wish to display any directory listings at all, you can simply disable directory listing by setting the following configuration:

```
<Directory />
    Options -Indexes
</Directory >
```

The Options directive tells Apache to disable all directory index processing.

> **Tip** It might also be a good idea to tell Apache to not follow symbolic links because such links can accidentally expose part of the disk space that you do not want to make public. To disable the following of symbolic links by Apache, set the Options **directive to** -FollowSymLinks.

Disabling default access

A good security model dictates that no default access exists, so get into the habit of permitting no access at first. Permit specific access only to specific directories. To implement no default access, use the following configuration segment in httpd.conf:

```
<Directory />
    Order deny,allow
     Deny from all
</Directory>
```

This disables all access first. Now, if you need to enable access to a particular directory, use the <Directory . . .> container again to open that directory. For example, if you want to permit access to /www/htdocs, add the following configuration:

```
<Directory "/www/htdocs">
    Order deny,allow
    Allow from all
</Directory>
```

This method — opening only what you need — is a preventive security measure and is highly recommended. Also, do not allow users to change any directory-wide configuration options using per-directory configuration file (.htaccess) in directories that are open for access.

Disabling user overrides

To disable overriding configuration settings using the per-directory configuration file (.htaccess) in any directory, do the following :

```
<Directory />
    AllowOverride None
</Directory>
```

This disallows user overrides and, in fact, speeds up your server, because the server no longer looks for the per-directory access control files (.htaccess) for each request.

The Apache configuration issues and solutions discussed here can help you to create a secure Web server. However, some administrators want to go a few steps farther (in the land of paranoia) when it comes to security.

The Sacrificial Lamb Configuration

In this configuration, the Web server is kept outside of the firewall and the internal LAN. The hosts in the internal LAN receive or transmit Internet packets through a firewall host. This way, the internal hosts are protected from outside attack (at least in theory). The Web server, on the other hand, is completely open to attack; which is why the configuration is called a *Sacrificial Lamb* configuration. Figure 18-3 shows the Sacrificial Lamb configuration.

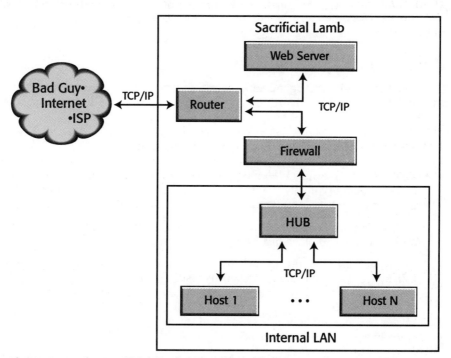

Figure 18-3: The Sacrificial Lamb network configuration

In this configuration, the following is true:

✦ The intruder cannot observe or capture network traffic flowing between internal hosts. Such traffic might include authentication information, proprietary business information, personnel data, and many other kinds of sensitive data.

✦ The intruder cannot get to internal hosts, or obtain detailed information about them.

The Sacrificial Lamb configuration guards against these two threats, and keeps the Web server isolated from the internal network and its traffic.

Tip   In this configuration, it is wise to turn off source routing at the router. This way, the Web server host cannot be used to forward packets to hosts in the internal network.

Caution   Some people like putting the Web server behind the firewall. In such a configuration, the firewall becomes the gateway for both the internal LAN and for Web traffic, and the firewall configuration becomes complex. I believe that such complexity can lead to security holes in the firewall, which defeats its purpose.

The Paranoid Configuration

This configuration is for Apache administrators who are paranoid about security. It is the most restrictive configuration among the configurations discussed in this chapter.

Here is what I consider paranoid configuration for Apache.

✦ **No Common Gateway Interface (CGI) script support.** As mentioned before, CGI scripts are typically the cause of most Web security incidents and therefore they have no place in a paranoid configuration.

✦ **No SSI support.** Similar to CGI scripts SSI pages are often problematic and therefore have no place in a paranoid configuration.

✦ **Allowing Web sites per user.** Using the `http://www.domain.com/~username` URL scheme introduces many security issues such as a user not taking appropriate cautions to reduce the risk of exposing file system information to the rest of the world; user mistakes making nonpublic disk areas of the server become publicly accessible; and the like. So per-user Web site has no place in a paranoid configuration.

✦ **No status information via Web.** Apache provides a status module that offers valuable status information about the server via the Web. This information can give clues to vandals if they have access to it. The paranoid way to make sure they don't have access to such information is to not have the module installed in the first place.

The paranoid configuration can be achieved by using the following configuration command:

```
./configure --prefix=/home/apache \
          --disable-module=include \
          --disable-module=cgi \
          --disable-module=userdir \
          --disable-module=status
```

After you have run the above configuration command from the `src` directory of the Apache source distribution, you can make and install Apache (in `/home/apache`) with paranoid configuration.

Tip Many paranoid administrators have been seen to run Apache on nonstandard ports such as 8080 or 9000. If you want to run Apache on such ports, change the `Port` directive in the `httpd.conf`. However, be warned that vandals usually use port scanner software to detect HTTP ports and that using nonstandard ports makes good users work harder because they have to type the :port number (`http://www.domain.com:port/`) at the end of the very first URL used to enter your Web site.

Protecting Your Web Contents

Your Web contents are your assets, and as such they need to be protected from vandalism and hack attacks. A poor or missing content publishing policy can result in security risks for your contents. In this section I discuss a content publishing policy with security focus. Also if some of your Web contents should not be indexed by Web search engines (that is, their robots) then you can use the robot or spider program control techniques discussed to be quite useful.

Content-publishing guidelines

Creating a content-publishing policy is one thing and enforcing it is another. After you have created your own publishing policy, discuss this with the people who should be using it. Get their feedback on each policy item and, if necessary, refine your policy to make it useful.

Contents publishers and script developers should know and adhere to the following guidelines:

✦ Whenever storing a content file, such as an HTML file, image file, sound file, video clip, and so on, the publisher must ensure that the file is readable by the Web server (that is, the username specified for `User` directive). No one but the publisher-user should should be permitted write access to the files and directory.

✦ Any file or directory that can not be displayed directly on the Web browser because it contains information that is indirectly accessed by using an application or script should not be located in a `DocumentRoot`-specified directory. For example, if one of your scripts needs to access a data file that should not be directly accessed from the Web, do not keep the data file inside the document tree. Keep the file outside the document tree and have your script access it from there, because even if there is no link to these files from any other viewable content, it may still be accessible to others.

✦ Any temporary files created by dynamic-content generators, such as CGI applications, should reside in a single subdirectory where the generators have write access. This directory must be kept outside the content area to ensure that a bug in the application does not mistakenly wipe out any existing content file. In other words, do not have a Web server-writable directory within your document tree. This ensures that a bug in a script does not accidentally write over an existing file in the document tree.

✦ To enforce clear copyright on the content, there should be both visible and embedded copyright notices on the content pages. The embedded copyright message should be kept at the beginning of a document, if possible. For example, in an HTML file, you can use a pair of comment tags to embed the copyright message at the beginning of the file. For example, `<!-- Copyright (c) 2001 by YourCompany; All rights reserved. -->` can be embedded in each page. If you plan to update your copyright messages often, you might consider an SSI solution using the `#include` directive.

✦ If you have a great deal of graphical content (images) that you want to protect from copyright theft, consider using watermarking technology. This technology invisibly embeds information in images to protect the copyright. The idea is that if you detect a site using your graphical contents without permission, you might be able to verify the theft by looking at the hidden information. If the information matches your watermark ID, you can clearly identify the thief and proceed with legal action. The strength of the currently available watermarking tools is questionable, as many programs can easily remove the original copyright owner's watermarks. This technology is worth investigating, however, if you are concerned about your graphical content.

Protecting your contents from robots and spiders

If you're serious about protecting your Web content, you should be aware of Web spiders and robots. All search engines, such as Yahoo!, AltaVista, Excite, and Infoseek use automated robot applications that search Web sites and index contents. This is usually desirable, but on occasion, you might find yourself wanting to stop these robots from accessing a certain part of your Web site(s).

If content in a section of your Web site expires frequently (daily, for example), you do not want the search robots to index them. Why not? Well, when a user at the search engine site finds a link to the old content and clicks it to find out the link does not exist, the user will not be happy. That user might then go to the next link without going to your site again.

There will be other times when will you want to disable indexing of your content (or part of it). These robots can have intended and unintended effects on the network and Web sites that they traverse. On occasion, search robots have overwhelmed Web sites by requesting too many documents too rapidly. Efforts are under way to create Internet standards of behavior for Web robots. The current version, the Robot Exclusion Protocol, enables Web site administrators to place a robots.txt file on their Web site indicating where robots should not go. For example, a large archive of bitmap images would be useless to a robot that is trying to index HTML pages. Serving these files to the robot is a needless use of resources both at your server's end and at the robot's end.

The current Robot Exclusion Protocol is a voluntary one, and an etiquette is evolving for robot developers as experience is gained through the deployment of robots. Most popular search engines abide by the protocol.

When a compliant Web robot visits a site called www.somesite.com, it first checks for the existence of the URL http://www.somesite.com/robots.txt.

If this URL exists, the robot parses its contents for directives that instruct the robot how to index the site. As a Web server administrator, you can create directives that make sense for your site. Note that there can only be a single /robots.txt on a site. This file contains records that may look like the following:

```
User-agent: *
Disallow: /cgi-bin/
Disallow: /tmp/
Disallow: /~sam/
```

The first directive, User-agent, tells the robot the following directives should be considered by any robots. The following three directives, Disallow, tell the robot not to access the directories mentioned in the directives. Note that you need a separate Disallow line for every URL prefix that you want to exclude—you cannot use the following:

```
Disallow: /cgi-bin/ /tmp/ /~sam/
```

Also, you may not have blank lines in a record because blank lines are used to delimit multiple records. Regular expressions are not supported in either the User-agent or Disallow lines. The * in the User-agent field is a special value that means any robot. Specifically, you cannot have lines such as these:

```
Disallow: /tmp/*
```

or

```
Disallow: *.gif
```

Everything not explicitly disallowed is considered accessible by the robot (some example configurations follow).

Excluding all robots

To exclude all robots from the entire server, use the following configuration:

```
User-agent: *
Disallow: /
```

Permitting all robots complete access

To permit all robots complete access, use the following configuration:

```
User-agent: *
Disallow:
```

Note   You can create the same effect by deleting the `robots.txt` file.

Excluding a single robot

To exclude a single robot called `WebCrawler` from accessing the site, use the following configuration:

```
User-agent: WebCrawler
Disallow: /
```

Allowing a single robot

To allow a single robot called `WebCrawler` to access the site, use the following configuration:

```
User-agent: WebCrawler
Disallow:

User-agent: *
Disallow: /
```

Disallowing a single file

To disallow a single file called `/daily/changes_to_often.html` from being indexed by robots, use the following configuration:

```
User-agent: *
Disallow: /daily/changes_to_often.html
```

Note   Currently, there is no `Allow` directive for robots.

Logging and Security

Good Web administrators closely monitor server logs, which provides clues to unusual access patterns. In this section I discuss how you can protect your log files from unauthorized access and also what to do when you detect unusual access in your log files.

Caution   Logs are great, but if the vandals can modify them, they are useless. So be sure to protect log files. I recommend keeping log files on their own partition where no one but the root user has access to make any changes.

CustomLog and ErrorLog

By using the `CustomLog` and `ErrorLog` directives (which I describe in Chapter 8), Apache allows you to log access requests that are successful and access requests that result in an error in separate log files. For example:

```
CustomLog /logs/access.log common
ErrorLog /logs/error.log
```

The first directive, `CustomLog`, logs each incoming request to your Web site and the second directive, `ErrorLog`, only records the requests that generated an error condition. The `ErrorLog` file is a good place to monitor closely to see what problems are being reported by your Web server. You can use fancy log analysis programs such as Wusage (`www.boutel.com`) to routinely analyze and monitor log files.

Make sure that the directories specified by `ServerRoot`, `CustomLog`, and `ErrorLog` directives cannot be written to by anyone but the `root` user. You do not need to give Apache user/group read or write permission in log directories. Enabling anyone other than the `root` user to write files in the log directory could lead to a major security hole. To ensure that only `root` user has access to the log files in a directory called `/logs`, follow these steps:

1. Change the ownership of the directory and all the files within it to root user and root group using the following command :

   ```
   chown -R root:root /logs
   ```

2. Change the directory's permission using the following command:

   ```
   chmod -R 750 /logs
   ```

What to do if you see unusual access in your log files

If you notice unusual access, such as someone trying to supply unusual parameters to your CGI scripts, you should consider that a hostile attempt and investigate the matter immediately. Here is a process that you can use in such matter:

1. Get the complete URL that was used in the attempt to fool a CGI script.

2. If you didn't write the script, ask the script author about what happens when someone passes such URL (that is, parameters within the URL after ?) to the script. If there is a reason to be concerned, proceed forward or stop investigating at this point, but make a note of the IP address in a POSSIBLE-ATTACKS.txt file along with the URL and time and date stamp.

3. If the URL makes the script do something it should not, consider taking the script offline until it is fixed so that such URL cannot pose a threat to the system.

4. Use the host program to detect the host name of the vandal's IP address. Sometimes host will not be able to find the host name. In such a case, try traceroute and identify the ISP owning the IP address.

5. Do a whois domain lookup for the ISP and find technical contact information listed in the whois output. You might have to go to a domain register's Web site to perform the whois lookup if you do not have the whois program installed. Try locating an appropriate domain register from the www.internic.net site.

6. Send an e-mail to the technical contact address at the ISP regarding the incident and supply the log snippet for their review. Write your e-mail in a very polite and friendly manner. Remember that the ISP at the other end is your only line of defense at this point. Politely request a speedy resolution or response.

7. If you can't take the script offline because it is used heavily in your Web site by others, you can ban the vandal from using it. Say, you run your script under the script alias ext, which is setup as:

```
ScriptAlias /ext/ "/some/path/to/cgi/scripts/"
```

Change the above to:

```
<Location /ext>
    SetHandler cgi-script
    Options -Indexes +ExecCGI
    AllowOverride None
    Order allow,deny
    Allow from all
    Deny from 192.168.1.100

    </Location>
```

Replace 192.168.1.100 with the vandal's IP address. This configuration will run your script as usual for everyone but the user on the IP address given in the Deny from line. However, if the vandal's ISP uses dynamically allocated IP addresses for it's customers, then locking the exact IP address will not be useful because the vandal can return with a different IP address. In such case, consider locking the entire IP network. For example, if the ISP uses the 192.168.1.0 network, you remove the .100 from the Deny from line to block the entire ISP. This is a drastic measure and might block a lot of innocent users at the ISP from using this script. Exercise caution when considering whether to block everyone at the ISP.

8. Wait a few days for the ISP to respond. If you do not hear from it, try to contact the ISP via its Web site. If the problem persists, contact your legal department to determine what legal actions you can take to require action from the ISP.

Securing Your CGI Implementation

Most Web security experts agree that the greatest security risk factors are the scripts or applications being run on the Web server to produce dynamic contents. Because CGI scripts are generally responsible for creating dynamic contents, they often cause most of the damage. This section focuses on security risks associated with CGI scripts and shows how you can reduce such risks.

Fending off CGI Risks with smart programming

According to SANS (www.sans.org), CGI script-related security risks ranks second on their top ten Internet security issues list. However, CGI is not inherently insecure; it is poorly written CGI scripts that are a major source of Web security holes. Actually, the simplicity of the CGI specification makes it easy for many inexperienced programmers to write CGI scripts. These inexperienced programmers, being unaware of the security aspects of internetworking, create applications or scripts that work, while also creating unintentional back doors and holes in the system. The following sections discuss first the types of risks that CGI applications or scripts create, and then discuss solutions for these risks.

Note   The terms *CGI application* and *CGI scripts* are used interchangeably.

Information leaks

Many CGI scripts can be fooled by vandals to leak information about users or resources available on the Web server. Such a leak helps vandals to break into a system. The more information a vandal has about a system, the better the vandal is at breaking into the system. For example, if this URL is used to display /doc/article1.html page using the showpage.cgi script:

```
http://unsafe-site.com/cgi-
bin/showpage.cgi?pg=/doc/article1.html
```

a vandal might try something like:

```
http://unsafe-site.com/cgi-bin/showpage.cgi?pg=/etc/passwd
```

which will display the /etc/passwd (user password file) for the entire system. This only works if the showpage.cgi author did not protect the script from such leaks.

Consumption of system resources

A poorly written CGI script can be used by a vandal to make a server consume system resources such that the server becomes virtually unresponsive. For example, this URL allows a site visitor to view a list of classifieds advertisements in a Web site:

```
http://unsafe-site.com/cgi-bin/showlist.pl?start=1&stop=15
```

The start=1 and stop=15 parameters are used to control the number of records displayed. If the showlist.pl script only relies on the supplied start and stop values, then a vandal can edit the URL and supply a larger number for the stop parameter to make showlist.pl display a larger list then usual. So what? Well, a vandal can use this knowledge and overload the Web server with requests that take longer to process, which makes real users wait and possibly makes them move to a competitor's site.

Spoofing of system commands via CGI scripts

In many cases, vandals have succeeded in tricking an HTML form-based mailer script to run a system command or to give out confidential system information. For example, say that you have a Web form that users use to sign up for your services or to provide you with feedback. Most sites with such a Web form send a thank-you note to the user via an e-mail. A CGI script is used to process the form. The script might be doing something similar to the following to send the e-mail:

```
system("/bin/mail  -s $subject $emailAddress < $thankYouMsg");
```

The system call runs the /bin/mail mail program and supplies it the value of variable $subject as the Subject: header, the value of variable $emailAddress as the e-mail address of the user, and redirects the contents of the file named by the $thankYouMsg variable. This works and no one should normally know that your application uses such system calls. However, vandals are always trying to break things, and so a vandal interested in breaking your Web site might look into everything that the vandal has access to and try entering irregular values for your Web form. For example if a vandal enters vandal@emailaddr < /etc/passwd; as the e-mail address, the script will be fooled into sending the /etc/passwd file to the vandal-specified e-mail address!

> **Tip**
>
> If you use system() function in your CGI script, you should use the -T option in your #!/path/to/perl line to enable Perl's taint-checking mode. You should also set the PATH (environment variable) using set $ENV{PATH} = '/path/to/commands/you/call/via/system' to increase security.

User input makes certain system calls unsafe

Certain system calls are unsafe to use in CGI script. For example, in Perl (a widely used CGI programming language) such a call could be made using the system(), exec(), piped open(), and eval() functions. Similarly, in C the popen() and system() functions are potential security hazards. All of these functions/commands typically invoke a subshell (such as /bin/sh) to process the user command.

Even shell scripts that use system() or exec() calls are likely to open a port of entry for vandals. Back-tick quotes, available in shell interpreters and Perl for capturing the output of programs as text strings, are also dangerous.

To illustrate the importance of careful use of system calls, consider this innocent-looking Perl code segment:

```perl
#!/usr/bin/perl -w
#
# Purpose: to demonstrate security risks in
# poorly written CGI script.
#
# Get the domain name from query string
# environment variable.
#

my $domain = $ENV{'QUERY_STRING'};

# Print the appropriate content type.
# Because whois output is in plain text,
# we choose to use text/plain as the content-type here.
#
print "Content-type: text/plain\n\n";

# Here is the bad system call:
system("/usr/bin/whois $domain");

# Here is another bad system call using back-ticks:
#
# my $output = `/usr/bin/whois $domain`;
#
# print $output;

exit 0;
```

This little Perl script is supposed to be a Web-based WHOIS gateway. If this script is called whois.pl, and if it is kept in the cgi-bin directory of a Web site called unsafe-site.com, a user can call this script as follows:

```
http://unsafe-site.com/cgi-bin/script.pl?domain=anydomain.com
```

The script will take the anydomain.com as the $domain variable via the QUERY_STRING variable, and launch the /usr/bin/whois program with the $domain value as the argument. This returns the data from the WHOIS database that InterNIC maintains. This is all very innocent and good, but the script is a disaster waiting to happen. Consider the following line:

```
http://unsafe-site.com/cgi-bin/script.pl?domain=nitec.com;ps
```

This does a WHOIS lookup on a domain called nitec.com and also provides the output of the Unix ps utility that shows process status. This reveals information about the system that should not be available to the requesting party. Using this technique, anyone can learn a great deal about your system. For example, replacing the `ps` command with `df` (a common Unix utility that prints a summary of disk space) enables anyone to determine what partitions you have and how full they are. This security hole could pose a great danger.

What is the lesson? It is not to trust any input, and not to make system calls an easy target for abuse. How to achieve these goals is the topic that is addressed in the next section.

User can modify hidden data in HTML pages

As you might already know, HTTP is a stateless protocol. Many Web developers keep state information or other important data in cookies, or temporary files, or using so called hidden tags. Because a user can turn off cookies and because creating unique temporary files per user is cumbersome, hidden tags are commonly used. A hidden tag looks similar to the following:

```
<input type=hidden name="datakey" value="dataValue">
```

For example:

```
<input type=hidden name="state" value="CA">
```

Here the hidden tag stores "state=CA," which can be retrieved by the same application in a subsequent call. Hidden tags are common in multiscreen Web applications. Because the user can manually change hidden tags, they should not be trusted. There are two ways of protecting against altered data: the developer can verify the hidden data before each use, or the developer can use a security scheme to ensure that data has not be altered by the user. The CGI script shown in Listing 18-2, demonstrates the use of the RSA Data Security MD5 message digest algorithm to protect hidden data.

Note   The details of the MD5 algorithm are defined in RFC 1321.

> ### Listing 18-2: **hidden-md5.eg**
>
> ```perl
> #!/usr/bin/perl -w
> #
> # Purpose: This script demonstrates the use of
> #          MD5 message digest in a multiscreen
> #          Web application.
> #
> # CVS: $Id$
> #
> ###############################################################
>
> use strict;
> ```

```perl
use CGI qw(:standard);
use Digest::MD5;

my $query = new CGI;

# Call the handler subroutine to process user data

&handler;

# Terminate
exit 0;

sub handler{

    #
    # Purpose: Determine which screen to display
    #          and call the appropriate subroutine to
    #          display it.
    #

    # Get user-entered name (if any) and e-mail address
    # (if any) and initialize two variables using given
    # name and e-mail values. Note: first time we will
    # not have values for these variables.

    my $name    = param('name');
    my $email    = param('email');

    # Print the appropriate Content-Type header and
    # also print HTML page tags
    print header,
        start_html(-title => 'Multi-Screen Web Application
Demo');

    # If we do not have value for the $name variable,
    # we have not yet displayed screen one so show it.
    if ($name eq ''){

        &screen1;

    # If we have value for the $name variable but the
    # $email variable is empty then we need to show
    # screen 2.
    } elsif($email eq '') {

        &screen2($name);

    # We have value for both $name and $email so
    # show screen 3.
```

Continued

Listing 18-2 *(Continued)*

```perl
    } else {

        &screen3($name, $email);

    }

    # Print closing HTML tag for the page
    print end_html;

}

sub screen1{
    #
    # Purpose: print an HTML form that asks the
    # user to enter his or her name.
    #

    print h2("Screen 1"),
            hr({-size=>0,-color=>'black'}),
                start_form,
                'Enter name: ',
                textfield(-name => 'name', -size=>30),
                submit(-value => ' Next '),
                end_form;

}

sub screen2{
    #
    # Purpose: print an HTML form that asks the
    # user to enter her email address. It also
    # stores the name entered in the previous screen.
    #

    # Get the name
    my $name  = shift;

    # Create a MD5 message disgest for the name
    my $digest = &create_message_digest($name);

    # Insert the digest as a new CGI parameter so
    # that we can store it using CGI.pm's hidden()
    # subroutine.
    param('digest', $digest);

    # Now print the second screen and insert
    # the $name and the $digest values as hidden data.
    print h2("Screen 2"),
```

```
                hr({-size=>0,-color=>'black'}),
                start_form,
                'Enter email: ',
                textfield(-name => 'email', -size=>30),
                hidden('name'),
                hidden('digest'),
                submit(-value => ' Next '),
                end_form;
    }

    sub screen3{
        #
        # Purpose: Print a message based on the
        # data gathered
        # in screen 1 and 2. However, print the message
        # only if the entered data has not been altered.
        #

        # Get name and email address
        my ($name, $email) = @_;

        # Get the digest of the $name value
        my $oldDigest = param('digest');

        # Create a new digest of the value of the $name variable
        my $newDigest = &create_message_digest($name);

        # If both digests are not same then (name) data has been
    altered
        # in screen 2. Display an alert message and stop processing
        #in such case.
        if ($oldDigest ne $newDigest){
            return (0, alert('Data altered. Aborted!'));
        }

        # Since data is good, process as usual.
        print h2("Screen 3"),
              hr({-size=>0,-color=>'black'}),
              p('Your name is '. b($name) .
              ' and your email address is '. b($email) . '.'),
              a({-href=>"$ENV{SCRIPT_NAME}"},'Restart');
    }

    sub create_message_digest{
        #
        # Purpose: Create a message digest for the
        #          given data. To make the digest hard
        #          to reproduce by a vandal, this subroutine
        #          uses a secret key.
```

Continued

Listing 18-2 *(Continued)*

```perl
    #
    my $data = shift;

    my $secret = 'ID10t' ;    # Change this key if you like.

    # We need the following line to tell Perl that
    # we want to use the Digest::MD5 module.
    use Digest::MD5;

    # Create a new MD5 object
    my $ctx = Digest::MD5->new;

    # Add data
    $ctx->add($data);

    # Add secret key
    $ctx->add($secret);

    # Create a Base64 digest
    my $digest = $ctx->b64digest;

    # Return the digest
    return $digest;
}

sub alert{
  #
  # Purpose: Display an alert dialog box
  #          using Java Script.
  #

  # Get the message that we need to display
  my $msg = shift;

  # Create a java script that uses the alert()
  # dialog box function to display a message
  # and then return the browser to previous screen.
  print <<JAVASCRIPT;

  <script language="JavaScript">
   alert("$msg");
   history.back();
  </script>

JAVASCRIPT

  }
```

Listing 18-2 is a simple multiscreen CGI script that asks the user to enter a name in the first screen, then asks the user to enter an e-mail address in the next screen, and finally it prints out a message. When the user moves from one screen to another, the data from the previous screen is carried to the next screen using hidden tags. This script works as discussed in the following paragraphs.

At the very beginning of the script, two external modules — CGI and Digest::MD5 — are used. The first one is the most popular CGI module that makes writing CGI scripts in Perl very easy. The second module provides us with an interface to the MD5 digest algorithm.

The script first creates a CGI object called $query. It then calls the handler() subroutine for each request. The handler() subroutine is the driver of the script. Look inside the handler() subroutine and you will see that it assigns user-entered name and e-mail fields (collected from a Web form) to $name and $email, respectively. Then it prints a Content-Type header message using the header() method and creates the start of an HTML document using the start_html() method found in CGI module.

If the user has not yet entered a name, this routine displays screen 1 by using the screen1() subroutine. If the $name variable does have a value, the handler() subroutine displays screen 2 by using the screen2() subroutine. When both $name and $email have values, the screen3() subroutine is used to display screen 3. Finally, the routine prints out closing tags for the page by using the end_html() method found in the CGI module.

Now look at the screen1() subroutine, which is quite simple. It simply displays a Web form that has a field called name that the user needs to fill out. Note that the entire Web form is created using the start_form(), textfield(), submit(), and end_form() methods found in CGI module. The form's action is not defined, which means that the script that generated the Web form is called. In other words, when the screen 1 form is displayed and a user enters his or her name and clicks Submit, the same script is called with name field set to user-defined data.

The screen2() subroutine takes the global $name variable as an argument and uses the create_message_digest() subroutine to create a MD5 digest called $digest for the user-entered name. The digest is than added to the CGI object using the param('digest', $digest), which is then entered into the screen 2 Web form using the hidden('digest') method found in CGI module. The screen 2 Web form is created using the start_form(), textfield(), hidden(), submit(), and end_form() methods found in CGI module. The hidden('argument') method simply creates an <input type=hidden name=argument value=value_found_in_CGI_object_for_argument> tag. The purpose of creating the digest and of hiding it in the Web form along with the name is that this allows us to determine whether the hidden name field was altered.

When the screen3() subroutine is called, it takes global variable $name and $email as arguments. It also assigns local variable $oldDigest to the hidden digest stored in the CGI object. Then it creates a new digest by calling the create_message_ digest() subroutine using the value of the $name variable. It then compares the old and the new digests to determine whether the name field was altered in screen 2. Remember that a name was entered in screen 1 and it was hidden using the HTML hidden tag in screen 2. So, there was a chance that someone could have altered the name value in transit.

If the digests do not match, an alert message is printed using the alert() subroutine, which displays a JavaScript pop-up message. Otherwise, the name and the e-mail address are printed on the screen.

The most interesting subroutine is the create_message_digest(). It takes anything as an argument and uses the Digest::MD5 object called $ctx to add the given data and a secret pass phrase (stored in $secret) using the Digest::MD5 object's add() method. Then it creates a Base64 MD5 digest using the b64digest() method, which is returned to the calling subroutine.

When the CGI script is first run, it produces a screen that asks the user to enter his or her name. After the user enters his or her name, the user continues to the next screen, where the user is asked to enter an e-mail address. The HTML source of this screen is shown in Listing 18-3.

Listing 18-3: **HTML Source for Screen 2 of hidden-md5.eg**

```
<!DOCTYPE HTML PUBLIC "-//IETF//DTD HTML//EN">
<HTML>
  <HEAD>
   <TITLE>Multi-Screen Web Application Demo</TITLE>
  </HEAD>

 <BODY>
  <H2>Screen 2</H2>
  <HR SIZE="0" COLOR="black">
  <FORM METHOD="POST"
         ENCTYPE="application/x-www-form-urlencoded">

  Enter email:
  <INPUT TYPE="text"
         NAME="email"
         SIZE=30>

  <INPUT TYPE="hidden"
         NAME="name"
         VALUE="Cynthia">

  <INPUT TYPE="hidden"
         NAME="digest"
         VALUE="IzrSJ1LrsWlYHNfshrKw/A">

  <INPUT TYPE="submit"
```

```
        NAME=".submit"
        VALUE=" Next ">

    </FORM>
    </BODY>
</HTML>
```

The hidden data are stored using the following lines:

```
<INPUT TYPE="hidden"
       NAME="name"
       VALUE="Cynthia">

<INPUT TYPE="hidden"
       NAME="digest"
       VALUE="IzrSJlLrsWlYHNfshrKw/A">
```

The first hidden data tag line stores `name=Cynthia` and the second hidden data tag line stores `digest=IzrSJlLrsWlYHNfshrKw/A`. The second piece of data is the message digest generated for the name entered in screen 1. When the user enters an e-mail address in the second screen and continues, the final screen is displayed.

However, before the final screen is produced, a message digest is computed for the name field in screen 1. This digest is compared against the digest created earlier to verify that the value entered for the name field in screen 1 is not altered in screen 2. Because the MD5 algorithm creates the same message digest for a given data set, any differences between the new and old digests will raise red flags and the script will display an alert message and refuse to complete processing. In other words, if a vandal decides to alter the data stored in screen 2 (shown in Listing 18-3) and submits the data for final processing, the digest mismatch will allow the script to detect the alteration and take appropriate action. In your real-world CGI scripts (written in Perl), you can use the `create_message_digest()` subroutine to create a message digest for anything.

Tip   You can download and install the latest version of Digest::MD5 from CPAN using `perl -MCPAN -e shell` **command followed by a** `install Digest::MD5` **command at the CPAN shell prompt.**

Keeping user input secure

As you can see, most of the security holes created by CGI scripts are caused by inappropriate user input. The following section discusses a few common problems and solutions.

There are two approaches to ensuring that user input is safe:

✦ Scanning the input for illegal characters and to replace or remove them. For example, for the whois.pl script, you can add the following line:

```
$domain =~ s/[\/ ;\[\]\<\>&\t]//g;
```

This removes illegal meta-characters. This is a common but inadvisable approach, as it requires that the programmer be aware of all possible combinations of characters that could cause trouble. If the user uses input not predicted by the programmer, there is the possibility that the program may be used in a manner not intended by the programmer.

✦ Defining a list of acceptable characters and replacing or removing any character that is *not* acceptable. The list of valid input values is typically a predictable, well-defined set of manageable size.

I prefer the second approach above, since it does not require the programmer to trap all characters that are unacceptable, leaving no margin for error. The recommended approach requires only that a programmer ensure that acceptable characters are identified; thus the programmer can be less concerned about the characters an attacker may try in an attempt to bypass security checks.

Building on this concept, the whois.pl program presented earlier could be sanitized to contain *only* those characters allowed; for example:

```perl
#!/usr/bin/perl -w
#
# Purpose: This is a better version of the previous
# whois.pl script.
#
# Assign a variable the acceptable character
# set for domain names.
#
my $DOMAIN_CHAR_SET='-a-zA-Z0-9_.';

# Get the domain name from query string
# environment variable.
#
my $domain = $ENV{'QUERY_STRING'};

# Now remove any character that does not
# belong to the acceptable character set.
#
$domain =~ s/[^$DOMAIN_CHAR_SET]//g;

# Print the appropriate content type.
# Because whois output is in plain text, we
# choose to use text/plain as the content-type here.
#
print "Content-type: text/plain\n\n";

# Here is the system call:
```

```
system("/usr/bin/whois $domain");

# Here is another system call using back-ticks:
#
# my $output = `/usr/bin/whois $domain`;
#
# print $output;

exit 0;
```

The $DOMAIN_CHAR_SET variable holds the acceptable character set, and the user-input variable $domain is searched for anything that does not fall in the set. The unacceptable character is removed.

The best way to go about user input is to establish rules for each input (that is, what you expect and how you can determine what you have received is acceptable). If you are expecting an e-mail address as input (rather than just scanning it blindly for shell meta-characters) for example, use a regular expression such as the following to detect the validity of the input as a possible e-mail address:

```
$email = param('email-addr');

if ($email=~ /^[\w-\.]+\@[\w-\.]+$/) {
    print "Possibly valid address."
  }
else {
    print "Invalid email address.";
  }
```

Just sanitizing user input is not enough. You need to be careful about how you invoke external programs (for example, there are many ways in which you can invoke external programs in Perl). Some of these methods include using back-ticks to capture the output of an external program, such as:

```
$list = '/bin/ls -l /etc';
```

This captures the /etc directory listing. Or, you can open a pipe to a program, such as:

```
open (FP, " | /usr/bin/sort");
```

You can also invoke an external program and wait for it to return with system():

```
system "/usr/bin/lpr data.dat";
```

or you can invoke an external program and never return with exec():

```
exec "/usr/bin/sort < data.dat";
```

All of these constructions are risky if they involve user input that may contain shell meta-characters. For `system()` and `exec()`, there's a somewhat obscure syntactic feature that enables you to call external programs directly rather than going through a shell. If you pass the arguments to the external program as separate elements in a list rather than in one long string, Perl will not go through the shell and shell meta-characters will have no unwanted side effects. For example:

```
system "/usr/bin/sort","data.dat";
```

You can take advantage of this feature to open up a pipe without going through a shell. Calling the character sequence `-|` forks a copy of Perl and opens a pipe to the copy. Then, the child copy immediately forks another program using the first argument of the `exec` function call.

To read from a pipe without opening a shell, you can do something similar with the sequence `-|`:

```
open(GREP,"-|") || exec "/usr/bin/grep",$userpattern,$filename;
while (<GREP>) {
  print "match: $_";
  }
close GREP;
```

These forms of `open()` are more secure than the piped `open()` and, therefore, you should use these whenever possible.

Note that there are many other obscure features in Perl that enable you to call an external program and to lie to it about its name. This is useful for calling programs that behave differently depending on the name by which they were invoked.
The syntax is:

```
system $real_name "fake_name","argument1","argument2"
```

One trick used by vandals is to alter the `PATH` environment variable so that it points to the program they want your script to execute, rather than to the program you're expecting. You should invoke programs using full pathnames rather than relying on the `PATH` environment variable. That is, instead of this fragment of Perl code:

```
system("cat /tmp/shopping.cart.txt");
```

use this:

```
system "/bin/cat" , "/tmp/shopping.cart.txt ";
```

If you must rely on the `PATH` variable, set it yourself at the beginning of your CGI script, as follows:

```
$ENV{'PATH'}="bin:/usr/bin:/usr/local/bin";
```

Even if you don't rely on the PATH variable when you invoke an external program, there's a chance that the invoked program will; therefore, you need to include the previous line toward the top of your script whenever you use taint checks. You have to adjust the line for the list of directories that you want searched. Also, in general, it's not a good idea to put the current directory (.) into the path.

Wrapping CGI Scripts

The best way to reduce CGI-related risks is not to run any CGI scripts at all; however, in the days of dynamic Web content, this is unrealistic. Perhaps you can centralize all CGI scripts in one location and closely monitor their development to ensure that they are well-written.

In many cases, especially on ISP systems, all users with Web sites want CGI access. In this situation, it might be a good idea to run CGI scripts under the user ID (UID) of the user who owns the CGI script. By default, CGI scripts that Apache runs use the Apache UID. If you run these applications using the owner's UID, all possible damage is limited to what the UID is permitted to access. In other words, a bad CGI script run with a UID other than the Apache server UID can damage only the user's files. The user responsible for the CGI script will become more careful, because the possible damage will affect his or her content solely. In one shot, you get increased user responsibility and awareness and, simultaneously, a limited area for potential damage. To run a CGI script using a UID other than the Apache server, you need a special type of program called a *wrapper,* which enables you to run a CGI script as the user who owns the file rather than as the Apache server user. Some CGI wrappers do other security checks before they run the requested CGI scripts. The following sections discuss two popular CGI wrappers.

suEXEC

Apache comes with a support application called suEXEC that provides Apache users with the ability to run CGI and SSI programs under UIDs that are different from the UID of Apache. suEXEC is a setuid wrapper program that is called when an HTTP request is made for a CGI or SSI program that the administrator designates to run as a UID other than that of the Apache server. When such a request is made, Apache provides the suEXEC wrapper with the program's name and the UID and GID. suEXEC runs the program using the given UID and GID.

Before running the CGI or SSI command, the suEXEC wrapper performs a set of tests to ensure that the request is valid. Among other things, this testing procedure ensures that the CGI script is owned by a user who is allowed to run the wrapper and that the CGI directory or the CGI script is not writable by anyone but the owner. After the security checks are successful, the suEXEC wrapper changes the UID and the group ID (GID) to the target UID and GID via setuid and setgid calls, respectively. The group-access list is also initialized with all groups in which the user is a member. suEXEC cleans the process's environment by establishing a safe execution PATH (defined during configuration), as well as by passing through only those variables whose names are listed in the safe environment list (also created during configuration). The suEXEC process then becomes the target CGI script or SSI command and executes. This may seem like a lot of work — and it is — but this provides a great security coefficient, as well.

Configuring and installing suEXEC

If you are interested in installing suEXEC support in Apache, run the `configure` (or `config.status`) script as follows:

```
./configure --prefix=/path/to/apache \
            --enable-suexec \
            --suexec-caller=httpd \
            --suexec-userdir=public_html
            --suexec-uidmin=100 \
            --suexec-gidmin=100
            --suexec-safepath="/usr/local/bin:/usr/bin:/bin"
```

Here is the detailed explanation of this configuration:

✦ `--enable-suexec`: Enables suEXEC support.

✦ `--suexec-caller=`*httpd*: Change *httpd* to the UID you use for the `User` directive in the Apache configuration file. This is the only user who will be permitted to run the suEXEC program.

✦ `--suexec-userdir=`*public_html*: Defines the subdirectory under users' home directories where suEXEC executables are to be kept. Change *public_html* to whatever you use as the value for the `UserDir` directive, which specifies the document root directory for a user's Web site.

✦ `--suexec-uidmin=100`: Defines the lowest UID permitted to run suEXEC-based CGI scripts. In other words, UIDs below this number won't be able to run CGI or SSI commands via suEXEC. Look at your `/etc/passwd` file to make sure that the range you chose does not include the system accounts that are usually UIDs below 100.

✦ `--suexec-gidmin=100`: Defines the lowest GID permitted to be a target group. In other words, GIDs below this number won't be able to run CGI or SSI commands via suEXEC. Look at your `/etc/group` file to make sure that the range you chose does not include the system account groups that are usually UIDs below 100.

✦ `--suexec-safepath="/usr/local/bin:/usr/bin:/bin"`: Defines the PATH environment variable that gets executed by suEXEC for CGI scripts and SSI commands.

Enabling and testing suEXEC

After you install both the suEXEC wrapper and the new Apache executable in the proper location, restart Apache, which will write a message similar to this:

```
[notice] suEXEC mechanism enabled (wrapper: /usr/local/sbin/suexec)
```

This tells you that the suEXEC is active. Now, test suEXEC's functionality. In the httpd.conf file, add these lines:

```
UserDir public_html
AddHandler cgi-script  .pl
```

The first directive (UserDir) sets the document root of a user's Web site to be ~*username*/public_html, where *username* can be any user on the system. The second directive associates the cgi-script handler with the .pl files. This is done so that Perl scripts with .pl extensions can run as CGI scripts. For this test, you will need a user account. In this example, I use the host wormhole.nitec.com and a user called kabir. Copy the script shown in Listing 18-4 to a file called test.pl and put it in a user's public_html directory. In my case, I put the file in the ~kabir/public_html directory.

Listing 18-4: **A CGI Script to Test suEXEC Support**

```perl
#!/usr/bin/perl
#
# Make sure the preceding line is pointing to the
# right location. Some people keep perl in
# /usr/local/bin.

my ($key,$value);
print "Content-type: text/html\n\n";
print "<h1>Test of  suEXEC<h1>";

foreach $key (sort keys %ENV){
    $value = $ENV{$key};
    print "$key = $value <br>";
    }
exit 0;
```

To access the script via a Web browser, I request the following URL: http://wormhole.nitec.com/~kabir/test.pl.

A CGI script is executed only after it passes all the security checks performed by suEXEC. suEXEC also logs the script request in its log file. The log entry for my request looks as follows:

```
[2001-03-29 16:00:22]: uid: (kabir/kabir) gid: (kabir/kabir) cmd: test.pl
```

If you are really interested in knowing that the script is running under the user's UID, insert a sleep command (such as sleep(10);) inside the foreach loop, which will slow the execution and allow you to run commands such as top or ps on your Web server console to learn the UID of the process running test.pl. You also can change the ownership of the script by using the `chown` command; try to access the script via your Web browser after changing ownership, and see the error message that suEXEC logs. For example, when I change the ownership of the `test.pl` script in the `~kabir/public_html` directory as follows:

```
chown root test.pl
```

I get a server error, and the log file shows the following line:

```
[2001-03-29 16:00:22]: uid/gid (500/500) mismatch with directory (500/500) or
program (0/500)
```

Here, the program is owned by UID 0, and the group is still `kabir` (500), so suEXEC refuses to run it, which means suEXEC is doing what it is supposed to do.

To ensure that suEXEC will run `test.pl` in other directories, I created a `cgi-bin` directory in `~kabir/public_html` and put `test.cgi` in that directory. After determining that the user and group ownership of the new directory and file are set to user ID `kabir` and group ID `kabir`, I accessed the script by using the following command:

```
http://wormhole.nitec.com/~kabir/cgi-bin/test.pl
```

If you have virtual hosts and want to run the CGI programs and/or SSI commands using suEXEC, you must use User and Group directives inside the `<VirtualHost . . .>` container. Set these directives to user and group IDs other than those the Apache server is currently using. If only one, or neither, of these directives is specified for a `<VirtualHost>` container, the server user ID or group ID is assumed.

For security and efficiency reasons, all suEXEC requests must remain within either a top-level document root for virtual host requests or one top-level personal document root for userdir requests. For example, if you have four virtual hosts configured, you need to structure all of your virtual host document roots off of one main Apache document hierarchy to take advantage of suEXEC for virtual hosts.

CGIWrap

CGIWrap is similar to the suEXEC program insofar as it permits users to use CGI scripts without compromising the security of the Web server. CGI programs are run with the file owner's permission. In addition, CGIWrap performs several security checks on the CGI script and is not executed if any checks fail.

Nathan Neulinger writes CGIWrap; the latest version of CGIWrap is available from the primary FTP site at `ftp://ftp.cc.umr.edu/pub/cgi/cgiwrap/`. CGIWrap is used via a URL in an HTML document. As distributed, CGIWrap is configured to run user scripts that are located in the `~/public_html/cgi-bin/` directory.

Configuring and installing CGIWrap

CGIWrap is distributed as a gzip-compressed tar file. You uncompress it by using gzip and extract it by using the `tar` utility.

Run the `Configure` script, which prompts you to answer many questions. Most of these questions are self-explanatory. Also note that there is a feature in this wrapper that differs from suEXEC. It enables you to create allow and deny files that can be used to restrict access to your CGI scripts. Both of these files have the same format, as shown in the following:

```
User ID
mailto:Username@subnet1/mask1,subnet2/mask2. . .
```

You can either have a single username (nonnumeric UID) or a user `mailto:ID@subnet/mask` line where one or more subnet/mask pairs can be defined. For example, if the following line is found in the allow file (you specify the filename),

```
mailto:kabir@192.168.1.0/255.255.255.0
```

user kabir's CGI scripts are permitted to be run by hosts that belong in the 192.168.1.0 network with netmask 255.255.255.0.

After you run the `Configure` script, you must run the `make` utility to create the CGIWrap executable.

Enabling CGIWrap

To use the wrapper application, copy the CGIWrap executable to the user's `cgi-bin` directory. This directory must match the directory that you specified in the configuration process. The simplest way to get things going is to keep the `~username/public_html/cgi-bin` type of directory structure for the CGI script directory.

After you copy the CGIWrap executable, change the ownership and permission bits as follows:

```
chown root CGIWrap
chmod 4755 CGIWrap
```

Create three hard links or symbolic links called `nph-cgiwrap`, `nph-cgiwrapd`, and `cgiwrapd` to CGIWrap in the `cgi-bin` directory as follows:

```
ln [-s] CGIWrap cgiwrapd
ln [-s] CGIWrap nph-cgiwrap
ln [-s] CGIWrap nph-cgiwrapd
```

On my Apache server, I specified only the cgi extension as a CGI script; therefore, I renamed my CGIWrap executable to `cgiwrap.cgi` to get it to work. If you have similar restrictions, you might try this approach or make a link instead.

Now, execute a CGI script as follows:

```
http://www.yourdomain.com/cgi-bin/cgiwrap/username/scriptname
```

To access user kabir's CGI script `test.cgi` on the `wormhole.nitec.com` site, for example, I would use the following:

```
http://wormhole.nitec.com/cgi-bin/cgiwrap/kabir/test.cgi
```

If you want to see debugging output for your CGI, specify `cgiwrapd` instead of `cgiwrap`, as in the following URL:

```
http://www.yourdomain.com/cgi-bin/cgiwrapd/username/scriptname
```

If the script is an nph-style script, you must run it using the following URL:

```
http://www.yourdomain.com/cgi-bin/nph-cgiwrap/username/scriptname
```

Hiding clues about your CGI scripts

When a vandal scans a Web site for possible holes, the vandal looks for little things that provide clues about the underlying hardware and software used for the Web site. So, the fewer clues you provide about your system, the greater the chance that your Web site will not become the vandal's next victim. There are several ways to hide some of the important details that could become clues.

Use a nonstandard script alias

Use of cgi-bin alias is very popular. As soon as you see a URL with cgi-bin you know the site runs CGI scripts of some sort. This alias is set using the `ScriptAlias` directive in Apache's `httpd.conf` file. For example:

```
ScriptAlias /cgi-bin/ "/path/to/real/cgi/directory/"
```

But only few people realize that you can use anything to create an alias like this. For example:

```
ScriptAlias /apps/ "/path/to/real/cgi/directory/"
```

Now the `apps` in a URL serves the same purpose as `cgi-bin`. So, if you use something similar to:

```
ScriptAlias /dcon/ "/path/to/real/cgi/directory/"
```

it certainly will confuse some vandals because dcon, or whatever you really use, is nonstandard. Also, remember that many vandals use automated programs to scan Web sites for features and other clues. A nonstandard script alias such as the above is not likely to be incorporated in any automated program.

Use nonextension names for your CGI scripts

Many sites boldly showcase what type of CGI scripts they run. For example:

```
http://www.domain.com/cgi-bin/show-catalog.pl
```

the above URL provides two clues about the site. First, it tells us that the site supports CGI scripts, and second, that the site runs Perl scripts as CGI scripts. If the above site instead used:

```
http://www.domain.com/ext/show-catalog
```

it is harder to determine anything about the site. Use of the .pl or .cgi extension should be avoided because these extensions provide clues about your system. To change an existing a script's extension from .pl, .cgi, and so on to a non-extension name, simply rename the script. You do not need to change or add any new Apache configuration for switching to nonextension names.

Like CGI scripts, SSI scripts pose a few security risks. They are discussed below.

Using CGI Scanners

CGI scanners are used to scan a Web server for CGI script-related vulnerabilities. There are two scanners that I like: cgichk.pl and Whisker.

cgichk.pl

This is a simple CGI scanner written in Perl. You can download the source from www.packetstorm.securify.com. When run from the command line using perl cgichk.pl command, it asks you to enter a host name for the Web server you want to scan and a port number (default 80). You can also choose to log the results in a file.

cgichk.pl first checks the HTTP protocol version being used by the Web server. For example, the following sample session shows that cgichk.pl is scanning a host called rhat.nitec.com.

```
CGI scanner [in Perl] v1.1

Host: rhat.nitec.com
HTTP Port [80]:
Log Session?(y/n)y
Log File [rhat.nitec.com.scan]:
```

```
Press [enter] to check the httpd version...

HTTP/1.1 200 OK
Date: Tue, 27 Mar 2001 04:50:47 GMT
Server: Apache/2.0.14 (Unix)
Last-Modified: Mon, 26 Mar 2001 20:23:13 GMT
ETag: "1ba42-1000-c65eee40"
Connection: close
Content-Type: text/html; charset=ISO-8859-1
```

After it detects the protocol version, cgichk.pl will ask you to press the enter key to start checking for CGI vulnerabilities. The following output is a sample scan for CGI security issues on rhat.nitec.com Web server running Apache 2.0.

```
Searching for UnlG - backdoor      : Not Found
Searching for THC - backdoor       : Not Found
Searching for phf                  : Not Found
Searching for Count.cgi            : Not Found
Searching for test-cgi             : Not Found
Searching for nph-test-cgi         : Not Found
Searching for nph-publish          : Not Found
Searching for php.cgi              : Not Found
Searching for handler              : Not Found
Searching for webgais              : Not Found
Searching for websendmail          : Not Found
Searching for webdist.cgi          : Not Found
Searching for faxsurvey            : Not Found
Searching for htmlscript           : Not Found
Searching for pfdisplay            : Not Found
Searching for perl.exe             : Not Found
Searching for wwwboard.pl          : Not Found
Searching for www-sql              : Not Found
Searching for view-source          : Not Found
Searching for campas               : Not Found
Searching for aglimpse             : Not Found
Searching for glimpse              : Not Found
Searching for man.sh               : Not Found
Searching for AT-admin.cgi         : Not Found
Searching for filemail.pl          : Not Found
Searching for maillist.pl          : Not Found
Searching for jj                   : Not Found
Searching for info2www             : Not Found
Searching for files.pl             : Not Found
Searching for finger               : Not Found
Searching for bnbform.cgi          : Not Found
Searching for survey.cgi           : Not Found
Searching for AnyForm2             : Not Found
Searching for textcounter.pl       : Not Found
Searching for classifields.cgi     : Not Found
Searching for environ.cgi          : Not Found
Searching for wrap                 : Not Found
Searching for cgiwrap              : Not Found
Searching for guestbook.cgi        : Not Found
```

```
Searching for edit.pl           : Not Found
Searching for perlshop.cgi      : Not Found
Searching for anyboard.cgi      : Not Found
Searching for webbbs.cgi        : Found!
Searching for environ.cgi       : Not Found
Searching for whois_raw.cgi     : Not Found
Searching for _vti_inf.html     : Not Found
Searching for service.pwd       : Not Found
Searching for users.pwd         : Not Found
Searching for authors.pwd       : Not Found
Searching for administrators    : Not Found
Searching for shtml.dll         : Not Found
Searching for shtml.exe         : Not Found
Searching for args.bat          : Not Found
Searching for uploader.exe      : Not Found
Searching for rguest.exe        : Not Found
Searching for wguest.exe        : Not Found
Searching for bdir - samples    : Not Found
Searching for CGImail.exe       : Not Found
Searching for newdsn.exe        : Not Found
Searching for fpcount.exe       : Not Found
Searching for counter.exe       : Not Found
Searching for visadmin.exe      : Not Found
Searching for openfile.cfm      : Not Found
Searching for exprcalc.cfm      : Not Found
Searching for dispopenedfile    : Not Found
Searching for sendmail.cfm      : Not Found
Searching for codebrws.asp      : Not Found
Searching for codebrws.asp 2    : Not Found
Searching for showcode.asp      : Not Found
Searching for search97.vts      : Not Found
Searching for carbo.dll         : Not Found
Server may have CGI vulnerabilities.
```

Notice the line in bold. The scan found a potential CGI security risk. The webbbs.cgi script can be abused by script kiddies and wanna-be hackers to break into the system. If your scan identifies one or more security risks, consider removing the scripts or updating them with appropriate fixes.

Whisker

Whisker is a Perl-based CGI scanner that I like a lot. You can download the source distribution from www.filesearch.ru. After it is downloaded, extract the source in a directory and run the whisker.pl script as perl whisker.pl -h *hostname*. For example, perl whisker -h rhat.nitec.com command runs the scanner on the Apache Web server running on the named host. The result is shown below:

```
= Host: rhat.nitec.com
= Server: Apache/2.0.14 (Unix)

+ 200 OK: HEAD /cgi-bin/webbbs.cgi
+ 200 OK: HEAD /manual/
+ 200 OK: HEAD /temp/
```

Interestingly, the scan output uses HTTP status codes such as 200, 303, 403, and 404 to indicate security risks For example, the above scan result shows that there are three potential risks found (200) on the server. If you want more information run whisker with the `-i` and `-v` options. For example, the `perl whisker.pl -h www.domain.com -i -v` command runs it on `www.domain.com`. Here is a sample scan output:

```
= - = - = - = - = - =
= Host: www.domain.com
- Directory index: /

= Server: Apache/1.3.12 (Unix) mod_oas/5.1/

-   www.apache.org
+ 302 Found: GET /scripts/
+ 403 Forbidden: GET /cgi-bin/
+ 200 OK: HEAD /cgi-bin/upload.pl
+ 403 Forbidden: HEAD /~root/
+ 403 Forbidden: HEAD /apps/
+ 200 OK: HEAD /shop/
+ 200 OK: HEAD /store/
```

Notice that there are a few `200 OK` lines which means that exploitation of resources exist; `403` states that access to an exploitable resource is denied but it still exists — this is both good and bad. It is good because currently as the server is configured, the exploitable resource is not accessible but if in the future the configuration changes, the exploitable resource might become available and that's why `403` is both good and bad news. The `302` lines indicate false positives. This occurs because many servers are configured to respond with a custom error message when a requested URL is missing, which generates a 302 HTTP status code.

You can also use `-I` n (where $n = 0$ to 9) option to enable evasive mode for evading Intrusion Detection System (IDS) on the Web server. If you use any IDS solution, you can also test your IDS effectiveness. For example, if your IDS knows about `/cgi-bin/phf` (a known CGI risk) then using `-I 1` will attempt to trick your IDS into using URL encoding so that the `/cgi-bin/phf` request is sent in an encoded URL instead of directly using `/cgi-bin/phf` in the request. Similarly, `-I 2` will try to confuse an IDS using an extra `/./` pattern in the URL. For details, run whisker without any argument.

Reducing SSI Risks

If you run external applications using SSI commands such as `exec`, the security risk is virtually the same as with the CGI scripts. However, you can disable this command very easily under Apache, using the `Options` directive as follows:

```
<Directory />
  Options IncludesNOEXEC
</Directory>
```

This disables `exec` and includes SSI commands everywhere on your Web space; however, you can enable these commands whenever necessary by defining a directory container with narrower scope, for example:

```
<Directory />
  Options IncludesNOEXEC
</Directory>

<Directory "/ssi">
    Options +Includes
    SetOutputFilter INCLUDES
</Directory>
```

This configuration segment disables the `exec` command everywhere but in the `/ssi` directory.

Also avoid using the `printenv` command, which prints out a listing of all existing environment variables and their values. For example, the command:

```
<--#printenv -->
```

displays all the environment variables available to the Web server. Displaying such information in a publicly accessible page will certainly give away clues to the vandals. So, use this command only when you are debugging SSI calls and not in a production environment.

There are a lot of configuration and policy decisions (what to allow and how to allow it) that you have to make to ensure Web security. Many become frustrated after implementing a set of security measures because they do not know what else they need to do to further enhance security. After you have implemented a set of measures such as controlled CGI and SSI requests as explained in the preceding material, you should focus your efforts on logging.

✦　　✦　　✦

Securing Apache with SSL

Only a few years ago, the Internet was still what it was initially meant to be — a worldwide network for scientists and engineers. By virtue of the Web, however, the Internet is now a network for everyone. These days, it seems as though everyone and everything is on the Internet. It is also the new economy frontier; thousands of businesses, large and small, have set up e-commerce sites to open doors to customers around the world. Customers are being cautious, however, because they know that not all parts of Internet are secured.

To eliminate this sense of insecurity in the new frontier, Netscape Communications (now a subsidiary of AOL Time Warner) invented a security protocol that ensures secured transactions between the customer's Web browser and the Web server. Netscape named this protocol as Secured Socket Layer (SSL). Quickly SSL found its place in many other Internet applications such as e-mail, remote access, etc. Because SSL is now part of the foundation of the modern computer security infrastructure, it is important for you to know how to incorporate SSL into your Apache server.

Apache does not ship with any SSL support by default. However, you can compile and install an SSL module for Apache to enable SSL capabilities. There are two open-source solutions available for Apache: mod_ssl and Apache-SSL. Both of these solutions use an open-source implementation of SSL called OpenSSL. In this chapter I discuss how you can compile and install OpenSSL and then set up Apache with either mod_ssl or Apache-SSL.

Introducing SSL

Using both symmetric and asymmetric encryption schemes (which are described in the "Understanding encryption" section later in this chapter), Netscape developed the open, nonproprietary protocol called Secured Socket Layer (SSL) to provide data encryption, server authentication, data integrity, and client authentication for TCP/IP-based communication. Figure 19-1 shows how SSL interacts with applications.

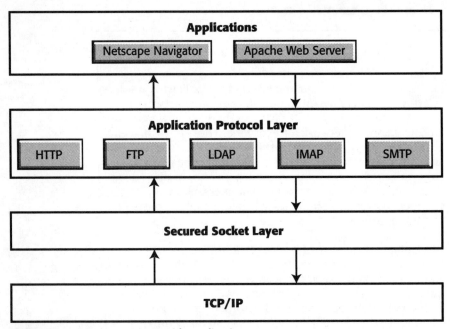

Figure 19-1: SSL interactions with applications.

The SSL protocol runs above TCP/IP and below higher-level, application-layer protocols such as HTTP, FTP, IMAP, and so on. It uses TCP/IP on behalf of the application-layer protocols, and in the process allows an SSL-enabled server to authenticate itself to an SSL-enabled client, allows the client to authenticate itself to the server, and allows both machines to establish an encrypted connection. The next section provides a closer yet simplified look at how SSL works.

How SSL Works

The foundation of SSL is encryption. SSL defines how and what type of encryption is used to secure network communication. In the following sections I discuss the different types of encryption and their applications in SSL.

Understanding encryption

When data travels from one point of the Internet to another, it goes through a number of computers such as routers, gateways, and other network devices. For example, when a visitor to a Web site at www.nitec.com enters his or her credit card number in an HTML form found on the site, it is quite possible that the information travels on a path similar to the one shown in Figure 19-2.

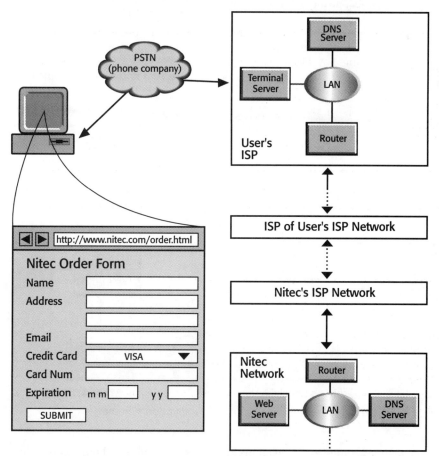

Figure 19-2: Data traveling from one point to another on the Internet.

As you can see from the figure, the data must travel through many nodes, so there's a chance it can be intercepted by someone at one of these nodes. Although data packets travel at a very high speed (usually milliseconds), interception is still a possibility. This is why we need a secured mechanism for exchanging sensitive data. This security is achieved through encryption.

Technically speaking, *encryption* is the mathematical encoding scheme that ensures that only the intended recipient can access the data; it hides the data from eavesdroppers. Encryption schemes are widely used to restrict access to resources. For example, if you log onto a Unix or Windows 2000/NT system, the passwords or keys that you use are typically stored in the server computer in an encrypted format. On most Unix systems, a user's password is encrypted and matched with the encrypted password stored in an /etc/passwd file. If this comparison is successful, the user is given access to the requested resource. Two kinds of encryption schemes are available:

✦ **Symmetric encryption:** This scheme is similar to the keys and locks you probably use on a daily basis. You unlock your car with a key, and also lock it with the same key. Similarly, in symmetric encryption, a single key is used for both locking and unlocking purposes. Figure 19-3 shows an example of such a scheme.

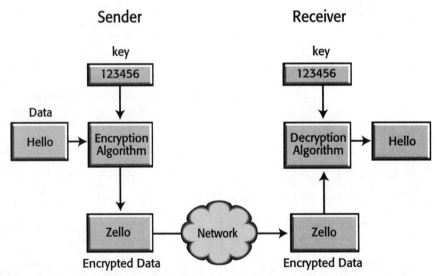

Figure 19-3: An example of a symmetric encryption scheme.

Because a single key is used in this scheme, all involved parties must know what this key is to make the scheme work.

✦ **Asymmetric encryption:** Asymmetric encryption works a bit differently from symmetric encryption, as its name suggests. With this scheme, there are two keys: a public key and a private key. The extra key is the public key—hence this scheme is also known as public key encryption. Figure 19-4 shows an example of how this encryption scheme works.

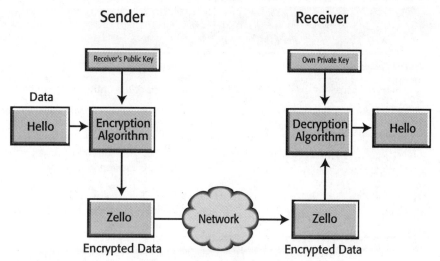

Figure 19-4: An example of the asymmetric encryption scheme.

✦ As the figure shows, when data is encrypted with the public key, it can only be decrypted using the private key, and vice versa. Unlike symmetric encryption, this scheme does not require that the sender know the private key that the receiver needs to unlock the data. The public key is widely distributed, so anyone who wants to initiate a secure data communication can use it. The private key is never distributed; it is always to be kept secret.

Understanding certificates

A *certificate* is encrypted information that associates a public key with the true identity of an individual, a server, or some other entity, known as the subject. It also includes the identification and signature of the issuer of the certificate. The issuer is known as a Certificate Authority (CA). Such a certificate may contain other information such as serial number, the period of time when the certificate is valid, and so on, which helps the CA to manage certificates. Using an SSL-enabled Web browser such as Netscape Navigator and Microsoft Internet Explorer, you can view a server's certificate quite easily. The entity being identified in a certificate is represented using distinguished name fields, which are defined in the X509 standard. Table 19-1 shows the distinguished name fields in a certificate.

	Table 19-1	
	Distinguished Name Fields	
DN Field:	*Abbreviation*	*Meaning*
Common Name	CN	Name of the entity being certified
Organization or Company	O	Entity is associated with this organization
Organizational Unit	OU	Entity is associated with this organization unit
City/Locality	L	Entity is located in this city
State/Province	ST	Entity is located in this state or province
Country	C	Name is located in this country (2-digit ISO country code)

The certificate is usually transmitted in binary or encoded text format.

Certificate-based transactions

In an SSL-based transaction, as shown in Figure 19-5, the server sends a certificate to the client system.

A well-known vendor, known as a Certificate Authority (CA), typically issues a certificate. The certificate is encrypted using the Certificate Authority's private key. The client decrypts the certificate using the public key of the Certificate Authority.

Because the certificate contains the server's public key, the client can now decrypt any encrypted data sent by the server. At this point, the server sends a piece of data identifying itself as the entity mentioned in the certificate. The server then creates a digest message of the same data it sent to identify itself earlier. The digest is encrypted using the server's private key. The client now has the certificate from a known CA stating what the server's public key should be, an identity message from the server, and an encrypted digest message of the identity message.

Using the server's public key, the client can decrypt the digest message. The client then creates a digest of the identity message and compares it with the digest sent by the server. If there is a match, this means the server is who it claims to be. Why? Well, the server initially sent a certificate signed by a known CA, so the client is absolutely sure to whom this public key belongs. However, the client needed proof that the server that sent the certificate is who it claims to be, so the server sent a simple identification message along with a public key encrypted digest of the same message. If the server hadn't had the appropriate private key, it would have been unable to produce the same digest that the client computed from the identification message.

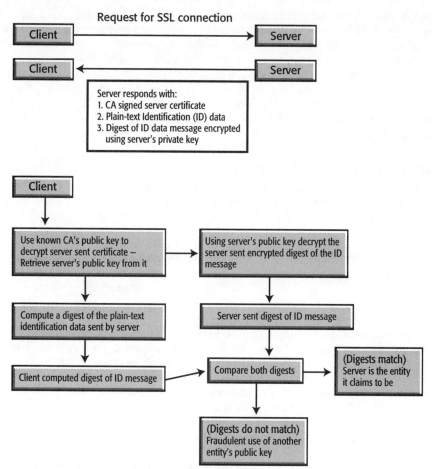

Figure 19-5: An example of an SSL transaction.

If this seems like a complex matter, it is—and it doesn't end here. The client can now send a symmetric encryption key to the server by encrypting it using the server's public key. The server can then use this new key to encrypt data and transmit it to the client. Why do that? Well, it turns out that symmetric encryption is much faster than asymmetric encryption. You can look at it this way: asymmetric encryption (private/public keys) is used to safely transmit a randomly generated symmetric key from the client to the server; this key is later used to provide a fast, secured communication channel.

If an impostor sits between the client and the server system, and is capable of intercepting the data being transmitted, will it be able to do damage? Well, it doesn't know the secret symmetric key that the client and the server are using, so it cannot determine the content of the data; however, it can introduce garbage in the data by injecting its own data into the data packets.

To avoid this, the SSL protocol allows for the use of a message authentication code (MAC). A MAC is simply a piece of data that is computed by using the symmetric key and the data to be transmitted. Because the impostor does not know the symmetric key, it can't compute the correct value for the MAC. For example, a well-known cryptographic digest algorithm called MD5, which was developed by RSA Data Security, Inc., can be used to generate 128-bit MAC values for each data packet to be transmitted. The computing power and time required to successfully guess the correct MAC value this way is almost nonexistent. SSL makes secure commerce possible on the Internet.

Defining Certificate Authority

A CA is a trusted organization that issues certificates for both servers and clients (that is, users). To understand the need for such an organization, consider the following scenario.

A client wants to securely access a Web application on your extranet Web server. The client uses HTTPS protocol to access your extranet server, for example, `https://extranet.domain.com/login.servlet`.

The client's Web browser initiates the SSL connection request. Your extranet Web server uses its private key to encrypt data it sends to the client's Web browser, which decrypts the data using your Web server's public key. Because the Web server also sends the public key to the Web browser there is no way to determine whether the public key is authentic. In other words, there is nothing to stop a malicious computer hacker from intercepting the information from your extranet server and sending the hacker's public key to your client. That's where the CA comes into play. A CA would issue you a certificate after verifying information regarding your company in the offline world. This server certificate is signed by the CA's own public key, which is well known. In such a case, when the Web browser receives the server certificate, it can decrypt the certificate information using the well-known CA's public key. This ensures that the server certificate is authentic. The Web browser can then verify that the domain name used in the authentic certificate is the same one it is communicating with.

Similarly, if you needed to ensure that the client is really who the client says it is, you could enforce a client-side certificate restriction, which enables you to turn the entire transaction into a closed-loop secured process.

The idea is that if each party has a certificate that validates the other's identity, that confirms the public key, and that is signed by a trusted agency, then they both will be assured that they are communicating with whom they think they are communicating.

There are two types of Certificate Authority: commercial CA and self-certified private CA.

Commercial CA

A commercial CA's primary job is to verify other commercial or nonprofit companies that want to establish their authenticity in the Internet. After a CA verifies the offline authenticity of a company by checking various legal records such as official company registration documents or certificate of incorporation, official letters from top management of the company, and so on, the CA can sign the certificate. There are only a few commercial CAs. Verisign (www.verisign.com) and Thawte (www.thawte.com) are the best-known CAs. Verisign has acquired Thawte Consulting.

Self-certified, private CA

A private CA is very much like the root-level commercial CA. It is self-certified. However, a private CA is typically used in a LAN or WAN environment, or inexperimenting with SSL. For example, a US university with a WAN that interconnects departments might decide to use a private CA instead of a commercial one. As long as you are not expecting an unknown user to trust your private CA, you can use it. In the following section, I show you how to create a private CA for your organization. Thereafter, I show you how to get a certificate from a commercial CA or to create your own CA to certify your servers and clients.

Setting up SSL for Apache

You have two open-source choices when it comes to using SSL with Apache. You can use the mod_ssl module or Apache-SSL distribution. Both of these solutions require OpenSSL, which is an open-source implementation of the SSL library. In this section I discuss how you can set up OpenSSL and both mod_ssl and Apache-SSL solutions for Apache.

SSL choices

The OpenSSL Project is an open-source community collaboration to develop commercial-grade SSL, Transport Layer Security (TLS), and full-strength general-purpose cryptography library packages. The current implementation of SSL is also called OpenSSL. OpenSSL is based on the SSLeay library developed by Eric A. Young and Tim J. Hudson. The OpenSSL software package license allows the software to be used for both commercial and noncommercial purposes freely.

There are two freely available OpenSSL packages for use with Apache:

✦ The OpenSSL-based Apache-SSL patches found at www.apache-ssl.org.

✦ The OpenSSL-based mod_ssl module for Apache found at www.modssl.org.

Both of these choices lead to the same functionality. Some people prefer Apache-SSL and some prefer mod_ssl. They both work but differ in code styles, documentation, and some minor features. I am biased toward mod_ssl because I like Ralf S. Engelchall's other modules such as mod_rewrite.

Setting up OpenSSL

The OpenSSL package found at `www.openssl.org` is needed for both Apache-SSL and `mod_ssl` solutions for bringing SSL to Apache Web server. In this section, you learn how to set up OpenSSL for your Unix system. I use a Linux system to illustrate. The OpenSSL Web site offers the OpenSSL source in a gzip-compressed tar file. The latest version as of this writing is `openssl-0.9.6.tar.gz`.

OpenSSL prerequisites

Before you starting the compilation process, you must ensure that your system meets the OpenSSL prerequisites. The OpenSSL source distribution requires that you have Perl 5 and an ANSI C compiler. This chapter assumes that you have installed both Perl 5 and gcc (C compiler) when you set up your Linux system.

Getting OpenSSL

SSL had been available in commercial Linux software such as Stronghold, an Apache-based, commercial Web Server for many years. However, because of some patent and U.S. export restrictions there were no open-source versions of SSL for Linux for a long time. The Open SSL Project now provides a Linux version of SSL, which you can download from the official OpenSSL Web site at `www.openssl.org/source`.

Tip   OpenSSL binaries are currently shipped with the Red Hat Linux distribution in RPM packages. So you can either use the RPM version supplied by Red Hat Linux or you can download the source distribution, compile, and install it.

I prefer that security software be installed from source distribution downloaded from authentic Web or FTP sites. I assume that you prefer to do the same. Thus, the following section discusses the details of compiling and installing OpenSSL from the official source distribution downloaded from OpenSSL Web site.

Note   If you must install OpenSSL from the RPM, use a trustworthy, binary RPM distribution such as the one found on the official Red Hat CD-ROM. To install OpenSSL binaries from a RPM package, run the `rpm -ivh openssl-packagename.rpm` command.

Compiling and installing OpenSSL

Compiling OpenSSL is a very simply task; just follow these steps:

1. Log in to your Linux system as root from the console.

2. Copy the OpenSSL source tar ball into `/usr/src/redhat/SOURCES` directory.

3. Extract the source distribution by running the `tar xvzf openssl-version.tar.gz` command. For example, to extract the `openssl-0.9.6.tar.gz` file, run the `tar xvzf openssl-0.9.6.tar.gz` command. The `tar` command creates a directory called `openssl-version`, which, for my example, is `openssl-0.9.6`.

4. You can delete the tar ball at this point if disk space is an issue. However, I recommend that you delete it only after OpenSSL is successfully compiled and installed.

5. Change your current directory to be the newly created directory.

At this point feel free to read the README or INSTALL files included in the distribution. Before compiling the software, you should configure the installation options. To install OpenSSL in the default /usr/local/ssl directory, run:

```
./config
```

However, if you must install it in a different directory append --prefix and --openssldir flags to the above command. For example, to install OpenSSL in the /opt/security/ssl directory, the command line is:

```
./config --prefix=/opt/security
```

There are many other options that you can use with the config or Configure script to prepare the source distribution for compilation. These options are discussed in Table 19-2.

Table 19-2
Configuration Options for Compiling OpenSSL

Configuration Options	Purpose
--prefix=DIR	Installs OpenSSL in DIR directory. Subdirectories such as DIR/lib, DIR/bin, DIR/include/openssl are created The configuration files are stored in DIR/ssl unless you use the --openssldir option to specify this directory.
--openssldir=DIR	Specifies the configuration files directory. If the --prefix option is not used, all files are stored in this directory.
rsaref	This option will force building of the RSAREF toolkit. If you wish to use RSAREF toolkit, make sure you have the RSAREF library (librsaref.a) in your default library search path.
no-threads	This option disables support for multithreaded application.
threads	This option enables support for multithreaded application.
no-shared	This option disables creation of shared library.
shared	This option enables creation of shared library.
no-asm	This option disables use of assembly code in the source tree. Use this option only if you are experiencing problem in compiling OpenSSL.

Continued

Table 19-2 *(Continued)*

Configuration Options	Purpose
386	Use this only if you are compiling OpenSSL on an Intel 386 machine. Not recommended for newer Intel machines.
no-<cipher>	OpenSSL uses many cryptographic ciphers such as bf, cast, des, dh, dsa, hmac, md2, md5, mdc2, rc2, rc4, rc5, rsa, and sha. If you wish to not include a particular cipher in the compiled binaries, use this option.
-Dxxx, -lxxx, -Lxxx, -fxxx, -Kxxx	These options allow you to specify various system-dependent options, for example, Dynamic Shared Objects (DSO) flags such as -fpic, -fPIC, and -KPIC, to be specified on the command line. This way OpenSSL libraries can be compiled with Position Independent Code (PIC), which is needed for linking it into DSOs.

Most likely you won't need to add any of these options to compile OpenSSL. However, if you have problem compiling it, you might have to try some of these options with appropriate values. For example, if you can't compile because OpenSSL complains about missing library files, try specifying the system library path using the -L option.

After you have run the config script without any errors, run the make utility. If the make command is successful, run make test to test the newly built binaries. Finally, run make install to install OpenSSL in your system. If you have a problem compiling, try to understand the cause of the problem. In most cases, the problem is caused by library file mismatch when trying to install the latest version of software like OpenSSL in a very old Linux system. Or the problem might be caused by an option you specified in the command line. For example, if you do not have the RSAREF library (it is not included in the Red Hat Linux distribution) installed on your system and you are trying to use the rsaref option, the compilation will fail when trying to build the binaries. So make sure that you know what you are doing when using specific options. If you still can't resolve the problem, try searching on the OpenSSL FAQ page at www.openssl.org/support/faq.html for a solution. Or, simply install the binary RPM package for OpenSSL.

Choosing the mod_ssl module for SSL support

You should use mod_ssl only if you choose not to use Apache-SSL to bring SSL support. This module can be used as a DSO module for Apache and it also works with the Windows platform.

Compiling and installing mod_ssl

To compile and install this module, follow these steps:

1. Download the latest source distribution of the mod_ssl module from `www.modssl.org`. Extract the source in a directory.

2. As root, run the `Configure` script as follows from the newly created `mod_ssl-version` directory.

   ```
   ./configure --with-apache=../httpd_version
   ```

   Make sure you replace `../httpd_version` with the appropriate path to your Apache source distribution directory. For example, if you installed the `mod_ssl` **source** in `/usr/local/src/mod_ssl-2.9.0-2.0.19` directory, and Apache source distribution in `/usr/local/src/httpd_2.0.19` directory, then run the following command from `/usr/local/src/mod_ssl-2.9.0-2.0.19` directory:

   ```
   ./configure --with-apache=../httpd_2.0.19
   ```

3. Set an environment variable called SSL_BASE to point to the OpenSSL directory in your system. For example, if you are using the bash shell you can run export SSL_BASE=`path_to_openssl` where `path_to_openssl` should be replaced with actual path to OpenSSL installation directory.

4. Go to the top-level Apache source directory and run the `configure` script using the `--enable-module=ssl` option along with all the other usual options you need for Apache. If you have already compiled Apache, you can use `config.status --enable-module=ssl` to reuse all your previous command-line options automatically.

   Tip

   If you plan to use `mod_ssl` **as a shared module, then use** `--with-apxs --enable-shared=ssl -enable-so` **instead of** `--enable-module=ssl` **with the** `configure` **script.**

5. Compile and install the Apache server with `mod_ssl` support by using `make` command.

6. If you do not have a server certificate, you can create a dummy certificate by using the `make certificate TYPE=dummy` command.

7. Run `make install` to install the `mod_ssl`-enabled Apache server. If you created the server certificate in step 6, it will be copied to the `conf` subdirectory of your Apache server installation path.

8. If Apache is running, stop it by using the `/usr/local/bin/apachectl stop` command and restart Apache with HTTPS protocol support by using the `/usr/local/bin/apachectl startssl` command.

Configuring Apache for mod_ssl-based SSL

If you compile `mod_ssl` with Apache after you have already built Apache once, the SSL-related configuration directives are stored in `httpd.conf.default` instead of in `httpd.conf`. Basically, when you add `mod_ssl` on an existing Apache server, the `httpd.conf` file is preserved. You must manually configure the SSL-related directives by copying necessary information from `httpd.conf.default`. In the following material, I assume that you are adding `mod_ssl` to a preexisting Apache system by recompiling Apache with `mod_ssl` support as shown in the previous section. To configure Apache for SSL by using `mod_ssl`, follow these steps:

1. If you installed `mod_ssl` as a shared module, then add the following line in `httpd.conf`:

   ```
   AddModule ssl_module moduleslibssl.so
   ```

2. Modify `httpd.conf` so that it includes these directives:

   ```
   <IfDefine SSL>
       Listen 80
       Listen 443
   </IfDefine>
   ```

   This `<IfDefine>` container tells Apache to consider the enclosed directives only if Apache was started with `-DSSL` option or `apachectl startssl` was used. In SSL mode, Apache is told to listen for connection on the standard HTTP port 80 and also on the standard HTTPS port 443.

3. Add the following lines in `httpd.conf` to tell Apache to add two MIME types for `.crt` and `.crl` extensions. The first extension denotes a certificate file and the second denotes a certificate revocation list (CRL) file. These two lines ensure that Apache sends the appropriate header when sending files with these extensions.

   ```
   <IfDefine SSL>
       AddType application/x-x509-ca-cert  .crt
       AddType application/x-pkcs7-crl      .crl
   </IfDefine>
   ```

4. Add the following lines to the `httpd.conf` to define the SSL session cache database path, the cache timeout value, the SSL mutex file path used by SSL-enabled children to communicate, the SSL random-seed-generation method, the SSL log path, and the SSL log level information.

   ```
   <IfModule mod_ssl.c>

       SSLPassPhraseDialog builtin

       SSLSessionCache dbm:/usr/local/apache/logs/ssl_scache
       SSLSessionCacheTimeout 300

       SSLMutex file:/usr/local/apache/logs/ssl_mutex

       SSLRandomSeed startup builtin
   ```

```
SSLRandomSeed connect builtin

SSLLog /usr/local/apache/logs/ssl_engine_log
SSLLogLevel info
```

```
</IfModule>
```

5. Create a catch-all default virtual host configuration in `httpd.conf` as shown below:

```
<IfDefine SSL>

    <VirtualHost _default_:443>

        DocumentRoot path_to_ssl_document_root
        ServerName ssl_server_hostname

        SSLEngine on

        SSLCipherSuite
ALL:!ADH:!EXPORT56:RC4+RSA:+HIGH:+MEDIUM:+LOW:+SSLv2:+EXP:+eN
ULL
        SSLCertificateFile conf/ssl.crt/server.crt

        SSLCertificateKeyFile conf/ssl.key/server.key

    </VirtualHost>

</IfDefine>
```

This `_default_` virtual host prevents any SSL request (on port 443) from being served by the main server. It catches all SSL requests that cannot be mapped to any of the other virtual hosts that are defined in `httpd.conf`.

- You should change the *path_to_ssl_document_root* to the appropriate document root for the SSL server. You can use the same document root as you use for your HTTP (port 80) site.

- The server name *ssl_server_hostname* needs to be set as appropriate. You can use the same hostname for both HTTP and HTTPS.

- The `SSLEngine` directive enables the SSL module for this virtual host.

- The `SSLCipherSuite` defines the cryptographic ciphers that can be used in this virtual host.

- The `SSLCertificateFile` directive defines the path to the server certificate file. Make sure the path is correct for your site.

- The `SSLCertificateKeyFile` defines the key file for the certificate. Again, make sure you have the appropriate path defined here.

6. If you run mod_perl scripts, CGI scripts, SSI, or PHP pages and would like to have access to the standard SSL/TLS-related environment variables (prefixed by SSL_), then you must explicitly instruct Apache to create these variables for mod_perl, CGI, SSI, or PHP requests. Use SSLOptions +StdEnvVars to tell Apache to generate the SSL_* environment variables for these requests. However, it is a very good idea to enable this option in a <File> container as shown below:

```
<Files ~ "\.(pl| cgi|shtml|php)$">
    SSLOptions +StdEnvVars
</Files>
```

Here the SS_* environment variables are only created for files with .pl (Perl scripts) or .cgi (typical CGI scripts) or .shtml (SSI pages) or .php (PHP ages). You can put this <File> container within the virtual host defined in step 5.

7. Similarly, if you use the standard /cgi-bin/ alias for CGI scripts, you can turn on SS_* environment creation for it using the following <Directory> container:

```
<Directory "physical_path_to_cgi_bin_directory">
    SSLOptions +StdEnvVars
</Directory>
```

Make sure you replace *physical_path_to_cgi_bin_directory* with the actual path to the CGI directory.

8. Start Apache using the /usr/local/apache/bin/apachectl startssl command.

Choosing Apache-SSL instead of mod_ssl for SSL support

The Apache-SSL source patch kit can be downloaded from the www.apache-ssl.org Web site. The Apache-SSL source patch kit turns Apache into a SSL server based on either SSLeay or OpenSSL.

Compiling and installing Apache-SSL patches for Apache

You need to make sure that you have installed OpenSSL on your system. The following material discusses how to compile and install Apache with Apache-SSL patches.

The following material assumes that you have installed OpenSSL in the /usr/local/ssl directory and that you have extracted the Apache source tree into /usr/local/src/httpd_*version* directory. For example, the Apache source path for Apache 2.0.16 would be /usr/local/src/httpd_2.0.16. To set up Apache for SSL support, follow these steps:

1. As root change the directory to the Apache source distribution (/usr/local/src/httpd_*version*) directory.

2. Copy the Apache-SSL patch kit (apache_*version*+ssl_*version*.tar.gz) file in the current directory and extract it using the tar xvzf apache_*version*+ ssl_*version*.tar.gz command.

3. Run patch -p1 < SSLpatch to patch the source files.

4. Change directory to src and edit the Configuration.tmpl file to have the following lines along with other unchanged lines.

```
SSL_BASE=/usr/local/ssl
SSL_APP_DIR= $(SSL_BASE)/bin
SSL_APP=/usr/local/ssl/bin/openssl
```

5. Change back your current directory to src by running the cd .. command.

6. Run the ./configure command with any command-line arguments that you typically use. For example, if you want to install Apache in /usr/local/ apache, run this script with the --prefix=/usr/local/apache option.

7. Run the make && make install command to compile and install Apache.

This compiles and installs both standard (httpd) and SSL-enabled (httpsd) Apache. Now you need to create a server certificate for Apache.

Creating a certificate for the Apache-SSL server

To create a temporary certificate to get going quickly, follow these steps:

1. Change directory to the src (for example /usr/local/src/httpd_ *version*/src) subdirectory of your Apache source distribution.

2. After you are in the src directory, run the make certificate command to create a temporary certificate for testing purposes only. The make certificate command uses the /usr/local/ssl/bin/openssl program to create a server certificate for you. You will be asked a few self-explanatory questions. Here is an example session of this command:

```
ps > /tmp/ssl-rand; date >> /tmp/ssl-rand; \
RANDFILE=/tmp/ssl-rand /usr/local/ssl/bin/openssl req -config
../SSLconf/conf/ssleay.cnf \
-new -x509 -nodes -out ../SSLconf/conf/httpsd.pem \
-keyout ../SSLconf/conf/httpsd.pem; \
ln -sf httpsd.pem ../SSLconf/conf/`/usr/local/ssl/bin/openssl
\
x509 -noout -hash < ../SSLconf/conf/httpsd.pem`.0; \
rm /tmp/ssl-rand
Using configuration from ../SSLconf/conf/ssleay.cnf
Generating a 1024 bit RSA private key
.................++++++
.......................................................++++++
writing new private key to '../SSLconf/conf/httpsd.pem'
-----
You are about to be asked to enter information that will be
incorporated
into your certificate request.
```

```
What you are about to enter is what is called a Distinguished
Name or a DN.
There are quite a few fields but you can leave some blank
For some fields there will be a default value,
If you enter '.', the field will be left blank.
-----
Country Name (2 letter code) [GB]:US
State or Province Name (full name) [Some-State]:California
Locality Name (eg, city) []:Sacramento
Organization Name (eg, company; recommended) []:MyORG
Organizational Unit Name (eg, section) []:CS
server name (eg. ssl.domain.tld; required!!!)
[]:shea.evoknow.com
Email Address []:kabir@evoknow.com
```

The certificate called `httpsd.pem` is created in the `SSLconf/conf` subdirectory of your Apache source distribution.

You are now ready to configure Apache.

Configuring Apache with Apache-SSL

When you ran `make install` in the "Compiling and Installing Apache-SSL Patches for Apache" section, it created an `httpsd.conf` file in the `conf` subdirectory of your Apache installation directory. For example, if you used the `--prefix=/usr/local/apache` to configure Apache, you will find the `httpsd.conf` file in `/usr/local/apache/conf` directory. You need to rename it to `httpd.conf` using the `mv /usr/local/apache/conf/httpsd.conf /usr/local/apache/conf/httpd.conf` command. Make sure you replace `/usr/local/apache/conf` with the appropriate pathname if you installed Apache in a different directory.

You have two choices when it comes to using SSL with Apache. You can either enable SSL for the main server or you can enable it for one or more virtual Web sites. Here I show you how to enable SSL for your main Apache server and I also discuss what you need to do to enable SSL for a virtual Web site. Follow these steps to modify the `httpd.conf` file:

1. By default Web browsers will send SSL requests to port 443 of your Web server, so if you wish to turn the main Apache server into a SSL-enabled server, change the `Port` directive line to:

    ```
    Port 443
    ```

2. Add the following lines to tell Apache how to generate random data needed for encrypting SSL connections:

    ```
    SSLRandomFile file /dev/urandom 1024
    SSLRandomFilePerConnection file /dev/urandom 1024
    ```

3. If you wish to reject all requests but the https (that is, SSL requests), insert the following directive:

    ```
    SSLRequireSSL
    ```

4. To enable SSL service, add the following directive:

```
SSLEnable
```

5. By default the cache server used by SSL-enabled Apache is created in the `src/modules/ssl` directory of the Apache source distribution. Set this directory as shown here:

```
SSLCacheServerPath \
/path/to/apache_version/src/modules/ssl/gcache
```

6. Add the following directives to enable the cache server port and cache timeout values:

```
SSLCacheServerPort logs/gcache_port
SSLSessionCacheTimeout 15
```

7. Now you need to tell Apache where you are keeping the server certificate file. If you created the server certificate by following the OpenSSL installation instructions earlier , your server certificate should be in `/usr/local/ssl/certs` directory. However, if you decided to temporarily use the test certificate (created by using the `make certificate` command discussed earlier), then your test certificate is in `/path/to/apache_version/SSLconf/conf` directory and it is called `httpsd.pem`. Set the following directive to the fully qualified path of your server certificate as shown here:

```
SSLCertificateFile \
/path/to/apache_version/SSLconf/conf/httpsd.pem
```

8. Set the following directives as shown and save the httpd.conf file:

```
SSLVerifyClient 3
SSLVerifyDepth 10
SSLFakeBasicAuth
SSLBanCipher NULL-MD5:NULL-SHA
```

9. To SSL-enable a virtual host called `myvhost.Evoknow.com` on port 443, I need the following configuration:

```
Listen 443
<Virtualhost myvhost.evoknow.com:443>
  SSLEnable
  SSLCertificateFile /path/to/myvhost.certificate.cert
</Virtualhost>
```

Your SSL-enabled Apache server is ready for testing.

Testing your SSL connection

After you start the Apache server with the `/usr/local/apache/bin/apachectl startssl` command, you should be able to access your SSL site by using `https://localhost/` or `https://your_server_hostname/` from local (on the Web server itself) or remote Web clients.

Note   Most people forget to use `https` and use `http` when testing their SSL server and panic when they don't see an SSL connection (usually displayed by a small lock icon in the status bar of most popular Web browsers).

Getting a Certificate

Before you can use Apache with SSL (via `mod_ssl` or Apache-SSL), you must create appropriate server certificate. You can get a server certificate from a commercial certificate authority or you can create your own certificate authority and then create certificates for your own servers and clients. The latter method is typically used for a large organization that wants to manage certificates between campuses internally.

Getting a server certificate from a commercial CA

To get a signed certificate from a commercial CA, you must meet its requirements. There are two types of requirements:

You (the requester) must prove that you are the entity you claim to be.

You must submit a Certificate Signing Request (CSR) in electronic form.

The first requirement is usually met by following the CA's guidelines for verifying individuals or organizations, so you must consult with your chosen CA to learn how to proceed. Typically, if you are planning on getting your Web server certified, be prepared to submit copies of legal documents, such as business registration or incorporation papers. Alternatively, you can create a CSR using OpenSSL.

The very first step in creating a CSR is to create a private key for your server. Then you need to create a certificate signing request that needs to be sent to a commercial certificate authority. After you have been approved by a commercial certificate authority you can install the certificate on your server and use SSL with Apache. I discuss these steps in detail in the following sections.

Generating a private key

To generate an encrypted private key for a Web server host called `www.domain.com` run:

```
openssl genrsa -des3 -out www.domain.com.key 1024 -rand
/dev/urandom
```

When you run this command, you are asked to enter a pass phrase (that is, a password) to encrypt the private key with it. Because the private key is encrypted using the `des3` cipher, you are asked to enter the pass phrase every time your server is started. If this is undesirable, you can create a nonencrypted version of the private key by removing the -des3 option in the above command line. I highly recommend that you use an encrypted private key to ensure a high-level of security. After all, you do not want someone else with access to your server to be able to see your private key. Listing 19-1 shows the content of the www.domain.com.key file.

Listing 19-1: **The Content of www.domain.com.key File**

```
-----BEGIN RSA PRIVATE KEY-----
Proc-Type: 4,ENCRYPTED
DEK-Info: DES-EDE3-CBC,C48E9F2F597AF968

47f4qGkVrfFfTNEygEs/uyaPOeAqksOnALtKUvADHKL7BhaB+8BrT/Haa7MHwEzU
jjaRd1XF1k1Ej3qH6d/Zl0AwVfYiAYvO1H3wQB2pllSuxui2sm7ZRkYUOpRMjxZI
/srHn/DU+dUq11pH3vJRw2hHNVjHUB0cuCszZ8GOhICa5MFGsZxDR+cKP0T2Uvf5
jlGyiMroBzNOQFOv8sqwZoSOsuKHU9ZKdA/Pcbu+fwyDWFzNfr8HPNTImlaMjGEt
i9LWZikzBW2mmaw79Pq6xSyqL+7dKXmiQL6d/bYiHOZUYHjMkJtqUp1fNXxJd4T6
kB8xVbvjPivo1AyvYKOqmmVQp7WDnEyrrYUZVyRuOa+1O50aTG2GnfSy32YGuNTY
lMB3PH5BuocSRp+9SsKKTVoWOaO1nORtgVk/EZTO2Eo94qPcsZes6YyAwY4fFVAw
gG/G3ZJCPdjBI2YLmvhua3bvp9duc5CXmKDxOO49VvjbEB/yvi9pLbuj8KuAt4ht
fZcZB94wxrR/EMGODs2xgNhH+SwEf5Pc/bPUMRCq/Ot6F/HJ47jVnUf17tdtoTT7
UbQQVyAsr9tKSFzsRKMOGBO4VoenkD5CzUUF3iO/NaXSs/EFu9HG1ctWRKZEVIp/
MSJBe3jYDXbmeGdQGNJUExpY64hv1XoNdOpAJk0E622o2a11raFus12PotNvWYdI
TShgoIHSmNgQQLCfssJH5TABKyLejsgQy5Rz/Vp3kDzkWhwECOhI42p0S8sr4GhM
6YEdASb51uP3ftn2ivKshueZHpFOvS1pCGjnEYAEdY4QLJkreznM8w==
-----END RSA PRIVATE KEY-----
```

Generating a certificate signing request

Now you need to generate the CSR using your private key as follows:

```
openssl req -new -key www.domain.com.key -out www.domain.com.csr
```

If you encrypted the private key earlier, you are asked to enter the pass phrase for the private key. Enter the appropriate pass phrase. Then, you are asked to enter country name, state, city, organization name, organization unit/department name, common name (that is, your name if the certificate request is for yourself, or your server's hostname), e-mail address and some optional information such as a challenge password and an optional company name.

At this point, you need to submit your CSR to a CA such as Thawte. Because the certification process involves verification of your individual or business identity documents, it might take a few days to a few weeks or even months before you receive your certificate. The following section uses Thawte as the chosen CA.

If you are in a rush to get the certificate to get started with testing or have some other reason why you need a temporary certificate fast, ask your CA. It might have a way to provide you with a temporary, untrusted certificate. For example, Thawte will let you submit your CSR via the Web for a temporary certificate, which you will receive in minutes via e-mail.

After you get the server certificate from a commercial CA, you can install the certificate file per their instructions. This step is usually quite simple. You are likely to be asked to copy the file into a directory and restart the server.

If you are not interested in getting a signed certificate from a commercial CA, you can create your own CA and certify entities such as servers or users at any time. I show you how in the following section.

Creating a private certificate authority

As stated earlier, private self-signed certificates are not suitable for Internet use in the sense that users at large should not trust such certificates. However, if you want to be able to issue internal, company-wide certificates to your departments and do not want the hassle of going through the third-party commercial CA verification, you must use a private CA.

Note   It might be possible to get a cross-linked certificate for your private CA from a commercial CA. In such a case, your private CA will be chained to the commercial CA and thus everyone should trust any certificate that you issue. However, the commercial CA might limit your certificate-granting authority to your own organization to ensure that you do not compete with the CA.

Follow these steps to create a private self-certified CA using OpenSSL:

1. Download the latest version of the `ssl.ca-version.tar.gz` script distribution from the user-contributed software section (`www.openssl.org/contrib`) of the OpenSSL Web site. Extract this file to a directory of your choice. A subdirectory called `ssl.ca-version` will be created. You will find a set of `sh` scripts in the directory.

2. Run the `new-root-ca.sh` script to create a self-signed root certificate for your private CA. You will be asked to enter a pass phrase. This pass phrase is required for signing future certificates.

3. To create a server certificate, run the `new-server-cert.sh www.domain.com` script to create a server's private and public key. You will be asked to enter distinguished name fields for the new server certificate. The script will also generate a CSR, which you can send to a commercial CA later if you so choose.

4. Run the `sign-server-cert.sh` script to approve and sign the server certificate you created using the `new-server-cert.sh` script.

5. Run the `new-user-cert.sh` script to create a user certificate. When signed by a commercial certificate authority, user certificates can be used with a Web browser to authenticate users to remote services. However, user certificates are not commonplace because of a lack of understanding about them and a lack of available client and server software.

6. Run the `sign-user-cert.sh` script to sign a user certificate. Also, run the `p12.sh` script to package the private key, the signed key, and the CA's public key into a file with `.p12` extension. This file can then be imported into applications such as e-mail clients for use.

Now you are ready to make use of OpenSSL with various applications. OpenSSL is an integral part of security. The more you use OpenSSL, the more you will find it easy to incorporate in many services.

Accessing SSL pages

If you installed Apache in the `/usr/local/apache` directory, run the `/usr/local/apache/bin/httpsdctl start` command to start the SSL-enabled Apache server. If you get an error message, check the log file for details. A typo or a missing path in the `httpd.conf` file is a common cause of error so watch out for them. After the server is started, you can access it using the HTTPS protocol. For example, to access an SSL-enabled Apache server called `shea.evoknow.com`, I can point a Web browser to `https:/shea.evoknow.com`. If you are using the test certificate or a homegrown CA-signed certificate the Web browser will display a warning message stating that the certificate could not be verified. This is normal because a known CA has not signed the certificate. You should accept the certificate and browse your SSL-enabled Web site.

✦   ✦   ✦

Running Apache on Windows

Apache 2 on Windows platform is more stable then ever before. This part is dedicated to Apache on Windows platform. I show you how to install and configure Apache on Windows platforms, and how to use the few Windows-only Apache directives.

Installing and Running Apache for Windows

◆ ◆ ◆ ◆

In This Chapter

System requirements for running Apache on Windows

Installing Apache on Windows

Starting, stopping, and restarting Apache

◆ ◆ ◆ ◆

Although Apache has been ported to the Windows platform for a long time, Apache 2.0 is the first version that can take advantage of native Windows system calls. All previous versions of Apache used a POSIX abstraction layer that degraded performance when Apache ran on Windows. Now Apache can finally compete head-to-head with other native Web servers such as Microsoft IIS and Netscape Enterprise server.

In this chapter, you learn about the system requirements for running Apache under popular Windows platforms such as Windows XP, Windows 2000, Windows NT, and Windows 9x/ME; you also learn to install Apache and to configure it so that you can get up and running fast.

System Requirements

Apache requires that you have TCP/IP enabled on your Windows system. You should make sure that you have the latest TCP/IP stack (Winsock) for your Windows platform. Users of Windows 2000 with TCP/IP enabled can install Apache without any other Windows-specific requirements. Users of Windows NT 4.0 should ensure that the latest service packs are installed.

Windows 2000 Advanced Server is the ideal platform for running a production-grade Apache Web server. Windows 2000 Advanced Server is tuned for network services, so it should yield the best performance for Apache along with other Internet services.

Note   I used the Windows 2000 Advanced Server as the Windows platform for the Windows-specific chapters of this book.

You also need Microsoft Installer version 1.10 or above to install Apache. Windows 2000 and Windows ME both have Microsoft Installer built-in. For other versions of Windows, you have to consult your manuals or visit the Microsoft Web site for details.

Downloading Apache for Windows

Apache for Windows is available for downloading as either a source distribution or a binary distribution. Unfortunately, unlike most Unix platforms, Windows does not ship with development capabilities such as a standard C compiler like GCC. So the only people who can actually compile Apache are Windows developers who have development tools such as the Microsoft Visual Studio. For most people, the binary distribution is the only viable download option. Although gcc *is* on Windows, the Apache source does not compile with the Windows version of gcc.

The official download site for the Windows Apache binary files is `http://httpd.apache.org/dist/httpd/binaries/win32/`. The binary distributions are named `httpd_version-win32-no_src-rnumber.msi` (for example, `httpd_2_0_16-win32-no_src-r1.msi`). The source distributions are named `httpd_version-win32-wint_src.msi`. Download the latest, stable binary distribution.

Note   If you are a Windows developer who plans to download and compile a source distribution of Apache, then you can download the zipped version of the source distribution instead of the `.msi` installer version. You will need an unzip program such as PKUNZIP from PKWARE or WinZip to extract the source files, which have MS-DOS line endings. Do not download the source distributions that end with `.tar.gz` or `.tar.Z` because these are Unix packages with line endings only suitable for Unix platforms.

Installing Apache Binaries

Double-clicking on the `httpd_version-win32-no_src.msi` file you downloaded starts Microsoft Installer and the Apache installation. Click Next to start the installation. You will be asked a series of questions, which are discussed below.

1. Read and accept the license shown in Figure 20-1.

   You must click on the radio button labeled "I accept the terms in the license agreement" to enable the Next button. Click Next to continue to the next screen.

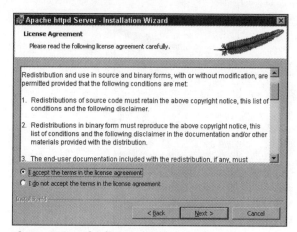

Figure 20-1: The license agreement

2. A screen similar to Figure 20-2 will appear. This screen displays the latest information (README). Browse the information, and when you are ready, click Next to continue.

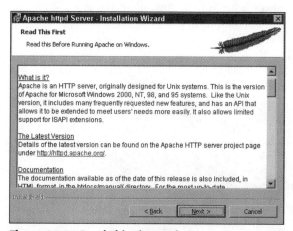

Figure 20-2: Read This First notice

3. The next screen is similar to Figure 20-3, and asks you to enter the network domain name, server name, and administrator's e-mail address. By default, the installer determines the names from your current Windows settings. Change the defaults if appropriate. Do not change server name or domain name without actually having the appropriate DNS and network configuration for the host. In other words, you cannot arbitrarily choose a domain name or server's host name. This information must be valid for the host you are installing Apache on. Click Next to proceed.

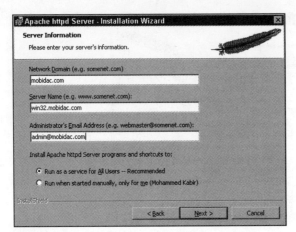

Figure 20-3: Entering your server information

4. Choose whether you wish to install Apache by using the Complete (all program features are installed, which uses the most disk space) or the Custom (only selected programs and files are installed) installation as shown in Figure 20-4. I recommend that you choose the custom installation option because it enables you to know more about what is being installed. You can always choose everything in custom installation to get a complete install.

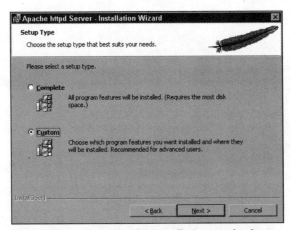

Figure 20-4: Choosing the installation method

5. If you chose to do a custom installation, you will see a screen similar to that shown in Figure 20-5. A tree of options is displayed. You can click on each item to decide whether or not you wish to install it.

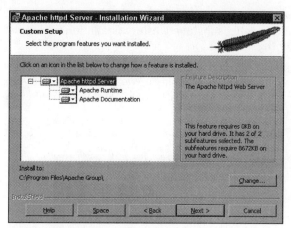

Figure 20-5: Customizing Apache for your site

For example, clicking on the Apache httpd Server item brings up the option menu shown in Figure 20-6.

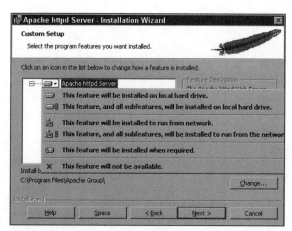

Figure 20-6: The installation option menu

Choose to install the feature (i.e. Apache server) to local hard disk or on a network drive. If disk space is an issue and you do not want the online documentation, you can choose not to install the documentation by clicking on that option to deselect this feature.

By default Apache is installed in the `C:\Program Files\Apache Group` directory. To change this, click on the Change button and enter a different directory in the next dialog window, and then click OK to return to this screen. Click Next to continue.

6. The installer shows a screen stating that it is ready to install Apache. Click Next and wait while Apache is installed. After installation is complete, click Finish to terminate the installer.

By default, the installer starts Apache, so you should be able to view the default Web site on your system by using a Web browser. Point your browser to `http://localhost` or `http://127.0.0.1` and you should see a Web site similar to that shown in Figure 20-7.

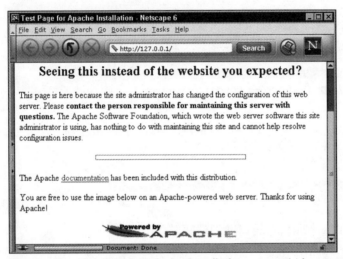

Figure 20-7: The default Web site installed on your Windows system.

Running Apache

You run Apache under Windows either from the command-line on a console window, or as a service under Windows 2000 or Windows NT systems. On Windows 2000 or NT systems, you should run Apache as an automated service. In fact, the default installation will detect your Windows and elect to install it as a service for these two platforms.

Note   On Windows 9x systems, there is no good way to run Apache as a service. The best approach for the 9x platform is to run Apache in a console window.

Running Apache automatically as a Windows service

The installer program automatically detects your Windows platform and installs Apache as a service on Windows 2000 and NT systems. On Windows 2000 (or NT systems), to run Apache automatically (or not) whenever the server is rebooted, do the following:

1. Choose Start ⇨ Settings ⇨ Control Panel ⇨ Administration Tools ⇨ Services to display a screen similar to the one shown in Figure 20-8.

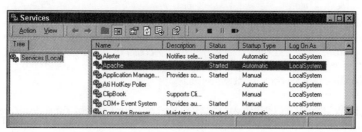

Figure 20-8: Running Apache automatically on reboot.

2. Double-click on the service name "Apache" and a dialog box appears, as shown in Figure 20-9.

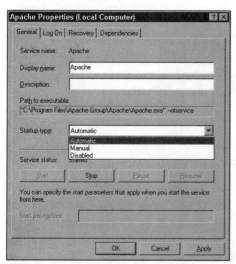

Figure 20-9: Configuring the Apache service.

3. Under the General tab you will see a drop-down menu labeled Startup type. Select Automatic (for automatic startup on reboot), Manual (for operator-assisted startup on reboot), or Disabled (to disabled on reboot) option.

4. If you wish to start or stop the Apache service, click on the appropriate button.

5. By default, Apache runs using the local system account under Windows 2000 or Windows NT. If you wish to change this user ID to another one, click on the Log On tab and choose the This account option. Then enter the appropriate username and password. Make sure this username and password is a valid user credential on your Windows network.

Note By default Apache runs as the LocalSystem ("System") account, which is a very powerful local account that is not associated with any username or password. This account cannot be used to log in to the machine or to connect to other machines on the same Windows network. If you choose to change the user for Apache service, make sure that you create an appropriate user account that can act as a service (that is, act as part of the operating system), log on as a service, backup and restore files and directories, has read access to document root, and that has read, write, and delete access to Apache log directories. The default username should be sufficient for most systems.

6. Under Windows 2000 Advanced Server, to define an action when Apache service fails, select the Recovery tab and choose appropriate actions for first, second, and subsequent failures. For example, you can choose to restart the service or reboot the machine automatically when Apache service fails, or even to run an external program to do something useful such as page the administrator. Figure 20-10 shows that when Apache service first fails to run, it will restart automatically, on second failure the server will automatically reboot, and for any subsequent failures a program will page the system administrator.

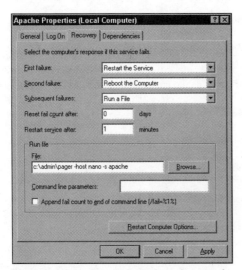

Figure 20-10: Recovery options for Apache service on Windows 2000 Advanced Server

7. After the service is configured, click Apply to finish the setup.

You can also start or stop Apache service at any time from the console by using `net start apache` or `net stop apache`, command respectively.

Note Unlike many Windows services, Apache logs its errors in its own error log file. The default is `logs/error.log`, which is found within the default `C:\Program Files\Apache Groups\Apache` directory. Only the errors that occur during the initial startup of the Apache service are logged in the `Event Log` facility available under Windows 2000 and NT.

Managing Apache from the Start menu

By default Apache installer will add menu items in Windows Start menu that you can use to start, restart, and stop Apache as follows:

- ✦ To start Apache, choose Start ⇨ Programs-Apache httpd Server ⇨ Control Apache Server ⇨ Start.

- ✦ To restart Apache, choose Start ⇨ Programs-Apache httpd Server ⇨ Control Apache Server ⇨ Restart.

- ✦ To stop Apache, choose Start ⇨ Programs-Apache httpd Server ⇨ Control Apache Server ⇨ stop.

- ✦ You can also edit and test the `httpd.conf` configuration file as follows:

- ✦ To edit the `httpd.conf` file, choose Start ⇨ Programs-Apache httpd Server ⇨ Configure Apache Server ⇨ Edit Configuration.

- ✦ To test the `httpd.conf` file, choose Start ⇨ Programs-Apache httpd Server ⇨ Configure Apache Server ⇨ Test Configuration. This is equivalent to running the `Apache -t` command from the Apache binary directory. A console window will pop up and you will be able to see the status of the configuration syntax.

Managing Apache from the command-line

If you do not run Apache as a service, you can start, stop, or restart Apache from a console (often called a DOS window) by using the following commands.

- ✦ To start Apache, run `Apache -k start` from the Apache binary directory, which is `C:\Program Files\Apache Group\Apache` by default.

- ✦ To gracefully restart Apache, run `Apache -k restart` from the Apache binary directory, which is `C:\Program Files\Apache Group\Apache` by default.

- ✦ To stop Apache, run `Apache -k stop` from the Apache binary directory, which is `C:\Program Files\Apache Group\Apache` by default. You can also use `Apache -shutdown` command to do the same.

- ✦ To run Apache with a nondefault configuration file, specify the file name by using the `-f` option. For example, to run Apache by using `c:\test\new-httpd.conf`, run the `Apache -f "c:\test\new-httpd.conf" -k start` command from the directory with the Apache binaries in it.

Running multiple Apache services

Under Windows, Apache normally runs only two processes: one to service all the HTTP requests using multiple threads and a second process to monitor the first process. If the first dies, the second process (the one responsible for monitoring the first) will restart the first process.

However, you can still run multiple primary Apache servers that use different `httpd.conf` files from the command-line of the Apache binary directory (the default is `C:\Program Files\Apache Group\Apache`) as follows:

```
Apache -f "path_to_httpd.conf"
```

For example, you can create two primary Apache services, one that responds to port 80 and one that responds to port 8080, by creating two `httpd.conf` files. You can run each of these services by using the above command. However, on Windows 2000 or NT systems, a default Apache service is already installed, so you can simply modify the `C:\Program Files\Apache Group\Apache\conf\httpd.conf` to reflect the port change and save it as another file. Then you only have to run one Apache instance using the above command. The default Apache configuration can still run on port 80.

To create a new Apache service, run the following command from the Apache binary directory (the default is `C:\Program Files\Apache Group\Apache`):

```
Apache -n new_service_name -f "path_to_httpd.conf" -k install
```

Running this command installs a new service called *new_service_name*, which will use the *path_to_httpd.conf* path.

You can also remove an existing Apache service by using the `Apache -n existing_service_name -k uninstall` command.

✦   ✦   ✦

Configuring Apache for Windows

The majority of the information found in the previous chapters does apply to Apache on Windows. However, there are certain differences between Apache for Windows and Apache for Unix because of the underlying differences in how Unix systems and Windows systems work. This chapter discusses those differences.

Windows httpd.conf Syntax

The `httpd.conf` file for a Unix system and Windows system differ because of how Windows treats pathnames. The differences are:

✦ On Windows systems, directory and filenames in a path are separated by backslashes. For example, `c:\temp` is a valid directory path. However, Apache internally still uses a forward slash as the path separator, so you still have to use the forward slash. For example, `c:/temp` is correct in the `httpd.conf` file but `c:\temp` is not.

✦ The Windows path often includes whitespaces. For example, `c:\Program Files\Apache Group\Apache\htdocs` is an acceptable path in Windows world. When using such path names in the `httpd.conf` file, double quote the entire path. For example:

```
ServerRoot "C:/Program Files/
Apache Group/Apache"
```

Here, the `ServerRoot` directive is set to point to the `C:/Program Files/Apache Group/Apache` directory.

Tuning Apache for Performance

Apache on Windows was multithreaded even before Apache 2.0. This is because Windows systems such as Windows 2000 and Windows NT perform better with threads than they perform with a bunch of child processes constituting a service.

On Windows systems, Apache runs using only two processes. A parent process monitors a child process, which is responsible for servicing all requests using multiple threads.

To control how many simultaneous requests Apache can serve under Windows, you need to tune the `ThreadsPerChild` directive. See Chapter 4 for details on this directive. This directive controls the number of threads that can be created by the sole Apache child process responsible for all requests. The default value of 50 should be fine for most sites.

If you require a higher response rate, make sure you have the appropriate system resources such as sufficient RAM and a fast CPU to backup your rate requirements. According to the source code for the `winnt MPM` module, you should be able to set this to a maximum of 4096 threads. Most likely, a number below 256 is more appropriate for most Web sites.

The `MaxRequestsPerChild` directive limits the number of requests that a child process can handle (see Chapter 4 for details on this directive). Because a single child processes all the requests via threads under Windows, this directive should be either set to a very high number or to 0, which means the child process will never exit.

Testing Apache Configuration

Whenever you change the `httpd.conf` file, you can run the following command from the Apache binary directory (`C:\Program Files\Apache Group\Apache` by default) to determine whether you have created any syntax errors.

```
Apache -t
```

You can also choose Start ⇨ Programs ⇨ Apache httpd Server ⇨ Configure Apache Server ⇨ Test Configuration option to do the same.

If an error is found, you can fix it before restarting the server with the `Apache -k restart` command.

Managing Apache with Comanche

If you are primarily a Windows user, then you might be wondering where the GUI administration program for Apache is. Sorry, Apache does not come with one. But there are plenty of third-party works-in-progress and even commercial ones that you can find out about at http://gui.apache.org.

However, Comanche (*CO*nfiguration *MAN*ager for Apa*CHE*) is the one that I like the best because it is multiplatform, nonintrusive, extensible, and very easy to set up. You can download Comanche from http://www.covalent.net/projects/comanche/.

After you have downloaded the binary distribution for Comanche, extract it and simply click on the executable icon to start configuring Apache. When the comanche.exe program is run, a small window with a button labeled Comanche appears as shown in Figure 21-1.

Figure 21-1: The Comanche main window

Click on the button labeled Comanche to start Comanche. You should see a screen similar to the one shown below in Figure 21-2.

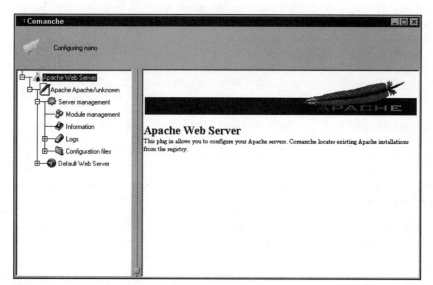

Figure 21-2: Configuring Apache with Comanche

You can click on the tree elements on the left to select different configuration options. For example, clicking on the Default Web Server option at the bottom of the left tree menu shows a screen similar to that shown in Figure 21-3.

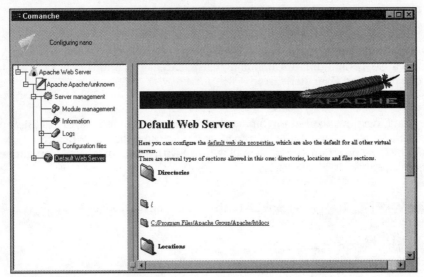

Figure 21-3: The default Web server configuration

Clicking on the default Web site properties link on the right brings up the actual configuration screen.

Here you can configure using Basic configuration, Module management, Server identification, Server options, Environment, Indexing, Proxy, Apache Jserv Settings, Alias, or CGI Settings options from the tree menu.

For example, to change the Port directive to a nondefault value (that is, other than 80) you can expand the Basic Configuration suboption tree and click on the Listening option to set it to a value such as 8080 as shown in Figure 21-4.

Similarly, to create a CGI script alias called /cgi-bin/ to point to "C:/Program Files/Apache Group/Apache/cgi-bin/" directory, I can expand the Alias option tree and click on the CGI option and use the Add button to add the alias as shown in Figure 21-5.

The newly created alias appears on the main Alias CGI screen.

Tip   When configuring the default Web server or a new virtual host you can quickly access options without expanding the Default Web Server option on the left by selecting and right-clicking it as shown in Figure 21-6.

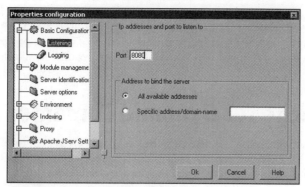

Figure 21-4: Setting Port directive to 8080

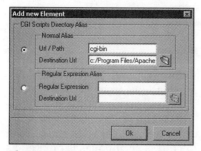

Figure 21-5: Setting a CGI script alias

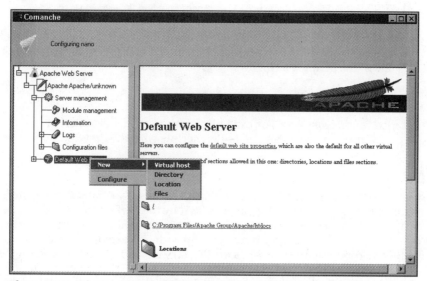

Figure 21-6: Shortcut for configuring default Web server or a virtual host

As you can see, once you get used to navigating the left option tree and know what features can be created, enabled, or disabled, you can use this tool to manage Apache from a GUI. However, do keep in mind that Comanche is a work in progress. Use it now and keep an eye open for updated versions as they become available.

Configuring Apache for Dynamic Contents

Like the Unix versions of Apache, you can use Apache on Windows to generate dynamic contents using CGI, PHP, SSI scripts. However, there are some differences in configuration for some of the dynamic contents generation solutions, which are discussed in this section.

Note Most of the directives discussed here are also discussed in Chapters 4 and 5. You can find all the syntax options in these chapters.

Running Perl-based CGI scripts

To run Perl-based CGI scripts with Apache on Windows, you must installed Perl on your system. You can download Perl for Windows from `http://www. activestate.com`.

After you have installed Perl properly, you can configure Apache to run CGI scripts using the `ScriptAlias` directive as usual. Typically, a script alias is created as follows:

```
ScriptAlias /cgi-bin/  "C:/Program Files/Apache Group/Apache/cgi-bin/"
```

You can also enable CGI scripts in a directory using the `Options ExecCGI` directive. Now, for Apache to invoke the appropriate Perl interpreter you must make sure the very first line of the script is as follows:

```
#!drive:/path_of_perl_interpreter
```

This is called the *shebang line*. For example, if you have installed Perl in `c:\perl\bin` directory, you can create Perl scripts with the first line set to:

```
#!c:/perl/bin
```

There is another way you can invoke Perl for CGI scripts. By default Perl registers `.pl` extension with Windows Registry to be executed by the Perl interpreter. If you set `ScriptInterpreterSource registry` directive in the main server configuration part of `httpd.conf`, you can now run any script with `.pl` extension properly. Apache will get the interpreter path from Windows Registry instead of the first shebang line.

Cross-Reference Read Chapter 12 for details on many other CGI-related issues that still apply to Apache on a Windows platform.

Running mod_perl scripts

To run `mod_perl` scripts, you must install the `mod_perl` module. You will need Perl installed on your system before you can install `mod_perl` binary module so make sure you have the latest Perl for Windows from `http://www.activestate.com`.

After you have installed Perl, you can run the following command from the command-line to download and install `mod_perl` module:

```
ppm install http://theoryx5.uwinnipeg.ca/ppmpackages/mod_perl-version.ppd
```

For example, to install the 1.25 version of `mod_perl`, run:

```
ppm install http://theoryx5.uwinnipeg.ca/ppmpackages/mod_perl-1.25_1.3.19.ppd
```

During the installation process you will be asked to enter the fully qualified path name of the Apache modules directory. The prompt displayed by the installation process is shown below:

```
Which directory should mod_perl.so be placed in?
    (enter q to quit) [C:/Apache/modules]
```

If you have installed Apache in the default `C:\Program Files\Apache Group\ Apache` directory, enter `C:\Program Files\Apache Group\Apache\modules`. The `mod_perl.so` module should be installed in this directory.

Now you need to add the following directive in `httpd.conf` to load the `mod_perl.so` module.

```
LoadModule perl_module modules/mod_perl.so
```

You should also set the `PATH` variable in `httpd.conf` as follows:

```
PerlSetEnv PATH "C:\WINNT\system32;C:\WINNT;C:\perl;C:\perl\bin\"
```

I assume that you installed Windows in `C:\WINNT` and the `system32` directory in `C:\WINNT\system32`, and that you have installed Perl in `C:\perl` directory and the Perl interpreter is stored in `C:\perl\bin` directory. If any of these assumptions, which are the defaults for Windows 2000 or NT systems, are incorrect, please change accordingly.

Note The `Windows` directory is either `C:\WINDOWS` (for Windows 9x) or `C:\WINNT` (for Windows 2000 and Windows NT systems) by default. If you are not sure, open a console screen (often called a DOS window) and enter the `echo %windir%` command to display the value of `windir` environment variable, which points to the Windows OS directory. You can also run the `set` command at the prompt to display all other environment variables such as `path`, which usually include both the `OS` directory and `system32` directory.

To load a set of `mod_perl` modules at startup use a startup script called `startup.pl` (you can use any other name as well) with the following directive:

```
PerlRequire "Drive:/your_path:startup.pl"
```

Don't forget to change *Drive:/your_path/startup.pl* to the real path for `startup.pl`. In `startup.pl`, load your modules by using the `use module_name ();` Perl statements. For example, the following `startup.pl` script loads the CGI module, the `DBI` (database independent interface) module, and the `Apache::DBI` module that allows caching database connections:

```
#!c:/perl/bin/perl

use CGI ();
use DBI ();
use Apache::DBI ();
```

Cross-Reference   Read Chapter 16 for details on many other mod_perl related matters that still apply to Apache on Windows platform. Remember, to download modules from CPAN you have to use the ppm command instead of the `perl -MCPAN -e shell` command used in Chapter 16. For example, to install the `Apache::DBI` module, you must run:

```
ppm install http://theoryx5.uwinnipeg.ca/ppmpackages/Apache-DBI.ppd
```

Similarly, to install `Apache::ASP`, you must run

```
ppm install http://theoryx5.uwinnipeg.ca/ppmpackages/Apache-ASP.ppd
```

Running PHP scripts

To run PHP scripts with Apache under Windows, follow these steps:

1. Download the latest PHP binary distribution from `http://www.php.net/distributions/`.

2. Extract the distribution in the `c:\php` directory. Copy the `c:\php\php4ts.dll` to the Windows system32 directory. For Windows 2000 and NT systems, the default is `C:\WINNT\system32`. Also copy the `C:\php.ini-dist` to the Windows directory, which on Windows 2000 or NT is `C:\WINNT` by default.

3. The default `php.ini` will work for most sites, but if you wish, you can edit it. By default, PHP on Windows platform has MySQL and ODBC support built-in, so you do not need to enable any extensions for it. However, you should look at the `;extension=module_name.dll` lines and to determine whether you need to enable any of the lines. For example, if you are planning on using the GD library (which is used for generating PNG images) with PHP, then you will need to uncomment the `;extension=php_gd.dll` line by removing the leading semicolon character.

4. Add the following lines to `httpd.conf`:

```
LoadModule php4_module c:/php/sapi/php4apache.dll
AddType application/x-httpd-php .php
AddType application/x-httpd-php .php4
```

5. Restart the Apache Web server from the console by using the `net stop apache` command followed by the `net start apache` command.

6. Place a small PHP script called `hello.php` as listed below in the document root directory of your Web server.

```
<html>
  <head>
    <title>Hello World from PHP</title>
  </head>
<body>
  <?php echo "Hello World from PHP"; ?>
</body>
</html>
```

7. Test the script by running the `http://your_server_name/hello.php` command. If you see a "Hello World from PHP" message you have successfully configured PHP.

Now you can follow the instructions in Chapter 15 to create PHP scripts for your Web site.

Running ISAPI extensions with mod_isapi

Apache for Windows is compiled with `mod_isapi` by default. This module enables Apache to load Internet Server Application Programming Interface (ISAPI) based applications that are written in any language, so that they can run via Apache. ISAPI was originally intended for Microsoft Internet Information Server (IIS); Apache implements ISAPI by using the `mod_isapi` module. However, Apache currently only allows ISAPI extensions, thus, ISAPI filters do not work with Apache. To use an ISAPI extension (usually DDL, or Data Definition Language), add the following line to your `httpd.conf` file:

```
AddHandler isapi-isa .dll
```

This enables Apache to load an ISAPI extension program that has a .dll extension. The `mod_isapi` module has the following directives.

ISAPIReadAheadBuffer

The `ISAPIReadAheadBuffer` directive sets the maximum size of the read-ahead buffer, which is made available to ISAPI extension DLLs. For example, when data that extends past the default 49152 bytes need to be read, the `ReadClient` callback method needs to be used.

> **Syntax:** ISAPIReadAheadBuffer *size*
>
> **Default setting:** ISAPIReadAheadBuffer 49152
>
> **Context:** Server config

ISAPILogNotSupported

The ISAPILogNotSupported directive enables or disables logging of all unsupported feature requests from ISAPI extension DLLs. This is only useful to isolate a problem related to an ISAPI extension that is not behaving properly.

> **Syntax:** ISAPILogNotSupported On | Off
>
> **Default setting:** ISAPILogNotSupported on
>
> **Context:** Server config

ISAPIAppendLogToErrors

The ISAPIAppendLogToErrors directive enables or disables the storing of requests from ISAPI extension DLLs in the error log.

> **Syntax:** ISAPIAppendLogToErrors On | Off
>
> **Default setting:** ISAPIAppendLogToErrors Off
>
> **Context:** Server config

ISAPIAppendLogToQuery

The ISAPIAppendLogToQuery directive enables or disables logging of query data to server's access log.

> **Syntax:** ISAPIAppendLogToQuery On | Off
>
> **Default setting:** ISAPIAppendLogToQuery Off
>
> **Context:** Server config

UserDir in Windows

Apache currently does not work with Windows user accounts and therefore it cannot detect home directories for Windows users. If you wish to provide Web sites for users, the following workaround can be used:

1. Choose a directory to be the top-level home directory for all users. For example, you can create a directory called C:\home and use it for this purpose.

2. Now create a subdirectory for each user in this top-level directory. Name each of these directories using each user's username. For example, if you have a user called `john`, create `C:\home\john`.

3. Add the following configuration to `httpd.conf`:

```
<IfModule mod_userdir.c>
    UserDir "C:/home/"
</IfModule>
```

4. Set permissions for each user directory (`C:/home/`*username*) so that individual users on your system can read and write files in their respective Web directories.

5. Restart the Apache server.

   Now you can access user Web sites by using `http://your_server_name/`
   `~username`. For example, `http://your_server_name/~john` will access the
   `C:/home/john` directory.

✦   ✦   ✦

Tuning for Performance and Scalability

◆ ◆ ◆ ◆

◆ ◆ ◆ ◆

Like any good application, Apache can be fine-tuned beyond the initial configuration for higher performance. In this part, I show you how to speed up Apache by tuning the configuration, and you will also learn how to create a scalable Web server network using multiple Apache Web server systems.

Speeding Up Apache

CHAPTER

22

If I were asked to write the simplest mathematical formula for performance, I would write `Performance = f(hardware, software, network, content)`, which in English means that performance is a function of hardware, software, network, and content. Although this is a very broad statement, it highlights that performance of a Web server cannot be improved without ensuring that your hardware (that is the server computer), software (Apache server, Web applications, operating system), network (bandwidth, latency), and content (size, type) are tuned.

This chapter discusses how to tune these aspects of performance so that you can improve overall system performance.

Using High-Performance Hardware

Apache runs on a variety of computers. Although the architecture may vary greatly, the hardware components that cause performance bottlenecks are virtually the same.

Note   By the way, because you're reading a chapter on performance, I assume that your current Apache system is a modern machine. If you told me that you use a PC clone as your Web server and were concerned about performance, I would assume that you have a Pentium class computer and not an i386-based system.

CPU

When analyzing your hardware performance needs, the very first question you should ask yourself is this: "Do I need a fast CPU for my Apache computer?" The answer depends on how you use your Apache server.

If the server serves mostly static HTML pages, chances are good that your CPU will not be a significant performance factor. On the other hand, if you generate a lot of dynamic content using Server-Side Includes (SSIs), CGI scripts, and so on, your Apache server is likely to make good use of a fast processor. In such a case, getting a faster processor is advisable.

How fast is fast enough? There is no such thing as fast enough: The faster, the better! You should know, however, that just getting a fast CPU won't do you any good if you deal with a high volume of dynamic content. The most likely candidate for a performance bottleneck in such a scenario is RAM (discussed in the next section).

RAM

You can never have enough RAM, but RAM costs money. The question then becomes how much RAM is going to give you the best performance for the money? You can answer this question by monitoring your system on a regular basis during load. For example, on most Unix systems, you can run utility programs to monitor your system performance. Figure 22-1 shows the output of one such widely available Unix utility called top.

```
rhat server - SecureCRT                                              _ □ ✕
  4:35pm  up 10 days, 20:54,  5 users,  load average: 0.00, 0.01, 0.00
115 processes: 113 sleeping, 1 running, 0 zombie, 1 stopped
CPU states:  1.0% user,  9.6% system,  0.0% nice, 89.2% idle
Mem:    387312K av,  366304K used,   21008K free,   56276K shrd,  234152K buff
Swap:   265064K av,    2680K used,  262384K free                    85128K cached

  PID USER     PRI  NI  SIZE  RSS SHARE STAT %CPU %MEM   TIME COMMAND
29164 root      19   0  1060 1060   816 R    10.7  0.2   0:01 top
    1 root       0   0   532  532   468 S     0.0  0.1   0:06 init
    2 root       0   0     0    0     0 SW    0.0  0.0   0:00 kflushd
    3 root       0   0     0    0     0 SW    0.0  0.0   0:08 kupdate
    4 root       0   0     0    0     0 SW    0.0  0.0   0:00 kpiod
    5 root       0   0     0    0     0 SW    0.0  0.0   0:00 kswapd
    6 root     -20 -20     0    0     0 SW<   0.0  0.0   0:00 mdrecoveryd
   45 root       0   0     0    0     0 SW    0.0  0.0   0:00 khubd
  366 root       0   0   560  560   460 S     0.0  0.1   0:00 syslogd
  376 root       0   0   404  400   332 S     0.0  0.1   0:00 klogd
  391 rpc        0   0   568  564   476 S     0.0  0.1   0:00 portmap
  407 root       0   0     0    0     0 SW    0.0  0.0   0:00 lockd
  408 root       0   0     0    0     0 SW    0.0  0.0   0:00 rpciod
  418 rpcuser    0   0   724  724   612 S     0.0  0.1   0:00 rpc.statd
  433 root       0   0   424  420   360 S     0.0  0.1   0:00 apmd
  487 nobody     0   0   600  592   480 S     0.0  0.1   0:00 identd
  494 nobody     0   0   600  592   480 S     0.0  0.1   0:00 identd
  495 nobody     0   0   600  592   480 S     0.0  0.1   0:00 identd
  499 nobody     0   0   600  592   480 S     0.0  0.1   0:00 identd
```

Figure 22-1: Output of the top program

A program such as top shows a great deal of information about a running system. In this particular sample output, the computer is using almost all of its physical memory (256MB), but has not yet used any of its virtual memory.

Note   If you are running Apache on a Windows platform, use the Task Manager program to monitor memory, virtual memory, and CPU usage.

Another program that you can use on most Unix systems to check on your system's virtual memory use is vmstat. Figure 22-2 shows a sample output of a vmstat session on the same computer as the last example. When you see your Web server computer making use of virtual memory—that is, swap space—you have a memory shortage! This is a good time to invest in RAM.

```
rhat server - SecureCRT
[root@rhat tomcat]# vmstat 1
   procs                    memory    swap      io     system         cpu
 r  b  w   swpd   free   buff  cache si  so   bi  bo   in   cs  us sy id
 0  0  0   2680  21156 234152 85144  0   0    0   0    14   11   0  0  8
 0  0  0   2680  21156 234152 85144  0   0    0   0   107  114   1  1 98
 0  0  0   2680  21156 234152 85144  0   0    0   0   107  119   1  1 98
 0  0  0   2680  21156 234152 85144  0   0    0   0   107  114   1  1 98
 0  0  0   2680  21156 234152 85144  0   0    0   0   107  122   1  1 98
 0  0  0   2680  21156 234152 85144  0   0    0   0   107  115   1  1 98
 0  0  0   2680  21156 234152 85144  0   0    0   0   107  119   1  1 98
 0  0  0   2680  21156 234152 85144  0   0    0   0   107  115   1  1 98
```

Figure 22-2: Output of the vmstat program

If buying more memory is not an option, or if you think you already have plenty, then you need to look at ways to reduce your RAM usage.

Hard drive

The next piece of hardware you should consider as a major factor in your Web server's performance is the hard drive. A Web server spends a great deal of time accessing hard drives, and because hard drives are still very slow, they are often the primary cause of lousy performance.

Hard drives are generally the limiting factor in a system's performance. Therefore, choosing the right hard drive for your system is important. Generally speaking, there are three drive technologies that you want to consider, including the following:

✦ **EIDE/IDE/ATA:** EIDE/IDE/ATA are the most common types of hard drives. They are also the cheapest of the three major types that I discuss in this section. They are also the worst performers and are typically used in a house or desktop environment where massive drive I/O is not common. Fortunately, EIDE drives are becoming faster, so this is not a stagnant technology.

✦ **SCSI:** SCSI rules in the server market. A server system without SCSI drives is unthinkable to me and to many other experienced server administrators.

✦ **Fiver Channel disks:** The Fiver Channel disk is the hottest and youngest drive technology, but it is not widely used because of high price and interconnectivity issues. However, Fiver Channel drives are taking market share from SCSI in the enterprise or high-end storage arena. If you need Fiver Channel disks, you should consider a very high-end drive subsystem, such as a storage area network (SAN) or a storage appliance.

Note   In this chapter I assume that you are an EIDE or SCSI user.

Comprehending the acronyms

Choosing a hard drive for a system (desktop or server) becomes unnecessarily difficult because of the flux of buzzwords in the drive technology market. Table 22-1 defines common acronyms and terms to help you understand the differences between the various technologies, which often get buried under marketing hoopla.

Table 22-1 Common Acronyms or Terms for Hard Drive Technology		
Common Acronym or Term	*Meaning*	*Standard Name*
IDE	Integrated Disk Electronics	ATA -1
ATA	AT Attachment. ATA is the superset of the IDE specifications.	
Fast-IDE or Fast-ATA	Second-generation IDE	ATA-2
EIDE	Enhanced IDE — It provides support for larger drives, more drives (four instead of two), and for other mass storage units such as tapes and CD-ROM.	ATA-3
UltraDMA/33 or UDMA/33	By using a fast direct memory access (DMA) controller, this type of drive provides faster and less CPU-intensive transfer rates.	ATA-4
ATAPI	ATA Packet Interface — It is a protocol used by EIDE tape and CD-ROM drives; similar in many respects to the SCSI protocol.	

Common Acronym or Terms	Meaning	Standard Name
SCSI or narrow SCSI	Small Computer System Interface — The initial implementation of SCSI was designed primarily for narrow (8-bit), single-ended, synchronous or asynchronous hard drives and was very limited relative to today's SCSI. It includes synchronous and asynchronous data transfers at speeds up to 5MB/second.	SCSI-1
Fast SCSI or Fast-10	Fast SCSI uses 10 MHz bus instead of 5 MHz bus used in narrow SCSI. On an 8-bit (narrow) SCSI-bus this increases the theoretical maximum speed from 5MB/second to 10MB/second. On a 16-bit (wide) bus can have a transfer rate up to 20MB/second.	SCSI-2
Ultra or Fast-20 SCSI	Synchronous data transfer option, which allows up to 20 MHz data clocking on the bus and for 40MB/second for the 16-bit (wide) bus, which is called Ultra Wide SCSI	SCSI-3
Ultra 2 or Fast-40 SCSI	Synchronous data transfer option, which allows up to 40 MHz data clocking on the bus and 80MB/second for the 16-bit (wide) bus, which is called Ultra2 Wide SCSI.	SCSI-3

Most people either go with IDE/EIDE hard drives or with SCSI drives. Only a few keep both types in the same machine, which is not a problem.

Tips on choosing a hard drive

Hard drive performance is critical to a Web server, and therefore you should consider high-end SCSI disk controllers and drives if you plan to run a high demand Web service. The reliability of your hard disks is also very important; a disk failure can be a very time-consuming and catastrophic event to recover from. Following are few tips to remember when choosing hard disks for your Web server.

✦ **Make sure your Web server is using a high-end SCSI drive controller with a set of high-end SCSI drive drives.** The latest ultrawide SCSI drives are your best choice. It's a good idea to use multiple drives on your Web server — for example, you shouldn't keep your operating system and Web data on the same drive. Use at least two drives: one for the operating system and another for data. Keeping operating-system-specific software out of the way of the Web server is a good security measure as well.

✦ **Disks are also a common point of failure.** If you are concerned about drive failure, consider backing up your data on a regular basis. If you can afford to get Redundant Array of Inexpensive Disks (RAID) subsystems, it's worth looking into. RAID is essentially a group of smaller drives that act in concert to mimic a larger drive. If one of the drives fails, the others take up the slack until the failed drive can be replaced. Using RAID subsystems could mean high-performance drive I/O and reasonable data security for your Web server.

✦ **Don't get fooled into a slow hard drive.** Many people buy their PC servers from vendors who lure them into package deals that tend to feature a large IDE or EIDE drive. I highly recommend that you avoid using IDE/EIDE drives for your Web server if you expect the server to function as more than a toy.

Tuning your EIDE/IDE hard drives in Linux

If you do not use Linux for your Apache server, you can skip this section. Regardless of your decision to go with SCSI or IDE drives, you must consider using multiple drives if you are serious about performance. At minimum, you should use two drives — one for operating systems and software and a second drive for data. For Web servers, I recommend a minimum of three drives, using the third drive for the logs generated by the Web sites hosted on the machine. Keeping drive I/O spread on multiple devices ensures that wait time is minimized.

Tip   If you have the budget for it, you can use fiber channel drives or go for a storage area network (SAN) solution. The latter is typically used by enterprises with high data storage demands. You can also go with hardware/software RAID solutions, which are discussed in this chapter.

You can get better performance out of your modern EIDE drive. First, you must determine how your drive is performing prior to any tuning, so you need a tool to measure the performance of the current state of your drive subsystem. The `hdparam` tool is just right for the job; you can download the source distribution of this tool from `http://metalab.unc.edu/pub/Linux/system/hardware`. You compile and install it as follows:

1. As root, extract the source distribution into a suitable directory such as `/usr/local/src`. For example, I ran the `tar xvzf hdparm-3.9.tar.gz` command in `/usr/local/src` to extract the `hdparam` Version 3.9 source distribution.

2. Change to the newly created subdirectory and run the `make install` command to compile and install the `hdparam` binary and the manual page. By default, the binary is installed in `/usr/local/sbin` directory and is called `hdparam`.

Caution Because `hdparam` enables you to change the behavior of your IDE/EIDE drive subsystem, it can sometimes cause the system to hang as a consequence of improper use or misconfiguration. I highly recommend that you back up your data before using `hdparam`. Also, it is a very good idea to experiment with `hdparam` in single-user mode so that no other user is using the hard drive when you are working on it. You can reboot your system and force it to go to single-user mode by entering `linux single` at the lilo prompt during boot up.

Checking your hard drive settings with hdparam

After you have installed the `hdparam` tool, you are ready to investigate the state of your drive subsystem performance. Assuming that your IDE or EIDE hard drive is `/dev/hda`, run the following command to check the state of your hard drive configuration:

```
hdparm /dev/hda
```

You should see output similar to this:

```
/dev/hda:
multcount     =  0 (off)
I/O support   =  0 (default 16-bit)
unmaskirq     =  0 (off)
using_dma     =  0 (off)
keepsettings  =  0 (off)
nowerr        =  0 (off)
readonly      =  0 (off)
readahead     =  8 (on)
geometry      = 2494/255/63, sectors = 40079088, start = 0
```

As you can see, most everything in this default mode is turned off. Some of these defaults need to be changed to enhance your drive's performance. Before proceeding further, more information is needed from the hard drive. Run the following command:

```
hdparm -i /dev/hda
```

The above command displays the drive identification info (if any) that was available during the last time you booted the system. You make use of some of the information displayed by this command later. Here, the command reports the model, configuration, drive geometry (cylinders, heads, sectors), track size, sector size, buffer size, supported DMA mode, PIO mode, and so on. Using the following command tests the drive subsystem:

```
/dev/hda:
 Model=WDC WD205AA, FwRev=05.05B05, SerialNo=WD-WMA0W1516037
 Config={ HardSect NotMFM HdSw>15uSec SpinMotCtl Fixed DTR>5Mbs FmtGapReq }
 RawCHS=16383/16/63, TrkSize=57600, SectSize=600, ECCbytes=40
 BuffType=DualPortCache, BuffSize=2048kB, MaxMultSect=16, MultSect=16
 CurCHS=16383/16/63, CurSects=16514064, LBA=yes, LBAsects=40079088
```

```
IORDY=on/off, tPIO={min:120,w/IORDY:120}, tDMA={min:120,rec:120}
PIO modes: pio0 pio1 pio2 pio3 pio4
DMA modes: mdma0 mdma1 *mdma2 udma0 udma1 udma2 udma3 udma4
```

Here the command reports the model, configuration, drive geometry (cylinders, heads, sectors), track size, sector size, buffer size, supported DMA mode, PIO mode, and so on. Now lets test the disk sub-system using the following command:

```
/usr/local/sbin/hdparm -Tt /dev/hda
```

You will see results similar to this:

```
/dev/hda:
 Timing buffer-cache reads:   128 MB in  1.01 seconds = 126.73 MB/sec
 Timing buffered disk reads:  64 MB in 17.27 seconds = 3.71 MB/sec
```

Of course, your numbers will vary based on your drive and controller subsystem. However, this is the untuned state of your drive subsystem. The -T option tells hdparm to test the cache subsystem (that is, the memory, CPU, and buffer cache). The -t tells hdparm to report stats on the drive (/dev/hda) by reading data not in the cache. Run this command a few times and taken an average of the MB/sec reported for your drive. This is roughly the performance state of your drive subsystem. In this example the 3.71 MB/sec is the read performance, which is quite low.

Tuning multiple sector mode for your hard disk

Review the hdparm -i /dev/hda command output and look for MaxMultSect value. In this example, it is 16. Recall that the hdparm /dev/hda command showed that multcount value to be 0 (off). This means that multiple sector mode (that is IDE block mode) is turned off.

Note   *Multiple sector mode* is a feature of most modern IDE hard drives. It allows the drive to transfer multiple drive sectors per I/O interrupt. By default it is turned off. However, most modern drives can perform 2, 4, 8, or 16 sector transfers per I/O interrupt. So, if you set this mode to the maximum possible value for your drive, which is shown by the MaxMultiSect value, you should see throughput increase of anywhere from 5 percent to 50 percent or more. Also, you will reduce the operating system overhead by 30 to 50 percent.

In this example the MaxMultiSect value is 16 so we can use the -m option of hdparm tool to set this and see how performance increases. Run the following command:

```
/usr/local/sbin/hdparm -m16 /dev/hda
```

Running the performance test by using the `hdparam -tT /dev/hda` command displays the change. For the example system, the change is as follows:

```
/dev/hda:
 Timing buffer-cache reads:   128 MB in  1.01 seconds = 126.73 MB/sec
 Timing buffered disk reads:  64 MB in 16.53 seconds =  3.87 MB/sec
```

The performance of the drive has gone up from 3.71 MB/sec to 3.87 MB/sec. Not much but not bad. Perhaps you will see a change similar to this as well. Chances are you can do lot better than that with your drive if your drive and controller are fairly new. You can probably achieve 20 to 30MB/second! Be forewarned, however, that when poking around with `hdparam` you might damage your data, so, as mentioned before, back up your data before playing with the drive hardware-specific options discussed below.

If `hdparam` reported that the I/O support setting is 16-bit for your system and you have a fairly new (one or two years old) drive subsystem, you should try 32-bit I/O support. You can set this using the `-c` option for `hdparam`. This option has three values:

0—Enables default 16-bit I/O support

1—Enables 32-bit support

3—Enables 32-bit support with a special synchronization sequence required by many IDE/EIDE chipset. It is also the value that works well with most systems.

Set the options as follows:

```
/usr/local/sbin/hdparm -m16 -c3 /dev/hda
```

Notice the `-m16` option from earlier was used and that `-c3` to enable 32-bit I/O support was added. Running the program with `-t` option shows the following results:

```
/dev/hda:
 Timing buffered disk reads:  64 MB in  8.96 seconds =  7.14 MB/sec
```

The performance of the drive subsystem practically doubled!

Enabling Direct Memory Access (DMA) for your hard disk

If your drive supports direct memory access (DMA), you might be able to use the `-d` option, which enables DMA mode.

Typically, `-d1 -X32` options or `-d1 -X66` options are used together to take advantage of the DMA capabilities of your drive subsystem. The first set of options (`-d1 -X32`) enables the multiword DMA mode2 for the drive and the next set of options (-d1 -X66) enables UltraDMA mode2 for drives that support UltraDMA burst timing feature. These options can dramatically increase your drive performance. I have seen 20 MB/sec transfer rates with these options on various new EIDE/ATA drives.

There is another option, -u1, that can be very useful for increasing overall system performance. This option enables the drive driver to unmask other interrupts during processing of a drive interrupt, which means that the operating system can attend to other interrupts, such as the network I/O or serial I/O, while waiting for a drive-based data transfer to finish.

There are many other options that you can set and experiment with by using hdparam; however, be very cautious about most of the options because there is a good chance that you may corrupt data. Always backup data before playing with the hdparam tool. Also, after you have found that a set of options work well, you should put the hdparam command with options in the /etc/rc.d/rc.local script so that they are set every time you boot the system. For example, I have added the following line in the /etc/rc.d/rc.local file in one of my newer Linux systems:

```
hdparm -m16 -c3 -u1 -d1 -X66   /dev/hda
```

Now that you have tuned your hard drive for better performance, let's look at how you can tune the file system that acts as the interface to your drives. Because Red Hat Linux uses the ext2 file system, I discuss tuning issues for it in the "Tuning Linux's ext2 File System" section below.

Ethernet card

The last piece of hardware that resides in your computer system and can have an impact on your server performance is the network adapter card. I assume that your Web server is going to be connected to an Ethernet network somewhere. The adapter card you use should be of reasonably high quality and fast. For example, if the Ethernet network to which you are hooking up your Web server handles either 10Mbps or 100Mbps nodes, get a 100Mbps adapter card from a brand-name vendor.

The rest of the hardware that may become a factor in your server performance is discussed in the network section of this chapter.

Tuning Linux's ext2 File System

You can skip this section if you do not use Linux for Apache server. It is not the greatest file system in the world, but it works reasonably well. For years the ext2 file system has been the de facto file system for Linux, and so that's the file system I cover in this book.

Changing the block size of the ext2 filesystem

One of the ways you can improve the ext2 file system's performance is by changing the default block size from 1024 to a multiple of 1024 (usually less than 4096) for servers with mostly large files. To find out what kind of files you have on a particular ext2 partition do the following:

1. As root, change to the top directory of the ext2 partition.

2. Run the following commands, which really comprise a small script that uses the `find` and `awk` utilities. This command-line script will display all the files and their sizes and finally provide you with a total and average size of the entire partition.

```
find . -type f -exec ls -l {} \; | \
awk 'BEGIN {tsize=0;fcnt=1;} \
{ printf("%03d File: %-060s size: %d bytes\n",fcnt++, $9,
$5); \
tsize += $5; } \
END { printf("Total size = %d\nAverage file size = %.02f\n",
\
tsize, tsize/fcnt); }'
```

3. After you know the average size of the file system, you can determine whether you should change the block size. If you discover that your average file size is 8192, which is 2×4096, you can change the block size to 4096.

4. Unfortunately, you cannot alter the block size of an existing ext2 file system without rebuilding it. So, you have to back up all your files from the file system and then rebuild the file system by using the `/sbin/mke2fs /dev/partition -b 4096` command. For example, if you have backed up the `/dev/hda7` partition and want to change the block size to 4096, use the `/sbin/mke2fs /dev/hda7 -b 4096` command.

Note

Changing the block size to a higher number than the default (1024) may yield significant performance in raw read speed because of a reduced number of seeks and also because the `fsck` session during boot may be faster, because there may be less file fragmentation, and for other reasons. However, increasing the block size blindly (that is, without knowing the average file size) can result in wasted space. If the average file size is 2010 bytes on a system with 4096 byte blocks, each file will waste on an average 2086 bytes (4096 – 2010)! So know your file size before messing with the block size.

Tuning the ext2 file system with e2fsprogs

The default ext2 file system can be tuned using the e2fsprogs suite. In this section, I will discuss how you can install this suite of programs and use them in tuning, performing routine checks, and repairing your disks.

Installing e2fsprogs

To tune the ext2 file system, you need to install the `e2fsprogs` utility package as follows:

1. Download the `e2fsprogs-version.src.rpm` (replace `version` with the latest version number) source distribution from `www.rpmfind.net`. I downloaded the `e2fsprogs-1.19-0.src.rpm` package. You can also get the source from the e2fsprogs project site at `http://e2fsprogs.sourceforge.net`. su to root.

2. Run the `rpm -ivh e2fsprogs-version.src.rpm` command to extract the source into a `/usr/src/redhat/SOURCES/` directory. The source RPM drops a `e2fsprogs-version.tar.gz` file that needs to be extracted using the `tar xvzf e2fsprogs-version.tar.gz` command. This creates a subdirectory called `e2fsprogs-version`.

3. Change to the new subdirectory.

4. Run `mkdir build` to create a new subdirectory and then change to that directory.

5. Run `../configure` script to configure the source tree.

6. Run the `make` utility to create the binaries.

7. Run the `make check` command to ensure that everything is built correctly.

8. Run the `make install` command to install the binaries.

After you have installed the `e2fsprogs` utilities you can start using them as discussed in the following sections.

Tuning your file system with tune2fs

You can use the `tune2fs` utility to tune various aspects of an ext2 file system.

Caution   You should never apply the ext2 utilities on a mounted ext2 and you should always back up your data whenever you are modifying anything belonging to a file system.

The following section discusses how to use the `tune2fs` utility (part of the `e2fsprogs` package) to tune an unmounted ext2 file system called `/dev/hda7`. If you one or more of the settings discussed below, don't forget to change the partition name (`/dev/hda7`) to the appropriate name. First, let's look at what `tune2fs` shows as the current settings for the unmounted `/dev/hda7` by running the following command:

```
/sbin/tune2fs -l /dev/hda7
```

The output should be similar to this:

```
tune2fs 1.19, 13-Jul-2000 for EXT2 FS 0.5b, 95/08/09
Filesystem volume name:    <none>
Last mounted on:           <not available>
```

```
Filesystem UUID:            5d06c65b-dd11-4df4-9230-a10f2da783f8
Filesystem magic number:    0xEF53
Filesystem revision #:      1 (dynamic)
Filesystem features:        filetype sparse_super
Filesystem state:           clean
Errors behavior:            Continue
Filesystem OS type:         Linux
Inode count:                1684480
Block count:                13470471
Reserved block count:       673523
Free blocks:                13225778
Free inodes:                1674469
First block:                1
Block size:                 1024
Fragment size:              1024
Blocks per group:           8192
Fragments per group:        8192
Inodes per group:           1024
Inode blocks per group:     128
Last mount time:            Thu Feb 15 17:51:19 2001
Last write time:            Thu Feb 15 17:51:51 2001
Mount count:                1
Maximum mount count:        20
Last checked:               Thu Feb 15 17:50:23 2001
Check interval:             15552000 (6 months)
Next check after:           Tue Aug 14 18:50:23 2001
Reserved blocks uid:        0 (user root)
Reserved blocks gid:        0 (group root)
First inode:                11
Inode size:                 128
```

The settings that I discuss in the list below are bolded above:

✦ `Errors behavior`: This setting dictates how the kernel behaves when errors are detected in the file system. There are three possible values for this setting—`continue`, `remount-ro` (readonly), `panic`. The default setting is to continue running even if there is an error.

✦ `Mount count`: The number of time you have mounted this file system.

✦ `Maximum mount count`: This means that after the maximum number of read/write mode mounts the file system will be subject to a `fsck` checking session during the next boot cycle.

✦ `Last checked`: This setting shows the last date on which a `fsck` check was performed. The check interval for two consecutive fsck sessions.

✦ `Check interval`: This is only used if the maximum read/write mount count is not reached during the interval. In other words, if you don't unmount the file system for 6 months, then even though the mount count will be only 2, the `Fsck` check will be forced because the file system exceeded the check interval.

✦ `Next check after`: This is the next `fsck` check date.

✦ Reserved block UID and reserved block GID: These settings show which user and group has ownership of the reserved portion of this files system. By default the reserved portion is to be used by root (UID = 0, GID = 0).

Tip

On an unmounted file system such as /dev/hda7, you can change the maximum read/write mount count setting to be something more suitable for your needs by using the -c option with tune2fs. For example, /sbin/tune2fs -c 1 /dev/hda7 will force fsck check on the file system every time you boot the system. You can also use the -i option to change the time-based fsck check enforcement schedule. For example, the /sbin/tune2fs --i7d /dev/hda7 command ensures that fsck checks are enforced if the file system is remounted in read/write mode after a week. Similarly, the /sbin/tune2fs --i0 /dev/hda7 command disables the time-based fsck checks.

Checking and repairing an ext2 file system with e2fsck

In case you have a corrupt ext2 file system, you can use the e2fsck utility to try to fix it. To check a partition by using e2fsck, you must unmount it first and run the /sbin/e2fsck /dev/device command where /dev/*device* is your hard drive. For example, to force fsck check on a device called /dev/hda7, use the /sbin/e2fsck -f /dev/hda7 command. Such a check might display output as shown here:

```
e2fsck 1.19, 13-Jul-2000 for EXT2 FS 0.5b, 95/08/09
Pass 1: Checking inodes, blocks, and sizes
Pass 2: Checking directory structure
Pass 3: Checking directory connectivity
Pass 4: Checking reference counts
Pass 5: Checking group summary information
/dev/hda7: 12/1684256 files (0.0% non-contiguous), 52897/3367617 blocks
```

The e2fsck utility will ask you repair questions, which you can avoid by using the -p option.

Tuning Your Operating System

Apache runs on many different operating systems. You should consult your operating system's user's manual for details on how to fine-tune it for higher performance. Because Apache on Linux platform is the most popular combination, I discuss how you can tune Linux for higher performance. If you do not use Linux, you should skip this section.

If you have installed the Red Hat-supplied vanilla kernel, chances are it is not optimized for your system. Typically, when you install a vendor-provided kernel, it is created to support the majority of installation scenarios. For example, a vanilla kernel might have both EIDE and SCSI drive support when you might only have need for the SCSI support or the EIDE support. This is why it is a good idea to start with a vendor-provided kernel to boot your system up and as soon as you can find some time, go through a custom kernel compilation and installation process, which is what is the subject of this chapter.

Compiling and installing a custom kernel

The goal of building a custom kernel is to fine-tune your kernel to just fit your needs. Thanks to the Linux kernel developers, creating a custom kernel in Linux is a piece of cake. Linux kernel is modular in design, which means that most everything you want can be installed as separate kernel modules. But recompiling your kernel is beyond the scope of this book. If you need to know how to recompile your kernel, see http://www.kernel.org for details.

Tuning your system for demanding Web applications

A lean and mean kernel is likely to be a good candidate for running demanding applications that make heavy use of your resources. In my experience, such applications are often not suitable for vanilla kernel or other resource configurations.

For example, a multithreaded mail server can open up thousands of files from the message queue and simply run out of file handles or start up too many threads to reach the system's simultaneous process capacity. These two issues come up so frequently that I will show you how to overcome them.

Controlling the max number of open file handles

A *file handle* is a system resource that points to an opened file. Any system can only have a certain number of open file handles. The maximum number of file handles that can be opened simultaneously often controls how your system behaves in high-load scenarios. In the following sections, I discuss how you can determine and set the maximum file handles for Linux-based Web servers.

Distribution and Kernel Version Confusion

Many people new to Linux can be confused because the distribution and kernel versions are different. For example, I am often asked why I talk about Linux 2.4 when what is available in the market is 7.x. Thanks to popular distributions such as Red Hat Linux, many newcomers think that the Red Hat Linux 7.x *distribution* is the latest *version* of Linux, and that by association everything within that distribution is also 7.x. 2.4 is the latest version of the Linux kernel, and so whenever I speak of 2.4, I say "Linux kernel 2.4" to be as clear as possible.

Determining your system's file handle limit

To determine the number of file handles that you can have for the entire system, run the `cat /proc/sys/fs/file-mx` command. You should see a number such as 4096 or 8192. To increase the number of file handles (often called file descriptors) to nnn, simply add the following lines to your `/etc/rc.d/rc.local` script:

```
# Don't forget to replace nnn with an appropriate number
echo  nnn > /proc/sys/fs/file-max
```

For example:

```
echo  10240 > /proc/sys/fs/file-max
```

Here the system-wide file handles will now total 10240 (10K).

Setting the per-processor file handle limit

Setting the per-process file handle limit to 8192, for example, will ensure that when a user logs in that the user can open as many as 8,192 files from within a program under the user's control. To set the per-process file handle limit, do the following:

1. Edit the `/etc/security/limits.conf` file and add the following lines to it:

   ```
   *        soft      nofile  1024
   *        hard      nofile  8192
   ```

2. Make sure that your `/etc/pam.d/system-auth` file has a line such as the following:

   ```
   session  required  /lib/security/pam_limits.so
   ```

Allowing users to run fewer processes

To allow users to run fewer processes, for example, 8,192 at most, add the following lines to the `/etc/security/limits.conf` file.

```
*       soft    nproc   4096
*       hard    nproc   8192
```

Note   This setting will apply to both processes and the child threads that each process opens. You can also configure how much memory a user can consume by using soft- and hard-limit settings in the same file. The memory consumption is controlled using `data`, `memlock`, `rss`, `stack`, and similar directives. You can also control the CPU usage of a user. See the comments in the file for details.

Making your Apache Server software lean and mean

When you're sure you have a lean-and-mean operating system running on your powerful hardware, you can start looking at other software "places" for performance bottlenecks. How about the Apache server itself? Could it be a bottleneck for your Web service? It sure can. If you did not custom compile and built your Apache server from the source, you might have unnecessary modules built into Apache that are taking up memory and wasting your system resources.

Knowing What Resources One User Can Use

Every system has a finite number of system resources available. Being able to control how many resources can be used by a single user is important so that you can limit or extend their resource capacity as needed. To see what kind of system resources a user can consume, run `ulimit -a` (assuming you are using the bash shell). A sample output is shown below (the open file handles and max user processes lines are in bold):

```
core file size (blocks)      1000000
data seg size (kbytes)       unlimited
file size (blocks)           unlimited
max locked memory (kbytes)   unlimited
max memory size (kbytes)     unlimited
open files                   1024
pipe size (512 bytes)        8
stack size (kbytes)          8192
cpu time (seconds)           unlimited
max user processes           12287
virtual memory (kbytes)      unlimited
```

As mentioned in Chapter 2, there are two ways to get Apache. You can either download a binary distribution and install it onto your system, or you can compile your own Apache binary and install it. The latter method is highly recommended because it enables you to fine-tune Apache from the start. Look at the binary you currently have and determine whether you need all the things it has to offer. Run a command such as

```
httpd -l
```

which reveals all the modules that have been built into your current Apache executable. If you see something you don't need, remove it by running the `configure` script with appropriate command-line options. For example, if you do not plan on using CGI scripts or SSIs, you can safely remove those options from Apache by first running the following command from the source distribution directory:

```
./configure --prefix=/usr/local/apache \
            --disable-cgi --disable-cgid \
            --disable-include
```

and then recompiling and reinstalling Apache with the `make && make install` command. If your operating system allows you to remove unnecessary symbolic information from executables and then strip them off, then you can save some more memory. For example, the following command

```
strip httpd
```

discards symbols from `httpd` under Linux. This makes the size of the executable a bit smaller, which results in RAM savings for each `httpd`.

If you think your Apache executable (`httpd`) is as lean and mean as it can be but you still suspect the bottleneck is within Apache, then take a close look at your Apache configuration files. Some Apache directives are expensive in terms of performance, and they are usually the ones that require domain name resolution, system calls, drive I/O, and process manipulation. Apache configuration tuning is discussed in the "Tuning the Apache Configuration" section.

Tuning Your Network

After you have your server hardware, operating system, and the Apache server itself tuned for performance, the next typical area of bottleneck is the network itself.

To tune your network you must know the network architecture. Most Web servers are run from an Ethernet network—be it at the office network or at a co-location facility in an ISP. How this network is configured makes a great deal of difference. For example, if you have an Apache server connected to an Ethernet hub, which is, in turn, connected to other hubs that are connected to either workstations or servers, you have a great breeding environment for major bottlenecks. Each machine sees all the traffic on the network, thus the number of packet collisions increases, and network slow-down is more common. However, such a bottleneck is easily remedied by using network switches in place of hubs.

No special hardware is needed on the devices that connect to an Ethernet switch. The same network interface used for shared media 10Base-T hubs will work with an Ethernet switch. From that device's perspective, connecting to a switched port is just like being the only computer on the network segment.

One common use for an Ethernet switch is to break a large network into segments. While it is possible to attach a single computer to each port on an Ethernet switch, it is also possible to connect other devices such as a hub. If your network is large enough to require multiple hubs, you could connect each of those hubs to a switch port so that each hub is a separate segment. Remember that if you simply cascade the hubs directly, the combined network is a single logical Ethernet segment.

Using fast Ethernet

The traditional Ethernet is 10MB/sec, which simply is not enough in a modern business environment that includes e-mail-based communication, Internet access, video conferencing, and other bandwidth-intensive operations. The 100MB/sec Ethernet is the way to go. However, 100 MB/sec or "fast" Ethernet is still quite expensive if you decide to go with fast switches as well. I recommend that you move toward a switched fast Ethernet from now on unless you have already done so. The migration path from 10MB/sec to 100MB/sec can be quite expensive if you have a lot of computers in your network. Each computer in your network must have a 100MB/sec-capable NIC installed, which can be expensive in terms of cost, staff, and time. For a large LAN with several hundred users or more, you should do the upgrade one segment at a time. You can start by buying 10/100MB dual-speed NICs, which will enable you to support your existing 10MB/sec and your upcoming 100MB/sec infrastructure seamlessly.

Using fast Ethernet hand-in-hand with switching hardware can bring a high degree of performance to your LAN. You should definitely consider this option if possible. If you have multiple departments to interconnect, consider an even faster solution between the departments: The emerging Gbit/sec Ethernet standard is very suitable for connecting local area networks together to form a wide area network (WAN).

Understanding and controlling network traffic flow

Understanding how your network traffic flows is the primary key in determining how you can tune it for better performance. Take a look at the network segment shown in Figure 22-3.

Knowing your hubs from your switches

The major difference between an Ethernet hub and switch is that each port on a switch is its own logical segment. A computer connected to a port on an Ethernet switch has a full set of bandwidth ascribed to it and need not contend with other computers. A main reason for purchasing a switch over a hub is for its address-handling capabilities. Whereas a hub will not look at the address of a data packet and just forward data to all devices on the network, a switch is supposed to read the address of each data packet and correctly forward the data to the intended recipient(s). If the switch does not correctly read the packet address and correctly forward the data, it has no advantage over a hub. The following table lists the major differences between hub and switch.

Ethernet Hub	*Ethernet Switch*
Total network bandwidth is limited to the speed of the hub, that is, a 10Base-T hub provides a 10MB bandwidth, no matter how many ports exist.	Total network bandwidth is determined by the number of ports on the switch. that is, a 12-port 100MB switch can support up to 1200MB/sec bandwidth — this is referred to as the switch's maximum aggregate bandwidth.
Supports half-duplex communications limiting the connection to the speed of the port, that is, 10MB port provides a 10MB link.	Switches that support full-duplex communications offer the capability to double the speed of each link from 100MB to 200MB.
Hop count rules limit the number of hubs that can be interconnected between two computers.	Allows users to greatly expand networks; there are no limits to the number of switches that can be interconnected between two computers.
Cheaper than switches.	More expensive than hubs but price/performance is worth the higher price.

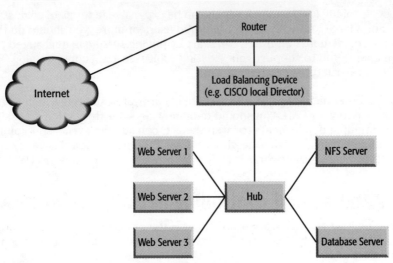

Figure 22-3: An inefficient Web network

Here, three Web servers are providing Web services to the Internet and they share a network with an NFS server and a database server. What's wrong with this picture? Well, several things are wrong. First, these machines are still using dumb hubs instead of a switch. Second, the NFS and database traffic is competing with the incoming and outgoing Web traffic. If a Web application needs database access in response to a Web request, it generates one or more database requests, which, in turn, takes away from the bandwidth available for other incoming or outgoing Web requests, effectively making the network unnecessarily busy or less responsive.

How can you solve such a problem? By using a traffic-control mechanism, of course! First determine what traffic can be isolated in this network. Naturally, the database and NFS traffic is only needed to service the Web servers. In such a case, NFS and database traffic should be isolated so that they do not compete with Web traffic. Figure 22-4 shows a modified network diagram for the same network.

Here, the database and the NFS server are connected to a switch that is connected to the second NIC of each Web server. The other NIC of each Web server is connected to a switch that is, in turn, connected to the load-balancing hardware. Now, when a Web request comes to a Web server, it is serviced by the server without taking away from the bandwidth of other Web servers. The result is a tremendous increase in network efficiency, which trickles down to a more positive user experience.

After you have a good network design, your tuning focus should shift to applications and services that you provide. Depending on your network load, you might have to consider deploying multiple servers of the same kind to implement a more responsive service. This is certainly true for the Web. The next section discusses how you can employ a simple load-balancing scheme by using a DNS trick.

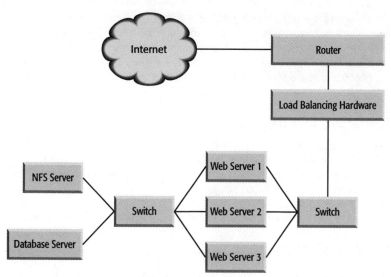

Figure 22-4: An improved Web network

Balancing load using the DNS server

The idea is to share the load among multiple servers of a kind. This typically is used for balancing the Web traffic over multiple Web servers. This trick is called *round-robin Domain Name Service.*

Suppose that you have two Web servers, www1.yourdomain.com (192.168.1.10) and www2.yourdomain.com (192.168.1.20) and you want to balance the load for www.yourdomain.com on these two servers using the round-robin DNS trick. Add the following lines to your yourdomain.com zone file:

```
www1    IN    A 192.168.1.10
www2    IN    A 192.168.1.20

www     IN    CNAME    www1
www     IN    CNAME    www2
```

Restart your name server and ping the www.yourdomain.com host. You will see the 192.168.1.10 address in the ping output. Stop and restart pinging the same host, and you'll see the second IP address being pinged, because the preceding configuration tells the name server to cycle through the CNAME records for www. In other words, the www.yourdomain.com host is both www1.yourdomain.com and www2.yourdomain.com.

Now, when someone enters www.yourdomain.com, the name server gives out the first address once, then gives out the second address for the next request, and keeps cycling between these addresses.

Caution A disadvantage of the round-robin DNS trick is that the name server has no way of knowing which system is heavily loaded and which is not—it just blindly cycles. If one of the servers crashes or becomes unavailable for some reason, the round-robin DNS trick still returns the broken server's IP on a regular basis. This could be quite chaotic, because some people will be able to get to the site and some won't.

Using load-balancing hardware

If your load demands smarter load distribution and checking your server's health is important, your best choice is to get a hardware solution that uses the new director products, such as Web Director (`www.radware.com`), Ace Director (`www.alteon.com`), or Local Director (`www.cisco.com`).

Figure 22-5 shows a Web network, which consists of two CISCO Local Directors; a set of proxy servers; Apache Web servers; `mod_perl`, PHP, Java Servlet application servers; and database servers.

All Web domains hosted in this network come to a virtual IP address that resolves to the Local Director. The Local Director uses its configuration and server health information, which it collects, to determine where to get the contents from. The second Local Director simply works as a standby in case the primary fails. Local Director enables you to do a stateful recovery when two Local Directors are connected via a special cable. If the primary fails, then the secondary can take over without anyone in the outside world knowing anything or receiving any errors.

Tip If you are serious about the reliability of your Web network, ensure that you have no single point of failure. For example, if you use a database server, make sure you have another that is replicating the data as close to real-time as possible so that you can recover from a database crash.

Tuning the Apache Configuration

After you have configured the hardware, operating system, network, and the Apache software itself (all of these processes are discussed earlier in this chapter), you are ready to tune the Apache configuration. The following sections discuss several tuning options that you can easily apply to increase server performance.

Minimizing DNS lookups

If the `HostnameLookups` directive is set to `On`, Apache will perform DNS lookup for each request to resolve IP address to a host name. This can degrade your server performance greatly. So, you should seriously consider not using host lookups for each request. Set `HostnameLookups` to `Off` in `httpd.conf`

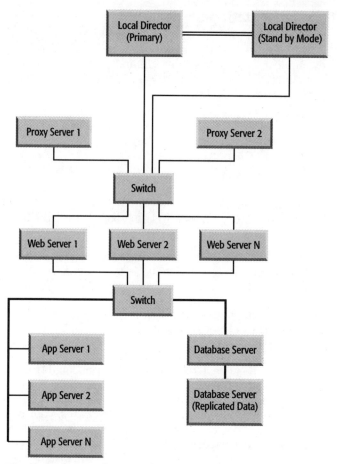

Figure 22-5: A Web network that uses Local Director for load balancing.

If you must resolve IP addresses to host names for log-processing purposes, use the logresolve tool instead. See Chapter 8 for details.

Speeding up static file serving

Although everyone is screaming about dynamic Web content that is database-driven or served by fancy application servers, the static Web pages are still there. In fact, dynamic contents are unlikely to completely replace static Web pages in the near future, because serving a static page is usually faster than serving a dynamic page. Some dynamic-content systems even create dynamically and periodically generated static Web pages as cache contents for faster delivery. This section discusses how you can improve the speed of static page delivery by using Apache and the Linux kernel HTTP module.

Reducing drive I/O for faster static page delivery

When Apache gets a request for a static Web page, it performs a directory tree search for .htaccess files to ensure that the requested page can be delivered to the Web browser. For example, if an Apache server running on www.nitec.com receives a request such as http://www.nitec.com/training/linux/sysad/intro.html, Apache performs these checks:

```
/.htaccess
%DocRoot%/.htaccess
%DocRoot%/training/.htaccess
%DocRoot%/training/linux/.htaccess
%DocRoot%/training/linux/sysad/.htaccess
```

%DocRoot% is the document root directory set by the DocumentRoot directive in the httpd.conf file. So, if this directory is /www/nitec/htdocs, then the following checks are made:

```
/.htaccess
/www/.htaccess
/www/nitec/.htaccess
/www/nitec/htdocs/.htaccess
/www/nitec/htdocs/training/.htaccess
/www/nitec/htdocs/training/linux/.htaccess
/www/nitec/htdocs/training/linux/sysad/.htaccess
```

Apache looks for the .htaccess file in each directory of the translated (from the requested URL) path of the requested file (intro.html). As you can see, a URL that requests a single file can result in multiple drive I/O requests to read multiple files. This can be a performance drain for high-volume sites. In such cases, your best choice is to disable .htaccess file checks all together. For example, when the following configuration directives are placed within the main server section (that is not within a VirtualHost directive) of the httpd.conf file, it will disable checking for .htaccess for every URL request.

```
<Directory />
    AllowOverride None
</Directory>
```

When the above configuration is used, Apache will simply perform a single drive I/O to read the requested static file and therefore gain performance in high-volume access scenarios.

Reducing system calls and drive I/O for symbolic links

On Unix and Unix-like systems running Apache, symbolic links present a danger. By using an inappropriately placed symbolic link, a Web user can view files and directories that should not be available via Web. This is why Apache offers a way for you to disable symbolic links or only follow a symbolic link if the user ID of the symbolic matches the server's own. For example, the following configuration in the main server section (that is, outside any virtual host configuration) of `httpd.conf` will instruct Apache not to follow symbolic links, effectively disabling all symbolic link access via Web.

```
<Directory />
   Options -FollowSymLinks
</Directory>
```

Unfortunately, this comes with a significant performance price. For each request, Apache performs an additional system call, `lstat()`, to ensure that it is not violating your don't-follow-symbolic-link policy.

To increase performance while having symbolic links and good security, do the following:

1. Find a way to not use any symbolic links on your Web document tree. You can use the `find your_top_web_directory -type 1 -print` command to find all the existing symbolic links in your top Web directory; then you can figure out how to avoid them.

2. Use the following configuration in the main server section of `httpd.conf` to enable symbolic links:

```
<Directory />
   Options FollowSymLinks
</Directory>
```

3. If you must disable symbolic links, consider narrowing the directory scope with a specific directory name. For example, if you want to disallow symbolic links in a directory called `my_dir` but allow symbolic links everywhere else (for performance), you can use this configuration:

```
<Directory />
   Options FollowSymLinks
</Directory>

<Directory /my_dir>
   Options -FollowSymLinks
</Directory>
```

4. Similarly, you can use the `SymLinksIfOwnerMatch`:

```
<Directory />
   Options FollowSymLinks
</Directory>

<Directory /my_dir>
   Options -FollowSymLinks +SymLinksIfOwnerMatch
</Directory>
```

Here Apache will follow symbolic links in the `/my_dir` directory if their owner ID matches the server's user ID.

Tuning your configuration using ApacheBench

Apache server comes with a tool called ApacheBench (ab), which is installed by default in the bin directory of your Apache installation directory. By using this nifty tool, you can tune your server configuration.

Depending on your multiprocessing module (MPM) choice (prefork, threaded, perchild) you have to tune the values for the following default configuration:

```
<IfModule prefork.c>
    StartServers            5
    MinSpareServers         5
    MaxSpareServers        10
    MaxClients             20
    MaxRequestsPerChild     0
</IfModule>

<IfModule threaded.c>
    StartServers            3
    MaxClients              8
    MinSpareThreads         5
    MaxSpareThreads        10
    ThreadsPerChild        25
    MaxRequestsPerChild     0
</IfModule>

    <IfModule perchild.c>
    NumServers              5
    StartThreads            5
    MinSpareThreads         5
    MaxSpareThreads        10
    MaxThreadsPerChild     20
    MaxRequestsPerChild     0
    </IfModule>
```

Tuning these directives randomly is not a good idea. Because your Web site and its traffic pattern and applications are likely to be different from other sites, there is no one-size-fits-all formula to calculate appropriate values for these directives. I will show you a technique, however, that uses ApacheBench to determine the appropriate values.

Caution   You should use the ApacheBench tool on a system (or on multiple systems) different than the Web server itself, because trying to do benchmarking on the same server using a client/server model will give you false information. The benchmark tool, ab, itself takes away resources from the server and therefore tampers with your results. So, you must run ab on a different machine. I recommend you run ab on multiple machines to better simulate loads.

Note   You will have to compile Apache on other machines to get the ab binary installed on a non-Web server system. You can install a binary RPM of Apache on such system and uninstall it after your tuning is over. See Chapters 2 and 3 for details on how to install and configure Apache.

Determine a goal for your server. Make an estimate (or guess) of how many requests you want to be able to service from your Web server. Write it down in a goal statement such as, "I wish to service *N* requests per second."

Restart your Web server and from a system other than the Web server, run the `ab` command as follows:

```
./ab -n number_of_total_requests \
     -c number_of_simultaneous_requests \
     http://your_web_server/page
```

For example:

```
./ab -n 1000 -c 50 http://www.domain.com/
```

The `ApacheBench` tool will make 50 concurrent requests and a total of 1,000 requests. Sample output is shown below:

```
Server Software:        Apache/2.0.16
Server Hostname:        localhost
Server Port:            80

Document Path:          /
Document Length:        1311 bytes

Concurrency Level:      50
Time taken for tests:   8.794 seconds
Complete requests:      1000
Failed requests:        0
Total transferred:      1754000 bytes
HTML transferred:       1311000 bytes
Requests per second:    113.71
Transfer rate:          199.45 kb/s received

Connnection Times (ms)
              min   avg   max
Connect:        0     0     5
Processing:   111   427   550
Total:        111   427   555
```

Notice that `Requests per second` is `113.71` for accessing the home page of the `http://www.domain.com` site. Change the concurrent request count to a higher number and see how the server handles additional concurrent load.

Now change the values for the `MaxClients`, `ThreadsPerChild`, `MaxThreadsPerChild`, and so on based on your MPM, restart Apache, and apply the same benchmark tests by using `ab` as before. You should see your `Requests per second` go up and down based on numbers you try. As you tweak the numbers by changing the directive values, make sure you record the values and the performance so that you can determine what is a good setting for you.

Caching for Speed

Caching Web contents is not a new concept. Most busy Web sites implement caching by using proxy servers or another mechanism. Here I discuss two options from which you can choose. You should also look into the proxy capabilities of Apache by using the mod_proxy module discussed in Chapter 10.

Caching frequently used files in memory with mod_fcache

The mod_fcache module for Apache caches a given file type in memory. The cached files are stored in the server's main memory space and are accessible to all the Apache child processes. You can download this module from www.fractal.net/mod_fcache.tm. To compile and install this module, follow these steps:

1. As root, extract the module source by using the tar xvzf mod_fcache.tar.gz command and copy the newly created directory to the modules subdirectory of your Apache source distribution. For example, if you have installed Apache source in /usr/local/src/httpd_2.0.16 and fcache in /usr/local/src/fcache, then you can copy the module files using cp -r /usr/local/src/fcache /usr/local/src/httpd_2.0.16/modules command.

2. Change the directory to the modules/fcache subdirectory of the Apache source distribution. Take a look at the config.m4 file and see if anything needs to be changed for your system. Most likely you do not have to make any changes. If you do, you should know who you are.

3. Run autoconf. to configure everything.

4. Change the directory back to the top-level Apache source distribution and run the Apache configure script with all the options you normally use (see config.status file) and the --enable-fcache option.

5. Compile and install Apache as usual using make && make install command.

6. Restart the Apache Web server by using the /usr/local/httpd/apachectl restart command.

Now you are ready to use this module. To cache GIF images that are served from a directory called *common_images*, for example, you use the following configuration segment in httpd.conf:

```
<Directory /common_images>
    fcache                    On
    fcache_CacheTypes         image/gif
    fcache_MaxSize            10240
    fcache_RecomputeTables    600
</Directory>
```

Some things to note about the above segment:

✦ `fcache` turns on the caching module.

✦ `fcache_CacheTypes` directive sets the MIME type for caching. The sample configuration sets this to `image/gif`. If you wish to cache all types of images, you can use `image/*` instead.

✦ `fcache_MaxSize` sets the size of the cache. Here the memory cache is set to 10MB (1024KB × 10). Remember that you must have plenty of memory to cache files.

✦ `fcache_RecomputeTables` directive sets the time in seconds to recompute the cache tables. The default of 10 minutes is sufficient for most purposes.

Tip To view cache statistics, you can create the following configuration:

```
<Location /fcache-stats>
    SetHandler fcache-stats-handler
</Location>
```

and then go to the `http://your_web_server/fcache-stats` page.

Getting slick with the Squid proxy-caching server

Squid is an open-source HTTP 1.1-compliant proxy-caching server that you can use to enhance your users' Web-browsing experience. You can download the latest stable Squid source distribution from `www.squid-cache.org`.

Ideally, you want to run the proxy-caching server with two network interfaces. One interface connects it to the Internet gateway or the router and the other one connects it to the internal network.

Tip Disabling IP forwarding on the proxy-caching system ensures that no one can bypass the proxy server and access the Internet directly.

The following sections discuss installing and configuring Squid.

Compiling and installing Squid proxy-caching server

To compile and install Squid, follow these steps:

1. As root, extract the source distribution using the `tar xvzf suid-version.tar.gz` (where `version` is the latest version number of the Squid software).

2. Run the `./configure --prefix=/usr/local/squid` command to configure Squid source code for your system.

3. Run `make all; make install` to install Squid in `/usr/local/squid` directory.

After you have installed Squid, you need to configure it (see the next section).

Configuring Squid

To configure Squid, follow these steps:

1. Create a group called `nogroup` by using the `groupadd nogroup` command. This group will be used by Squid.

2. Run the `chown -R nobody:nogroup /usr/local/squid` command to give the ownership of the `/usr/local/squid` directory and all its subdirectories to `nobody` user and to the group called `nogroup`. This enables Squid (running as `nobody` user) to create cache directories and files and to write logs. Modify the `/usr/local/squid/etc/squid.conf` file as discussed in the following steps.

3. Decide which port you want to run the proxy-cache on. Because most sites run proxy-cache on 8080, I use this value here. Add the following line in `squid.conf`:

   `http_port 8080`

   This tells Squid to listen to port 8080 for proxy requests.

   Tip   If you prefer a different port, use it here. Be sure not to use a port that is already in use by another server. Ideally, you want to use port numbers above 1024 to avoid collision with standard services, but if you know you are not running a Web server on port 80 and want to run your proxy-cache on that port, you can do so. Also, a quick way to check whether a port is available is to run `telnet localhost` *portnumber* command where *portnumber* is the port number you want to use for proxy-cache. If you get a connection failure message, the port is currently not in use.

4. You need to define where you want to keep the cache data. Define the following line in the `squid.conf`:

   `cache_dir ufs /usr/local/squid/cache 100 16 256`

   This tells Squid that you want to store the cache data in `/usr/local/squid/cache`. If you have a very large user base that will use this proxy-cache, it is a very good idea to have multiple cache directories spanning different drives. This reduces drive I/O-related wait because multiple, independent drives are always faster than a single drive.

5. Default Squid configuration does not allow any connection from anywhere; this is a security feature often known as "deny everyone, allow only those who should have access." So, you have to create an access control list (ACL) that enables your network to access to the proxy-cache. For example, if your network address is `192.168.1.0` with subnet `255.255.255.0`, then you can define the following line in `squid.conf` to create an ACL for your network:

   `acl local_net src 192.168.1.0/255.255.255.0`

6. Squid needs to know that you want to allow machines in `local_net` ACL to have access to the proxy-cache, which you do by adding the following line in `squid.conf` just before the `http_access deny all` line:

```
http_access allow local_net
```

7. You need to tell Squid the username of the cache manager user. If you want to use webmaster@*yourdomain.com* as the cache manager user, define the following line in squid.conf:

```
cache_mgr webmaster
```

8. To tell Squid the user and group it should run as, add the following lines in `squid.conf`:

```
cache_effective_user nobody
    cache_effective_group nogroup
```

Here Squid is told to run as the `nobody` user and to use permissions for the group called `nogroup`.

9. Save the `squid.conf` file and run the following command to create the cache directories:

```
/usr/local/squid/squid -z
```

Gentlemen, start your Squid

After configuring Squid, you can run the `/usr/local/squid/bin/squid &` command to start Squid for the first time. You can verify it is working in a number of ways:

✦ Squid shows up in a `ps -x` listing.

✦ Running `client www.nitec.com` dumps Web page text to your terminal.

✦ The files `cache.log` and `store.log` in the `/usr/local/squid/logs` directory show Squid to be working.

✦ Running `squid -k check && echo "Squid is running"` tells you Squid is active.

Now for the real test: If you configure the Web browser on a client machine to use the Squid proxy, you should see results. In Netscape Navigator, select Edit ⇨ Preferences and then select Proxies from within the Advanced category. By selecting Manual Proxy Configuration and then clicking View, you can specify the IP address of the Squid server as the http, FTP, and Gopher proxy server. The default proxy port is 3128, so unless you have changed it in the `squid.conf` file, place that number in the port field.

Note   If you use Microsoft Internet Explorer, you can set Squid server as your http, FTP, and Gopher proxy by choosing Tools ⇨ Internet Options ⇨ Connections ⇨ LAN Settings. Then click the Use a proxy server option which enables the Advanced button. Click the Advanced button and enter the Squid server and port number in appropriate entry boxes for HTTP, FTP, and Gopher. Click OK a few times to close all the dialog boxes.

You should now be able to browse any Web site as if you had no proxy. You can double-check that Squid is working correctly by checking the log file `/usr/local/squid/logs/access.log` from the proxy server and making sure the Web site you were viewing is in there.

Tweaking Squid to fit your needs

Now that you have Squid up and running, you can customize it to fit your needs. Ultimately, a tool such as Squid should be completely transparent to your users. This "invisibility" removes the users from the complexity of administration and enables them to browse the Web as if there were no Web proxy server. Although I do not detail how to do that here, you may refer to the Squid Frequently Asked Questions at `http://squid.nlanr.net/Squid/FAQ/FAQ.html`. Section 17 of this site details using Squid as a transparent proxy.

Note   This section shows you the basics to using Squid as a Web proxy. Squid has many features above and beyond those discuss here. If you are interested in making Squid function beyond the basics, visit the Squid Web page at `http://squid.nlanr.net`.

Setting rules for Squid

By default, Squid does not restrict your users from accessing any sites. You can define rules in your `squid.conf` file to set access control lists and to allow or deny visitors according to these lists; for example:

```
acl BadWords url_regex foo bar
```

By adding the preceding line, you have defined an ACL rule called `BadWords` that matches any URL containing the words `foo` or `bar`.

Note   This applies to `http://foo.deepwell.com/pictures` and `http://www.thekennedycompound.com/ourbar.jpg` because they both contain words that are members of `BadWords`.

By adding the following:

```
http_access deny BadWords
```

to `squid.conf`, you block your users from accessing any URLs that match this rule.

Caution   Almost every administrator who uses word-based ACLs has a story about not examining all the ways in which a word can be used. You should realize that if you ban your users from accessing sites containing the word "sex," you are also banning them from accessing `www.buildersexchange.com` and any others that may fall into that category.

Changing Squid's cache memory settings

You can control the amount of Web pages that Squid keeps in the cache memory.

Going with Redirector instead of Rules

If you find yourself managing a large list of "blacklisted" sites in the `squid.conf` file, you should think of using a type of program called a *redirector*. Large lists of ACL rules can begin to slow a heavily used Squid proxy. By using a redirector to do this same job you can improve on Squid's efficiency of allowing or denying URLs based on filter rules. You can get more information on Squirm, a full-featured redirector that works with Squid, from `www.senet.com.au/squirm`.

The `cachemgr.cgi` file comes in the Squid distribution. It is a CGI program that enables you to view statistics about your proxy as well as shut down and restart Squid. It requires only a few minutes of your time to install, but it gives you explicit details about how your proxy is performing. If you'd like to tune your Web cache, this tool will help.

For example, by adding the line

```
cache_mem  16 MB
```

you allow Squid to use 16MB of memory to hold Web pages in memory. By trial and error you may find you need a different amount.

Caution

The `cache_mem` is not the amount of memory Squid consumes; it only sets the maximum amount of memory Squid uses for holding Web pages, pictures, and so forth. The Squid documentation says that you can expect Squid to consume up to three times this amount.

Writing Squid logs in Apache Log format

Apache writes logs in Common Log Format (CLF). If you have an Apache log analysis tool, wouldn't it be nice to be able to parse Squid log using the same tool? You can, by letting Squid write logs in CLF format.

By using the line

```
emulate_httpd_log on
```

the files in `/var/log/squid` are written in a form similar to the Web server log files. This arrangement enables you to use a Web statistics program such as Analog or Webtrends to analyze your logs and to examine the sites that your users are viewing.

Avoiding negative caching

If you type in a URL and find that the page does not exist, chances are that page won't exist anytime in the near future. By setting `negative_ttl` to a desired number of minutes, as shown in the next example, you can control how long Squid remembers that a page was not found in an earlier attempt. This is called *negative caching*.

```
negative_ttl 2 minutes
```

Negative caching isn't always a good thing. The default is five minutes, but I suggest lessening this to two minutes or possibly to one minute, if not disabling it all together. Why would you do such a thing? You want your proxy to be as transparent as possible. If a user is looking for a page that the user knows exists, you don't want a short lag time between the URL coming into the world and your user's ability to access it.

Using mod_backhand for a Web server farm

If you have a cluster of Web servers (that is, a Web server farm) and would like to redirect requests among the servers using a native Apache module, consider using mod_backhand. For example, if you have a Web server farm that consists of three similarly configured Apache servers and would like to distribute high-load CGI or mod_perl requests to whichever is not busy at the time of the request, you can make good use of this module. The module uses resource status information from all the servers in the cluster, and redirects requests to the server that is more ready than the others to service a specific request.

Here is how you can download, compile, install, and configure this module with Apache.

1. Download the module source from http://ww.backhand.org/mod_backhand.

2. As root, extract the source distribution in a directory. Run ./precompile *path_to_apache_source* command from the newly created mod_backhand subdirectory. Remember to change the path_to_apache_source to the actual Apache source distribution path.

3. Configure Apache source using --enable-backhand or --enable-modules= backhand option and all your usual options with configure script from the Apache source distribution directory.

4. Run make && make install as usual.

5. Add the following configuration segment to your httpd.conf:

```
<IfModule mod_backhand.c>
    UnixSocketDir /var/backhand/backhand
    MulticastStats 192.168.1.254:4445
    AcceptStats 192.168.1.0/24
</IfModule>
```

The above sample configuration assumes that your IP broadcast address is 192.168.1.254 and that you have a class C network, 192.168.1.0/24, which hosts all your Web servers. Make sure you change these IP addresses per your network. The UnixSocketDir must be only accessible to the Apache user.

Note   The mod_backhand module uses the Ethernet broadcast address or IP multicast address to announce resource status from each server. The above example uses the Ethernet broadcast address; you can use the multicast address instead.

Now you need to decide which directory you want to load balance (that is, redirect) between all your Web servers. Typically, this is the CGI directory. For example, the following configuration shows that `/www/mysite/cgi-bin` is to be placed under `mod_backhand`'s control:

```
<Directory "/www/mysite/cgi-bin">
     Backhand byAge
     Backhand byRandom
     Backhand byLogWindow
     Backhand byLoad
</Directory>
```

6. Restart the Apache Web server using `/usr/local/apache/bin/apachectl restart` command.

7. Repeat all of the above steps for each Web server.

The `mod_backhand` module creates a daemon process that facilitates gathering and transmission of resource statistics within the Web server cluster. To ensure that this daemon gets a fair share of the system resources, run it with a high priority. For example you can use the `renice` utility found in most Unix and Unix-like systems to set its priority to `-20`.

Note   There are other `mod_backhand`-specific tuning issues that you need to consider when using this module. Visit `www.backhand.org/mod_backhand` for more information.

Tuning Web Applications

Web applications are usually the primary performance culprits. Ill-configured or ill-written applications can take servers down to their knees quite easily. It is very important to ensure that your Web applications are not causing problems. This section discusses several tricks that you can use to minimize Web application-related problems. However, because Web applications can be written in many languages using many types of architecture, it is impossible to cover all types of Web applications. So, the discussion here is limited to Perl-based Web application issues.

Speeding up mod_perl scripts

The `mod_perl` scripts speed up your Web application performance because they are loaded once and can be run any time without reloading. The following tricks might make your `mod_perl` scripts run even faster or be more performance-friendly.

Preloading your mod_perl modules

If you use a lot of `mod_perl` modules for your Web sites, consider preloading the modules by using the `PerlRequire` directive in `httpd.conf`. Simply, create a Perl script that loads your common modules. For example, following is a simple Perl script called `startup.pl` that loads a few modules that I often use.

```
#!/usr/bin/perl
use CGI ();
use Apache::DBI ();
use Digest::MD5 ();

1;
```

The empty parentheses disable default importing of module variables until needed. This saves memory space because you might not need all the features of all the modules that you preload. This script can now be preloaded at server startup by using the PerlRequire /path/to/startup.pl directive.

When you preload modules using a script such as startup.pl, the child processes can at least share a lot of code pages used by these modules, which saves RAM, helping your system's health.

Caching database connections

If you use Perl DBI to access relational databases from your mod_perl scripts, you can increase the performance of your database connectivity significantly by changing a single line of code. If, in your mod_perl scripts, you are currently using the use DBI; call to use the DBI module directly, then change this to use Apache::DBI;, which will cache database connections for your application and increase performance significantly. There are several other programming techniques that you should consider as well:

✦ If you connect to the same database for each request, then consider opening the connection to the database outside the request handler. For example:

```
sub handle {
   my $r = shift;

   my $q = new CGI;

   my $id = $q->param('id');

   # Connect to database

   my $dbh;

   eval {

     $dbh = DBI->connect($dataSource,
                         $dbUser,
                         $dbPassword, { AutoCommit => 1 }) ||
            die;
   };

   if ($@) {
       # die "Can't connect to database $DBI::errstr";
       # connect failed do something
```

```
            print STDERR "Can not connect to $dataSource \n";
            print STDERR "DB2 Server Error: $DBI::errstr \n";
    }

   my $statement = "SELECT myfield from mytable where ID =
$id";

   my $sth   = $dbh->prepare($statement);

   my $rv           = $sth->execute;

   if (! $rv ) {

        # No record found. Do something
   }


   while ( my @fields = $sth->fetchrow_array){

        print STDOUT "ID $id shows: ", join(',', @fields),
"<br>";

   }

   $sth->finish;

}
```

Notice that the database connection is performed within the handle, which can be performed outside the handler because the same database and user credentials are used for the connection.

✦ If possible prepare SQL statements once and reuse prepared statements to save time. The previous example can be written more efficiently as shown here:

```
my $APP_RUN_COUNT = 0;
my ($dbh, $sth);


sub init {

   eval {

     $dbh = DBI->connect($dataSource,
                         $dbUser,
                         $dbPassword, { AutoCommit => 1 }) ||
            die;
   };

   if ($@) {
        # die "Can't connect to database $DBI::errstr";
        # connect failed do something
```

```
            print STDERR "Can not connect to $dataSource \n";
            print STDERR "DB2 Server Error: $DBI::errstr \n";
        }


    }

my prepare_statement {
    my $dbh = shift;

    my $statement = "SELECT myfield from mytable where ID =
?";
    $sth = $dbh->prepare($statement);

}


sub handle {
    my $r = shift;

    if ($APP_RUN_COUNT++ == 0) {

        init();
        prepare_statement();

    }

    my $q    = new CGI;

    my $id   = $q->param('id');

    my $rv   = $sth->execute($id);

    if (! $rv ) {

        # No record found. Do something
    }


    while ( my @fields = $sth->fetchrow_array){

        print STDOUT "ID $id shows: ", join(',', @fields),
"<br>";

    }

    $sth->finish;

}
```

Here the handler method calls init() and prepare_statement() routines
to create global database and statement handles once for the entire life cycle
of the child-server process. This makes the script much more efficient than
the previous version.

Running mod_perl applications on a partial set of Apache children

When you start using many mod_perl scripts, you will notice that your Apache child-server processes become larger in size. You can witness this phenomenon by using the top command. Now, as long as you have plenty of RAM you should be fine. However, no one ever has enough RAM, and so it is a good idea to not rely on having lots of memory as the solution and to consider how you can address this problem more effectively.

If you find that Apache child processes are becoming larger and larger because many mod_perl scripts are being loaded into them, consider having a dedicated script server that only serves dynamic contents. Figure 22-6 shows how this can work.

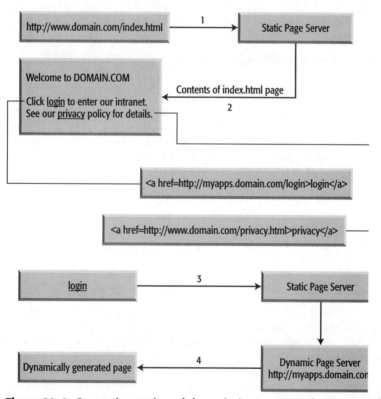

Figure 22-6: Separating static and dynamic (mod_perl script-generated) contents

When a user requests the home page of a site called www.domain.com, the Apache server responsible for static pages returns the index.html page to the client. The page contains embedded links for both static and dynamic contents. The figure shows two such links: <u>login</u> and <u>privacy</u>. When the end-user clicks on the <u>login</u> link it requests `http://myapps.domain.com/login`, which is a different Apache server than the `www.domain.com` server. In fact, these two should be two different Linux systems in the ideal world. However, not everyone can afford to split the dynamic and static contents like this, so this solution is not appropriate for everyone.

If you must keep the `mod_perl` and static contents on the same Linux system that runs Apache, you can still ensure that fat Apache child processes are not serving static pages. Here is a solution that I like:

1. Compile and install the `mod_proxy` module for your Apache Web server.

2. Copy your existing `httpd.conf` file to `httpd-8080.conf` and modify the Port directive to be `Port 8080` instead of `Port 80`. Remove all `mod_perl`-specific configurations from `httpd.conf` so that all your `mod_perl` configurations are in `httpd-8080.conf` file.

3. Modify the `httpd.conf` file to have the following proxy directives:

   `ProxyPass /myapps http://127.0.0.1:8080/myapps`

   You can change *myapps* with whatever you like. If you do change this, make sure that you also change it in any other location where it is mentioned in this discussion. Here the Apache server serving static pages is being told that all requests to the `/myapps` URL are to be serviced via the proxy module, which should get the response from the Apache server running on the same Linux system (`127.0.0.1` is the localhost) but on port 8080.

4. Add the following configuration in `httpd-8080.conf` to create a `mod_perl` script location.

   ```
   <Location /myapps>
       SetHandler perl-script
       PerlHandler MyApp1
   </Location>
   ```

   Don't forget to change *MyApp1* to whatever your script's name is.

5. If you have `KeepAlive On` in `httpd-8080.conf`, change it to `Off`. This ensures that Apache does not keep the connection open for `KeepAliveTimeout`-specified number of seconds in the hope of serving new clients from the same TCP connection.

6. Start (or restart) the Apache server (listening on port 80) as usual by using the `apachectl` command. However, you have to start the Apache on port 8080 by using the `/usr/local/apache/bin/httpd -f /usr/local/apache/conf/httpd-8080.conf` command. This assumes that you have installed the `/usr/local/apache` directory; if that is not so, make sure you change the path.

Now you have two Apache parent daemons (that is, run as root) running two sets of child processes where one services static pages and uses the proxy module to fetch the dynamic mod_perl script pages by using the ProxyPass directive. This allows you to service the static pages using a set of child servers that are not running any Perl code whatsoever. On the other hand, the server on port 8080 only services dynamic requests; thus, you effectively have a configuration that is very performance-friendly.

Going with FastCGI instead of mod_perl

Scripts running under mod_perl run fast because they are loaded within each child-server's code space. Unlike its CGI counterpart, a mod_perl script can maintain a persistent connection to an external database server. This means that database-driven dynamic content generation becomes fast with mod_perl scripts.

However, a new problem introduces itself if you run a very large Web server. When you run 50 or more Apache server processes to service many simultaneous requests, it is possible for Apache to eventually open up that many database connections and to keep each connection persistent for the duration of each child. Say that you run a Web server system through which you run 50 Apache child processes so that you can service approximately 50 requests per second and you happen to have a mod_perl-based script that opens a database connection in the initialization stage. As requests come to your database script, Apache services such requests by using each of its child processes and thus opening up 50 database connections. Because many database servers allocate expensive resources on a per-connection basis, this could be a major issue on the database side.

For example, when making such connections to a IBM Universal Database Server (UDB) Enterprise Edition running on a remote Linux system, each Apache child has a counterpart connection-related process on the database server. If such environment uses load-balancing hardware to balance incoming requests among a set of mod_perl-enabled Apache Web servers, there is likely to be a scenario when each Web-server system, which is running 50 Apache child processes, has all of the child processes opened and connected to the database server. For example, if such an environment consists of 10 Web servers under the load-balancing hardware, then the total possible connections to the database server is 10×50, or 500 connections, which might create an extensive resource load on the database server.

One possible solution for such a scenario is to find a way to have the database time-out idle connections, make the mod_perl script code detect stale connections, and have the code reinitiate connection. Another solution is to create a persistent database proxy daemon that each Web server uses to fetch data from the database.

Fortunately, FastCGI or Java Servlets has a more native solution for such problems and should be considered for heavily used database-driven applications. The next section discusses another performance-boosting Web technology called FastCGI.

Like mod_perl scripts, FastCGI applications run all the time (after the initial loading) and therefore provide a significant performance advantage over CGI scripts. Table 22-2 explains the differences between a FastCGI application and a mod_perl script.

 Cross-Reference   To learn more about FastCGI, see Chapter 14.

	Table 22-2	
Difference Between a FastCGI Application and mod_perl Scripts		
Topic	*FastCGI Applications*	*mod_perl Scripts*
Apache platform dependent	No. FastCGI applications can run on non-Apache Web servers such as IIS, Netscape Web Server, and the like.	Yes. Only Apache supports mod_perl module.
Perl only solution	No. FastCGI applications can be development in many languages including C, C++, and Perl.	Yes
Runs as external process	Yes	No
Can run on remote machine	Yes	No
Multiple instances of the application/script are run	Typically, a single FastCGI application is run to respond to many requests that are queued. However, if the load is high, multiple instances of the same application are run.	Number of instances of mod_perl script that run is equal to the number of child Apache server processes.
Wide support available	Yes. However, I sometimes get the impression that FastCGI development is slowing down but I can't verify this or back this up.	Yes. There are a great deal of mod_perl sites on the Internet and support via Usenet or Web is available.

Topic	FastCGI Applications	mod_perl Scripts
Database connectivity	Because all requests are sent to a single FastCGI application, you only need to maintain a single database connection with the back-end database server. However, this can change when Apache FastCGI process manager spawns additional FastCGI application instances because of heavy load. Still, the number of FastCGI instances of an application is likely to be less than the number of Apache child processes.	Because each Apache child process runs the `mod_perl` script, each child can potentially have a database connection to the back-end database. This means that you can end up with hundreds of database connections from even a single Apache server system.

✦   ✦   ✦

Creating a High-Availability Network

In this chapter, you learn about design considerations for building a Web network. A Web network is a network of Web server nodes that create a Web service. For example, Yahoo! uses a large number of Web servers, application servers, and database servers to create a multitude of Yahoo! Web services.

If you have decided to integrate the Web into your business, you must consider a Web solution that can grow beyond a single Web server or a shared Web drive space on an ISP. A Web network is one solution. In this chapter, you learn to use proven networking and system management concepts regarding design considerations for building successful Web network. Although the chapter focuses on Apache-on-Linux-based solutions, most of the solutions are applicable to other platforms as well.

Features of a High-end Web Network

A high-end Web network serves thousands to millions of pages per day. To serve a large number of Web requests it must have these features:

✦ **Reliable DNS servers.** If your Domain Name Service (DNS) servers are down, no one can easily access your Web sites. So, reliable DNS is a big consideration in Web network design.

✦ **Load-balanced Web access.** Users connect to one or more Web servers, which are automatically selected based on system loads, and availability.

✦ **A manageable storage architecture.** Anyone considering a Web network is likely to have a large amount of content, which needs to be made available on all the Web servers in a reliable and manageable manner. Having many Web servers and managing each server's hard drives can be a nightmare without proper planning and solid storage architecture.

✦ **Efficient back-end networks.** Large Web sites run many applications and perform zillions of database queries, as well as many other back-end tasks, to produce high-quality, personalized content for their visitors. Therefore a solid back-end network is a must. A *back-end network* is a network that is not accessible for Web visitors but serves as the backbone for keeping each server updated and synchronized with the latest contents. Back-end networks also allow administrator to perform various system administration tasks such as backup, software upgrade, and so on.

✦ **High degree of security.** Designers must pay close attention to security concerns when designing Web networks because hackers often target Web networks that are easy to break in and use them as platforms for attacking other sites. This can result in serious legal hassle.

Enhancing DNS Reliability

When a site's DNS is down, it is unreachable by most users. Yes, if you know the IP address of a Web site you can probably access it, but most people don't even know how to find out what a Web site's IP address is, so expecting users to visit while your DNS is down is unrealistic.

This is why two DNS servers are required for registering new domains. However, you should consider this requirement as the absolute minimum and you should use more than two servers to increase redundancy and the reliability of your DNS service. Following is the DNS strategy that I often recommend:

✦ Deploy at least two DNS servers for your Web site(s) as required by most domain name registers, and preferably more than two.

✦ Deploy an off-site secondary DNS server. This means that if your local DNS server goes out, the off-site secondary DNS server should still be reachable. For example, if your primary DNS server sits on a network that is temporarily out of order, the off-site secondary server will respond and direct traffic to the appropriate resources. If you do not wish to deploy an off-site DNS server and maintain it yourself, consider using services such as secondary.com.

✦ Use at least one dedicated DNS server if possible because systems that run multiple services are more likely to be down frequently than the one that runs a single service.

✦ Run local DNS cache if any of your Web applications require that the DNS IP address be resolved to host names. For example, there are commercial banner advertisement systems that use the IP address that matches demographics by performing asynchronous DNS lookups. These types of applications can benefit greatly from DNS caching.

✦ Use monitoring software on a routine basis to ensure that DNS data is correct and available.

Load Balancing Your Web Network

The purpose of having multiple Web server nodes in a Web network is to balance load among them to ensure a high-degree of performance and stability. There are two primary ways of balancing loads among servers: round-robin DNS and hardware load balancers. Both methods are discussed in the following sections.

Distributing HTTP requests with Round-Robin DNS

The Round-Robin DNS solution is recommended only if a hardware-based load-balancing solution is unavailable. Round-Robin DNS is a mechanism for cycling through a list of Web server IP addresses for a single Web host name.

Suppose that you have two Web servers, www1.yourdomain.com (192.168.1.10) and www2.yourdomain.com (192.168.1.20), and you want to balance the load for www.yourdomain.com on these two servers by using the Round-Robin DNS trick. Just follow these steps:

1. Add the following lines to your yourdomain.com zone file:

```
www1   IN  A 192.168.1.10
www2   IN  A 192.168.1.20

www    IN  CNAME  www1
www    IN  CNAME  www2
```

2. Restart your DNS server and ping the www.yourdomain.com host. You will see the 192.168.1.10 address in the ping output.

3. Stop pinging and then start pinging the same host, and you'll see the second IP address being pinged, because the preceding configuration tells the name server to cycle through the CNAME records for www. In other words, the www.yourdomain.com host is both www1.yourdomain.com and www2.yourdomain.com.

When someone enters www.yourdomain.com, the name server gives out the first address once, then gives out the second address for the next request, and keeps cycling between these addresses.

A disadvantage of the round-robin trick is that the DNS server has no way of knowing which system is heavily loaded and which is not—it just blindly cycles. If one of the servers crashes or becomes unavailable for some reason, the round-robin DNS trick still returns the broken server's IP on a regular basis. This means that some people will be able to access the sites and some won't.

Distributing HTTP requests with hardware load balancers

Hardware load balancers are very common these days. A hardware load-balancing solution is typically much smarter than the Round-Robin DNS solution discussed in the previous section. A hardware load-balancing device can implement various ways to monitor each of the Web server's network load, performance, and availability by using response time, by number of requests sent, and by making self-generated HTTP test requests. Consequently, these devices offer a greater control for your load-balancing scheme.

Some of the load-balancing devices also enable you to create server pools in which some servers have higher priority over others. For example, if you have a Pentium 4 1.3 GHz system with 2GB of RAM and a Pentium III 550 MHz system with 512GB of RAM, you can give higher priority to the Pentium 4 system because it's more powerful and more likely to be capable of servicing many more requests than the Pentium III system. Local Director (CISCO) and Web Director (Radware) are hardware load-balancing solutions that have worked well for me.

Figure 23-1 shows a simple load-balanced solution in which each client request comes to the load-balancing hardware.

The load balancer decides which Web server node to use to service the request and passes the request to the most suitable Web server, which responds to the request as usual. The selection criteria for the Web server can be dependent on priority, availability, and reliability.

Avid readers will notice that this solution has a single point of entry into the Web network. For example, requests for `http://www.domain.com` must come to the load balancer, which internally translates this request to a request for service by a Web server node on the network. Figure 23-2 shows an example load-balanced Web network.

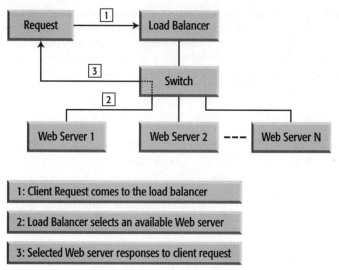

1: Client Request comes to the load balancer

2: Load Balancer selects an available Web server

3: Selected Web server responses to client request

Figure 23-1: A simple load-balancing solution

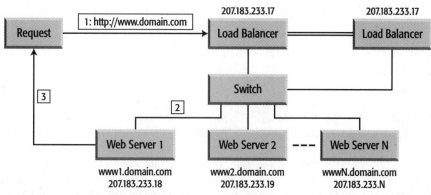

Figure 23-2: A sample load-balancing solution for `www.domain.com`

A request for `http://www.domain.com` is sent to the load balancer because `www.domain.com` resolves to the IP address of the load balancer. In other words, you must set up the DNS record to point `www.domain.com` to your load balancer system. The load balancer then decides which of the `www[1-N].domain.com` Web servers will respond to the request.

Looking at Figure 23-2, you may notice that there is a second load-balancer connection to the internal Web network switch, as well as a direct connection between the primary load balancer (on the left) and the secondary load balancer (on the right). The direct connection is typically a crossover network cable or a RS232 serial connection. This connection is used between the hardware devices to maintain states. In other words, the secondary load balancer tracks each of the operations performed by the primary load balancer. If the primary load balancer becomes unavailable because of a hardware failure, the secondary load balancer starts responding to the same IP address as the primary and takes over the job. The crossover connection ensures that the secondary load balancer has access to the state of the network and is therefore able to restore current state of connections between the site and the clients.

Also note that if you use the NAT translation facility of your load-balancing hardware (if it is equipped with this feature), you do not need routable IP addresses for each of your Web servers.

Managing Web Storage

As a Web network developer you must have a clear and defined storage strategy. Proper management of storage is critical for Web networks. There are many technologies to consider, and many performance issues to address in creating solid storage architecture for your Web network. This section discusses some of the major storage technologies, as well as hands-on performance techniques, to boost your storage performance under a Linux platform.

RAID, SAN, or Storage Appliances

Redundant Array of Inexpensive (or Independent) Disks (RAID), Storage Area Network (SAN), or storage appliances are the most commonly used storage technologies. They all promise either to increase reliability or to increase reliability and performance. Choosing the right solution for your needs requires a better understanding these technologies, which are discussed in the following sections.

Hardware RAID

A hardware RAID solution typically uses SCSI drives with an internal RAID controller card. No matter which RAID (hardware or software) you use, you will have to pick a RAID level that is suitable for your needs. The most common RAID levels are 1 and 5. RAID 1 is purely drive mirroring. If you want to use drive -mirroring RAID 1 and want to have 100GB of total space, you need to invest in 200GB of drive space. Although RAID levels 2 through 4 are available, RAID 5 is almost always the best choice. If you use N devices with the smallest device being size S, the size of the entire array is (N-1)*S. This missing space is used for parity (redundancy) information. It is recommended that you use same size media to ensure that drive space is not wasted because the smallest disk among the N disk is used to calculate available disk space under RAID 5.

Storage Area Networking (SAN)

Storage Area Networking (SAN) is the new holy grail of storage solutions. Companies such as EMC, IBM, Compaq, and Storage Networks are the SAN providers. Typically, a SAN solution consists of dedicated storage devices that you place in a fiber channel network and the storage is made available to your Linux systems via dedicated switching hardware and fiber-channel interface cards. Generally speaking, SAN is for the enterprise world and not yet ready for small- to mid-range organizations.

However, if you colocate your Linux systems in a well known data center such as the centers provided by large ISPs such as Exodus and Globix, chances are that you will find SAN as a value-added service. This might be one way to not pay for the expensive SAN hardware, yet still have access to it. I know of storage networks that provide such services in major ISP locations. They also have fiber rings throughout the U.S., which means you can make your drives in New York appear in California with negligible latency.

Storage appliances

These days there is special-purpose hardware for everything, so storage appliances (which are dedicated storage systems) are not strangers to network/system administrators. Today, you can buy dedicated storage appliances that hook up to your 10 or 100 or 1000Mbits Ethernet and provide RAIDed storage services. These devices are usually remotely managed over the Web. They are fairly good for small- to mid-range organizations and often very easy to configure and manage.

Tuning your hard drives

No matter what type of storage solutions you choose for your Web network, you will have to deal with hard drives. Chances are you will use either Fiber Channel, SCSI, or IDE drives to implement your storage solutions. In fact, SCSI and IDE are the most common types of hard drives in today's computing world. SCSI drives and SCSI controllers are much more expensive than IDE drives because they provide greater performance and flexibility. IDE or the enhanced version of IDE called EIDE drives are more commonplace in the personal and drive I/O nonintensive computing. The difference between the SCSI and IDE world is that SCSI drive controllers handle most of the work of transferring data to and from the drives, whereas the CPU itself controls IDE drives. So, on a busy system SCSI drives don't add as much load on the CPU as IDE drives do. Also, SCSI drives have wider data transfer capabilities, whereas IDE drives are still connected to the system via 16-bit bus. If you need high performance, SCSI is the way to go. Buy brand-name SCSI adapters and ultrawide, 10K RPM or faster SCSI drives and you have done pretty much all you can do to improve your drive subsystem.

Tip Of course if you have the budget for it, you can use fiber channel drives or go for a SAN solution. The latter is typically used by enterprises with high data-storage demands. You can also go with hardware/software RAID solutions, which are discussed in this chapter.

Regardless of your decision to go with SCSI or IDE drives, you must consider using multiple drives if you are serious about performance. At minimum, you should use two drives—one drive for operating systems and software and the other drive for data. For Web servers, I generally recommend a minimum of three drives. The third drive is for the logs generated by the Web sites hosted on the machine. Keeping drive I/O spread over multiple devices ensures that wait time is minimized.

If you have a modern ultrawide SCSI drive set up for your Linux system, you are already ahead of the curve and should be getting good performance out of your drives.

Getting hdparam

To get better performance out of your modern EIDE drive, you must first determine how your drive currently performs before doing any tuning. So, you need a tool to measure the performance state of your drive's subsystem. The hdparam tool is just right for the job; you can download the source distribution for this tool from http://metalab.unc.edu/pub/Linux/system/hardware/. To compile and install the hdparam tool, follow these steps:

1. su to root.

2. Extract the source distribution in a suitable directory such as /usr/local/src. For example, I ran the tar xvzf hdparm-3.9.tar.gz command in /usr/local/src to extract the hdparam version 3.9 source distribution.

3. Change to the newly created subdirectory and run the make install command to compile and install the hdparam binary and the manual page. By default, the binary is installed in the /usr/local/sbin directory and it is called hdparam.

Because hdparam enables you to change the behavior of your IDE/EIDE drive subsystem, it can sometimes cause the system to hang because of improper use or misconfiguration. I highly recommend that you back up your data before using hdparam. Also, it is a very good idea to experiment with hdparam in single-user mode. You can reboot your system and force it to go to single-user mode by entering linux single at the lilo prompt during boot up.

Gauging your drive's performance

After you have installed the hdparam tool, you are ready to investigate the state of your drive subsystem performance. Assuming that your IDE or EIDE hard drive is /dev/hda, run the following command to see the state of your hard drive configuration:

```
hdparm /dev/hda
```

You should see output similar to the following:

```
/dev/hda:
multcount     =  0 (off)
I/O support   =  0 (default 16-bit)
unmaskirq     =  0 (off)
using_dma     =  0 (off)
keepsettings  =  0 (off)
nowerr        =  0 (off)
readonly      =  0 (off)
readahead     =  8 (on)
geometry      = 2494/255/63, sectors = 40079088, start = 0
```

As you can see, most everything in this default mode is turned off. You can change some of these defaults to possibly enhance your drive performance. Before proceeding further, however, you need more information from the hard drive. Run the following command:

```
hdparm -i /dev/hda
```

This command will return information similar to the following:

```
/dev/hda:

 Model=WDC WD205AA, FwRev=05.05B05, SerialNo=WD-WMA0W1516037
 Config={ HardSect NotMFM HdSw>15uSec SpinMotCtl Fixed DTR>5Mbs FmtGapReq }
 RawCHS=16383/16/63, TrkSize=57600, SectSize=600, ECCbytes=40
 BuffType=DualPortCache, BuffSize=2048kB, MaxMultSect=16, MultSect=16
 CurCHS=16383/16/63, CurSects=16514064, LBA=yes, LBAsects=40079088
 IORDY=on/off, tPIO={min:120,w/IORDY:120}, tDMA={min:120,rec:120}
 PIO modes: pio0 pio1 pio2 pio3 pio4
 DMA modes: mdma0 mdma1 *mdma2 udma0 udma1 udma2 udma3 udma4
```

The above command displays the drive identification information (if any) that was available the last time that you booted the system. You make use of some of this information later. The command reports the model, configuration, drive geometry (cylinders, heads, sectors), track size, sector size, buffer size, supported DMA mode, PIO mode, and so on. To test the drive subsystem, run the following command:

```
/usr/local/sbin/hdparm -Tt /dev/hda
```

You will see results similar to the following:

```
/dev/hda:
 Timing buffer-cache reads:   128 MB in  1.01 seconds = 126.73 MB/sec
 Timing buffered disk reads:   64 MB in 17.27 seconds = 3.71 MB/sec
```

Of course, your numbers will vary based on your drive and controller subsystem. However, this is the untuned state of your drive subsystem. The -T option tells hdparm to test the cache subsystem (that is, the memory, CPU, and buffer cache).

The -t option tells hdparam to report stats on the drive (/dev/hda) by reading data not in the cache. Run this command a few times and take an average of the MB/sec reported for your drive. This is roughly the performance state of your drive subsystem. In this example, the 3.71MB/sec is the read performance, which is quite low.

Improving your drive's performance

Now let's try to improve the performance of your drive. Go back to the hdparam -i /dev/hda command output (see the previous section if you've no idea what I'm referring to) and look for MaxMultSect value. In this example, it is 16. The hdparam /dev/hda command showed the multcount value as 0 (off). This means that multiple sector mode (that is, IDE block mode) is turned off.

The multiple-sector mode is a feature of most modern IDE hard drives. It enables the drive to transfer multiple drive sectors per I/O interrupt. By default, it is off. However, most modern drives can perform 2, 4, 8, or 16 sector transfers per I/O interrupt. So, if you set this mode to the maximum possible value for your drive, which is shown by the MaxMultiSect value, you should see a throughput increase of anywhere from 5 percent to 50 percent or more. Also, you will reduce the operating system overhead by 30 to 50 percent. In this example, the MaxMultiSect value is 16, so we can use the -m option of the hdparam tool to set this and to see whether performance increases. Run the following command:

```
/usr/local/sbin/hdparm -m16 /dev/hda
```

Now run the performance test using the hdparam -tT /dev/hda command to see the change. For the example system, the change is as follows:

```
/dev/hda:
 Timing buffer-cache reads:   128 MB in  1.01 seconds = 126.73 MB/sec
 Timing buffered disk reads:  64 MB in 16.53 seconds =  3.87 MB/sec
```

The performance of the drive has risen from 3.71 MB/sec to 3.87 MB/sec. Not much, but not bad. You are likely to see a change similar to this. Chances are you can do much better than that with your drive if your drive and controller are fairly new. You can probably achieve 20 to 30 MB/sec! Be forewarned, however: when poking around with hdparam you might damage your data, so always backup your data before playing with the more drive hardware-specific options discussed below.

If hdparam reported that the I/O support setting is 16-bit for your system, and you have a fairly new (one or two years old) drive subsystem, you should try 32-bit I/O support. You can set this by using the -c option for hdparam, which has three values:

0 — Enables default 16-bit I/O support.

1 — Enables 32-bit support.

3 — Enables 32-bit support with a special synchronization sequence required by many IDE/EIDE chipset. It is also the value that works well with most systems.

You set the options as follows:

```
/usr/local/sbin/hdparm -m16 -c3 /dev/hda
```

Notice that the -m16 option was used as well as the -c3 option to enable 32-bit I/O support. Running the program with the -t option shows the following results:

```
/dev/hda:
 Timing buffered disk reads:  64 MB in  8.96 seconds =  7.14 MB/sec
```

As you can see, the performance of the drive subsystem practically doubled! However, you should be able to improve performance even more. For example, if your drive supports direct memory access (DMA) you might be able to use the -d option, which enables DMA mode.

Typically, -d1 -X32 options or -d1 -X66 options are used together to take advantage of the DMA capabilities of your drive subsystem. The first set of options (-d1 -X32) enables the multiword DMA mode2 for the drive, and the next set of options (-d1 -X66) enables UltraDMA mode2 for drives that support the UltraDMA burst timing feature. These options can dramatically increase your drive's performance. I have seen 20 MB/sec transfer rates with these options on various new EIDE/ATA drives.

There is another option, -u1, which can be very useful for increasing overall system performance. This option enables the disk driver to unmask other interrupts during processing of a disk interrupt, which means that the operating system can attend to other interrupts such as the network I/O, serial I/O, and so on, while waiting for a disk-based data transfer to finish.

There are many more hdparam options that you can set and experiment with; however, be very cautious about most of the options because there is a good chance that you may corrupt data. Always back up data before playing with hdparam tool. Also, after you have found that a set of options works well, you should put the hdparam command with those options in the /etc/rc.d/rc.local script so that they are set every time you boot the system. For example, I added the following line to the /etc/rc.d/rc.local file in one of my newer Red Hat Linux systems:

```
hdparm -m16 -c3 -u1 -d1 -X66   /dev/hda
```

Now that your hard drive is tuned for better performance, let's look at how you can tune the file system that acts as the interface to your disks. Because Linux uses the ext2 file system, I will discuss tuning issues for that file system in the next section.

Tuning ext2 Filesystem

For years the ext2 file system has been the de facto file system for Linux. It is not the greatest file system in the world, but it works reasonably well. One of the ways you can improve the ext2 file system's performance is by changing the default block size from 1024 to a multiple of 1024 (usually less than 4096) for servers with mostly large files. Let's look at how you can change the block size.

Changing the block size of the ext2 file system

To find out what kind of files (in terms of size) you have on a particular ext2 partition do the following:

1. su to root and change to the top directory of the ext2 partition.

2. Run the following command, which is really a small script that uses the find and awk utilities. This command-line script displays all the files and their sizes, and finally provides a total and average size of the entire partition.

```
find . -type f -exec ls -l {} \; | \
awk 'BEGIN {tsize=0;fcnt=1;} \
{ printf("%03d File: %-060s size: %d bytes\n",fcnt++, $9,
$5); \
tsize += $5; } \
END { printf("Total size = %d\nAverage file size = %.02f\n",
\
tsize, tsize/fcnt); }'
```

3. After you know the average size of the file system you can determine whether you should change the block size. Say you find out your average file size is 8192, which is 2 × 4096. You can change the block size to be 4096.

4. Unfortunately, you cannot alter the block size of an existing ext2 filesystem without rebuilding it. So, you have to backup all your files from the filesystem and then rebuild it using the /sbin/mke2fs /dev/partition -b 4096 command. For example, if you have backed up the /dev/hda7 partition and want to change the block size to 4096, use the /sbin/mke2fs /dev/hda7 -b 4096 command.

Note   Changing the block size to a higher number than the default (1024) may yield significant performance in raw read speed as a result of a reduction in the number of seeks, as well as a potentially faster fsck session during boot, less file fragmentation, and the like. However, increasing the block size blindly (that is, without knowing the average file size) can result in wasted space. If the average file size is 2010 bytes on a system with 4096-byte blocks, each file will waste on average 2086 bytes (4096 – 2010)! So know your file size before messing with the block size.

Installing e2fsprogs to tune ext2 file system

To tune the ext2 file system, you need to install the e2fsprogs utility package as follows:

1. Download the e2fsprogs-version.src.rpm (replace version with the latest version number) source distribution from www.rpmfind.net. I downloaded the e2fsprogs-1.19-0.src.rpm package. You can also get the source from the e2fsprogs project site at http://e2fsprogs.sourceforge.net. su to root.

2. Run the `rpm -ivh e2fsprogs-version.src.rpm` command to extract the source into a `/usr/src/redhat/SOURCES/` directory. The source RPM drops a `e2fsprogs-version.tar.gz` file, which needs to be extracted with the `tar xvzf e2fsprogs-version.tar.gz` command. This creates a subdirectory called `e2fsprogs-version`.

3. Change to the new subdirectory `e2fsprogs-version`.

4. Run `mkdir build` to create a new subdirectory and then change to that subdirectory.

5. Run `../configure` script to configure the source tree. Then run the `make` utility to create the binaries. Then run `make check` to ensure that everything is built correctly. Finally, run the `make install` command to install the binaries.

After you have installed the e2fsprogs utilities you can start using them as discussed in the following section.

Using the tune2fs utility for file-system tuning

You can use the `tune2fs` utility to tune various aspects of a ext2 file system. However, you should never apply the ext2 utilities on a mounted ext2 and always back up your data whenever you are modifying anything belonging to a file system. In this section, I discuss how to use the `tune2fs` utility (which is part of the e2fsprogs package) to tune an unmounted ext2 file system called `/dev/hda7`. If you use one or more of the settings discussed below, don't forget to change the partition name (`/dev/hda7`) to the appropriate name. First, run the following command to determine what `tune2fs` shows as the current settings for the unmounted `/dev/hda7`:

```
/sbin/tune2fs -l /dev/hda7
```

The output should be something similar to the following:

```
tune2fs 1.19, 13-Jul-2000 for EXT2 FS 0.5b, 95/08/09
Filesystem volume name:   <none>
Last mounted on:          <not available>
Filesystem UUID:          5d06c65b-dd11-4df4-9230-a10f2da783f8
Filesystem magic number:  0xEF53
Filesystem revision #:    1 (dynamic)
Filesystem features:      filetype sparse_super
Filesystem state:         clean
Errors behavior:          Continue
Filesystem OS type:       Linux
Inode count:              1684480
Block count:              13470471
Reserved block count:     673523
Free blocks:              13225778
Free inodes:              1674469
First block:              1
Block size:               1024
Fragment size:            1024
```

```
Blocks per group:         8192
Fragments per group:      8192
Inodes per group:         1024
Inode blocks per group:   128
Last mount time:          Thu Feb 15 17:51:19 2001
Last write time:          Thu Feb 15 17:51:51 2001
Mount count:              1
Maximum mount count:      20
Last checked:             Thu Feb 15 17:50:23 2001
Check interval:           15552000 (6 months)
Next check after:         Tue Aug 14 18:50:23 2001
Reserved blocks uid:      0 (user root)
Reserved blocks gid:      0 (group root)
First inode:              11
Inode size:               128
```

The settings discussed in the following list are bolded above.

✦ The is `Errors behavior` setting dictates how the kernel behaves when errors are detected on the file system. There are three possible values for this setting: continue, remount-ro (read only), and panic. The default setting is to continue even if there is an error.

✦ The `Mount count` setting is the number of time you have mounted this file system.

✦ The `Maximum mount count` setting means that after the maximum number of read/write mode mounts (in this case, 20) the file system is subject to an fsck checking session during the next boot cycle.

✦ The `Last checked` setting shows the last date at which an fsck check was performed.

✦ The `Check interval` setting shows the time difference for two consecutive fsck sessions. The check interval is only used if the maximum read/write mount count is not reached during the interval. In other words, if you don't unmount the file system for 6 months, then even though the mount count will be only 2, the fsck check will be forced because the file system exceeded the check interval.

✦ The next fsck check date is shown in `Next check after` setting.

✦ The `Reserved blocks uid` and `Reserved blocks gid` settings show which user and group has ownership of the reserved portion of this file system. By default, the reserved portion is to be used by superuser (UID = 0, GID = 0).

On an unmounted file system such as /dev/hda7, you can change the maximum read/write mount count setting to be something more suitable for your needs by using the -c option with tune2fs. For example, /sbin/tune2fs -c 1 /dev/hda7 will force an fsck check on the file system every time you boot the system. You can also use the -i option to change the time-based fsck check enforcement schedule.

For example, the `/sbin/tune2fs --i7d /dev/hda7` command ensures that fsck checks are enforced if the file system is remounted in read/write mode after a week. Similarly, the `/sbin/tune2fs --i0 /dev/hda7` command disables the time-based fsck checks.

Checking and repairing your file system by using the e2fsck utility

If you have a corrupt ext2 file system, you can use the `e2fsck` utility to try to fix it. To check a partition by using `e2fsck`, you must unmount it first and then run the `/sbin/e2fsck /dev/device` command where `/dev/device` is your disk drive. For example, to force an fsck check on a device called `/dev/hda7`, use the `/sbin/e2fsck -f /dev/hda7` command. Such as check might display output as shown here:

```
e2fsck 1.19, 13-Jul-2000 for EXT2 FS 0.5b, 95/08/09
Pass 1: Checking inodes, blocks, and sizes
Pass 2: Checking directory structure
Pass 3: Checking directory connectivity
Pass 4: Checking reference counts
Pass 5: Checking group summary information
/dev/hda7: 12/1684256 files (0.0% non-contiguous), 52897/3367617 blocks
```

The `e2fsck` utility will ask you repair questions that you can avoid by using the `-p` option.

Increasing reliability with journaling file systems for Linux

The new buzz in the Linux filesystem arena is the journaling file system. A *journaling file system* is simply a transaction-based file system. Each file system activity that changes the file system is recorded in a transaction log. In the event of a crash, the file system can replay the necessary transactions to return to a stable state in a very short time. This is a technique that many widely used database engines, such as IBM DB2 and Oracle, use to ensure that the file system is always in a known and recoverable state.

The problem with the ext2 file system is that in the unfortunate event of a crash, the file system can be in such an unclean state that it might be corrupt beyond any meaningful recovery. The fsck program that is used to check and potentially repair the file system often cannot do much to fix such problems. With a journaling file system such a nightmare is a thing of the past! Because the transaction log records all the activities in the file system, a crash recovery is fast and data loss is minimal.

Note　A journaling file system does not log data in the log; it simply logs meta-data related to disk operations, so replaying the log only makes the file system consistent from the structural relationship and resource allocation point of view. So some small data loss is possible. Also, logging is subject to the media errors like all other activity. Thus, if the media is bad, journaling won't help much.

The journaling file system is new to Linux but has been available for other platforms. Although journaling file-system support is very new to Linux, it has received a lot attention from the industry that is interested in using Linux in the enterprise; thus, journaling file systems will mature in a fast track. I highly recommend that you start using this flavor of the journaling file system on an experimental level and become accustomed to its sins and fancies.

There are several flavors of experimental journaling file system available today. ReiserFS is discussed in this section because it is included with Linux kernel 2.4.1 (or above), but I would be remiss if I did not list the other major journaling file systems that are also available. They are

✦ **IBM's JFS open source for Linux.** JFS has been ported from AIX, IBM's own operating system platform, but it is still not quite ready for production use. You can find more information on JFS at `http://oss.software.ibm.com/developerworks/opensource/jfs`.

✦ **Red Hat's own ext3 file system ext2 +, which has journaling capabilities.** It is also not ready for prime time. You can download the alpha release of ext3 at `ftp://ftp.linux.org.uk/pub/linux/sct/fs/jfs/`.

✦ **ReiserFS, developed by Namesys, which is currently included in the Linux kernel source distribution.** It is more widely used than the other journaling file systems for Linux. So far, it appears to be leading the journaling file system arena for Linux. ReiserFS was developed by Hans Reiser, who secured development funding from commercial companies such as MP3, BigStorage.com, SuSe, and Ecila.com. These companies all need better, more flexible file systems yesterday, and can immediately channel early beta user experience back to the developers. You can find more information on ReiserFS at `www.namesys.com`.

Caution   As of this writing, the ReiserFS file system cannot be used with NFS without patches, which are not officially available for the kernel 2.4.1 or above yet.

✦ **XFS journaling file system, developed by Silicon Graphics, Inc. (SGI).** You can find more information on XFS at `http://oss.sgi.com/projects/xfs/`. XFS is a fast, solid 64-bit file system, which means that it can support large files (9 million terabytes) and even larger file systems (18 million terabytes).

Compiling and installing ReiserFS

Before you can use ReiserFS, you need to compile and install it. Follow these steps to compile and install ReiserFS (reiserfs) support in Linux kernel 2.4.1 or above:

1. Get the latest Linux kernel source from `www.kernel.org` and extract it in `/usr/src/linux-version` directory as root, where `version` is the current version of the kernel. The following steps assume that the latest kernel is 2.4.1.

2. Run `make menuconfig` from the `/usr/src/linux-2.4.1` directory.

3. Select the Code maturity level options submenu and, by using the spacebar, select the Prompt for development and/or incomplete code/drivers option. Exit the submenu.

4. Select the File systems submenu. By using the spacebar, select Reiserfs support to be included as a kernel module and exit the submenu.

> **Note** Don't choose the Have reiserfs do extra internal checking option under the ReiserFS support option. If you set this to yes, then reiserfs will perform extensive checks for internal consistency throughout its operation, which will make it very slow.

5. Ensure that all other kernel features that you use are also selected as usual.

6. Exit the main menu and save the kernel configuration.

7. Run the `make dep` command to as suggested by the menuconfig program.

8. Run `make bzImage` to create the new kernel. Then run `make modules` and `make modules_install` to install the new modules in the appropriate locations.

9. Change the directory to `arch/i386/boot`. If your hardware architecture is Intel, you have to replace `i386` and possibly need further instructions from a kernel how-to documentation to compile and install your flavor of the kernel. I assume that the majority of readers' systems are i386-based and continue.

10. Copy the `bzImage` to `/boot/vmlinuz-2.4.1` and edit the `/etc/lilo.conf` file to include a new configuration such as the following:

    ```
    image=/boot/vmlinuz-2.4.1
            label=linux2
            read-only
            root=/dev/hda1
    ```

11. Run the `/sbin/lilo` command to reconfigure `lilo` and then reboot your system. At the `lilo` prompt enter **linux2** and boot the new kernel. If you have any problem, you should be able to reboot to your standard Linux kernel, which should be default automatically. After you have booted the new kernel, you are now ready to use ReiserFS (reiserfs).

Mounting the ReiserFS file system

Because ReiserFS (reiserfs) is still in the "experimental" category, I highly recommend that you use it on a noncritical aspect of your system. Ideally, you want to dedicate an entire disk or one or more partitions for ReiserFS so that you can safely use it and see how you like it.

To use ReiserFS with a new partition called `/dev/hda7`, do the following:

1. As root ensure that the partition is set as Linux native (83) by using `fdisk` or another disk-partitioning tool.

2. Create a ReiserFS (reiserfs) file system on the new partition by using the `/sbin/mkreiserfs /dev/hda7` command.

3. Next create a mount point for the new file system. For example, I can create a mount point called `/jfs` by using the `mkdir /jfs` command.

4. Finally, mount the file system by using the `mount -t reiserfs /dev/hda7 /jfs` command. Now you can access it from `/jfs` mount point.

To see how a journaling file system stacks up against an ext2 file system, you can use the benchmark in the following section.

Benchmarking ReiserFS

This material assumes that you have created a brand-new ReiserFS file system on `/dev/hda7` and can mount it on `/jfs`.

 Caution

To do this benchmark, you must not store any data in this partition. So, back up everything you have in `/jfs` because you will erase everything on `/jfs` in this process.

To benchmark ReiserFS, follow these steps:

1. Create a shell script called `reiserfs_vs_ext2.bash` in the `/tmp` directory. This script is listed in Listing 23-1.

Listing 23-1: /tmp/reiserfs_vs_ext2.bash

```
#!/bin/bash
#
# This script is created based on the file_test script
# found in the homegrown benchmark found at http://www.namesys.com
#

if [ $# -lt 6 ]
then
        echo Usage: file_test dir_name device nfiles size1 size2 log_name
        exit
fi

TESTDIR=$1
DEVICE=$2
LOGFILE=$6

/bin/umount $TESTDIR
/sbin/mkreiserfs $DEVICE
mount -t reiserfs $DEVICE $TESTDIR


echo 1. reiserfs 4KB creating files ...
```

```
echo "reiserfs 4KB create" $3 "files of size: from " $4 "to" $5  > $LOGFILE
(time -p ./mkfile $TESTDIR $3 $4 $5)>> $LOGFILE 2>&1
echo done.
sync
df >> $LOGFILE

/bin/umount $TESTDIR
/sbin/mke2fs $DEVICE -b 4096
mount -t ext2 $DEVICE $TESTDIR

echo 2. ext2fs 4KB creating files ...
echo "ext2fs 4KB create" $3 "files of size: from " $4 "to" $5  >> $LOGFILE
(time -p ./mkfile $TESTDIR $3 $4 $5)>> $LOGFILE 2>&1
echo done.
sync
df >> $LOGFILE

/bin/umount $TESTDIR
```

2. Also, download a small C program called `mkfile.c`, developed by the ReiserFS team, to `/tmp`, from `www.namesys.com/filetest/mkfile.c`.

3. From the `/tmp` directory, compile `mkfile.c` by using the `gcc -o mkfile mkfile.c` command.

4. Change the permission of the `reiserfs_vs_ext2.bash` and `mkfile` programs by using the `chimed 755 reiserfs_vs_ext2.bash mkfile` command.

5. Run the following command from the `/tmp` directory as root:

   `./reiserfs_vs_ext2.bash  /jfs /dev/hda7 100000 1024 4096 log`

6. You will be asked to confirm that you want to lose all data in `/dev/hda7`. Because you have already emptied this partition for testing, say yes and continue. This test will create 100,000 files in a variety of sizes, ranging from 1K to 4K in both ReiserFS (reiserfs) and ext2 file systems by creating each of these two file systems in `/dev/hda7` in turn. The results will be recorded in the `/tmp/log` file. Here is a sample `/tmp/log` file:

```
reiserfs 4KB create 100000 files of size: from  1024 to 4096
real 338.68
user 2.83
sys 227.83
Filesystem            1k-blocks      Used Available Use%
Mounted on
/dev/hda1             1035660     135600    847452   14% /
/dev/hda5             4134868    2318896   1605928   60% /usr
/dev/hda7            13470048     332940  13137108    3% /jfs
ext2fs 4KB create 100000 files of size: from  1024 to 4096
real 3230.40
user 2.87
sys 3119.12
```

```
Filesystem              1k-blocks       Used Available Use%
Mounted on
/dev/hda1                1035660      135608    847444  14% /
/dev/hda5                4134868     2318896   1605928  60% /usr
/dev/hda7               13259032      401584  12183928   4% /jfs
```

Notice that to create 100K files of size 1K to 4K, ReiserFS (reiserfs) took 338.68 real-time seconds; ext2 took 3230.40 real-time seconds. So ReiserFS (reiserfs)'s performance is quite nice.

Sharing drive space with NFS server

Although you can share static content via a network file system (NFS), earlier I recommended using local copies of the static files instead. Files stored on a local drive will yield a much faster access time than any network storage solution unless you choose a high-end SAN solution.

I highly recommend that you put only files that need to be shared, that change frequently, or that must use the same data across all Web nodes on a NFS partition. For example, your Web applications can be shared over all nodes so that you have a single copy of all the software. However, more importantly the data that these applications create should be shared. For example, if you have a CGI script that writes disk-session data for a shopping cart, when the user makes the next request the load-balancing scheme that you use might direct the user to a different Web server on your network, which means that the session data has to be available to the other Web server or else the user will have to restart her shopping cart.

Create a single directory in which you keep all your must-share data. For example, create /www/cgi-data as your CGI script data directory on the NFS server. You can create subdirectories for each CGI application and configure each application to write to its own directory within /www/cgi-data. Then, mounting this directory via NFS will make it available to all Web servers in the network. The following sections show you how.

Setting up an NFS server

An NFS server needs to run a program called portmapper (also called portmap or rpc.portmap), which is usually started by an rc script. To check whether portmapper is already running, use the following command:

```
ps auxw | grep portmap
```

It turns out that under RedHat Linux, portmapper is automatically started by the /etc/rc.d/rc3.d/S40portmap script (that is, the /etc/rc.d/init.d/portmap.init script) so there is no need to manually start it.

The next step is to modify the /etc/exports file to tell the system what file systems or directories need to be exported to NFS clients. Because XC News only needs the

`/www/cgi-data` directory exported to the Web servers, the export file on the `ns.xcnews-lan.com` host looks like this:

```
/www/cgi-data  www1.xcnews-lan.com(rw) www2.xcnews-lan.com(rw)
```

This line tells the NFS server to allow both `www1.xnews-lan.com` and `www2.xcnews-lan.com` read and write access to the `/www/cgi-data` directory.

 Note The syntax for the exports file may not be the same for all brands of Unix.

The next programs that must run are mountd (rpc.mountd) and nfsd (rpc.nfsd). These two programs are also started automatically from rc scripts in `/etc/rc.d/rc3.d`. Whenever a change is made to the `/etc/exports` file, however, these two programs need to be told about this change. A script called `exportfs` can restart these two programs, as follows:

```
exportfs
```

If `exportfs` is missing on a system, then a script such as the following can be used instead:

```
#!/bin/sh
killall -HUP /usr/sbin/rpc.mountd
killall -HUP /usr/sbin/rpc.nfsd
echo re-exported file systems
```

This script uses the killall program found on most Linux systems; if it is not available, you can always run a `ps` command, find the PID for these processes, and manually perform a `kill -HUP` for each process. Now to make sure both mountd and nfsd are running properly, run a program called rpcinfo, as follows:

```
rpcinfo -p
```

The output looks like this:

```
program vers    proto    port
100000   2      tcp      111       rpcbind
100000   2      udp      111       rpcbind
100005   1      udp      635       mountd
100005   2      udp      635       mountd
100005   1      tcp      635       mountd
100005   2      tcp      635       mountd
100003   2      udp      2049      nfs
100003   2      tcp      2049      nfs
```

This shows that portmapper, mountd, and nfsd have announced their services and are working fine. Before setting up the client side of NFS on the Web servers, it is important to make sure security issues are addressed, as I discuss in the next section.

Server security issues

The portmapper, in combination with nfsd, can be fooled, making it possible to get to files on NFS servers without any privileges. Fortunately, the portmapper Linux uses is relatively secure against attack, and can be made more secure by adding the following line in the /etc/hosts.deny file:

```
portmap: ALL
```

The system will deny portmapper access for everyone. Now the /etc/hosts.allow file needs to be modified as follows:

```
portmap: 192.168.1.0/255.255.255.0
```

This enables all hosts from the 192.168.1.0 network to have access to portmapper-administered programs such as nfsd and mountd.

Caution   Never use host names in the portmap line in /etc/hosts.allow because use of host name lookups can indirectly cause portmap activity, which will trigger host name lookups in a loop.

Another security issue on the server side is whether to allow the root account on a client to be treated as root on the server. By default, Linux prohibits root on the client side of the NFS to be treated as root on the server side. In other words, an exported file owned by root on the server cannot be modified by the client root user. To explicitly enforce this rule, the /etc/exports file can be modified as follows:

```
/www/cgi-data    www1.xcnews-lan.com(rw, root_squash) www2.xcnews-lan.com(rw,
root_squash)
```

Now, if a user with UID 0 (the root user) on the client attempts to access (read, write, or delete) the file system, the server substitutes the UID of the server's "nobody" account. This means that the client root user can't access or change files that only the server root can access or change.

Tip   To grant root access to an NFS file system, use the no_root_squash option instead.

At this point the NFS server is set up and secure, so now let's set up the NFS client hosts.

Setting up an NFS client

By default, Red Hat Linux supports NFS file systems, so there is no need to mess around with the kernel. To mount the /www/cgi-data directory exported by the ns.xnews-lan.com host, add the following line to the /etc/fstab file for both of the Web servers:

```
ns.xcnews-lan.com:/www/cgi-data         /www/cgi-data       nfs
```

This line automatically mounts the `/www/cgi-data` directory when any of the Web servers is rebooted.

Next, create the `/www/cgi-bin` directory on both systems and manually mount the directory using the mount command, as follows:

```
ns.xcnews-lan.com:/www/cgi-data          /www/cgi-data       nfs
```

 Caution One typical NFS mounting problem occurs because many developers forget to run exportfs (that is, `restart rpc.mountd` and `rpc.nfsd`) after they modify the `/etc/exports` file on the NFS server.

Unmounting an NFS file system is exactly the same as unmounting the local file system. Note that it is also possible to enhance NFS client security by not trusting the NFS server too much. For example, you can disable suid programs to work off the NFS file system with a `nosuid` option. This means that the server's root user cannot make a suid-root program on the file system, log in to the client as a normal user, and then use the suid-root program to become the root on the client, too. It is also possible to forbid execution of files on the mounted file system altogether with the `noexec` option. You can enter these options in the options column of the line that describes your NFS mount point in the `/etc/fstab` file.

At this point, the file distribution scheme and the NFS-based CGI data directory are both ready. It is time to configure Apache and to make sure it is secured.

The primary bottleneck in a NFS environment is the disk I/O speed of the NFS server. The disk I/O speed is dependent on what kind of disk subsystem you use with your NFS server. For example, running a NFS server using IDE disks will not yield great performance versus running a server with ultrawide SCSI drives that have high RPM rates. The maximum number of I/O operations per second will dictate how well your NFS server performs. I have used an Intel Xeon 500 system with 10 ultrawide SCSI disks in RAID 5 as a NFS server for approximately 50 users with great success.

After you have decided on a good disk subsystem such as a RAID 5 using an array of 10K RPM ultrawide SCSI disks with a disk controller that has a large built-in disk cache, your next hardware bottleneck is the network itself. Isolating high-bandwidth traffic into its own network is a good way to reduce performance loss. So, I recommend that you connect your NFS server(s) to your NFS clients by using a dedicated 100Mbits Ethernet of it's own. In other words, create a NFS backbone that only moves NFS packets. This will result in a high-performance NFS network.

The software configuration options that can help you to tune your NFS server are addressed in the following sections.

Optimizing read/write block size

The default read and write block size for NFS is 4096 bytes (4K), which might not be optimal for all situations. You can perform a test to determine whether changing the block size will improve performance. Here is how you perform such a test.

This test assumes that you have a NFS server running on a Linux system and also have a Linux-based NFS client system. The test also assumes that the client mounts a file system called /mnt/nfs1 from the NFS server.

1. su to root on the NFS client machine.

2. First, you need to know the total amount of memory your system has. You should know the default because it is your system, but if you don't remember too well, you can run the cat /proc/meminfo command to view the memory information for your system. This produces a display similar to what is shown here:

```
        total:     used:     free:  shared: buffers:  cached:
Mem:  263720960 260456448  3264512 30531584 228245504
6463488
Swap: 271392768  6209536 265183232
MemTotal:    257540 kB
MemFree:       3188 kB
MemShared:    29816 kB
Buffers:     222896 kB
Cached:        6312 kB
BigTotal:         0 kB
BigFree:          0 kB
SwapTotal:   265032 kB
SwapFree:    258968 kB
```

3. The total amount of system memory is shown under the column heading total:; divide this number by 1,048,576 (1024×1024) to get the total (approximate) memory size in megabytes. In the above example, this number is 251MB. Interestingly, total memory is never reported accurately by most PC system BIOSs, thus you have to round-off the number based on what you know about the total memory. In my example, I know that the system should have 256MB of RAM, thus I will use 256MB as the memory size in this test.

4. Now change directory to a currently mounted /mnt/nfs1 NFS file directory. Run the du command to check whether you have at least 512MB (2 × total RAM) of free space available on the NFS directory. If you don't, you cannot continue with this experiment.

5. The next task is to measure the write performance of your current NFS setup by writing a 512MB (16K/block × 32,768 blocks) file called 512MB.dat in the /mnt/nfs1 directory by using the following command:

```
time dd if=/dev/zero \
       of=/mnt/nfs1/512MB.dat \
       bs=16k count=32768
```

This command runs the time command, which records execution time of program named as the first argument. In this case, the dd command is being timed. The dd command is given an input file (using if option) called /dev/zero. This file is a special device that returns a 0 (zero) character when read. In other words, if you open this file for reading, it will keep returning a 0 character until you close the file. This gives us a easy source to fill out an output file (specified using the `of` option) called `/mnt/nfs1/512MB.dat`; the dd command is told to use a block size (specified using `bs` option) of 16K and write a total of 32,768 blocks (specified using the `count` option). Because 16K/block times 32,768 blocks equals 512MB, you will create the intended file. After this command is executed, it will print a few lines such as the following:

```
32768+0 records in
32768+0 records out
1.610u 71.800s 1:58.91 61.7% 0+0k 0+0io 202pf+0w
```

Here the dd command has read 32,768 records from the `/dev/zero` device and also wrote back the same number of records to the `/mnt/nfs1/512MB.dat` file. The third line states that the copy operation took 1 minute 58.91 seconds. Write this line in a text file as follows:

```
Write, 1, 1.610u, 71.800s, 1:58.91, 61.7%
```

Here you are noting that this was the first (1) write experiment.

6. To measure the read performance of your current NFS setup, you can simply read the 512MB file you created in step 5 and see how long it takes to read it back. To read it back and to time the read access, run the following command:

```
time dd if=/mnt/nfs1/512MB.dat \
        of=/dev/null \
        bs=16k count=32768
```

Here the dd command is timed again to read the `/mnt/nfs1/512MB.dat` file as input and output the file contents to `/dev/null`, which is the official bottomless bit bucket for Linux. As before, you should record the time used in the same file you wrote down the read performance record. For example, the read test using the above command displayed the following output on my system.

Record the third line as follows:

```
Read, 1, 1.970u, 38.970s, 2:10.44, 31.3%
```

Here you are noting that this was the first (1) read experiment.

7. Now remove the `512MB.dat` file from `/mnt/nfs1` and unmount the partition by using the `umount /mnt/nfs1` command. The unmounting of the NFS directory ensures that disk caching does not influence your next set of tests.

8. Repeat the write and read back test (steps 5 to 7) at least five times. You should have a set of notes as follows:

```
Read, 1, 1.971u, 38.970s, 2:10.44, 31.3%
Read, 2, 1.973u, 38.970s, 2:10.49, 31.3%
Read, 3, 1.978u, 38.971s, 2:10.49, 31.3%
Read, 4, 1.978u, 38.971s, 2:10.49, 31.3%
Read, 5, 1.978u, 38.971s, 2:10.49, 31.3%

Write, 1, 1.610u, 71.800s, 1:58.91, 61.7%
```

```
Write, 2, 1.610u, 71.801s, 1:58.92, 61.7%
Write, 3, 1.610u, 71.801s, 1:58.92, 61.7%
Write, 4, 1.610u, 71.801s, 1:58.92, 61.7%
Write, 5, 1.611u, 71.809s, 1:58.92, 61.7%
```

9. Now calculate the average read and write time from the fifth column (shown in bold).

The first phase of this test is now complete. You discovered the average read and write access time for a 512MB file. For the second phase of the test, follow these steps:

1. Unmount the /mnt/nfs1 directory on the NFS client system using umount /mnt/nfs1 command.

2. Modify the /etc/fstab file on the NFS client system such that the /mnt/nfs1 file system is mounted with the rsize=8192, wsize=8192 options as shown below.

   ```
   nfs-server-host:/nfs1 /mnt/nfs1 nfs \
   rsize=8192, wsize=8192 0 0
   ```

3. Remount the /mnt/nfs1 directory by using the mount /mnt/nfs1 command.

4. Perform steps 4 to 9 of the first phase of the experiment.

5. Compare the read and write access averages of phase 1 and phase 2 of the test. If the results in phase 2 (this part) of the test look better, then changing of the read and write blocks increased your NFS performance. If not, remove the rsize=8192, wsize=8192 options from the line in /etc/fstab. Most likely the read and write block size change will increase NFS performance. You can also experiment with other block sizes. It is advisable that you use multiples of 1024 for block size because 1024 is the actual file system block size. Also, do not use numbers larger than 8192 bytes. If the block size change works for you, keep the rsize=8192, wsize=8192 (or whatever you find optimal via further experimentation) in the /etc/fstab line for the /mnt/nfs1 definition.

Setting the appropriate Maximum Transmission Unit

The Maximum Transmission Unit (MTU) value determines how large a single packet transmission can be. If the MTU is set too small, NFS performance suffers greatly. To discover the appropriate MTU setting, do the following:

1. su to root on the NFS client system.

2. Run the tracepath *nfsserver*/2049 command where *nfsserver* is your NFS server's hostname. The command will report the MTU for the path.

3. Check out the current MTU for the network interface that is used to access the NFS server. You can simply run the ifconfig command to list information about all your up and running network interfaces.

4. If you see that your MTU setting for the appropriate network interface is not the same as the one reported by the `tracepath` command, use `ifconfig` with the `mtu` option to set it. For example, the `ifconfig eth0 mtu 512` command sets the MTU for network interface eth0 to 512 bytes.

Running the optimal number of NFS daemons

By default, you run eight NFS daemons. If you want to see how heavily each nfsd thread is being used, run the `cat /proc/net/rpc/nfsd` command. The last ten numbers on the `th` line in that file indicate the number of seconds that the nfsd thread usage was at that percentage of the maximum allowable. If you have a large number in the top three deciles, you may wish to increase the number of nfsd instances. To change the number of NFS daemons started when your server boots up, do the following:

1. As root, stop nfsd by using the `/etc/rc.d/init.d/nfs stop` command if you are currently running it.

2. Modify the `/etc/rc.d/init.d/nfs` script so that `RPCNFSDCOUNT=8` is set to an appropriate number of NFS daemons.

3. Restart nfsd by using the `/etc/rc.d/init.d/nfs start` command.

Controlling socket input queue size

By default, Linux uses a socket input queue of 65535 bytes (64KB). If you run 8 NFS daemons (nfsd) on your system, each daemon gets 8K buffer to store data in the input queue. You should increase the queue size to at least 256KB as follows:

1. As root, stop nfsd by using the `/etc/rc.d/init.d/nfs stop` command if you are currently running it.

2. Modify the `/etc/rc.d/init.d/nfs` script so that just before the NFS daemon (nfsd) is started with the `daemon rpc.nfsd $RPCNFSDCOUNT` line, the following lines are added:

```
echo 262144 > /proc/sys/net/core/rmem_default
echo 262144 > /proc/sys/net/core/rmem_max
```

3. Immediately after the `daemon rpc.nfsd $RPCNFSDCOUNT` line add these lines:

```
echo 65536 > /proc/sys/net/core/rmem_default
echo 65536 > /proc/sys/net/core/rmem_max
```

4. Restart NFS daemon by using the `/etc/rc.d/init.d/nfs start` command.

   Now each NFS daemon started by the `/etc/rc.d/init.d/nfs` script will use 32K buffer space in the socket input queue.

Monitoring packet fragments

The Linux kernel controls the number of unprocessed UDP packet fragments it can handle using a high-to-low range. When unprocessed UDP packet fragment size reaches the high mark (usually 262144 bytes or 256K), the kernel throws away the incoming packet fragments. In other words, when UDP packet fragments reach the high mark, packet loss starts. The loss of packet fragments continues until the total unprocessed fragment size reaches a low threshold (usually 196608 bytes or 192K).

Because NFS protocol uses fragmented UDP packets, the above high-to-low threshold used by Linux matters a great deal in NFS performance. You can view the current value of your high threshold size by running the `cat /proc/sys/net/ipv4/ipfrag_high_thresh` command. Similarly, you can view the low threshold value by running the `cat /proc/sys/net/ipv4/ipfrag_low_thresh` command. You can change the high values by running the `echo high-number > /proc/sys/net/ipv4/ipfrag_high_thresh`, and similarly, running the `echo low-number > /proc/sys/net/ipv4/ipfrag_low_thresh` changes the low number.

Replicating contents among Web servers

Typically, content is developed and placed on a single (master) server and then is distributed to all the other Web servers that participate in the Web network. In this section I discuss a tool called `rdist`, which allows you to distribute contents from one Linux system to others.

Using rdist to distribute files

The rdist program enables you to maintain identical copies of files over multiple hosts. It uses either the rcmd function calls or the remote shell (rsh) to access each of the target host computers.

The easiest way to get rdist working is to create a common account on all the machines involved and create `.rhosts` files for each target Web server system so that the common user on the name server host is allowed to run rsh sessions. For this purpose, create a user called `httpd` on all three systems involved. On each of the Web server systems, add a `.rhosts` file in the home directory of the `httpd` user. This file contains the host name of the rdist server in a single line.

The `.rhosts` file must be owned by the root user and be read-only for everyone else. This allows a user called `httpd` on the rdist server to run remote shell sessions on each Web server system. If you have created a back-end network as instructed in previous sections, you should use the rdist server's host name associated with the back-end network interface, which enables you to keep the rdist-generated file traffic in the back-end network; thus, the packets will not compete with your Web traffic. The next step is to create a distfile for rdist. A distfile is a text file that contains instructions for rdist on how to perform the file distribution task. Listing 23-2 shows one such distfile, `rdist_distfile`.

Listing 23-2: **rdist_distfile**

```
# Distfile for rdist
#
# This is used to distribute files from ns.domain.com
# to www[12].domain.com systems
#
# $Author$ (kabir@nitec.com)
# $Version$
# $Date$
# $Id$

# List all the hosts that need to be updated.
# The list is created using user@hostname entries where each
# entry is separated by a whitespace character.
#
HOSTS = (httpd@www1.domain.com httpd@www2.domain.com)

# List the directories that need to be updated.
#
FILES = (/www)

# list the directories that need to be excluded from
# the update process.
EXCLUDE_DIR = (/www/cgi-data/    /www/apache /www/secured)

# Here are the commands:
# Install all directories listed in FILES for all hosts
# listed in HOSTS except for the directories that are
# listed in EXCLUDE_DIR
#
${FILES} -> ${HOSTS}
  install ;
  except ${EXCLUDE_DIR};
```

This is really a very simple distfile. It defines a variable called HOSTS that has two entries as values: httpd@www1.domain.com and httpd@www2.domain.com. This tells rdist to use the httpd user account on both www1.domain.com and www2. domain.com for connection. The next variable, FILES, defines the files and directories for rdist to distribute. This script assumes that the staging server keeps all the files in the /www directory or partition. You can change this path or add multiple paths (separated by space).

The third variable is EXCLUDE_DIR. This variable is set to list all the files and directories that we want to exclude from getting distributed. The values that you see in the example are important. The first directory, /www/cgi-data/, is the CGI data directory to which all CGI scripts write their data. This directory will be exported to the Web server hosts via NFS, so it does not need to be copied onto each Web server via rdist. The /www/apache directory is where makesite writes the /www/apache/conf/httpd.conf file, which needs to be copied because each Web server has its very own Apache configuration file in the local /www/apache directory. The final value is /www/secured, which is used by the secured server as the document root and needs to be copied onto the Web servers. The rest of the file describes a simple command:

```
${FILES} -> ${HOSTS}
    install ;
    except ${EXCLUDE_DIR};
```

This command takes all the files and directories that the FILES variable points to and installs them on the hosts indicated by the HOSTS variable. It also tells rdist to exclude the files and directories specified by the EXCLUDE_DIR variable. To run rdist (as httpd), use the following command from the command line:

```
/usr/bin/rdist -p /usr/sbin/rdistd \
               -oremove,quiet \
               -f /usr/local/rdist/ rdist_distfile
```

The -p option specifies the location of the rdistd program needed by rdist; the -o option specifies that one or more options are to follow — in this case, remove and quiet. The remove option tells rdist to remove any extraneous files found in the target system in target directories. This provides an easy method for maintaining an identical copy of the staging area on each Web server. The quiet option tells rdist to be as quiet as possible during the operation. The final option, -f, specifies the location of the distfile.

To reduce human error in running this command, create an sh script called rdistribute.sh, as shown in Listing 23-3.

Listing 23-3: **rdistribute.sh script**

```
#!/bin/sh
#
# This script runs rdist to update Web servers via the
# non-routable lan domain.com. The script is run
# by cron at a fixed interval.
#
# /etc/rc.d/rc.local starts the script to clean up
# left-over tempfiles that might have been left
# at shutdown. This process also removes the
# log file.
#
# $Author$ (kabir@evoknow.com)
# $Version$
# $Id$
# $Date$
# $Status
```

```
##############################################################

RDIST=/usr/bin/rdist
RDISTD=/usr/sbin/rdistd
DIST_FILE=/usr/local/rdist/rdist_distfile
RDIST_OPTIONS=remove,nochkgroup,nochkmode,nochkowner,quiet
RDIST_LOCK_FILE=/tmp/rdist.lck
RDIST_LOG_FILE=/tmp/rdist.log
TOUCH_BIN=/bin/touch
DATE=`date`

# If the script is called with an argument, then
case "$1" in
  boot)
  # Because the argument is 'boot,' the script is being
  # called at system start-up, so remove all old lock
  # files and logs.
  echo -n "Cleaning up rdistribute.sh tmp files: "
    rm -f $RDIST_LOCK_FILE
      rm -f $RDIST_LOG_FILE
  echo "complete."
  exit 0;
  ;;

  # Because the argument is 'restart,' the script
  # needs to clean up as if the system just booted.
  restart)
  $0 boot
  ;;

esac

# If the lock file exists, then don't do anything.
if [ -f $RDIST_LOCK_FILE ]; then
   exit 0
fi

# Otherwise, create the lock file using touch
$TOUCH_BIN $RDIST_LOCK_FILE

# Run rdist
$RDIST -p $RDISTD -o$RDIST_OPTIONS -f $DIST_FILE

# Remote the lock file
rm -f $RDIST_LOCK_FILE

# Write the time and date in the log file
echo $DATE >> $RDIST_LOG_FILE

# Exit the script

  exit 0
```

This script is smart enough to detect in progress the `rdistribute.sh` process by using a lock file, which can tell when a previous `rdistribute.sh` is already in progress and continuing. This can happen when a large number of files are being updated over multiple servers. The script also accepts an argument called boot that can be used to clean up the lock file and the log file it creates during the boot process. The script should be called from `/etc/rc.d/rc.local` as follows:

```
/usr/local/rdistribute.sh boot
```

This script can be scheduled to run by a cron entry in `/etc/crontab`. For example, to run this script at 10-minute intervals, the following cron entry can be added in `/etc/crontab`:

```
0,10,20,30,40,50 * * * * httpd  /usr/local/rdistribute.sh > /dev/null
```

The cron daemon will run the script as `httpd`.

Creating a RAM-based file system

You can create a temporary, small file system in RAM for high-speed access. The reason this is a small file system is because, by default, the maximum amount of RAM that ramfs can use is one-half of the total RAM on your system. So, if you have 2GB of RAM, ramfs can only use 1GB. Because I haven't yet seen systems with more than 4GB of RAM, even 2GB ramfs is really small compared to today's large drive-based file systems. The ramfs is perfect for many small files that need to be accessed fast. For example, I use ramfs for a set of small images used in a heavily accessed Web site.

Enabling a RAM-based file system

To use ramfs, you must enable ramfs support in the kernel as follows:

1. Get the latest Linux kernel source from `www.kernel.org` and extract it into `/usr/src/linux-version` directory as root, where `version` is the current version of the kernel. For this material, I assume that this is 2.4.1.

2. Select the File systems submenu. By using the spacebar, select Simple RAM-based file system support to be included as a kernel module and exit the submenu.

3. Ensure that all other kernel features that you use are also selected as usual.

4. Exit the main menu and save the kernel configuration.

5. Run the `make dep` command to as suggested by the menuconfig program.

6. Now run `make bzImage` to create the new kernel. Then run `make modules` and `make modules_install` to install the new modules in appropriate location.

7. Change the directory to `arch/i386/boot`. If your hardware architecture is Intel, you have to replace `i386` and may also need further instructions from the kernel how-to documentation to compile and install your flavor of the kernel. I assume that the majority of readers' systems are i386-based and continue.

8. Copy `bzImage` to `/boot/vmlinuz-2.4.1` and edit the `/etc/lilo.conf` file to include a new configuration such as the following:

```
image=/boot/vmlinuz-2.4.1
        label=linux3
        read-only
        root=/dev/hda1
```

9. Run the `/sbin/lilo` command to reconfigure `lilo` and reboot your system. At the `lilo` prompt enter **linux3** and boot the new kernel. If you have any problem, you should be able to reboot to your standard Linux kernel, which should be the default.

10. After you have booted the new kernel, you are now ready to use ramfs. Create a directory called `ramdrive` by using the `mkdir /ramdrive` command.

11. Now mount the ramfs file system with the `mount -t ramfs none /ramdrive` command.

You are all set; you can now write files to `/ramdrive` as usual.

Caution

Be forewarned that when the system is rebooted, or when you unmount the file system, all contents will be lost. This is why it should be a temporary space for high-speed access. Also, note that because ramfs is really not a block device, programs such as df and du cannot see it. You can verify that you are really using RAM by running the `cat /proc/mounts` command and finding an entry such as the following:

```
none /ram ramfs rw 0 0
```

Tip

You can specify options using `-o` option when mounting the file system, just like mounting a regular drive-based file system. For example, to mount the ramfs file system as read-only, you can use the `-o ro` option. You can also specify special options, such as `maxsize=n` where *n* is number of kilobytes to allocate for the file system in RAM; `maxfiles=n` where *n* is the number of all files allowed in the file system; and `maxinodes=n` where *n* is the maximum number of inodes (default is 0 = no limits).

Making use of the RAM-based file system

If you run a Web server, you will have many uses for a RAM-based file system. Elements such as common images and files on your Web site that are not too big (no more than a few KB) can be kept in the ramfs file system. You can write a simple shell script to copy the contents from their original location on each reboot. Listing 23-4 is a simple script that does that.

Listing 23-4: **make_ramfs.sh**

```
#!/bin/sh
#
# Simply script to create a ramfs file system
# on $MOUNTPOINT (which must exists).
#
# It copies files from $ORIG_DIR to $MOUNTPOINT
# and changes ownership of $MOUTPOINT to
# $USER and $GROUP
#
# Change values for these variables to suit
# your needs.

MOUNTPOINT=/ram
ORIG_DIR=/www/commonfiles

USER=httpd
GROUP=httpd

MOUNTCMD=/bin/mount
CHOWN=/bin/chown
CP=/bin/cp

echo -n "Creating ramfs file system in $MOUNTPOINT ";
$MOUNTCMD -t ramfs none $MOUNTPOINT
echo "done.";

echo -n "Copying $ORIG_DIR to $MOUNTPOINT ... ";
$CP -r $ORIG_DIR $MOUNTPOINT
echo "done.";
echo -n "Changing ownership to $USER:$GROUP for $MOUNTPOINT ...";
$CHOWN -R $USER:$GROUP $MOUNTPOINT
echo "done.";
```

To use this script on your system, do the following:

1. Create make_ramfs.sh in your /usr/local/scripts directory. Create the /usr/local/scripts directory if you don't have one.

2. Edit /etc/rc.d/rc.local file and append the following line to it:

   /usr/local/scripts/make_ramfs.sh

3. Create a directory called ram by using the mkdir /ram command. If you keep the files you want to load in RAM in any location other than /www/commonfiles, then modify the value for the ORIG_DIR variable in the script. For example, if your files are in the /www/mydomain/htdocs/common directory, then set this variable to point to this directory.

4. If you run your Web server by using a username or group other than `httpd`, then change the `USER` and `GROUP` variable values accordingly. For example, if you run Apache as `nobody` (user and group), then set `USER=nobody` and `GROUP=nobody`.

5. If you are using Apache Web server, create an alias in your `httpd.conf` file such as the following:

```
Alias /commonfiles/  "/ram/commonfiles/"
```

Whenever Apache Web server needs to access `/commonfiles/*`, it will now use the version in the RAM, which should be substantially faster than the files stored in the original location. Remember that the RAM-based version will disappear whenever you reboot or unmount the file system. So never update anything there unless you also copy the contents back to a drive-based directory.

Caution
If you mounted a ramfs file system by using a command such as `mount -t ramfs none /ram` and copied contents to it and later reran the same mount command, the rerunning of the same command wipes out the contents and remounts the ramfs. The `/proc/mounts` file shows multiple entries for the same mount point, which causes a problem when unmounting the device. If you must regain the memory for another use, you have to reboot. It is hoped that this will be fixed soon.

Creating a Reliable Back-end Network

A typical Web network consists of a set of Web servers, proxy servers, application servers, databases servers, and the like. In most cases, only the Web servers and proxy servers (if any) need to be in the front-end of the Web network. Figure 23-3 shows an example Web network with a front-end and back-end network.

Each Web server node has two network interfaces. One interface is connected to the front-end network 207.183.233.0/24 and the other one is connected to the back-end network 192.168.1.0/24. The front-end network consists of the Web servers and the load-balancing hardware; the back-end network consists of the Web servers, application servers, and the database servers.

When a request comes to the active (primary) load balancer, the following chain of actions are performed:

✦ The load balancer determines the best Web server to service the request and passes the request to appropriate Web server.

✦ The Web server decides whether the request requires any additional resources. For example, if the request is to run an application on the application server, the Web server selects the appropriate application server and/or database server and perform the tasks necessary to complete the request.

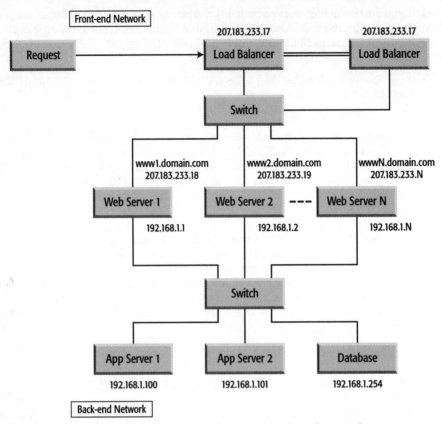

Figure 23-3: A Web network with both front- and back-end network

When a request comes to the active (primary) load balancer, the following chain of actions is performed:

✦ The load balancer determines the best Web server to service the request and passes the request to appropriate Web server.

✦ The Web server decides whether the request requires any additional resources. For example, if the request is to run an application on the application server, the Web server selects the appropriate application server and/or database server and perform the tasks necessary to complete the request.

The application server(s) and database server(s) do not need to be accessible directly via the Web because only the Web servers in the front-end network contact them. This ensures good security and therefore it is a good idea to use a non-routable 192.168.x.x network address for all back-end networks attached to a Web network.

However, a large Web network requires that the application servers and the database servers be load balanced as well, otherwise the application or database usage becomes a major bottleneck for very busy sites. Figure 23-4 shows a highly balanced Web network that uses load-balancing hardware for both front-end and back-end networks.

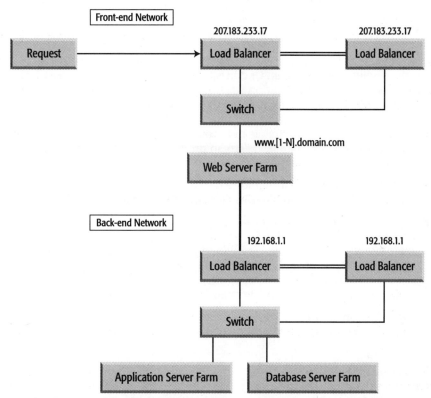

Figure 23-4: A Web network with both front-end and back-end load balancers

Fortifying Your Web Network

Hackers find Web networks or any cluster of nodes that comprise an Internet service to be ideal candidates for attacks. This is because if they can break into a network of computers, the network can be used as a launching pad for attacks on other systems. Basically, a poorly secured, yet well-connected (high bandwidth) Web network provides hackers with a great resource for attacking others. This can result in serious problems for Web network administrators. Therefore, it is critical that you perform all the preventive measures that you can to reduce the risk of being attacked. See Chapter 18 for details on how to secure your Web server. This section provides additional security-related information that is suitable for Web networks, as well as for a single-server system.

Using Tripwire to protect your Web contents

In a great move toward open-source software, Tripwire released Tripwire Open Source, Linux Edition, under the General Public License (GPL). Simply speaking, Tripwire is a file and directory integrity checker that creates a database of signatures for all files and directories and stores them in a single file. When Tripwire is run again, it computes new signatures for current files and directories and compares them with the original signatures stored in the database. If there is a discrepancy, the file or directory name is reported along with information about the discrepancy.

Now you can see why Tripwire can be a great tool for helping you determine which files were modified in a break-in. Of course, for that you have to ensure the security of the database that the application uses. When setting up a new server system, many experienced system administrators do the following in the given order:

1. Ensure that the new system is not attached to any network to guarantee that no one has already installed a Trojan program, virus program, or other danger to their system's security.

2. Run Tripwire to create a signature database of all the important system files, including all the system binaries and configuration files.

3. Write the database to a recordable CD-ROM. This ensures that an advanced bad guy cannot modify the Tripwire database to hide Trojans and to prevent the program from identifying modified files. Administrators who have a small number of files to monitor often use a floppy disk to store the database. After writing the database to the floppy disk, the disk is write-protected and, if the BIOS permits, the hard drive is configured as a read-only device.

4. Set up a cron job to run Tripwire on a periodic basis (daily, weekly, monthly) such that the application uses the CD-ROM version of the database.

Getting Tripwire

Red Hat Linux comes with the binary Tripwire RPM file. However, you can always download the free (LGPL) version of Tripwire from a RPM mirror site such as the `http://fr.rpmfind.net`. I downloaded the Tripwire source code and binaries from this site by using `http://fr.rpmfind.net/linux/rpm2html/search.php?query=Tripwire`. The source RPM that I downloaded was missing some installation scripts so I downloaded the source again from the Tripwire Open Source development site at `http://sourceforge.net/projects/tripwire/` site. The source code I downloaded was called `tripwire-2.3.0-src.tar.gz`. You might find a later version there by the time you read this.

Compiling Tripwire

This section shows you how to compile, configure, and install Tripwire from the `tripwire-2.3.0-src.tar.gz` file. When following these steps, be sure to replace the version number with the version of Tripwire you downloaded.

Note If you wish to install Tripwire from the binary RPM package, simply run the `rpm -ivh tripwire-version.rpm` command from the directory where the Tripwire RPM is located. You still need to configure Tripwire by running `twinstall.sh`. Run this script from the `/etc/tripwire` directory and skip to step 7 in the following section.

To compile from the source distribution, do the following:

1. As root, extract the tar ball using the `tar xvzf tripwire-2.3.0-src.tar.gz` command. This will create a subdirectory called `/usr/src/redhat/SOURCES/tripwire-2.3.0-src`. Change your current directory to the `/usr/src/redhat/SOURCES/tripwire-2.3.0-src/src` directory.

2. Run the `make release` command to compile all the necessary Tripwire binaries. This takes a little bit of time, so do it just before a coffee break. After Tripwire is compiled, you need to install the binaries. Change your directory to `/usr/src/redhat/SOURCES/tripwire-2.3.0-src/install`. Copy the `install.cfg` and `install.sh` files to the parent directory with the `cp install.* ..` command.

3. Before running the installation script, you might need to edit the `install.cfg` file, which is shown in Listing 23-5. For example if you are not a vi editor fan and camp in the emacs world, you need to change the `TWEDITOR` field in this file to point to emacs instead of to `/usr/bin/vi`. I do not recommend changing the values for the `CLOBBER`, `TWBIN`, `TWPOLICY`, `TWMAN`, `TWDB`, `TWDOCS`, `TWSITEKEYDIR`, or `TWLOCALKEYDIR` settings. However, you might want to change the values for the `TWLATEPROMPTING`, `TWLOOSEDIRCHK`, `TWMAILNOVIOLATIONS`, `TWEMAILREPORTLEVEL`, `TWREPORTLEVEL`, `TWSYSLOG`, `TWMAILMETHOD`, and `TWMAILPROGRAM`.

Listing 23-5: install.cfg

```
#
# install.cfg
#
# default install.cfg for:
# Tripwire(R) 2.3 Open Source for Linux
#
# NOTE:   This is a Bourne shell script that stores installation
#         parameters for your installation. The installer will
#         execute this file to generate your config file and also to
#         locate any special configuration needs for your install.
#         Protect this file, because it is possible for
#         malicious code to be inserted here.
#
# This version of Tripwire has been modified to conform to the FHS
# standard for Unix-like operating systems.
```

Continued

Listing 23-5 *(continued)*

```
#
# To change the install directory for any tripwire files, modify
# the paths below as necessary.
#
#=========================================================

# If CLOBBER is true, then existing files are overwritten.
# If CLOBBER is false, existing files are not overwritten.
CLOBBER=false

# Tripwire binaries are stored in TWBIN.
TWBIN="/usr/sbin"

# Tripwire policy files are stored in TWPOLICY.
TWPOLICY="/etc/tripwire"

# Tripwire manual pages are stored in TWMAN.
TWMAN="/usr/man"

# Tripwire database files are stored in TWDB.
TWDB="/var/lib/tripwire"

# Tripwire documents directory
TWDOCS="/usr/doc/tripwire"

# The Tripwire site key files are stored in TWSITEKEYDIR.
TWSITEKEYDIR="${TWPOLICY}"

# The Tripwire local key files are stored in TWLOCALKEYDIR.
TWLOCALKEYDIR="${TWPOLICY}"

# Tripwire report files are stored in TWREPORT.
TWREPORT="${TWDB}/report"

# This sets the default text editor for Tripwire.
TWEDITOR="/bin/vi"

# TWLATEPROMTING controls the point when tripwire asks for a password.
TWLATEPROMPTING=false

# TWLOOSEDIRCHK selects whether the directory should be monitored for
# properties that change when files in the directory are monitored.
TWLOOSEDIRCHK=false

# TWMAILNOVIOLATIONS determines whether Tripwire sends a no violation
# report when integrity check is run with --email-report but no rule
# violations are found.  This lets the admin know that the integrity
# was run, as opposed to having failed for some reason.
TWMAILNOVIOLATIONS=true

# TWEMAILREPORTLEVEL determines the verbosity of e-mail reports.
```

```
TWEMAILREPORTLEVEL=3

# TWREPORTLEVEL determines the verbosity of report printouts.
TWREPORTLEVEL=3

# TWSYSLOG determines whether Tripwire will log events to the system log
TWSYSLOG=false

####################################
# Mail Options - Choose the appropriate
# method and comment the other section
####################################

####################################
# SENDMAIL options - DEFAULT
#
# Either SENDMAIL or SMTP can be used to send reports via TWMAILMETHOD.
# Specifies which sendmail program to use.
####################################

TWMAILMETHOD=SENDMAIL
TWMAILPROGRAM="/usr/lib/sendmail -oi -t"

####################################
# SMTP options
#
# TWSMTPHOST selects the SMTP host to be used to send reports.
# SMTPPORT selects the SMTP port for the SMTP mail program to use.
####################################

# TWMAILMETHOD=SMTP
# TWSMTPHOST="mail.domain.com"
# TWSMTPPORT=25

###############################################################################
# Copyright (C) 1998-2000 Tripwire (R) Security Systems, Inc. Tripwire (R) is a
# registered trademark of the Purdue Research Foundation and is licensed
# exclusively to Tripwire (R) Security Systems, Inc.
###############################################################################
```

4. Run the ./install.sh command. This command walks you through the installation process. You will be asked to press the Enter key to accept the GPL licensing agreement and to agree to the locations where files will copied.

5. After the files are copied, you will be asked to enter a site pass phrase. This pass phrase is used to encrypt the Tripwire configuration and policy files. Enter a strong pass phrase (that is, one that is not easily guessable and that is at least eight character long) to ensure that these files are not modified by any unknown party. Next, choose a local pass phrase. This pass phrase is used to encrypt the Tripwire database and report files. Again, choose a strong pass phrase here.

6. Enter the site pass pharse and the installer signs the configuration file using your pass pharse. A clear-text version of the Tripwire configuration file is created in /etc/tripwire/twcfg.txt. The encrypted, binary version of the configuration file, which is what Tripwire uses, will be stored in /etc/tripwire/tw.cfg. The clear-text version is created for your inspection. The installer recommends that you delete this file manually after you have examined it.

7. Enter the site pass phrase so that the installer can use it for signing the policy file. The installer creates a clear-text policy file in /etc/tripwire/twpol.txt and the encrypted version is kept in /etc/tripwire/tw.pol. You will learn to modify the text version of the policy file later and be able to create the binary, encrypted version, which is what Tripware uses.

That's all there is to getting the software installed.

Configuring Tripwire policy

The policy file defines rules that Tripwire uses to perform integrity checks. Each rule defines which files and directories to check and what type of checks should be performed. Additionally, each rule can include information such as name and severity. Syntax for a rule is as follows:

```
(attribute=value attribute=value ...)
{

  /path/to/a/file/or/directory      -> mask;

}
```

Table 23-1 shows the list of available attributes and their meanings.

<table>
<tr><th colspan="2">Table 23-1
List of Available Attributes</th></tr>
<tr><th>Attribute</th><th>Meaning</th></tr>
<tr><td>rulename=name</td><td>This attribute associates a name to the rule. It makes Tripwire reports more readable and easy to sort by named rules.</td></tr>
<tr><td>emailto=e-mailaddress</td><td>When a rule is violated, the e-mail address given as value for this attribute receives a violation report.</td></tr>
<tr><td>severity=number</td><td>This attribute allows you to associate a severity level, that is, level of importance, to a rule. This makes Tripwire reports easier to manage.</td></tr>
</table>

Attribute	Meaning
recurse=true | false	This attribute determines whether a directory is automatically recursed or not. If set to true (or –1), all subdirectories are recursed; on the other hand, if it is set to false (or 0), the subdirectories are not traversed. Any numeric value in the range of –1 to 1000000 (excluding –1 and 0) dictates the depth of subdirectories that are recursed. For example recurse=3 means that subdirectories up to level 3 depth are recursed.

This is an example rule:

```
(Rulename= "OS Utilities", severity=100)
{
  /bin/ls        -> +pinugtsdrbamcCMSH-l;
}
```

Here the rule being defined is called the "OS Utilities" rule; it has a severity rating of 100, which means that violation of this rule would be considered a major problem; the +pinugtsdrbamcCMSH-l properties of /bin/ls is checked. Table 23-2 shows the meaning of each of these property/mask characters.

Table 23-2
Property/Mask Characters Used in a Tripwire Policy File

Property or Mask	Description
a	Access timestamp of the file or directory
b	Number of blocks allocated to the file
c	Inode timestamp
d	ID of the disk where the inode resides
g	Owner's group
i	Inode number
l	File is increasing in size
m	Modification timestamp
n	Inode reference count or number of links
p	Permission bits of file or directory
r	ID of the device pointed by an inode belonging to a device file

Continued

Table 23-2 *(continued)*

Property or Mask	Description
s	Size of a file
t	Type of file
u	Owner's user ID
C	CRC-32 value
H	Haval value
M	MD5 value
S	SHA value
+	Record and check the property followed by this character
-	Ignore the property followed by this character

Another way to write the previous rule is

```
/bin/ls -> +pinugtsdrbamcCMSH-1 (Rulename= "OS Utilities", severity=100);
```

However, the first method is preferred because it allows you to group many files and directories under a single rule. For example,

```
SEC_CRIT   = +pinugtsdrbamcCMSH-1;

(Rulename= "OS Utilities", severity=100)
{
  /bin/ls            -> $(SEC_CRIT);
  /bin/login         -> $(SEC_CRIT);
  /bin/ls            -> $(SEC_CRIT);
  /bin/mail          -> $(SEC_CRIT);
  /bin/more          -> $(SEC_CRIT);
  /bin/mt            -> $(SEC_CRIT);
  /bin/mv            -> $(SEC_CRIT);
  /bin/netstat       -> $(SEC_CRIT);
}
```

Here all the listed utilities fall under the same policy. Note the use of the SEC_CRIT variable, which is defined before it is used in the rule. This variable is set to +pinugtsdrbamcCMSH-1 and substituted in the rule statements using $(SEC_CRIT). This enables you to define a single variable with a set of properties that can be applied to a large group of files and/or directories. When you want to add or remove properties, you simply change the mask value of the variable; the change is reflected everywhere the variable is used. There are some built-in variables that are shown in Table 23-3.

Table 23-3
Built-in Variables for the Tripwire Policy File

Variable	Meaning
ReadOnly	+pinugtsdbmCM-rlacSH. **Good for files that should remain read-only.**
Dynamic	+pinugtd-srlbamcCMSH. **Good for user directories and files which are dynamic in terms of changes.**
Growing	+pinugtdl-srbamcCMSH. **Good for files that grow in size.**
Device	+pugsdr-intlbamcCMSH. **Good for device files.**
IgnoreAll	-pinugtsdrlbamcCMSH. **Checks whether the file exists but does not check anything else.**
IgnoreNone	+pinugtsdrbamcCMSH-l. **Opposite of** IgnoreAll. **Checks all properties.**

When creating a rule, you must consider the following:

✦ Do not create multiple rules that apply to the same file or directory. For example:

```
/usr                  -> $(ReadOnly);
/usr                  -> $(Growing);
```

Tripwire will complain about the above policy.

✦ The most specific rule will be honored. For example:

```
/usr                  -> $(ReadOnly);
/usr/local/home       -> $(Dynamic);
```

When checking a file /usr/local/home/filename, the properties substituted by the variable $(Dynamic) are checked.

If you create or modify rules, you need to run the /usr/sbin/twadmin --create-polfile /etc/twpol.txt command to generate the encrypted /etc/tripwire/tw.pol policy file. You will be asked to enter the site pass phrase needed to sign (that is, encrypt) the policy file.

Creating the Tripwire database

Before you initialize the Tripwire database file, be absolutely certain that hackers have not already modified the files on your current system. This is why the best time to create this database is when your system has not yet been connected to the Internet or to any other network. After you are certain that your files are untouched, run the following command:

```
/usr/sbin/tripwire --init
```

This command applies the policies listed in the /etc/tripwire/tw.pol file and creates a database in var/lib/tripwire/k2.intevo.com.

After you have created the database, move it to a read-only medium such as a CD-ROM or a floppy disk that is write-protected after copying, if possible.

Protecting Tripwire itself

Hackers can modify the Tripwire binary (/usr/sbin/tripwire) or the /etc/tripwire/tw.pol policy file to hide traces of their work. To help prevent this, you can run the /usr/sbin/siggen utility to create a set of signatures for these files. To generate a signature for the /usr/sbin/tripwire binary, run the /usr/sbin/siggen -a /usr/sbin/tripwire command.

You will see something similar to the following on the screen:

```
-------------------------------------------------------------------
Signatures for file: /usr/sbin/tripwire

CRC32       BmL301
MD5         BrP2IBO3uAzdbRc67CI16i
SHA         F1IH/HvV3pb+tDhK5weOnKvFUxa
HAVAL       CBLgPptUYq2HurQ+sTa5tV
-------------------------------------------------------------------
```

You can keep the signature in a file by redirecting it to a file. For example, /usr/sbin/siggen -a /usr/sbin/tripwire > /tmp/sig.txt stores the signature in /tmp/sig.txt file. . You should print out the signature as well. Do not forget to also generate a signature for the siggen utility itself. If you ever get suspicious about Tripwire not working correctly, run the siggen utility on each of these files and compare the signatures. If any of them do not match, you should not trust those files; instead, you should replace them with new copies and launch an investigation of how the discrepancy happened.

Running Tripwire to detect integrity in interactive mode

To run in interactive mode run the /usr/sbin/tripwire --check --interactive command. In this mode, a report file is generated and loaded in the preferred editor. The summary part of an example Tripwire report generated by this command is shown in Listing 23-6.

Listing 23-6: **Tripwire report**

```
Tripwire(R) 2.3.0 Integrity Check Report

Report generated by:        root
Report created on:          Fri Dec 22 02:31:25 2000
Database last updated on:   Fri Dec 22 02:13:44 2000

===================================================================
```

```
Report Summary:
============================================================================

Host name:                k2.intevo.com
Host IP address:          172.20.15.1
Host ID:                  None
Policy file used:         /etc/tripwire/tw.pol
Configuration file used:  /etc/tripwire/tw.cfg
Database file used:       /var/lib/tripwire/k2.intevo.com.twd
Command line used:        /usr/sbin/tripwire --check --interactive


============================================================================
Rule Summary:


----------------------------------------------------------------------------
  Section: Unix File System
----------------------------------------------------------------------------

Rule Name                     Severity Level   Added   Removed  Modified
--------                      --------------   -----   -------  --------
    Invariant Directories         66            0        0        0
    Temporary directories         33            0        0        0
*   Tripwire Data Files           100           0        0        1
    Critical devices              100           0        0        0
    User binaries                 66            0        0        0
    Tripwire Binaries             100           0        0        0
*   Critical configuration files  100           0        0        1
    Libraries                     66            0        0        0
    Shell Binaries                100           0        0        0
    File System and Disk Administraton Programs
                                  100           0        0        0
    Kernel Administration Programs 100          0        0        0
    Networking Programs           100           0        0        0
    System Administration Programs 100          0        0        0
    Hardware and Device Control Programs
                                  100           0        0        0
    System Information Programs    100          0        0        0
    Application Information Programs
                                  100           0        0        0
    Shell Releated Programs       100           0        0        0
    Critical Utility Sym-Links    100           0        0        0
    Critical system boot files    100           0        0        0
    System boot changes           100           0        0        0
    OS executables and libraries  100           0        0        0
    Security Control              100           0        0        0
    Login Scripts                 100           0        0        0
    Operating System Utilities    100           0        0        0
    Root config files             100           0        0        0

Total objects scanned:  14862
Total violations found:  2
```

There are two violations, which are marked with the * sign to the left of the lines. The first violation occurred for the `Tripwire Data Files` rule. The report also states that there is another violation for the `Critical configuration files` rule. In both cases, a file was modified that should not have been modified. The Object Summary section of the report shows the following lines:

```
===========================================================================
Object Summary:
===========================================================================


-----------------------------------------------------------------
# Section: Unix File System
-----------------------------------------------------------------


-----------------------------------------------------------------
Rule Name: Tripwire Data Files (/etc/tripwire/tw.pol)
Severity Level: 100
-----------------------------------------------------------------

Remove the "x" from the adjacent box to prevent updating the database
with the new values for this object.

Modified:
[x] "/etc/tripwire/tw.pol"

-----------------------------------------------------------------
Rule Name: Critical configuration files (/etc/cron.daily)
Severity Level: 100
-----------------------------------------------------------------

Remove the "x" from the adjacent box to prevent updating the database
with the new values for this object.

Modified:
[x] "/etc/cron.daily"
```

As you can see, Tripwire shows exactly which files where modified and what rules these files fall under. If these modifications are okay, the 'x' marks (denotes section) can be left in the appropriate sections of the report and the editor exited. Tripwire will update the database. For example, if I leave the x marks on for both files, the next time the integrity checker is run, it will not find these violations because the Tripwire database was updated to account for these modified files. However, if one of the above modifications was not expected and looks suspicious, Tripwire has done its job!

Tip   If you wish to view a report from the /var/lib/tripwire/report **directory, you can run the** /usr/sbin/twprint -m r --twrfile reportfilename **command at any time.**

Running Tripwire to detect integrity in an automated manner

You can also run Tripwire as a cron job by creating a small script such as the one shown in Listing 23-7.

> ### Listing 23-7: /etc/cron.daily/tripwire-check

```
#!/bin/sh
HOST_NAME=`uname -n`
if [ ! -e /var/lib/tripwire/${HOST_NAME}.twd ] ; then
   echo "***    Error: Tripwire database for ${HOST_NAME} not found.    ***"
   echo "*** Run "/etc/tripwire/twinstall.sh" and/or "tripwire --init". ***"
else
    test -f /etc/tripwire/tw.cfg &&  /usr/sbin/tripwire --check
fi
```

This script checks whether the Tripwire database file exists; if it does exist, the script then looks for the configuration file and when it is found, the /usr/sbin/ tripwire command is run in a noninteractive mode. This results in a report file and if you have configured one or more rules using the emailto attribute, e-mails are sent to appropriate person(s).

Updating the Tripwire database

You need to update the Tripwire database whenever you have a change in the file systems that will generate false warning absent the database being updated. For example, if you modify a configuration file or remove a program that Tripwire is "watching" for you, Tripwire will generate a violation report. Therefore, whenever you change something intentionally, you have to update the database either by reinitializing the database with the /usr/sbin/tripwire --init command or by using the /usr/sbin/tripwire --update command to simply update the database. The update method should save you a little bit of time because it does not have to re-create the entire database.

Similarly, when you change the Tripwire policy file /etc/tripwire/twpol.txt, you need to update the database. Again, instead of reinitializing the entire database by using the --init option, you can instruct the program to apply policy changes and to update the database with the /usr/sbin/tripwire --update-policy /etc/tripwire/twpol.txt command.

After you have created a tripwire database, it needs to be updated every time you update your policy file. Instead of reinitializing the database every time you change (or experiment) with your policy file, you can run the tripwire --update-policy /etc/tripwire/twpol.txt command to update the database. This saves a significant amount of time.

Getting tripwire report by e-mail

If you use the `emailto` attribute in rules you can receive violation (or even nonviolation) reports from Tripwire. This is especially useful if you are running Tripwire checks as a cron job (see the "Running Tripwire to Detect Integrity in an Automated Manner" section earlier in this chapter).

Before you can get e-mail from Tripwire, you must configure the e-mail settings in the `/etc/tripwire/twcfg.txt` file and rebuild the configuration file with the `/usr/sbin/twadmin --create-cfgfile /etc/tripwire/twcfg.txt` command. The settings that control e-mail are explained in Table 23-4.

Table 23-4
E-mail Settings for the Tripwire Configuration File

Attribute	Meaning
`MAILMETHOD =` `SMTP	SENDMAIL`	Default: `MAILMETHOD = SENDMAIL` This attribute is used to set the mail delivery method that Tripwire uses. The default enables Tripwire to use the Sendmail daemon, which must be specified by using the `MAILPROGRAM` attribute discussed later. Because most popular Sendmail alternative mail daemons such as qmail and postoffice, work very much like Sendmail, you can still set this to `SENDMAIL` and specify the path to your alternative daemon using the `MAILPROGRAM`. However, if you do not run a Sendmail or a Sendmail-like daemon on the machine on which you run the Tripwire program, you can set this attribute to `SMTP` and specify the `SMTPHOST` and `SMTPPORT` number attribute. Assuming that the `SMTPHOST` allows your system to relay messages, Tripwire will connect to the host via the SMTP port and deliver messages, which will be delivered later to the appropriate destination by the host.
`SMTPHOST = hostname |` `IP Address`	Default: none This attribute enables you to specify the host name of a mail server. Use this only if you do not have mail capabilities in the same system in which Tripwire runs. You can look up the mail server IP or host name by using the `nslookup -q=mx yourdomain` command.
`SMTPPORT = port number`	Default: none This attribute specifies the TCP port number of the remote mail server. Typically, this should be set to 25. You only need this if you set `MAILMETHOD` to `SMTP`.

Attribute	Meaning
`MAILPROGRAM = /path/to/ mail/program`	**Default:** `MAILPROGRAM = /usr/sbin/ sendmail -oi -t` This attribute specifies the mail daemon path and any arguments that you need to supply to run it. This attribute only makes sense if you are using `MAILMETHOD = SENDMAIL`.
`EMAILREPORTLEVEL = 0 - 4`	**Default: EMAILREPORTLEVEL = 3** This attribute specifies the level of information reported via email. Leave the default as is.
`MAILNOVIOLATIONS = true | false`	**Default:** `MAILNOVIOLATIONS = true` If you wish to not receive e-mail when no violation is found, set this to `false`.

To test your e-mail settings, you can run Tripwire by using the `/usr/sbin/ tripwire -m t -email` *your@emailaddr* command. Don't forget to change the *you@emailaddr* to your own e-mail address.

Securing Apache using the Linux Intrusion Detection System (LIDS)

Root is the source of all evil. The previous statement probably only makes sense to the Unix/Linux system administrators of the world. Once an unauthorized root access is confirmed, damage control seems hopeless or at the mercy of the intruder.

In a plain-vanilla Linux system, several subsystems are typically unprotected. The file system is often left as open as the wild, wild, West. There are many important files, such as the `/bin/login`, in the system, that hackers exploit frequently because they are not protected. If a hacker breaks in, the hacker can upload a modified version of the login program as `/bin/login` to allow him or her free access to the system in the future. But the fact of the matter is that files (that is, programs) such as `/bin/login` files do not need to change frequently (if at all); therefore, they must not be left unprotected. Like the file system, the running processes are also unprotected. Many processes run with the root privileges, which means that when they are exploited using tricks such as buffer overflow, the intruder gains full root access to the system.

Reducing the power of the root user enhances system security. LIDS does that. It actually does quite a few other things. It implements a very low-level security model in the kernel to provide security protection, incident detection, and incident response capabilities. For example, LIDS can:

✦ Protect important files and directories from unauthorized access on your hard drive no matter what local file system they reside on. Chosen files and directories can be protected from modifications by the root user, which means that an unauthorized root access will not turn the intruder into the super evil we all fear.

✦ Protect important processes from being terminated by anyone including the root user. Again, this reduces root user capabilities.

✦ Prevent raw I/O operations from unauthorized programs. It can also protect a hard drive's master boot record (MBR).

LIDS can detect when someone scans your system using port scanners and can inform the system administrator via e-mail of the scan. LIDS can also notify the system administrator whenever it notices any violation of imposed rules. When someone violates such a rule, LIDS can log detailed messages about the violations in LIDS-protected, temper-proof log files. In fact, LIDS can not only log and send e-mail about detected violations, it can immediately shut down the user's interactive session!

LIDS is a kernel patch and a suite of administrative tools that enhances security from within the very kernel of the Linux operating system. Because in the LIDS security model the subject, object, and access type all are in the kernel, it is called a reference monitor. The LIDS project Web site is `www.lids.org/about.html`.

LIDS enables Linux system to run a customized kernel and you must have the latest kernel source from a reliable kernel site such as `www.kernel.org`. After you have downloaded and extracted the kernel into `/usr/src/linux`, download the LIDS patch for the specific kernel that you want to use. For example, if you are using kernel 2.4.1, make sure you download the LIDS patch from the LIDS project Web site. Typically the LIDS patch and administrative tool package is called `lids-x.x.x.y.y.y.tar.gz` where `x.x.x` represents the LIDS version number and `y.y.y` represents the kernel version (for example, `lids-1.0.5-2.4.1`). I use LIDS 1.0.5 for kernel 2.4.1 in the instructions below. Make sure you change the version numbers as needed. Extract the LIDS source distribution into the `/usr/local/src` directory with `tar xvzf lids-1.0.5-2.4.1.tar.gz` command from the `/usr/local/src` directory. Now you are ready to patch the kernel.

Note   Make sure that `/usr/src/linux` points to the latest kernel source distribution that you downloaded. You can simply run `ls -l /usr/src/linux` to see which directory the symbolic link points to. If it points to an older kernel source, remove the link using `rm -f /usr/src/linux` and relink it using `ln -s /usr/src/linux-version /usr/src/linux` where *version* is the kernel version you downloaded. For example, `ln -s /usr/src/linux-2.4.1 /usr/src/linux` links the latest kernel 2.4.1 source to `/usr/src/linux`.

Patching, compiling, and installing the kernel with LIDS

To compile LIDS for your system you need to recompile the Linux kernel after you apply the LIDS patch. This process is described below:

1. As root, extract the LIDS patch package into a suitable directory of your choice. I usually keep source code for locally compiled software in my /usr/local/src directory. For these steps, I assume that you do the same; if you do not use the same directory, make the appropriate modifications to the instructions. So, from the /usr/local/src directory, run the tar xvzf lids-1.0.5-2.4.1.tar.gz command. This will create a new subdirectory called lids-1.0.5-2.4.1.

2. Change the directory to /usr/src/linux and run the patch -p < /usr/local/src/lids-1.0.5-2.4.1.patch command to patch the kernel source distribution.

3. From the /usr/src/linux directory run the make menuconfig command to start the menu-based kernel configuration program. You can also use the make config or make xconfig commands to configure the kernel, but I prefer the first one and assume you use it as well.

4. From the main menu select the Code maturity level options submenu and choose the Prompt for development and/or incomplete code/drivers option by pressing the spacebar key. Exit this submenu.

5. Go to the General setup submenu and select the Sysctl support and exit the submenu.

6. From the main menu, select the Linux Intrusion Detection System submenu, which only appears if you have completed steps 4 and 5. This submenu should be listed at the bottom of the main menu and therefore you might have to scroll down a bit.

7. From the LIDS submenu select the Linux Intrusion Detection System support (EXPERIMENTAL) (NEW) option. You will see a list of options as shown below.

```
(1024)    Maximum protected objects to manage (NEW)
(1024)    Maximum ACL subjects to manage (NEW)
(1024)    Maximum ACL objects to manage (NEW)
(1024)    Maximum protected processes (NEW)
 [ ]      Hang up console when raising a security alert (NEW)
 [ ]      Security alert when executing unprotected programs
before sealing LIDS (NEW)
 [ ]      Try not to flood logs (NEW)
 [ ]      Allow switching LIDS protections (NEW)
 [ ]      Port Scanner Detector in kernel (NEW)
 [ ]      Send security alerts through network (NEW)
 [ ]      LIDS Debug (NEW)
```

8. The default limits for managed objects, protected objects, ACL subjects/objects, and protected processes should be fine for most systems. So leave them as is.

9. If you want LIDS to disconnect the console when a user violates a security rule, then select the `Hang up console when raising a security alert` option.

10. LIDS is enabled during boot up process so it is likely that you will run other programs before it. If you wish to issue a security alert when a program is executed before LIDS protection is enabled, select the `Security alert when execing unprotected programs before sealing LIDS` option. When you select this option, you will have a chance to also choose to disable execution of unprotected programs all together by using the `Do not execute unprotected programs before sealing LIDS` option. I do not recommend that you disallow unprotected programs completely during boot up unless you are absolutely certain that everything (that is, all the utilities, daemons, and so on) that you want to run during boot are protected and will not stop the normal boot process.

11. Enable the `Try not to flood logs (NEW)` option and leave the default 60-second delay between logging of two identical entries to conserve the sanity and the size of the log file.

12. (Optional) Select the `Allow switching LIDS protections` option if you want to allow switching of LIDS protection. If you do, you can customize this further by selecting the value for `Number of attempts to submit password`, or `Time to wait after a fail (seconds)`, or `Allow remote users to switch LIDS protections`, or `Allow any program to switch LIDS protections`, or `Allow reloading config. file`. My preferences are shown below.

    ```
    [*]     Allow switching LIDS protections (NEW)
    (3)     Number of attempts to submit password (NEW)
    (3)     Time to wait after a fail (seconds) (NEW)
    [*]     Allow remote users to switch LIDS protections (NEW)
    [ ]     Allow any program to switch LIDS protections (NEW)
    [*]     Allow reloading config. file (NEW)
    ```

13. You definitely want to select the `Port Scanner Detector in kernel` option so that you can detect port scans by potential intruders and the `Send security alerts through network` option. Leave the default values for the second option as is.

14. Save your kernel configuration and run the following commands to compile the new kernel and its modules (if any).

    ```
    make depend
    make bzImage
    make modules
    make modules_install
    ```

Caution

If you are not compiling a newer version of the kernel than what is running on the system, you should back up the /bin/modules/*current-version* directory, where *current-version* is the current kernel version. For example, if you are compiling version 2.4.1 and you already have 2.4.1 running, then you should run the cp -r /lib/modules/2.4.1 /lib/modules/2.4.1.bak command to backup the current modules. In case of a problem with the new kernel, you can delete the broken kernel's modules and rename this directory to its original name.

15. Now copy the newly created /usr/src/linux/arch/i386/boot/bzImage kernel image to /boot/vmlinuz-lids-1.0.5-2.4.1 by using the cp /usr/src/linux/arch/i386/boot/bzImage /boot/vmlinuz-lids-1.0.5-2.4.1 command.

16. Add to the /etc/lilo.conf file:

```
image=/boot/vmlinuz-lids-1.0.5-2.4.1
        label=lids
        read-only
        root=/dev/hda1
```

If /dev/hda1 is not the root device, make sure you change it as appropriate.

17. Run /sbin/lilo to reconfigure lilo.

The kernel part of the configuration is complete and LIDS configuration can be done.

Compiling, installing, and configuring LIDS

To compile and install the LIDS administrative program lidsadm, follow these steps:

1. Assuming you have installed the LIDS source in the /usr/local/src directory, change to /usr/local/src/lids-1.0.5-2.4.1/lidsadm-1.0.5.

2. Run make; make install commands to install the lidsadm program in /sbin and to create the necessary configuration files (lids.cap, lids.conf, lids.net, lids.pw) in /etc/lids.

3. Run the /sbin/lidsadm -P command and enter a password for the LIDS system. This password is stored in the /etc/lids/lids.pw file in RipeMD-160 encrypted format.

4. Run the /sbin/lidsadm -U command to update the inode/dev numbers.

5. Configure the /etc/lids/lids.net file. Following is a simplified version of the default /etc/lids/lids.net file:

```
MAIL_SWITCH= 1
MAIL_RELAY=127.0.0.1:25
MAIL_SOURCE=lids.sinocluster.com
MAIL_FROM= LIDS_ALERT@lids.sinocluster.com
MAIL_TO= root@localhost
MAIL_SUBJECT= LIDS Alert
```

  • The MAIL_SWITCH option can be 1 or 0, where 1 turns on the e-mail alert function and 0 turns it off. Leave the default as is.

- The MAIL_RELAY option should be set to the IP address of the mail server that LIDS should use to send the alert message. If you run the mail server on the same machine that you are configuring LIDS for, leave the default as is. The port number, 25, is the default SMTP port and should be left alone unless you are running your mail server on a different port.

- The MAIL_SOURCE option should be set to the host name of the machine being configured. Change the default to the appropriate host name of your system.

- The MAIL_FROM option should be set to an address that tells you from which system the alert is coming. The default should be changed to reflect the host name of your system. You do not need to create a real mail account for the from address to be useful.

- The MAIL_TO option should be set to the e-mail address of the administrator of the system being configured. Because the root address, root@localhost, is the default administrative account you can leave it as is.

- The MAIL_SUBJECT option is obvious and should be changed as needed.

6. To see what is protected by default, run the /sbin/lidsadm -L command, which should show output similar to the following:

```
LIST
        Subject            ACCESS TYPE      Object
        ------------------------------------------------
            Any File          READ              /sbin
            Any File          READ              /bin
            Any File          READ              /boot
            Any File          READ              /lib
            Any File          READ              /usr
            Any File          DENY          /etc/shadow
          /bin/login          READ          /etc/shadow
             /bin/su          READ          /etc/shadow
            Any File          APPEND            /var/log
            Any File          WRITE         /var/log/wtmp
      /sbin/fsck.ext2         WRITE            /etc/mtab
            Any File          WRITE            /etc/mtab
            Any File          WRITE               /etc
    /usr/sbin/sendmail        WRITE     /var/log/sendmail.st
          /bin/login          WRITE      /var/log/lastlog
            /bin/cat          READ           /home/xhg
            Any File          DENY          /home/httpd
      /usr/sbin/httpd         READ          /home/httpd
            Any File          DENY         /etc/httpd/conf
      /usr/sbin/httpd         READ         /etc/httpd/conf
    /usr/sbin/sendmail                     WRITE
/var/log/sendmail.st
      /usr/X11R6/bin/XF86_SVGA    NO_INHERIT      RAWIO
      /usr/sbin/in.ftpd                READ       /etc/shadow
      /usr/sbin/httpd NO_INHERIT              HIDDEN
```

Because you are not likely to have /home/xhg (the home directory of the author of LIDS) you can remove the configuration for it by using the

`/sbin/lidsadm -D -s /bin/cat -o /home/xhg` command. You can leave everything else as is because you can later change them as needed.

7. Add the following line to the `/etc/rc.d/rc.local` file to seal the kernel during the end of the boot cycle:

`/sbin/lidsadm -I`

8. Reboot the system and choose the LIDS enable kernel by entering `lids` at the `lilo` prompt. When the system boots up and runs the `/sbin/lidsadm -I` command from the `/etc/rc.d/rc.local` script, it will seal the kernel and the system will be protected by LIDS.

Administering LIDS

Except for the `/etc/lids/lids.net` file, you must use the `/sbin/lidsadm` program to modify the LIDS configuration files `/etc/lids/lids.conf`, `/etc/lids/lids.pw`, and `/etc/lids/lids.cap`.

The `/etc/lids/lids.conf` file stores the Access Control List (ACL) information. The `/etc/lids/lids.cap` file contains all the capability rules for the system. You can configure which capability you want to enable or disable on the system by editing this file with the `/sbin/lidsadm` command. You can just set + in front of the capability name to enable the system or - to disable the capability.

The `/etc/lids/lids.net` file configures the mail setup needed for sending alert e-mails. You can use a regular editor such as vi, emacs, or pico, to edit this file.

If you need to stop LIDS to perform system administration tasks, then you should use `/sbin/lidsadm -S -- -LIDS` or `/sbin/lidsadm -S -- -LIDS_GLOBAL` command. You will also need to provide the LIDS password to switch off LIDS. After you make any changes in a LIDS configuration file with the `lidsadm` command, reload the updated configuration into the kernel by running the `/sbin/lidsadm -S -- + RELOAD_CONF` command.

To add a new ACL to the `/etc/lids/lids.conf` file, you use the `/sbin/lidsadm` command as follows:

`/sbin/lidsadm -A  [-s subject] [-t | -d | -i] -o object -j TARGET`

The options in the command above are explained in the following list:

✦ The `-A` option tells the `/sbin/lidsadm` program to add a new ACL.

✦ The `-s subject` option specifies a subject of the ACL. A subject can be any program such as `/bin/cat`. When you do not specify a subject, the ACL will apply to everything.

✦ The `-t`, `-d`, `-i` options are not typically needed.

✦ The `-o object` option is used to specify the name of the object, which can be a file, a directory, or a capability. Each ACL requires a named object.

✦ The `-j` *TARGET* option specifies the target of the ACL. When the new ACL has a file or directory as the object, the target can be `ob` `READ`, `WRITE`, `APPEND`, `DENY`, and `IGNORE`. If the object is a Linux capability, the target can be only `INHERIT` or `NO_INHERIT`, which defines whether the object's children can have the same ability or not.

Protecting files and directories

You can use `lidsadm` to protect important files and directories. You can make a file or directory read-only, control write access, control append mode file access, and deny access. LIDS provides the following type of protection for a file or directory.

✦ `READ`—makes file or directory read-only

✦ `WRITE`—allows modifications of the file or directory

✦ `IGNORE`—ignores all other protection set for a file or directory

✦ `APPEND`—allows adding to the file

✦ `DENY`—all access to the file or directory is denied

Making files or directory read-only

To make a file called `/path/filename` read-only run:

```
/sbin/lids -A -o /path/filename -j READ
```

To make a directory called `/mypath` read-only run:

```
/sbin/lids -A -o /mypath -j READ
```

Notice that because you do not specify a subject in any of the above commands, the ACL applies to all programs. So no program can write to the above-mentioned file or directory. If you specify a subject then the command only applies to the named file or directory.

Denying access to a file or directory

To deny access to a file called `/etc/shadow` run:

```
/sbin/lids -A -o /etc/shadow -j DENY
```

After the above command is run and the LIDS configuration is reloaded, you can run commands such as `ls -l /etc/shadow` and `cat /etc/shadow` to see whether you can access the file. None of these programs will see the file because you implicitly specified the subject to be all the programs in the system. However, if you need to allow a program such as `/bin/login` to access the `/etc/shadow` file, you can give it read access by creating a new ACL such as

```
/sbin/lids -A -s /bin/login -o /etc/shadow -j READ
```

Allowing append-only access

Typically, programs only need append-only access to critical system logs such as /var/log/messages or /var/log/secure. You can enable append-only mode for these two files with the following commands:

```
/sbin/lids -A -o /var/log/messages -j APPEND
/sbin/lids -A -o /var/log/secure -j APPEND
```

Allowing write-only access

To allow a program called /usr/local/apache/bin/httpd to be able to write to a protected directory called /home/httpd, run the following commands:

```
/sbin/lids -A -o /home/httpd -j DENY
/sbin/lids -A -s /usr/local/apache/bin/httpd -o /home/httpd -j READ
```

Deleting an ACL

To delete all the ACL rules, run the /sbin/lidsadm -Z command. To delete individual ACL rule, simply specify the subject (if any) and/or the object of the ACL. For example, if you run the /sbin/lidsadm -D -o /bin command, all the ACL rules with /bin as the object is deleted. However, if you run the /sbin/lidsadm -D -s /bin/login -o /bin command, only the ACL that specifies /bin/login as the subject and /bin as the object is deleted.

Caution   Specifying the -Z or the -D option without any argument deletes all your ACL rules.

A good file and directory protection scheme

In this section I show you a good protection schema that you can use with LIDS. This schema allows you to make the /boot directory (or partition) read only, which means that kernel cannot be modified by intruders; it makes the system library directory /lib, root user's home directory /root, system configuration directory /etc, system daemon binaries directory /sbin and /usr/sbin, standard binaries directory /usr/bin and /bin read-only as well. It also only allows append operations for files in /var/log directory, which ensures that log files are not destroyed by any intruders. This configuration is shown below:

```
# Make the /boot directory or partition read-ony
/sbin/lidsadm -A -o /boot  -j READ

# Make the system library directory read-only
# This protects the lib/modules as well
/sbin/lidsadm -A -o /lib  -j READ

# Make the root user's home directory read-only
/sbin/lidsadm -A -o /root -j READ

# Make the system configuration directory read-only
```

```
/sbin/lidsadm -A -o /etc -j READ

# Make the daemon binary directory read-only
/sbin/lidsadm -A -o /sbin -j READ

# Make the other daemon binary directory read-only
/sbin/lidsadm -A -o /usr/sbin -j READ

# Make the general binary directory read-only
/sbin/lidsadm -A -o /bin -j READ

# Make the other general binary directory read-only
/sbin/lidsadm -A -o /usr/bin -j READ

# Make the general library directory read-only
/sbin/lidsadm -A -o /usr/lib -j READ

# Make the system log directory append-only
/sbin/lidsadm -A -o /var/log -j APPEND

# Make the X Windows binary directory read-only
/sbin/lidsadm -A -o /usr/X11R6/bin -j READ
```

In addition to protecting your files and directories by using the above technique, LIDS can use the Linux Capabilities to limit the capabilities of a running program (that is, process). In a traditional Linux system, the root user (that is, user with UID and GID set to 0) has all the "Capabilities" or the ability to perform any task by running any process. LIDS uses Linux Capabilities to break down all the power of the root (or processes run by root user) into pieces so that you can fine-tune what a specific process can or cannot do. To find out more about what Linux Capabilities are available, see the `/usr/include/linux/capability.h` header file. Table 23-5 lists of all Linux Capabilities and their status (turned on or off) in the default LIDS Capabilities configuration file `/etc/lids/lids.cap`.

Table 23-5
List of Linux Capabilities

Capability ID	Capability Name	Meaning	Status in /etc/lids/ lids.cap
0	CAP_CHOWN	Allow/disallow the changing of file ownership	Allow
1	CAP_DAC_OVERRIDE	Allow/disallow override of all DAC access restrictions	Allow
2	CAP_DAC_READ_SEARCH	Allow/disallow override of all DAC restrictions regarding read and search	Allow

Capability ID	Capability Name	Meaning	Status in /etc/lids/lids.cap
3	CAP_FOWNER	Allow/disallow the following restrictions that the effective user ID shall match the file owner ID when setting the S_ISUID and S_ISGID bits on a file; that the effective group ID shall match the file owner ID when setting such bit on a file	Allow
4	CAP_FSETID	Allow/disallow access when the effective user ID does not equal owner ID	Allow
5	CAP_KILL	Allow/disallow sending of signals to processes belonging to others	Allow
6	CAP_SETGID	Allow/disallow changing of the GID	Allow
7	CAP_SETUID	Allow/disallow changing of the UID	Allow
8	CAP_SETPCAP	Allow/disallow the transferring and removal of current set to any PID	Allow
9	CAP_LINUX_IMMUTABLE	Allow/disallow the modification of immutable and append-only files	Disallow
10	CAP_NET_BIND_SERVICE	Allow/disallow binding to ports below 1024	Disallow
11	CAP_NET_BROADCAST	Allow/disallow broadcasting/listening to multicast	Allow

Continued

Table 23-5 *(continued)*

Capability ID	Capability Name	Meaning	Status in /etc/lids/ lids.cap
12	CAP_NET_ADMIN	Allow/disallow network administration to perform interface configuration, administer IP firewalls, set up masquerading, set up IP accounting, set up debug option on sockets, modify routing tables, set up arbitrary process/process group ownership on sockets, bind any address for transparent proxying, set up Type Of Service (TOS), set up promiscuous mode, etc.	Disallow
13	CAP_NET_RAW	Allow/disallow use of raw sockets	Disallow
14	CAP_IPC_LOCK	Allow/disallow locking of shared memory segments	Allow
15	CAP_IPC_OWNER	Allow/disallow IPC ownership checks	Allow
16	CAP_SYS_MODULE	Allow/disallow insertion and removal of kernel modules	Disallow
17	CAP_SYS_RAWIO	Allow ioperm(2)/iopl(2) to access CAP_SYS_CHROOT chroot(2)	Disallow
18	CAP_SYS_CHROOT	Allow/disallow chroot system call	Disallow
19	CAP_SYS_PTRACE	Allow/disallow ptrace	Allow
20	CAP_SYS_PACCT	Allow/disallow configuration of process accounting	Allow
21	CAP_SYS_ADMIN	Allow/disallow various system administration tasks.	Allow
22	CAP_SYS_BOOT	Allow/disallow reboot	Allow

Capability ID	Capability Name	Meaning	Status in /etc/lids/ lids.cap
23	CAP_SYS_NICE	Allow/disallow changing of process priority using the nice command.	Allow
24	CAP_SYS_RESOURCE	Allow/disallow setting of system resource limit	Allow
25	CAP_SYS_TIME	Allow/disallow setting of system time	Allow
26	CAP_SYS_TTY_CONFIG	Allow/disallow pseudo-terminal (TTY) configuration	Allow
27	CAP_MKNOD	Allow/disallow the privileged aspects of mknod() system call.	Allow
28	CAP_LEASE	Allow/disallow taking of leases on files	Allow
29	CAP_HIDDEN	Allow/disallow hiding of a process from rest of the system	Allow
30	CAP_INIT_KILL	Allow/disallow programs the capability of killing children of the init process (PID = 1)	Allow

The default settings for the above Linux Capabilities are stored in /etc/lids/lids.cap file as shown in Listing 23-8.

Listing 23-8: /etc/lids/lids.cap

```
+0:CAP_CHOWN
+1:CAP_DAC_OVERRIDE
+2:CAP_DAC_READ_SEARCH
+3:CAP_FOWNER
+4:CAP_FSETID
+5:CAP_KILL
+6:CAP_SETGID
+7:CAP_SETUID
+8:CAP_SETPCAP
-9:CAP_LINUX_IMMUTABLE
```

Continued

Listing 23-8 *(continued)*

```
-10:CAP_NET_BIND_SERVICE
+11:CAP_NET_BROADCAST
-12:CAP_NET_ADMIN
-13:CAP_NET_RAW
+14:CAP_IPC_LOCK
+15:CAP_IPC_OWNER
-16:CAP_SYS_MODULE
-17:CAP_SYS_RAWIO
-18:CAP_SYS_CHROOT
+19:CAP_SYS_PTRACE
+20:CAP_SYS_PACCT
-21:CAP_SYS_ADMIN
+22:CAP_SYS_BOOT
+23:CAP_SYS_NICE
+24:CAP_SYS_RESOURCE
+25:CAP_SYS_TIME
+26:CAP_SYS_TTY_CONFIG
+27:CAP_MKNOD
+28:CAP_LEASE
+29:CAP_HIDDEN
+30:CAP_INIT_KILL
```

The + sign enables the capability and the - sign disables it. For example, in the above listing, the last Linux Capability called `CAP_INIT_KILL` is enabled, which means that a root-owned process could kill any child process (typically daemons) created by the `init` process. You use a text editor to enable or disable the Linux Capabilities.

Protecting your system by using LIDS-managed Linux Capabilities

You can use LIDS-provided capabilities to protect your system. In this section, I show you how to take advantage of the Linux Capabilities managed by LIDS. You will see how you can protect daemons (such as Apache Web server) from being killed by the root user, how to hide processes from programs like `ps`, how to disable raw access to devices, and how to protect the ext2 immutable flag.

Protecting daemons from being killed by root

Typically, daemon processes, such as the Sendmail mail transport agent and Apache Web server, are started by the `init` process. If you wish to protect them from being killed by the root user, modify the `CAP_INIT_KILL` settings in `/etc/lids/lids.cap` to be:

```
-30:CAP_INIT_KILL
```

After you have reloaded the LIDS configuration (by using the `/sbin/lidsadm -S -- + RELOAD_CONF` command) or rebooted the system and sealed the kernel (by using the `/sbin/lidsadm -I` command in the `/etc/rc.d/rc.local` script), you (as root) will not be able to kill the `init` children. This ensures that even if your system is compromised and an intruder gains root privileges, the intruder cannot kill the daemons and replace them with Trojan versions.

Hiding processes from everyone

By default, the `CAP_HIDDEN` capability is turned on in the `/etc/lids/lids.cap` configuration file. You can hide a process from everyone by using the following command:

```
lidsadm -A -s /path/to/binary -t -o CAP_HIDDEN -j INHERIT
```

where `/path/to/binary` is the fully qualified path to the executable that you want to hide when running. For example, to hide the Apache server process `/usr/local/apache/bin/httpd` when running, simply run the following command:

```
lidsadm -A -s /usr/local/apache/bin/httpd -t -o CAP_HIDDEN -j INHERIT
```

This labels the process as hidden in the kernel and it cannot be found using any user-land tools such as `ps` or `top`, or even exploring files in the `/proc` file system.

Disabling raw device access by processes

Normally, only special processes need access to raw devices. So it is a good idea to disable accesses to raw devices and to enable access to them as needed, which conforms to the overall security concept of "close all, open only what you need."

The raw device access is controlled with the `CAP_SYS_RAWIO` capability, which is disabled by default in `/etc/lids/lids.cap` configuration file. If it was enabled, processes could access `ioperm/iopi`, `/dev/port`, `/dev/mem`, `/dev/kmem`, and other raw block devices. For example, when this capability is off (as in default) the `/sbin/lilo` program cannot function properly because it needs raw device-level access to the hard drive.

But some special programs, such as `XF86_SVGA`, might want this capability to run properly. In this case, you can add the program to the exception list as follows:

```
lidsadm -A -s /usr/X11R6/bin/XF86_SVGA -t -o CAP_SYS_RAWIO -j INHERIT
```

This gives `XF86_SVGA` the capability of `CA_SYS_RAWIO`, whereas other programs are unable to obtain `CAP_SYS_RAWIO` capability.

Disabling network administration tasks

By default, the `CAP_NET_ADMIN` capability is turned off, which means that a network administrator (typically the root user) can no longer perform the following network administration tasks:

✦ Configuring the Ethernet interface

✦ Administering IP firewall, masquerading, and accounting

✦ Setting debug option on sockets

✦ Modifying routing tables

✦ Setting arbitrary process/process group ownership on sockets

✦ Binding to any address for transparent proxying

✦ Setting Type of Service (TOS)

✦ Setting promiscuous mode

✦ Clearing driver statistics

✦ Multicasting

✦ Setting the read/write of device-specific registers

The default setting is highly recommended. If you do need to perform one of the above tasks, simply turn off LIDS temporarily with the `/sbin/lidsadm -S -- -LIDS` command.

Protecting the Linux immutable flag for files

The ext2 file system has an extended feature that enables you to flag a file as immutable. This is done with the `chattr` command. For example, the `chattr +i /path/to/myfile` turns `/path/to/myfile` into an immutable file. A file with the immutable attribute cannot be modified or deleted or renamed, nor can it be symbolically linked. However the root user is able to change the flag by using the `chattr -i /path/to/myfile` command. You can protect immutable files even from the superuser (root) by disabling the `CAP_LINUX_IMMUTABLE` capability. Note that the `CAP_LINUX_IMMUTABLE` is disabled by default in `/etc/lids/lids.cap`.

Detecting scanners

If you have enabled the built-in port scanner during kernel compilation as recommended in the LIDS installation section discussed earlier, you can detect port scanners. This scanner can detect half-open scan, SYN stealth port scan, Stealth FIN, Xmas, or Null scan, among others. Tools such as `nmap` and Satan or Saint can be detected by the detector. It is useful when raw socket (CAP_NET_RAW) is disabled.

Note   When `CAP_NET_RAW` is turned off some user-land scanners based on sniffing will not work properly. But the kernel-based scanner provided by LIDS does not use any socket, which makes it more secure. You might want to consider using the LIDS supplied scanner.

Responding to an intruder

When LIDS detect a violation of any of the ACL rules, it can respond to the action by following method.

✦ **Logging the message.** When someone violates an ACL rule, LIDS will log a message using the kernel log daemon (`klogd`).

✦ **Sending e-mail to the appropriate authority.** LIDS can send e-mail when a violation occurs. This feature is controlled by the `/etc/lids/lids.net` file, which is discussed in Step 5 of the "Compiling, installing, and configuring LIDS" section earlier in this chapter.

✦ **Hanging up the console.** If you enabled this option during kernel patching for LIDS as discussed in Step 9 in the LIDS installation section, the console will be dropped when a user violates a ACL rule.

Another similar system to LIDS is the OpenWall project (`www.openwall.com/linux`). The OpenWall project contains some security features that are different from those found in LIDS, and one particular OpenWall patch makes the stack area of a process nonexecutable. You should take a look at this work-in-progress project.

✦   ✦   ✦

HTTP 1.1 Status Codes

For each request from a Web client, the Web server must return to the client an HTTP status code, which consists of a three-digit number. A Web client can attempt to understand the server's response by looking at this status code, sent in the HTTP Status-Line header. The code is accompanied by a short phrase, called a *reason phrase,* which is intended to provide a brief explanation for the user. For example, an HTTP Status-Line header might look like this:

```
HTTP/1.1 404 Not Found
```

Here, 404 is the status code and Not Found is the reason phrase. On a typical Web client, a Web browser will display the Not Found phrase in the browser window. Five different classes of status codes are available from the latest HTTP 1.1 specifications; these classes are discussed in the following sections.

Informational Status Codes (100–199)

The purpose of this type of status code is to let the client know that the server is in the process of fulfilling a request. These status codes are only informational; the client does not have to act on any of them. Note that HTTP 1.0 does not define 1xx status codes, so 1xx status codes must not be sent to HTTP 1.0 clients. The currently defined 1xx status codes are:

100 Continue—The server sends this code to let the client know it is ready to receive the rest of the request.

101 Switching Protocols—The server sends this code when it is willing to switch the application protocol

to one specified in an Upgrade request header provided by the client. Switching should take place only if the new protocol provides an advantage over the existing one. For example, the client may request that the server use a newer HTTP protocol than what it is currently using. In such a case, the server should switch if possible.

Client Request Successful (200–299)

A returned status code in the range 200–299 indicates that the client's request was successfully received and accepted. The currently defined 2*xx* status codes are:

200 OK—The server succeeded in processing the request, and the requested document is attached.

201 Created—The server successfully created a new URI, specified in a Location header.

202 Accepted—The request was accepted for processing, but the server has not yet completed processing it.

203 Non-Authoritative Information—The metainformation in the response header did not originate with the server; it was copied from another server.

204 No Content—The request is complete, but no new information needs to be sent back. The client should continue to display the current document.

205 Reset Content—The client should reset the current document. This is useful when an HTML form needs to be reset to clear all existing values of input fields.

206 Partial Content—The server has fulfilled the partial GET request for the resource. This code is used to respond to Range requests. The server sends a Content-Range header to indicate which data segment is attached.

Request Redirected (300–399)

Status codes in the range 300–399 are sent to a client to let it know it needs to perform further action to complete the request. The currently defined 3*xx* status codes are:

300 Multiple Choices—The requested resource corresponds to a set of documents. The server can send information about each document with its own specific location and content negotiation information so that the client can choose one.

301 Moved Permanently—The requested resource does not exist on the server. A Location header is sent to redirect the client to the new URL. The client directs all future requests to the new URI.

302 Moved Temporarily — The requested resource has temporarily moved. A Location header is sent to redirect the client to the new URL. The client continues to use the old URI in future requests.

303 See Other — The requested resource is found in a different location indicated by the Location header, and the client should use the GET method to retrieve it.

304 Not Modified — The server uses this code to respond to the If-Modified-Since request header. This indicates that the requested document has not been modified since the specified date, and that the client should use its cached copy.

305 Use Proxy — The client should use a proxy, specified by the Location header, to retrieve the requested resource.

307 Temporary Redirect — The requested resource is temporarily redirected to a different location. A Location header is sent to redirect the client to the new URL. The client continues to use the old URI in future requests.

Client Request Incomplete (400–499)

The status codes in the range 400–499 are sent to indicate that the client request is incomplete and that more information is needed to complete the resource request. The currently defined 4xx status codes are:

400 Bad Request — The server detected a syntax error in the client request.

401 Unauthorized — The request requires user authentication. The server sends the WWW-Authenticate header to indicate the authentication type and realm for the requested resource.

402 Payment Required — This code is reserved for future use.

403 Forbidden — Access to requested resource is forbidden. The client should not repeat the request.

404 Not Found — The requested document does not exist on the server.

405 Method Not Allowed — The request method used by the client is unacceptable. The server sends the Allow header stating what methods are acceptable to access the requested resource.

406 Not Acceptable — The requested resource is not available in a format that the client can accept, based on the Accept headers received by the server. If the request was not a HEAD request, the server can send Content-Language, Content-Encoding, and Content-Type headers to indicate which formats are available.

407 Proxy Authentication Required — Unauthorized access request to a proxy server. The client must first authenticate itself with the proxy. The server sends the Proxy-Authenticate header indicating the authentication scheme and realm for the requested resource.

408 `Request Time-Out`—The client has failed to complete its request within the request timeout period used by the server. However, the client can repeat the request.

409 `Conflict`—The client request conflicts with another request. The server can add information about the type of conflict along with the status code.

410 `Gone`—The requested resource is permanently gone from the server.

411 `Length Required`—The client must supply a Content-Length header in its request.

412 `Precondition Failed`—When a client sends a request with one or more If. . . headers, the server uses this code to indicate that one or more of the conditions specified in these headers is false.

413 `Request Entity Too Large`—The server refuses to process the request because its message body is too large. The server can close connection to stop the client from continuing the request.

414 `Request-URI Too Long`—The server refuses to process the request because the specified URI is too long.

415 `Unsupported Media Type`—The server refuses to process the request because it does not support the message body's format.

417 `Expectation Failed`—The server failed to meet the requirements of the Expect Request header.

Server Errors (500-599)

The status codes in the range 500–599 are returned when the server encounters an error and cannot fulfill the request. The currently defined 5xx status codes are as follows:

500 `Internal Server Error`—A server configuration setting or an external program has caused an error.

501 `Not Implemented`—The server does not support the functionality required to fulfill the request.

502 `Bad Gateway`—The server encountered an invalid response from an upstream server or proxy.

503 `Service Unavailable`—The service is temporarily unavailable. The server can send a Retry-After header to indicate when the service may become available again.

504 `Gateway Time-Out`—The gateway or proxy has timed out.

505 `HTTP Version Not Supported`—The version of HTTP used by client is not supported.

◆　　◆　　◆

Understanding Regular Expressions

A *regular expression* is typically composed of both normal and special characters to create a pattern. This pattern is used to match one or more substrings or to match an entire string. For example:

```
([a-z]+)\.([a-z])\.([a-z]+)
```

is a regular expression that matches www.idgbooks.com, www.apache.org, and so on. The special characters used in a regular expression are often called metacharacters. Table B-1 shows the commonly used meta characters.

Table B-1
Commonly Used Meta Characters

Meta Characters	Purpose
.	Matches any character (except newline character)
^	Matches the start of the string
$	Matches the end of the string
\b	Matches a word boundary
x?	Matches 0 or 1 x's, where x is any regular expression
x*	Matches 0 or more x's
x+	Matches 1 or more x's
foo|bar	Matches one of foo or bar
[abc]	Matches any character in the set abc
[A-Z]	Matches any character in the range A to Z.
[^xyz]	Matches any single character not in the set xyz
\w	Matches an alphanumeric character (for instance, [a-zA-Z0-9_])
\s	Matches a whitespace character
\t	Tab character
\n	Newline character
\r	Return character
\f	Form-feed character
\v	Vertical tab
\a	Bell character
\e	Escape character
\077	Octal char
\x9f	Hex char
\c[	Control char
\l	Lowercase next char
\L	Lowercase till \E
\U	Uppercase till \E
\E	End case modification
\Q	Uppercase next char
\u	Quote metacharacters till \E

If you need to use a metacharacter as a normal character in the regular expression, you can use the \metachar format to take away the special meaning. An example of this is \\$, which is a regular dollar sign character. The standard quantifiers used in regular expressions are shown in Table B-2.

Table B-2
Standard Quantifiers

Quantifier	Meaning
*	Match 0 or more times
+	Match 1 or more times
?	Match 1 or 0 times
{n}	Match exactly *n* times
{n,}	Match at least *n* times
{n, m}	Match at least *n* but not more than *m* times

A | character is treated as an OR operator. A pair of parentheses ( ) enables you to define the area used for the search match strings in a regular expression. A pair of square brackets [ ] creates a character class or range.

Let's revisit the first example again:

```
([a-z]+)\.([a-z])\.([a-z]+)
```

As mentioned before, this expression can be used to match strings such as www. hungryminds.com. The first [a-z]+ specifies that one or more characters in the a to z range is needed to match the group specified by the first pair of parentheses. If a match is found, whatever is matched can be accessed using $1. There are three pairs of parentheses in this expression. The first pair (starting from the left) is $1, the second one is $2, and the third one is $3. Notice that \ is used to escape the dot (.) metacharacter between the groups.

Here are two more examples:

✦ ^foo\.htm$ — This will match a string foo.htm. It would not match afoo.htm because the ^ metacharacter is used to specify that the matching string must start with the f character. It also would not match foo.html because the $ metacharacter is used to specify that the matching string must end with the m character.

✦ `^www\.([^.]+)\.host\.com(.*)` — This will match a string, such as `www.username.host.com STATUS=java` and the $1 will be assigned to host and $2 will hold everything followed by the `www.username.host.com` part of the string. The $2 will hold `STATUS=java`.

✦ ✦ ✦

Online Apache Resources

This appendix lists Web sites, Usenet newsgroups, and mailing-list addresses that relate to Apache that you may find useful.

Free Resources

Just like Apache, many of the best resources for Apache are available free on the Internet. The following sections describe some of these free Internet resources for Apache.

Web sites

Following are some of the better Apache Web sites:

Official Apache Web site — www.apache.org

Apache Module Registry — http://modules.apache.org

Apache/Perl Integration Project — http://perl.apache.org

Apache-SSL — www.apache-ssl.org

Jakarta Project — http://jakarta.apache.org

Apache GUI Project — http://gui.apache.org

Apache Today — www.apachetoday.com

Apache Week — www.apacheweek.com

Usenet newsgroups

Usenet newsgroups are excellent resources for anyone interested in learning from the personal experiences and expertise of people from all over the world. When you hit a problem with Apache, a CGI script, or a Java servlet, chances are someone out there also has hit that problem. Searching the Usenet for answers is a common research process for most successful system administrators. If you have access to a Usenet server via your ISP, then you can access and post to any public newsgroups.

If you do not have Usenet access via your ISP, you can always use Google Groups at http://groups.google.com. Google Groups enable you to browse all Usenet newsgroups and to post to them. If you wish to perform complex searches, you can use the http://groups.google.com/advanced_group_search.

Avoid creating unnecessary discussions (called *flame wars*) by posting questions such as, "Is IE better than Netscape Navigator?" because different people have different personal preferences, and they often get in the way of objective analysis of such topics. Ask constructive questions, and don't forget to answer if you can.

Web server-related newsgroups

These news groups are very good sources for information on various Web servers. You can ask questions or follow discussions on Apache in appropriate platform-specific group here. For example, if you run Apache for Windows, then you can ask questions in the comp.infosystems.www.servers.ms-windows group.

comp.infosystems.www.servers.mac

This newsgroup holds discussions of Web servers for the Macintosh (MacOS) platform. Subjects include configuration questions/solutions, security issues, directory structure, and bug reports.

comp.infosystems.www.servers.misc

This newsgroup discusses Web servers for other platforms, such as Amiga and VMS, as well as other platforms. Subjects include configuration questions/solutions, security issues, directory structure, and bug reports.

comp.infosystems.www.servers.ms-windows

This newsgroup covers Web servers for the MS Windows and NT platforms. Subjects include configuration questions/solutions, security issues, directory structure, and bug reports.

comp.infosystems.www.servers.unix

This newsgroup discusses Web servers for UNIX platforms. Subjects include configuration questions/solutions, security issues, directory structure, and bug reports.

Authoring-related newsgroups

News groups in this category deals with Web content authoring tools and techniques. You can ask questions or follow discussions on CGI programming, HTML tags, images, and the like.

comp.infosystems.www.authoring.cgi

This newsgroup discusses the development of Common Gateway Interface (CGI) scripts as they relate to Web-page authoring. Subjects include how to handle the results of forms, how to generate images on the fly, and how to put together other interactive Web offerings.

comp.infosystems.www.authoring.html

This newsgroup discusses HyperText Markup Language (HTML) as it relates to Web-page authoring. Subjects include HTML editors, formatting tricks, and current and proposed HTML standards.

comp.infosystems.www.authoring.images

This newsgroup discusses the creation and editing of images as they relate to Web-page authoring. Possible subjects include how best to leverage the image-display capabilities of the Web and common questions and solutions for putting up image maps.

comp.infosystems.www.authoring.misc

This newsgroup covers miscellaneous Web-authoring issues that are not covered by the other `comp.inforsystems.www.authoring.*` groups. Subjects include the use of audio and video and so on.

comp.infosystems.www.authoring.site-design

This newsgroup covers site design issues. You can learn about good and bad site designs that others have used.

comp.infosystems.www.authoring.stylesheets

This newsgroup covers style sheets that are used in Web-page development.

comp.infosystems.www.authoring.tools

This newsgroup discusses Web tools, ranging from authoring tools that enable you to create Web contents to full-blown Web-publishing engines.

Web browser-related newsgroups

If you are interested in Web browsers on various platforms, you can browse or post questions in the newsgroups in this category.

comp.infosystems.www.browsers.misc

This newsgroup covers Web browsers for all other platforms. Subjects include configuration questions/solutions, external viewers (helper applications), and bug reports. Included platforms are Amiga, DOS, VMS, and Unix text-mode.

comp.infosystems.www.browsers.mac

This newsgroup talks about Web browsers for the Macintosh platform. Subjects include configuration questions/solutions, external viewers, and bug reports.

comp.infosystems.www.browsers.ms-windows

This newsgroup discusses Web browsers for the MS Windows and NT platforms. Subjects include configuration questions/solutions, external viewers (helper applications), and bug reports.

comp.infosystems.www.browsers.x

This newsgroup discusses Web browsers for the X Window System. Subjects include configuration questions/solutions, external viewers, and bug reports.

Announcements newsgroups

News groups in this category are used by various groups to announce software releases, security alerts regarding Web software, and other matters of importance. You should not post to any of these news groups unless you have information to announce that is related to a group.

comp.infosystems.www.announce

This is a newsgroup in which new, Web-related resources can be announced.

Other WWW newsgroups

News groups in this category are Web advocacy groups and groups related to matters that do not fall under any of the other categories.

comp.infosystems.www.advocacy

This newsgroup is for comments, arguments, debates, and discussions about which Web browsers, servers, external-viewer programs, and other software is better or worse than any other.

comp.infosystems.www.misc

`comp.infosystems.www.misc` provides a forum for general discussion of WWW-related topics that are not covered by the other newsgroups in the hierarchy. This group is likely to include discussions about future changes in the Web's structure and about protocols of the Web that affect both clients and servers.

Perl newsgroups

Because Perl is used heavily in CGI, mod_perl, and FastCGI programming, the following Perl newsgroups can be quite beneficial.

comp.lang.perl.announce

New releases, FAQ, and new modules are announced here.

comp.lang.perl.misc

This newsgroup is devoted to discussions about Perl; it includes everything from bug reports to new features to history, humor, and trivia. This is the best source of information about anything Perl related, especially what's new with Perl 5.

Mailing lists

If you would like to receive Apache announcements about the Apache Foundation and its activities, subscribe to the announce-subscribe@apache.org. Remember that this is not a discussion mailing list. It is simply used by the Apache Foundation to announce newsworthy matters. Please do not post questions or comments there.

If you are interested in Apache conferences, which are a great resource for serious Apache administrators, you can subscribe to the announce-subscribe@ apachecon.com list. This is also an announcement list and not suitable for posting any questions or comments.

If you are interested in topics related to new Apache developments, then you can subscribe to new-httpd-subscribe@apache.org.

You can also subscribe to http://groups.yahoo.com/group/new-httpd, which is a Yahoo! group dedicated to Apache server.

Commercial Resources

A growing number of Apache users (especially corporate users) are always looking for commercial resources that offer Apache software or services. Some well-known commercial resources for Apache are:

Stronghold — www.c2.net

Covalent Raven — http://raven.covalent.net

Rovis — www.rovis.com/warpaint/

Other Related Resources

There are many Web sites that will benefit a Web developer or administrator. A short list of such resources is provided here.

WWW Consortium — www.w3.org/

Netcraft Survey Report Web site — www.netcraft.co.uk/Survey/

Server Watch — www.serverwatch.com

Search Engine Watch — www.searchenginewatch.com

Browser Watch — www.browserwatch.com

Web Compare — www.webcompare.com

Web Developer — www.webdeveloper.com

Web Reference — www.webreference.com

Electronic Commerce on Internet — http://e-comm.internet.com

ISP Buyer's Guide — www.TheList.com

Internet News — www.InternetNews.com

CGI Specification — http://hoohoo.ncsa.uiuc.edu/cgi/interface.html

FastCGI Web site — www.fastcgi.com

Perl Language Site — www.perl.com

Perl Mongers — www.perl.org

What's on the CD-ROM?

The CD-ROM that accompanies this book contains many great software programs and files that will save you a lot of time as you work this book. To navigate the CD-ROM quickly, use a file browser program such as File Manager under X Windows systems or Windows Explorer under Windows systems.

To view the contents of the CD-ROM, Unix and Linux users must mount the CD-ROM using the `mount` command. Windows users simply need to insert the CD-ROM in the CD-ROM drive and refresh (press F5) their Windows Explorer window.

The following sections describe what you can find on the CD.

Apache Server Distribution

The latest release version of the Apache server source distribution is included in this CD. We have also included a binary distribution of the Apache server for Windows 2000/NT/9*x* platforms because these operating systems do not come with appropriate C compiler and other development tools that are needed to compile and build Apache on the Windows platform.

Note The CD-ROM that accompanies this book includes software developed by the Apache Software Foundation (`http://www.apache.org`).

Book Chapters in Searchable PDF Format

All the chapters of the book are also included in PDF format so that you can search and print information from it for your own use only. We have included Acrobat Reader 5.0 for Windows platforms in the CD for your convenience.

 Note   Unix/Linux users must use Acrobat Reader for the respective platform instead of any other PDF readers, which might not work with searchable PDF documents.

Sample Book Scripts in Text Format

All sample scripts developed by the author are included on the CD in text format. Copy each script from appropriate directory and modify as you need to.

 Note   Make sure you turn on execute permission for the Web server user to run these scripts via Apache.

MySQL

MySQL is a free relational database server that is widely used as the database server for Web applications. MySQL database server version is included in the CD. Both Linux (and Unix) and Windows versions of the server are included in this directory. To learn about how to install the MySQL database on your system, visit `http://www.mysql.com` for details.

OpenSSL

OpenSSL is the open-source implementation of the Secure Socket Layer (SSL) protocol. The OpenSSL source distribution is needed by Apache-SSL distribution and `mod_ssl` module for Apache. The OpenSSL source distribution is included on the CD.

 Note   The CD-ROM that accompanies this book includes software developed by Ben Laurie for use in the Apache-SSL HTTP server project.

PHP

The PHP source distribution is included in the CD. To install PHP on your Unix/Linux system, follow the instructions in Chapter 15.

Note The CD-ROM that accompanies this book includes software written by the PHP Development Team.

Perl and Related Modules

The source distribution of the Perl scripting language is included on the CD. To install Perl on your Unix/Linux system, extract the source distribution in a directory such as /usr/local/src on your hard disk and read the INSTALL file for details.

Note Windows 2000/NT/9x users should download the binary distribution from http://www.activeperl.com instead.

The Perl modules that are included in the CD are HTML::Template, Config::IniFiles, LWP, CGI, MIME::Lite, MIME::Lite::HTML, DBI, DBD::MySQL, and FCGI. Extract any of these modules in a directory such as /usr/local/src and read the INSTALL and/or README file for detailed installation instructions.

Also, the source distribution of the mod_perl Apache module is also included in the CD. For info about how to install mod_perl on your system, see Chapter 16.

Tomcat

The Java servlet container software called Tomcat is included on the CD. See Chapter 17 for details on how to install Tomcat on your system.

Troubleshooting

If you have difficulty installing or using any of the materials on the companion CD, try the following solutions:

✦ **Turn off any anti-virus software that you may have running.** Installers sometimes mimic virus activity and can make your computer incorrectly believe that it is being infected by a virus. (Be sure to turn the anti-virus software back on later.)

✦ **Close all running programs.** The more programs you're running, the less memory is available to other programs. Installers also typically update files and programs; if you keep other programs running, installation may not work properly.

✦ **Reference the ReadMe:** Please refer to the ReadMe file located at the root of the CD-ROM for the latest product information at the time of publication.

If you still have trouble with the CD, please call the Hungry Minds Customer Care phone number: (800) 762-2974. Outside the United States, call 1 (317) 572-3994. You can also contact Hungry Minds Customer Service by e-mail at `techsupdum@hungryminds.com`. Hungry Minds will provide technical support only for installation and other general quality control items; for technical support on the applications themselves, consult the program's vendor or author.

Index

Continued

Continued

Hungry Minds, Inc.
End-User License Agreement

READ THIS. You should carefully read these terms and conditions before opening the software packet(s) included with this book ("Book"). This is a license agreement ("Agreement") between you and Hungry Minds, Inc. ("HMI"). By opening the accompanying software packet(s), you acknowledge that you have read and accept the following terms and conditions. If you do not agree and do not want to be bound by such terms and conditions, promptly return the Book and the unopened software packet(s) to the place you obtained them for a full refund.

1. **License Grant.** HMI grants to you (either an individual or entity) a nonexclusive license to use one copy of the enclosed software program(s) (collectively, the "Software") solely for your own personal or business purposes on a single computer (whether a standard computer or a workstation component of a multi-user network). The Software is in use on a computer when it is loaded into temporary memory (RAM) or installed into permanent memory (hard disk, CD-ROM, or other storage device). HMI reserves all rights not expressly granted herein.

2. **Ownership.** HMI is the owner of all right, title, and interest, including copyright, in and to the compilation of the Software recorded on the disk(s) or CD-ROM ("Software Media"). Copyright to the individual programs recorded on the Software Media is owned by the author or other authorized copyright owner of each program. Ownership of the Software and all proprietary rights relating thereto remain with HMI and its licensers.

3. **Restrictions On Use and Transfer.**

   (a) You may only (i) make one copy of the Software for backup or archival purposes, or (ii) transfer the Software to a single hard disk, provided that you keep the original for backup or archival purposes. You may not (i) rent or lease the Software, (ii) copy or reproduce the Software through a LAN or other network system or through any computer subscriber system or bulletin-board system, or (iii) modify, adapt, or create derivative works based on the Software.

   (b) You may not reverse engineer, decompile, or disassemble the Software. You may transfer the Software and user documentation on a permanent basis, provided that the transferee agrees to accept the terms and conditions of this Agreement and you retain no copies. If the Software is an update or has been updated, any transfer must include the most recent update and all prior versions.

4. **Restrictions on Use of Individual Programs.** You must follow the individual requirements and restrictions detailed for each individual program in Appendix D of this Book. These limitations are also contained in the individual license agreements recorded on the Software Media. These limitations may include a requirement that after using the program for a specified period of time, the user must pay a registration fee or discontinue use. By opening the Software packet(s), you will be agreeing to abide by the licenses and restrictions for these individual programs that are detailed in Appendix D and on the Software Media. None of the material on this Software Media or listed in this Book may ever be redistributed, in original or modified form, for commercial purposes.

5. Limited Warranty.

(a) HMI warrants that the Software and Software Media are free from defects in materials and workmanship under normal use for a period of sixty (60) days from the date of purchase of this Book. If HMI receives notification within the warranty period of defects in materials or workmanship, HMI will replace the defective Software Media.

(b) HMI AND THE AUTHOR OF THE BOOK DISCLAIM ALL OTHER WARRANTIES, EXPRESS OR IMPLIED, INCLUDING WITHOUT LIMITATION IMPLIED WARRANTIES OF MERCHANTABILITY AND FITNESS FOR A PARTICULAR PURPOSE, WITH RESPECT TO THE SOFTWARE, THE PROGRAMS, THE SOURCE CODE CONTAINED THEREIN, AND/OR THE TECHNIQUES DESCRIBED IN THIS BOOK. HMI DOES NOT WARRANT THAT THE FUNCTIONS CONTAINED IN THE SOFTWARE WILL MEET YOUR REQUIREMENTS OR THAT THE OPERATION OF THE SOFTWARE WILL BE ERROR FREE.

(c) This limited warranty gives you specific legal rights, and you may have other rights that vary from jurisdiction to jurisdiction.

6. Remedies.

(a) HMI's entire liability and your exclusive remedy for defects in materials and workmanship shall be limited to replacement of the Software Media, which may be returned to HMI with a copy of your receipt at the following address: Software Media Fulfillment Department, Attn.: *Apache Server 2 Bible*, Hungry Minds, Inc., 10475 Crosspoint Blvd., Indianapolis, IN 46256, or call 1-800-762-2974. Please allow four to six weeks for delivery. This Limited Warranty is void if failure of the Software Media has resulted from accident, abuse, or misapplication. Any replacement Software Media will be warranted for the remainder of the original warranty period or thirty (30) days, whichever is longer.

(b) In no event shall HMI or the author be liable for any damages whatsoever (including without limitation damages for loss of business profits, business interruption, loss of business information, or any other pecuniary loss) arising from the use of or inability to use the Book or the Software, even if HMI has been advised of the possibility of such damages.

(c) Because some jurisdictions do not allow the exclusion or limitation of liability for consequential or incidental damages, the above limitation or exclusion may not apply to you.

7. U.S. Government Restricted Rights.
Use, duplication, or disclosure of the Software for or on behalf of the United States of America, its agencies and/or instrumentalities (the "U.S. Government") is subject to restrictions as stated in paragraph (c)(1)(ii) of the Rights in Technical Data and Computer Software clause of DFARS 252.227-7013, or subparagraphs (c) (1) and (2) of the Commercial Computer Software - Restricted Rights clause at FAR 52.227-19, and in similar clauses in the NASA FAR supplement, as applicable.

8. General.
This Agreement constitutes the entire understanding of the parties and revokes and supersedes all prior agreements, oral or written, between them and may not be modified or amended except in a writing signed by both parties hereto that specifically refers to this Agreement. This Agreement shall take precedence over any other documents that may be in conflict herewith. If any one or more provisions contained in this Agreement are held by any court or tribunal to be invalid, illegal, or otherwise unenforceable, each and every other provision shall remain in full force and effect.

Version 2, June 1991

Copyright © 1989, 1991 Free Software Foundation, Inc.

59 Temple Place, Suite 330, Boston, MA 02111-1307, USA

Everyone is permitted to copy and distribute verbatim copies of this license document, but changing it is not allowed.

Preamble

The licenses for most software are designed to take away your freedom to share and change it. By contrast, the GNU General Public License is intended to guarantee your freedom to share and change free software — to make sure the software is free for all its users. This General Public License applies to most of the Free Software Foundation's software and to any other program whose authors commit to using it. (Some other Free Software Foundation software is covered by the GNU Library General Public License instead.) You can apply it to your programs, too.

When we speak of free software, we are referring to freedom, not price. Our General Public Licenses are designed to make sure that you have the freedom to distribute copies of free software (and charge for this service if you wish), that you receive source code or can get it if you want it, that you can change the software or use pieces of it in new free programs; and that you know you can do these things.

To protect your rights, we need to make restrictions that forbid anyone to deny you these rights or to ask you to surrender the rights. These restrictions translate to certain responsibilities for you if you distribute copies of the software, or if you modify it.

For example, if you distribute copies of such a program, whether gratis or for a fee, you must give the recipients all the rights that you have. You must make sure that they, too, receive or can get the source code. And you must show them these terms so they know their rights.

We protect your rights with two steps: (1) copyright the software, and (2) offer you this license which gives you legal permission to copy, distribute and/or modify the software.

Also, for each author's protection and ours, we want to make certain that everyone understands that there is no warranty for this free software. If the software is modified by someone else and passed on, we want its recipients to know that what they have is not the original, so that any problems introduced by others will not reflect on the original authors' reputations.

Finally, any free program is threatened constantly by software patents. We wish to avoid the danger that redistributors of a free program will individually obtain patent licenses, in effect making the program proprietary. To prevent this, we have made it clear that any patent must be licensed for everyone's free use or not licensed at all.

The precise terms and conditions for copying, distribution and modification follow.

Terms and Conditions for Copying, Distribution, and Modification

0. This License applies to any program or other work which contains a notice placed by the copyright holder saying it may be distributed under the terms of this General Public License. The "Program", below, refers to any such program or work, and a "work based on the Program" means either the Program or any derivative work under copyright law: that is to say, a work containing the Program or a portion of it, either verbatim or with modifications and/or translated into another language. (Hereinafter, translation is included without limitation in the term "modification".) Each licensee is addressed as "you".

Activities other than copying, distribution and modification are not covered by this License; they are outside its scope. The act of running the Program is not restricted, and the output from the Program is covered only if its contents constitute a work based on the Program (independent of having been made by running the Program). Whether that is true depends on what the Program does.

1. You may copy and distribute verbatim copies of the Program's source code as you receive it, in any medium, provided that you conspicuously and appropriately publish on each copy an appropriate copyright notice and disclaimer of warranty; keep intact all the notices that refer to this License and to the absence of any warranty; and give any other recipients of the Program a copy of this License along with the Program.

You may charge a fee for the physical act of transferring a copy, and you may at your option offer warranty protection in exchange for a fee.

2. You may modify your copy or copies of the Program or any portion of it, thus forming a work based on the Program, and copy and distribute such modifications or work under the terms of Section 1 above, provided that you also meet all of these conditions:

a) You must cause the modified files to carry prominent notices stating that you changed the files and the date of any change.

b) You must cause any work that you distribute or publish, that in whole or in part contains or is derived from the Program or any part thereof, to be licensed as a whole at no charge to all third parties under the terms of this License.

c) If the modified program normally reads commands interactively when run, you must cause it, when started running for such interactive use in the most ordinary way, to print or display an announcement including an appropriate copyright notice and a notice that there is no warranty (or else, saying that you provide a warranty) and that users may redistribute the program under these conditions, and telling the user how to view a copy of this License. (Exception: if the Program itself is interactive but does not normally print such an announcement, your work based on the Program is not required to print an announcement.)

These requirements apply to the modified work as a whole. If identifiable sections of that work are not derived from the Program, and can be reasonably considered independent and separate works in themselves, then this License, and its terms, do not apply to those sections when you distribute them as separate works. But when you distribute the same sections as part of a whole which is a work based on the Program, the distribution of the whole must be on the terms of this License, whose permissions for other licensees extend to the entire whole, and thus to each and every part regardless of who wrote it.

Thus, it is not the intent of this section to claim rights or contest your rights to work written entirely by you; rather, the intent is to exercise the right to control the distribution of derivative or collective works based on the Program.

In addition, mere aggregation of another work not based on the Program with the Program (or with a work based on the Program) on a volume of a storage or distribution medium does not bring the other work under the scope of this License.

3. You may copy and distribute the Program (or a work based on it, under Section 2) in object code or executable form under the terms of Sections 1 and 2 above provided that you also do one of the following:

a) Accompany it with the complete corresponding machine-readable source code, which must be distributed under the terms of Sections 1 and 2 above on a medium customarily used for software interchange; or,

b) Accompany it with a written offer, valid for at least three years, to give any third party, for a charge no more than your cost of physically performing source distribution, a complete machine-readable copy of the corresponding source code, to be distributed under the terms of Sections 1 and 2 above on a medium customarily used for software interchange; or,

c) Accompany it with the information you received as to the offer to distribute corresponding source code. (This alternative is allowed only for noncommercial distribution and only if you received the program in object code or executable form with such an offer, in accord with Subsection b above.)

The source code for a work means the preferred form of the work for making modifications to it. For an executable work, complete source code means all the source code for all modules it contains, plus any associated interface definition files, plus the scripts used to control compilation and installation of the executable. However, as a special exception, the source code distributed need not include anything that is normally distributed (in either source or binary form) with the major components (compiler, kernel, and so on) of the operating system on which the executable runs, unless that component itself accompanies the executable.

If distribution of executable or object code is made by offering access to copy from a designated place, then offering equivalent access to copy the source code from the same place counts as distribution of the source code, even though third parties are not compelled to copy the source along with the object code.

4. You may not copy, modify, sublicense, or distribute the Program except as expressly provided under this License. Any attempt otherwise to copy, modify, sublicense or distribute the Program is void, and will automatically terminate your rights under this License. However, parties who have received copies, or rights, from you under this License will not have their licenses terminated so long as such parties remain in full compliance.

5. You are not required to accept this License, since you have not signed it. However, nothing else grants you permission to modify or distribute the Program or its derivative works. These actions are prohibited by law if you do not accept this License. Therefore, by modifying or distributing the Program (or any work based on the Program), you indicate your acceptance of this License to do so, and all its terms and conditions for copying, distributing or modifying the Program or works based on it.

6. Each time you redistribute the Program (or any work based on the Program), the recipient automatically receives a license from the original licensor to copy, distribute or modify the Program subject to these terms and conditions. You may not impose any further restrictions on the recipients' exercise of the rights granted herein. You are not responsible for enforcing compliance by third parties to this License.

7. If, as a consequence of a court judgment or allegation of patent infringement or for any other reason (not limited to patent issues), conditions are imposed on you (whether by court order, agreement or otherwise) that contradict the conditions of this License, they do not excuse you from the conditions of this License. If you cannot distribute so as to satisfy simultaneously your obligations under this License and any other pertinent obligations, then as a consequence you may not distribute the Program at all. For example, if a patent license would not permit royalty-free redistribution of the Program by all those who receive copies directly or indirectly through you, then the only way you could satisfy both it and this License would be to refrain entirely from distribution of the Program.

   If any portion of this section is held invalid or unenforceable under any particular circumstance, the balance of the section is intended to apply and the section as a whole is intended to apply in other circumstances.

   It is not the purpose of this section to induce you to infringe any patents or other property right claims or to contest validity of any such claims; this section has the sole purpose of protecting the integrity of the free software distribution system, which is implemented by public license practices. Many people have made generous contributions to the wide range of software distributed through that system in reliance on consistent application of that system; it is up to the author/donor to decide if he or she is willing to distribute software through any other system and a licensee cannot impose that choice.

   This section is intended to make thoroughly clear what is believed to be a consequence of the rest of this License.

8. If the distribution and/or use of the Program is restricted in certain countries either by patents or by copyrighted interfaces, the original copyright holder who places the Program under this License may add an explicit geographical distribution limitation excluding those countries, so that distribution is permitted only in or among countries not thus excluded. In such case, this License incorporates the limitation as if written in the body of this License.

9. The Free Software Foundation may publish revised and/or new versions of the General Public License from time to time. Such new versions will be similar in spirit to the present version, but may differ in detail to address new problems or concerns.

   Each version is given a distinguishing version number. If the Program specifies a version number of this License which applies to it and "any later version", you have the option of following the terms and conditions either of that version or of any later version published by the Free Software Foundation. If the Program does not specify a version number of this License, you may choose any version ever published by the Free Software Foundation.

10. If you wish to incorporate parts of the Program into other free programs whose distribution conditions are different, write to the author to ask for permission. For software which is copyrighted by the Free Software Foundation, write to the Free Software Foundation; we sometimes make exceptions for this. Our decision will be guided by the two goals of preserving the free status of all derivatives of our free software and of promoting the sharing and reuse of software generally.

No Warranty

11. BECAUSE THE PROGRAM IS LICENSED FREE OF CHARGE, THERE IS NO WARRANTY FOR THE PROGRAM, TO THE EXTENT PERMITTED BY APPLICABLE LAW. EXCEPT WHEN OTHERWISE STATED IN WRITING THE COPYRIGHT HOLDERS AND/OR OTHER PARTIES PROVIDE THE PROGRAM "AS IS" WITHOUT WARRANTY OF ANY KIND, EITHER EXPRESSED OR IMPLIED, INCLUDING, BUT NOT LIMITED TO, THE IMPLIED WARRANTIES OF MERCHANTABILITY AND FITNESS FOR A PARTICULAR PURPOSE. THE ENTIRE RISK AS TO THE QUALITY AND PERFORMANCE OF THE PROGRAM IS WITH YOU. SHOULD THE PROGRAM PROVE DEFECTIVE, YOU ASSUME THE COST OF ALL NECESSARY SERVICING, REPAIR OR CORRECTION.

12. IN NO EVENT UNLESS REQUIRED BY APPLICABLE LAW OR AGREED TO IN WRITING WILL ANY COPYRIGHT HOLDER, OR ANY OTHER PARTY WHO MAY MODIFY AND/OR REDISTRIBUTE THE PROGRAM AS PERMITTED ABOVE, BE LIABLE TO YOU FOR DAMAGES, INCLUDING ANY GENERAL, SPECIAL, INCIDENTAL OR CONSEQUENTIAL DAMAGES ARISING OUT OF THE USE OR INABILITY TO USE THE PROGRAM (INCLUDING BUT NOT LIMITED TO LOSS OF DATA OR DATA BEING RENDERED INACCURATE OR LOSSES SUSTAINED BY YOU OR THIRD PARTIES OR A FAILURE OF THE PROGRAM TO OPERATE WITH ANY OTHER PROGRAMS), EVEN IF SUCH HOLDER OR OTHER PARTY HAS BEEN ADVISED OF THE POSSIBILITY OF SUCH DAMAGES.

End Of Terms And Conditions